KT-591-072

THE BUILDINGS OF ENGLAND
EDITOR: NIKOLAUS PEVSNER
ASSISTANT EDITOR: JUDY NAIRN

BE 41
GLOUCESTERSHIRE:
THE VALE AND THE FOREST OF DEAN
DAVID VEREY

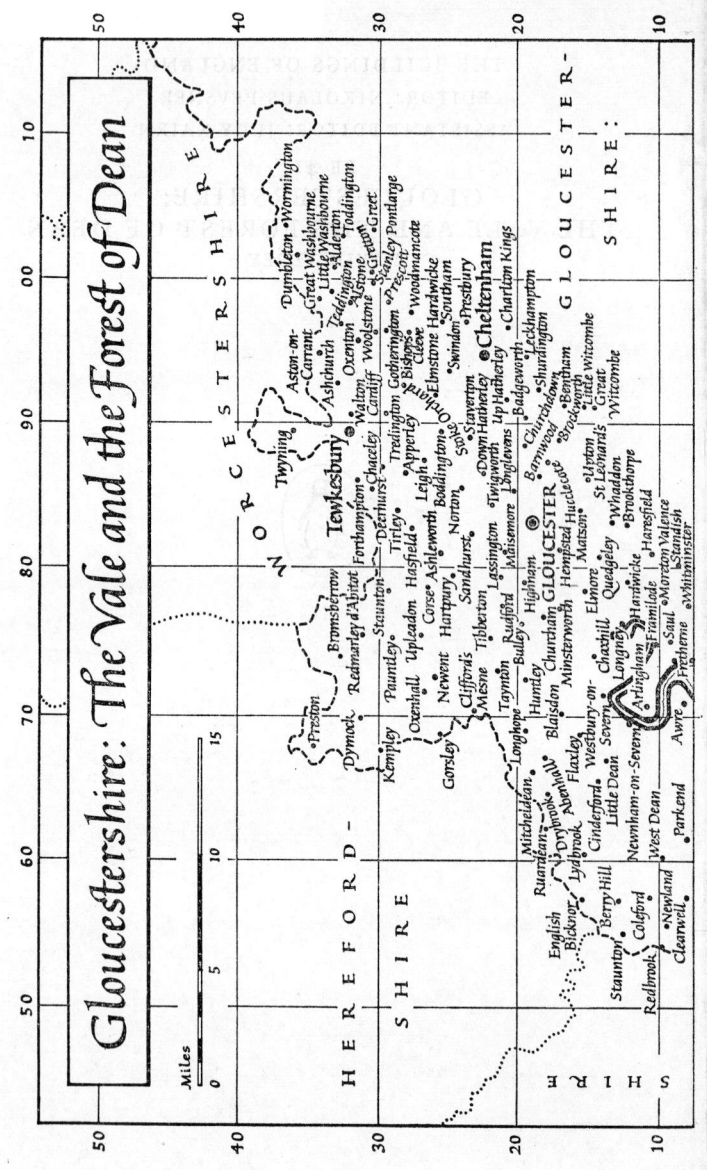

Gloucestershire: The Vale and the Forest of Dean

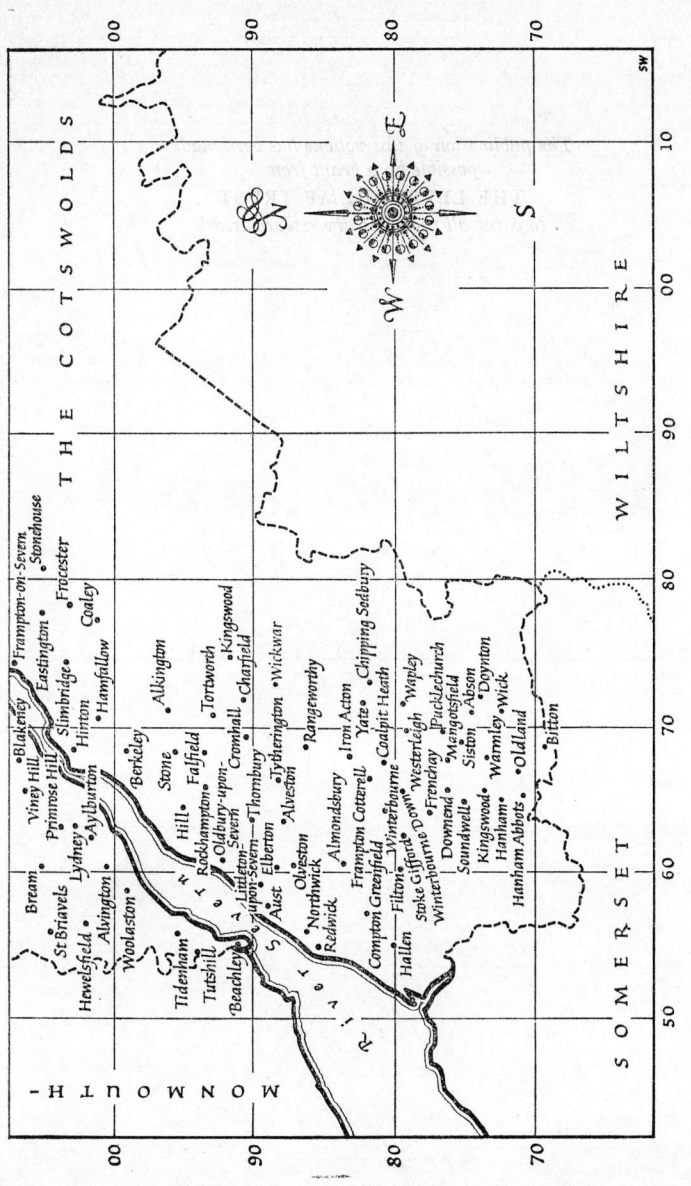

*The publication of this volume has been made
possible by a grant from*
THE LEVERHULME TRUST
to cover all the necessary research work

Gloucestershire

2

THE VALE AND THE FOREST OF DEAN

BY

DAVID VEREY

★

PENGUIN BOOKS

Penguin Books Ltd, Harmondsworth, Middlesex, England
Penguin Books Inc., 7110 Ambassador Road, Baltimore, Md 21207, U.S.A.
Penguin Books Australia Ltd, Ringwood, Victoria, Australia

—

First published 1970

—

Copyright © David Verey, 1970

Made and printed in Great Britain
by William Clowes and Sons, Limited, London and Beccles
Gravure plates by Harrison & Sons Ltd
Set in Monotype Plantin

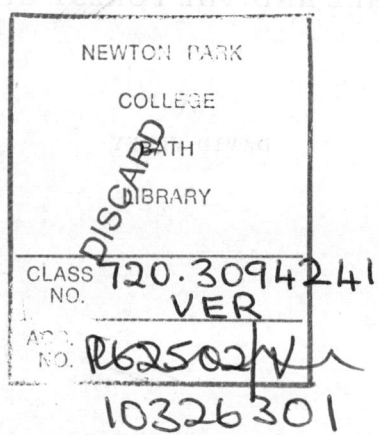

NEWTON PARK

COLLEGE

BATH

LIBRARY

CLASS
NO. 720.3094241
VER

ACC.
NO. R62502/V

10326301

This book is sold subject to the condition
that it shall not, by way of trade or otherwise,
be lent, resold, hired out, or otherwise circulated
without the publisher's prior consent in any form of
binding or cover other than that in which it is
published and without a similar condition
including this condition being imposed
on the subsequent purchaser

To
JOAN EVANS

To
JOAN EVANS

CONTENTS

Map References

★

The numbers printed in italic type in the margin against the place names in the gazetteer of the book indicate the position of the place in question on the index map (pages 2–3), which is divided into sections by the 10-kilometre reference lines of the National Grid. The reference given here omits the two initial letters (formerly numbers) which in a full grid reference refer to the 100-kilometre squares into which the country is divided. The first two numbers indicate the *western* boundary, and the last two the *southern* boundary, of the 10-kilometre square in which the place in question is situated. For example Frenchay (reference *6070*) will be found in the 10-kilometre square bounded by grid lines 60 and 70 on the *west* and 70 and 80 on the *south*; Deerhurst (reference *8020*) in the square bounded by grid lines 80 and 90 on the *west* and 20 and 30 on the *south*.

The map contains all those places, whether towns, villages, or isolated buildings, which are the subject of separate entries in the text.

EDITOR'S FOREWORD

As the editor of The Buildings of England *and the author of most of the volumes, I can only thank David Verey for having undertaken the labour of love of writing these two volumes on Gloucestershire. No one could be better qualified than he, and whereas I always go to my counties as an outsider, he lives in Gloucestershire, has done the listing of the buildings of Gloucestershire for the Ministry of Housing and Local Government, and has written the Shell Guide to Gloucestershire. He did all the library preparation for the 900 pages of the Gloucestershire volumes of* The Buildings of England *himself. He knows the houses, inside and out, far better than ever I do in my counties, and so the result has a completeness which few of the other volumes can match. All I did about Gloucestershire was to visit with Mr Verey's text more than sixty places. In many of them I strengthened medieval detail a little. Only for Tewkesbury and Gloucester Cathedral did I add more, but everything of course in agreement with Mr Verey.*

FOREWORD

To begin with, a note on the division between the two volumes. The most natural division of the county seemed to be along the line of the Cotswold escarpment, which roughly meant dividing the book into one volume for hill places (c) and one for Vale and Forest (v). It is in a way unfortunate that this was necessary at all, for obvious reasons, and also because there are borderline cases (particularly near Bristol) about which it was difficult to be precise. However, this division seemed better than trying to have a North and South Gloucestershire which, if at all convenient, could only be so east of the Severn.

There is not overmuch published material on Gloucestershire apart from the Transactions of the Bristol and Gloucestershire Archaeological Society, *and these deal with hardly anything post-Reformation. Until recently there has been an almost complete absence of Victoria County History volumes; but I am obliged to the Editor, Mr C. R. Elrington, who allowed me access to unpublished material, though in the end vol. VI and probably another have easily beaten me to it. I am most deeply indebted to Mr Irvine Gray, of the County Records Office, who patiently answered tiresome questions and frequently volunteered the most useful information, and not less to his staff, and to the staff of the City Library where the Diocesan records are kept. I am grateful to the owners of historic houses who have allowed me to see the reports of the Ministry of Public Building and Works, and to the many others who have allowed me to look over their homes. So many individuals have helped me that it is not possible to acknowledge them all; but I particularly wish to thank the Rev. B. F. L. Clarke, who accompanied me on several summer journeys and from whose great knowledge I derived much benefit, and Mr James Lees-Milne, Mr Howard Colvin, Mr John Harris, Mr Robert Sherlock, Mr Norman Jewson, Dr Mark Girouard, Mr Anthony Symondson, Mr Anthony Mitchell, Mr Nigel Temple, Mr T. H. B. Burrough, Miss Isabel Kirby, Mr B. Tingle, Canon J. E. Gethyn-Jones, Canon R. J. Mansfield, Dr Paul Thompson, Dr K. M. Tomlinson, Mr Peter Price, Mrs Jennifer Tann, Mr Lionel Walrond, Mrs Shirley Bury, Miss E. de Haas, Mr John Craig, and also to put on record the inspiration I received from the late Mr W. I. Croome in his exemplary knowledge of and care for the churches of Gloucester-shire. I also have to thank many of the practising architects in the county for answering my questions specially: Mr B. J. Ashwell, Lord Falconer, Major H. Stratton-Davis, Mr David Stratton-Davis, Mr R. W. Paterson, L. W. Barnard & Partners, Mr E. A. Roiser, and Col. Eric Cole. I have received very helpful suggestions from the Dean of Gloucester about the cathedral and I am also grateful to Dr Joan Evans for her unfailing interest in everything Gloucestershire, and to Mr William Dreghorn for everything geo-logical, and to Miss Anne Warren-Swettenham, and to my daughters Veronica and Davina, and finally to Mrs Gillian Beeston, without whose impeccable typing the task of writing this book would have been very much harder.*

Limitations of inclusion are the same as in other volumes, except that all churches of the Church of England have been included up to the present day. Movable furnishings in houses are excluded, and of furnishings in churches (with exceptions) bells, chests, chairs, early decorated coffin lids, incised slabs, church plate not of silver or gold, most church plate after c.1830, and churchyard and village crosses if no more than the base and a minor part of the shaft is preserved, all are as usual excluded. An attempt however has been made to include Royal Arms, hatchments, and interesting post-Reformation brasses.

References from the Goodhart-Rendel index of Victorian churches have usually been given in full in the text. Acknowledg-ment is here paid to Mr Geoffrey Spain's index from C19 technical journals, and to Mr Peter Ferriday's index of Victorian church restorations.

We would as usual be grateful to readers for writing in about any omissions or errors they may spot.

It is also necessary to point out to those readers who may expect to find Bristol included in the Gloucestershire volumes that they will not do so. It has already been published in the volume for North Somerset.

INTRODUCTION

WHEN the Romans left Britain, the Saxon invaders began to settle in the plains. These areas had been deliberately avoided by the earlier Neolithic and Iron Age tribes because they had no tools capable of working the heavy clay soil. They therefore kept to districts like the Cotswolds, which had much lighter soils, and where the forest cover was thinner. The Saxons of course had better ploughing implements, and so were able to work the heavy Lias clays of the plains. At the same time, they looked around for dry sites for their homes, and these they found wherever there were deposits of sand. This theory works to a certain extent in Gloucestershire; anyway Deerhurst (v),* where there are the most important Saxon remains in the county, is situated in the Severn plain. The earlier West Saxon settlement was practically restricted to the upper Thames valley, with some extension northwards along the affluent valleys in the southern Cotswolds such as at Bibury (c), seven miles from Cirencester, although the name Bibury is no older than the early c8, and is named from Earl Leppa's daughter Beage, and *burh*, denoting a settlement. The southern part of the Severn valley also has in its place-names some evidence of a West Saxon background. Both Gloucester (v) and Cirencester (c) were captured by the Saxons in 577. Somerford Keynes (c) is very close to the now extensively worked gravel pits in the upper Thames valley, and the Ampneys are not far distant. Coln Rogers, Daglingworth, and Duntisbourne Rouse are in the valleys of the tributaries of the Thames, though they are really in Cotswold country, with Edgeworth, Miserden, and Winstone even more so (all c). These are the places whose churches retain Anglo-Saxon features, facts in no way necessarily indicative of the general situation of Anglo-Saxon settlement. The Domesday picture in fact shows that the whole county (apart from the Bisley area, the Cotswold scarp, and the Forest of Dean) had been fairly evenly developed.

During excavations of Cirencester Abbey (c) in 1965 it

---

* As this Introduction refers to both Gloucestershire volumes, places in that on *The Vale and the Forest of Dean* are distinguished (v) and those in *The Cotswolds* (c).

became apparent that the abbey church covered the foundations of an earlier, pre-Conquest church. This probably c8 church was found to be apsidal at the E end with a nave and side chapels or porticus. The internal width of the nave was about 20 ft and the porticus 7 ft. The overall length of the church was 180 ft. Among the surviving examples of Saxon churches this would be the longest, with the possible exception of the foundations now buried beneath York Minster. The foundations at Cirencester are of massive re-used Roman stones. The Saxons buried important persons just S of the altar, and a tomb was found in this position, thought to be that of Reinbald, Chancellor to Edward the Confessor. The position of the tomb agreed with the description of it given by Leland in 1536 when he visited the abbey, as being in 'the great body of the church', which implies the nave. When the abbey nave had been built over the site of the Saxon church, this tomb lay in the middle of that nave.

CHURCH ARCHITECTURE

ANGLO-SAXON. Apart from Escomb in County Durham, and St Lawrence's church at Bradford-on-Avon, Odda's Chapel at Deerhurst (v) is perhaps the most complete small Anglo-Saxon church now standing, although its existence so near the famous church of St Mary was quite unknown until 1885. The chapel is precisely dated to 1053–6, and is of course very much later than St Mary's church, an Anglo-Saxon monument of the first order, though difficult to date with certainty. However, a monastery is known to have existed in 804, and H. M. and J. Taylor believe that the nave, the lower part of the W porch, and the E surviving side chapels represent the remains of a church that was standing at that time. Anyway there is evidence in the fabric for three stages of building prior to the Danish raids towards the end of the C9. The apse with its strip-work and sculpture is ascribed to the post-Danish restorations of the early C10. Here is a genuine sculptural creation in the Angel, excellently carved, and the face full of expression. The font is about the same date or a little earlier. There is a stone preserved at Elmstone Hardwicke (v) with similar double spiral ornament. At Bibury (c), which must have been built on an imposing scale and may have been a minster, are the surviving carved imposts of the tall chancel arch, and gravestones, of the Ringerike style. Another piece of Saxon sculpture is to be found in the chapter house of

Gloucester Cathedral (v). This is a roundel of Christ, which according to Dr Joan Evans sets Gloucestershire in the main current of European art somewhere about 950. Nor does it stand alone. Professor Talbot-Rice has written of the remarkable relief of a standing Christ holding a long-stemmed cross, now built into the s wall of the tower at Beverston church (c). There are c11 sculptured reliefs at Daglingworth. Somerford Keynes (c) c 7 first appears in history in 685; so if the little N doorway is of this date, and it could perfectly well be, it is earlier than the interesting carved stone of two monsters' heads which Clapham has assigned to the first half of the c11. At Newent (v) is a fragment of a c9 cross shaft of the Mercian type, and a funerary tablet of the c11. We have evidence enough that Gloucestershire must have been endowed with very many Saxon churches. The Saxons however were now dispossessed, and replaced by Norman lords who instigated a huge programme of church-building.

NORMAN. There can be little doubt that the county is one of the richest in respect of surviving Norman architecture. On the grandest scale we have Gloucester Cathedral and Tewkesbury Abbey (both v), where the almost exact comparison, even to dimensions, of the tall cylindrical piers and short arches of the v 9 nave arcades clearly points to fashion and imitation. It was a & fashion which was at first restricted to the West Country, or to 10 be more exact the counties of Gloucester and Worcester. Talbot-Rice explains this 'love of inordinately tall columns' as being the 'result of a return to ideas prevalent in Saxon times when tall narrow interiors were favoured'. He goes on to say in the *Oxford History of English Art*, that the disposition of Tewkesbury is especially interesting, for there were four instead of the usual three storeys; the same was true of Pershore. M. Jean Bony in the *Bulletin monumental* (1937) has shown that these English examples antedate the earliest known on the continent, which is at Tournai c.1110. The building of the presbytery at Tewkesbury, begun after 1087, now survives only in regard to the cylindrical piers and the respond walling adjoining the central tower. The piers now stand 13½ ft above the pavement of the presbytery, that is up to the c14 moulded capitals, below which they have not been altered. On the ambulatory side the c14 aisle vaults spring from late c11 corbels, 2 ft below the c14 capitals on the presbytery side. Sir Alfred Clapham has pointed out that there can be only one logical explanation: that here there must have been a combined main arcade and tribune. 'This system involves the springing of the main arcade from the rear or aisle half of the face of the cylindrical pier in two or more recessed orders and forming together a wall of rather more than half the thickness of the main side walls of the presbytery. Above the main arcade was the open arch or arches of the tribune, above the level of the aisle vault; the openings were of the same thickness as the main arcade below. The presbytery face of the cylindrical piers was at the same time carried up and finished with a capital at the level of the springing of the arches of the tribune, and an arch was thrown across in advance of the face of this second stage, thus restoring to their full thickness the main side-walls of the superstructure. The scheme thus included in appearance, if not in actual fact, the colossal order of the nave arcade, the cylindrical piers in the presbytery being presumably the same height as those of the nave; they supported a superior arcade which enclosed the main and tribune arches below, which thus became architecturally subordinate to the main double storey. Above this we may accept the triforium-arcade and clerestorey from the surviving work in the transept.'

VI3
&
14

At Tewkesbury too the western arch and the central tower are two of the noblest works of the period in all England. On the smaller scale riches are no less; for on the Cotswolds there is hardly a church which has not, in some surviving feature, the proof that it was once Norman, and very many are outstanding examples of the style both for the quality and for the quantity of what survives. Gloucestershire has in fact exactly one hundred churches for which it can be claimed that they are Norman in essence to this day, and of these, sixty are situated on the Cotswold plateau. Before the Conquest, Edward the Confessor had made regulations for the conduct of the woollen industry. By 1082 the first wool-merchants' guild in England was started at Burford, just over the county border, and Flemish weavers came to England in the wake of the Conqueror. The wool-trade was to become the backbone of the wealth and revenue of England, because the English obtained a monopoly. One reason was that there were no wolves in England, so the sheep were safe; and moreover Gloucestershire in the Cotswolds had not only the finest sheep but also the finest sheep-runs. Other advantages enjoyed by the district in a time when there were hardly any roads were the excellent communications left by the Romans, and the presence of superb building-stone everywhere to hand in the oolitic limestone. Taking all these factors into consideration, it is perhaps not altogether surprising that the Cotswolds retain such an impressive group of Norman churches.

First of all there is a small group of Cotswold churches, five in all (and all c), which have no E window: Notgrove, Aston Blank, Baunton, Winstone, and Brimpsfield. Do they represent the rare unaltered survival of an early plan which is of Celtic origin ? A narrow rectangular nave with lateral entrances and a small square-ended chancel is traced to the Celtic missionaries who built a shelter for the altar, their converts at first following the pagan habit of worshipping in the open air. Later the converts would add their larger shelter up against the priest's, which of course would not hitherto have required a window. This was now a building which had to be readily defensible against intruders and designed to offer few points of entry. Windows were small, and where other Early Norman E walls survive, as at Elkstone, Edgeworth, Tarlton, Hampnett, and Clapton (all c), c16 the E window is an insignificant opening which plays no part in the architectural design. W. I. Croome concluded that the five blind E walls must be the unusual survival in the hills and in small remote places, of a practice common before the E window began to develop.

The apsidal E end, found in Normandy and in France generally, did not usually supplant the rectangular form favoured by native craftsmen in this country. In fact Sir Alfred Clapham thought that Dymock (v) was the only Norman parish church in England to possess a polygonal apsidal E end with five sides, though only slight evidence for this still exists on the external face of the s wall. Dymock, of course, is not one of the group of vII Cotswold churches and belongs more to a Herefordshire Border group, called by the Rev. J. E. Gethyn-Jones the Dymock School of Sculpture. Other Gloucestershire churches of this school are at Kempley and Pauntley (both v); they are of early date, and have certain distinguishing motifs such as the capitals which are carved with large tongued or stepped volutes, and the tympana enriched with the Tree of Life.

Several Norman churches retain that rare feature, a stone-vaulted chancel. They are Hampnett (c), Rudford (v), Aven- c16 ing (c), Elkstone (c), and Kempley (v). At Coln St Dennis (c) c15 there is a pier in each of the corners which once must have supported a vault, while at Blockley (c) there is a three-bay chancel with the preparations for vaulting still visible. The plan with a central tower, or a simple nave and chancel divided by a tower, survives in several instances. One of the most complete examples is at Avening (c), which has a rib-vaulted crossing; Coln St Dennis has no transepts, and neither does Elkstone, where the tower was rebuilt at the w. Central tower and transepts v15 & 17 exist at Bishop's Cleeve (v), a church with many splendid Norman features besides, and at Brockworth (v) with its magnificent tower arches. English Bicknor (v) had a central tower once, as did the other two similar Norman churches on the periphery of the Forest of Dean (both v), St Briavels, and Staunton (near Monmouth) where it survives. Other examples are at Great c3 Rissington, Leonard Stanley, South Cerney, Withington, Stowell (all c), and St Mary de Crypt, Gloucester (v).

SCULPTURED TYMPANA are to be found among the Cotswold churches at Ampney St Mary, Stratton, Harnhill, Little Barrington, Lower Swell, Eastleach Turville, Elkstone, Quenington, and South Cerney (all c), and there is a tympanum incorporated in new masonry at Dowdeswell (c) depicting the seven-branch candlestick of Zachariah. The subject at Elkstone (c) is a Majesty with the Evangelists' emblems, the Agnus Dei, and the Hand of God. The design is unsophisticated when compared with the conventional ornament, and the beak-heads on the arch. At Quenington there are two tympana; that on the s doorway, the Coronation of the Virgin, is like the one at Elkstone, with vigorous naïve carving filling the space awkwardly. Here too the arch has many beak-heads. The subject of c14 the other is the Harrowing of Hell. At Little Barrington and Eastleach Turville there are Majesties with supporting angels making more of a composition. At Lower Swell and Stratton the subject is the Tree of Life, with variations, and at Ampney St Mary there is a curious, primitive design said to be the Lion of Righteousness. Harnhill has the Archangel Michael fighting a dragon. Of plain tympana with recessed panels there are many more examples, bearing conventional diaperings, star, fish-scale, honeycomb, and lozenge, such as at Farmington, Saintbury, Southrop, Winstone, and Condicote (all c); Broadwell (c) has a Maltese Cross.

v12   At Ruardean (v) in the Forest of Dean is a well-preserved St George and the Dragon which belongs to the Herefordshire School of Norman sculpture. Moreton Valence (v), in the Gloucester vale, also has an Archangel fighting a dragon. Across the river at Upleadon (v) is a crude Agnus Dei, and Preston near Dymock (v) has an Agnus Dei too. One in Gloucester (v) is at St Mary de Crypt. The Herefordshire workshop had a diversity of sources, and Ruardean's must be West French. As we have seen, the tympana at Dymock and Kempley have the Tree of Life. Siston (v) in the Bristol quarter also has a Tree of Life tympanum.

In the s tympanum at Quenington there is a little domed Heavenly Mansion, like the aedicule in the spandrels of the arches on the FONT at near-by Southrop (both C). The Southrop c12 font is unique in the county in that it has figure sculpture far in advance of anything else, probably owing to the gradual penetration of the influence of French art. The figure sculpture has more freedom than that on the font at Rendcomb (C), which c11 resembles the one in Hereford Cathedral with its figures in an arcade, and a band of Greek-key pattern above. A copy of another font of the Rendcomb type exists at Mitcheldean (v). Generally speaking however, Norman architecture in Gloucestershire does not possess figure sculpture as is found in Herefordshire, except on the capitals at Leonard Stanley, and the wooden Crucifix at c10 South Cerney (both C). Certain places however, such as Bishop's Cleeve (v), show strong Viking influence, with their long dragons and dragon-heads as corbels, or stops to hoodmoulds. Elkstone (C) also has dragon-head stops, and in the quadripartite vault of the chancel there is a boss which looks like a pierced buckle binding four grotesque masks together. Elkstone, together with one or two others such as Barnsley (C), retains its Norman corbel-table carved with grotesque heads. The best example of beak-head ornament is round the s doorway at Windrush (C); c13 but it is a rare feature. Other examples in the Cotswolds are at Elkstone, Quenington, South Cerney, and at Sherborne in the doorway of a cottage where once was a Norman chapel. Many churches retain their Norman doorways with rich ornament, Late Norman chevron mouldings and Transitional features merging into the Gothic style; for instance the s doorway at Little Barrington (C) has keeled jamb shafts with stiff-leaf capitals, and an arch of three orders deeply cut with chevron and lozenge ornament, and a hoodmould of dogtooth broken at the centre by a grotesque head. At Withington (C) the s doorway is also a particularly fine example of Late Norman work, with three orders of chevron mouldings and a hoodmould of daisies ending in dragon-heads.

Many churches retain their Norman arcades, or parts of them, with narrow aisles, like the ones at St Briavels (v). On the whole, signs of an early date are square or rectangular piers, unmoulded arches, and capitals not yet decorated with many scallops. A little later round piers with square abaci became the rule. The development then goes from the square abacus to the round abacus, from multi-scalloped to trumpet-scalloped, and from these to rocketed and stiff-leaf capitals, from the unmoulded to the single-step, to the slightly chamfered, and so to the fully double-chamfered arch. And of course from the round arch to the pointed arch; but there are all kinds of overlap.

Two Norman churches in the county have hexagonal towers, c 8 Swindon (v) and Ozleworth (c), but the latter is altogether peculiar, and may have been the nave with an apse to the E and narthex to the w. Anyway in the w wall is an early c13 pointed arch with an inner order carried on short round corbel shafts. This inner order is carved with deeply undercut and pierced chevrons, a unique decoration, comparable only to the vaulting v18 ribs in St Mary's Gateway, Gloucester (v); it is what Dr Joan Evans was referring to when she said*: 'It is significant that one of the characteristic local things is the modulation of Norman dog's tooth and beak mouldings into a Gothic form.'

The THIRTEENTH CENTURY was a period of serious Border warfare in which the w part of Gloucestershire suffered. On the other hand it was also a period when the clergy were undergoing a revival of asceticism and were desirous of setting up a more emphatic distinction between themselves and the laity. The consequence was a general rebuilding of chancels, or at any rate lengthening of them, thus creating a new E wall, usually with three lancet windows for the Trinity. What could be quite arresting was groups of lancets connected by external and internal arcading and string-courses. Again more instances are to be found in the peaceful and prosperous Cotswolds, particularly c17 charming examples surviving at Wyck Rissington and Cherington. Other good chancels are at Bibury, Eastleach Turville, Shipton Oliffe, Icomb, Meysey Hampton, Little Rissington (all c), and Almondsbury (v). This form of chancel survived in the c19, as it found favour with the Ecclesiological Society, and there are many Victorian triple-lancet E ends. Thirty Cotswold churches have notable E.E. features, but there are not so many in the rest of the county.

Three churches however are outstanding. Berkeley (v) has a v23 w end influenced by Bristol fashion, with a window of five round-headed lancets, and three pointed-arched openings below. v21 The nave arcades have clustered keel-moulded shafts with & 22 deeply undercut stiff-leaf capitals of the second quarter of the c13. The rather earlier arcades at Slimbridge (v) are even finer, v20 having compound piers and variously and exquisitely carved capitals. The third church is Teddington (v), which has late c13

* Presidential address to the Bristol and Gloucestershire Archaeological Society, 1962.

work moved there from Hailes Abbey (c) in 1567, and made into
the w window and tower arch. Here we have a far better indication of what Hailes was like than from anything left on the site,
for this is part of the ambulatory of the Cistercian abbey of
*c.*1271–7. Most of the Early Gothic architecture in Gloucestershire was lost with the destruction not only of Hailes but also the
abbeys of Cirencester (c), Winchcombe (c), Kingswood (v), and
Flaxley (v), though the vaulting of the naves of Gloucester and
Tewkesbury (both v) probably represent the style well enough.

A feature which perhaps can be considered typically Cotswold
is the c13 stone bellcote, though of course both gable and
sanctus bellcotes are also found all along the stone belt. Fine
examples exist at West Littleton, Acton Turville, Boxwell, c18
Harescombe, and Shipton Oliffe (all c), which have spirelets and
pinnacles. Preston's (c) is later, and is open with two tiers and
space for three bells, while Shorncote (c) has space for two bells
and a pierced quatrefoil above. Some c19 copies were made
such as the one on *Charles Hansom*'s Roman Catholic church at
Nympsfield (c). Up to the c14 a primitive form of saddleback or
gabled tower was quite often used, as at Eastleach Turville (c),
Syde (c), and Brookthorpe (v). Those at North Cerney, Bagendon, Duntisbourne Rouse, and Duntisbourne Abbots (all c) are
later additions.

The DECORATED STYLE is hardly represented on the Cotswolds at all, except for the usual window insertions of plain
character, such as those at Little Badminton (c), plainer still after
the Black Death in 1348, and in one or two places, notably at
Eastleach Martin sometimes called Bouthrop (c), where the N c20
transept is a c14 addition and has very beautiful Dec windows,
and at Stow-on-the-Wold (c), which has a c14 chancel with
ogee-arched piscina and sedilia. At Longborough (c) there is a
fine early c14 s transept which has a large window with reticulated tracery and pretty buttresses. At Minchinhampton (c) too
the s transept is Dec, also with a beautiful s window, and sup- c21
ported on the E and W by many buttresses holding up a stone-
vaulted roof, which has ribs perhaps not unlike the stone arch
in the porch at Todenham (c). Todenham was almost wholly
rebuilt in the early c14, and has many splendid features including flowing tracery in the E window, and an arcade of pointed
arches without capitals. The chancel at Meysey Hampton (c) c23
was greatly enriched in the c14, and has a geometrical Dec E
window with a double border of ballflower ornament. Ballflower
decoration however is not plentiful on the hills, but the delight-

ful lowside window in the s chapel at Coberley (c), which is quatrefoil in shape, has an edging of ballflower, and a small window at Temple Guiting (c) as well as the piscina there are so decorated.

To find extensive evidence of EARLY FOURTEENTH CEN-TURY building we have to go either to Gloucester Cathedral and
v26 Tewkesbury Abbey (both v) (for the monastic churches were
& more independent of trade-cycles), or into the Vale of Severn to
30
v 4 Standish, Badgeworth, Cheltenham, and Bishop's Cleeve (all v),
v24 or across the river to Newland (v), beyond the wool district, where almost every type of c14 window tracery can be studied, and where the convolutions of the Dec style seem to be Celtic in quality. The s aisle in the cathedral has window tracery of *c*.1318, resembling exotic butterflies, everywhere budding with ball-flower. 'There too', says Dr Joan Evans, 'the elaborate but-tresses, with niches and pinnacles and statues, give the building something of the quality of a metal shrine.' Equally memorable, if not more so, is the N chapel at Badgeworth, built *c*.1314, with four windows and a doorway all profusely enriched with ball-flower both inside and outside, and there is ballflower round the
v25 windows in the chancel at Bishop's Cleeve too. Standish, how-ever, which is almost contemporary, has no ballflower decora-tion, and the beautiful tracery of the E window is more flowing.

This was also the great period for spire building. Most of them show a local characteristic, very slender and narrow at the base,
v 4 with roll-mouldings at the angles. The Standish (v) spire is broached and graceful. Other c14 spires in the neighbourhood include Slimbridge, Stone, and Haresfield (all v), and the Cheltenham group consisting of St Mary's parish church, Leck-hampton, and Shurdington (both v). Cheltenham (v) parish church also has a notable rose window. There are spires at Staunton, near Newent, at Ruardean, and a detached one at Westbury-on-Severn (all v). c14 spires on the Cotswolds (all c) are to be found at Bisley, Rodmarton, Saintbury, Sapperton, Notgrove, Stroud, Siddington, Sherborne, Stanton, and Toden-ham. The spires at Dowdeswell and Aldsworth are later, and the one at Painswick later still; but generally spires went out of fashion as the c14 advanced. The ones at Kemble and Tetbury have been rebuilt.

The next period of expanding wealth was the LATE FOUR-TEENTH CENTURY and the whole of the FIFTEENTH CEN-TURY. In the Cotswolds, churches are usually either much earlier than *c*.1300 or pure Perp when English medieval architecture had settled down to its final phase. The final phase however lasted a very long time, for it began in Gloucester v31 Cathedral (v) in 1331–7 and went on without much change for -3 two hundred years. The beginnings of the Perp style are discussed in the introduction to the cathedral. It probably took some time for the new fashion to spread, and early dating of even a near-by church like St Mary de Crypt is difficult. There is hardly a medieval church in the county which shows no trace of Perp work, and on the Cotswolds the yields of the wool entirely remodelled great churches like Cirencester, Northleach, c27, Chipping Campden, Fairford, Winchcombe, Lechlade, Ched- 35, worth, and Rendcomb (all c), and large numbers were given at 39 least Perp towers. The buttresses of the Gloucestershire towers of the c15 and c16 are set diagonally at the angles, not parallel with the main walls, and the string-courses are carried boldly across the buttresses instead of dying out behind them. In the later examples there is an exuberance of surface ornament expressed in almost excessive panelling. The mid-c15 tower of Gloucester Cathedral (v) might have appeared even more impressive had the elaborate panelling been more restrained, at least in the lower portions, but the elaboration of the coronet is beyond criticism, with its pierced battlements and pinnacles, which were copied at Thornbury (v), and at St Stephen, Bristol, v57 and elsewhere outside the county. There is an Early Perp tower at Coates (c), built before 1361. Other notable towers are at c22 Coberley (c), Compton Abdale (c), Elmstone Hardwicke and c36 Leigh (both v), Kempsford (c), Oxenton (v), Gloucester St Nicholas (v), and Wotton-under-Edge (c). Splendid towers were c26 also built in the Bristol quarter at Bitton, Yate, Chipping Sod- v36 bury, Abson, Westerleigh, and Wickwar (all v). It is worth v38 noting that since the money was the people's it was also the & naves and chapels which were rebuilt, older work often surviving 35 in the chancels.

In medieval times, when roads were almost non-existent, the junction of the great Roman roads Ermine Street and Fosse Way gave Cirencester (c) a big advantage over many other places. For the first two hundred years that we have any record of commerce here it was based entirely upon wool, that is from 1300 to 1500, or a bit after, without a break. Cirencester like Northleach was a great wool-market. In some ways it was rather a frustrated market, as the merchants were under the thumb of the abbot, who had the manorial rights, owned the market, and charged tolls on every sack of wool sold. For this reason the townsfolk never acquired self-government, nor were they able to form the usual trade guilds. Shortly after 1400 they started to build the c27 great W tower. The arms on either side of the W door are those of the Augustinian abbey of Cirencester and King Henry IV, who died in 1413. The tower showed signs of instability and had to be buttressed by two huge spur-buttresses on the N and on the S. This meant rebuilding the W walls of both aisles and their windows, which are therefore one hundred years earlier than the rest of the nave but in the same Perp style. They had also meant to crown the tower with a spire and had built the squinches to carry it. They are still there, but in view of the warning of risks the project was abandoned when the tower was finished c.1430. After this St Edmund's Chapel, the Trinity Chapel, and the Lady Chapel were remodelled, and finally St Catharine's Chapel c46 in 1460, and this was completed in 1508, by one of the last abbots, Hakebourne, who set up the splendid fan-vaults, and whose initials and mitre are carved in the pierced parapet above c40 the E end of the nave. The great S porch was built c.1490 by the abbey upon its own land and for its own purposes as a kind of secular business office. The biggest job of all however, the c47 reconstruction of the nave, was carried out at the opening of the C16, by the parishioners, those merchants of the town whose arms and trademarks we see carried by the carved angels above the great piers of the arcade. They crowned this splendid work with its lofty arches and great walls of glass outside and above with that beautiful pierced battlement which runs all round the roof, and which had only two rivals, and those on royal works – the battlements of King Henry VII's Chapel, Westminster, and St George's Chapel, Windsor. The greatest of the Cotswold 'wool' churches was therefore the result of the combined efforts of abbey and town, and was hardly completed before the civil and religious upheavals of the Reformation in England put a stop for over a century to practically all work of church building. This and the other 'wool' churches have in essentials remained unchanged ever since.

The building of the churches at Northleach, Chipping Campden, and Fairford (all C) is associated with the names of Fortey, Grevel, and Tame respectively, all rich wool-merchants in the C15. Gloucestershire benefactors did not lack for master masons of first-rate quality, and there was certainly an unknown genius at work at Northleach and Chipping Campden, who took the Perp style and made it into something different and entirely individual. This 'twist' is based on the concave or hollow moulding which is part of the universal Perp style, and was exaggerated in other places by other masons, such as the designers of some fonts in the West Riding of Yorkshire. In these two Cotswold churches (and to a lesser degree at Cirencester and Winchcombe) the piers of the arcades have pronounced in-turned curves, so clear and crisp that they have the quality associated with classical Greece. The capitals of the piers follow the plan with their several mouldings, thus producing a shape unlike anything else, except quite fortuitously the roof of a Chinese pagoda. These churches also have another peculiarity in the fashion for placing a window above the chancel arch. This occurs at Northleach, Chipping Campden, and Cirencester, and also at North Cerney in the small three-light imitation which is now blocked.

North Cerney (c) also has a passage squint between the s transept and the chancel high enough for a man to walk through. At Sevenhampton, Beverston, and Stanton (all c) the passage connects a n transept, and, being very low, seems to have been made for a child acolyte. At Icomb, Tormarton, and Bledington (all c) these are on the s, and at Bledington the passage also connects the little chantry chapel. Bledington in the c15 must have had the most highly skilled mason-sculptors available, for the church abounds with pedestals and nodding-ogee-arched c37 canopies for images. Chantry chapels were generally gorgeous additions in Perp times, and at Tewkesbury we have as splendid examples as anywhere in England; two c14 and one c15, stone-screened and fan-vaulted. At Berkeley (v) the Lords of Berkeley built their mortuary chapel divided by a stone screen from the chancel, and there is also a most rare c15 stone screen under the v55 chancel arch. At Aldsworth (c) the n aisle has exceptionally good-quality and rich carving of c.1500, and at Eastington (v) the s aisle was greatly enriched by the Duke of Buckingham before 1521. At Cold Ashton (c) the entire church was rebuilt between 1508 and 1540.

A curious Late Perp feature of the central group of Cotswold churches is a niche on the E wall of the porch, rarely found elsewhere in England. They occur at Aldsworth, all three Ampneys, Barnsley, Baunton, Bibury, both the Eastleach churches, Haselton, Kempsford, Little Barrington, Notgrove, Salperton, Winson (all c), and elsewhere. At Great Rissington (c) there is a late c15 sculptured Crucifixion re-set in this position in the porch. At Coberley (c) a Crucifixion is preserved in the chancel, and this may have originated as a porch carving. There seems to be no proof, however, of exactly what these niches or cupboards were for. Some of them are rebated for doors or shutters or a grille, and the one at Aldsworth has a pierced stone cresset to hold lights and a narrow flue for the smoke, so it may be a Poor Soul's Light or Chantry.

Having attempted to trace the history of church building in Gloucestershire up to the Reformation, this would be a suitable moment to review the MONASTIC BUILDINGS in the county. Most writers quote the medieval saying, 'As sure as God is in Gloucestershire', with varying interpretations as to what it means, from the Blood of Christ erstwhile at Hailes Abbey, to the supposedly quite extraordinary number of monastic foundations, parish churches, and chapels. The Cotswolds had three great abbeys (all C), Augustinian at Cirencester, Benedictine at Winchcombe, both with mitred abbots, and the third at Hailes, Cistercian; the latter was at one time the most popular place of pilgrimage in the West of England. The Benedictines in the great abbey of St Peter, Gloucester (V), of course also had a mitred abbot. The Benedictine monasteries had their origin before the beginning of the C9. Gloucester (according to the *Victoria County History*, vol. II) was founded *c.*681, Tewkesbury (V) about 715, and Winchcombe (C) in 798. Of the smaller houses of the order, Deerhurst (V) was founded *c.*804. The priories of Newent (V), Horsley (C), and Brimpsfield (C) were cells of Benedictine monasteries in Normandy in the reign of William the Conqueror. Leonard Stanley (C) was founded between 1121 and 1129. Before the middle of the C12 the Augustinians had three important houses. In 1131 they took the place of the secular canons in Cirencester (C). Lanthony, Gloucester (V), started in 1136, and Augustinians appeared at St Oswald, Gloucester (V), *c.*1150. The Cistercian abbey at Flaxley (V) was founded between 1148 and 1154, Hailes (C) in 1246, and Kingswood near Wotton-under-Edge (V) *c.*1139. Preceptories of the Knights Templars and Hospitallers were established at Guiting and Quenington (both C) before the end of the C12. In Gloucester (V) there are the two Friaries, Black Friars, founded *c.*1239, and Grey Friars *c.*1230; both have been beautifully restored recently by the Ministry of Public Building and Works.

Of all the other monasteries there survive the church of St Peter's Abbey as it is now Gloucester Cathedral, and the church of Tewkesbury Abbey now a parish church (both V); but at Winchcombe and Cirencester (both C) there is nothing above ground, except a gatehouse at Cirencester. Lanthony and St

Oswald's still possess a very few scant ruins. Part of Flaxley is incorporated in a house, Hailes has been excavated and has some walls still standing, Kingswood has a gatehouse, and so does v62 Quenington. Monks are still to be found near Gloucester at Prinknash Abbey (c), which was a house of Abbot Parker of St Peter's Gloucester before the Dissolution and was reoccupied by Benedictines in 1928. There is also the Dominican Priory at Woodchester (c) founded in 1845.

POST-REFORMATION churches hardly exist before the reign of Queen Anne. One of the exceptions seems to be the rebuilding of the tower at Teddington (v) in 1567 with the use of material from Hailes Abbey. There have also been those who believed that the fan-vaulting in St Catharine's Chapel at Ciren- c46 cester (c) was originally put up in the cloisters of the Augustinian abbey, and was brought there only after the Dissolution; but in this case it seems unlikely that, when Henry VIII had granted the abbey to a layman on the condition that every building was to be destroyed, any recipient would have dared to disobey. At Naunton (c) the chancel, nave, and N aisle were all rebuilt in the c16. At Whittington (c) there was considerable Tudor work imposed on a Norman building. The famous spire at Pains-wick (c) was built in 1632. Taynton church (v) was rebuilt by order of Parliament in 1647-8, and the nave at Newent (v) was rebuilt in 1675-9.

With the coming of the EIGHTEENTH CENTURY several towers had to be completely rebuilt, and they must all be con-sidered examples of Gothic Survival rather than Revival – in fact it would be a perfectly reasonable question to ask whether the Gothic style ever died in Gloucestershire vernacular archi-tecture. The first of the towers is at Bishop's Cleeve (v), rebuilt in 1700 by *James Hill* of Cheltenham. The nave arcade here had already been altered and given c17 arches. The second is at Dursley (c), rebuilt in 1707-9 by *Sumsion* of Colerne, because the original tower collapsed. At Somerford Keynes (c), however, a new Perp Gothic tower was built in 1710-13, as the original had been merely a timber-framed belfry. *Thomas Woodward* rebuilt the tower at Blockley (c) in 1725-7. The Gothic Survival Perp tower at Frampton-on-Severn (v) was built in 1735. Redmarley d'Abitot tower (v) was built in 1738. The *Bryan* brothers rebuilt the tower at Great Witcombe (v) in 1749-52. The detached tower at Berkeley (v) now dates from 1750-3. The only c18 classical tower in the county is that of Bourton-on-the-Water (c), c79 built by *William Marshall* in 1784. On the other hand the nave

and s transept at Sapperton (c) are classical and were built in the
time of Queen Anne. Kingswood church, near Wotton-under-
Edge (v), was built in 1723, but has since been altered. The N
aisle at Chalford (c), with a classical arcade, was built in 1724,
and the Yate Chapel at Bromsberrow (v) in 1725. The only complete Early Georgian classical church in the diocese is in
Gloucester (v), St John, built by *E. & T. Woodward* of Chipping
Campden in 1732–4. The nave at Hill (v) was rebuilt in 1759. A
Georgian chancel arch survives at Didbrook (c), and at Stoke
Gifford (v) there is an C18 N arcade with classical fluted piers as
well as the chancel arch, and the 'Duchess of Beaufort's Room'
complete with fireplace. The church at Hawling (c) was mostly
rebuilt in Georgian classical *c.*1764, and the small church at
Poole Keynes (c) *c.*1770–5. One or two spires were rebuilt too,
v37 such as the one at Mitcheldean (v) *c.*1760, and the top of the one
at Painswick (c) in 1763, but these are more in the nature of
repairs. Many more churches may have been given Georgian
fenestration which has not survived; this is known to be the case
at Barnsley (c). However at Temple Guiting there are Georgian
windows inside Perp surrounds, there is a Venetian window in
the N transept, the tower was rebuilt, and on the monument of
the Rev. George Talbot, who died in 1785, it is stated that the
fabric was 'substantially repaired and beautified at his sole
expense'. The only two full-blown classical churches are both
connected with great houses: Great Badminton (c) built in 1785
by *Charles Evans*, and Dodington (c) designed in 1799 by *James
Wyatt*. Apart from these two and St John, Gloucester (v), it
cannot be claimed for the county that there is very much
Georgian classical church architecture. There is however a very
interesting, large, and beautiful example of early Gothic Revival
c78 at Tetbury (c), built in 1781 by *Francis Hiorn*. The nave at
Alderley (c) was rebuilt *c.*1802 as a broad auditorium and an
apsidal sanctuary, with Gothick windows with intersecting
tracery.

Notable Georgian or earlier NONCONFORMIST CHAPELS are
v73 mostly near Bristol: the Unitarian Church and Friends Meeting
House at Frenchay, the old Baptist Chapel at Hanham, the
Whitefield Tabernacle at Kingswood, and the Congregational
Chapel at Whiteshill, Winterbourne (all v). At Stroud (c) there
is the fine Congregational Chapel of 1837 and another of the
same date is at Rodborough (c). There is a Lady Huntingdon
Chapel in Cheltenham (v) and another at Woodmancote (v).

About one hundred and twenty churches were newly built in

the NINETEENTH CENTURY in Gloucestershire. In 1820 one
million pounds was voted by Parliament for new churches. In
Gloucestershire the places expanding at that time were Cheltenham (v), and to a lesser extent Gloucester itself (v), Stroud (c),
the Forest of Dean, and the outskirts of Bristol. The first church
to be built in Cheltenham was Holy Trinity in 1820–3 in a kind
of Soanian Gothic by Soane's pupil *Underwood*. This was followed in 1825 by St James, Suffolk Square, begun by *Jenkins*,
who designed the pretty Gothic, and finished by *Papworth* who
engineered the large roof-span and staggered the pews in the
same way and at the same time, 1828–30, as he was building
St John, Berkeley Street. St John had a large galleried auditorium, with an extraordinary trefoil-shaped ceiling of enormous
span, having wood panels overlaid with fretwork, with perforated
zinc plates for ventilation, and a lovely dripping valance, bargeboard style, on the E wall. The church was demolished in
December 1967. Papworth's pews however found a home at St
Mark, Woodmancote, Dursley (c), and other furnishings went
to St Luke, Cheltenham. In 1827 Joseph Pitt commissioned
Forbes to build St Paul in neo-Greek style; this must be the last [v82]
of the very few classical churches in the diocese. In 1838–40 the
Jearrad brothers built Christ Church, another galleried audito- [v83]
rium in Gothic style. The churches of this date in Gloucester (v)
are Christ Church, 1822 by *Rickman & Hutchinson*, to serve the
Spa there, and St James, 1837–41 by *Sampson Kempthorne* for
the poorer classes. There is one in Stroud (c), Holy Trinity of
1838 by *Thomas Foster* of Bristol, and round Bristol we have
Christ Church, Hanham, 1842 by *Foster*, St Anne, Oldland,
1829, also by *Foster*, and the church at Frenchay, 1834 by
Rumley (all v). There are several others in the Stroud area: at
Whiteshill (c) *Foster* built a church in 1839–41, but this time it
is neo-Norman, the beginning of the next fashion. *Foster* also
rebuilt Rodborough (c) in 1842. Slad church (c) was designed
by *Charles Baker* of Painswick in 1831, and Cainscross, Stroud (c),
in 1835–7 by the same; but both have been altered. Oakridge (c)
was built in 1837, by *Robert Stokes*. Horsley (c), 1838–9, is
another by *Rickman*. There is also a group of churches inside
the Forest of Dean. Berry Hill (v) was built in 1816 by *Richard
James*, who also designed the delightful church at Parkend (v) in
1822, and one at Coleford (v) long since demolished. St John,
Cinderford (v), was built in 1844 by *Edward Blore*. Gothic
buildings were generally structurally unconvincing up to *c*.1840,
when the change came with Pugin. *A. W. N. Pugin* was born in

1812, almost contemporary with the other architectural giants, Scott in 1811, and Butterfield in 1814, but unlike most Victorian architects, who lived to an enormous old age, Pugin died young, in 1852; not, however, before he had set the trend for church architecture throughout the Victorian age. The Catholic Emancipation Act had been passed in 1829, and the Oxford Movement within the Church of England began in 1833 – the latter resulting in a demand for a return to the internal arrangements of the medieval Gothic church. At the age of twenty-two Pugin had been converted to the Roman Catholic faith, but his writings had greater influence within the Church of England. Pugin is not the accredited designer of any building in Gloucestershire, although in 1845–6 he made plans for the Dominican monastery and chapel at Woodchester (c), for a client, William Leigh, who allowed these plans to be used by another architect, *Charles Hansom*, in September 1846, against Pugin's wishes. The church at Woodchester Priory is in every way thoroughly Puginesque.

Within the Church of England, the organization of the Gothic Revival was the work of the Cambridge Camden Society, soon to be known as the Ecclesiological Society, who published a list of favoured architects as well as laying down all sorts of rules as to what was acceptable and what was not. Among certain sections of the clergy in Gloucestershire the ground must have been fallow to receive such instructions, for it should not be forgotten that the very seeds of the Oxford Movement were sown in the vicarage at Southrop by John Keble and his friends, including Isaac Williams, as long ago as c.1825. One of the architects acceptable to the Ecclesiological Society was *J. P. Harrison* of Oxford, and he was chosen by Thomas Keble to design the new church at Bussage (c), in 1846, largely built from the subscriptions of Oxford undergraduates. Harrison also rebuilt the nave at Barnsley (c) in 1843–7 for Canon Howman. About this time John Keble left Fairford and went to Hampshire, where Harrison rebuilt the church at Hursley for him in 1848. Another Gloucestershire church by Harrison is at Warmley (v), 1849. None of these works is particularly distinguished, and it is said that the Tractarians did not specially mind about architecture; but, unlike Newman, they had now at least swallowed the Pugin doctrine that Gothic is Christian, and certainly in two of these cases were replacing classical (if not pagan) architecture with Harrison's approved brand of Gothic.

Far more significant architecturally was what was going on at Coalpit Heath (v) in 1844–5; for here *Butterfield* was building

his first church, lychgate, and vicarage. The vicarage must be v93
regarded as a turning point in architectural history, when one
realizes it was fifteen years earlier than Webb's Red House. It
has an ample gabled roof, a tall battered chimneybreast, a c 13-
looking porch, and elevations resulting directly from the plan;
a trend-setter for the secular Gothic style. To quote Professor
Hitchcock, 'the irregularities of massing and window placement
are only those which the convenient disposition of the rooms
makes necessary. As an expression of the asceticism of the Early
Tractarian parsons it could hardly be bettered'.

The neo-Romanesque fashion which prevailed in the forties
and fifties is well exemplified. The best example is St Peter,
Cheltenham (v), by *Daukes*, 1847–9. A late one is at Batsford (c),
by *Poulton & Woodman*. Other examples are the Unitarian
Church in Cheltenham by *R. Abraham*, Coleford Baptist Chapel
(v) by *Searle*, Apperley church (v), 1856 by *F.C. Penrose*, Frami-
lode church (v), 1854 by *Francis Niblett*, Tresham church (c),
1855 by *J. J. Rowland*, Brimscombe church (c), 1840, St
Thomas, Northwick (v), also 1840, and Frampton Mansell (c),
1844. A freak of the period is the clerical amateur architects.
Lower Cam (c) was designed by the *Rev. George Madan* in 1844,
Hillsley (c) by the *Rev. B. Perkins* in 1851, and the *Rev. W. H.
Lowder* restored Bisley church (c) in 1862. *Lowder* also restored
Miserden in 1866 and Ozleworth in 1873 (both c).

All the top Victorian church architects are represented in the
county. Besides Coalpit Heath, *Butterfield* finished the church at
Wick (v), in 1850, which had been begun by *Charles Dyer* a few
years earlier, and it looks very much as if he had been concerned
in the restoration of Driffield (c) in 1863. He also built Poulton
church (c) in 1873. *Sir George Gilbert Scott* built churches at
Watermoor, Cirencester (c), in 1850–1, Flaxley (v) in 1856, and
All Saints, Gloucester (v), in 1875, besides of course playing a
part in the restorations of the cathedral (v), Tewkesbury
Abbey (v), Cirencester parish church (c), and Sudeley Castle
chapel (c). *Clutton & Burges* built Hatherop (c) in 1854–5. *G. E.
Street* designed Whelford church in 1864, having altered Kempsford in 1858 (both c). He also built Winterbourne Down
church (v) in 1858. He restored Prestbury (v) in 1864 and rebuilt
Toddington (v) in 1873–9. *J. L. Pearson* rebuilt Stinchcombe in v96
1855, Daylesford in 1860, and North Nibley chancel in 1861 c95
(all c). *S. S. Teulon* built churches at Woodchester (c), Huntley v97
(v), and Nympsfield (c) in 1861–4, having altered Kingscote (c)
in 1851, Uley church (c) in 1857–8, and the chancel at Newing-

ton Bagpath (C) in 1858. Teulon, like Pugin, was a Londoner of French descent born in 1812. The Ecclesiologists in general approved of him. He seems to have been a devout family man who was only wild in his working drawings, and very wild he could be. He attempted to create new forms out of medieval precedent, and many of his churches have Gothic tracery never seen before or since. It is this quality which makes him attractive today, and not his more orthodox designs. Huntley is a fine example of the former, Woodchester of the latter.

Another character who had a good connexion in the county is *Henry Woodyer*, who was born in 1816, educated at Eton and Oxford, and became one of Butterfield's only two pupils. He was a distinguished-looking man, tall, rather spare, always attired in an easy-fitting blue serge suit, loose shirt collar, and crimson silk tie. His soft black hat, rather wide in the brim, bore a small steel brooch in front. During inclement weather a long dark Inverness cloak was worn. A most picturesque figure often smoking an extremely fragrant cigar, he lived the life of a country gentleman in Surrey and had an intense dislike of anything which savoured of professionalism. This was the architect the cultured Thomas Gambier-Parry employed to design his
v95 church at Highnam (v) in 1847, and whose combined achievement – for *Gambier-Parry* painted the internal polychromy – has been described by Goodhart-Rendel as the fulfilment of the Pugin ideal. Woodyer also designed Upton St Leonard's (v) chancel in 1849, the church at Lydbrook (v) in 1851, St Luke, Tutshill (v), in 1853, the chancel at Mitcheldean (v) also in 1853, restored Quedgeley (v) in 1856, completely rebuilt Minsterworth (v) in 1870, and gave Windrush (C) a new chancel in 1874.

G. F. Bodley first appears in Gloucestershire in connexion with Bussage (C), where he added the s aisle in 1854. In 1855-7
c93 he built the church at France Lynch (C) at the very beginning of
c94 his French-Gothic period, which found fulfilment at Selsley (C) in 1862. He restored King's Stanley in 1876, and Leonard Stanley in the 1880s (both C).

William White restored Bream in 1860 and Newland in 1861 (both v). At the time White complained in an address to the R.I.B.A. of the perverseness of the workmen employed at Newland, who, 'in answer to his remonstrances for acting contrary to express orders, in dressing down all the little inequalities of the masonry, told him that anyway they had erred on the right side'. It seems that this must quite often have been the case when a distinguished London architect undertook the restoration of a remote country church and the workmen were not properly supervised, and this may be the explanation of many relentless restorations – not that Newland appears to be a particularly bad case.

Sir T. G. Jackson rebuilt Bourton-on-the-Water (c) during the seventies and nineties, and restored Iron Acton (v) in 1878–9.

Thomas Henry Wyatt, architect of the Salisbury Diocese, designed and restored churches on the Wiltshire border (all c): Acton Turville, 1853, West Littleton, 1855, Shipton Moyne, 1864–5, Long Newnton, and St Michael, Didmarton, 1872.

Lewis Vulliamy rebuilt Lasborough in 1861–2 and restored Beverston in 1844 (both c). *Benjamin Ferrey* rebuilt Lower Slaughter (c) in 1867. *James Brooks* restored Meysey Hampton (c) in 1872–4. *Ewan Christian* designed Viney Hill in 1867, and St Matthew, Cheltenham, in 1878–9 (both v).

Of the local church architects during the Victorian period *John Middleton* was the most prolific, and (with the possible exception of *Benjamin Bucknall*, that brilliant follower of Viollet-le-Duc and designer of the chapel at Woodchester Park) the most talented. Middleton, who had been trained in the North by J. P. Pritchett, came to Cheltenham about 1860. He built no less than five churches in Cheltenham (v): St Mark, 1862; All Saints, his masterpiece, 1868; St Philip, Leckhampton, 1870; St Stephen, 1873; Holy Apostles, Charlton Kings, 1878. Middleton also built Clearwell church for the Countess of Dunraven in 1866, Oxenhall in 1865, the chancel at Twyning in 1867–8, and Walton Cardiff in 1869 (all v). His churches were therefore all built within a short space of time, and are all rather alike, showing Middleton's predilection for contrasting coloured stones and textures and High Victorian Gothic detail. Of All Saints, Goodhart-Rendel went so far as to say it was 'a splendid example of what Sir Gilbert Scott was always aiming at and never achieved, complete Gothic self assurance and Victorian punch'. Many of the interiors were subsequently greatly enhanced by the beautiful wrought-iron screens designed by his partner *Prothero*, the architect of Cheltenham College Chapel. The interior of Christ Church was altered by his son, *J. H. Middleton*, a learned archaeological professor and the friend of Morris, and his partners *Prothero & Phillott*.

Another prolific local architect, also far from being without interest, but of an earlier vintage, was *Francis Niblett*, who was born in 1814, a son of the owner of Haresfield Court. He

restored Slimbridge church (v) in 1845. Despite his sincere belief
in the ideals of the Cambridge Camden Society, the moguls of
The Ecclesiologist slated his work and he was never an 'in' architect with them. His rebuilding in 1849 of St Peter, Frocester (v),
now demolished except for the tower, upset them, and he
remained for ever on their black list. His best-known and most
remarkable church is Fretherne (v), built in 1847. In that same
year he also built St Mark, Gloucester (v). He added the N aisle
to Upton St Leonard's (v) in the 1850s, and built Framilode
church (v) in neo-Norman in 1854; but for the church at
Redmarley d'Abitot (v), rebuilt in 1854-5, he chose Gothic
again.

   Samuel Whitfield Daukes was born in 1811, and was articled to
Pritchard of York, and so, like Middleton, came from the North
of England; but at least twenty years earlier, because by c.1839
Daukes had bought the Park estate in Cheltenham as a speculation. Everyone agrees that his neo-Norman church, St Peter, is
really a great success. This was finished in 1849, the year in
which he was building St Paul's College, which has equally
well-composed massing and elevations, and three years after his
best-known achievement, the Royal Agricultural College and
Chapel at Cirencester (c), built in 1846 with his partner *Hamilton*. In 1844 *Daukes & Hamilton* restored St Mary de Crypt,
Gloucester (v), and in 1848 they built St Saviour, Tetbury (c).
There are two small later churches by Daukes, Falfield (v) of
1860, and Edge (c) of 1865. *James Medland* came to Gloucester
as chief assistant to Daukes, and when Daukes went to London
the firm became *Hamilton & Medland*. Nailsworth church (c)
was built by Medland's son in 1898-1900. *Capel Nankivell Tripp*,
the architect of St Paul, Gloucester (v), was a pupil of Medland's.

   The most obvious local architectural family dynasty was that
of the Wallers. *Frederick Sandham Waller* was born in 1822, and
was articled to *Thomas Fulljames* in 1839. *J. P. St Aubyn*, his
senior by seven years, was also a pupil of Fulljames, but Waller
became Fulljames's partner and early in his career was given
work on restoring the cathedral. Waller had a hunting accident,
and Fulljames deputized for him as architect to the Dean and
Chapter from December 1862 until 10 January 1866. Fulljames
and Waller added the N aisle to Hasfield church in 1850, and
built Down Hatherley in 1860 (both v). Twigworth (v) was
built by Fulljames in 1842-4 and altered by the Waller firm in
1891. F. S. Waller lived till 1905. His son *Frederick William*

Waller was born in 1846, and married Jessica Oriana, daughter of Professor T. H. Huxley. The firm restored very many churches in the diocese, often under the name of *Waller & Son*. Unfortunately they were rather inclined to scrape the interiors of plaster. Incidentally Waller & Son designed the building for Lloyds Bank which still survives in St James's Street, Piccadilly. F. W. Waller died in 1933, and the architect member of the third generation, *Noel Huxley Waller*, was born in 1881 and died in 1961. The two churches built entirely new by Waller & Son were St John, Coleford, in 1880, and Oldbury-upon-Severn in 1899 (both v). The firm, under *Bernard Ashwell*, still looks after the cathedral. On occasion the Wallers worked in association with *Sidney Gambier-Parry*, a son of Thomas Gambier-Parry of Highnam, and a professional architect who lived at Duntisbourne Rouse. The churches he did on his own at Bentham and Tidenham Chase (both v) in 1888 are very disappointing; however his restorations of Cranham (c) and Bulley (v) are good.

The best Victorian NONCONFORMIST CHAPELS are in Cheltenham (v): the Synagogue, 1837–9 by *W. H. Knight*, the Unitarian church built in 1844 neo-Norman, the Salem built in 1844 Gothic, and Cambray 1855 Italianate. In Gloucester (v), the Baptist Chapel is by *C. G. Searle* (so is the earlier one at Coleford (v); 1858 Romanesque). Southgate Congregational Chapel, c.1865, is by *Francis Niblett*, and the Whitefield Presbyterian Church, 1871, by *Medland & Son*.

Of the churches built in the TWENTIETH CENTURY the most interesting early ones are the Arts and Crafts church at Kempley (v) by *Randall Wells*, 1903, All Saints, Uplands, v99 Stroud (c), by *Temple Moore*, 1908–10, and St Paul's College Chapel, Cheltenham (v), by *Hodgson Fowler*, 1909–10. The thirties produced St Oswald, Coney Hill, Gloucester, by *Ellery Anderson*, 1939, Holy Trinity, Longlevens, by *Harold Stratton-Davis*, 1935, and St Barnabas, Gloucester, by *Cachemaille Day*, 1939–40 (all v). Since the war there have been St John, Churchdown (v), by *David Stratton-Davis*, 1957, under the influence of John Buonarotti Papworth, St Aidan, Cheltenham (v), by *W. L. Barrow*, 1959, Lechlade Convent chapel (c), by *Eric Cole*, 1960, St Aldate, Gloucester (v), by *Robert Potter & Richard Hare*, v 1964, St Michael, Cheltenham (v), by *David Stratton-Davis*, 101 1965–6, and two Roman Catholic churches, St Thomas More, Cheltenham, c.1967, and Stonehouse, 1966 (both v), by *Peter Falconer*.

CHURCH FURNISHINGS

Starting with FONTS: there is a Saxon font at Deerhurst (v).
The evidence for its early date – late C9 – was provided by Sir
Alfred Clapham, who compared the double spiral ornament
with an almost identical form on a pendant found in the
Trewhiddle hoard, which is dated by accompanying coins as not
later than 875. He also records that the trumpet-spiral disappeared from English manuscripts about the middle or end of
the C9.

There are at least sixty Norman fonts in the county. Of these
the most interesting perhaps are a group of six lead bowls
probably dating from the closing years of the C12, and all
probably made locally from the same mould. They belong to the
v16 churches at Frampton-on-Severn, Oxenhall, Sandhurst, Siston,
Tidenham, and Lancaut near Tidenham (all v); the latter is now
a ruin, and the font is in the Lady Chapel in Gloucester Cathedral. The decoration is in *alto relievo*, and consists of a band of
foliage at the top and bottom, and an arcade in between with
figures and scrolls alternately. There are two different figures
three times repeated, except that the Sandhurst and Lancaut
fonts are smaller, having only eleven and ten arcades respectively, with two scroll patterns coming together at Sandhurst.
In addition to these six there are three other lead fonts (though of
much later date) in Gloucestershire, making nine out of a total
of thirty in the whole of England and Wales.

Of the stone Norman fonts by far the most interesting is that
c12 of Southrop (c), *c.*1160 (of which there is a variant at Stanton
Fitzwarren, Wiltshire), showing the Virtues and Vices, standing
as figures in trefoil-headed niches which have attractive aedicules
or Heavenly Mansions in the spandrels, and a splendid, free
c11 swirling pattern above. At Rendcomb (c) is another carved font,
this one with twelve compartments in an arcade, containing
figures, similar to the font in Hereford Cathedral. There are or
were two other similar fonts in Gloucestershire, at Newnham-
on-Severn (v), and at Mitcheldean (v), where it is now largely a
replica. They are the product of a local Late Norman school of
sculpture. It is quite probable that such a font as Rendcomb's
never had supports when it was originally made for adult
baptism. The tall cylinder at Siddington (c) would never have
required a pedestal. Cherington (c) has a tub-shaped bowl with
a circular pedestal only 12 in. high standing on a low, massive,

circular base. At Duntisbourne Abbots (c) the bowl is carved
with trilobed foliage, at St Briavels (v) with curious horizontal
scallops. The majority of our Norman fonts however are plain,
and large numbers must have been destroyed in the c15, when
the fashion for making new ones was at its height.

We have also a few examples from the years between. The c13
fonts at Bibury and Tormarton (both c), though very different,
both have square bowls, at Bibury notably decorated with panels
of intersecting tracery; at Ozleworth and Todenham (both c)
they are circular, and at Chipping Sodbury (v), Hailes (c), and
Whittington (c) octagonal. In the first quarter of the c13
detached shafts were largely used; at Bibury they are octagonal
and set at each corner. Later, clusters of engaged pillars were
used, as at Ozleworth, Tormarton, and Boxwell (all c).

Coeval with the Dec period, from the late c13, fonts became
pedestal and octagonal. Beautiful c14 fonts exist at Longborough (c), St Bartholomew, Churchdown (v), Staunton near
Coleford (v), Whaddon (v), Longney (v), Leighterton (c),
Shurdington (v), and at Tewkesbury (v), which has ballflower
on the pedestal; but here the octagonal bowl is c19. However,
comparatively few fonts were made in the c13 and c14; but in
the Perp period a great many were carved, and there are at least
seventy examples in the county. Many of them are very much the
same, with their octagonal bowls carved with quatrefoils and
rosettes. Others show considerable originality. Abenhall's (v) is
octagonal, each face of the bowl being enriched with lozenges
containing quatrefoils. The chamfer has eight heater-shaped
shields bearing devices of the Free Smiths and Free Miners of
the Forest of Dean, as well as nobler arms. At Northleach (c) a
large human head is carved on the centre of each face of the
octagonal bowl, most of them men with long wavy hair and
drooping moustaches. The chamfer has angels playing musical
instruments. The chamfer at Adlestrop (c) is also carved, with
geometrical patterns, foliage, a head of corn, a mask, and a
shield. There is a beautiful bowl at Upper Slaughter (c), no
longer used. Barnwood (v) has a richly decorated bowl with
demi-angels with wings, vested in albs and holding heater-
shaped shields, foliage, and roses. This is one of the last and was
probably given by Abbot Parker. Medieval font covers have not
survived.

Of post-Reformation fonts there is an interesting Tudor
pedestal with the Royal Arms of 1583 at Westbury-on-Severn (v).
The three lead fonts already referred to (all v) are c16 and c17.

The one at Haresfield has been thought to be Gothic; but it does not seem to have that appearance and looks C17. Down Hatherley's bowl is Tudor, and that of Slimbridge was made in 1664. There are several fonts dating from the Restoration of Charles II in 1661, including those at Painswick (C), dated 1661, Taynton (V), Sevenhampton (C), and Mickleton (C), also dated 1661. Winchcombe's font (C) is dated 1634 and has its pretty original cover. Leonard Stanley (C) also has a nice cover to an early C18 font.

PULPITS. There are a quite remarkable number of surviving medieval stone pulpits even for a largely stone district,
c41 twenty in fact, only equalled by Somerset. At Cirencester,
c42 North Cerney, Northleach, Chedworth, Naunton (all C), and Cromhall (V) are the finest examples of the Perp type which rests upon a slender stone stem; and at Chipping Sodbury (V) and Cold Ashton (C) we have the uncommon form bracketed out from a wall, and approached by steps cut in the wall. Others are at Ampney Crucis (C), Aylburton (V), Colesbourne (C), Cowley (C), Hawkesbury (C), Rangeworthy (V), Staunton near Coleford (V), Thornbury (V), Turkdean (C), Westerleigh (V), Lasborough (C),
v49 and Winson (C), and at Iron Acton (V) there is the graceful and elaborate out-of-door pulpit or preaching cross.

On the other hand WOODEN MEDIEVAL FURNISHINGS have not survived in Gloucestershire to any considerable extent. The most notable exception must be the C14 CHOIR STALLS in Gloucester Cathedral (V). Many churches, such as Alderton, Ashleworth, and Awre (all V), possess wooden chests; but these, like bishop's chairs and bells, have not been noted in this volume. There is an interesting C15 BELL FRAME at Twyning (V). There are C15 wooden PULPITS or parts of pulpits at Elmstone Hardwicke (V), Evenlode (C), Mitcheldean (V), and Stanton (C); but the county has suffered the almost total disappearance of the churches' once splendid ROOD SCREENS. It is thought to have been the hot reforming zeal of Bishop Hooper which produced their so widespread removal. The most complete Late Perp wooden screens to survive are at Fairford and Rendcomb (both C). At Cirencester (C) too there are several; part of the rood screen survives, though it has been altered, and it shows the Midland characteristic of an insertion of pierced carving between the transom and solid panels below, as does the
c28 more complete screening round the Garstang Chapel. The screen at near-by Somerford Keynes (C) also has this Midland characteristic with quatrefoil piercings in its bottom section.

A good screen survives at Ashchurch (v), and parts at Awre (v), v40 Coates (c), Beverston (c), Elmstone Hardwicke (v), Hailes (c), and English Bicknor (v). The only surviving stone rood screen v55 is the one at Berkeley (v). The curious returned stalls in stone at Ampney St Mary, the mutilated brackets on the jambs of the chancel arch at Bagendon, and some indications at Little Barrington (all c) suggest that we may once have had yet other instances of this substitution of the abundant stone for the more usual wood.

The stone parclose screen of the Holy Trinity Chapel at Cirencester (c) should belong to the same category as the stone screens round the chantry chapels at Tewkesbury and Gloucester (both v), which should be thought of as architecture rather than furnishings. The stone encouraged the sculptors too, though most of their work has been lost to the Puritans. The former grace of the empty niches is revealed when, as on the porch at Northleach (c), the IMAGES are miraculously undisturbed. So we can only imagine the splendours of the medieval altar. However, a considerable number of MENSAE have survived, and the sacristy at Northleach has an ALTAR *in situ* apparently undisturbed. There are three more which are complete with their substructures, though reconstructed. Daglingworth (c) has a small Norman altar (now a credence in the N chancel wall), Forthampton (v) an early C13 altar on four pillars, and North Cerney (c) one of the same date but different, being supported by five slabs of stone. Tewkesbury Abbey (v) has a mensa 13ft 8in. long, Northleach chancel (c) one 10ft long. There are three at Newland (v). Others in use are at Edgeworth, Farmcote, and Shipton Sollars (all c).

Medieval WALL PAINTING is well represented in the Romanesque frescoes at St Mary, Kempley (v), of c.1130–40; these have long been recognized as some of the most beautiful in England. The theme in the chancel is the Glorification of Christ taken from Revelation and occupying the central portion of the tunnel vaulted roof; N and s are the Apostles. At Stowell (c) also there is part of a Romanesque painting with somewhat similar Apostles. Another complete scheme of painting is at Stoke Orchard (v), of c.1190–1220, depicting the life of St James of Compostela. At Ampney St Mary (c) there are, besides some C12 masonry patterns, the very interesting C13 or C14 paintings intended to teach that labour on the Sabbath is wounding to Christ. There are also traces of early wall paintings at near-by Ampney Crucis (c). Better preserved are those in the parish church at Hailes (c), particularly the early C14 paintings of St Catherine and St Margaret. There is a fairly well preserved C14 c25 St Christopher at Baunton (c). Other places with fragments of wall painting are Berkeley (v), Cirencester (c), St Nicholas at Oddington (c), Oxenton (v), and the Trinity Chapel, Tewkesbury (v).

Several churches possess medieval embroideries, that OPUS ANGLICANUM which won for our broiderers a world-wide reputation. In most examples the former vestments have been cut up and converted into frontals or palls, as at Cirencester, Buckland, and Northleach (all c); but at Baunton (c) we have a complete frontal of the C15, quite unaltered, with its embroidered subjects appliqué upon alternate panels of red and yellow silk damask, and at Chipping Campden (c) we have a treasure unique in England, the C15 frontal of the high altar, complete with its upper frontal or dorsal. Campden also has a C15 cope of velvet embroidered with powdered coronets and stars, the orphreys showing saints under canopies, all in its full original form. Other examples are at Winchcombe (c), Minsterworth (v), and Little Dean (v).

The thought of medieval STAINED GLASS in Gloucesterc45 shire must bring Fairford (c) to mind at once. Here we have a Late Perp church with the usual complement of windows including a clerestory all filled with the exceedingly beautiful original glass which was made for the church at the time of its building, c.1500, by *Barnard Flower*, Master Glass Painter to Henry VII.

At Rendcomb (c) the glass, though fragmentary, is interesting for being a little later than Fairford and showing Renaissance details. Chronologically these windows come last; the earliest v44 medieval glass in the county is probably at Arlingham (v), where the saints on plain ruby grounds date from c.1340 and are similar to the exquisite St Catherine at Deerhurst (v). There is, however, some glass in St Mary, Sudeley Castle (c), which is v42 said to be C13. The most complete selection and the most beauti-& ful is the glass in the clerestory of the presbytery at Tewkes- 43 bury (v), which is of c.1340. The great E window in the cathedral contains by far the largest quantity of early glass. This is of c.1350. Most glass to survive is C15. The E window at Cirencester (c) has glass of c.1480. There is very interesting glass at Bledington (c) c.1470, Buckland (c) c.1475 (and also in the rectory), and at Bagendon, Coln Rogers, Dyrham (all c), Frampton-on-Severn (v), Iron Acton (v), North Cerney (c),

Stanton (c), Hailes (c), Temple Guiting (c), and Tortworth (v), v56
where there is a portrait of Edward IV.

Chipping Campden (c) has a late c15 latten eagle LECTERN.

For the century after the Reformation PLATE must come first.
Very few churches have anything earlier. The famous Gloucester
Candlestick, early c12 German work, is in the Victoria and
Albert. At Fairford (c) there is a mazer bowl of 1480–90, and
Cold Ashton (c) has a paten which is pre-Reformation. Some
sixty-eight churches have Elizabethan plate. As in neighbouring
Wiltshire, the majority of chalices and patens were made in 1576,
or thereabouts, anyway between 1569 and 1579. According to
the Rev. J. T. Evans's survey of *Church Plate in Gloucestershire*
Cirencester (c) has the most interesting set of church plate in
England. The principal and most ancient treasure is the secular
gilt cup with cover surmounted by the Boleyn family badge. c48
The design is Renaissance. The hallmark shows it to have been
made in London in 1535 which was the last year of Queen Anne
Boleyn's ill-fated reign, and the cup no doubt then came into
the possession of her daughter, afterwards Queen Elizabeth I.
It was given to the Queen's physician, Dr Richard Master, in
1561, and was afterwards given to the parish. Cirencester also
has a pair of the finest known examples of the early post-
Reformation chalice. They are hall-marked 1570, but are in the
style of the time of Edward VI. Of equal interest is the pair of
jug-shaped flagons, of 1576, the finest of their type, though there
is another pair in the county at Rendcomb (c); 1592.

There is some c16 STAINED GLASS in one of the windows
in the cathedral cloisters, mostly heraldry, which is what they
then excelled in; some of it is Royal and some to do with the
family of Brydges, Lords Chandos of Sudeley, who also owned
Prinknash. This came from Prinknash (c), where the chapel
retains a c16 window of the Nine Choirs of Angels. There is
also some glass of this period at Sudeley Castle (c).

ELIZABETHAN FURNISHINGS are rare. There is a good HOLY
TABLE at Barnsley (c) with bulbous legs. Jacobean PULPITS
have survived in many instances, such as at Oddington (c),
Shipton Sollars (c), Abson (v), Windrush (c), and elsewhere.

The best examples of c17 and c18 furnishings in medieval
churches are at St Lawrence, Didmarton (c), Little Wash- c67
bourne and Great Washbourne (v), Driffield (c), Teddington (v) c55
(1655), Farmcote, Temple Guiting, Buckland (all c), and &
Bishop's Cleeve (v) (Jacobean musicians' gallery). There are v63
fine ORGAN CASES at Tewkesbury Abbey (v), in the cathedral (v)

1665, at Wotton-under-Edge (C), given in 1726, Winchcombe (C), *c*.1735, and Newent (V), *c*.1740. At Standish (V) the PEWS are by
c78 *Anthony Keck*, 1764. Tetbury (C) of 1781 is complete with all its neo-Gothic furnishings, chandeliers, and an altar picture by *Benjamin West*. At Dowdeswell (C) there are two GALLERIES approached by outside staircases, one at the W for the manor and one in the N transept for the rectory. Most churches were given these appendages but few survive. There is a W gallery at North Cerney (C) with only an external stair, and the Sezincote pew at Longborough (C) has only an external door.

VICTORIAN FURNISHINGS are everywhere. It is worth mentioning *G. F. Bodley*'s choir stalls in the church at Selsley (C), and *James Brooks*'s choir stalls still preserved at Northleach (C), and *Street*'s at Kempsford (C), all superb in their way. The carved oak reredos at Almondsbury (V) is by *C. E. Ponting*, 1891, and Ponting is also responsible for the excellent woodwork at Down Ampney (C), just as *Sir Ninian Comper* is at Stanton (C). The early C20 Arts and Crafts movement is represented in the furnishings at St Edward, Kempley (V), by *Gimson* and the *Barnsleys*, and at Chalford (C) by *Peter Waals* and *Norman Jewson*, the communion rails at Broad Campden (C) by *C. R. Ashbee*, and the wrought-iron chandelier at Saintbury (C) also by
c103 *Ashbee*, 1911. *F. C. Eden* did much work at North Cerney (C), and at Iron Acton (V) and Minchinhampton (C), and *Stephen Dykes-Bower* in the cathedral and at Standish (V), Eastington (V), and elsewhere. *Peter Falconer*'s screen at Turkdean (C) of 1949 is also noteworthy.

Victorian STAINED GLASS exists in most churches. Particularly spectacular is the glass by *Clayton & Bell* at Daylesford (C), *Alexander Gibbs* at Driffield (C), *Burlison & Grylls*'s E window at Dursley (C), *Willement*'s heraldic windows at Great Badminton (C), more *Willement* at Haresfield (V), Thornbury (V), Barnsley (C), and elsewhere, *David Evans* at Upton St Leonard's (V), the rose-window in Cheltenham parish church (V) by *Wailes*, more *Wailes* in Gloucester Cathedral (V) and Stow-on-
c98 the-Wold (C), excellent glass by *William Morris & Co.* at Selsley (C), *Hardman* at Cirencester (C) and in the cathedral (V), *Kempe* at Bourton-on-the-Water (C), etc., *Walter Tower*'s E window at Redbrook (V), *Comper* at Eastington (V), Stanton (C), Whaddon (V), and Rangeworthy (V), *Powell* at Tortworth (V), *Bewsey* at Iron Acton (V) and St Lawrence, Stroud (C), *Eden* at North Cerney (C), *Henry Payne* at Chipping Campden and Turkdean (both C), *H. J. Stammers* at Sandhurst (V), and *Geoffrey*

Webb at Shipton Sollars (C); though this brings examples well into the present century and must inevitably be a somewhat subjective selection.

CHURCH MONUMENTS

One of the earliest monuments must be the effigy in Gloucester Cathedral (v) presumed to represent Abbot Serlo, though it is not earlier than *c.*1280. Also in the presbytery and also C13, but quite different, is the wooden effigy of Robert Duke of Nor- v27 mandy, though both these characters died in the C12. At Old Sodbury (C) there is a stone military effigy of *c.*1240. The Knight at Bishop's Cleeve (v) is a little later. There are some early tombs in the s ambulatory at Tewkesbury Abbey (v); Abbot Alan who died in 1202, the biographer of Thomas Becket, has the only monument in E.E. style. The Purbeck marble coffin slab of Abbot Forthington † 1254 has a diminutive figure within the head of a floriated cross in low relief. The ogee canopy is ornamented with ballflower. At St Briavels (v) is an early C14 carved slab with a head in relief and a form of ballflower ornament. At English Bicknor (v) are two female effigies with their gowns caught up under their arms, typically early C14; one may be a heart-burial. Another heart-burial is at Coberley (C), where a small bust of a Knight † 1295 holds a heart. At Cirencester (C) is now preserved the coffin lid of a priest, Walter de Cheltenham † 1306, with a head in relief, a floriated cross, and inscription; this was luckily excavated from the abbey church in 1965.

The C14 produced the most magnificent series of monuments at Tewkesbury (v), second only to those at Westminster. The three chantry chapels close to the high altar, two late C14 and one early C15, are the culmination of the series which includes the recumbent effigies of Hugh Despencer † 1348 and Elizabeth Montacute (under a canopy which can be compared with that of Edward II in the cathedral) and the tomb of Sir Guy de Brien, the lady's second husband. The murdered King's effigy at Gloucester (v) is London work of *c.*1330. There are also very v28 fine effigies at Coberley (C), e.g. Sir Thomas Berkeley, † *c.*1352 but earlier, and by the same hand as the effigies at Leckhampton (v) of Sir John Giffard † 1327 and his Lady. Other splendid Berkeley tombs are at Berkeley church (v), including Thomas Lord Berkeley † 1361 and his wife, on their castellated v29 Gothic tomb-chest. And there is the Berkeley tomb-chest at Wotton-under-Edge (C) with marvellous brasses of *c.*1392.

Other C14 effigies are to be found at Minchinhampton, Long-borough, Whittington (all C), Newland (V), Pucklechurch (V), Shipton Moyne (C), and Winterbourne (V), and at Old Sodbury (C) a late C14 wooden effigy of a Knight. Usually the nearer to Bristol the more skilful the sculptor. The effigies of the Lancastrian Knight and Lady in the S aisle of the cathedral (V) are very early C15.

Perhaps the most interesting monuments of the C15 are the brasses, and these mostly belong to the wool-merchants at Chipping Campden, Cirencester, Northleach, and Lechlade (all C). The earliest brass is that of a Lady at Winterbourne (V). This is of c.1370. Other C15 brasses are to be seen at Deerhurst (V) (Sir John Cassey, c.1400), Dyrham (C) (Sir Maurice Russell † 1416), Newland (V), and Rodmarton, Sevenhampton, Tormarton, and Blockley (all C).

v50   The most splendid C15 monument must be the Beauchamp chantry chapel at Tewkesbury (V) of c.1430; but another of con-
v52 siderable richness exists in Berkeley church (V), that of James Lord Berkeley † 1463 and his son. There are also C15 effigies in the cathedral (Abbot Seabroke † 1457) and at Ebrington (C), Icomb (C), and Newland (V) (the Forester of Fee, c.1457); at Iron Acton (V) there are incised slabs, and at Elmore (V) the incised line portrait of a Knight.

Brasses continued to be made in the early C16; a priest at Blockley (C), † 1510, others at Berkeley (V), Bisley (C), Cold Ashton (C), St Mary, Cheltenham (V), Dowdeswell (C), Eastington (V), Fairford (C), St Mary de Crypt, Gloucester (V), Kempsford (C), Mitcheldean (V), Minchinhampton (C), Newent (V), Northleach (C), and Olveston (V), and after the Reformation a Philip and Mary brass at Whittington (C).

There are few early indications of the coming of the Renaissance in church monuments; however the tomb of Thomas Throckmorton † 1568 at Tortworth (V) does spring to mind, for here we have Gothic merging into classical, and the tomb-chest bearing the Lygon effigies at Fairford (C), which is of c.1560, is decorated with strapwork. At Sapperton (C) there is a monument by *Gildo* of Hereford with a Renaissance canopy dated 1574. The monument to Sybil Clare † 1575 at Twyning (V) is far more sophisticated. At Almondsbury (V) the tomb of Edward Veele † 1577 is in a Renaissance setting, as is that of George Wynter † 1581 at Dyrham (C). The Lloyds at Ampney Crucis (C), † 1584, have a Renaissance canopy, fluted columns, and strapwork. Effigies in the little church at Farmcote (C) have a simple

Renaissance canopy c.1590, and the Trye monument at Hardwicke (v) is admirable country work in the Renaissance manner.
There the date of death is 1591. Another Renaissance monument
is that of Thomas Smythe † 1593 at Chipping Campden (c).
A couple of late brasses are perhaps worth mentioning here, one
at Yate † 1590, and a Lady † 1605 in a four-poster bed at
Wormington (both v).

The beginning of the C17 was a period of prosperity and
much domestic re-building, and the county has its fair share of
monuments. *Samuel Baldwin* of Stroud was active, and quite a
successful imitator of the Southwark workshops. He did monuments in the cathedral (v) to the daughters of the bishop, † 1622 v64
and † 1623, one the effigy of a lady lying on her side. There is
also the half-length upright effigy of Alderman John Jones
which did come from Southwark. Baldwin made the kneeling
effigy of Henry Brydges † 1615 at Avening (c), the recumbent
effigies of Lord and Lady Berkeley at Berkeley (v) † 1615, the
Kingston monument at Miserden (c) † 1614, and kneeling
effigies of the Partridges † 1625, another at St Lawrence,
Stroud (c), those of Dr Seaman and his wife at Painswick (c)
† 1623, and the Bridges monument in the Lady Chapel at c56
Cirencester (c). At St Nicholas, Gloucester (v), there are the
effigies of Alderman Wallton and his wife, she in a tall hat like
Mrs Bridges of Cirencester. The bust of William Ferrers † 1625
at Ashchurch (v) is London work, and so is that of John Roberts
† 1631 in Tewkesbury Abbey (v). At Broadwell (c) are the alabaster effigies of Herbert Weston † 1635 and his wife kneeling
at a prayer desk, typical of the period. These people were
tradesmen or lesser gentry. Grander are the de la Bere recumbent effigies at Bishop's Cleeve (v) † 1636; a large and costly v65
monument more in the style of *Nicholas Stone*, and indeed perhaps by him, is that with the marble effigies of Lord and Lady c58
Campden † 1629 at Chipping Campden (c). Other monuments
of this sort are those of Alderman Blackleech and his wife † 1639
in the cathedral (v), and Sir William and Lady Sandys, c.1640,
at Miserden (c), both possibly by *Edward Marshall*. There is a
monument at Withington (c), dated 1651, which is signed by
Marshall. At Sapperton (c) the kneeling effigies of Sir Henry
Poole † 1616 and his family, under a great Renaissance edifice, c57
are thought to be London work. *Peter Bennier* is said to be the
sculptor of the bust of Charles Cocks at Dumbleton (v), † 1654,
and the bust of Sir Christopher Guise at Brockworth (v). The
shrouded figures of Edward Noel, Viscount Campden, and his

wife at Chipping Campden (C) are signed by *Joshua Marshall* and dated 1664, and according to Gunnis this is his finest work. Other attractive monuments at Campden are the busts of Penelope Noel † 1633 by *Francesco Fanelli* and of Lady Anne Noel † 1636. At near-by Longborough (C) are the recumbent effigies of Sir William Leigh † 1631 and his wife on a black and white marble monument. There are one or two monuments by *Thomas Burman*, an artist of considerable merit; these include the busts of Sir John and Lady Keyt † 1662 at Ebrington (C), and the shrouded upright effigy of John Dutton at Sherborne (C) signed and dated 1661. At Cirencester (C) there is the reclining effigy of Sir Thomas Master † 1680, a life-size figure in dishabillé and wig. An earlier be-wigged reclining figure is that of Robert Straung at Somerford Keynes (C), and a later one is Sir Robert Atkyns † 1711 at Sapperton (C). At the very end of the century comes the great *Grinling Gibbons* monument at Great Badminton (C) to the first Duke of Beaufort † 1699.

The C18 has provided a great many charming and attractive tablets in our churches, though really outstanding C18 monuments inside the churches are scarce; however, before passing the year 1700 in our survey, we must have a look at the churchyards, which are second to none in the country. Elmore (V), in the Gloucester vale, has the most notable examples of table-tombs with sculpture of great accomplishment and imagination. In fact it is quite a mistake to think that good stone table-tombs are only found on the hills. At Dumbleton (V) in the Vale of Evesham there are some remarkable headstones with Resurrection scenes. Little Dean (V) in the Forest has magnificent headstones with carvings of many subjects, some of them whole figures in high relief. Ruardean (V) also has some good headstones. Quite intriguing symbolism is frequently used. At Newnham (V) there are thirteen angels on one stone. On the whole however the best churchyards are found on the Cotswolds with their many stone quarries. Painswick churchyard (C) is deservedly the best known, with table-tombs of all shapes, even like silver tea-caddies, many belonging to the families of the masons themselves. Some Cotswold oolitic limestones carve very well but have poor resistance to weather, and it is quite customary to have engraved lettering on small brass plaques attached to the stone. Many are treated thus at Painswick. These Cotswold brasses are little known and have qualities deriving from intaglio prints. They are found widespread in the district. One of them at Barnsley (C) is signed by a Painswick artist and com-

memorates a young man who was drowned in a place where
there is no more water than is found in a dew-pond:

> O Death how sudden was Thy stroke,
> The nearest union Thou has broke,
> Nor gave me time to take my leave
> Of my dear parents left to grieve;
> The watery wave which stopped my breath
> For want of help, soon caused my death.

They make good use of the medium in evolving complex and
highly decorative letter forms. There are some very nice ones at
Miserden and Kings Stanley (both c). They have also been used
in modern times, as on the grave of Ernest Gimson † 1919 at
Sapperton (c). Inscriptions on the stone itself are now often inde-
cipherable; but the churchyards are rich in survivals because the
limestone allowed such deep cutting. There are fine table-tombs
and headstones in many places, particularly so at Alderley,
Bibury, Brimpsfield, Broadwell, Cowley, Harescombe, Kingscote,
Bisley, Bourton-on-the-Water, Oddington, Windrush, and
Winson (all c).

There are not many great Georgian monuments inside
Gloucestershire churches. The county was not the home of great
Whig families; by far the grandest people were the Beauforts, and
they were Tories. At Great Badminton church (c) there are
Rysbrack's statues of the second and third Dukes of Beaufort in c81
Roman costume (1754), and the fourth Duke likewise. At Blockley
(c) we have the monuments of the Rushouts of Northwick Park
with busts by *Rysbrack*, and at Sherborne (c) Sir John Dutton, a c80
full-length figure by *Rysbrack*, 1749. At Great Barrington (c) there
is the monument to the Bray children † 1720 by *Christopher Cass*, c68
the most interesting of its date in the county. In this church too
is the bust of Countess Talbot † 1787 by *Nollekens*, who also did c82
work at Arlingham (v) and Batsford (c) and the busts of Earl and
Countess Bathurst at Cirencester (c). There is a medallion profile by *Henry Scheemakers* at Mickleton (c), † 1729, and a bust
by *Horsnaile* at Dowdeswell (c), † 1734. *Peter Scheemakers* did
the monument to Mrs Snell † 1746 in St Mary de Crypt, v75
Gloucester (v), and *Thomas Scheemakers* one at Temple Guiting (c) † 1785. At Lechlade (c) there is an excellent work († 1769)
by *Nicholas Read*. The splendid monument at Upton St
Leonard's (v) is by the talented local sculptor *John Ricketts
the Younger*, commemorating Sir Thomas Snell † 1745. The
Ricketts family did a quantity of works in the neighbourhood.
The tablet to William Little in the cathedral (v) is an important

piece with a fine bust; this is signed by John the elder, who died in 1734. The *Bryans* are another family of mason sculptors who did tablets all over the county. They originally came from Painswick. At near-by Cranham (C) there are some very charming examples of local Cotswold Baroque tablets, very rustic, painted stone, with putti holding wooden palms and trumpets. These are of c.1738. Another good but very local sculptor was *Pearce* of Frampton-on-Severn; he did tablets at Stone, Longney, Moreton Valence, Slimbridge, and Whitminster (all V). Another was *Franklin* of Stroud. *Daw* of Berkeley also signs tablets in this area, but he is much duller. Large numbers of beautiful tablets were done by the Bristol family of *Paty*, notably at Alderley, Upper Slaughter, Tetbury, Blockley (all C), Wickwar and Lydney (both V), and many other places far from the Bristol quarter. There are many examples of *Thomas King* of Bath, and a few by *W. Stephens* of Worcester. Other well-known sculptors who worked in the county include *Rossi*, at Adlestrop (C), † 1817, and at Cirencester (C) two years later. *Flaxman* was responsible v77 for Mrs Morley's monument in the cathedral (1784) and that of her sister at Newent (both V). *Richard Westmacott Sen.* signs a c83 life-size angel at Sherborne (C) in 1791, and in the same church *J. Bacon* signs a tablet in 1794. *J. Bacon Jun.* did the monument at Sherborne to Princess Bariatinsky † 1807 and another at Alderley (C) † 1817. *Sir Francis Chantrey* also has a tablet at Alderley; † 1818. Later C19 monuments include the bust of Sir Onesiphorus Paul and the statue of Jenner, by *Sievier* in the cathedral (V), the recumbent effigy of Queen Katherine Parr by *J. B. Philip*, 1859, at Sudeley (C), the recumbent effigy of Lady c92 de Mauley, by *Raffaelle Monti*, 1848, at Hatherop (C), a recumbent effigy † 1880 by *Gaffin* at Weston-sub-Edge (C), and another of R. S. Holford † 1892 at Westonbirt (C). *Henry Wilson*, the v architect, is well represented in the cathedral in the monument 100 to Canon Tinling † 1897. In more modern times there are several inscriptions by *Eric Gill*, notably at Stanway (C), where also there is sculpture by *Alexander Fisher*.

SECULAR ARCHITECTURE

The earliest domestic building still in use must be Berkeley Castle, though its origin in 1067 was no doubt primarily military, and it is essentially a C14 castle, the whole of the interior v47 & 48 having been remodelled between 1340 and 1350. It is largely

built of tufa, that hard vermiculated limestone found at Dursley (C), where it is grey; but at Berkeley (V), owing to the per-
colation of iron, the walls are a blend of pink and red, grey and
buff and brown. Beverston Castle (C) is C13 and is still partly
inhabited. St Briavels Castle (V) retains its splendid C13 keep-
gatehouse, and the domestic range including a C13 fireplace. The
C12 castle at Thornbury (V) was rebuilt c.1511, a palace, with v61
Tudor garden inside the curtain wall. Sudeley Castle (C) is not
older than the C14, with Royal apartments added by Richard III
in the C15. There was a Norman castle at Kempsford (C) of
which nothing survives, and of course Gloucester Castle (V) also
has disappeared completely. The Norman castle at Brimpsfield (C)
was on a different site from the castle demolished in the C14, of
which only a few stones remain. Apart from the castles a few
other Norman domestic buildings survive. At Horton Court (C)
the N wing is the remains of a prebendal house of c.1140, and
there is a Norman doorway at Southrop Manor (C). The most
complete survival is the Old Deanery at Gloucester (V), which
was the Norman abbot's living quarters, with three large square
chambers one upon the other. There is a Norman vaulted
chamber under the Fleece Hotel at Gloucester, and a C12 undercroft at Bury Court, Redmarley (V). The undercroft at Turkdean
Rectory Farmhouse (C) is later, C14 or C15.

The Rectory at Bishop's Cleeve (V) is the oldest and most
splendid parsonage in Gloucestershire, dating from the C13.
Buckland Rectory (C) comes next and may in part be almost as c32
old, but it is chiefly noted for its C15 hall. Standish Vicarage (V)
does not appear to be earlier than the C15. There are slight
remains of a priest's house at Coln Rogers (C) which may be C14.
The priest's house at Elkstone (C) survives. It dates from the C14
and has its upper hall roof. Frocester Court (V) has a built-in C14
hall, and the barn was built c.1300. This is the earliest complete v46
barn in the county, and one of the best preserved in England.
There is part of a barn of about this date at Calcot, near Newing-
ton Bagpath (C). The tithe barn at Hartpury (V) is possibly C14,
and the one at Southam (V) late C14 or early C15. There is also
a notable barn at Stanway (C) built in the C14 for the Abbot of
Tewkesbury. There are many splendid stone-built barns on the
Cotswolds, such as the remains of the mid-C15 barn at Sudeley
Castle, the medieval barn next to Syde church, the barn at
Farmcote probably part of a grange of Hailes Abbey, the C15
barn at Postlip, and many more later ones such as at Taddington
near Stanway which is dated 1632, and the beautiful group at

Ablington, near Bibury (all c). In the Vale a notable later barn is that at Taynton House (v), dated 1695.

c29   One of the oldest small manor houses must be Daneway House at Sapperton (c), which dates from before 1300. Forthampton Court belonged to Tewkesbury Abbey and has a hall of c.1380. Leckhampton Court also has a c14 hall (both v). Field Court at Quedgeley (v) has a formerly open hall of the c14 or c15.

c31 There must be many medieval timber-framed buildings in the Gloucester Vale. Farley's End Farmhouse, at Elmore (v), has four cruck-framed bays, of which the two middle bays once formed an open hall. Field House at Awre (v) has four bays of crucks. Corse Court (v) has splendid crucks, as do several of the cottages and farms in the scattered parish of Sandhurst (v). At Ashleworth (v) there is a very fine group of c15 stone buildings: the

v3 Court which dates from c.1460, the barn built between 1481 and 1515, and the church. There is also a timber-framed manor house in the parish of the same date. Sometimes in the wide Severn valley we find houses partly of stone and partly timber-framed, such as the modest Manor Farm at Alderton (v), or Brockworth Court (v), which was built for the last Prior of Lanthony, and has a magnificent barn with nine bays of crucks. This is symbolic of the wealth behind the Perp church building. The only house known to have belonged to one of the famous Cotswold wool-

c30 merchants is Grevel's house at Chipping Campden (c). He died in 1401. Down Ampney House (c), on the Wiltshire border, has a c15 open hall of four bays. Other random examples are Icomb Place (c) dating from c.1420, Little Sodbury Manor (c), c15, and Wanswell Court at Hamfallow (v) with a hall of c.1450–60. The

v59 New Inn in Gloucester (v) was built for pilgrims c.1457, as no doubt was the George Hotel at Winchcombe (c), c.1525. Prinknash (c) was enlarged by Abbot Parker, c.1514; there is an oriel window with a fan-vault, and the bust of Henry VIII as a young man of c.1510. By far the grandest early c16 building is Thorn-

v61 bury Castle (v). Had it been completed by the Duke of Buckingham, who lost his head in 1521, it would no doubt have been one of the finest houses in England, with huge bay windows resembling Henry VII's Chapel, Westminster. Most of these buildings are found in the vale or on the foothills or banks of the Cotswolds. For centuries the whole of the uplands remained open sheep-walks – that tract of 'high wild hills and rough uneven ways' complained of by Shakespeare's Earl of Northumberland on his way to Berkeley Castle, and characterized, after inclosure, in a still severer way by the later traveller Cobbett.

The latter on leaving Cirencester says: 'I came up hill into a country, apparently formerly a down or common, but now divided into large fields by stone walls. Anything so ugly I have never seen before.' After ten miles, 'all of a sudden,' he says, 'I looked down from the top of a high hill into the Vale of Gloucester. Never was there, surely, such a contrast in this world. This hill is called Birdlip . . . All below is fine . . .'. This had not been the opinion of the Romans judging from the number of villas round Cirencester, nor is it so today, when the Cotswolds are a popular residential, though very carefully preserved, area. In Tudor times the former prejudices generally prevailed; but what Cobbett would not have realized, if his visit was of short duration, is that the charm of this limestone country lies not in the bleakness of the open wolds but in the intimacy of the small valleys of its rivers, the Windrush, Leach, Coln, and Churn. Here Tudor, Elizabethan, and Jacobean houses abound.

It was unfortunate that the coming of the RENAISSANCE to England coincided with the Reformation, which cut us off so thoroughly from Italian culture. The first little building of the new era in Gloucestershire may well be the Ambulatory at Horton Court (C), situated on the foothills towards Bristol. This was built by one William Knight after he had been sent to Rome in 1527 to promote King Henry's divorce. It looks like an Italian loggia, though the arcade still has flat four-centred Gothic arches. Newark Park, Ozleworth (C), is said to have been built with the stones from Kingswood Abbey (V), demolished c.1540. Only the E front survives from that period, but it is interesting because it has a central bay with fluted columns of Renaissance c49 character. The Renaissance style and motifs took a long time to make any headway, and the Gothic style never died out in Gloucestershire, surviving rather than being revived in the C18; even today local authorities demand that new building is traditional (which roughly means steeply-pitched roofs and not flat). Most LATE ELIZABETHAN AND JACOBEAN houses however have a little Renaissance detail, either round the door or on a fireplace, mixed with strapwork, a form of ornament which came from France via the Netherlands. The term C16/17 is frequently used in the text descriptions and means between 1550 and 1650 where differences in style are slight or non-existent. There must be at least a hundred quite sizeable manor-type houses of this period surviving in the county. One of the largest is Sherborne House (C), which was built c.1551 for Thomas Dutton, a friend of Sir William Sharington of Lacock. The house was rebuilt in the C19 but apparently keeping the original form, and if this is so, it is Gloucestershire's one pure Early-Renaissance-style building. Later and rather different is the rebuilding of the Outer Court at Sudeley Castle (c) c.1572, by Lord Chandos, in a style that resembles Kirby Hall, Northamptonshire. Southam Delabere (v) was built between 1512 and 1547 on a courtyard plan, by the son of Richard III's Constable at Sudeley. The interiors have later enrichments; one fireplace shows the arms of de la Bere impaling Huddleston, referring to a marriage earlier than 1554. This has caryatids, strapwork, and typical attempts at Renaissance motifs. The panelling in several instances has a cornice with the dragon frieze, but in one room with winged angels. The decoration is similar but not so grand at Elmore (v). Elmore Court was built between 1564 and 1588 by John Guise (whose family owned the manor in 1262 and still do, in uninterrupted male succession). Renaissance forms are just beginning to creep in, but the motifs are strapwork, caryatids, friezes of dragons, and what can be called Anti-Renaissance. John Guise's wife came from Hasfield Court (v), which also has interior features of this period or a little earlier. They were married in 1564. Chavenage, in the parish of Horsley (c), is dated 1576 but is probably older; the main staircase is still the stone-newel type usually found in C15 houses. The hall chimneypiece, which is Renaissance in character, is however as late as 1608. Whittington Court (c) was probably begun before 1556 but is now only half its original size. The mullioned windows have Renaissance pediments, and there is a later Renaissance chimneypiece. Stowell Park (c) was rebuilt c.1600 and has a panelled drawing room with an arcaded dado with tiers of Doric and Ionic pilasters. The old town hall at Stroud (c) appears to be late C16 and has a mixture of Gothic and Renaissance motifs. Ablington Manor, Bibury (c) (where in 1898 Arthur Gibbs wrote *A Cotswold Village*, the first and best book to popularize the Cotswolds), was built in 1590 according to the inscription on the porch, which is interesting, as it has a gable and pinnacles in true Gothic style underneath which are carved Elizabethan portrait heads set between the triglyphs of a Renaissance frieze. Siston Court (v) was built before 1598 round three sides of a square, with tall octagonal towers crowned with ogee-shaped roofs in the two corners of the open court. This is in the Bristol quarter. Bradley Court, near Wotton-under-Edge (c), of 1567, also has two projecting staircase towers. The only large house of this period to survive on the Forest side of the river is Naas House at Lydney (v). Built by a

London merchant, it remains unrestored. The date 1573 appears
on a door. There is a hexagonal cupola. The above houses are
thought to be the most important and certainly the largest Elizabethan houses in the county, but they are stylistically difficult to
date. For instance it has hitherto been supposed that Cold Ashton Manor (c), built by a Mayor of Bristol, was in the lead of
fashion c.1570, instead of being rather behind it c.1629. Some
houses have been altered so much at so many different periods
that it is difficult to say this is Elizabethan more than anything
else. Such a one is Owlpen (c), perhaps the most romantic of all. c50
Marjery Owlpen (or Ollepen) married John Daunt in 1464, and
their arms are painted on the wall of the hall which is said to have
been built c.1540. The Cotswold Elizabethan manor house and
its yew trees is a nostalgic symbol for anyone who has known and
loved this part of the West of England and been separated from
it during the world wars of this century. The drawings of F. L.
Griggs of Chipping Campden have given the romance visible
and literary form. Owlpen in its remote and beautiful valley near
the Severn estuary is the epitome of romance.

The coming of James I to the throne of England made little
difference to the style of building. Stanton Court (c) and the
Greenway at Shurdington (v) are similar, with projecting gables
and angle towers, like Siston but on a smaller scale. There are
so many houses of this period that it is perhaps invidious to men-
tion any except the innovators. However, among the traditional
houses of quality are Bibury Court (c), 1621, Ampney Park,
Ampney Crucis (c), c.1625, Ashley Manor, Aston-sub-Edge (c),
Dixton Manor at Alderton (v), Upper Dowdeswell (c), Matson (v), Miserden (c), Somerford Keynes Manor (c), Elberton (v),
a whole group round Bisley (c) in that most beautiful and unspoiled countryside of woods and valleys, such as Solomons
Court at Bournes Green, the Lypiatts, Lower Througham, and
Througham Slad, more at Painswick such as the Court House,
Humphrys End at Randwick, Hazleton Manor at Rodmarton,
lots of houses in Cirencester, Chipping Campden, and Winchcombe, Snowshill Manor, Temple Guiting Manor Farm, Dough-
ton Manor, Lower and Upper Dean Manors at Turkdean, Upper
Slaughter, Upper Swell, Lasborough Manor, Postlip Hall,
Withington Manor, Southfield Mill House at Woodchester, and
Wick Court (this in the Vale). The traditional timber-framed
houses worth mentioning, all of course in the Vale, are many in
Tewkesbury, The Grove at Taynton, Woodmancote Manor
(partly stone), Preston near Dymock, the Great House at Has- v66

field, and the few which have been preserved in Gloucester itself. Chipping Campden Manor (c), built by Sir Baptist Hicks *c*.1613, must have been a full-blown Renaissance building, but only the c54 pavilions and lodges survived the Civil War. Innovators scarcely exist since Fairford Park (c) has been pulled down, but there is the Manor House at Lower Slaughter (c) which may be as early as 1640. Built by *Valentine Strong*, the master mason of Taynton, Oxfordshire, it is four-square in the manner of Coleshill, but on c61 a much more modest scale. Lodge Park, Sherborne (c), was built between 1640 and 1655 probably by Valentine Strong from c60 a design by *John Webb*. The s front at Stanway House (c) was c59 built about 1640, and the extraordinary gatehouse could be the work of Valentine Strong's father Timothy, if it is as early as v67 1630. Highnam Court (v) is something quite different from these Cotswold houses. Situated on the w bank of the Severn in flat, low-lying country opposite Gloucester, it is a large rectangular house built of brick with stone dressings about 1658. Hempsted House (v), formerly a rectory, and even nearer Gloucester, is a curious house dated 1671, built of brick with a stone porch combining an ogee arch and strapwork. Secluded and charming is the late c17 house at Cassey Compton in the parish of Withington (c). It is shown by Kip to have been much larger than it now is, with hipped roofs and mullioned and transomed cross windows typical of the William and Mary period. The newer part of Roberts House, Siddington (c), is an example of the small William and Mary straight-up house without gables, but with two-light mullioned and transomed windows, and dormers. Inside, the elaborately chamfered beams are similar to many in Cirencester. The troubles of the Civil War were over and there was a great boom in building. There was a revival of the wool trade (corpses had to be buried in wool) and the cloth trade was expanding. Painswick (c) has many houses of this period. Medford House, Mickleton (c), is the perfect example of the transition from the vernacular Cotswold style to Queen Anne Classical. Exquisite small examples of Queen Anne at Painswick are the Vicarage and Dover House. Others are the Manor House at Poulton, and Wadfield near Sudeley (both c). Nether Lypiatt (c) of 1702–5 is the most charming of all. Of the larger houses the w c62½front of Northwick Park, Blockley (c) is dated 1686. Badmin-
& 63 ton (c) was mostly built by 1691, and Dyrham's w front (c) in 1692. Of the fifty-eight houses illustrated by Kip (probably from paintings by Knyff) in Atkyns's *Present State of Gloucestershire* in 1712, twenty-eight have variations of the Dutch water-

garden. Remains of Dyrham's can still be seen, and there is a
drawing by *Talman* for a Baroque waterfall; but only the one at
Westbury-on-Severn (v) completely survived the later fashions.
The E front at Dyrham (1698–1704) is by *Talman* too.

We now come to the EIGHTEENTH CENTURY. The most
interesting houses of the early Georgian years are those reflecting
the Baroque tendencies of Vanbrugh and Archer before Lord
Burlington put a stop to them. These are, among others, the
wings at Sandywell Park, Dowdeswell (C), possibly *c*.1720,
Barnsley Park (C), 1720–31, and Frampton Court, Frampton- c71
on-Severn (v), 1731–3. *Burlington*'s own remodelling of Northwick Park, Blockley (C), took place in 1732. It was surely his c72
protégé *Kent* who did work at Barrington Park, Great Barrington (C), in 1736–8, though private documents, if they exist,
have not become available; and to *Kent* in the early 1740s is now
fairly attributed the whole of the Georgian embellishments at c70
Badminton (C) including the pediment, the cupolas, and the
pavilions, as well as the Worcester Lodge, seen from the house c73
at the end of the Three Mile Ride. The park at Cirencester (C) is
even grander; it is the finest example in England of a 'pre-
landscape' layout.

Not only is elaborate plasterwork to be found at Barnsley and c69
Barrington (both C), but also, and often Rococo, in lesser houses
like Ladybellegate House in Gloucester (v) and The Beacon in v7
Painswick (C); Highnam (v) must also be mentioned in this con- c76
nexion, and Upton House, Tetbury Upton (C), of 1752, and
Stoke Park, Stoke Gifford (v), of *c*.1760.

At the same time the GOTHIC REVIVAL had begun at Clearwell Castle (v) in *c*.1740, at Adlestrop Park (C) in *c*.1759 (by c77
Sanderson Miller), and in the orangery at Frampton Court (v), at v76
Field Place, Stroud (C), and Stout's Hill, Uley (C). The classical
façade of Frenchay Manor (v), datable to 1736, however, is of the
type common in Bristol and Bath with the upper floors emphasized by pilasters. In fact there is a distinguished group of
Georgian houses at Frenchay. Another group exists, but more
scattered, in the Chalford area (C), like St Mary's Mill House and
Skaiteshill, though this is rather later. Horsley House (C) is
small, elegant, and in the Adam style, like Atcombe Court,
Woodchester (C), and a great many others built by the successful
clothiers, near Stroud. In the Painswick district (C) there is
Pitchcombe House of *c*.1740, and Brownshill Court of *c*.1777,
built by the same clothier family as they grew richer.

The cloth for which Gloucestershire had become famous was

superfine broadcloth, a high-quality fabric. After fulling, the warp and weft of the cloth were invisible. Much was sold 'white' for export. If it was dyed in Gloucestershire it was usually done after fulling, and Stroudwater reds were famous as early as the c15. Serge-makers were recorded in Tetbury (c) before 1635 and in Dursley in 1691. Spanish cloth was first made at Uley (c) and became important in Kingswood (v). The clothier's mark was required by statute in the reign of Henry VIII. It was a matter of pride; an example of one survives carved on a fireplace in Salmon's Mill House, Stroud (c). Another is carved on the brass of Edward Halyday in Minchinhampton church (c). Cirencester and Tetbury (both c) were the great wool markets. Fulling mills rapidly increased in number along the Cotswold scarp streams during the c16. Leland describes Thornbury (v), Wickwar (v), Wotton-under-Edge (c), Alderley (c), and Dursley (c), all as pretty clothing towns. Even as far afield as Bibury on the Coln there was a fulling mill at Arlington (c), recorded in 1638 and again in 1713; but it is not known when cloth manufacture ceased here. Most of these mills became merely corn mills as the cloth industry intensified round Stroud. Few early mills survive, as they were rebuilt in the normal course of events, so there are only a few examples of pre-factory-system mills such as Cap Mill, Painswick, and Egypt Mill, Nailsworth (both c). Many cottages contained a large enough room to house a loom, but weavers' windows such as exist in the North of England are absent. In the early c19 clothiers began installing looms in their mills. Unlike weavers' cottages, workshops in mills can be recognized by long weavers' windows in the upper storeys. The Sapperton Canal Tunnel (c), joining Thames and Severn, was built c.1789 with a classical entrance at one end and Gothic revival at the other. Stanley Mills, King's Stanley (c), were built in classical style with Venetian windows in 1812–13, and an c90 internal structure of cast-iron Doric columns. There are many examples of early c19 mills, which were built on a much larger scale. Extensions were vertical, and stone was usually used. Welsh slates became a common roofing material after the cutting of the Stroudwater and Thames–Severn Canals. Ebley (c) (afterwards enlarged by *Bodley*) and St Mary's Mills are perhaps the most elegant.

c86   At the opposite end of the county Daylesford (c) was being built for Warren Hastings, beginning in 1787, by *S. P. Cockerell*; a forerunner of Sezincote but not in the Indian style, which was c89 used at Sezincote c.1805 and had never been used in England before. We are now with the grander merchants. Dodington Park (C) of 1796–1816 was built by *James Wyatt* for Christopher Codrington, who had business interests in the West Indies. Another house by Wyatt is Lasborough Park (C) of 1794; this is castellated. Two Georgian country houses were enlarged by *Basevi*, Painswick House and Gatcombe Park (both C). Several not very distinguished houses were built by *Sir Robert Smirke* – Hardwicke in 1818, Sedbury Park, Tidenham, c.1825, and the Judges' Lodgings, Gloucester, as well as the Shire Hall in 1816 (all V). There was a good line in prisons; Little Dean Gaol was built in 1791 and Gloucester completed after 1790 (both V). The Gloucester–Berkeley Ship Canal was opened in 1827, designed by *Telford* and *Mylne*, who was responsible for the little neo-Greek canal houses which look like temples. The Royal visit to Cheltenham (V) which started off the spa was in 1788. *Papworth* was building extensively there in 1825. His layout for Montpellier and Lansdown represents the first planned garden-estate. Examples of landscaping during the C18 include the work of *Kent* at Barrington Court, Great Barrington (C), *William Emes* at Northwick, Blockley (C), and Fairford (C), *Capability Brown* at Dodington (C), possibly *Thomas Wright* at Stoke Gifford (V) and *Humphry Repton* at Adlestrop (C); Cirencester Park has already been mentioned, as has Badminton (both C). Papworth took the whole process another step forward by closely relating the house to the garden; the garden overflowed into the house; hence the vogue for conservatories and French windows. His publications, *Rural Residences*, etc., were influential. At about the same time a few miles N of Cheltenham the amateur architect *Charles Hanbury-Tracy* was building a picturesque Gothic mansion at Toddington (V), evidently under the influence of Uvedale Price and Richard Payne Knight, the Oxford colleges, and the publications of the elder Pugin.

There were no large-scale urban developments in Gloucestershire during the VICTORIAN ERA, except at Cheltenham (V), which is in great part Early Victorian, and in Gloucester itself (V). There are also the Chartist houses at Corse (V), a piece of socialist planning of 1847; certainly nothing comparable with what went on in the North of England and elsewhere. In fact this was a period of stagnation in places like Cirencester (C), which by c.1800 had anyway been reduced to relying on the stage-coach and inn to provide employment; agriculture now was their only *raison d'être*. The town hall at Tewkesbury (V) was enlarged by *Medland*, who also provided the excellent façade to the Corn

Hall in Cirencester (c) in 1862 and the splendid entrance to the
Eastgate Street Market in Gloucester (v) in 1856, with their fine
realistic sculptures. The city has agreed to the latter's re-
erection, if its removal from its present site is required. Apart
from these charming but minor undertakings there are no
Victorian public buildings of any special interest, and certainly
none to compare with the earlier ones in Cheltenham: the Pittville Pump Room of 1825–30, *Papworth*'s Montpellier Rotunda,
and *Underwood*'s Masonic Hall.

Victorian country houses there are, however. Dumbleton
Hall (v) was designed in 1830 by *George Stanley Repton*, who
was also employed at Spring Park, Lord Ducie's original house
at Woodchester (c). This house was demolished by William
Leigh when he bought the Woodchester estate and commis-
sioned *Pugin* to rebuild it. After Pugin retired from the scene,
Benjamin Bucknall built the existing (unfinished) mansion of
Woodchester Park, the best but least-known Victorian house in
Gloucestershire and unfortunately inhabited only by bats.
Bucknall is known as the translator into English of Viollet-le-
Duc, whose rational theory of architecture revolutionized design;
construction must always be apparent, there is nothing to hide.
Bucknall's careful pursuit of the precepts of Viollet-le-Duc
translated into the Cotswold stone idiom has produced original
buildings and a truly functional use of stone. A smaller house
by him is Tocknells House, near Painswick (c). Having disposed
of his probably comfortable Georgian house at Spring Park,
Lord Ducie now, in 1849, employed *S. S. Teulon* to build an
enormous and what must have been an excruciatingly uncom-
fortable house at Tortworth (v), the first sight of which was so
terrifying to guests that it was found necessary to write WEL-
COME on the entrance. On the other hand no Victorian family
could have been more anxious not to be disturbed by the cries of
their children, for the room in the top of the tower was planned
as a nursery. Lord Ducie, like his friend Mr Holford at Westonbirt (or Elwes at Colesbourne; both c), was a great tree-man, of
his arboretum was originally as good as that at Westonbirt.
Here Holford's house by *Vulliamy* is a 'copy' of Elizabethan
Wollaton Hall. This was a worthy setting for the princely
entertaining which took place there. The Victorian terraced
gardens are still kept up by Westonbirt School. Vulliamy's chief
but dull smaller house in the county is Rosehill, Alderley (c), of
1860, and *Teulon*'s is Huntley Manor (v) of 1862, very spiky like
the coniferous trees all round. Hatherop Castle (c) was rebuilt

by *Clutton* in 1850-6, in an English historical style, and Rend-comb (c) by *P. C. Hardwick* in 1863 in the Italianate. *Anthony Salvin* did a good job of restoration at Thornbury Castle (v) in 1854, and *Sir George Gilbert Scott* at Sudeley Castle (c) the same year. *J. L. Pearson*'s house, Quarwood, Stow-on-the-Wold (c), has virtually been destroyed. Amongst the work of local archi-tects it is perhaps worth mentioning Tibberton Court (v), which was made to look Italianate by *James Medland* in 1852, Foscombe near Ashleworth (v) built by *Thomas Fulljames* c.1860 in Dec Gothic, and Haresfield Court (v) by *Francis Niblett* in the 1860s, again enlarged in 1892-3 by *Waller & Son*.

This brings us to later Victorian mansions. Lechlade Manor (c) was built by *J. L. Pearson* in 1872-3, the SE wing at Lypiatt Park (c) by *T. H. Wyatt* in 1876, Batsford (c) in 1888-92 by *George & Peto*, Edgeworth (c) in 1899 by *Sir E. George*, and Forthampton (v) c. 1891, by *Philip Webb*. A few other miscel-laneous Victorian buildings are of interest, like the factory by *G. F. Bodley* at Ebley, Stroud (c), and his school at Bisley (c), 1854, Highnam Vicarage (v) by *Woodyer*, 1852, the old rectory, Wickwar (v), by *George Devey*, 1864, the Tyndale Monument, North Nibley (c), by *S. S. Teulon*, 1866, Raymeadow Farm, Tod-dington (v), by *W. E. Nesfield*, 1876, Redesdale Market Hall, Moreton-in-Marsh (c), by *Sir E. George*, 1887, and the Art School at Stroud (c) by *J. P. Seddon*, 1890-9. The philanthropic vogue for erecting memorial drinking fountains produced some charming little buildings like the gabled water-troughs at Bisley (c) built in 1863, and the drinking fountain at Mickle-ton (c) designed by *Burges* in 1875; one in memory of a member of the Tractarian Prevost family at Stinchcombe (c) also comes to mind.

The EARLY TWENTIETH CENTURY provided many Cots-wold style country houses for well-to-do clients who now lived in this county because of its unspoiled nature and sporting facilities. This coincided with the Arts and Crafts Movement, and the post-Ruskin interest in the building materials readily available. *Sir Guy Dawber*, who had learned all about Cotswold stone when working under *Sir Ernest George* at Batsford (c), was building houses on his own at the turn of the century, such as Hartpury House (v), near Gloucester, and several in the North Cotswolds like the Old Stone House at Oddington, Hill Place at Lower Swell, Eyford Park, and Burdocks at Fairford. *Sir Edwin Lutyens* altered Stonehouse Court (v) in 1906, and Miserden Park (c) in 1920. He built Abbotswood at Lower Swell (c) in

1902, and later the War Memorial there, and Copse Hill and cottages at Upper Slaughter (c) in 1906–9. Willersey House (c), 1912, is by *A. N. Prentice*, and Fox Hill *c.*1914, by *J. L. Ball.*
102 *Detmar Blow* built Hilles, Harescombe (c), for himself, *c.*1914. Ilsome Farmhouse, Tetbury (c), is by *M. Chesterton, c.*1922. A great deal of architectural work was done in Cirencester (c) over a period of some forty years by *Vincent Alexander Lawson*, a civil engineer who as a young man had come to the district to prepare a plan to convert the Thames–Severn Canal into a railway between Stroud and Cirencester. He died in 1928. Meanwhile Chipping Campden (c) had become the centre of a Guild of Handicrafts. *Charles Robert Ashbee* was born in 1863, was in Bodley's office in 1887, and had become so involved in the Ruskinian philosophy of craftsmanship and honest work that he founded a Guild of Handicrafts in 1888 in the East End of London, which he moved to Campden in 1902. In all one hundred and fifty men, women, and children, nearly all of them Londoners, came, among them about fifty working guildsmen. Of these *George Hart* the silversmith still works in the old Silk Mill they took over, now with his son and grandson.* The influence of Ashbee and later of *Frederick Landseer Griggs* has left a lasting impression on Campden. Griggs built his own house in the traditional Cotswold manner. It was later bought by Sir Frank Brangwyn.

Ernest Gimson, however, is the name to conjure with. He was what W. R. Lethaby called an 'idealist individualist'. Gimson met William Morris at Leicester in his father's house in 1884. Morris probably suggested that Gimson should enter the office of J. D. Sedding, which was next door to the headquarters of Morris & Co. in London. He soon got put on the committee of the Society for the Protection of Ancient Buildings, and so for years was in close contact with Philip Webb, and others of the coterie like Lethaby, and Emery Walker, and also Sydney Cockerell and Detmar Blow, who as young men had travelled with Ruskin. In London too he met the brothers *Ernest and Sidney Barnsley* from Birmingham, the former in Sedding's

* *George Hart* has made silver for a great many Gloucestershire churches as well as other places all over the world. The following churches in Gloucestershire have work by him besides the cathedral: Batsford, Charlton Kings, Cheltenham parish church, St Stephen's and St Luke's, Bourton-on-the-Water, Great Rissington, Amberley, Daglingworth, Weston-sub-Edge, Chipping Campden, Ebrington, Tewkesbury, Minchinhampton, Hawling, Miserden, Oddington, Stow-on-the-Wold, Northleach, Blockley, Dean Close School Chapel, Cheltenham, and Prinknash Abbey.

office and the latter in Norman Shaw's. Lethaby writes: 'It is a curious fact that this Society, engaged in an intense study of antiquity, became a school of rational builders and modern building.' Not only did Gimson design but he also learnt the crafts of modelled plaster-work and furniture-making. The Art-Workers Guild was established in 1884, and made the Arts and Crafts Exhibition Society possible in 1888. Gimson exhibited furniture in 1890, and the short-lived Kenton & Co. was formed. His work included the ebony stalls inlaid with ivory in St Andrew's Chapel in Westminster Cathedral. Gimson and the Barnsleys now moved to Pinbury Park in the Cotswolds, described by Alfred Powell at that time as a 'mystery land of difficult hills and deeply wooded valleys dividing the Vale of White Horse from the Severn and the Welsh borderland'. It proved the ideal place for their purpose. For the next twenty-five years they lived and worked here and at Sapperton. The country was a necessity to Gimson. He absorbed everything in nature around him. Socially he was all the time 'drawing together and invigorating whatever threads of true village life were still discernible'. His time was largely taken up with making designs for his cabinet-makers, such as *Peter Waals*, the Dutch foreman, whose standard of workmanship was so high that everything had to be as near perfect as possible, and for his blacksmiths, the best of whom was *Alfred Bucknell*, the brilliant son of a local wheelwright. Gimson's gospel was that of William Morris, of healthy enjoyment for all in making useful and beautiful things; but he could never follow Morris into the ways of mass-production, and so his furniture was expensive and only within the reach of the well-to-do. However, the demand was there, so much so that he had little time for architecture. He built a house for himself at Sapperton, but it has been seriously damaged by fire, and he altered Waterlane House near Bisley. The addition which he built on to Pinbury, and which contains the drawing room with his beautiful stone chimneypiece, modelled plaster ceiling, and splendidly proportioned bay-window looking out towards the great yews of the Nun's Walk, is his architectural memorial. He died aged fifty-four in 1919, just in time not to see the shattering of his Utopia. It would be nice to be able to stop this Introduction here, and on further consideration there seems to be no valid reason for not doing so, for in spite of so much technical progress there is little to report except that we now have a Motorway over the Severn and two Atomic Power Stations alongside. Apart from the many obvious advantages accruing to the dis-

c
101

v
102
&
103

trict by these developments, aesthetically too they are most important additions. This cannot be said of the skyscraper which appeared in the centre of Cheltenham (v) in 1968. It has the unfortunate effect of dominating everything around, and has completely spoiled the scale of the perfectly landscaped town, so greatly admired hitherto.

READING LIST

The first item to be entered in a reading list must be the *Transactions of the Bristol and Gloucestershire Archaeological Society*, begun in 1876, and with now some eighty-seven volumes. The *Victoria County History* published vol. II in 1907, and then nothing till vol. VI came out in 1965, edited by C. R. Elrington. The county is well served with ancient histories. Sir Robert Atkyns's marvellous history *The Ancient and Present State of Gloucestershire*, published in 1712, with seventy-three copper plates by Kip, must be an inexhaustible source of wonder and interest. *A Collection of Gloucestershire Antiquities* by Samuel Lysons, 1804, has one hundred and ten plates which are of the greatest possible interest to the historian. *Historical, Monumental, and Genealogical Collections relative to the County of Gloucester*, by Ralph Bigland, 1791, has splendid plates engraved by Bonnor. Then there are *A New History of Gloucestershire*, by Samuel Rudder, 1779, printed in Cirencester, with plates of country houses engraved by Bonnor, and others; *The History and Antiquities of Gloucester* by Thomas Rudge, 1803; *Abstracts of Records and Manuscripts respecting the County of Gloucester* by T. D. Fosbrook, 1807; *Picturesque and Topographical Account of Cheltenham* by T. D. Fosbrook, 1826; Griffith's *New Historial Description of Cheltenham*, 1826; *History of Cheltenham* by John Goding, 1863, and *A Handbook for Travellers in Gloucestershire*, John Murray, 1844 (third edition).

Twentieth-century publications are *The Little Guide*, revised by H. Stratton-Davis, 1949; *Cotswold Stone* by Freda Derrick, 1948; *Gloucestershire Studies* by H. P. R. Finberg, 1957; *A Physical, Social and Economic Survey and Plan for Gloucestershire* by Gordon E. Payne; *The Cotswolds*, by E. R. Delderfield, 1961. More specialized: *Old Cottages, Farmhouses, and other stone Buildings in the Cotswold District* by W. Galsworthy Davie and E. Guy Dawber, 1904; *The Church Plate of Gloucestershire*, by J. T. Evans, 1906; *Ancient Cotswold Churches* by Ulric Daubeny, 1921; *Old Gloucestershire Churches* by W. Hobart Bird, 1928;

A Cotswold Village by J. Arthur Gibbs, 1898; *Cheltenham* by
Bryan Little, 1952; *A History of Cheltenham* by Gwen Hart,
1965; *A History of Chipping Campden* by Christopher Whitfield,
1958; *Wotton-under-Edge* by E. S. Lindley, 1962; *Dymock Down
the Ages* by J. E. Gethyn-Jones, 1966; *Gloucestershire Woollen
Mills* by Jennifer Tann, 1967; *Geology Explained in the Severn
Vale and Cotswolds* by William Dreghorn, 1967; *Geology
Explained in the Forest of Dean and Wye Valley* by William
Dreghorn, 1968; *Ernest Gimson, His Life and Work*, by W. R.
Lethaby, Aldred Powell, and F. L. Griggs, 1924; *By Chance I
did Rove*, by Norman Jewson. This is a wide list of local reading;
but of course many books of a much broader connotation have
direct bearing on the architecture of the county.

GEOLOGY AND BUILDING MATERIALS

Gloucestershire is a magnificent county for the geologist; many
of the principal varieties of English rock can be found within a
radius of fifty miles from Gloucester. The Palaeozoic rocks crop
out in the Forest of Dean, where we have carboniferous and
Devonian rocks in abundance and not far away the Silurian
rocks of May Hill. Northwards we come to the pre-Cambrian
crystalline rocks of the Malverns, which are at least seven
hundred million years old. The Mesozoic rocks, comprising the
Triassic, Jurassic, and Cretaceous, are displayed in the Severn
Vale, the Cotswolds, and the chalk hills near Swindon across
the border in Wiltshire. When the shire of Gloucester was first
constituted in the C9 no attention was paid to natural or geo-
graphical boundaries, and a purely artificial unit was created of
some eight hundred thousand acres, comprising at least three
different kinds of landscape. Anyone who cares to go to Haresfield Beacon (v), 3 m. NW of Stroud, can see for himself what has
happened. Looking W, in the middle distance the Severn makes
a vast loop round Arlingham (v), and then broadens out as the
tidal water flows down to pass under the new Bridge and meet
the Wye at Chepstow. Beyond it rise the wooded scarps of Old
Red Sandstone which form the E edge of the Forest of Dean.
In the foreground, 700 ft below, lies the Vale of Berkeley with
its old timber-framed dairy-farms and orchards, extending into
the Vale of Gloucester further to the N, and the Bristol
quarter to the S. Haresfield Beacon juts out into the Vale. To the
S there is a view of Stinchcombe Hill (C), a similar headland.

Viewed from the other side of the river, the Cotswold scarp, or edge, is impressive not for its height, since at its highest point at v2 Cleeve Hill (C) it is only 1,083 ft, but for its length. For about fifty miles as the crow flies from Dyrham to Dover's Hill near Chipping Campden, the great cliff presents a virtually unbroken skyline. It is the w edge of a limestone plateau, which dipping always gently to the E or SE merges finally into the clay plains of Oxford. The receding Cotswold scarp has left several detached outliers such as Robin's Wood Hill and Churchdown (v). At Haresfield we have a bird's-eye view of the three landscapes, Forest, Vale, and Wold.

The Forest of Dean is a plateau of which the rim is formed by resistant Old Red Sandstone. Within it three lofty ridges, each running almost due N and S, break up the surface with such effect that it would be hard to find a level area of more than two hundred acres. The syncline is composed of three series of rocks, the Old Red Sandstone outer ring, massive carboniferous limestones, followed by the central part of our saucer filled with Coal Measures, sandstones, and shales. The Old Red Sandstone (Devonian) is a thick red sandstone – a good building stone (e.g. Hereford Cathedral). The limestones, blue-grey to buff, give rise to the magnificent scenery of the Wye Gorge at Symond's Yat and at Chepstow. The Coal Measures country is the heart of Dean and is mainly forested, making it without doubt the prettiest coalfield in Britain. For nearly 2,000 years the Forest of Dean has been a source of excellent iron-ore deposits, which are found in pockets in the Carboniferous Limestone, in particular the Crease Limestone.

The clay Vales of Gloucester, Berkeley, and the Severn in general stretch almost from Bristol to Worcester, and the foundation is composed of the softer rocks of the Trias and Lower Jurassic. It is the Blue Lias Clay which dominates the Vale of the Severn in Gloucestershire. This blue clay, often more than 700 ft thick, is pre-eminently pasture land; on the other hand it has its economic uses for bricks and tiles, and in some places these are still made, e.g. at Stonehouse (v). Although the clay lowlands suffer from excessive dampness in winter, in places there are patches of superficial sand deposits; only 10 to 20 ft in thickness, they gave the early Saxon settlers dry sites for their villages (e.g. Twyning and Cheltenham, both v). The general name for the interglacial deposit is Cheltenham Sands.

The limestone of the Cotswolds is composed of small rounded grains of calcium carbonate packed together like the roe of a fish.

From this resemblance the stone is called oolite, meaning egg-stone. The Inferior Oolite, so called because it is the lower and older stratum of this limestone, is tilted upwards at its western edge. There it forms the Cotswold scarp, and it includes all the highest points. Further E it dips under the Great Oolite, the newer rock which extends across into Oxfordshire. Some beds of Great Oolite provide fine-grained stone, called freestone, which can be cut or carved very easily when freshly quarried, but hardens on exposure.

Others provide thin layers of rock which can be split by exposure to frost, thus producing the stone tiles which have always till now been used for roofing, and are called Stonesfield or Cotswold slates, though they are not slate in the geological sense. The correct term should be 'tilestone', for it is in fact a sandy limestone which splits nicely into thin layers; an alternative name would be fissile limestone, meaning that it foliates like the leaves of a book. A tilestone with a continuous groove at the back indicates that it was made in medieval times. Grooving was probably only done on large tilestones to carry the great weight on the oak beams. A hole was also made for the insertion of a wooden peg to hang it on. The earliest example of the use of the Great Oolite Tilestone is in the Neolithic long barrow at Belas Knap, Sudeley (C), of c.2000 B.C., but in this case it was used for drystone walling. The Romans used tilestone for roofing their villas and they gave them pointed ends. A modern example of the re-use of Roman tiles is on a summer house at Water-combe House, Bisley (C). At Chipping Campden (C) the roofs of medieval buildings are particularly well preserved. They are carefully graduated, and the huge stone tiles at the bottom of the roofs often weigh 50lb. or more, requiring enormous oak beams. Their weight is one of the reasons for the decline of the stone tile industry, and the only way to obtain them now is to buy them off some old unwanted barn, or to apply to Collyweston in Northamptonshire, where they are still being produced.

Throughout the Middle Ages, Vale dwellers found that the tough Quartz Conglomerate from the Devonian rocks of the Forest made excellent millstones for both cider and grain. The best stone that Dean can produce today is the famous Pennant Sandstone found in the Coal Measures series. It is also found on the other side of the river, NE of Bristol. This sandstone has a great range of colour, from blue-grey to yellow, and the well-known Bixhead Quarries near Cannop Ponds are very busy even today exporting stone for public buildings as far afield as London.

Tufaceous limestone is found near Dursley, and was used at Berkeley Castle (v).

There is no doubt that much of the beauty of the Cotswolds lies in its stone churches and other old buildings made out of oolite. It can shade from yellow, through cream to deep brown. The variations in colour are due to an iron mineral called Limonite, so that in some areas where the rock is richer in this iron (more ferruginous) we can get deeper yellows and browns, as for example the famous yellow Guiting stone (c). Guiting stone is still quarried at Coscombe and has good weathering qualities. One special feature of oolitic limestone is that the fossils in it are very finely comminuted. If this were not so, frost would soon etch the fossils out, leaving cavities in the rock causing it to crumble. The matrix of some oolitic limestones is rather soft or contains cross-bedding, and we can see in many old buildings where the stone has crumbled and weathered much more quickly than in others. In the upper divisions of the Inferior Oolite some of the limestones have irregular bedding, so that it is possible to pull out ragged slabs of stone called ragstones, or 'presents', and pendles, which the medieval shepherds found very useful for enclosing their enormous sheep runs, and which have been used ever since for drystone walls. They are still produced at Huntsman's Quarry, Naunton (c). Today in some quarries, such as Westington at Chipping Campden, and Farmington (both c), the oolite is sawn into blocks of ashlar for indoor use such as fireplaces, or special requirements of restoration like replacing stone mullions for windows, and of course particularly for the whole range of church restoration, and it seems that this is still an economic use for natural stone in the Cotswolds. The future of Cotswold building-stone quarries is not very bright, though everyone interested must hope that Coscombe Quarry and every other natural building-stone quarry such as Tetbury (c) should continue to do well, because high labour costs make a large degree of mechanization necessary. It has unfortunately been discovered that it is far more economical to crush the stone, mix it with cement and other colouring ingredients such as sand, and so produce a reconstructed stone to any required shape.

In *The Pattern of English Building*, Mr Alec Clifton-Taylor writes: 'Nothing is more striking about Cotswold buildings than the visual accord which they achieve with the landscape in which they are placed. . . . In the Cotswolds the buildings themselves, even the barns, are of such high quality that at every turn it is they that we notice first. The landscape here plays second fiddle: it is the background, the mise-en-scène, the frame. That is why, for those who cherish our building heritage, the Cotswolds occupy a special place, and why any development proposals affecting this region cannot be too carefully scrutinized.'

Cotswold stone has been extensively used for making roads in the past, but for heavy motor traffic it is not hard enough. The hardness of a rock is measured by its crushing power (for example most Cotswold stone will crush to powder when the pressure exceeds about 8,000 lb. per square inch); but the tough carboniferous limestones of the Chepstow area have a crushing power of over 40,000 lb. per square inch, so there we have very active quarries producing road metal for the new motorways. It can be safely stated that from the point of view of economic geology the most valuable materials within the county are the sands and gravels that lie as scattered superficial deposits in the Severn and Thames valleys. About fifty thousand years ago an ice sheet occupied the Midlands, and the melt waters from the ice became great rivers depositing sands and gravels southwards. In places the gravels are up to 20 ft in thickness, and the most important workings are near Beckford, Whitminster, and Twyning in the Severn area, and at South Cerney and Fairford on the Upper Thames.

INTRODUCTION TO THE PREHISTORIC REMAINS

BY L. V. GRINSELL

The earliest evidence of human settlement in Gloucestershire so far found occurs in the form of flint implements, usually hand-axes, of the Acheulian phase of the LOWER PALAEOLITHIC period, which have been found in the gravels of tributaries of the Severn, especially at Barnwood (v), and in those of the Upper Thames and its tributaries, where they have been recorded from Bourton-on-the-Water, Lechlade, Meysey Hampton, and Poole Keynes (all c), together with animal remains of the period.

The MESOLITHIC period may be represented by microlithic flint implements, which have been found in various parts of the Cotswolds, especially in the Stroud region and on Tog Hill near Bristol; it is uncertain to what extent these microlithic cultures survived into the Neolithic period.

The NEOLITHIC period (c. 3000–1700 B.C.)* was notable for the introduction of agriculture and pasture, of pottery-making, and of the art of grinding and polishing implements of flint and stone. It is strongly represented on the Cotswolds. The daily life of the period is illustrated by large numbers of leaf-shaped flint arrow-heads which imply the use of the bow and arrow for hunting and warfare; the Royce Collection alone includes more than a thousand leaf-arrowheads from the small area between Stow-on-the-Wold and the Slaughters (all c). Axe-heads, often ground or polished, used largely for digging and woodland clearance, are sometimes found on and around the Cotswolds. They are of either flint or stone. The flint used in prehistoric times on the Cotswolds for implements was ultimately derived from the chalk downs of Wessex. The Marlborough Downs would have been the nearest source of supply; but if the earlier Cotswold long barrows owe their origin to impulses from North-Western France, and the shale beads from the Eyford (Upper Slaughter) and Notgrove long barrows (both c) were of shale from Kimmeridge, it is possible that some of the flint may have come from the chalk downs of Dorset. Application of the techniques of implement petrology to the examination of the stone axe-heads from Gloucestershire has shown that four stone axes and three flakes (the latter from the Nailsworth (c) area) are of material from the stone-axe working sites at Graig Lwyd near Penmaenmawr in Caernarvonshire: a fact of particular interest in view of the presence of chambered long barrows of Cotswold–Severn type such as Capel Garmon and Maen Pebyll in the region of the Conway Valley within a few miles of the Graig Lwyd axe factories. Six of the Gloucestershire stone axe-heads are from greenstone working-sites in Cornwall, and four from the axe factory sites around Great Langdale in Westmorland. Neolithic pottery from the county includes both Windmill Hill (earlier) and Peterborough (later) bowls, as well as some rare pottery spoons from a long barrow on Cow Common, Swell (c).

Little is known of Neolithic settlement sites in Britain generally. Pits containing Late Neolithic material have, however, been examined at Bourton-on-the-Water and on Lower Knapp Farm, Cam – both (c) and both low-lying sites in contrast to the distribution of the burial-sites of the period.

* The dates here given may need to be pushed back by some 500–300 years between the Neolithic and the Late Bronze Age if the proposed correction of radiocarbon dating by Bristlecone-pine tree-ring dating gains general acceptance.

Architecturally, the only visible remains of the Neolithic period in the county are the long barrows, all of which are on the Cotswolds. They were essentially collective tombs, and although the records seldom permit precise statements on the number of individuals represented by the bones found, it is believed that Hetty Pegler's Tump, Uley, contained about twenty-eight human skeletons, and Belas Knap, near Winchcombe, about thirty-eight (both c). These long barrows fall into two main groups: true-entrance (or 'terminally chambered') long barrows, and false-entrance (or 'laterally chambered') long barrows. The former contain a true entrance at the larger (eastern) end, leading to a central gallery with burial-chambers off-set from this gallery in pairs (called by Glyn Daniel 'transepted gallery graves'). The number of pairs of burial-chambers in the Cotswold examples still accessible is either one (Nympsfield) or two (Hetty Pegler's Tump and Notgrove; all c). Hetty Pegler's Tump is the only roofed example of this type on the Cotswolds still accessible. Similar though more rudimentary forms of tomb are known in the Pornic region in North-Western France, from which area the Cotswold examples may have been ultimately derived.

The false-entrance (or 'laterally chambered') long barrows have a dummy entrance, and burial-chambers entered from the sides of the mound. The finest visible example is Belas Knap, restored about 1930 by the Ministry of Works; others are Windmill Tump, Rodmarton (c), with two opposed burial-chambers having porthole entrances (at present filled in to protect them from winter frosts and other hazards). The only porthole-entrance burial-chamber now to be seen in Gloucestershire is that NW of Avening (c), which was removed from a local long barrow in 1806.

The Cotswold long barrows are of far more than local importance: they form the major element in the Severn–Cotswold Group of chambered long barrows, first described as such by Glyn Daniel.

About 1900/1800 B.C., a group of predominantly round-headed people reached Britain, mainly from the Rhineland and the Low Countries but perhaps partly from France, and these people are known as the BEAKER FOLK from the pottery beakers associated with them. They buried their dead in what were essentially single graves, sometimes apparently flat, but often beneath round barrows as distinct from the earlier long barrows. The Beaker folk came into southern Britain in two main waves, one with bell-beakers (type B beakers), and the other with long-necked beakers (type A beakers).

Only about a dozen beakers (or parts of them) are so far known from Gloucestershire; although both bell-beakers and long-necked beakers occur among them, almost all the Gloucestershire beakers are degenerate. This strongly suggests that the Neolithic people who built the Cotswold long barrows delayed the intrusion of the Beaker folk. The large number of barbed-and-tanged flint arrowheads found especially on the eastern fringe of the Cotswolds (there are 3,142 in the Royce Collection alone) could well be evidence of efforts of the considerable numbers of Beaker folk in the Oxford region and the Upper Thames valley to gain a footing on the Cotswolds. The round-headed skull of a young man, found in the blocking of Belas Knap long barrow, if of a Beaker man, as is most likely, shows the fate of those Beaker folk who did succeed in penetrating Cotswold long barrow territory. On the other hand, the siting of several round barrows in immediate proximity to long barrows, as at Belas Knap, Sudeley, Cow Common, Swell, Bown Hill, Woodchester, Colnpen, Coln St Dennis, Eyford Hill, Upper Slaughter (all c), and elsewhere, suggests eventual intermingling.

There are about 350 known round barrows in the county; the former existence of some others is attested by field names. Some of these would have been Beaker period but most of them are BRONZE AGE. This number is small compared with Wiltshire (2,200) and Dorset (1,800), and there is no doubt that the Bronze Age occupation of Gloucestershire was slight compared with the Neolithic. Nearly all the Gloucestershire round barrows are on the Cotswolds; but there are a few in the valley of the Lower Wye, and a few formerly existed at Frampton-on-Severn (v) and perhaps elsewhere in the Severn valley. Not many reach impressive proportions; but examples at Bitton (v), Nan Tow's Tump, Didmarton (c), Wyck Beacon, Wyck Rissington (c), and the group of about eight in Hull Plantations, Longborough (c), are among the more noteworthy. The (destroyed) round barrow at Ivy Lodge near Woodchester (c) yielded a degenerate necked (type A) beaker. The best-known grave group came from a round barrow at Snowshill (c), in which a burial (probably male) with grooved bronze dagger, tanged bronze dagger or spearhead, bronze pin, and stone axe-hammer were found in 1881; these are now in the British Museum.

An important factor concerning the Bronze Age in Gloucestershire is the evidence of trade between Ireland and Wessex via the Severn estuary and the Bristol Avon. This is attested by the finding of decorated flanged axes of Irish origin in a small hoard from Westbury-on-Trym, and other implements of Irish origin such as a socketed spearhead from Bristol; also probably the gold-covered 'sun-disc' from a round barrow on Lansdown above Bath. Use was probably made of much of this route for transporting the 'blue-stones' from the Prescelly Hills in Pembrokeshire to Stonehenge. Irish bronze implements from Gloucestershire proper include decorated flanged axes from Newent (v) and Whittington (c), and two socketed spearheads from Rodborough (c). Occupation of the county in the later Bronze Age seems to have been very slight; but a hoard of eight socketed axes (five claimed as of Welsh type) from Bourton-on-the-Water (c) suggests a continued use of the Lower Severn as a prehistoric thoroughfare. Heavy stone axe-hammers from the working-site in the region of Corndon Hill, on the Shropshire–Montgomeryshire border, found at Cromhall (v) and Saltford (Bristol Avon), were probably traded down the Severn.

From about 550/500 B.C. onwards, the earliest IRON AGE peoples reached Gloucestershire. One group of immigrants (Iron Age A) seems to have moved up the Severn and gained a foothold on Kings Weston Hill N of Bristol, where their pottery and other material have been identified at a small defensive enclosure and with cremations in round barrows. These people also left their traces in the Severn valley near Gloucester and Cheltenham (v), on Cleeve Hill (c), and in the N Cotswold hill-forts of the Knolls, Oxenton (v), and Shenberrow, Stanton (c), s of Broadway. They also reached the Cotswolds from the E: their pottery was found on the old turf-line beneath the rampart at Salmonsbury, Bourton-on-the-Water; and some of the more slender univallate earthworks, probably primarily pastoral, in the E part of the Cotswolds may have been built by them.

There were three main phases of Iron Age B (La Tène) culture in Britain. The earliest (c3 B.C.) does not appear to have reached Gloucestershire. The next, largely a fusion of A and first B elements, reached South Gloucestershire around 150 B.C. Its characteristic linear-tooled pottery has been found at the Knolls, Oxenton, the bivallate fort of Salmonsbury, where this culture continued until the Belgic phase of occupation superseded it around 25 B.C., and at a few apparently undefended Iron Age sites in the county. This is the period from which probably date the iron currency-bars, about 147 of which have been found at

Salmonsbury, and 394 at Meon Hill hill-fort just over the border of Gloucestershire into Warwickshire. The univallate hill-fort of Lydney (v) yielded finds of this culture; and so did Bury Hill camp, Winterbourne (v), N of Bristol, a bivallate hill-fort. The tendency of the people of this culture to build bivallate hill-forts with closely set ramparts may also be illustrated by those at Painswick (not yet excavated) and Shenberrow, Stanton (both c), when more fully explored.

The final B culture (100/75 B.C. until about A.D. 43/50) is distinguished by stamped pottery, including the so-called 'duck-stamped' ware. On present evidence its distribution in Gloucestershire is limited to the area between the Severn and the W scarp of the Cotswolds. This pottery has so far been found at the Knolls hill-fort, Oxenton (v), at Beckbury hill-fort, Temple Guiting (c), and at certain apparently undefended sites in the county. N of Gloucestershire it has been found at Bredon Hill, Worcestershire, and other hill-forts in the Wye Valley and that of its tributary the Lugg, including Sutton Walls near Hereford: this indeed is the classic region for this pottery. Stamped wares of this type occur also in the Iberian peninsula and Brittany, and either the pottery or the idea of making it is believed to have been brought by immigrants from the Iberian peninsula via Brittany, the Cornish coast, and the Bristol Channel; indeed Dr Kathleen Kenyon suggested that the English varieties be called 'Bristol Channel B ware'.* The Iberian bronze figurine from Aust Cliff (v), now in the British Museum, although perhaps later in date but still pre-Roman, is another illustration of the use of this route. Some of the univallate hill-forts between the Severn and the Cotswolds may well date from this phase, but none of them has yet been excavated.

Of the three phases of Iron Age C, only the latest is known to be represented in Gloucestershire; and it covers the period from about 25 B.C. well into the Early Roman period (about A.D. 50/60). By the beginning of this period, if not earlier, the tribe settled in Gloucestershire E of the Severn and its environs was known as the Dobunni, probably identical with the Bodunni of Dio Cassius, and from now onwards they can conveniently be called the Belgic Dobunni.

There may first (around 25 B.C.) have been a tribal capital with mint for uninscribed coins in South Gloucestershire, per-

---

* The substance of this account of 'duck' pottery may need modification in the light of current investigations by Dr P. S. Peacock of Birmingham University, to appear in *Proc. Prehist. Soc.*, vol. XXXIV for 1968 (1969).

haps at Minchinhampton Bulwarks (C), an elaborate system of earthwork defences, probably originally combined with woodland, resembling those at Bagendon (C; see below); both systems of earthworks have their closest parallels in the territory of their eastern neighbours and (at that time) allies, the Catuvellauni of Hertfordshire and Essex, then under Cunobelin. The finding of Belgic Dobunnic pottery on the old land surface beneath the rampart at Amberley Camp, Minchinhampton, shows that earthwork to have been built either then or later.

About A.D. 10, another tribal capital was founded, at Bagendon: a series of earthworks combined with a wooded scarp, enclosing some 200 acres, about 3 miles NNW of Cirencester. This included a mint for coining in silver, and for producing base coin in bronze. The Bagendon settlement was an important centre for trade and industry, especially for metalworking; iron from the Forest of Dean, lead and silver from Mendip, and other metals were within their reach. The inhabitants lived in huts with stone floors and foundations, half-timbered and wattle-and-daub walls, and thatched roofs, and obtained luxury goods such as red glazed wares from Italy and southern France, and glass from the eastern Mediterranean. The NE Belgic Dobunni also occupied Salmonsbury near Bourton-on-the-Water (C).

About A.D. 20–30, the uninscribed Dobunnic coinage was followed by the issue of gold and silver coins inscribed ANTED and EISU.

After the death of Cunobelin (A.D. 41), the alliance between the Belgic Dobunni and the Catuvellauni became disturbed because of the aggressive policies of his sons Caratacus and Togodomnus. Bodvoc, leader of the NE Belgic Dobunni, was pro-Roman and came to terms with the Roman invaders in Kent in A.D. 43; the coins inscribed with his name bear lettering in a far more Roman style than any of the other inscribed coins of the Dobunni. The settlement at Bagendon was within the next decade or two superseded by Corinium Dobunnorum, the Roman tribal capital (now Cirencester; C). As coins of Bodvoc have not yet been found at Bagendon but have been found at Cirencester, Bodvoc himself may have moved early to the new capital.

After the death of Cunobelin, the SW Belgic Dobunni became opposed to Rome, separated from the rest of the tribe, and appointed their own coin-issuing kings – certainly Corio (c. A.D. 43) and probably Comux (c. A.D. 47). Either at or before the conquest they spread into NE Somerset.

The extended female burial with decorated bronze mirror and other objects (Gloucester City Museum), found on Birdlip Hill (c) in 1879, has been dated *c.*A.D. 20–5. The mirror is similar to that from Desborough (Northants), and both find-spots are significantly on the Jurassic route from Lincolnshire s w over the Cotswolds into NE Somerset: a route dating from before the Iron Age, which increased in importance during that period, and was later closely followed by the Roman Fosse Way. The Belgic Dobunni normally cremated their dead, and cremations of the period have been identified from Bagendon and Barnwood.*

ROMAN GLOUCESTERSHIRE

BY BARRY CUNLIFFE

In the years following A.D. 43 the Roman army swept rapidly across Gloucestershire, snuffing out all resistance and driving dissidents w into Wales. For a while it seems that imperial policy was to hold only part of Britain, creating a frontier zone across the country based for part of its course on the line of the river Severn. It is to this period, *c.*43–9, that the earliest group of Roman forts and the initial road-grid in Gloucestershire belong. The main artery of the defensive system was the Fosse Way,

---

* A word must here be said regarding the principles on which the sites have been selected for the gazetteer. Only the most notable long and round barrows have been included; and preference has been given to those which are most worth visiting. A complete list, with full references, was published in *Transactions of the Bristol and Gloucestershire Archaeological Society*, vol. 79 (1961). Selection of Iron Age hill-forts was much more difficult, because of major differences in recent assessments by the Ordnance Survey Archaeology division, as reflected in their *Map of Southern Britain in the Iron Age* (1962), the work of the Royal Commission on Historical Monuments (in its preliminary stages for the Cotswolds) and of the writer. The general principle has been to exclude sites that are almost destroyed or for other reasons barely worth visiting, and sites that are considered doubtful. A warning must here be given regarding the use of the terms univallate, bivallate, and multivallate as applied to the number of ramparts. Many hill-forts are univallate on one side and bivallate on the others; and some are partly multivallate. Again, if there is a small counterscarp outside the ditch of an otherwise univallate hill-fort, it is generally so-called; if the counterscarp assumes larger proportions, the hill-fort can perhaps better be described as bivallate. For these reasons no two independent surveys of the hill-forts of a region will be absolutely consistent in such details. The writer gratefully acknowledges the help received from Dr Isobel F. Smith of the RCHM, but would add that the final decisions have always been his own, and have sometimes differed from those so far made by that body.

which served both as a means for rapidly deploying troops and as a base to which the main supply routes from the s could be linked. The principal road junction within the area of modern Gloucestershire was at Cirencester (c), where roads from Colchester and London converge on the Fosse. It is hardly surprising that so important a site was defended by a military garrison housed in a sequence of forts which were several times rebuilt and re-sited. The 18-mile wide strip of land lying between the Fosse and the E bank of the Severn was, at this stage, regarded as a military zone, laced on its w fringe by another road running approximately parallel to the Fosse and linking a further group of forts, of which two are known to fall near or within our area, one at Sea Mills (Bristol), at the confluence between the Avon and the Trym, the other in the Kingsholme suburb of Gloucester (v). These early forts, and others which may yet be discovered, seem to have been defended by contingents of auxiliaries; two, the *ala Indiana* and the *ala Thracum*, are known to have served at Cirencester, and a cohort of Thracians was probably housed at Kingsholme at this time.

The geography of Western Britain and the warlike character of those still unconquered, soon showed that entrenchment behind the Fosse line was an inefficient and impracticable policy. Thus by 49 a new forward drive was initiated, but before large sections of the army could be committed to campaigning far into the territory of the Silures in South Wales, certain preparations had to be made. One of the most far-reaching was that the Legio XX was brought up from Colchester and housed in a new legionary fortress built at Gloucester, where it was to remain for many years. But gradually, as hostilities moved further W and then N, the army pulled out of Gloucestershire; the fort at Cirencester was evacuated some time after A.D. 60, but it was not until thirty years later that the military presence at Gloucester was finally removed. Civilian development proceeded rapidly. The site of the old fortress at Gloucester was retained by the government and a colonia, a chartered town for the settlement of veterans, was laid out within the military fortifications, enclosed by a new stone wall. Its name, colonia Nervia Glevensium, shows that its foundation date lay during the reign of Nerva in A.D. 96–8. Yet in spite of these auspicious beginnings Gloucester does not appear to have thrived; true, many simple mosaics and a monumental façade have been found within its walls and an official tile-making industry belonging to the town was exporting its produce widely within the region, but in sheer size and grandeur

Gloucester was soon outstripped by the spectacular growth of Cirencester, where civil development had begun at least a generation earlier. By the end of the C2 the town defences were enclosing an area of 240 acres (five times as large as Gloucester), and its great forum and basilica was second in size only to London. Within the walls wealthy town houses abounded. In the C4 a change in status from a cantonal capital to a seat of provincial government gave an added boost to an already vigorous growth.

The growth of Cirencester must have been largely dependent upon the wealth of the region over which it ruled, but as yet all too little is known of the surrounding countryside. Villas, many of them extremely rich, cluster round the town, but of their growth and economic basis we are still largely ignorant, and practically no work has been done on the problems of the peasant settlement pattern. It is, however, fair to say that by the C4 great wealth had accumulated in the hands of a few, sufficient to provide luxurious mansions and patronage for a lively school of mosaicists based, presumably, upon Cirencester.

The end came very gradually. In Cirencester recent excavations have shown that the forum was kept clean well into the C5, but eventually civilized government disintegrated so far as to allow dead bodies to lie unburied in the gutters. In the countryside several villas can be shown to be functioning in the C5, and indeed the building of the elaborate shrine to Nodens, at Lydney (v), towards the end of the C4 implies a stability adequate to provide not only the money for the building but also a sufficient supply of pilgrims.

GLOUCESTERSHIRE

THE VALE AND THE FOREST OF DEAN

*

ST MICHAEL. A medieval church of red sandstone, prettily situated on the edge of the Forest of Dean. Perp SW tower of two stages with diagonal buttresses on the W, and a stair-vice on the S. On the W wall is a shield carved with the arms of the free miners. Chancel, nave, S aisle, and S porch. The S arcade is C14, and was longer, now having only two bays and half a third; octagonal piers. Nave roof old, with a kind of queen-post truss. Flowing tracery in the chancel N window. – FONT. Mid-C15. Octagonal bowl with a large band of quatrefoils in lozenges, and below, incised shields with free-miners' and smiths' emblems, as well as more noble arms, Buckingham, Warwick, and Serjeaunt. – STAINED GLASS. The window on the N of the nave by *Bryans*, 1911. – Jumbled fragments of good C14 glass, possibly St Catherine, in the N chancel window. – PLATE. Paten, 1731 by *Richard Pargeter*; Chalice, 1733 by *Jacob Margas*. – MONUMENTS. Brass to Richard Pyrke † 1609 and his wife in comtemporary clothes, plus two sons whose dates of death have not been filled in. – Baroque tablet in the chancel to the Pyrkes, early C18; full of character.

ST JAMES. The pretty W tower, like that at Bitton but not so 38 grand, is Perp. Angle-buttresses, gargoyles, battlements with pinnacles, and a staircase-turret round which the string-course continues, though not round the buttresses, as at Bitton. The middle battlement each side has a niche; in that on the E side is a sculptured figure. Buttresses with crocketed pinnacles; the stair-turret is surmounted by a kind of pyramid and ball. W doorway with fleurons round the architrave, and a crocketed ogee hood with angel-stops carrying shields. S doorway C12, with roll-mouldings and scalloped capitals. N doorway also Norman, but blocked up; the wall to the E was rebuilt c.1600. Nave windows late C16 or early C17. The E window is an E.E. triple lancet. On the E wall, externally, is an inserted phallic figure, probably not pre-Conquest. There is also an anthropophagus on the S face of the tower; the victim's feet rest on the string-course and his calves are grasped by the dragon's hands. Inside, the walls are limewashed, and the nave has a wagon roof. – FONT. Perp, with octagonal bowl enriched with arcading, quatrefoils, and flowers, on an arcaded shaft. – PULPIT. Of c.1630, with a sounding-board. – ALTAR TABLE. Of c.1600. – In the nave is a DADO of C18 pew ends. – The SEATS date from the restoration of 1901; good CHOIR STALLS, perhaps by *Ponting*. – Parts of the medieval SCREEN are preserved, not *in situ*. – PLATE. Chalice and two-handled Dish, 1630–70; Paten Cover, 1698.

ACTON HALL *see* HAMFALLOW

0030

ALDERTON

St MARGARET. Chancel, nave, S aisle, N and S porches, and W tower. Restored in 1890–2 by *Knight & Chatters*. All the interior walls are scraped. Mostly C14, with Perp embattled tower and S aisle with embattled parapet. The N wall of the nave seems to have been rebuilt in 1890; but there is an image niche in the splay of the Perp NE window. C14 nave arcade of three bays with octagonal piers and capitals and arches of two chamfered orders; the chancel arch also has two chamfered orders. The low tower arch dies off into the responds. Either side of the chancel arch are mutilated C14 image niches with ogee-arched heads. E window of the S aisle Dec. Chancel windows possibly C18. S porch early C18 with a stone roof; N porch C19. In the chancel is a C14 PISCINA and CREDENCE SHELF with cinquefoil head, in front of which is a recently made-up stone CREDENCE TABLE. Over the S doorway is a mutilated image. – FONT. Rectangular scalloped Norman bowl. It has the corners cut off and now presents the appearance of an octagon, with a fine pedestal having rounded corner shafts and capitals formed from the chamfer of the bowl. – STAINED GLASS. E window by *Geoffrey Webb*, 1928. – CHEST. Medieval, with good ironwork. – PLATE. Chalice, Paten, and Flagon, 1841. – MONUMENT. Rev. Henry Higford † 1795. Pedimented white marble tablet on the S wall of the chancel.

METHODIST CHAPEL. 1899. Red brick with lancet windows.

OLD RECTORY. Built c.1840. Faced in stucco with a stone cornice. Two storeys, regular windows. The new rectory was built in 1962, by *Roiser & Whitestone*, in the garden of the old, in modern style with picture windows. On the blank reconstructed-stone gable end, over the entrance, is an Oberammergau figure of St Margaret.

In the village there is considerable rebuilding, including council houses carefully built of reconstructed stone; but several timber-framed and stone cottages survive with thatched or stone roofs, mixing the traditions of the Vale and the Cotswolds. MANOR FARMHOUSE is a much altered medieval hall of two bays and a cross passage; two massive arch-braced collarbeam trusses survive. W of the screens passage is a two-storeyed cross-wing, probably of the C16, with a gable-end of close-studded timbering with later brick infilling. Ground floor faced in stone. The hall was largely rebuilt in stone and divided into two storeys in the early C17, with gables and mullioned windows, on to which was added, c.1800, a Georgian front facing the garden. BARN. C17, timber-framed. The GARDENERS ARMS, opposite the Manor Farm, also combines stone and timber-framing. It has a tall timbered gable facing the street, oversailing at the first floor, with a Cotswold stone roof.

DIXTON MANOR, 2 m. SW. C16, but partly demolished at the beginning of the C19. What remains is a four-bay gabled stone house facing W, of three storeys, with all the fenestration sashed in the early C18. At the NE corner is a three-storeyed porch with four gables all having finials like the other gables of the house; over the porch entrance, which has a four-centred-arched head, is an inscription 'John Hugeford, 1555'. Inside, a C16 staircase with moulded balusters and square newels. Early C18 panelling in the drawing room.

ALKERTON *see* EASTINGTON

ALKINGTON   7090

A civil parish in the Berkeley vale, consisting mostly of scattered farms, with a group of Georgian houses at NEWPORT on the A38 Gloucester–Bristol road. GOLDWICK FARM, 1 m. E, is of 1816. Stone-built with a Regency veranda, and contemporary staircase with turned balusters. BAYNHAM COURT FARM, C18, of three bays and two storeys, has attic cheese-room openings under the eaves, characteristic of the 'Double Gloucester' cheese-producing district.

EARTHWORK, at Damery. Probably medieval; a medieval schist hone found here c.1950 is in the Bristol City Museum.

6080   ALMONDSBURY

ST MARY. A possession of St Augustine's Abbey, Bristol. Cruciform, with a C13 central tower surmounted by a very fine lead broach-spire, transepts, chancel, nave with N and S aisles, and N porch. This porch has Norman features, including an entrance doorway of three plain orders and jamb shafts with scalloped capitals. It is two-storeyed, with the upper chamber carried on a quadripartite rib-vault springing from C14 corbel heads, and with a round-arched light. Four-bay nave, rebuilt in 1834, and the Norman arcades removed. The E.E. crossing and chancel were also extensively restored; the E.E. screen across the W arch is a C19 innovation, and most of the lancet windows in the chancel are C19, but the triple lancets at the E end certainly existed, though they had to be re-opened. The chancel has a rib-vault supporting an upper chamber, with moulded ribs springing from half-shafts of Purbeck marble with foliated capitals and corbel heads. Lancet windows with moulded inner arches and painted Purbeck shafts with foliated capitals. In the S wall is an original E.E. DOUBLE PISCINA with a trefoil head; also two plain AUMBRIES. The transepts are entered from the aisles under half-arches which buttress the tower. The S transept has a trefoil-headed PISCINA, and both have triple lancet windows. – FONT. Norman square bowl with scalloped edge on a cylindrical pedestal and rectangular plinth. – REREDOS. Carved oak, by *C. E. Ponting*, 1891. – STAINED GLASS. E window 1849, by *O'Connor*. – CHANDELIER. 1905. – ROYAL ARMS. – HATCHMENT. 1779, with the arms of Bromley-Chester. – PLATE. Paten, 1712 by *Nathaniel Lock*. – MONUMENTS. In the S transept, Edward Veele † 1577 and his wife. Recumbent stone effigies resting on a tomb-chest with portraits of their children in a Renaissance setting of fluted Ionic pilasters. The canopy also has Renaissance details and is carried by fluted Corinthian columns, and surmounted by heraldry. – Hugh Ivy † 1630. Jacobean tablet. – John Maronne † 1711. Painted stone classical tablet erected by a Frenchman who has inscribed that his sins were the cause that God took the life of his children. – Thomas Chester † 1763. Large monument with a mourning female and a gadrooned sarcophagus. – Catherine Parrott † 1781. Slate tablet. – Elizabeth Chester † 1799, by *C. Rossi*. – Emma Chester-Master † 1834, by *W. Tyley*. – Margaret Lippincott † 1845. White marble tomb-chest by *Tyley*.

COTTAGE HOSPITAL AND INSTITUTE. 1891 by *C. E. Ponting*. Brick, with stone dressings, and Renaissance and Queen Anne details in the manner of Norman Shaw. Tower with cupola.

COURT FARMHOUSE, NW of the church. This is all that remains of the old manor. It appears to be Tudor.

KNOLE PARK, ½ m. SW. Apart from the C15 tower, which must have been built as a vantage-point overlooking the Severn, the house was built c.1570 by Thomas Chester, Mayor of Bristol. Additions were made shortly after it was built, so that all its elevations are irregular, and the exterior remains much as it always was, though many of the windows have been altered and there is a modern porch near the base of the tower. The tower retains much of its oak newel staircase, but generally the interior of the house has lost most of its original features. It was bought by a speculative builder in 1931, and has small rustic-style houses, built since then, coming almost up to the front door.

OVER COURT, 1½ m. SW. The original house is said to have been built c.1345, but the existing building, now ruinous, is Elizabethan, with gables and mullioned windows. Interior altered in the C19. Detached rusticated ARCHWAY of mid-C18 date, with a pediment surmounted by an obelisk standing on a scrolled plinth.

GAUNTS EARTHCOTT, 2 m. E. A hamlet. The MANOR HOUSE is C16, with a datestone 1605 on one of the gables. Beautiful, many-gabled roof. Contemporary staircase. Garderobe. Two-storey gabled porch. Gateposts with large ball finials. Also GREEN FARM, C17, two gables, three storeys, and five bays, and COURT FARM, a small farmhouse with remains of a medieval chapel with a trefoil-headed window, but all much altered.

UPPER HEMPTON FARM, 1 m. S. Porch dated 1657.

THE PORTICO, Hempton Lane, Patchway. 1735. Twin-pedimented ashlar house with Corinthian pilasters, moved from Frenchay c.1920. Roman Doric porch.

The parish is now cut up by the new motorways.

ALMONDSBURY INTERCHANGE. Joining the M4 and M5 Motorways is the first four-level interchange in Britain. Opened in 1966; architect, *R. E. Slater*. On the Almondsbury–Tor-

marton section of the M4 twenty-four excellent bridges were
built by 1966, sixteen designed by *R. A. Downs* and *S. C. Brown*
of the Gloucestershire County Council, and eight by *Harry
Brompton & Partners*.

9030   ALSTONE

ST MARGARET. Chancel, nave, N aisle, S porch, and central
wooden bell-turret. S porch dated 1621. Late Norman S doorway with jamb shafts with scalloped capitals and abaci with
dogtooth ornament, a plain tympanum over a band of dogtooth, a chevron-moulded arch, and pellets on the hood-mould.
Chancel arch with Norman responds and shafts with scalloped
capitals and abaci as on the S door; the pointed arch is later.
Perp N arcade of three bays. The windows are possibly all C17,
except in the chancel, which has two E.E. lights at the E end
Norman PISCINA. Squints N and S of the chancel arch. The
walls are scraped; the church was restored in 1880, and the
roofs renewed. – FONT. Massive plain octagonal C14 bowl
resting on a chamfered octagonal base. – STAINED GLASS.
Medieval fragments in a SW window. – FURNISHINGS. C17
bench ends, and PULPIT with linenfold panels. – English style
ALTAR. – PLATE. Elizabethan Chalice. – MONUMENT. John
Darke † 1805. Tablet with Ionic columns and broken pediment.
In the village are several C17 timber-framed farmhouses.

6080   ALVESTON

ST HELEN. 1885 by *Henry Lloyd*. Dec, of rock-faced stone, with
nave, chancel, and embattled pinnacled W tower. – FONT. Norman. Plain rectangular bowl with three scallops to each face,
on a cylindrical pedestal. Removed from the old church.
– STAINED GLASS. Three-light window on the N side by
Joseph Bell, 1938. – ROYAL ARMS. Early Victorian. – HATCH-
MENT. 1844. – DECALOGUE. Late C17 or early C18.
OLD CHURCH, in a formerly circular churchyard. The Perp
tower survives, with a portion of the N wall of the nave including a probably Norman rather than Saxon plain round-headed
doorway with a diaper moulding and carved imposts.
OLD CHURCH FARMHOUSE. C16–17, of rubble, with moulded
mullioned and transomed windows with stone relieving arches,
some elliptical windows, diagonal chimneys, and Jacobean details inside. Formerly much larger.

STREET FARMHOUSE. Date-stone 1628.

THE GROVE is a Late Georgian stucco house; there is a rather earlier house opposite.

SHIP HOTEL. Originally C17–18, but much enlarged and modernized since c.1960.

EARTHCOTT GREEN FARM, 2 m. SE. C17, with two gables and diagonal chimneys.

ALVINGTON 6000

ST ANDREW. E.E. to Dec church, drastically restored in 1858 and in 1890, when the N vestry was built. Most of the geometrical Dec windows were renewed, and the exterior has a C19 appearance. E.E. W tower with later embattled parapet. The S aisle is about as broad as the nave, and there is a S porch and S chapel to the chancel. Arcade between nave and aisle of three bays with octagonal piers and Early Dec capitals carved with foliage. The responds, also carved with foliage, have the beginnings of slender shafts, corbelled off. The entrance to the rood stair remains, and the chancel has one small Norman light on the N. Squint to the S chapel. Chancel arch C19. – FONT. C19 octagonal bowl, with a stone reading desk on one side, and supported on granite shafts. – REREDOS. C19, carved stone. – PLATE. Chalice and Paten Cover, 1675. – MONUMENTS. Sir Robert Woodrof † 1602. Stone tablet. – Mary Medcalfe † 1768. Stone and marble tablet. – Sarah Lawrence † 1771. Marble tablet. – William Clarkson † 1803, by *Wood* of Bristol. – Thomas Baker † 1808. Painted stone and slate tablet. – George Watkins † 1832, by *William Price* of Chepstow. – Hon. Anne Noel † 1851. Marble tablet by *Reeves* of Bath.

The village is bisected by the Gloucester–Chepstow road.

ALVINGTON COURT may be on the site of a grange of Lanthony Priory, but little remains even of the Elizabethan house, except a large central chimney.

CLANNA, 1 m. NW. The C19 mansion was demolished after the Second World War, but farm buildings, cottages, garden houses, and ornaments survive, all c.1890.

APPERLEY 8020

HOLY TRINITY. 1856 by *F. C. Penrose*. Romanesque, of brick with stone and pink terracotta dressings. Two-light windows divided by stone piers with lozenge-shaped piercings above. The eaves cornice has stone corbels. This was when Penrose was a young man; he returned as an old man *c.*1890, and spoilt it by adding a small W campanile making a tiny porch below, and an apse like the nave in style but with pointed windows. 'Poor, silly Penrose', writes Goodhart-Rendel. – STAINED GLASS. Windows N and S in the sanctuary, 1914 and 1925 by *Whitefriars Glass Works*. – CHURCHYARD. Headstone of Hornton stone to Algernon Strickland † 1938, with lettering by *Eric Gill*.

APPERLEY COURT. By *John Collingwood*, after 1817. Regency-style brick house faced in stucco. Two storeys, seven bays, with central Ionic porch and wrought-iron veranda the whole length of the ground floor. Inside, a nice elliptical staircase, plastered cornices, and good doorcases of Regency pattern. Billiard room added by *Prothero & Phillott* in 1898.

APPERLEY HALL. C16 timber-framed house with brick infilling and a stone roof. One gable has a finial consisting of a 'bear with ragged staff', the badge of the Earl of Warwick.

The village has several half-timbered houses. OAK FARMHOUSE has the date 1772 in a gable-end. APPERLEY HOUSE is early C19 with Gothick glazing in the ground-floor windows and a Tuscan portico.

ARLE *see* CHELTENHAM, p. 155

7010   ARLINGHAM

ST MARY. C14. Nave, chancel, W tower, and S porch. Tower with an open panelled parapet, diagonal buttresses, and Dec bell-openings. All the windows are Dec; the E window has reticulated tracery. Sanctus bellcote on the E gable of the nave. Chancel arch with three plain chamfered orders. The floors are stone-flagged, and the walls and roofs plastered. In the chancel is a PISCINA and CREDENCE SHELF with cinquefoil head. The church was restored *c.*1868 by *H. James* of Gloucester. The N vestry is dated 1864. – FONT. Perp. Octagonal, with panelled stem. – ALMSBOX. Late C17 or early C18. Hexagonal, with gadroon and leaf mouldings. – PULPIT. Panelled oak, probably C18. – READING DESK with carved panel; late C17. – PEWS. Panelled. Early C19. – CHANDELIERS. A pair, made in Bristol, 1772 by *William Wasbrough*. – STAINED GLASS. Some of the oldest glass in Gloucestershire in two windows on the N side of the nave, of *c.*1340, by an individual and local hand; comparable with the St Catherine at Deerhurst. In the first window are the figures of St John and St Mary on plain ruby grounds, and under canopies with borders. In the tracery a figure of St Catherine holding a wheel. The next window, also of two lights, has a crowned female saint and St Margaret, standing on a double-headed dragon. Remains of an entirely different c15 series in the chancel sw window: St Philip (about half restoration) and St James (more than half restored). Below St Philip the arms of Berkeley, and below St James a modern coat (Hodges). These are the only two figures left of a series of apostles with creed scrolls, remains of which are in two tracery lights in the nave. – N window in the chancel by *Clayton & Bell*, 1886. – E window by *Clayton & Bell*. – PLATE. Chalice, 1720 by *Joseph Clare*; Flagon, 1753; Almsplate, 1753; Almsdish, 1780. – MONUMENTS. Thomas Hodges † 1784, by *Ricketts* of Bath. Classical marble tablet. – Thomas Hodges † 1780, also by *Ricketts*. – Nathaniel Rogers † 1798, by *Pearce* of Frampton. – Charles Yate † 1738. Rococo monument. – John Yate † 1758. With classical sculpture. – Mary Yate † 1777, by *Nollekens*. Sculptured mourning female. – Priscilla Bromwich † 1805, by *Millard* of Gloucester. – CHURCHYARD. A good collection of monuments and tombstones in Forest stone.

Arlingham is situated in a remote loop of the Severn, where the river travels nine miles to progress one.

WICK COURT, 1½ m. w. c16 or earlier. Timber-framed rear wing, covered in roughcast, on to which is added a c17 brick house of three storeys with five gables set close together, mullioned and transomed windows, and a two-storey gabled porch. The doors have their original wrought-iron fittings. c17 staircase with turned balusters. Ornamental plaster ceiling and chimneypiece in a bedroom.

ASHCHURCH

ST NICHOLAS. Like two other Norman churches in the neighbourhood of Tewkesbury, Forthampton and Twyning, this church has an unusually long and narrow nave. All that remains is the fabric of the s wall, with the outer order of a doorway of the second half of the c12, with chevron ornament, and a contemporary window with cable-moulding. The short chancel is the same width as the nave, but it was probably rebuilt in the c13. N aisle added in the late c13 the full length of the nave, with an arcade of six bays, later supported by flying buttresses. The w tower latest c14, with an embattled parapet and diagonal buttresses with crocketed and panelled pinnacles. The s porch has windows and details resembling those of the tower, and an upper chamber. The doorway has been made to fit under the Norman arch. c15 clerestory with embattled parapet and Late Perp or Tudor windows. The survival of the Perp ROOD SCREEN is perhaps the church's most interesting feature (such screens being particularly rare in Gloucestershire owing to the deprivations of Bishop Hooper), much restored though it is. The roofs generally are ancient, that in St Thomas's Chapel in the N aisle having a painted Tudor frieze at wall-plate level with portraits and initials. The walls are scraped, the floor stone-flagged. – FONT. Plinth and pedestal c14; pillar and octagonal bowl c16. – Jacobean HOLY TABLE in St Thomas's Chapel. – SCREEN of c17 domestic panelling below the organ. – The framing of the BENCH ENDS and the moulded top rails are old, but not the traceried panels. – ROYAL ARMS of George I. – STAINED GLASS. E window by *Hardman*; other windows mostly by *Kempe*. – PLATE. Chalice, Elizabethan; Paten, 1664. – MONUMENTS. William Ferrers † 1625. London work of painted stone; bust, heraldry, and good lettering. – Brass to Robert Barker † 1671, with coat of arms.

NORTHWAY COURT, ¾ m. N. A neat c18 brick front with dentil cornice and parapet, two storeys, and three windows with enriched keystones; central door with fanlight.

FIDDINGTON MANOR, 1¾ m. S. Timber-framed house with gables at the back, and close-set studding. The front is symmetrical, with stone chimneys at either end with diagonal stacks. It was the house of William Ferrers, *see* above. – DOVECOTE. Very fine c17 stone building with four gables and a cupola. The copings and kneelers carry splendid carved finials. An inscription bears the date 1637.

ASHCHURCH RAILWAY STATION. Buff brick and Gothic cast iron.

ASHLEWORTH

3 The church, the Court, and the magnificent tithe barn form a group of rare interest and charm. The village is ½ m. away to the w.

ST ANDREW AND ST BARTHOLOMEW. Ashleworth was in the lordship of Berkeley when the church was granted to the Abbey of St Augustine at Bristol, in 1154, by Robert Fitzharding. It has work of all periods. The earliest part which survives is a portion of the N wall of the nave which is faced internally with herringbone masonry and is not pre-Conquest, but c.1100. In it are the rere-arches of a Norman window and doorway. Chancel rebuilt in the C13. Simple chancel arch. In the N wall is a single lancet light and a pretty group of three lancets, behind which has been added a C19 vestry. The lower stages of the W tower are C14 and have bold diagonal buttresses and ogee-headed single-light windows in each stage. The top stage has gargoyles and a spire. In the mid C15 the S aisle was added with the nave arcade, and soon afterwards the chancel S chapel was built and the chancel widened on the S. N porch early C16 or later. The N doorway has a four-centred arched head outside; the DOOR itself is old and has good early iron hinges. E window C15 with C19 tracery. Arch between chancel and chapel like those in the nave but wider and flatter. Blocked squint S of the chancel arch. AUMBRY on the E wall, and a C15 trefoil-headed PISCINA in the S wall. The C14 priest's door was reset in the S chancel chapel, and in the S wall is an ogee-arched trefoil-cusped PISCINA with ballflower ornament of the first quarter of the C14. The E window is C15, and, like that in the chancel, has an external hood-mould with stops and a relieving arch over, similar to those on the Court. The chapel is separated from the aisle by a much restored wooden SCREEN of the C15. On the E side are remains of a canopy, and in the NW angle is the rood-loft stair. Over the E end of the aisle the roof is boarded, with moulded ribs and carved bosses. The upper part of the W wall of the aisle has a board with the ROYAL ARMS of Elizabeth I. This woodwork was probably originally fixed on top of the Perp screen at the E end of the aisle, or even over the rood loft, and may have a Doom or earlier PAINTING underneath. All the roofs are C15 of the trussed-rafter type with curved struts and moulded tiebeams. N transept added in 1869, with a re-set Perp window on the E. – FONT. C19. – HOLY TABLE and COMMUNION RAILS. C17. – READING DESK. Panel with the sacred monogram, and date 1635. – PULPIT. Jacobean, but much restored. – BENCHES. Some have linen-fold panels. – Primitive oak CHEST. – STAINED GLASS. E window 1865 by A. Gibbs. – The C15 S window has fragments of medieval glass. – PLATE. Chalice and Paten, 1773. – CHURCH-YARD CROSS. Probably late C14, except for the upper part of the shaft. The head has four niches with carved figures in relief; on one side a Crucifixion with the Virgin and St John, and on the other the Virgin and a supplicant; mutilated figures on the sides.

THE COURT. Built c.1460, the house is practically unspoiled. There have been a number of minor alterations to the exterior, chiefly to the windows, and some subdivisions internally, particularly in the hall, where an upper floor has been inserted and an attic floor above the solar; but the basic planning is intact, and there are very fine open timbered roofs in both hall and solar.

In plan the house is L-shaped, with the solar extending a little beyond the main range to the E, and with a stone newel staircase tucked into the corner between this extension and the main range. On the E elevation of the solar there are indications of further buildings, probably only minor. The staircase also looks as if it may have gone higher. The hall is marked on the outside by large traceried windows, two of which, one on each elevation, have been lengthened. In the s portion of the house (the kitchen end) the fenestration is intact, single and two-light windows, but the solar windows have been either restored or renewed; one is dated 1870. The hall windows have very delicately carved stops to their hood-moulds, and so have the entrances to the screens passage. The hall was originally a ground-floor hall, open to the roof, of four bays with arched-braced collar-trusses, three tiers of wind-bracing, and embattled wall-plates, exposed in what is now the upper floor. A similar roof above the solar. The stone newel staircase, which serves the solar, has been altered at its head, where there are two carved masks (the larger representing King Henry VI) though they are probably not in situ. In the room below the solar, the ceiling has large chamfered and moulded ceiling beams, and in the kitchen a very big fireplace. The house is built of limestone and had a thatched roof, but now has Broseley tiles.

TITHE BARN. According to Smyth, the chronicler of the Berkeleys, the barn was built during the time of Abbot Newland (1481–1515). It is of limestone with freestone dressings, 125 ft long and 25 ft wide, of ten bays, with queen-post roof-trusses and an immense stone slate roof. Diagonal buttresses, and two gabled transepts with curved wooden lintels.

Near by, on the Severn, is an old wharf, where there is a typical river-side public house, the BOAT INN. This dates from c.1830.

ASHLEWORTH MANOR. Abbot Walter Newbury of Bristol is said to have built the house as a summer residence at about the same date as the Court, i.e. c.1460, but it is totally different, being entirely of timber-frame construction. After 1542 it became the vicarage. It is E-shaped with an exceptionally rich and complete interior, though the N wing matching the original S wing is a C19 addition, and behind it is a further domestic addition of c.1904. W front with a two-storey gabled porch between the two gabled wings, with overhangs. Arched entrance doorway with enriched spandrels with sword-like leaves; the door itself has ancient ironwork, stud nails, and a small wicket-door. On the S side is another small ancient door. In the hall exposed heavy moulded beams and joists, and a large stone Tudor chimneypiece. S of the hall was one large room, now partitioned, with heavy moulded beams which at either end are carried diagonally into the corners. On the first floor over the hall is a room with moulded beams and a sloping plastered ceiling. In the attics the sloping floors are apparent, and the timber-framing of the thin walls shows on the inside similarly to the outer face; the roof-trusses have curved wind-braces. The house has recently been restored by *D. Stratton-Davis*.

Village green with rather nondescript houses, mostly of brick, but one timber-framed cottage with part of a cruck exposed at one end. The SCHOOL, of limestone, is dated 1842.

FOSCOMBE was designed by *Thomas Fulljames*,[*] c.1860, for himself. It is unspoiled Victorian fantasy, in an unsurpassed situation, commanding exquisite views in all directions. Fully Gothic, built of limestone with freestone dressings, it is large and irregular, with turrets and a castellated tower, and grouped chimneys. Most of the windows have Gothic tracery, there is a Gothic conservatory, and the house is enriched with realistic sculpture.

ASTON-ON-CARRANT

MANOR HOUSE. C16 and C17. Timber-framed, the main block with close-set studding. Carved frieze at eaves level, and a similarly carved bressumer supporting the overhang of the upper floor. Tudor doorway with enriched spandrels. On the E is a gabled cross wing; the W is refaced in stone, and has the date 1614 carved in the spandrel of the doorway.

OLD FORGE is a picturesque timber-framed cottage with a thatched roof.

---

[*] Fulljames died at Foscombe in 1871 or 1874, and is buried in Hasfield churchyard.

103 CHURCH (dedication unknown). Perp, with a noble w tower, nave, s porch, and chancel, restored in 1866 by *Pope & Bindon*. Tower with diagonal buttresses, an embattled parapet which is probably Tudor or later with ball-finials, and a stair-turret crowned with a dome. All the windows have Perp tracery, often inserted in older openings. The timber roofs of both nave and chancel are in the main C15 and have carved stone corbels. Chancel arch segmental, springing from Late Perp piers with crude carvings on the imposts. – FONT. C15 octagonal bowl with two small quatrefoils on each face supported on a circular shaft with a square buttress at each corner of the octagon. – PLATE. Chalice and Paten Cover, 1571. – MONUMENTS. Sir Samuel Astry † 1704, by *Edward Stanton*. – Richard Street † 1773, by *W. Paty*. – Elizabeth Weston † 1793, by *W. Paty*. Classical marble tablets.

103 SEVERN BRIDGE. Opened in 1966. Designed by *Sir Gilbert Roberts*, of *Freeman, Fox & Partners*, in conjunction with *Mott, Hay & Anderson*. The design differs from that of previous suspension bridges in that the torsionally stiff box combined with the inclined suspenders provides aerodynamic stability and does away with the need for a stiffening girder. The design provides economy by lightening the deck, which is itself cheaper and moreover enables savings to be made in the cables, towers, and substructure. The main span is 3,240 ft; the two side spans each 1,000 ft. Each of the two towers is 400 ft high. The bridge is a consummate expression of the civil engineer's art in that, although it appears so impossibly fragile in its lightness and grace, it is capable of carrying vehicles up to 200 tons in weight. A significant comparision may be drawn between it and Brunel's Clifton suspension bridge only ten miles away, for not only are both bridges of the same type, but each in its day represents a pinnacle of achievement in the ages of steel and wrought iron.*

* Professor James Sutherland, an impartial judge, wrote in *The Architectural Review* (CXL, 1966, p. 176, etc.) that the Severn Bridge is 'almost as far ahead of its forebears as the jet is in advance of the piston engine'. He refers to the points made in the text and also to the fact that, while having about the same size and capacity as the Forth Road Bridge (3,300 ft span; 1964), it weighs about a third less and was considerably cheaper, although the Forth Bridge had been admired by Americans for relative cheapness. The comparable American bridges are the George Washington Bridge in New York of 1931 (3,500 ft), the Golden Gate Bridge at San Francisco of 1937

MOTORPORT, by the Aust approach. 1964–6 by *Russell, Hodgson & Leigh*. The senseless term means a service area with restaurant, cafeterias, etc. The architecture is more restrained and less showy than that of most of such motorway areas.

IRON AGE HILL-FORT, in Vineyard Brake, just E of Elberton church. Stone-built and essentially univallate, with outer ditch and counterscarp varying in height. The rampart is *c.*6 ft high. There is a steep natural scarp on the N, where no certain indications of a rampart exist. The fort encloses about 2 acres.

AWRE   7000

ST ANDREW. Tucked away in a loop of the Severn, the church has altered little in form since it was built in the early 1200s, except for the addition of an embattled Perp W tower of three stages divided by moulded string-courses, with diagonal buttresses, and a stair-vice on the NE corner. C13 W doorway. Nave, N aisle, chancel, and S porch. N arcade of six bays with cylindrical piers with moulded capitals. Fine chancel arch with jamb shafts with floriated capitals, opening into a large E.E. chancel with a three-light E window divided by slender shafts. The E window in the N aisle has three lancets, jamb shafts, and a hoodmould with carved stops; the other windows in the aisle are alternately Perp and small lancets. On the N wall is a C13 tomb recess. Over the S door a niche with E.E. capitals. The Perp window over the porch entrance was presumably for a no longer existing priest's chamber. Restored by *Waller & Son* in 1875: heavy C19 trussed rafter roof in the chancel, restored boarded wagon roofs in the nave and N aisle, restored and plastered walls. – SCREEN. Of *c.*1500, the lower portion renewed with plain boarding. – REREDOS. 1892, carved by two ladies 'as a labour of love'. – FONT. C15, octagonal, two quatrefoils in panels over a trefoil, arcading below. – LIGHTS. Brass lampholders on stands. – CHEST. Enormous, ancient 'dug-out', said once to have been used for laying out bodies recovered from the Severn; now under the tower. – PLATE. Chalice and Paten Cover, 1576; Flagon, 1749 by *John Wirgman*. – MONUMENTS. Slate tablet of 1670. – Marble tablet to Archdeacon Sandiford † 1826, by *Henry Healey*. – CHURCHYARD. Good collection of Forest stones; multiple cherub heads, a local speciality.

(4,200 ft), the Mackinac Straits Bridge in Michigan of 1957 (3,800 ft), and the recent Verrezano Heights Bridge in New York (4,260 ft). The longest span in Europe is the Tagus Bridge in Portugal with 3,320 ft (1966).

There is no village, only scattered farms, most of which are long established.

FIELDHOUSE, ½ m. W. The oldest part is medieval and has four bays with splendid large cruck trusses. At the end and set at r. angles is a timber-framed C16 addition, part of which was built up in stone in 1856. Beyond this is a taller gabled timber-framed portion, probably C17. The C16 part has original panelled partitions on two floors, and the rooms have very fine moulded beams. Original front door with moulded wooden architrave. An outstanding survival, in unspoiled condition.

BOX FARMHOUSE, 1¼ m. NW. The house does not look much from the outside, but it is medieval in origin and was mentioned in the time of Edward III in connexion with a levy for the marriage of the Black Prince. Some of the walls are 9 ft thick.

POULTON COURT, 1¼ m. SW. A moated Tudor manor house, of stone, with gables, a three-storey gabled porch, and some mullioned windows. Panelled spiral staircase, carved Elizabethan overmantel, and a panelled bedroom inside.

HAGLOE HOUSE, 1¾ m. SW. Built c.1720. Brick, chamfered stone quoins, six windows with keystones, and a doorway with an enriched hood. The house contains a very fine contemporary staircase.

ETLOE HOUSE, 2½ m. SW. Date-stone 1730. Stone, with a partly hipped slate roof with dormers, and five windows with keystones and voussoirs.

LOWER ETLOE. C17, rubble, two gables, three storeys. The ground floor has mullioned windows with stone relieving arches; date-stone 1678.

GATCOMBE, 2¾ m. SW. A picturesque riverside hamlet where there is still a house named after Sir Francis Drake, who is said to have stayed here when the river was more navigable and he visited Sir William Wynter of Lydney, Queen Elizabeth's vice-admiral of the Fleet.

OAKLANDS PARK, 2 m. NW. Built c.1830 for one of the Crawshay family, who were colliery owners in the Dean. Classical, of rusticated stone. The ground-floor windows have rusticated quoins, keystones, and voussoirs, the first-floor windows freestone architraves with alternating triangular and segmental pediments. Venetian window over the porch. Crowning cornice. The return elevation has a bow window to full height with a splendid view.

CASTLE MOUND(?), at Bledisloe Farm. Recent excavation showed that it was occupied probably from the C12 onwards.

AYLBURTON

ST MARY. The church dates from the early C14, but was rebuilt in 1856 after being moved from its original site further up the hill. Nave, chancel, S aisle, S porch, and W tower. C14 S arcade of five bays. The S door has a C14 niche above it with a quatre-foiled, crocketed ogee arch, with pinnacles and figures either side. The window tracery shows development from E.E. to Dec. – FONT. C15. – PULPIT. C15. Stone, with five transomed sides carved with Perp panels. – STAINED GLASS. In the tracery of the E window of the S aisle fragments of medieval glass. – ROYAL ARMS of George III. – PLATE. Chalice, 1710. CROSS, in the village. C14; base and steps.

AYLESMORE COURT see ST BRIAVELS

BADGEWORTH

HOLY TRINITY. According to Atkyns, Gilbert de Clare, 10th Earl of Gloucester, was possessed of this manor in 1314; and in July 1315 a consecration took place in the church. It was a cell of the priory of Usk which was founded by the de Clares. Whatever existed before, the church was evidently altered c.1314, when the magnificent N chapel was built, presumably through the munificence of Gilbert de Clare.

The church now consists of a nave, chancel, N chapel, W tower, S porch, and S vestry. When the chancel was rebuilt in 1869, traces of an earlier building, such as blocks of tufa and broken shafts, were found in the walls. The nave is difficult to date but appears to have C13 features. S doorway with an unusual circular head. The S porch, otherwise rebuilt in the C19, has a trefoil-headed window over the entrance, which was perhaps an image niche. There must have been an altar in the S nave, as there is a trefoil-headed PISCINA and a tall image niche on its E wall. W window under the tower with reticulated tracery. Holy water stoup by the W door. Tower arch Perp (concave-sided imposts), and the upper stages of the tower also Perp, with an embattled parapet with Perp panels and gargoyles, and diagonal buttresses. The rebuilt E wall of the N chapel has a Perp window.

The N chapel is open to the nave through a three-bay arcade (octagonal piers, double-chamfered arches growing out of vertical pieces above the capitals). The walls are of fine ashlar, unlike the scraped rubble walls of the nave. The w window and three windows on the N, together with a doorway, are all profusely enriched with ballflower decoration both inside and outside, and many of the mouldings are as sharp as when first cut. Windows of two cinquecusped lights with a spherical triangle above, a typical motif of the late C13, conservative here in conjunction with ballflower and of course the recorded date 1314. Both nave and chapel have C14 wagon roofs with ribs and bosses and plaster infilling, the two E bays more elaborate, and all supported on stone corbels. The chancel is meant to follow the C14 Dec style, but does so in a very exaggerated and self-assured Victorian way. – STAINED GLASS. Medieval fragments in the tracery in the N chapel, and also in a window in the C19 vestry. – FONT. Scraped octagonal bowl. – COMMANDMENT BOARD, in the N chapel, inscribed: 'God save the Queen. 1591. James Elbrige. William Bub.' – HOLY TABLE. C17. – PULPIT. Made up, with linenfold panels. – SUNDIAL. 1645. – CHANCEL SCREEN. 1917. – PLATE. Chalice and Paten Cover, C17. – MONUMENTS. Coffin lid with incised foliated cross, used as a step to the S doorway. – William Hynson † 1667. Baroque coloured stone tablet. Twisted columns, open segmental pediment with two cherubs. – Sara Gwinnett † 1717. Country work, with a crude bust of the lady above the inscription tablet. Skulls below, cherubs above. – George Gwinnett Gough † 1756. Coloured marbles, good workmanship, snobbish inscription. – CHURCHYARD. Some C18 table-tombs, of the Bubb family. – CROSS. 1897, on an old base and steps.

MANOR HOUSE. An old timber-framed building by the churchyard, largely rebuilt c.1866 in the same style, with very elaborately carved bargeboards to the gables.

BADGEWORTH COURT AND LODGE. 1895 by *Paul Crompton*. Brick, Tudor style.

⁸⁰¹⁰

BARNWOOD

ST LAWRENCE. Norman nave, with a narrow N aisle with lean-to roof. Chancel rebuilt in 1874–8, with Dec windows, when the church was restored by *Ewan Christian* and *Waller*. The Perp w tower was built c.1514 for Abbot Parker, the last abbot of Gloucester, whose arms appear in the spandrel of the W doorway. It has three stages, diagonal buttresses, battlements and pinnacles. Also a Late Perp N chapel with a four-centred arched opening from the N aisle. The roof of the chapel appears to be original, with simple moulded and carved tiebeams. Over the E nave gable a large C14 Dec bellcote with an ogee crocketed canopy. The S side of the nave is restored, and has C19 Norman windows and a restored Norman doorway. The Norman N doorway is also restored, but has more original work. N porch C19. N arcade of three bays with round Norman piers and later chamfered pointed arches. The chancel arch has Norman jamb shafts, with enriched scalloped capitals and an E.E. arch. Small Norman window in the W wall of the aisle. The nave roof seems to be mostly C19, and has elaborate windbraces. Chancel PISCINA and SEDILIA C19. – FONT. Probably of c.1514. It has an octagonal bowl with shields held by winged angels, foliage, and roses, and a chamfered stem with niches. – STAINED GLASS. Mostly by *Hardman*: E window and three on the S of the nave with figured medallions, 1874. – Three-light window in the S aisle, by *Veronica Whall*, 1932. – SCULPTURE. Figure of the Good Shepherd; burnished gold, by *W. Butchard*.* – Other good fittings have lately been added, including a FONT COVER by *R. W. Paterson* and a fibre-glass Majesty by *Darsie Rawlins*. – PLATE. Paten, 1761; Chalice, 1761. – MONUMENTS. Beata Johnson† 1722, by *Stephen Reeve*. Classical marble tablet. – Elizabeth Whitehead † 1750, by *J. & J. Bryan*. Tablet with Rococo ornament. – Thomas Parker † 1800, by *Bryan*. Classical marble tablet with heraldry.

BARNWOOD COURT. C17 gabled house with an added Georgian front containing good interior fittings of both periods.

BARNWOOD HOUSE HOSPITAL. By *Giles & Gough*, c.1881, with additions of 1897 by *Waller*.

COUNTY MENTAL HOSPITAL, Coney Hill. 1881–3 by *Giles & Gough*.

PARISH ROOM. 1898 by *Walter B. Wood*.

BASE LANE COTTAGE *see* SANDHURST

BATTLEDOWN *see* CHARLTON KINGS

BAYNHAM COURT FARM *see* ALKINGTON

BEACH *see* BITTON

* Butchard was Comper's head decorator. He gilded the Blore stalls in Westminster Abbey in 1966.

8090

BEACHLEY

St JOHN. 1833 by *Foster & Okeley*. Nave, transepts, and sanctuary. The windows are lancets, except for a wooden cartwheel window at the w end over which there is a small bellcote. The sanctuary is paved in black and white marble. – STAINED GLASS. Some original coloured glass medallions remain in the windows. – MONUMENTS. Early to mid-C19 tablets by *Tyley* of Bristol.

There are one or two late C18 or early C19 houses. The great Severn road-bridge of 1966 (*see* Aust) passes almost overhead.

9010

BENTHAM

St PETER. 1888 by *S. Gambier-Parry*.[*] An ugly little church of rock-faced stone. Aisles and clerestory with small, squat lancet windows. Gabled belfry.

THE ELMS. Late C18, of ashlar, with slate roof and parapet. Two storeys. Two bay windows to full height, and a doorway with fluted pilasters, fluted frieze, and pediment.

BRIDGE MANOR FARM. The DOVECOTE is a small timber-framed building with half-hipped stone roof and lantern.

6090

BERKELEY

St MARY. Berkeley was the site of a pre-Conquest minster, which was suppressed by Earl Godwin. In the C12 the church was given to the Augustinian Abbey of Bristol. It remained an important church served by a number of clergy. In a document of 1338 ten chaplains are mentioned. The high ground occupied by the cemetery in which the church is set overlooks the castle, and formed part of the outer defences. The tower was placed on the N side of the churchyard to minimize danger if it should be captured. The present structure of the tower is a Gothic Survival rebuilding of 1750–3, and stands on the C15 plinth of the medieval tower. It was probably designed by the mason-builder *Clark*. Diagonal buttresses, embattled pierced parapet with pinnacles, and simple Gothic openings in the traditional manner.

The church is C12 in origin, with a reset Late Norman s doorway having jamb shafts with capitals including decorated

---

[*] Sidney Gambier-Parry, 1859–1948, architect, of Duntisbourne Rouse, was the youngest son of Thomas Gambier-Parry of Highnam.

trumpets and a moulded arch. Apart from this, the oldest part of the existing building is the nave, which has the original s clerestory with its range of broad windows of the second quarter of the C13, though the N side has been rebuilt as a blank wall. The chancel retains a single original lancet on the N; the strings at sill level indicate the extent of the mid-C13 building. To the E of the lancet is an early C14 window of three stepped lights above an inner tomb recess. s chancel windows Perp, except for one over-large one in the late C13 style which is most probably *Scott*'s. E window Perp too, of nine lights. The beautiful w end of the nave is mid-C13, and has five 23 graduated round-headed lancets with moulded hoods and slender shafts. Below are three pointed moulded arches with steep gables, jamb shafts, and a cusped and subcusped inner arch over the doorway, Bristol fashion. Aisles and lower part of the N porch C14. Aisle windows of three stepped lights with cinquefoiled heads, and with buttresses in between. They go well with the C13 work in the church. The buttresses on the s side have no set-offs, a sign usually of an earlier date. The porch has a rib-vault with ridge-ribs, above which is an upper chamber added c.1450. Ogee-arched entrance; parapet with trefoil-headed panels. E of the N aisle is a C14 sacristy with a small trefoil-headed window and a tiny quatrefoil opening. On the s side the Berkeley Chapel is Perp, mid-C15, with an elaborate ogee crocketed arch over the small priest's doorway 54 and the Berkeley arms held by angels. Parapet with carved enrichment and pinnacles.

The splendid seven-bay arcades have eight filleted shafts 21 with deeply undercut stiff-leaf capitals of c.1225–50. The bases 22 of the three easternmost piers are at a higher level, suggesting the existence of an enclosed choir for clergy. Very tall chancel arch of the same period, with shafts cut to allow for the insertion of the magnificent C15 Perp stone SCREEN. The screen 55 has a bold depressed two-centred arch subdivided into two four-centred arches and a higher, narrow two-centred arch for the doorway. Quatrefoils and daggers in the spandrels. The heraldic wooden cresting is an addition.* Rood-loft stairs on the N, trefoil-headed PISCINA on the s. Nave and aisles with Perp roofs supported on carved corbels. The slit recesses in the s wall were probably made to take the wall timbers of the original lean-to aisle roof. The fourth pillar to the E on the s

* The opening out of the stone panels at the base is a 'modern perversion' (Aymer Vallance).

side has a curious hood-mould corbel of two female gossips'
heads surmounted by a toad. The chancel, lengthened *c.*1300
to take the choir, was enclosed by a SCREEN of which the
remains survive at the base of the present structure. The
church was restored by *Pope & Bindon*, 1862, and by *Sir
George Gilbert Scott*, 1865–6. – Scott is responsible for the
preservation of the WALL PAINTINGS, which cover a considerable part of the interior of the church, and are mostly late
C13 patterns in red. Over the chancel arch is a fragment of a
Doom, showing Christ seated in judgement with upraised
hand. One of the capitals in the S arcade has pre-Reformation
gilding. On the r. of the E window of the S aisle a Tudor rose,
and above it a crown and the letters E.R. for Edward VI. The
painting in the chancel was restored in 1938 by *E. W. Tristram*.

There were three chantries in the church at the time of the
Reformation. The one at the E end of the S aisle has C14
SEDILIA and a CREDENCE. The Berkeley Chapel was built by
James, eleventh Lord Berkeley (1417–63). Perp stone screen,
squint to the high altar, and lierne-vault with carved bosses.
– FONT. Mid-C12 Norman rectangular bowl with a scalloped
bottom edge, supported on corner shafts with moulded
capitals and bases and keeled sides. – EASTER SEPULCHRE, on
the N side of the chancel. It dates from the second quarter of the
C14. – PULPIT. Stone, 1918, by *Sir Ninian Comper*. – RERE-
DOS. 1881, with heavy sculptured figures. – PILLAR PISCINA.
C12. At the W end, not *in situ*. – SCREEN. *See* above. – HOLY
TABLE in the S aisle; Elizabethan. – NORTH DOOR. C14, show-
ing marks of the siege of 1645. – TRIPTYCH in the N aisle by
Henry Payne, 1919. – STAINED GLASS. E window 1873 by
Hardman. – Rose window over the S door by *William Aikman*,
1927. – PLATE. Pair of Chalices, Salver, and Flagon, 1776. –
MONUMENTS. In the Berkeley mortuary chapel, James,
52 eleventh Lord Berkeley, † 1463, and his second son James.
Alabaster recumbent effigies resting on an alabaster tomb-chest
under a freestone canopy between the chancel and the Berkeley
Chapel. The difference in their ages is indicated by the different sizes of the effigies; both are in armour with Yorkist collars
of alternate suns and roses, and both heads rest on tilting hel-
mets. Tomb-chest adorned with a row of canopied niches containing figures of saints, and panels with quatrefoils. The S
side reaches to a lower level and has two rows of ogee-shaped
canopies separated by pinnacles. The canopy above the tomb
on the S side has thirteen canopied niches without figures,

divided by decorated pinnacles starting directly from the arch, which has diamond-shaped vaulting. – Henry, seventeenth Lord Berkeley, † 1615, and his wife, by *Samuel Baldwin* of Stroud (chapel E end). Alabaster recumbent effigies on a free-stone tomb-chest, under an alabaster canopy of Renaissance design. – The last Earl of Berkeley † 1942. Tablet by *Sir N. Comper* with heraldry flanked by figures of St George and St Francis. – Thomas, eighth Lord Berkeley, † 1361, and his [29] wife (nave S side). Recumbent effigies of alabaster, life-size, and resting on a large tomb-chest with embattled Gothic edge, the sides of which have panels with shields of arms within quatrefoils, and divided by strips of deep-blue glass, which were mostly renewed in 1864. This is the Lord Berkeley to whom Edward II was entrusted at the time of his murder. – Three diminutive Berkeley effigies probably representing heart burials (the bodies would be laid in St Augustine's Abbey, Bristol): two Ladies, end of the C13, and one Civilian, early C14 (on window sills in the S aisle). – Brass of William Freme † 1526, 1 ft 10 in. (sanctuary). – Ledger stones of John Hopton † 1681 and Stephen Jenner † 1754. – Tablets include James Bayley † 1712. – Nicholas Hickes † 1798, by *W. Paty*. – Betty Wiltshire † 1797, by *J. Pearce* of Frampton. – John Hickes † 1808, by *T. King* of Bath. – Mary Tratman † 1826, and several others by *Daw*. – Frederick Hickes † 1844 and William Ellis † 1855, both by *Tyley*. – CHURCHYARD. Table-tomb of Thomas Pearce, watchmaker, † 1665.

BERKELEY CASTLE. 'The castle is rose red and grey, red sand-stone and grey stone, the colour of old brocade . . . the coats of its hunt servants, not pink but canary yellow.'[*]

The present shell keep and the bailey to the SE probably represent the castle erected by Fitz Osborn, Earl of Hereford, shortly after 1067; the keep, certainly, is known to occupy the site of a truncated motte which was reduced in height, and the spoil used to raise the level within the enclosing walls of the shell keep in 1153. These form a retaining wall around the base of the motte some 60 ft high on the outside, with the interior 20 ft above the outer ground level. Up to this height it was clearly built first as a plain circular wall, to which four semicircular bastions were added which rise above this as one construction with the keep wall, open to the interior. One of the bastions has been obliterated by the C14 Thorpe Tower, and another by the gatehouse. The remaining two formed part of the buildings within the keep, of which no other trace now survives, except for the apse of the CHAPEL OF ST JOHN in the E bastion, where the body of the murdered King Edward II rested before burial in Gloucester Cathedral. The W part of the chapel is a modern reconstruction. Apse covered with a semi-dome with surface ribs springing from wall-shafts with cushion capitals. On the exterior of the shell the wall has pilaster buttresses, which occur only on the W and S sides. The external stair explains their absence on the SE side. The W side is a modern rebuild, and partly fills the breach made in the 1645 siege.

Slightly later than the shell keep, if not contemporary with it, is the curtain wall enclosing the inner bailey, built between 1160 and 1190. Only the SE stretch survives, the greater part taken up with the outer wall of the C12 Great Hall. The window embrasures, round-headed with keel-moulded architraves, can be seen within the present hall. Only the northernmost of these windows remains entire, though blocked up; the other two have been filled with medieval windows introduced from France by the eighth Earl of Berkeley in the 1920s. To the S and W of the hall the C12 curtain is lost in the C14 rebuilding, but to the N fragments survive to indicate that it ran much on the lines of the existing buildings. Internally there are few signs of the C12 buildings; at the N end of the hall, within the screens passage, is part of a C12 window, with a keeled jamb shaft and scalloped capital at a sufficiently low level to suggest a two-storey chamber block.

Berkeley is essentially a C14 castle, the whole of the interior having been remodelled between 1340 and 1350 by Thomas, Lord Berkeley, who died in 1361, although any work of this period in the shell keep has been destroyed. In the inner bailey, however, the C14 buildings survive with only minor alterations and additions. Against the E curtain, on the site of its C12 pre-decessor, stands the GREAT HALL. It is of six bays, with a double-pitched roof, and tiers of wind-bracing. On the court-yard side are four windows coming low to the floor, with straight heads and 'Berkeley' rere-arches and window seats in the embrasures. The 'Berkeley' arch is a distinctive feature, found also in Bristol. It is polygonal, with four or more straight sides enclosing a cusped inner arch with usually slightly ogee-shaped foils. The C15 stone fireplace at the SW was brought from Wanswell Court in the 1920s. At the N end of the hall is a PORCH with a kind of embryonic fan-vault, and outer and inner 'Berkeley' arches, leading into the screens passage, which has three service doors, each with a 'Berkeley' arch. The medieval screen was brought from Caefn Mably, Pembrokeshire. The service area has been much altered, but the KITCHEN is an irregular hexagon with fireplaces on three sides, and a medieval roof. The BAKEHOUSE is spanned by a pair of remarkable flat stone arches.

At the SW end of the hall a doorway with a very fine 48 'Berkeley' arch leads up steps to the C14 State Lodgings. The first room, now a morning room, was until 1923 the CHAPEL OF ST MARY. Three-sided apse at the E; otherwise of four bays, with a narrow aisle contrived in the thickness of the wall on the S, having transverse shoulder-arches. Arcade between the room and the aisle with ogee-headed openings with beautiful cusped and cinquefoiled inner arches. The fine original cambered timber ceiling springs from corbel heads, one representing two gossips and a toad like the one in the church. The painted decoration of the ceiling, restored by *Tristram*, includes Norman-French verses taken from John Trevisa's translation of Revelation, *c.*1357. The present fireplace and doorway are French importations of the last Earl of Berkeley. The fifth and westernmost bay was formerly occupied by the C15 wooden GALLERY now transferred to the adjoining Long Drawing Room. This has a projecting box or pew, carved with the arms of Henry VII, which, when it was in the chapel, was supported on Renaissance pillars, something more Gothic having now been substituted. There was formerly no central doorway at the other end of the Long Drawing Room, and the inner chamber was reached only by the charming octagonal lobby in the N angle. Beyond this lie the Berkeley family's private apartments, which date from the C14 and C15, and include the Great and Little State Bedrooms with their painted ceilings, their C15 and C16 fireplaces, and an American marble bathroom and other innovations of the 1920s. Below the State Lodgings was a suite now divided up, and its fenestration changed. This was entered from a large, vaulted lobby used later as a beer cellar, on which rests the floor of St Mary's Chapel. The inner GATEHOUSE retains its C14 form, with guard-rooms flanking the passage and two sets of chambers on the upper floors. Corbelled gallery on the inner side modern. The NE range must have been largely remodelled in the C16, though the internal arrangements have been lost in more modern alterations, and the window of the housekeeper's sitting room is another of Lord Berkeley's French innovations.

PARK HOUSE. Castellated eye-catcher seen from the castle, probably early C19, containing the kennels and offices. PARK LODGES are in much the same style, but later in date.

The small town of Berkeley has a fairly wide, straight street, with the HIGH STREET at r. angles and leading down to the w side of the castle. Most of the houses seem Georgian or refronted in the C18.

UNION CHAPEL. 1835.

TOWN HALL. Early C19, ashlar, moulded cornice and shaped parapet. Coupled pilasters either side, rusticated ground floor, semicircular-headed window in a recess on the first floor.

VICARAGE. Early C18. The home of Jenner, discoverer of vaccination. HUT in the garden, preserved as the place where Jenner carried out his vaccinations, of rustic construction and thatched.

BERKELEY ARMS HOTEL. C18, brick, three storeys and six bays. Windows with keystones and voussoirs. Central Hanoverian arched carriageway.

BERKELEY NUCLEAR POWER STATION. Begun c.1957 for the Central Electricity Board by *A.E.I.-John Thompson Nuclear Energy Co. John Laing & Son* and *Balfour Beatty & Co.* were responsible for the civil engineering work.

5010   BERRY HILL

CHRISTCHURCH. 1816. The first C19 church to be built in the Forest of Dean. Tower by *Richard James*, similar to those at Coleford and Parkend. Nave and equally broad N aisle. Chancel of 1885, apsidal, with Dec windows. – MONUMENT. Rev. P. M. Procter † 1822, by *Johnson*.

BIGSWEIR HOUSE *see* ST BRIAVELS

BIRDWOOD *see* CHURCHAM

9020   BISHOP'S CLEEVE

ST MICHAEL AND ALL ANGELS. About 1286 the Bishop of Worcester petitioned the Pope that he might make the churches under his patronage prebendal to the Benedictine College of Westbury-on-Trym. Apart from this there seems no evidence that there was ever a priory at Bishop's Cleeve, or that the church was ever anything other than a parish church; however the large size of the chancel has led people to suppose otherwise.

The Late Norman church had a nave with narrow aisles (evidence for which can be seen, though they have both been enlarged), a central tower and crossing with transepts, a splendid w end with turrets, and a s porch, all of which sur- 15 vive; but the chancel was rebuilt in the early c14. The style is Transitional in character, c.1160 to 1190. The turrets flanking the w doorway contain winding stairs which may have led to a narrow internal w gallery. They are crowned with pyramidal pinnacles and enriched with chevroned arcading. The thrust from the nave arcade has pushed the turrets out of the perpendicular, and the N turret has a large c15 buttress. The doorway is extremely rich with chevron mouldings including chevron at r. angles to the wall, the hood-mould ending in a beast's head à la Malmesbury and a serpent. The doorway is very similar to that at Leonard Stanley. s porch also with an exceptionally rich inner doorway, by the same hand as the w doorway, with beasts complete with entwined tails. The aisle side of the inner doorway has in the arch a kind of Norman ballflower. Hood-mould stops as little relief panels of animals. The walls of the porch have interlaced arcades supported on 17 slender shafts, each intersection having a trefoil-headed lower arch, and the whole is redolent of the transition to E.E. Quadripartite stone vault with ribs of a roll flanked by a projecting chevron. Above the porch an upper chamber, its window c13, i.e. later than the ground stage. Inside the chamber a well preserved section of the original Norman corbel-table. It is thus clear that the upper portion of the porch was detached from the main building prior to Perp times, when the curiously unstable ceiling was placed in the aisle halfway up to support the additional floor space above. It is a traceried roundel with ribs leading to it from w and E. Apart from the N transept the rest of the church externally has been rebuilt. Large w window Dec with reticulated tracery. Wide N aisle of the early c14, with windows with cusped intersecting tracery and an embattled parapet. The very long Dec chancel, rebuilt in the c14, has an eaves course enriched with pellets or embryo ballflower. The tracery in the great E window is c19, but the surround is original and is enriched with ballflower ornament. s priest's doorway also with ballflower de- 25 coration. The s transept was mostly rebuilt in the Dec period. Its s window (and the N window of the N transept) has enriched cusped intersecting tracery. The space between the s transept and the s porch is filled in with a Dec chapel which has Late

Perp windows. The central tower fell in 1696, and *James Hill* of Cheltenham was employed to rebuild it in 1700; it is traditional or Gothic Survival, with battlements and pinnacles.

Inside, Norman nave arcade of three bays with massive circular piers with renewed circular scalloped capitals, and C17 arches built when every second pier of the original six-bay arcade was removed. The E end of the E arch on both sides has some chevron at r. angles to the wall, the only part of the original arches to survive. The pointed chancel arch was rebuilt in 1700, but the archways either side leading from the original narrow Norman aisles into the transepts are *in situ*, and show much the same fine decoration as the S and W doorways. An additional motif appears in the decoration: crenellation. Above the two arches the pent-roof line of the original aisle roofs is visible. Small Norman window at the W end of the S aisle, and blocked Norman windows in the W walls of both transepts. The Dec S chapel has thin octagonal piers with small ballflower ornament on the capitals, and a Dec tomb recess with two orders of ballflower enrichment. In the S corner is a trefoil-headed DOUBLE PISCINA, so there must have been an altar. In the N aisle the cresting of the REREDOS of the Perp altar survives; it has a band of small quatrefoils and an embattled cornice.

The N transept is structurally Norman. In the S E corner is a blocked Norman doorway, rather pinched on the outside, as the chancel was broadened to the N when it was rebuilt, thus placing it off centre. In the E wall of the transept is an altar recess, and to the N of this a circular stair leads up to what apparently can only have been a gallery. Against the N and W walls is a most interesting stair which starts with stone steps and a balustrade, and then turns into a C15 ladder leading to the tower, with large wooden blocks for treads and a panelled wooden balustrade. Roof with C14 braced collar-beam trusses. In the S wall of the S transept a Dec tomb recess, cinquefoil with triple cusps and an ogee arch with ballflower and crockets. To the E of this is a restored PILLAR PISCINA. The splendid chancel is virtually unaltered since it was built in the C14. – WALL PAINTINGS. In the arch-splay of the Norman light on the S transept W wall is a bold conventional design in red, of foliated scrollwork with a border of large cubes at intervals; C13. – The N transept E wall has the remains of a Crucifixion painting in black and red; C14. – On the N aisle N wall later work in black, red, blue, and yellow, with part of an inscription in late black-letter; at the w end of this painting are faint conventional fish and water indicating there was once a St Christopher. – In the chamber over the s porch are some delightful paintings done by *Sperry*, the schoolmaster, in 1818, with the Rules of the Academy, a tiger, a lion, a skeleton, and battle scenes with elephants, illustrating I. Maccabees VI. – FONT. Probably made between 1570 and 1580; plain, octagonal, with no pedestal. – PULPIT. C17, with plain moulded wooden panelling. – HIGH ALTAR. A marble slab given in 1794; the triptych was painted by *J. Eadie Reid c.*1900. – COMMUNION RAILS modern, by *R. Paterson*. – WEST GALLERY. Extremely fine Jacobean musicians' gallery, luckily preserved when the church was restored, *c.*1900, by *Henry Prothero*. – PEWS. Some at the w end are Tudor. – CHEST. Ancient log chest with Norman locks. – STAINED GLASS. Fragments of C14 and C15 glass in the Norman w window of the s aisle. – SE window by *Powell*, 1911. – SW window, St Peter and St George, by *Burlison & Grylls*. – Central window in the s aisle by *J. Eadie Reid*, *c.*1890. – PLATE. Chalice, 1656; Paten Cover, 1656. – MONUMENTS. Knight, in the s transept, *c.*1270, i.e. earlier than the recess in which it now rests.* Recumbent effigy in freestone, dressed in a complete suit of chainmail and bearing a plain heater shield, but subjected to many coats of paint and scrapings. – Lady, *c.*1500 (s chapel). Recumbent effigy of freestone, dressed in contemporary costume, with winged angels at her head. – Richard de la Bere † 1636 and his wife (s chapel). A large and costly alabaster monument with two recumbent effigies on a tomb-chest. Back wall with two pairs of black detached columns, each pair separated by two small relief panels, Faith, Hope, Charity, and Peace. The wall between the columns, i.e. behind the effigies, has a segmental arch with shields and garlands under. Upper display of smaller black columns with statuettes of Justice and Strength, and heraldry, some of the ornamentation being gilded. Nice wrought-iron railings. – Edmund Bedingfield † 1695. Stone Baroque tablet in the chancel. – Catherine Norwood † 1711. Similar but smaller. – Thomas Beale † 1782. Classical stone and slate tablet. – Mary Smith † 1787, by *Bryan* of Gloucester. Classical marble; palm leaves. – R. L. Townsend † 1830. Draped urn by *Gardner* of Cheltenham. – Mary Ramus † 1809, by *Bowd* of

---

* The recess has an ogee top, ballflower, and openwork cusping and subcusping.

Cheltenham. White marble and heraldry. – Jane Reed. C17
slate tablet.

RECTORY. Probably the oldest and most splendid parsonage in
the county, built by the Bishop of Worcester. It retains its
original H-plan with solar and buttery wings. The date is
c.1250. In the hall a stone screen with three pointed chamfered
stone arches leading to kitchen, buttery, and pantry. The
central arch is wider; a fourth to the w is blocked by a later
door. At the upper end of the hall, visible from the solar cross
wing, a doorway at first-floor level has a two-centred arch and
segmental-pointed rere-arch to the solar, indicating an internal stair rising against the wall of the hall. The house was
altered in 1667 by Bishop Nicholson of Gloucester. Front
elevation with matching gables either end masking the cross
wings, which now have Venetian windows. The central part in
front of the hall, filled in in 1667, has an Ionic doorway and
hipped porch. The huge hipped roof of the main block
stretches right over the original medieval roof of the solar
cross wing, which has curved-braced, cambered collar-beams
forming a coved ceiling below. The service wing on the other
end is smaller.

Inside, the hall has been divided. The entrance part has a
nice early C18 fireplace with Roman Doric columns, enriched
with cornucopias and a 'furniture' picture in situ. It faces the
buttery screen, and behind it is a room with a Regency fireplace
and doorcases. Beyond this, in the cross wing under the solar,
is the dining room, which has C17 moulded beams where the
ceiling was heightened, presumably by Bishop Nicholson. C18
fireplace and wallpaper of 1836. Staircase also C17, with moulded balusters. C18 mural painting in an alcove on the landing.
The windows throughout appear to be C17 and have their
original ironwork and catches of the time of Charles II. In the
bedroom over the hall an ogee-arched bed recess. The front
bedroom of the solar wing, with its coved ceiling, has all its
walls covered with a very well preserved MURAL PAINTING
of 1810, depicting scenes and houses connected with the Townsend family, particularly one showing a bride arriving in a
carriage at Steanbridge House, Slad. A little Regency glass in
the Venetian window.

DOVECOTE in the garden. A rectangular, possibly C16,
stone-built double pigeon house retaining its dividing wall and
innumerable pigeon holes.

TITHE BARN, across the road from the rectory. This was at one time some 60 ft longer than its present length of about 75 ft. It probably dates from the early C15. Roof with arch-braced collar-beam trusses and curved wind-braces. The barn has now been converted into a hall and community centre.

PRIORY HOUSE, N of the church. Possibly C16, of stone, gabled, with mostly Georgian fenestration, though the side gable-end retains its mullioned windows.

EVERSFIELD HOUSE. A typical stone-built C16 or C17 house with steep gables and mullioned windows.

Several timber-framed cottages in the village, which has roads surrounding the large churchyard. A considerable amount of new building is going on everywhere, including a large new COMPREHENSIVE SCHOOL by *Peter Falconer*.

BITTON

ST MARY. The church possesses the most splendid Perp (late C14) tower in that part of Gloucestershire nearest to Bristol. It is a church of Anglo-Saxon origin on a Roman site, with a long aisleless Saxon nave, a chantry chapel of *c.*1300, and a late C14 chancel. It was a source of antiquarian interest in the C19 and was the subject of detailed study by its well-known vicar, the Rev. H. T. Ellacombe, who discovered that the nave was originally 5 ft longer than its present length of 95 ft. There were porticus near its E end, opening from the nave through big arches; that on the N wall has survived, though now blocked, and with its head mutilated by the insertion of a Dec window. A Norman arch in the vestry represents a N doorway inserted towards the W end, and a Late Norman doorway survives one bay further E on the S side. The arch in the vestry has one enriched trumpet and one leaf capital and an arch moulding of a roll and at intervals lozenges.

About 1299 Bishop Thomas de Bitton of Exeter built a chantry chapel on to the N of the nave, with six lancet windows on the N, all with cusped rere-arches, a splendid triple SEDILIA and PISCINA, and a W entrance with a triplet of doorway and two windows. This is advanced Bristol work and the culmination of the period *c.*1280–1300. It is now used as a Lady Chapel and was given a pre-stressed concrete roof in 1950. The tower, begun *c.*1371 (upper part later), is very satisfactory, with its diagonal buttresses, battlements and pinnacles, and a stair-vice with spirelet. The chancel was rebuilt about the same time. It has a stone vault with quite elaborate ribs, including ridge-ribs and tiercerons, and bosses with carved heads of Christ and the Virgin. The neo-Norman chancel arch was put up in 1847, destroying the Saxon arch to a great extent, but part of the SCULPTURE above is preserved. It is *in situ*, a massive stone carved with the feet of a very large rood. Below, on another stone, is the head of a serpent. The gable must have been very much higher. Also, if the rood is *in situ* and the porticus arch is, the nave must have been of spectacular width. From the similar roods at Bibury and Breamore one could deduce a date *c.*1000. The splendid hammerbeam nave roof, with its carved and gilded angels, was designed by the Rev. *H. N. Ellacombe* (the younger) and erected in 1860. – FONT. Perp. – REREDOS. Designed by *John Wood* the younger of Bath, 1760, in marble, and re-used by *Ellacombe*, who also designed the PEWS with different designs on each bench end. – STAINED GLASS. All by *Ward & Hughes*, pink and sentimental. – One window on the N by *Robinson* of Bristol, 1951. – Brass CANDELABRA and C19 brass candlesticks. – PLATE. Chalice, 1571; Flagon, 1694; Paten, 1821. – MONUMENTS. Two C13 sepulchral slabs, one with the effigy of a Knight, partly incised and partly in low relief, and the other with a Lady's head in low relief over a foliated cross. – Two small effigies, one of a chantry priest, and a tomb of *c.*1350, in pieces, all at the w end of the Lady Chapel. – Tablet in the porch to Ellacombe's servants, another in the chancel to the Rev. H. T. Ellacombe and three wives. – Tablet by *T. King* of Bath, 1812. – Tablets of 1657 and 1697.

The church is set in a large churchyard round which are planted some rare and splendid trees, some of which date from the time of H. N. Ellacombe, who wrote *In a Gloucestershire Garden*, and *In my Vicarage Garden and Elsewhere*, *c.*1893. The two Ellacombes between them were vicars for ninety-nine years.

The OLD VICARAGE stands hard by the churchyard. The house consists of a SE portion built in 1778; the SW part was enlarged and rebuilt in 1823. Some inscriptions are preserved; one has advice 'to my successor' by H. T. Ellacombe, 1835. The house was sold in 1951 and the new VICARAGE built in glaring red brick and given a clumsy concrete porch.

SCHOOL. 1830 by *H. T. Ellacombe*.

On the other side of the churchyard, the GRANGE is separated from it by a huge garden wall. The ground plan suggests a converted hall-house of which one wing was completely rebuilt in the C18 and the remainder considerably altered. It is said that John Wood the younger, of Bath, lived here. The outbuildings are early C18. – BARN. About a hundred yards W of the church; dated 1793.

FIELDGROVE. C18, of coursed rubble Pennant stone with a hipped slate roof. Symmetrical three-storey frontages. Portico with flat entablature on four Tuscan columns.

On the Bath–Bristol road, N side: WESLEYAN CHAPEL, 1834. Classical. KNIGHT'S FOLLY FARM. C17–early C18. Coursed rubble, two storeys, moulded mullioned windows with flat cornices over. Central door with fanlight. – On the S side: WHITE HART INN. C18, with five windows and plain stone architraves.

ROUND BARROW, on Barrow Hill, just W of the village. 32 yds in diameter, 7 ft high.

GOLDEN VALLEY MILL AND HOUSE, 1 m. N. On the site of one of William Champion's brass and copper foundries. A Georgian house, with a symmetrical three-storey elevation with three sash windows, ground-floor windows in two pairs, end pilasters, moulded cornice, and ashlar parapet. The mill is a taller four-storey building, with hoist openings to the first and second floors.

RAILWAY INN, Willsbridge. 1840. LONDONDERRY FARM-HOUSE, on the Willsbridge to Keynsham road, has a date inscription 1672; roughcast, gables with bargeboards, and sash windows in bolection surrounds with moulded sills. LOWER CULLYHALL FARMHOUSE, Ryedown Lane, is of the C17 and C18. Symmetrical two-storey front with seven windows in bolection surrounds, and moulded entablatures to the ground-floor windows, hipped pantile roof, and coved eaves cornice. Doorway with a large stone shell-hood on enriched scroll brackets. The garden forecourt has two pairs of rusticated stone GATEPIERS with ball finials.

UPTON CHENEY MANOR FARMHOUSE, ¾ m. NE. C16/17, L-shaped, and built of rubble. Frontage in two portions, stepping downwards from the r.; windows with moulded mullions and dripmoulds. The entrance from the road has a four-centred arch. The DOVECOTE is probably C16; square with gables. The front of UPTON HOUSE was rebuilt in 1857 in Tudor style with Gothic bellcote; but the rear has a wing with C18 features, such as early C18 sash windows with segmental heads and keystones. Also HOLLISTERS FARM-HOUSE, C17/18, with a door with bolection architrave and

hollow elliptical stone hood on heavy scroll brackets; CHET-
WYNDS, C17, picturesque, with oval windows in some gable
faces; and UPTON FARM, Mill Lane, C17, gabled and picturesque.

At Beach, 1 m. NE of Upton Cheyney, BEACH HOUSE, late C18
with a mansard roof, and Tuscan pedimented doorcase, the
two-storey ashlar front with grouped sash windows, plus an
additional Victorian wing; and BRITTONS FARMHOUSE, a
typical C17 gabled house with mullioned windows, dripmoulds, and relieving arches.

BLAISDON

ST MICHAEL. Rebuilt in 1867–9, by *F. R. Kempson* of Hereford,
in Forest stone with Bath stone dressings, except the tower,
which is Perp with diagonal buttresses, battlements, and an
apology for a spire. The church itself is E.E. and Dec, and
consists of a nave, chancel, N aisle, vestry, and S porch. Nave
and chancel arcades with elaborately carved capitals with
realistic flowers, leaves, animals, and birds. Encaustic tiles
survive. – STAINED GLASS. By *T. F. Curtis, Ward & Hughes*,
1912. – Window in the N aisle, 1931 by *A. J. Davies* of Broms-
grove. – MONUMENTS. Tablet in the chancel by *Cooke* of
Gloucester, c.1846. – Others by him are under the tower.

BLAISDON HALL. Of c.1894, Jacobean style, with tower; gatehouse and arch with date-stone. Now Salesian School (R.C.).

IRON AGE HILL-FORT (WELSHBURY), ¾ m. W of Flaxley.
Three ramparts on the W side, one on the E, covering about
13 acres.

BLAKENEY

ALL SAINTS. Originally early C18, rebuilt c.1820 by *Samuel
Hewlett*, with pointed windows and an embattled parapet; a
'barn' with huge windows and far too small tower. The sanctuary was built and the church restored in 1907. – FONT. A
much weathered C15 stoup is now used as font. – PLATE.
Chalice, 1669.

BAPTIST CHAPEL. 1874. E.E. style.

CONGREGATIONAL CHURCH. 1849. Inscribed 'Independent
Chapel'. Of stone, debased classical.

SWAN HOUSE (formerly an inn). C17, partly colour-washed
stone and partly timber-framed. Between it and the church
is an early C19 VICARAGE. MANCHESTER HOUSE is of the
C18, of stone, three storeys, three bays; some contemporary

panelling. The KINGS HEAD INN is C18, colour-washed stone, three bays with a pretty Venetian window in the centre on the first floor and bay windows either side on the ground floor. NIBLEY MILL, of the early C19, has an earlier cottage attached. HAWFIELD, on the road to Newnham, partly C17 and C18, has a wing added in 1922 by *Stanley Peach*.

HEWLERS FARMHOUSE, Brain's Green. C16, stone-built but partly faced in roughcast to imitate masonry. Three storeys, with stone and wood mullioned windows. Inside, C16 panelling, and an arched doorway.

HICKMAN'S COURT. Part of a C17 house.

BODDINGTON

8020

ST MARY MAGDALENE. A long nave, originally Norman, with a Norman N doorway, now leading into a modern vestry, and with one small Norman window to the W of it. S doorway C13, with a C14 porch retaining its original stone benches and stoup. The nave windows are mostly C14; but the walls have had constant restoration due to their marked tendency to move outwards owing to the clay foundations, which cause movement in dry weather. N side of the church heavily buttressed. Nave roof C14 with tiebeams which in some places have come away from the walls. Chancel much restored in 1876. All the walls inside are scraped, and a blocked doorway is visible immediately W of the S door; one of its quoins appears to be the re-used head of a small Norman window. W tower C13, but somewhat truncated, with a low roof. It has a sundial dated 1719. – FONT. Perp. – PULPIT. 1876, possibly by *John Middleton*. – COMMUNION RAILS. C17. – CHEST. 1676. – PLATE. Chalice and Paten (of Ruardean type), 1723. – MONUMENTS. John Arkell † 1818 by *Cooke* of Gloucester. – Robert Arkell † 1813 by *J. T. Whitehead* of Cheltenham. – Thomas Arkell † 1876 by *D. A. Bowd*.

BODDINGTON MANOR. On an old site, the present house was entirely remodelled and partly rebuilt *c.*1820 in Tudor style. It consists of a main block with a N wing. S front of 1, 1, 3, 2, 1 bays, with the main, more or less central block castellated. All the windows have stone mullions and transoms and dripmoulds. The house is built of a fine ashlar, and the E gable-end of the continuous Cotswold stone roof is stepped. On the N side a porch and a tower in the angle of the wing are late C19 additions. Ballroom added on the W in 1901. The drawing room contains an early C18 fireplace, not *in situ*. Overmantel with carved wooden Ionic columns, bolection frieze, and swags of fruit. Two C15 stone shields showing the arms of Tewkesbury Abbey and the Earls of Gloucester perhaps belong to an earlier house.

HAYDEN FARMHOUSE is C17, partly timber-framed and brick on a stone plinth. BODDINGTON MILL has machinery *in situ*.

BOWDEN HALL *see* UPTON ST LEONARD'S

BOX FARMHOUSE *see* AWRE

BRAIN'S GREEN *see* BLAKENEY

BREADSTONE *see* HAMFALLOW

6000

BREAM

St JAMES. 1860 by *William White*, though a church existed here in the early C16. The present building consists of a nave with four bays, N aisle, chancel, and SW bellcote. Chancel windows with plate tracery. The arcade has marble columns with very large stone capitals, carved with foliage, and pointed arches. The roof is a forest of king-posts and collars. N vestry added in 1891. On the chancel N side an old PISCINA or the head of a window made into one, possibly early C16. Below it a C19 credence shelf. – FONT. Post-Reformation octagonal bowl on a slender pillar. – PLATE. Chalice and Paten Cover, 1680; Chalice, Paten and Flagon, 1854 by *John Keith*, probably a Butterfield design.

NEW INN. C17, with mullioned windows, and a two-storey porch which has lost its gable. Chimneypiece with carved date-stone 1637. Restored in 1968.

BRIDGEYATE *see* SISTON

BROCKWEIR *see* HEWELSFIELD

8010

BROCKWORTH

St GEORGE. Dedicated in 1142 and given to Lanthony Priory, Gloucester. All that remains of this date is the central tower, though it has a C19 embattled top stage. The church was re-built in the C14, and consists of a nave with N aisle, S transept, S porch, and chancel. Dec windows, the E window with reticulated tracery. Splendid Norman tower arches of three orders, on the nave side of roll and chevron mouldings with jamb shafts with scalloped capitals, on the chancel side with chevron, roll, and outer mouldings, on huge half-cylindrical responds with cushion capitals. C14 N arcade of three bays with octagonal piers with ballflower round the capitals. The small S transept has a panelled wooden roof with carved bosses and a PISCINA with a chamfered pointed arch, the chancel a C14 PILLAR PISCINA. N vestry C19. – FONT. Norman, with a plain circular bowl. – REREDOS. C19; sculpture in niches. – SCREEN. C19 ironwork. – STAINED GLASS. E window by *William Wailes*, 1847. – PLATE. Chalice, 1677; Paten, 1680; Almsdish, 1778. – MONUMENTS. Sir Christopher Guise † 1670, by *Peter Bennier*. Marble Baroque monument with a bust, heraldry, and cherubs. – Susanna Colchester † 1811, by *James Cooke*. – William Roberts † 1808, by *Daniel Hewlett*. – John Jones † 1801, by *James Millard*.

BROCKWORTH COURT. The E wing was built for Richard Hart, the last prior of Lanthony, in 1534–9. In the N gable-end a bargeboard carved with quatrefoils, and cusping. Ground floor of stone with two Perp windows, one blocked, with concave mouldings, tracery, and dripmoulds with carved stops, and buttresses. Upper floor timber-framed, with close-set studding, and jettied out on a cove. Inside on the ground floor is a room, running N and S, with Perp details; moulded oak beams to the ceiling enriched with carved bosses, supported on elegant moulded wooden wall shafts. In the thickness of the wall in the NW corner a stone newel staircase leading to an upper hall, now ceiled in, which has its original roof with collars on moulded arched braces. Against the chimney in the N gable, high up, and now only visible in the attic, is a WALL PAINTING with the pomegranate badge of Katharine of Aragon, and the initials of Prior Richard Hart. C19 bay window in the S end of this wing. The main portion of the house is at r. angles, running E–W, and may be part of an earlier building. N front a continuation of the buttressed stone ground floor, with a four-centred arched entrance towards the W, and jettied-out close-set studding above. In one room a wall-plate or bressumer with embattled moulding. The projecting SW wing is C18. The wings are linked on the S by a two-storey C19 gallery or passage, with a neo-Tudor elevation. On the S a SUNK GARDEN with an C18 brick wall with stone quoins of alternating length, and a road bridge over the brook. The

BARN on the N of the house, probably C15, has nine bays with cruck trusses, and a stone roof.

Seen from the S, the church, house, and barn, standing on a slight rise in the ground, form an outstanding group.

Brockworth is now very much built-up, and has lost its identity as a village. There are two timber-framed cottages where Court Road joins the main road to Gloucester.

FACTORY of British Nylon Spinners. A conversion of a wartime aircraft factory. The main building was re-designed, and faced with pyluminized aluminium sheeting, by *J. Douglass Matthews & Partners*.

COOPER'S HILL HOUSE, 1½ m. S. C18. The front elevation, of two storeys and three bays, has a segmental porch with fluted Doric columns. Spectacular situation.

WELL CLOSE FARM. C17, with exposed timber-framing and stone roof.

7030

BROMSBERROW

ST MARY. The lower part of the W tower is stone-built, C13, with lancet windows; above is a timber-framed belfry rebuilt with a shingled spire in 1875, though the beam supporting it in lieu of a tower arch, at the W end of the nave, is dated 1502. Nave walls rebuilt in 1858, when the N aisle was added. C14 chancel, over-restored; both it and the N chapel have Decstyle windows with flowing tracery. Chancel arch with two plain chamfered orders. In 1725 the chancel N wall was opened with a rounded archway leading to the Yate mortuary chapel through wrought-iron gates. – FONT. Norman tub-shaped bowl. – LECTERN AND COMMUNION RAILS, c.1860, by *David Smith* of Ledbury. – STAINED GLASS. E window 1886, W lancet window, S chancel window, N and S nave windows 1887, all by *Kempe*. – The E window in the chapel contains fragments of medieval glass and C17 glass. – ROYAL ARMS of George III; 1779. – HATCHMENTS. – PLATE. Chalice and Paten Cover, 1588; Paten, 1781. – MONUMENTS. John Yate † 1749. Classical, with obelisk, urns, and heraldry. – Robert Yate † 1802, by *Millard*. – Cleaver Burland † 1801, by *Lewis* of Gloucester. – CHURCHYARD CROSS with C13 round head, a foliated cross on either face, mounted on a shaft in 1882.

RECTORY. Late Georgian, of brick, three storeys and three bays; three-light windows on the ground floor.

BROMSBERROW PLACE. A C17/18 farmhouse altered and enlarged in the C18; some rainwater-heads are dated 1768. Refaced in the early C19, in neo-Greek style. Stucco-faced entrance front with two storeys and 3–1–3 bays. Central portico with four detached fluted Doric columns. The central bay of the house is taller, and has a balustraded parapet, and a window with a pediment; the other windows have plain entablatures. On the l. large C18 brick STABLES, surmounted by a cupola. The LODGE is a *cottage orné* but has lost its thatch.

BROOKTHORPE

8010

ST SWITHIN. Mainly C13; N aisle added in 1892. C13 W tower with saddleback roof. E.E. chancel, fairly well preserved, with a single lancet E window. N of the E.E. chancel arch a rood stair, buttressed on the exterior, S of it a pointed-arched recess. On the wood cornice of the S porch a rudely carved chronogram commemorating the execution of Charles I. – FONT. C17, chalice-shaped. – REREDOS. Restored E.E. arcade. – PULPIT. C18 panelling. – PLATE. Chalice and Paten Cover, 1630. – MONUMENTS. Good wall tablet to George Venn † 1694. – Detmar Blow, the architect, † 1939. His name is carved on the splay of a cinquefoil-headed lancet window in the N side of the nave, by *Eric Gill*.

VICARAGE, S of the church. 1846 by *T. H. Wyatt & D. Brandon.*

BROOKTHORPE COURT, E of the church. C16 and C17, restored in the C19. Mostly stone, with gables and mullioned windows. Timber-framed central cross-wing with exposed framing in both gable-ends. The entrance on the N and a projecting stair-turret rebuilt in the C19. The BARNS on the NW are ancient.

MULBERRY TREE FARM. C16/17, faced in rubble or roughcast, with a Cotswold stone roof. The projecting gabled wing and a large gabled dormer have fine decorative stone finials. Mullioned windows with dripmoulds; moulded four-centred arched doorway.

COUNCIL HOUSES, on the Gloucester–Stroud road. By *C. D. Carus-Wilson*, in traditional cottage style.

BULLEY

7010

ST MICHAEL. Small Norman church with a chancel most tactfully rebuilt in 1886 by *S. Gambier-Parry* in unobtrusive Norman style. S doorway Norman with alternating stones of blue lias and sandstone, a very effective motif which is carried out throughout the church and was copied by Parry. Two orders of chevron moulding and an outer arch enriched with dogtooth, and a plain tympanum. The jamb shafts have affronted key-patterns, vertical lines, and volutes or leaf pattern on the capitals; the bases have spurs, as at Dymock. Norman nave w window, with two narrow rectangular lights above, two deeply splayed Norman windows on the N, and one very small light on the S. Chancel arch with two orders of chevrons and two jamb shafts with scalloped capitals, and a window above. Good Perp window on the S. Rounded apse and Norman-style windows. w bell-turret C19. – WALL PAINTING. Remains of C12 red painting in chevron pattern on the splays and jambs of the two Norman lights in the N nave wall. – FONT. Norman circular bowl with roll at top and bottom, supported on a heavy cylindrical shaft. – PLATE. Chalice, C17; Paten, 1761; Flagon, 1892.

BURY COURT *see* REDMARLEY D'ABITOT

CALLOW FARM *see* DYMOCK

CAMBRIDGE *see* SLIMBRIDGE

CHACELEY

ST JOHN THE BAPTIST. Apart from the Norman chancel arch, and the lower stages of the C13 tower, the church was generally rebuilt in the C14, when the S aisle was added. Chancel rebuilt from the bases of the windows upwards by *E. Christian*, who restored the church in 1882. The upper stage of the tower C14, with a small spire. The blue lias stone on the N of the nave so deteriorated that it has been patched up with brick. Chancel arch probably early C12, but of unusual design. The arch is enriched with intersecting zigzag moulding, with a grotesque keystone, under a double row of billet moulding, and supported on jamb shafts with scalloped capitals. Tower arch C15 with concave mouldings. The S arcade is most striking; it has four bays, octagonal piers, and a good series of corbel heads, mostly of men with hair curled in the fashion of the time of Edward II and III. C14 wagon roof in the aisle, and a C14 Dec PISCINA with a crocketed canopy. The walls of aisle and chancel are scraped. Chancel PISCINA with a cinquefoil head; double AUMBRY C14 Dec, but poorly executed. In the NE corner of the sanctuary a few medieval TILES. – FONT. C13 or early C14, octagonal, with the bowl and stem cut out of one block of stone. – BENCH ENDS. C15 with carved panels, mostly copies. – STAINED GLASS. C14 Crucifixion in the E window. –

Fragments of C14 glass in the S aisle E window. – DRUM with the Royal Arms of 1817. – STOCKS for three. – PLATE. Chalice, 1696. – MONUMENTS. In the chancel are three tablets by *W. & J. Stephens* of Worcester: Sarah Carne † 1807, Susanna Buckle † 1816, and another. – Thomas White † 1771. Slate tablet with incised lines and Rococo ornament. – William Buckle † 1803, by *Cooke*. – William White † 1807, by *Millard & Cooke*. – Noah Buckle † 1834, by *Cooke*.

CHACELEY HALL, ¾ m. W. C15 range running roughly E–W, with C16 additions on the N and S, all timber-framed on a stone base. All the timber-framing is similar in character, with close studding. The E gable has cusped bargeboarding, half of it original, of the C15. The bargeboard on the W gable, patterned with trails of vine, and the carved braces at eaves level belong to the C16 remodelling, although the jettied N gable added then has no such enrichment. One C16 window survives in the N addition; otherwise the windows are modern. The roof of the C15 range is almost complete, four bays, with arch-braced collars, upper and lower purlins, and curved wind-braces.

CHARFIELD

ST JOHN. 1881–2 by *W. W. Bethell*. Rough coursed rubble walls and ashlar dressings. Chancel, nave, N aisle with porch. Shingled belfry on the W gable, the timber frame of which is visible inside. The porch is also timber-framed. Square abaci and stiff foliage. Wrought-iron candle brackets. – STAINED GLASS. E window by *Heaton, Butler & Bayne*. – FONT. C15, from the old church. – PLATE. Chalice and Flagon, 1675. – CHURCHYARD CROSS commemorating a railway disaster in 1928.

ST JAMES, now redundant and disused. Chancel, nave, S aisle, arcade of four bays, N porch, W tower; all C15. Barrel roofs. Rood steps and squint all buried in the E end bay of the arcade. C13 PISCINA. The porch has an open parapet and a niche supported by a winged angel, diagonal buttresses, and a contemporary inscription. – STAINED GLASS. Fragments of medieval glass.

SCHOOL. 1894 by *W. W. Bethell*.

CHARFIELD MILLS. Large block with date-stone 1829.

CHARLTON KINGS

ST MARY. C15 Perp central tower with N and S transepts; nave with N and S aisles mostly rebuilt in 1877–8, though part of the s wall and s porch are Late Perp and part of the N wall dates from 1826; chancel rebuilt in 1878 by *John Middleton*; choir vestry enlarged in 1917. Tower of three stages, with diagonal buttresses on the lower two, and panelled angle pilasters terminating in pinnacles on the embattled, be-gargoyled top stage. The bell-openings have ogee heads with finials. Crossing arches of two orders with concave mouldings and a quadripartite stone tierceron vault. In the s transept springers of a vault, hidden by the present ceiling built in 1938; also a C14 PISCINA. The chancel PISCINA, now built into a window seat, is possibly earlier. – FONT. Tub-shaped, with bowl cut into an octagon and decorated with panels of C14 curvilinear tracery. – ROYAL ARMS, over the chancel arch. Of *c.*1826, in carved stone. – REREDOS. 1901 by *W. H. Fry*; marble and alabaster. – STAINED GLASS. W windows N and S by *Clayton & Bell*, 1880. – Three windows in the N aisle by *Curtis, Ward & Hughes*, 1911 and 1914. – PLATE. Paten, 1714. – MONUMENTS. Elizabeth Prinn † 1771 and John Whithorne † 1797, both by *Ricketts*. – Mrs Dodington Hunt † 1813, by *Thomas King* of Bath. – Martha Taylor † 1817, by *George Wood*. – Henry Campbell † 1823 and several others by *G. Lewis*. – Life-sized marble sculpture of the Angel of the Resurrection, no inscription, but a portrait and part of the rebuilding of the chancel in 1878 in memory of the mother of Sir Frederick Dixon-Hartland. – Boer War Memorial, 1902 by *W. H. Fry*.

HOLY APOSTLES. 1871 by *John Middleton*. Early Dec, taking full advantage of an up-standing, triangular site, and no expense spared. The exterior is faced in rusticated stone with correct Dec windows; the interior has a nave with five-bay arcades with pointed arches, deeply cut foliated capitals, Apostles in roundels in the spandrels (cf. All Saints, Cheltenham), and a very lofty, steep-pitched roof. The chancel arch has Middleton's usual band of two different coloured stones on short polished granite shafts supported by flying angels. In the chancel two-bay arcades, a five-sided apse with diapered walls, a stone and marble REREDOS, richly cusped windows, and a painted roof. – STAINED GLASS. Sanctuary windows by *Clayton & Bell*, 1875; also the w window. – Others by *G. Maile*. – LECTERN. Brass; decorated by *Rupertia Sanders*, 1870.

SCHOOL, complementary to the church and built in the point of the triangle to the w, by *Middleton*. Five-sided gabled end and bellcote.

Charlton Kings is a residential suburb of Cheltenham of long standing, now being filled in with more building. On the Cirencester road are the following houses:

LANGTON LODGE. Early C19 stucco villa. Two storeys, three bays, overhanging slate roof, and tetrastyle Tuscan portico.

CHARLTON HOUSE. Of c.1790. Rendered front with two segmental bows to full height, three storeys, cornice and parapet.

CHARLTON PARK. A late C18 brick house, as shown in Bigland in 1789, built for the Prinn family on to an earlier house. Three storeys and three, five, three bays, the central portion breaking forward. Modillion cornice and pediment. Large later additions. The drive has rusticated GATEPOSTS with eagles and urns.

BAFFORD HOUSE. Early C19, ashlar-faced, two storeys, one, three, one bays with Ionic pilasters to full height either side, and portico with Ionic columns. BAFFORD FARM is an old timber-framed house, picturesquely situated on the Chelt.

CUDNALL STREET. CHARLTON LODGE, faced in stucco, has a Doric porch and a long veranda on the return elevation. ELBOROUGH COTTAGE is a C17 timber-framed house, partly faced in roughcast, and with C19 Gothic windows.

CHARLTON PARK JUNIOR SCHOOL, London Road. Early C19 stucco house with Ionic pilasters to full height. Two storeys, four bays, and Doric porch with fluted columns.

ASHLEY MANOR (formerly THE OAKLANDS). Early C19, ashlar-faced, two storeys. s front with a central bow to full height with Corinthian columns and three windows, with one further window either side. w front of four bays with a classical porch. GAZEBO, in the grounds. Octagonal and faced in stucco with angle pilasters; inside, niches alternate with the windows.

BRIDGE HOUSE. Attractive early C19 stucco house of three storeys with three Gothick windows and a niche with a statue.

COURTFIELD. Stucco house of three bays, with pilasters and veranda.

KING'S HOUSE, School Lane. C16/17, timber-framed with first-floor projection. The date 1698 on a fireplace.

THE HEARNE, Hearne Road. Early C19, Tudor-Gothick, stucco-faced, with gables, Tudor windows, and a sundial with ogee crocketed hood-mould and finial. The Tudor doorway has hood-stops representing Elizabeth and Burleigh, under a light and charming *porte-cochère* with ornamental iron cresting and 'valance'.

EAST COURT, East End Road. Stucco-faced, of two storeys.

Five bays to the front, and a veranda supported by Ionic columns. Enlarged *c.*1960, as an old people's home, by *R. F. Fairhurst.*

COXHORNE, ½ m. SW, on the London road. A nice Georgian house, rendered. Two storeys. Five-bay front probably added *c.*1815; contemporary fittings.

BATTLEDOWN is a more recently developed area on the hill N of the old independent manor of Ashley. BATTLEDOWN MANOR of *c.*1900 is a stone house in Cotswold style.

GLENFALL, 1 m. W. Early C19, two-storey villa originally of three bays with windows set in arched recesses, but altered and enlarged *c.*1923 by *Sidney Barnsley*, who introduced excellent panelling and plasterwork. Attractive polygonal LODGE, with decorative wrought-iron fringe to its overhanging eaves.

7010

CHAXHILL

1½ m. E of Westbury-on-Severn

ST LUKE. 1894 by *Medland & Son.* Of brick, in E.E. school-chapel style. The apse is interrupted by an ugly gable.

CHAXHILL HOUSE. Early C19, stucco-faced, three storeys and three bays. Doorway with fanlight and an open pediment supported on three-quarter columns with feathered capitals.

NINNAGE LODGE. C18 or early C19.

9020

CHELTENHAM

INTRODUCTION

Shortly before the Reformation John Leland described Cheltenham as 'a longe towne havynge a Market. There is a brook on the South Syde of the Towne'. The original town consisted solely of the long High Street, which had a Booth Hall, Prison, High Cross, and Market House. Practically none of the medieval buildings have survived except the church.

In the C17 Cheltenham was still only a 'market town – about 350 families there'. A new source of livelihood had developed in the growing of tobacco. Although its cultivation had been declared illegal in 1619, local farmers persisted, with varied success, for another fifty years.

In a field at the back of the Chelt, on, or near, the site of the Princess Hall, in Cheltenham Ladies College, there was a spring which left a deposit of salts, and possessed purgative properties, discovered in 1718. A well was sunk near the spring. Henry

Skillicorne, a merchant captain from Bristol, married a wife whose property this was. He instituted a pumping system and built a brick structure over the well, later known as the Royal Old Well. In 1739 he planted an avenue with a double row of elms and limes, as a suitable approach to the new Spa from Church Meadow, crossing the Chelt by a rustic bridge. The Spa was off to a good start and then slumped. A Master of Ceremonies was appointed c.1781, and the Assembly Rooms (long since demolished) were built in the High Street, to the designs of *Henry Holland*. In 1786 a new authority was established by Act of Parliament appointing fifty-eight Commissioners, and changing the rural community into a paradise for the speculators who built the beautiful Regency town during the next sixty years. Skillicorne built a no longer surviving house in Bayshill for Lord Fauconberg, which, in 1788, housed the Royal Family during a five-week holiday. This unprecedented event made Cheltenham fashionable. It was a summer resort, unlike Bath, and *rus in urbe* was the fashion. Despite the intervention of the Napoleonic Wars, the town grew, with a population of 3,000 in 1801 increasing to 20,000 in 1826. In 1823 four to five hundred people were employed in the building trade, and contracts in hand for new houses amounted to £450,000. In 1801 the Enclosure Act freed much common land for building on the outskirts of the town. Henry Thompson, a Liverpool and London banker, bought four hundred acres, now the Lansdown and Montpellier estates. In 1804 he added a further thirty acres at the then enormous price of £14,000. Thompson opened his first spa in 1804 at Hygeia House (Vittoria House since 1813) (*see* p. 143). In 1809 he built the Montpellier Spa, a wooden cabin with a veranda. In 1817 the spa was often overcrowded, and *G. A. Underwood*, who had just left Sir John Soane's office, was employed to rebuild the pump room. The room (now Lloyds Bank) with its plain Doric colonnade survives. The Rotunda was not added till 1825-6, by Thompson's son Pearson, who employed *J. (B.) Papworth*.

In 1824 Papworth had paid a brief visit to Cheltenham to do a preliminary survey for a house for a Dr Shoolbred (Rosehill, situated near the racecourse). Pearson Thompson then asked him to prepare a scheme for the Lansdown estate. In the event this was only partially carried out; but Papworth had planned the first English garden city with houses set among formal avenues and gardens. Lansdown Road was built as shown in Papworth's 1825 plan, and the lay-outs of Lansdown Place, and Lansdown Crescent, were partially adhered to. Unfortunately part of the scheme had to be abandoned in 1825, owing to a local financial crisis caused by land speculation at Pittville. Economy without meanness was the motto after 1825. Although the facing was stone, to give the appearance of luxury, the balconies were of cast iron, an innovation which Papworth had recommended in *Rural Residences* as being cheaper. No attempt was made to give any coherence to the rear elevations, though Papworth always finished his end houses with a side porch; for a residence consisted of house and garden together. The interiors were decorated with simple marble fireplaces, mahogany door surrounds, and plaster friezes of fruits and foliage; the arrangement of the rooms could be varied. With the obvious exception of Thirlestaine House, Cheltenham's domestic interiors are not generally outstanding.

When the *Jearrads* took over all Thompson's enterprises in 1830, they dismissed Papworth, retaining his plans against his wishes, and without further payment. During Papworth's connexion with Thompson, he had produced a sewerage scheme, the first in the town, for the whole of Thompson's property. Thompson eventually emigrated to Australia, but not till 1849.

The contemporary Pittville development also failed to come up to Joseph Pitt's original expectations. However, what the speculative developers had achieved was a planned town, a garden city, which was something completely new in England. The broad tree-lined streets provided a perfect setting for the architecture of the Greek Revival, enhanced by the widespread use of decorative ironwork. The neo-Greek style continued well into the 1840s, as can be seen in Bayshill. The large houses built here by *Samuel Onley* are more residential in character, as the popularity of British spas declined with the fashion for continental travel. The chief legacy which Cheltenham derived from its spas was its popularity with retired Indian Army officers and colonial civil servants, a self-sufficient group who shared a common background, and enjoyed fox-hunting with the Berkeley hounds. Contemporaneously the town became a stronghold of Evangelism, partly due to the extraordinary influence of its vicar, the Rev. Francis Close. 'There are great spiritual advantages to be had in the town', says one of George Eliot's characters.* And there were soon great educational advantages, with the founding of public schools, for boys in 1841 and girls in 1854. Superimposed therefore on the neo-Greek domestic architecture are a great many Gothic Revival ecclesiastical and college buildings.

* *Middlemarch.* Bulstrode to his wife.

John Middleton,* who had been trained by J. P. Pritchett of Darlington, and married his daughter, came to Cheltenham about 1860. The field was wide open, and in the course of a few years he built no less than five new churches in the town, apart from altering a great many others in the neighbourhood, and adding large blocks on to Cheltenham College, and the Ladies College.

A list of architects working in Cheltenham in 1841 consists of *R. W. Jearrad, Paul & Sons, G. J. Engall, E. H. Shellard,* and *S. W. Daukes.* Jearrad died in 1861 and Paul in 1854. Other architects mentioned are *Samuel Onley,* who was active between 1847 and 1862, when he claimed: ' I have dug, during the last 15 years, enough brick earth to make a million bricks . . .'; *H. Dangerfield* who was Borough Surveyor, and was succeeded in 1862 by *D. J. Humphris;* and *W. H. Knight,* mentioned in connexion with a street development in 1858 as Paul & Knight, perhaps *C. Paul*'s son *R. Paul.*

Recent developments in Cheltenham are frankly disturbing. Cavendish House has set a completely new trend in the Promenade, as have the new shopping blocks in Pittville Street and Winchcombe Street. There are bad infillings with small boxes round the south of Pittville Park and there is a terrible row of bungalows just back from All Saints Road. The new Telephone Exchange in Oriel Road however is quite polite and in scale, but it would be a pity if development here meant the destruction of Oriel Lodge. A number of good houses are now in a derelict condition. Everything in the future depends on the Central Development Plan.

CHURCHES

ST MARY. The parish church, and the only medieval church in Cheltenham; it was a possession of Cirencester Abbey till the Dissolution. Cruciform; central tower and early C14 broachspire. The nave W wall with its buttresses and the piers supporting the arches under the tower may be as early as *c.*1170, but the arches are pointed Transitional work and the piers have slender E.E. shafts. Rib-vaulted crossing. Nave, N and S aisles, and the four-bay arcades with octagonal piers early C14, as is the remarkable rose window with its flowing cusped tracery on the E side of the N transept, and the lovely curvilinear N window adjacent to it. Arched tomb recesses in the N

---

* Not be confused with his son *John Henry Middleton,* the eminent orientalist and archaeologist, curator of the Fitzwilliam Museum, Cambridge, and close friend of William Morris.

transept and N aisle have ballflower enrichments. The chancel
was extended in the C14, and the window tracery N and S is
Dec, with a later E window, almost Perp, with a beautiful
broad horizontal band of large quatrefoils. Splendid canopied
PISCINA on the S side of the sanctuary, with sculptured
images and ogee arches, under an embattled top. The latest part
of the medieval church is the N porch, now used as a baptistery; Perp, with a lierne-vault under an upper chamber, which
was opened to the church when it was restored in 1851, by *H.
Dangerfield* and *D. J. Humphris*. The church was again restored
in 1877, by *Ewan Christian*. N vestry and S porch added in 1893.
– REREDOS. Of *c.*1915, designed by *Healing & Overbury*, executed by *Boulton*. – SANCTUS BELL. Probably C13; preserved
in the chancel. – ROYAL ARMS. George III. – STAINED
GLASS. Mostly by *Lavers, Barraud & Westlake*. Also includes
windows by *Heaton & Butler, Clayton & Bell, Hardman,
Joseph Bell*, and *Burlison & Grylls*. The rose-window is by
Wailes, 1876. – PLATE. Chalice, Paten, and Flagon, 1823 by
J. E. Terry. – MONUMENTS. Brass to William Grevil (2 ft 2 in.),
his wife and children. Early C16, restored in 1920. – In the S
aisle, a touching and beautiful inscription by John English to
his wife, † 1643, surmounted by a bold stone cresting. – Long
epitaph to the Skillicorne family, almost a history of the town.
– Several tablets of the C18, including a neo-Greek one to
Mrs Hughes † 1786, by *J. & J. Bryan*. – Large monument to
Sir William Myers, killed at Albuera in 1811, by *Oldfield &
Turner*. – Alexander Jaffray † 1818. Neo-Greek by *Wood*. –
Charles Jervis † 1826, by *P. Turnerelli*. Neo-Greek with
Christian symbolism. – The usual collection of tablets by *G.
Lewis*, including a broken column with a fallen Corinthian
capital, to Thomas Gray † 1835. – INCUMBENTS BOARD. By
John L. Jones, 1965. – CHURCHYARD. Always a focal point for
perambulation, linking the High Street with the Spa. One or
two, but not all, of the peculiar inscriptions attributed to the
tombstones survive, and some brass measuring-marks, once
used to check the length of rope sold in the market, can be
seen in the path to the E of the S porch.

ALL SAINTS, Pittville. 1868 by *John Middleton*; his finest church.
Of rusticated Cleeve Hill stone and Bath stone dressings, the
interior lined with Bath stone and bands of blue Forest stone.
The style is early French Gothic, with beautiful plate-
traceried windows. Clerestoried nave of five bays, N and S
transepts, lean-to aisles with porches, apsidal chancel, Lady

Chapel and organ chamber. The tower intended at the sw corner was never built; Middleton planned a 200-ft spire. In the w front a doorway with carved typanum by *A. B. Wall*. The interior is extremely rich and is Middleton's most sumptuous masterpiece. Nave arcades with alternate blue and white voussoirs supported on polished granite columns with boldly carved stone capitals, and statues under canopies in the spandrels; everything rich and proficiently designed. Chancel arch tall and nobly proportioned, so that the painted apsidal chancel roof is visible from the nave. Goodhart-Rendel described it as a 'splendid example of what Gilbert Scott was always aiming at and never achieved . . . complete Gothic self-assurance with Victorian punch'.

A lot of the fittings were designed by *H. A. Prothero*, e.g. the FONT COVER, 1896, consisting of elaborate foliated and gilded ironwork, the ORGAN CASE, the SOUNDING BOARD over the pulpit, and the chancel SCREEN, 1894, in the most delicate wrought iron, a medium in which Prothero excelled. The ROOD figures were made in Oberammergau. In 1898 Prothero designed the small apse for the Lady Chapel. – FONT. Caen stone, circular bowl supported on granite shafts, with alabaster carved panels; contemporary with the church. – PULPIT. Designed by *Middleton*, 1872; carved by *Boulton*. – LECTERN. Elaborate brass-work by *Hardman* of Birmingham. – STAINED GLASS. Rose window in the s transept designed by *Burne-Jones* and made by *Morris & Co.*, 1901. – Two two-light windows in the N transept by *Heaton, Butler & Bayne*. – Rose window at the w end by *Sir William Richmond*, 1897. – PLATE. Chalice and Paten, 1577; two Chalices, two Patens, and Flagon 1839 and 1841 by *J. & J. Angell*.

HOLY APOSTLES. *See* Charlton Kings.

CHRIST CHURCH, Malvern Road. 1838–40 by *R. W. & C. Jearrad*. Interior remodelled in 1888–93 by *J. H. Middleton, H. A. Prothero & Phillott*. Restored and redecorated with a new N chapel, which has a ciborium over the altar, by *R. W. Paterson* in 1956. The Jearrads designed the church in the E.E. style with a tall Perp tower, symmetrically placed in the centre of an elaborately gabled w end. The determination to give the building vertical emphasis, and the directness of approach, cannot fail to give the viewer a memorable impression. The details of crocket and finial are so weathered now that what was always a simple Gothic style is even simpler still. Goodhart-Rendel wrote irreverently: 'An outstanding fantasy in the style of a Staffordshire china ornament, that could stand on the largest chimneypiece in the world. There is also a tall Perpendicularish tower with a lamentable expression; you expect it to sob.'

At first the interior was merely fitted up as a preaching church with large galleries on three sides, supported on cast-iron columns, and facing a three-decker pulpit. From 1888 onwards the interior was altered; the domed apse was added at the E end by *J. H. Middleton* and his partners, and the paintings were done by *Sir William Richmond*, assisted by *J. Eadie Reid*. An attempt was made to make the church look like an Italian basilica: the iron columns supporting the gallery were encased in white marble, and the choir received a low coloured-marble screen with wrought-iron side screens, marble communion rail, and Renaissance sanctuary arch. The whole interior has been brought to admirable unity and lightness by a complete scheme of redecoration. – STAINED GLASS. By *Lavers & Westlake* and *Heaton, Butler & Bayne*. – MONUMENTS. All of much the same date and style, mostly by *Lewis* of Cheltenham; many with military trophies.

EMMANUEL, Ewlyn Road. 1936 by *H. Rainger*. Stone, with W bell-turret. Neo-Georgian windows but no E window. Wagon roof. – STAINED GLASS. W window by *Joseph Nuttgens*. – S chapel E window by *Geoffrey Webb*, 1942. – S window by *John Hardman*, 1949.

ST AIDAN, Princess Elizabeth Way. 1959 by *W. L. Barrow*. One of the newest churches in the diocese, making full use of modern materials and methods; the emphasis is on texture rather than solid and void, and the concrete frame is clearly visible, with patterned brick infilling.

ST GREGORY (R.C.), St James's Square. 1854–7 by *Charles Hansom*. Dec. Clerestoried nave, aisles, chancel, transepts, elegant tower and spire completed in 1861. Porch added in 1859 with stubby columns in lieu of jambs and a large foiled arch. – STAINED GLASS. By *Hardman*; very striking, with large circular frames going through two lights, both in the five-light sanctuary window, and in the transept window on the Epistle side (the church is not orientated normally, but has the chancel at the S end). The nave was extended to connect with the tower in 1877.

ST JAMES, Suffolk Square. Begun in 1825. Designed by *Edward Jenkins*, a local architect, in Regency Gothic. *J. (B.) Papworth**

* Papworth assumed the additional name of Buonarotti.

was appointed in an advisory capacity in 1828 because Jenkins was having difficulty with the enormous span of the roof. The church was completed in 1830. The exterior is typical of its date, but nothing mean; ashlar-faced, with nave, N and S aisles, and later Victorian sanctuary. The W end has octagonal buttresses terminating in castellated pinnacles, a gabled embattled parapet, and a Dec W window with a crocketed ogee-shaped hood-mould. The aisles are embattled, pinnacled, and buttressed. Single flat-pitched roof of considerable span, supported by slender stone-faced columns, quatrefoil in plan, with octagonal abaci like the top mouldings of a cornice, interesting in having Tudor arches all mixed up with the roof, springing directly from the columns, and with cast-iron trusses. Continuous gallery over aisles and W end. Original furnishings have not survived, though the PEWS are presumably *Papworth*'s, as they were staggered in the same way at St John's. – PLATE. Pair of Chalices, 1828; Flagon, 1828; two Patens, 1830 by *John Angell*. – MONUMENTS. A lot of very dull tablets by *G. Lewis* of Cheltenham, but at the E end of the S aisle a finely sculptured monument by *Peter Hollins* of Birmingham, [89] 1855, showing the death of a young officer at the siege of Sebastopol.

ST LUKE, St Luke's Road. 1854 by *F. W. Ordish*. Chancel enlarged in 1866 by *John Middleton*. Restored in 1888–9. The general scheme is normal, with biggish transepts with galleries, clerestoried, cruciform, with W tower and spire; but many details are delightfully peculiar. The spire is broached with ugly fat broaches, and the windows in the aisles have three lights with highly original, unorthodox, and complicated tracery, each one different. – REREDOS. Painted and gilded stone with realistic carving, designed by *Middleton*. – STAINED GLASS. E window by *Hardman*. – N and S by *Heaton & Butler*. – PLATE. Two Chalices, Paten, and Flagon, 1845.

ST MARK, Lansdown. 1862–7 by *John Middleton*. Good W tower with spire. Rich, competent, conventional Dec; but Middleton's least sumptuous, least effective, and earliest church in Cheltenham. Built of rusticated stone with Bath stone dressings. In 1888, huge congregational double transepts were added, covered with twin gabled roofs, the box gutters N to S being supported on tiebeams running E to W; so no arcade was needed under the valley. Arches and clerestory openings continue internally across the transepts. Nave arcades of five bays with cylindrical columns and round moulded capitals. –

STAINED GLASS. E window and those N and S in the chancel, good examples of *Kempe*. – Three-light window S nave, by *Abbott & Co.*, 1929. – Two-light window W of S aisle, by *John Hardman*, 1955. – PULPIT and FONT. Contemporary, with elaborate carving.

ST MATTHEW, Clarence Street. 1878–9 by *Ewan Christian*; one of his best works. A magnificent auditorium church canted into the chancel with cross-gabled aisles; admirable and handsome, the detail severe and good. Of stone; E.E. NW tower, the spire taken down in 1952.

ST MICHAEL, Whaddon Road, Lynworth. 1965–6 by *D. Stratton-Davis*. Hexagonal plan. Prefabricated laminated timber framework on six concrete piers. – FONT. Hexagonal, slate, with incised and relief decoration, by *E. M. Dinkel*. – DOORS. Engraved glass by *Dinkel*.

82 ST PAUL, St Paul's Road. 1827–31 by *John B. Forbes*. Built for the artisan classes of the town, in the poorer quarter. Very neatly designed, galleried and in one span, with a nice tetrastyle Ionic frontispiece and a tower with cupola top; all well detailed, and based on the Temple of Ilissus. – GALLERIES supported by cast-iron columns and panelled with Georgian mouldings. – Later fittings include a wrought-iron PULPIT which pulls out on runners, and a NORTH CHAPEL fitted up in 1932. It has a window with STAINED GLASS by *Edward Payne*, 1963, and good brass pendant LIGHTS, originally brackets.

ST PETER, Tewkesbury Road. 1847–9 by *Samuel Whitfield Daukes*. Romanesque. Goodhart-Rendel says: '. . . really a great success. The circular lantern tower on pendentives is beautiful inside and out. Correct Norman detailing in execution looks very well. Who cares if the chevrons inside are of plaster. Good stone work outside.' Cruciform with a large dome in the middle, the arches supported by Norman columns with scalloped cushion capitals, and abaci enriched with round pellet ornaments as big as apples, and gilded. All the interior is painted and gilded. – FURNISHINGS. 1910–13. – ROYAL ARMS. Elizabeth II. – PLATE. Paten, 1708; Paten, 1721; Flagon, 1734, by *Francis Spilsbury*; two Chalices, 1807.

ST PHILIP. *See* Leckhampton.

ST STEPHEN, St Stephen's Road, Tivoli. 1873 by *John Middleton*. Of rusticated stone with a tall nave, lean-to aisles, N porch, chancel, and transepts. The rather dull exterior is quite surpassed by the most successful and carefully detailed interior of the richest Dec. Nave arcades of six bays, with alternating white Bath stone and blue Forest stone voussoirs and supported by clustered columns with fine mouldings and waterholding bases. Clerestory with cinquefoil-headed windows, divided from each other by shafts which support the excellent timber wagon roof. The E window has nice geometrical tracery. The W wall of the nave is carved with the Apostles in niches, and a very florid arcade below. – Light Gothic iron SCREEN on the low marble wall under the chancel arch, and a splendid ROOD added in 1945. – The feeling of completeness in the design is unmarred by the Lady Chapel, an addition of 1919 by *L. W. Barnard*, as it is visually a separate entity.

HOLY TRINITY, Portland Street. 1820–3 by *George Allen Underwood*.* The church is of freestone on a now shaling sandstone plinth, in Soanian Gothic, with central W tower flanked by similarly buttressed but much lower towers, all with pierced parapets giving a well-proportioned vertical look. Simple Gothic windows, buttressed in between. Inside, a plain gabled nave or auditorium with galleried aisles N and S, and a W gallery on cast-iron columns. Five-bay arcades with four-centred arches and slender plastered piers. Unenlarged shallow sanctuary with small transepts either side. Alterations were made to the interior *c*.1877 by *John Middleton*. – FONT. 1879. – ORGAN. 1896 by *A. J. Price & Sons*. – CHOIR STALLS. 1916. – PLATE. Four Chalices of 1821 and 1822 and two of 1825; Flagon, 1819; two Patens, 1822. – MONUMENTS. The walls are crowded with tablets mostly by *G. Lewis* of Clarence Street, Cheltenham, one hundred and eighty one of them, and mostly to retired Indian civil servants and officers, for example Watkin Williams Massie, late of the Bengal civil service, † 1838, and one with a medallion profile of Colonel Warburton † 1836.

ST THOMAS MORE (R.C.). By *Peter Falconer & Partners*, *c*.1967.

ST MARY'S CEMETERY CHAPEL, Lower High Street. By *Charles Paul*, *c*.1830. Giant portico with Greek Doric columns *in antis*, and a frieze enriched with wreaths. The cemetery is now a public garden.

NONCONFORMIST CHAPELS

BETHEL BAPTIST CHAPEL, or CHRISTADELPHIAN HALL, Knapp Road. Date inscription 1820. Ashlar. Windows with semicircular heads under a large pediment.

* He had been an assistant in Sir John Soane's office in 1807–15, starting there at the age of 14. He died in Bath in 1829.

SALEM BAPTIST CHAPEL, Clarence Parade. 1844. Ashlar-faced, in pretty Gothick style. Ceiling lowered inside, so the effect of the galleries is spoiled.

CAMBRAY BAPTIST CHAPEL, Cambray Place. 1855 by *Dangerfield*. Italianate.

METHODIST CHAPEL, St George's Street. 1839. Ashlar; classical.

MORMON CHURCH OF JESUS CHRIST OF LATTER DAY SAINTS, Thirlestaine Road. 1964 by *John Graham*. Faced in buff-coloured brick, and glass, with deeply overhanging pitched roof.

NORTH PLACE CHAPEL (Countess of Huntingdon's Connexion). 1816. Classical, with Gothic windows and Doric portico. Galleries N, S, and W, on cast-iron columns. Gothic ORGAN CASE.

ST ANDREW'S PRESBYTERIAN CHURCH, Fauconberg Road. 1885 by *Thomas Arnold*. E.E. NW tower with spire. Rusticated stone, plate tracery, pitch-pine pews.

SYNAGOGUE, St James's Square. 1837–9 by *W. H. Knight*. Classical, stucco-faced; top lighting.

UNITARIAN CHURCH, Bayshill Road. 1844 by *R. Abraham*. Neo-Norman ashlar façade.

PUBLIC BUILDINGS

TOWN HALL, Imperial Square. Designed in 1901 by *F. W. Waller*, in the same heavy classical style as he had used for Lloyds Bank the previous year. Of stone. Three-bay pedimented front with a massive *porte-cochère*. The enormous Ballroom has five-bay arcades, with Corinthian columns supporting balconies over which are tunnel-vaults with domes; top-lit coved ceiling. Either side are ranges of lesser rooms.

85 MUNICIPAL OFFICES, The Promenade. Built *c.*1823. A great terrace, equal to any in Europe. Stucco-faced. Three storeys, basement, and attic, rusticated ground-floor treatment, and continuous first-floor veranda with fluted Ionic pilasters and semicircular-headed arches, with wrought-iron railings. Pediment over the central portion supported by four fluted Ionic columns with six similar pilasters either side; here the first-floor windows are in round-headed recesses with a continuous wrought-iron balcony. In 1916, the central seven houses were converted into Municipal Offices. Further extended since 1945 by *G. H. Ryland*, of *L. W. Barnard & Partners*,

to include thirteen terrace houses, it is now one of the finest municipal blocks in the country. New Mayor's Parlour and Council Chamber, *c.*1961.

GENERAL POST OFFICE, The Promenade. Built *c.*1823, by a portrait painter named *Millet*. It was first the Imperial Hotel, then in 1856 it became the Imperial Club, and in 1874 the Post Office. It is the central block of a symmetrical stucco terrace, with the centre and either end projecting slightly. The post office has three storeys and attic, nine bays, with four fluted Ionic pilasters through the upper floors, supporting the cornice and enriched parapet.

PUBLIC LIBRARY, Clarence Street. 1887 by *Knight & Chatters*. Victorian eclectic. The ART GALLERY was added in 1899, and the MUSEUM in 1907.

GENERAL HOSPITAL, Sandford Road. 1848–9 by *D. J. Humphris*. The last important building to be erected in the neo-Greek style. Entrance with central tetrastyle portico of giant fluted Ionic columns through the full height, supporting a pediment. E and W blocks designed in 1929 by *Charles Holden*. Recent additions since 1933 by *Healing & Overbury*. – SCULPTURE. The Good Samaritan by *Holme Cardwell*, of Rome, 1852. (Not *in situ* 1965.)

DELANCEY HOSPITAL, Charlton Lane. 1877 by *John Middleton*. Brick. Windows with plate tracery. Somewhat grim and forbidding. Addition of 1898 by *Middleton, Prothero & Phillott*.

PITTVILLE PUMP ROOM. 1825–30 by *John Forbes* for Joseph Pitt. Ashlar-faced, with a great colonnade of Ionic columns copied from Stuart and Revett's engravings of the Temple of Ilissus. Central bay of six columns to the front, with outer bays either side of two columns *in antis*, linked with the centre by two more columns. Parapet enriched with neo-Greek panelling. Surmounting the three projecting bays, and giving them the necessary further emphasis, are the recent statues of Aesculapius, Hygeia, and Hippocrates (the originals by *L. Gahagan* were removed). Above this are the central three-bay features of the main block, with pilasters, cornice, parapet, and small dome. Restored in 1951–62 by *R. W. Paterson*. The interior has beautiful elliptical arches and pendentives on fluted Ionic 88 columns, supporting a gallery, with further pendentives beneath the dome, all richly encrusted with paterae, and Greek 90 patterns. It is the culmination of the superb landscape gardening of Pittville, but as a building it perhaps demonstrates Forbes's limitations. It has not escaped criticism; Sir Hugh

Casson – alas, with some justification – called it 'stilted, high shouldered and rather graceless'.

MONTPELLIER PUMP ROOM AND ROTUNDA. *See* Lloyds Bank, Montpellier.

MASONIC HALL, Portland Street. 1820–3 by *G. A. Underwood*, and exactly contemporary with his Holy Trinity church, but far more successful. Underwood was himself a mason, and it must have been satisfactory to him to create such a mysterious-looking building, calculated to preserve the secrecy of the rites that went on within from the eye of the curious passer-by; altogether a happy commission for a young man who had been in Soane's office. The interior is said to contain much of its original furniture.

LANSDOWN RAILWAY STATION. 1840. Stucco façade of two storeys, with one–three–one bays and a central pediment. The Doric *porte-cochère* has been demolished, and only one fluted half-column remains to tell the tale.

POLICE STATION, Crescent Place. Of *c.*1820. Formerly the Clarence Hotel, so called after a visit from the future Queen Adelaide in 1827; it became the police station in 1859. Ashlar-faced, of four storeys plus basement and eight bays. Wrought-iron window guards on the first floor. Central stucco Ionic portico.

COUNTY POLICE STATION, Lansdown Road. 1965 by *R. F. Fairhurst*.

SCHOOLS

CHELTENHAM COLLEGE. Founded in 1841. The nucleus of the college buildings is the original range facing Bath Road, of 1841–3, by *J. Wilson* of Bath. Symmetrically planned, with a picturesque grading of levels stepping up to a central tower with detached octagonal turrets. The outline suffers somewhat from the loss of the pinnacles, recently taken down as unsafe. The style is Late Perp, with rather unimaginative tracery characterized by the multiplication of the standard vesica-shaped Perp unit. The virtue of the building lies in the bold handling of masses. The two great halls have been redecorated, one becoming a THEATRE and the other a LIBRARY, in classical taste, with a central portrait of the Queen; but in the middle the original staircase, with a Gothic cast-iron balustrade, survives.

In the 1850s further buildings were added to the E of the original range to form a quadrangle. Of these, the chief is the former chapel, now used as a DINING HALL. It is by *D. J. Humphris*, the exterior vaguely in the Eton and Kings tradition, with tracery continuing the theme of the earlier range. There is some ingenuity in the seven-light windows at either end (with, on the S, head-stops wearing mortar-boards), but on the whole the building is pedestrian in quality, and the quadrangle is now cluttered with nondescript later buildings.

The next addition to the S was in the 1860s, when *John Middleton* designed a range for the Junior School, still Perp but now of the C14 rather than the C15, although some of the same tracery motifs recur. The building has a semi-octagonal projection like half a chapter house, and an entrance tower with a figure in a niche; the handling of the detail is hard.

The present CHAPEL of 1896, by *H. A. Prothero*, is again in the Eton and Kings tradition, but ugly in proportion, and with little outbreaks of over-elaborate sculpture. The chapel is approached by an ingenious arrangement of fan-vaulted passages designed by *L. W. Barnard*, after the First World War. The whole adds to the art-historical interest of the group as illustrating differing interpretations of the Perp style during the course of the C19. – STAINED GLASS. Two superb windows on the S by *Louis Davis*, the last of the Pre-Raphaelites, and a window by *Powell* opposite, 1924. – E window by *Heaton, Butler & Bayne*. – The great REREDOS was designed by *Prothero*, and carried out by *Boulton & Sons*, introducing the figures of great men who had local connexions, like Jenner, Tyndale, and Raikes. – The PAINTINGS of the lunettes over the canopies of the stalls are by *J. Eadie Reid*. – MONUMENT to F. G. H. Myers † 1901, designed by *Prothero*, and carried out by *H. H. Martyn & Co*. Rising at the corner is a symbolic tree of life, a wild rose, beautifully carved in sycamore wood, with realistic brambles, birds and flowers.

GYMNASIUM BUILDING. 1864 by *F. H. Lockwood*. A long yellow brick building, flanked by towers with broach-spires; very nice. – MASTERS' DWELLINGS. By *Peter Falconer*, c.1966.

THIRLESTAINE HOUSE was begun in 1823, by *J. R. Scott*, an amateur architect. The wings were added in 1840 and 1845 for Lord Northwick, to house his collection of pictures. The original block has a giant order of pilasters, and facing the Bath Road, a noble neo-Greek Ionic portico; on the other side a single-storey *porte-cochère*, also in neo-Greek-Ionic, has been added, perhaps at the time when the wings were built. The

wings, not symmetrical, are articulated by blind windows and
inset panels in relief, with ingeniously top-lit rooms. Central
entrance hall aisled with two lines of Ionic columns and a
coved rosetted ceiling – like the Pittville Pump Room – a
Roman spatial idea expressed in Greek detail. Main staircase
with graceful scrolling on the iron balustrade, and pilasters
with anthemion capitals round the upper floor. The interior
detail of the main block modulates gradually from the purity of
the entrance hall to the still Grecian but rather more florid
work in the wings. It is interesting that Scott, the amateur,
brought to Cheltenham the Grecian style in its most learned
mode, before Forbes, the professional architect of Pittville.
The plain STABLE BLOCK behind the house, now converted
into dwellings, has lost the two 'Lysicrates' turrets which
Professor Richardson copied on the Jockey Club at Newmarket.
The Greek buildings, now happily the property of the College,
counterpoint their Gothic neighbours, with which they are
linked by open green lawns and cedar trees.

CHELTENHAM LADIES COLLEGE. Founded in 1854; but the
buildings are later in date, and have introduced an unsym-
pathetic architecture into the heart of Regency Cheltenham.
In 1873 the school moved to the present site from the former
Cambray House, and the first buildings were erected on the E
side of Old Well Walk, thus destroying one of Cheltenham's
best-known features. The earliest building was the LOWER
HALL, of brick faced with Cotswold stone, used in all subsequent additions; the style is Dec Gothic. In 1876 additions
were made by *John Middleton* which included the TOWER with
its rather French spire with sprocketed eaves, and now truncated at the tip. The MUSIC WING was built out at r. angles in
1881–2, and heightened and given dormer windows in 1898.
There followed considerable new building along Montpellier
Street by *Prothero c.*1889–90. Prothero's wing was much later
joined to Middleton's wing by a bridge designed by *L. W.
Barnard*. On the inside a wide marble corridor extends the
whole length. In 1896–8 additions were made by *E. R. Robson*
which included the extraordinary PRINCESS HALL, further up
Montpellier Street on the site of the old Theatre Royal, and
costing £20,000. Inside it has two tiers of wooden galleries
with Gothic fluted piers and segmental cusped cinquefoil
arches. In 1927 the GYMNASIUM was added to the S of the
Princess Hall, thus completing the aesthetic disaster along the
whole length of this part of Montpellier Street. The SCIENCE

WING, facing St George's Road, was built in 1904 of hard rusticated Cotswold stone in the Gothic style by *Waller & Son*. The latest addition in the Cotswold idiom is the large block built in Bayshill Road in 1936. However, the modern SCIENCE LABORATORY by *Brian Tait & Anthony Ault*, c.1960, is far politer to this street of Regency villas.

The interior decorations of the College provide a consistent theme in praise of great women: much STAINED GLASS by *Heaton, Butler & Bayne*; 'The Dream of Fair Women', a MURAL by *J. Eadie Reid* in the Princess Hall; a BUST of Dorothea Beale by *J. E. Hyett*, and one of Queen Victoria by *Countess Feodora Gleichen*. – MONUMENT, on the wall near the Oxford Staircase, with lettering by *Eric Gill*, c.1907, commemorating Dorothea Beale.

ST PAUL'S (TEACHERS' TRAINING) COLLEGE, St Paul's Road. 1849 by *S. W. Daukes*. The whole of his original work survives, and is not least among the notable buildings of Cheltenham. Certainly the best C19 Gothic work is to be found here, particularly the CHAPEL built in 1909–10 by *Hodgson Fowler* in the manner of Bodley. – STAINED GLASS. By *William Morris & Co. (Westminster)*, 1934 and 1935. – ROSEHILL is a detached part of St Paul's Training College, in Evesham Road. The original Regency house was designed by *J. (B.) Papworth*, in 1824. He also laid out the grounds – some of the trees may still survive – and paid particular attention to the views obtainable from the house, which has suffered much alteration in Victorian and later times. It is now surrounded by new College buildings.

DEAN CLOSE MEMORIAL SCHOOL.* 1884–6 by *Chatters & Smithson*. Red brick and Dutch gables. Successful modern buildings by *Rainger, Rogers & Smithson*. – CHAPEL. 1923 by *Eric Cole*. Gothic. Brick. Five bays with fine tall brick arches. – FONT. Made of silver, by *George Hart*.

PATE'S GRAMMAR SCHOOL FOR GIRLS, Pittville. By *S. E. Urwin*, c.1939.

GLOUCESTER COLLEGE OF ART, Pittville. 1964 by *R. F. Fairhurst*.

ST MARY'S COLLEGE, The Park. By *Hening & Chitty*, c.1960.

NORTH GLOUCESTERSHIRE TECHNICAL COLLEGE. By *S. E. Urwin*, c.1957.

CHELTENHAM GRAMMAR SCHOOL, Hester's Way. 1963 by *Chamberlin, Powell & Bon*.

* The poet James Elroy Flecker was educated here.

PERAMBULATIONS

PERAMBULATION A

Imperial Square; Promenade Terrace; Queen's Hotel; Montpellier Walk; the Rotunda; Lansdown Place, Crescent, Terrace, and Parade; Lypiatt Terrace; Suffolk Square; Montpellier Terrace, and Parade; Vittoria Walk; Trafalgar Street; Oriel Road; and Wolseley Terrace.

We start from the town hall, situated in the largest of the Cheltenham squares, with its fine ranges of terrace houses, built c.1834. Nos. 1 to 13 IMPERIAL SQUARE just opposite immediately afford a splendid introduction to the town with a foretaste of what is to come. The stucco elevations with their wrought-iron balconies, and cast-iron balcony fronts of 'double hearts', can be found all over Cheltenham. The very plain railings to the basement areas, worth noting for the delicacy of their design, and the swept hoods to the balconies, carrying right along the whole length of the terrace, are typical of the Cheltenham style. Turning l., the building next to the town hall is the NEW CLUB, built in 1874, and opened only to 'Visitors of approved rank in society'. Two storeys, and bays with large three-light windows under entablatures supported on carved stone brackets. The entrance is reached up a broad flight of steps, under a cast-iron, glazed veranda. We are now in the upper part of THE PROMENADE. Originally the buildings forming PROMENADE TERRACE were hotels and private houses with individual gardens in front of them, which have now become car-parks, and most of the houses are offices with flats above. The setting back of the Terrace and the triple 5 avenue of trees is a delightful amenity to the town. This happy marriage of fully grown forest trees with urbanity provides a fresh visual experience for many visitors. The lower terrace of this group has three storeys and a semi-basement, but each house, unlike those on the other sides of Imperial Square, has its own individual balcony, and a pilaster runs the whole height between it and its neighbour. The use of channelled joints in the stucco of the entrance floor gives a solidity to the base of the buildings which contrasts well with the delicacy of the wrought-iron balconies above. The first two pairs of houses, Nos. 121–127, seem almost identical, though in fact there are many little differences. They each have an unusual pseudo-Corinthian capital to their pilasters (similar to those on Brandon House, Painswick Road), and they each have attic-storey windows with inverted shafts; but the upper pair has its pilasters grouped in the centre, whereas on the lower they are placed on the terminal blocks. The capitals on SHERBORNE HOUSE and GLOUCESTER LODGE are a charming fantasy based on the Prince of Wales feathers. CLARENCE HOUSE is a delightful little house in an intimately domestic style. Pleasant individual hoods over each of the main ground-floor windows, which open on to a continuous balcony, with cast-iron railings of typical standard design of the late Regency period. Three-bay central portion of two storeys plus basement, with Ionic pilasters on the upper floor; lower one-bay wings extend either side.

There is an interesting trick here about the carriageway of the Promenade itself; at this upper point it is exactly double the width of the carriageway at the lowest end. This has the effect of making the centre of the town appear to be a long way from the Queen's Hotel, whereas the Promenade appears to be shorter than it is when seen from the other end. Also, Clarence House has only two storeys, yet the skyline remains almost constantly level; Nos. 121–127 give the key, by permitting the change of level with their attic floors above the main cornice, whilst the other buildings have all their windows below the cornice.

91 QUEEN'S HOTEL. Built in 1838 by the brothers *Robert W. Jearrad* and *Charles Jearrad*. It is a very strong design, and has a curious resemblance to some of the classical Russian buildings in old St Petersburg. Stucco-faced, four storeys, four, five, and four bays, with a central projecting giant Corinthian order supporting the pediment and rising from a horizontally channelled ground floor.

The road here has to curve round to avoid the hotel, which is built on the site of *Underwood*'s Sherborne Spa. Interesting treatment of the swept cornice of the houses in QUEEN'S CIRCUS, which successfully takes account of the rise in level of the road. This pattern could have been followed on the E side of Imperial Square with advantage, as the cornices there, except on the topmost house, are just chopped, and the result is not nearly so pleasant.

The first house in MONTPELLIER WALK is a branch of the NATIONAL PROVINCIAL BANK, formerly a chemist's shop and converted by *Eric Cole*. The Walk is a charming example of intimate classical architecture, designed by *W. H. Knight*
92 *c.*1840. The caryatid figures are painted terracotta – at least three of them, sculptured by *Rossi*, are – and these were used as models for the others, which were made in stone by *W. G. Brown*, of Tivoli Street. In some places the caryatids are 'out of step' with each other, stabilizing the design, which is stepped up, with a swept cornice and frieze of oak-leaves. The buildings are ashlar-faced, of two storeys, with attics behind a balustraded parapet. The shop fascias ought to be controlled for the sake of uniformity.

84 MONTPELLIER SPA (now occupied by Lloyds Bank) was built for Pearson Thompson, in 1817, by *G. A. Underwood*. In 1825 Thompson extended the accommodation, and laid out the gardens opposite. The problem for his architect *J. (B.) Papworth*

was to give the building distinction, and at the same time preserve Underwood's colonnaded room, which was too new to be pulled down, and too low to be really impressive. Papworth's solution is a masterpiece, providing Roman opulence inside the ROTUNDA, with a domed room lit after the manner of the Pantheon, and providing a feeling of spaciousness, while the outside harmonizes with the simple colonnade, and retains the appearance of small scale. As usual Papworth designed all the interior fittings personally to achieve a unity of all the parts. The Rotunda was completely refurbished in 1965 by *Llewelyn, Smith & Waters*. For some years there were no buildings in Montpellier Walk. *Papworth* designed the Montpellier Gardens in relation to the Rotunda, a combination of formal flower gardens, and winding paths leading through shrubs. The STATUE of William IV, by a self-taught stonemason, was erected in 1831 to commemorate his Coronation.

MONTPELLIER EXCHANGE. This is a pedestrians' walk behind BARCLAYS BANK. The delightful little wrought-iron balconies, with cast-lead ornaments and small hoods, are good examples of this decorative quality when applied to stucco buildings. The bank, built before 1825, was recently restored by *Eric Cole*. In the street a sentimental STATUE by *R. L. Boulton & Sons*, erected in 1914, of Edward VII holding a child by the hand, and further on, an iron LAMPSTAND in memory of General Gordon † 1885. On the r. is LAURISTON HOUSE, which has Tower of the Winds capitals, successfully used on the porch, but less so on the pilasters of the house under an over-massive cornice.

LANSDOWN PLACE. Begun in 1825, to the designs of *J. (B.) Papworth*. Designed in pairs, linked by recessed porches (though some have now been spoiled by building forward in front of the porches), the houses are faced in ashlar, and of great height – three storeys and a basement. Stables and coach-houses were crammed behind under towering cliffs of brickwork. No. 1, later the Montpellier Spa Hotel, and with the two adjacent houses now converted into flats, still retains its fine cast-iron staircase, and the original porch – much disguised – survives. The balconies were probably the first of cast iron to be used in Cheltenham, and they have the subsequently common 'double heart' motif. Turning r. at No. 14 one crosses the rather squalid mews and comes into LANSDOWN CRESCENT, which derives from the 1825 'circular plot' designs by *Papworth*. Although conceived as semi-detached houses as late as 1829, it is clear that the façade design is his, though it was the *Jearrads* who eventually built the huge convex Crescent. Since No. 1 was not finished until 1829, it is probable that No. 3 onwards were not built when Papworth was dismissed by the Jearrads in 1829/30. The façades, however, show remarkable uniformity in contrast to the variations of Lansdown Place, though the stuccoed surface of No. 1 was not repeated, and the pedimented windows and porch with columns *in antis* are more refined than those on the rest of the crescent. Papworth wrote on his drawing for No. 1, 'Balcony to a single window as used at Brighton.' This survives; but it was the only house in Cheltenham that Papworth did not face in stone, and it was in a ruinous condition in 1967. On the E side of Malvern Road is LANSDOWN TERRACE, indubitably the most original terrace in Cheltenham. No. 1 was built first, before Malvern Road was constructed. The 'Italian' villas, LANSDOWN COURT, were built at the same time, *c.*1830, the year that Papworth had to hand over to the Jearrads. In 1832 the terrace was 'rapidly advancing'. It is therefore possible that Papworth may have made designs for both No. 1 Lansdown Terrace* and for the 'Italian' villas; but if these houses were not begun before 1830, it is far more likely that they were entirely conceived by the Jearrads, who were also professional architects established in London. The style of the terrace is considerably more bold and three-dimensional than was usual with Papworth; furthermore the interiors lack the refinements found in Papworth's other buildings. Each house in the terrace has a charmingly designed classical portico to the main first-floor room, with pairs of Ionic columns supporting a pediment, and rising from a stone balcony. LANSDOWN COURT has similar balconies, though conceived in a completely different style. It has excellent proportions, and the bold overhang of the tower roofs, with their very solid lead rolls, makes a most satisfactory composition. Part of Lansdown Terrace, known as EVELYN COURT, was converted horizontally into flats, after 1918, by *P. R. Morley Horder*. LANSDOWN PARADE, 1838–41 by the *Jearrads*, is successful in an intimate way. The houses have some nicely detailed drawing-room cornices. Their ashlar fronts and Greek Doric porches look well with the triangular Green in front.

* It has been impossible to check the statement of the owner of No. 1 that Papworth's name appears on the deeds of his house. The Jearrads' names appear on the deeds of all the others.

Returning to, and crossing, Lansdown Road, we come to
LYPIATT ROAD with LYPIATT TERRACE on the r., which
is another forthright but later example of the symmetrical
'Italianate' style. On the l. are earlier (c.1832) detached classical houses, mostly similar, with Ionic porticoes. SUFFOLK
HOUSE FLATS were built in 1936, to the designs of *Eric Cole.*
SUFFOLK SQUARE. The terrace on the N side is probably the one
designed for Robert Morris by *Papworth,* in 1825. It was built
against an earlier house on the W, now called WILLOUGHBY,
which has a good tetrastyle Ionic porch and an interesting
pattern of glazing bars to the inner doorway. The Terrace was
designed to have attached Corinthian columns centrally as well
as at the ends, but when built, the central columns were
omitted, and the pavilions at the ends were given pediments,
not intended by Papworth. Leaving by St James's church, also
partly by *Papworth,* and going down SUFFOLK PARADE, turn
r. into MONTPELLIER TERRACE, which relies solely on
pleasant proportions for its effect, and was built before 1825.*
Turn l. into MONTPELLIER PARADE. The villas on the l.
were built c.1823, or earlier. WESTAL, a villa on the r., is of a
standard '*Papworth*' design, as is the house at the top facing
down this street. Facing us at the crossroads at the bottom is
CLAREMONT LODGE, an intriguing design, about which
Nathaniel Lloyd once said, 'This should be preserved as a
national monument.' The three blank windows over the
colonnaded porch, with its four little bull's-eye windows,
form a masterly composition, but it is a later addition to the
house. Very delicate cornice on the E façade, over the excellent
wrought-iron work of the balcony; but here again the top
storey above the cornice is an addition, as can be seen from an
original 'Furniture' picture, over a fireplace in the house,
which shows it as it was before the improvements. The
original house was probably built c.1800, and the additions not
till after 1834. On the corner of VITTORIA WALK is the
REGENT HOTEL, designed as a house for Pearson Thompson
by *J. (B.) Papworth* in 1825. It is the prototype of the small
Papworth type of house of three bays, with three-light windows – and segmental recesses above – either side of the front
door. Further along Vittoria Walk on the r. is VITTORIA
HOUSE, the original Spa opened in 1804 by Pearson Thompson's father. The exterior has not been greatly altered. It is
rectangular, with a bow in the centre of each long elevation,

* No. 91 is inscribed as the birthplace of Edward Wilson in 1872.

and completely surrounded by a colonnaded veranda. The next house was FARNLEY LODGE, now Y.M.C.A., another very early C19 house, with a pleasant detached tetrastyle Ionic portico. At the S end of the small road running parallel to Vittoria Walk on the W, called TRAFALGAR STREET, NELSON COTTAGE, one of three forming a little terrace lying back behind small gardens. It represents an aspect of Regency Cheltenham, and so of the England of the Napoleonic Wars, easily overlooked. The cottages, built c.1806, were part of a modest detached speculation. The Prince Regent was entertained some doors down, at Lindsay Cottage (it has now disappeared), in 1808. ROCK COTTAGE, a cottage orné built of tufa, vermiculated coloured rocks, and shells, of three storeys with a coved eaves cornice, is said to have been occupied by Nelson's Captain Hardy.

87 ORIEL ROAD. ORIEL TERRACE was built in 1824, with pleasant details and ironwork. ORIEL LODGE* appears on the 1825 map, and could be by *E. Jenkins*, the original architect of St James's church, since the Gothic styles are so similar. The symmetrical front, with its central projecting gable, has an oriel window over the tierceron-vaulted porch. Retracing our steps towards the town hall, on the l. is WOLSELEY TERRACE, c.1834; mostly two storeys plus a basement. The ground floor has a raised balcony; nice crisp decoration and fluted Ionic pilasters in stucco.

PERAMBULATION B

Bath Road; Sandford Public Gardens; London Road; Priory Parade; Oxford Parade; Berkeley Place; Cambray Place; Rodney Terrace; High Street; Regent Street; The Promenade.

This perambulation enters the BATH ROAD by Oriel Terrace. On the r. is ORIEL PLACE, also a comparatively early terrace, existing in 1825. Stucco-fronted houses, their pilasters with the incised neo-Greek lines often used by Papworth, though this terrace is too early for him. On the l. the MONTPELLIER BATHS, built by Henry Thompson at the very beginning of the C19, with three Doric entrances and a central feature with acroterion, and the Cheltenham coat of arms, presumably added when the baths were altered in 1869 by *Edward Holmes*. Turn to the r. into Bath Parade and l. by Sandford Public Gardens, in which the river Chelt can be seen to advantage.

* Threatened with demolition, 1969.

This part of the town was not developed till Victorian times. Turn r. in the LONDON ROAD, sometimes called UPPER HIGH STREET. The terraces here were all in existence by 1820. OXFORD BUILDINGS and PRIORY BUILDINGS are faced in ashlar, with three storeys and basements, and pretty wrought-iron window guards or verandas. THE PRIORY, where Wellington stayed in 1828, was a larger house with a giant Corinthian order; but it was stupidly demolished in 1968. Set back from the road are the splendid terrace houses of PRIORY PARADE and OXFORD PARADE, with particularly good wrought-iron work. Beyond this are the semi-detached stucco blocks of SPRING GROVE and HERONDEN, c.1832. Beyond again, and further set back, are the earlier and smaller houses of QUIETWAYS and KEYNSHAM BANK. Most of the houses on the opposite side of the road, by which the perambulation returns, were not built till Early Victorian times, though the cul-de-sac called PRIORY PLACE, leading towards the Chelt, has one or two cottages, such as the ashlar-faced BIBURY COTTAGE, which are shown on the 1826 map. PRIORY LAWN is a picturesque Gothick cottage. BERKELEY PLACE, developed before c.1820, is ashlar-faced, with four storeys and basement. The doors have fanlights; wrought-iron verandas on the first floor. The houses face the cedar trees in the garden of the BELLEVUE HOTEL. Continuing along the HIGH STREET, there is little to be noted. Turn l. into BATH ROAD and r. into BATH STREET, and thus to CAMBRAY PLACE, which has a terrace on the N side, built by 1820, of three-storey, three-bay stucco houses with first-floor wrought-iron verandas. This is a cul-de-sac leading to the ugly flats which were built in 1930 on the site of CAMBRAY HOUSE, once let to the Duke of Wellington by its eccentric owner Colonel Riddell. Through the passage on the r. of the flats to RODNEY ROAD. RODNEY TERRACE existed by 1832. The houses on the NW end were demolished in 1964 to give place to the new buildings of the Eagle Star Insurance Company. Returning towards the High Street, on the l. is RODNEY LODGE, built in 1809 for Robert Hughes. Stucco-faced. Good Ionic porch and fluted pilasters, running through two floors, with acanthus-leaf capitals. On the return elevation an attractive two-storey bow with overhanging roof. Beyond this is the classical Baroque LLOYDS BANK, built in 1900 on the site of the old Assembly Rooms by *Waller & Son*. Dome on the corner. Turning l. in the HIGH STREET, the PLOUGH

HOTEL is on the l. The inn, in existence in the C16, was always the most important in the town. Long, symmetrical, early C19 stucco front, of four storeys and twelve bays. The High Street generally has always been subject to constant change, and is now thoroughly commercialized. Turn l. into REGENT STREET. The EVERYMAN THEATRE was built in 1891, by *Frank Matcham*. (All the original theatres have disappeared.) R. and then l. into the PROMENADE, which was first laid out in 1818, by the landowners Samuel Harward and Thomas Henney, as a tree-lined avenue from the Colonnade, in the High Street, to the Sherborne Spa. Before this, it was an 'uncultivated marsh'. This development gave the Promenade the character it has since maintained. Within a few years buildings had been begun on the w side, and in 1826 they were completed, including the great group of terrace houses which have been cleverly converted into the present Municipal Offices (*see* p. 132), and the Imperial Hotel, now the General Post Office (*see* p. 133). These buildings are the vital features of the Promenade. On the opposite side are a heterogeneous collection of Victorian shops, many of which are being rebuilt. FOUNTAIN. 1893. Sculpture of Neptune drawn by sea-horses, by *R. L. Boulton & Sons*, in Portland stone. Bronze STATUE of Edward Wilson † 1912, by *Lady Scott*, 1914.

PERAMBULATION C

St George's Road; Bayshill; Royal Parade; Queen's Parade; Parabola Road; St George's Place; St James's Square; Clarence Street; Royal Crescent; Clarence Parade; North Street and Place; Portland Street; Pittville Street.

Leave the Promenade by ST GEORGE'S ROAD, which is not shown on the 1834 map; so the terraces here, and the large houses on BAYSHILL, are all part of the Early Victorian development, though the style remains almost universally Greek.

On the r. is ROYAL WELL TERRACE, stucco-faced, two storeys plus attic and basement, three bays to each house. The end houses project slightly and have round-headed windows on the ground floor, and straight-headed windows above, just the opposite way round to the rest of the terrace. Corinthian columns, and a continuous balcony on the first floor. Doors with nice fanlights and side-lights. On the return side is a recessed porch with Doric columns *in antis*. The next terrace on the r.,

BAYSHILL TERRACE, had pavilions either end and one in the centre, with six fluted Ionic columns, though the nearer two now only have stumps where the columns were. Beyond this the houses are later and later, starting with the Italianate villas of YORK TERRACE.* Opposite is BAYSHILL ROAD. The first house on the l. is the splendid FAUCONBERG HOUSE, built in 1847 for Charles Fowler by *Samuel Onley*, neo-Greek, but somehow resembling a lady by Winterhalter or Ingres. Two storeys, plus a tall attic storey and basement. The fluted Ionic pilasters rise through both floors, beautifully connected at the corners, and supporting a dentil cornice. Ground-floor windows with pediments on consoles. The portico has a smaller-scaled Ionic order. As it is known that Onley was the architect for this house, and also that he bought much of the Bayshill property including the Royal Old Wells, it is likely that he designed some, if not most, of the other houses now to be described.

FAUCONBERG VILLAS. Four similar houses, unmistakably Early Victorian, and at the same time so light and simple that they look as if they were made of cardboard. Painted stucco. Two storeys, basements, and dormer windows. Three bays, the architraves of the windows enriched with rosettes. Round-headed windows on the ground floor with carved keystones, and an ornamented string-course at first-floor level. Entrances at the sides. Opposite, PYATT'S HOTEL, rather dull and altered. The MILVERTON HOTEL, built as two semi-detached houses, but giving the appearance of one large villa, with a splendid pedimented Corinthian portico, and nine windows all crowned by a balustraded parapet, could well be by *Onley*. BAYSHILL HOUSE is again stucco, and with the same balustraded parapet. Two storeys plus basement. Five windows, the central three set back behind two fluted Ionic columns *in antis*, the outer windows of three lights. The next villa, THE LIMES and MARYMEDE, is almost exactly the same. On the l. is a Cotswold interruption from the Ladies' College, and then one of the most charming of all Cheltenham's terraces, ROYAL PARADE. It is faced in a particularly beautifully coloured ashlar. Two storeys and basement, with a

* Much further along St George's Road, beyond the range of this perambulation, is ALPHA HOUSE, a plain late C18 cottage faced in stucco with two storeys and five windows. A plaque on this house states: 'Edward Jenner, 1749–1823, discoverer of vaccination, lived here.' This is now disputed, as Jenner actually lived in St George's Place (*see* p. 149).

crowning cornice which sweeps up the hill. The doors are set
back in deep recesses, and the ground-floor windows have
entablatures supported on stone brackets carved with elegant
Greek motifs. The terrace ends with a detached house, in the
same style but beginning to look more Italianate. Opposite are
two more full-blown stucco houses. WINDSOR HOUSE has
Doric pilasters through its two floors supporting a cornice,
above which is a pilastered attic and cornice. The central
Roman-Doric portico has coupled columns and a pediment.
The SAVOY HOTEL has a central portion of five bays with
projections, and four Corinthian pilasters through two floors
and a modillion cornice. Attic storey with plain pilasters in the
centre. Central Corinthian portico, with four columns. Considerable later additions. Running across the top of Bayshill is
QUEENS PARADE, an ashlar-faced terrace of three storeys and
basement. The ground floor has horizontal grooving, and
round-headed windows in slight recesses. Doors with fanlights and side-lights. Verandas on the first floor. No. 1 projects and has four Corinthian columns through the upper
floors, and cast-iron double-heart window guards. Turn r. and
walk round PARABOLA ROAD, where most of the houses are
later in date and now belong to the Ladies' College. SIDNEY
LODGE, in OVERTON ROAD, is on the site of Lord Fauconberg's house where George III stayed. The existing house was
built in 1860 for Baron de Ferrières, in red brick with patterned
stone quoins and dressings, round-headed windows with
archivolts, keystones and scroll stops, and overhanging eaves.
Beyond this is ABBEYHOLME, built c.1865 by *John Middleton*
for himself, in French-Gothic style, an innovation for domestic
building in Cheltenham. Of rock-faced rusticated stone with
freestone dressings, Gothic windows, a steep-pitched tile roof
and tower, and a small oriel window projecting to a point.
Returning to St George's Road, cross into St George's Place
(*see* p. 149), and walk to ST JAMES'S SQUARE. On the l. is
ST GEORGE'S TERRACE, built after 1834. Stucco with
pilasters to full height. Modest, well-proportioned houses.
Continuing to the site of St James's station, built in 1847 but
now demolished, on the opposite side is a house occupied at this
exact time, 1846–50, by Tennyson. Three storeys plus basement, three bays, with a cast-iron balcony and window guards,
and channelled pilasters either side. Portico to the side with
fluted Doric columns. The next house, the VICTORIA HOME,
is by the same hand. Turn r. into CLARENCE STREET, passing

the MANCHESTER HOTEL on the l., a tall brick Georgian house, and the ELECTRICITY SOCIAL CLUB, a late C19 terracotta building on a rusticated stone plinth. The continuation of ST GEORGE'S PLACE is on the l. Jenner lived at No. 22, from 1805 to 1820. It is a three-storey, two-bay terrace house with wrought-iron balconies and a fanlight over the door. Almost opposite is No. 41, a small house where Fred Archer, the jockey, was born in 1857. To get to the ROYAL CRESCENT we must turn r. at CRESCENT PLACE with the back of the SALEM CHAPEL on the l. and the Police Station on the r. The Crescent is the earliest important terrace in Cheltenham. It was begun c.1806, and completed before 1810. Princess Victoria visited the Duke of Gloucester, at the end house, No. 18, in 1830. The plain astylar stucco façade is three-storeyed with basements. The houses are of three bays each, with pretty fanlit doorways and first-floor balconies. Inside, nice reeded doorcases with corner rosettes, and ornamental plaster cornices; in fact the interiors are a cut above most of the later ones in Cheltenham. The front of the Crescent is now ruined by the bus station, in the same way as St James's Square was once ruined by the railway. Adjacent is CRESCENT TERRACE, a good symmetrical stucco composition, with rusticated ground-floor treatment, and doors with segmental fanlights and side-lights. The end houses break forward slightly, and the central house has a pediment. The balancing block, PROMENADE HOUSE, is of two storeys and seven bays. Either side projects, with fluted pilasters to full height, and crowning pediments. Tetrastyle Doric portico with a frieze decorated with swags. CLARENCE PARADE takes us back to Clarence Street, and so on past the roundabout in the High Street, to NORTH STREET. ALBION VILLA (the Liberal Club), of c.1805, was built for Theodore Gwinnett, Clerk to the Commissioners (see p. 123). It is faced in stucco, with two storeys, and one–three–one bays. The central portion projects. Pediment with a fan ornament in the tympanum. The doorway, with its large fanlight, is set back in a wide and deep recess. The upper floor is supported by four Ionic columns. Straight on to NORTH PLACE. An unusual house, next the chapel, No. 11, is faced in ashlar, with ground-floor windows set in segment-headed recesses, wrought-iron window guards above, and panelled pilasters to full height, dying into the overhanging eaves without the benefit of a cornice. At r. angles is ST MARGARET'S TERRACE, built before 1825. These large houses are faced in ashlar, and have three storeys, plus attic and basement, with pilasters through the upper floors and again in the attic storey above the cornice. Magnificent wrought-iron balcony throughout on the first floor. Again the environment is spoiled by a bus station. Turn r. past the chapel into PORTLAND STREET, the link between Pittville and the town, and retrace your steps towards the High Street, where the back of the chapel is worth noticing. Presumably built as a house for the Countess of Huntingdon's chaplain, it is faced in ashlar with three storeys and two bays. Either side are two-storey wings with Roman Doric arcades. On the opposite side, No. 25 (formerly the Church of Christ Tabernacle) has a charming but ungrammatical neo-Greek panelled stone façade of three storeys and three bays, the upper windows round-headed. Good wrought-iron balcony on the first floor. The MASONIC HALL is on the r. PITTVILLE STREET has been rebuilt and commercialized.

Two further perambulations are recommended, one to the Pittville estate on the N, and the other to the Park on the S.

PERAMBULATION D

Winchcombe Street; Pittville Central Drive, Circus, and Lawn; Evesham Road; Wellington Square; and Clarence Square.

PITTVILLE. This estate on the N side of the High Street was developed by Joseph Pitt,* who played a very important part in the architectural history of Cheltenham. In the early 1820s Pitt began to develop the land which he had received under the Inclosure Act. The architect associated with him was the local *John Forbes*. The plan of the Pittville estate was published in 1826. It shows two central gardens, on each side of which was a road with terraces, varied with individual villas, and two squares, afterwards named after the Dukes of Clarence and Wellington. Beyond this was a third garden, with artificial lakes, and sloping up to the Pump Room, which was not completed till 1830. The building of Forbes's Pittville therefore exactly coincided with Papworth's Montpellier and Lans-

* In 1812 he was described as follows: 'Pitt used to hold gentlemen's horses for a penny, when, appearing a sharp lad, an attorney at Cirencester took a fancy to him and bred him to his own business. He soon scraped together a little money by his practise in the law, and by degrees entered into speculation. . . . Everything has thriven with him. He has now a clear estate of £20,000 a year . . .'. The same year he became Member of Parliament for Cricklade.

down. Expansion had reached saturation point. Thompson's financial difficulties in Lansdown were such that he had to sell out; Pitt continued with the development of his estate, but was unable to complete the original plan. The distance from the centre of the town proved to be another disadvantage.

The street leading directly from the High Street to the entrance of Pittville is WINCHCOMBE STREET, which crosses the artisan area of the C19, and has a rather transitional appearance, though some buildings would be well worth preserving, particularly COLUMBIA PLACE. This terrace, of c.1820–5, is faced in stucco and has two storeys plus basement. Continuous veranda on the ground floor of the main block, with square coupled pillars, and interesting cast-iron lotus and honeysuckle guards. Pedimented wings either end. Crossing into PITTVILLE CENTRAL DRIVE, on the r. is SEGRAVE PLACE, a dignified stucco terrace of three storeys and basement, horizontally channelled on the ground floor, and with an excellent continuous balcony with cast-iron anthemion decoration on the first floor. WESTON HOUSE is a detached villa with a pedimented Ionic portico. BERKELEY VILLAS are semi-detached, with seven bays and entrances either end; RODEN HOUSE and BERKELEY HOUSE are semi-detached with nine bays, and cast-iron balconies on the first floor. The turning on the r. leads to PITTVILLE CIRCUS, where APSLEY HOUSE, designed by a builder called *Cope*, who developed this neighbourhood c.1840, is an attractive building with a round castellated tower of three storeys rising adjacent to a Greek Doric porch. Continuing with the catalogue of Central Drive, the next house is KENILWORTH, two storeys plus attic and basement, one–three–one bays with Corinthian pilasters through both floors supporting a modillion cornice, and plain pilasters in the attic. Central stone portico with Corinthian columns *in antis*. Nos. 29–37 (odd numbers): a magnificent stucco terrace of three storeys and basement, and three bays each. The central and outside houses project slightly, the central house having two Ionic columns and *antae* through the first and second floors, and a continuous wrought-iron balcony at first-floor level. The drive is lined with silver birch trees, which contrast with the stucco like delicate wrought-iron work.

PITTVILLE LODGE. Excellently proportioned, with rusticated ground floor, first-floor pilasters, dentil cornice, side entrances, and a charming wrought-iron balcony. Nos. 45–53 (odd numbers) form another similar terrace. WIDDINGTON HOUSE is

less distinguished, but luckily the subject of a Building
Preservation Order. Nos. 59–67 (odd numbers) comprise the
third similar terrace. One would suppose that anyway the
terraces must have been designed by *Forbes*. REGENCY
LODGE, stucco, has horizontal grooving on both floors, and
plain pilasters with egg-and-dart-enriched capitals on the outsides. The windows are set in slightly projecting faces, three-
light on the ground floor divided by Corinthian pilasters, and
either side of a Corinthian portico. MALDEN COURT is an
interloper, in Tudor-Gothic style with ornamental bargeboards. The continuation of the drive is called PITTVILLE
LAWN. ELLINGHAM HOUSE is a large stucco villa with
pilasters to full height, and a wrought-iron veranda on the
return elevation. DORSET HOUSE is the most ambitious of the
neo-Greek villas, as the front elevation is repeated on the S
side, with two attached fluted Ionic columns *in antis*, the *antae*
capitals being enriched with egg-and-dart moulding, supporting a tall entablature and pediment, with acanthus-carved
finials. Horizontal channelling continues up to sill level of the
first-floor windows, which have stucco plaques above, enriched with anthemion. Presumably *Forbes* designed this
house, which shows more scholarship than some of the others.*
LAKE HOUSE and RAVENHURST is of considerable size, and
all the elevations are good. Two storeys; the attic storey has
been removed on the W side, which is of three bays, with fluted
Ionic columns in the centre with *antae* pilasters, and pilasters
either side of the outer bays. The windows have their own
pilasters and entablatures and blind balustrades on the first
floor.

The gardens in front of the Pump Room have stone bridges over
the artificial lake, of an accomplished and subtle design, by
Forbes, with balustraded parapets and urns. These were completed at the same time as the Pump Room, in 1830.

Returning along EVESHAM ROAD, where there is a rash of
horrible 'between the wars' houses facing the Central Drive
gardens, we come to some high terrace ranges, PITTVILLE
PARADE and BLENHEIM PARADE. On the r. are the two
squares, which possess an atmosphere of quiet and contain-
ment, as they are large enough but not too large. On the E and
N sides of WELLINGTON SQUARE are semi-detached houses,
and a small terrace, all stuccoed, and with Greek detail and

---

* *Forbes* was trained at the Royal Academy Schools, entering in 1815 at the
age of 20.

ornamental ironwork. The exception is on the NE corner, the
RECTORY, designed *c.*1870 by *John Middleton*, of brick with
different-coloured bands and arches, and unmoulded stone
dressings to the window openings, which have trefoil-headed
lights. The projecting gabled wing, dormers, and porch all
have ornamental bargeboards and steep-pitched roofs. On the
w side of the square a Tudor-Gothic-style terrace, with
heraldic devices carved on the stops of the dripmoulds, and
arched doorways with buttresses and crocketed pinnacles.
The s side has three blocks, the central one faced in ashlar with
individual window balconies. On the N and s of CLARENCE
SQUARE are stucco Regency terraces, on the w a terrace with
Tudor-Gothic-style details, and on the E LISLE HOUSE and
WELLESLEY COURT HOTEL form a stucco house of two
storeys with attic and basement, with five large fluted Ionic
pilasters through the ground and first floors, and a continuous
ground-floor wrought-iron balcony. There is also a terrace of
five houses. Pleasant, but not outstanding architecture.

PERAMBULATION E

Park Place; The Park; Painswick Road; Bath Road; and
Thirlestaine Road.

THE PARK. Best approched from Suffolk Square along PARK
PLACE. This street was developed by 1832, and consists mostly
of detached or semi-detached villas, nearly all with neo-Greek
detail, and some very much in the style of *Papworth*, who designed a house for a Captain Capel in Cheltenham. This house,
if built, has never been identified, though it could be one of at
least eight in the town. The two in Park Place which most
resemble it are Nos. 16 and 18.

As early as 1833, THE PARK was laid out by its owner
Thomas Billings as an oval tree-lined carriage drive enclosing
a central park, which for a short time became a zoological
garden. The estate was bought *c.*1839 by the architect *S. W.
Daukes*; however, most of the houses seem to have been built
by that time, and are still in the neo-Greek style of the rest of
Cheltenham. Daukes's own house, which he designed in
Tudor-Gothic and called TUDOR LODGE, has unfortunately
been demolished, though it is possible that he also designed
the Italianate lodge which stands sentinel at the entrance to the
Park, called CORNERWAYS. The first houses on the l. in
PARK DRIVE were the first to be built, and are shown on the

1834 map. ELLESMERE LODGE, a classical stucco villa, has a
Roman Doric portico. On the first floor the central window has
fluted Ionic pilasters either side, supporting a now mutilated
cornice and parapet. There follow a series of attractive villas
all very much alike: BENTON HOUSE, IRETON HOUSE,
GREENFIELDS, STONEGARTH, and OAKELEY. All have
pure Greek Doric porticoes, two storeys, three bays with three-
light windows on the ground floor, with variations, are faced in
ashlar or stucco, and have overhanging eaves. PARK LAWN
and SPRINGFIELD LAWN are large semi-detached houses,
faced in ashlar, with a tall entablature. Beyond this the houses
look more Victorian, and LONGFORD HOUSE is in the Italianate villa style. Interspersed are modern buildings, particularly
the NORTH GLOUCESTERSHIRE TECHNICAL COLLEGE, by
S. E. Urwin, and, inside the park, the new buildings of St
Mary's College (see p. 137). Turn l. into TIVOLI ROAD. Here
the houses furthest from the Park were built first. TIVOLI
LODGE and TIVOLI LAWN are like the Papworth prototype,
and are shown on the 1834 map. On the other hand, ST
OSWALDS, on the opposite side, is in the Strawberry-Hill–
Gothic style.

If it is desired to prolong the perambulation, turn r. in Andover
Road and r. again in PAINSWICK ROAD. Here, on the corner
of GRAFTON ROAD, is BRANDON HOUSE, which has the
same capitals to the pilasters as Nos. 121, 123, 125, and 127
The Promenade, and was presumably built c.1834. It is faced
in ashlar and has two storeys and five bays, and an imposing
portico with fluted columns and Tower-of-the-Winds capitals.
Grafton Road leads past humbler quarters to the now commercialized BATH ROAD. Turn l. towards the College. In
THIRLESTAINE ROAD, on the r., COLLEGE HOUSE, formerly
LAKE HOUSE, built before 1820 by R. Varden, the architect
and landscape gardener. Stucco-faced, with a portico with
coupled Ionic columns. Two bows and a wrought-iron
veranda to the side. A Regency fireplace has honeysuckle enrichments and detached columns. THIRLESTAINE HALL is a
classical stucco house with a Doric portico, and additional
wings, with a dome. Converted to offices by G. H. Ryland.

OUTER CHELTENHAM

The greatest modern development has taken place on the NW
between the Gloucester and Tewkesbury roads. ALSTONE

LANE leads directly into it. Here DERBY COTTAGE is a rare survival of the C16 or C17 and is timber-framed, with a Cotswold stone roof. The GLOUCESTERSHIRE MARKETING SOCIETY premises were designed in 1964 by *Peter Ryland*. UMBRELLA INN, Orchard Way, 1947–8, is by *G. H. Ryland*. SCOTT HOUSE and EDWARD WILSON HOUSE, Princess Elizabeth Way, are two four-storey blocks providing 204 flats, designed by *G. H. Ryland*, c.1950. The industrial development of Cheltenham is due to the pioneer work of Sir George Dowty. ARLE COURT is the headquarters of the Dowty Group. The house was built by *J. J. Rowland* in 1858, in Tudor-Gothic style, with much expensive carving. When the original Elizabethan house at Arle was demolished in 1880, much of its panelling is said to have been moved to the new house. The staircase has French historical figures, carved in wood, as finials.

CHIPPING SODBURY

7080

ST JOHN THE BAPTIST. Nothing earlier than the C13. Outwardly however the church appears to be entirely Perp or the work of *G. E. Street*, who did the restoration in 1869. The very large W tower is late C15 or early C16, and has four stages, with diagonal buttresses, a pierced embattled parapet, crocketed pinnacles, and gargoyles. The embattled S porch is enriched with three images, re-inserted in the C19. C15 nave with N and S aisles roofed with Pennant stone (not so durable as Cotswold), continued the full length of the church. E.E. chancel arch with two chamfered orders, supported on corbels with curious twisted terminals, which appear again in the large E.E. pier in the N chancel aisle. Here there are detached Purbeck shafts on the E and W sides, and corbels with twisted finials, instead of shafts, on the N and S. In the N chapel an E.E. PISCINA and a beautifully carved C15 image bracket. Perp nave arcades of four bays, those on the S with slightly ogee arches. In the N aisle two of the C13 capitals of the piers from the E.E. church are used as corbels for the C15 roof. N doorway C14, re-erected; S doorway dated 1526. Tierceron-vault under the tower. The interior walls of the church are limewashed. – PULPIT. C15, built into the wall of the N arcade. It was discovered by *Street*, who restored it rather drastically; a small stone fan-vault survives inside. – FONT. C13. Plain octagonal bowl on an octagonal shaft with a roll at the top and bottom. – STAINED GLASS. E window 1870 and E window of the S chapel 1905 by

Clayton & Bell. – PLATE. Chalice, two Patens, and Flagon, 1812. – MONUMENTS. A large stone slab with the incised figures of Richard Colmore † 1513 and his wife, represented in the civilian dress of the Tudor period under a double ogee-headed canopy. – Sir John Walshe, patron of William Tyndale, translator of the New Testament, who tutored his sons, 1522–4. Inscription and carved shields of heraldry.

The town is built either side of a broad street on a slight rise, well articulated, with buildings closing in where the HIGH STREET becomes ROUNCIVAL STREET. The lower end is called BROAD STREET, taking a sharp turn into HORSE STREET, at the bottom. The remains of the old CROSS are incorporated in the War Memorial, well sited here, and halfway up the High Street is a CLOCK TOWER, a memorial of 1871, surrounded by an arcade in Tudor style, added in 1948. The architecture of this fine street has perhaps been somewhat underrated compared with the small Cotswold towns, probably because of the inferior quality of the stone. There are as yet no serious blemishes; the houses stand well back and have considerable group value, without being in any way outstanding. CAMBRIAN HOUSE, Broad Street, is C18, three storeys, five bays, quoins, cornice, and pedimented Ionic portico. The TOWN HALL is C19 Dec Gothic. The GEORGE HOTEL, C17, has three steep gables with verges and finials and Georgian windows. Nos. 84 and 86, on the opposite side, are C16 with two unequal gables and windows with ovolo mullions. In HORSE STREET a range of tall C18 random-coursed stone houses with ashlar quoins, and architraves to the windows. The POST OFFICE is part of a building of three storeys and six bays with a crowning pediment. MELBOURNE HOUSE, early C18, three storeys, 2, 2, 2 bays, has a modillion cornice and central pediment with an *œil de bœuf* window in the tympanum. Two central first-floor windows emphasized with pediments; large pedimented porch in the centre with detached Ionic columns. Inside the house are early C18 panelling, chimneypieces, and stairs. Returning to the HIGH STREET, on the s side, Nos. 24 and 26 are Tudor with steep gables and small enriched oval windows, and a four-centred arched moulded stone doorway. On the N, No. 19 has a nice Early Georgian pedimented front. Nos. 9, 11, 13, 15, and 17 form a picturesque group with five gables with small openings in them. No. 7 is mid-C18, three storeys and three bays, with quoin pilasters to full height, and a two-storey Venetian-

windowed wing. No. 1 HIGH STREET partly closes the view
with a classical stucco façade. ROUNCIVAL HOUSE, of the
C18, has bay windows to the full height, either side of a
Venetian window, and a Tuscan porch.

Some of the side streets also have interesting houses, most notably
TUDOR HOUSE in HATTERS LANE, which is medieval. The
open hall with a timber roof of four bays survives. A large
early C15 stone archway in the hall may have led into a projecting wing. The house was altered c.1530 and in the C17 and
has features of both periods. It was restored in 1957 by *B. J.
Ashwell*.

IRON AGE HILL-FORT (SODBURY), on a hill 2 m. E, just W of
the A46, bisected by the boundary between Little Sodbury and
Sodbury parishes. Perhaps the finest on the Cotswolds after
Uleybury (*see The Buildings of England: Gloucestershire: The
Cotswolds*). Bivallate with widely spaced ramparts on all sides
except the W, where it is univallate above the scarp. Original
entrances perhaps at the NW and SW corners and in the middle
of the E side. The site covers about 22 acres.

CHURCHAM

7010

ST ANDREW. In 1876 the wooden spire, bells, and roof were
destroyed by fire, and the church was partly rebuilt in 1878
by *Waller & Son*. The existing spire is similar to the early C11
one at Sompting. H. M. Taylor however says when describing
Sompting that there is a persistent tradition that the spire was
modified in 1762 into its present form of a Rhenish helm. He
also says he knows of only one other example in England, that
at Flixton, Suffolk, which was rebuilt by Salvin in 1861 and
said to be a faithful copy of the original. In fact Teulon, in
1850, copied the Sompting spire when he built St Stephen,
Southwark, and it seems that Waller must have done the same
thing here, as Bigland (1791) says the church only had a 'low
spire'.

However, the church generally dates from Early Norman
times and has a very large chancel arch which, although much
restored, still retains original masonry. In the exterior of the S
wall of the nave, a fragment of a volute similar to the Dymock
capitals. S doorway restored; N rebuilt, Norman, though probably not facsimile; one Norman window survives on the N.
Above the N doorway is set a small piece of figure-sculpture
which, according to Baddeley, is Romano-British, probably

C3; it has been the cause of a considerable amount of speculative and inconclusive writing. – WALL PAINTING. The s doorway arch has remains of C12 or C13 painting in deep red on the soffit and moulding. – FONT. C15, octagonal bowl decorated with quatrefoils; the original pedestal is separate. The bowl of an earlier font is in the churchyard. – FURNISHINGS. C19 Renaissance-style panelling in the sanctuary. – STAINED GLASS. E window by *Wailes*. – PLATE. Chalice, Elizabethan; Paten, 1716 by *Nathaniel Lock*; Flagon, 1851. – MONUMENTS. William Harris † 1738. Tablet with heraldry. – Ann Phelps † 1843, one of a pair in neo-Norman style. – Richard Green † 1786. Painted stone tablet.

CHURCHAM COURT is a farmhouse close to the church, probably C17, with gables, and faced in stucco.

METHODIST CHAPEL, Birdwood, 2 m. w. C18/19. Brick, with six round-headed windows in two rows; gallery inside. The adjoining cottage has windows with round-headed lights. BIRDWOOD HOUSE is C18, brick-built, with chamfered stone quoins, three storeys, and three windows with keystones and voussoirs.

CHURCHDOWN

ST BARTHOLOMEW. Situated on the skyline on the steep edge of Chosen Hill, and of considerable landscape value. Nave, chancel, s aisle, N porch, and w tower. Norman nave with a Transitional s arcade of four bays with cylindrical piers and moulded capitals supporting chamfered pointed arches. s doorway E.E. with an inner Norman arch with enriched chevrons, perhaps moved from the N doorway, where the E.E. shafts in the porch stand on reversed Norman capitals. Three-storey porch, also E.E., with a rib-vault. On the walls are remains of graffiti of pre-Reformation date. Priest's chamber above with a fireplace, and a window opening into the church. Tower of 1601, with battlements and finials. The windows generally are Perp or Elizabethan. Chancel restored in 1880 by *Ewan Christian*. The s window is an early C17 adaptation of an earlier opening. PISCINA, moved from the s aisle into the chancel; with an octagonal basin and a credence shelf, a cinquefoiled head under a pointed arch supported on thin moulded jamb shafts. – FONT. C14. Octagonal bowl with panels decorated with shallow trefoil niches with richly crocketed canopies; the chamfered pedestal has trefoil-headed niches. – PULPIT. 1631, with Renaissance detail and sounding-board. – PEWS.

C17 and C18. – PLATE. Chalice, 1680; Paten, 1680; Flagon, 1796 by *Samuel Godbehere* and *Edward Wigan*. – MONUMENTS. Sir Robert Austen † 1743. Classical tablet with heraldry. – Built into the outside S wall of the church some sculptured figures from an Elizabethan table-tomb.

ST ANDREW. 1903 by *Walter B. Wood*. C19 in character. Nave, chancel, and sanctuary, short unfinished two-bay transepts, W baptistery, and N porch added by *D. Stratton-Davis*, 1964, with engraved glass doors by *E. M. Dinkel*. – FONT. C15. Octagonal bowl decorated with quatrefoils; octagonal pedestal with shallow niches. Brought from Great Witcombe. – STAINED GLASS. Side windows in the sanctuary by *Powell & Sons*. – Most of the windows have Art Nouveau glass of 1903. – Single-light S nave by *E. R. Payne*, 1962. – MONUMENT. Ralph Streatfield-James † 1916. Brass with military portrait.

ST JOHN. 1957 by *David Stratton-Davis*. A skilful adaptation of Regency style which meets modern requirements, practical and liturgical. The detail is everywhere of high quality. – VICARAGE in the same style.

METHODIST CHAPEL. 1902. Tower with short stone spire.

CINDERFORD

ST JOHN. 1844 by *Edward Blore*. Of rock-faced Forest stone with ashlar dressings and lined inside with brick. SW tower with small octagonal spire. Nave, N and S transepts, and chancel with painted apsidal sanctuary. Lancet windows. The WEST GALLERY is supported on cast-iron columns with cast-iron decoration in the balcony. – SCREEN. Good contemporary neo-C13 work. – STAINED GLASS. Windows in the sanctuary 1938, and triple lancet window in the S transept 1946, by *D. B. Taunton* of *Hardman*'s. – Two windows on the N by *Hugh B. Powell*, 1966. – MONUMENT. Tablet to Juliet Crawshay † 1848, by *Toleman* of Bristol.

ST STEPHEN. Nave 1890, chancel 1893, by *E. H. Lingen Barker* of Hereford. Clerestoried nave with N and S aisles, and four-bay arcades, in C13 style. Organ chamber and vestry 1896.

ST MICHAEL, Soudley. 1910. Small simple C13-style church with nave and sanctuary. – STAINED GLASS. Two outer lights of the E window by *Alfred L. Wilkinson*, 1937.

WESLEY CHURCH. 1849, Dec, with an elaborate hammerbeam roof with pendant bosses. – STAINED GLASS. Two two-light windows, one on the N and one on the S, by *Whitefriars*, 1960. – Two-light window on the N by *Goddard & Gibbs*, 1958.

BAPTIST CHAPEL. 1860. Neo-classical façade.

FOREST VALE IRON WORKS. 1867 by *E. J. Reynolds.*

CLINIC AND TRAINING CENTRE. By *Alan J. Ede,* of the County Architect's Department, *c.*1955.

COUNTY LIBRARY. By *R. F. Fairhurst, c.*1964.

At Soudley is a probable MOTTE.

CLANNA *see* ALVINGTON

5000

CLEARWELL

ST PETER. 1866 by *John Middleton* of Cheltenham for Caroline, Countess of Dunraven, replacing, but on a different site, a church of 1829 by *G. V. Maddox* of Monmouth. Nave, chancel, N and S aisles, and a tower with a spire 120 ft high. Of local red sandstone with white Bath stone dressings, late C13, or what is sometimes called 'French Gothic'. The interior a mixture of blue and red Forest stones with white Bath stone in horizontal stripes, which is particularly effective in the arcades. Much rich sculpture. Above the chancel arch panels with Alpha and Omega signs and a foliated cross with passion-flower terminations. In the chancel Derbyshire, Italian, and Irish marbles are blended with Serpentine. – REREDOS by *Hardman,* carved and gilded, with PISCINA and SEDILIA to match. Encaustic tiles on the floor. The roofs are painted with patterns throughout, and nearly all the pews have brass candlesticks. The church appears to have suffered very little, if any, alterations. – PULPIT. Of Caen stone and marbles with Forest stone base; the FONT equally elaborate. – STAINED GLASS. E window by *Hardman;* also the two windows on the S. – The E window in the S aisle by *Edward Payne,* 1959. – PLATE. Chalice, Paten and Flagon, 1855; Almsdish, 1755.

CLEARWELL CASTLE. Of *c.*1740 or earlier, Gothick, with battlements. Until 1908 known as Clearwell Court. The Throckmorton family lived here in the early C17, but their house was pulled down, and the new one built by Thomas Wyndham. Of Forest stone, which has survived a fire in 1929 and other unfortunate vicissitudes such as the removal of the roof and floors after the last war. Two-storeyed centre to the entrance front flanked by symmetrical three-storey towers, all with battlements alternately carved with the Wyndham lion. Diagonal buttresses in the two lower stages of the towers.

Mullioned and transomed windows with pointed-arched heads on the ground floor and elsewhere. The central doorway, which opens directly into the great hall, is approached up a double flight of steps with turned balusters; here and all along the basement are attractive round windows. The house is built on a sloping site, and the sides and back are irregular and romantic, partly owing to C19 additions in the same style. The library has a large bow window on the S, which appears at one time to have been used as a chapel. At the opposite end leading into the hall there are tall Ionic columns *in antis*, and this room, like many others, has a typical early C18 cornice and a splendid stone fireplace with carved overmantel of this date. At least seven original fireplaces survive, but perhaps the best is in the hall, which has carved hunting equipment in the frieze. That part of the castle which is now habitable has been turned into flats. The house was restored after the fire, and so many of the ceilings are facsimile rather than original. Between 1948 and 1954 the interior was largely ruined by speculators. There does not seem to have been any Gothick decoration inside, and the Baroque fireplaces are typical of the early C18. Immediately N of the castle a courtyard surrounded by embattled outbuildings and stables and pierced by an arched gateway with the Wyndham arms carved over the top. An outer curtain wall and gateway is similarly treated, but the lodges at either end are C19, and the iron gates bear the initials of the Countess of Dunraven. Facing this gateway a triangular green with three pairs of stone gateposts with ball-finials.

Near the castle is a large BARN, older than the present house. The village CROSS, C14, has five square steps, a tall base with carved niches, and a shaft and cross designed by *John Middleton* at the time he built the church.

BAYNHAMS, C16, timber-framed and partly stone-built, with fine joinery and panelling and gables with bargeboards, is however considerably restored. PLATWELL HOUSE has an C18 front with a pretty ogee-headed window over the door and a circular window above that. At the back it is largely Tudor. In the centre of the village the WYNDHAM ARMS, a C16/17 roughcast house with an overhanging timber-framed gable and mullioned windows. TUDOR COTTAGES have mullioned windows, and STANK FARMHOUSE an overhanging gable; so here is the nucleus of a Tudor village. The BETHEL CHAPEL, dated 1852, is classical and old-fashioned, but the MORTUARY CHAPEL, designed by *John Middleton* in 1867, is C13 and has a rose window and a bellcote. It is on the site of the old church, and is due to be demolished.

CLIFFORD'S MESNE
2 m. sw of Newent

7020

St PETER. 1882 by *E. S. Harris*. Stone, C13, with central bell-cote, nave, chancel, s porch, and s vestry. Simple and inoffensive. Scissor roof-trusses and pitch-pine pews.

COALEY

7000

St BARTHOLOMEW. Perp tower of four stages, with diagonal buttresses, embattled parapet with traceried panels, and remains of crocketed pinnacles. The rest of the church rebuilt Dec in 1854–8 by *Jacques & Son*. N arcade of five bays, with octagonal piers ornamented with ballflower round the abaci. – STAINED GLASS. E window of the N aisle by *Wailes*, 1856. – s window in the chancel by *Geoffrey Webb*, 1925. – A nave window by *Lavers & Westlake*, 1886. – PLATE. Chalice and Paten Cover, 1664. – MONUMENTS. Brass to Daniel Stayno † 1630. – Anna Underwood † 1802, by *Drewett*.

CHURCH COTTAGES. C19; ornamented with medieval corbel heads from the church.

TRENLEY HOUSE, Silver Street. Small C17 house with steep gables and oval windows.

WESTFIELD FARMHOUSE. C18, of brick, two storeys and five bays. Gateposts with stone acorn finials.

COALPIT HEATH

6080

St SAVIOUR. 1844–5 by *William Butterfield*. Splendidly built in imitative early C14 style. Nave, chancel, s porch, w tower, and narrow aisles, well proportioned and correctly designed, with considerable attention paid to details like the iron door-hinges. Henry-Russell Hitchcock, however, does not consider it a mature work of architecture: 'Only the stone LYCHGATE, with its simple forms and curious juxtaposition of angles, suggests the pungent sort of originality Butterfield's finest work was to display later.'

93 VICARAGE. 1845 by *Butterfield*. If the lychgate is his first masterpiece, the vicarage possibly shows the first appearance of functionalism, and looks forward to Webb, Nesfield, and Shaw in the 1860s. 'In many ways the house is more important

historically than the castles of Salvin, the palaces of Barry, and
the manor houses of Pugin.' The reason for this high-sounding
praise is really that it must be regarded as a turning-point in
architectural history, when one realizes that it was fifteen years
earlier than Webb's Red House. It has an ample gabled roof, a
tall battered chimneybreast, a c13-looking porch, and elevations resulting directly from the plan; a trend-setter for the
secular Gothic style.

COLEFORD   *5010*

ST JOHN. 1880 by *F. S. Waller*; one of his biggest and best
churches. Large nave of four bays; two-light windows with
plate tracery. Two-bay chancel with E.E. N and S transepts,
1885 by *S. Gambier-Parry*. Tall sanctuary with a three-sided
apse. The walls are limewashed. – REREDOS. Carved oak 1918
War Memorial, by *Sir Charles Nicholson*. – STAINED GLASS.
E window 1958 by *Francis Stephens*. – PLATE. Two Chalices,
two Patens, and Flagon, 1780.

TOWER of the former parish church. The church was built as an
octagon in 1821, by *Richard James*, and was similar to Parkend
church. It was restored by *William White* in 1862, but demolished (except the tower) in 1882. The tower resembles the
towers at Parkend and Berry Hill, and has diagonal buttresses,
simple Georgian Gothic openings, and an embattled parapet
with pinnacles.

CEMETERY with two MORTUARY CHAPELS. 1868.

SCOWLES CHAPEL, ¾ m. W. Small mid-c19 Anglican chapel,
with lancet windows – three at the E end – and a W bellcote.

INDEPENDENT CONGREGATIONAL CHAPEL. 1842. Stucco-
faced with a hipped roof and parapet. Two storeys and three
bays, the central bay breaking forward. Doric porch. Early
Victorian round-headed windows enclosing two round-headed
lights and a circle.

BAPTIST CHAPEL. 1858 by *C. G. Searle*. Romanesque, with
French-looking towers either side of the W gable. Steep
sprocketed roofs hung with fish-scale slates.

TOWN HALL. c17, rebuilt in 1866, of stone, on an irregular plan
and on an island site, with rather uninspired municipal enrichments. Hipped steep-pitched roof with stone eaves corbels,
and octagonal wooden turret.

Several Late Georgian houses in the town, particularly in the
MARKET PLACE. The ANGEL HOTEL has a nice early c19

stucco-faced front. Parapet, three storeys, three-light windows, with contemporary bay windows on the ground floor.
There are also some Late Georgian terrace houses at the
market end of the HIGH STREET, and BANK HOUSE in
BANK STREET has five bays with a central pediment, and a
round-headed central window. In NEWLAND STREET an
early C19 Gothic folly, like a miniature fortress, called ROCK
HOUSE; now rendered. WHITECLIFF HOUSE has another
decent early C19 front. In GLOUCESTER ROAD, POOLWAY
HOUSE is C17 with an C18 front of five bays and two storeys.
An original fireback is dated 1650. FOREST HOUSE on CIN-
DER HILL, early C19, was the home of David Mushet, who
was the first to produce good cast steel by the combined process of Bessemer & Mushet. This was done in an experimental
shed in the garden, which still exists.

FIRE STATION, POLICE STATION, AND MAGISTRATES
COURT. Designed by *Alan J. Ede*, of the County Architect's
Department, in the 1950s.

5080   COMPTON GREENFIELD

ALL SAINTS. C14 Dec w tower with w window and doorway,
three stages, diagonal buttresses, and embattled parapet;
otherwise Norman, though largely rebuilt in 1852 by *C. S.
Fripp* and restored in 1896 by *C. E. Ponting*. s doorway with the
most elaborate Late Norman mouldings. The hood-mould has
reptile-head stops, and there are three orders, chevron mouldings, double-key pattern, and an interlaced double chevron
deeply undercut in high relief; the jamb shafts have carved
capitals. Chancel arch Transitional, very pointed. Jamb shafts
with scalloped capitals. The interior walls are scraped, and the
arch to the N transept restored. Vestry by *P. Hartland Thomas*,
1924–5. – FONT. Perp. – ROYAL ARMS. – PLATE. Chalice and
Paten, 1731 by *Richard Bayley*. – MONUMENTS. Henry
Davis † 1851 and Emily, Lady Davis, † 1866, both by *Gaffin*.

HOLLYWOOD TOWER. *c.*1820. Ashlar. Cornice and parapet.
Two storeys and three bays with semicircular recesses, ornamented with carved draped spears over the ground-floor windows, and a semicircular Roman Doric portico. On the r. a
one-storey wing in the same style. The contemporary interior
fittings have the usual Regency motifs.

MANOR FARMHOUSE. C16/17 stone-built manor house, rather
tall and thin. Two-storey gabled porch with carved finial.

Most of the original oak doors survive, but other interior features have been removed.

CONEY HILL see GLOUCESTER, pp. 237, 238

COOPER'S HILL see BROCKWORTH

CORSE

7020

ST MARGARET. Mainly C14; a simple nave and chancel with W tower and spire. N porch timber-framed Tudor work; S porch now a vestry. Dec or Late Perp windows. Ceiled wagon roof to the nave, with moulded tiebeams and wall-plates. – FONT. Norman. Deep circular bowl with scallops and a band of cable and pellet moulding at the bottom. – MONUMENT. John Clark † 1787. Painted stone tablet.

CORSE COURT, immediately SW of the church. Medieval. The central section timber-framed, based on magnificent cruck trusses, originally an open hall running the full height of the interior. The dairy, which continues the line of the main block, is similarly of cruck construction. At the other end is a later gabled cross wing of two storeys, timber-framed, with a jettied-out first floor on the N. It was remodelled in the C17. The gable-end is plastered and carries a cartouche containing the arms of de Clare.

SNIGS END, 1½ m. N. Built c.1847, by Feargus O'Connor, the Chartist, as a settlement for industrial workers. The attractive PRINCE OF WALES INN was originally the school. Little single-storey cottages of brick or stone stand well back in their holdings. In MOAT LANE, one house bears on the trefoil over the door the inscription 'O'Connor Villa. June 12. 1848', which is the year and the month of the founder's bankruptcy. More of these houses at LOWBANDS, and in the adjoining parish of Staunton.

THE HAWTHORNS, near Staunton. C17 timber-framed farm-house with a contemporary staircase. A pane of glass is inscribed with the date 1627, similar to one at Great Cumber-wood, Tirley.

CROMHALL

6090

ST ANDREW. Nave, chancel, S aisle, S porch, and N tower. The exterior is rather dull, with too much dark pointing, and the N tower untypical, with four stages, Perp openings, and battle-ments. Its N doorway however has a good Dec ogee-shaped trefoiled arch, with a possibly original door and ironwork. The SOUTH DOOR is also ancient, with oak-traceried panels of C15 appearance. W window of the S aisle C14 with intersecting tracery and many cusps. The E end of the S aisle was a chapel and has a priest's doorway which looks Tudor but is dated 1745. Lofty Perp S arcade of four bays with octagonal piers. The chancel arch, with hollow mouldings and no capitals, is not central. Another Perp arch between the aisle and its chapel, now blocked with the organ, but retaining a trefoil-headed PISCINA. The roofs of nave and aisle are wagon-shaped, of four bays, the easternmost bays enriched with carved bosses. The church was restored in 1852, and the chancel roof is C19. C19 balcony of a former pew in the tower, now blocked. The walls are limewashed. – PULPIT, N of the chancel arch. Of stone, late C14, beautiful, chalice-shaped, with Perp panels; entered from behind by steps from the vestry. – FONT. Perp, octagonal, scraped and dull. – ROYAL ARMS. Georgian. – STAINED GLASS. E window by *Bell* of Bristol, 1854; particularly nasty. – PLATE. Two Chalices, 1788. – MONUMENTS. Nicholas Hickes † 1710. Provincial Baroque tablet. – Robert Webb † 1731. Classical marble. – Agnes Chisholme † 1798, by *W. Paty*. – Elizabeth Dyer † 1807 and another similar, coloured marbles, both by *Daw*. – Robert Codrington. Pretty tablet but no date, by *T. King*, of Bath.

SCHOOL. 1844. Two brass plates by *Willet*, of Bristol.

WOODEND, 1 m. NE. C17 gabled house with C18 features, altered in the C19.

HEATH END COURT, ¾ m. SE. Late C18, stuccoed, nine bays with central Gothick window, and turret.

THE GABLES, Talbot's End. Two-gabled C17 house with central two-storey porch, and moulded stone gateposts and finials.

IRON AGE HILL-FORT (BLOODY ACRE), on a hill SW of Tortworth Lake, ½ m. N. Bivallate on the W, trivallate on the SW, with a natural scarp elsewhere. The inner ramparts enclose about 9 acres, the outer ramparts about 12 acres. The site is covered with beeches planted c.1800.

CROOKES FARMHOUSE *see* NEWENT

DEERHURST

8020

8 ST MARY. The priory church is an Anglo-Saxon monument of the first order. A monastery is known to have existed here in

804, when Aethelric bequeathed lands to Deerhurst and referred to a *congregatio*. It is now thought that the nave, the slightly later lower part of the W porch, and the also slightly later two pairs of porticus extending N and S fairly far E, represent the remains of a church that was standing in 804; the later features, including the upper storeys of the W tower, the ruined chancel with an elongated polygonal apse rounded inside (cf. Brixworth), and a number of more elaborate arched openings, are the result of alterations or rebuildings of the church in the C10.

The church is built almost wholly of roughly coursed rubble, with appreciable areas of herringbone work. There is no long-and-short quoining; nor are there any pilaster strips, except on the apse. The earliest doorways and windows are of the simplest type, with megalithic jambs, and heads formed of single lintels or of pairs of stones sloped together to make triangles; but the later openings are arched with some precision, and the arches are outlined with characteristic Anglo-Saxon hood-moulds of plain, square cross-section which end on beasts' heads. Two openings in the tower and one in the S wall also have additional ornament above them in the form of boldly projecting stones like the figure-heads of wooden ships or *prokrossoi* (which appear also at Barnack, Northamptonshire, and at Alkborough, Lincolnshire).

The earliest church must have been a nave and a chancel without any adjuncts, since neither the W porch nor the two pairs of porticus are in bond with the main fabric. The W porch of two storeys was probably the first addition. It is much deeper than it is wide, and is divided by a cross-wall into two chambers. The doorways, however, are later. Next came the addition of the N and S porticus, each of two storeys. The third building stage, still of pre-Viking date, was the raising of the W porch to become three-storeyed, with its remarkable double triangular-headed E window into the nave. This has short fluted and reeded pilasters or pillars (a Carolingian motif; cf. Lorsch) and stepping-out abaci. Of the same build is the asymmetrically placed doorway with sloping sides lower down. It must have led to a wooden gallery, and a second such doorway in the porch cross-wall corresponds to it. At about the same time the side chapels were extended W by stages so as to flank the nave.

Following the Viking invasions, the church was restored in the C10. The W porch was raised to form a tower; and the apsidal chancel was probably rebuilt, with its stripwork panelling and sculptured ornament. At the same time the presumably simpler chancel arch was replaced by the present large and elaborate opening. It has big capitals of unique details and a hood-mould on beast stops. The same stops appear on one porch doorway and one doorway into the former cloister. Thus the building history provides an explanation of what is otherwise an illogical assortment of no less than thirty early and later Anglo-Saxon doorways and windows in a single

6 building. The amazingly tall narrow nave of the C8 can be compared with Northumbrian buildings like Monkwearmouth, Escomb, and Jarrow. The chancel arch is now blocked; the earliest porticus are still separated from the central space by walls in which their doorways have survived at two levels to show that the chapels were of two storeys, and the later porticus further W have been thrown together and opened to the nave by the demolition of their dividing walls and by the cutting of very good E.E. arcades through the originally continuous N and S walls of the nave. The arcades are of *c*.1200, three bays long and very similar in detail, though S seems a little later than N. S has striping of white and green stone (cf. the late C12

19 work at Worcester Cathedral). The capitals are of enriched trumpet-scallop varieties and also of early stiff-leaf. One capital has bold upright leaves. The arches are moulded. The arches from the Saxon porch to the W bays of the aisles are of the same time. The windows in the clerestory and aisles are Dec and very Late Perp; but herringbone masonry reaches right up into the clerestory walls. The church was restored in 1861–3 by *William Slater*, a pupil of Carpenter, and the nave roof dates from this time; a polite copy of a C15 roof, with original corbels.

SCULPTURE. In the W porch, Virgin and Child, possibly not finished, C8 and *in situ*. – On the ruined apse, at the S corner between structural pilaster strips, an angel, C10, *in situ* since the apse was built, and showing Byzantine influence (Talbot Rice). – FONT. Late C9.* Cylindrical bowl with a broad band of double trumpet-spiral ornament occupying about half its total height, with narrower bands of vine-scroll above and

---

* The evidence for its early date was provided by Sir Alfred Clapham, who compared the double spiral ornament with an almost identical form on a pendant found in the Trewhiddle hoard, which is dated by accompanying coins as not later than 875. He also records that the trumpet-spiral disappeared from English manuscripts about the middle or end of the C9.

below. The stem is cylindrical above and octagonal below. The octagonal part is plain, as if intended to be sunk into a socket, while the upper cylindrical part is elaborately decorated with alternating panels of which the first type is of double spirals like the bowl, while the second type shows a complicated pattern of interlacing. Its recent history is one of almost unbelievable good fortune. For an unknown period the bowl had been used as a washing tub in a farm, until in 1844 Bishop Wilberforce bought it for Longdon church, where it remained for twenty-five years. Then the stem was found at Apperley Court, and the two were re-united in Deerhurst church. – STAINED GLASS. In the s aisle w window on the l. good panel of St Catherine beneath a canopy, dating from c.1300–40; on the r. St Alphege, who was a monk here and was martyred by the Danes when he was Archbishop of Canterbury in 1012. This glass is of c.1450. The coat of arms in the tracery is that of de Clare, and the sun-in-splendour is the badge of the house of York. The kneeling figures are donors. – w window in the N aisle by *Wailes*, 1853. – N window in the N aisle by *Clayton & Bell*. – Splendid COMMUNION RAIL of c.1600. – SEATING in the sanctuary, keeping to the Puritan arrangement with seats E as well as on either side of the Holy Table. – The last eight PEWS at the w end of the s aisle are C15. The other pews date from the restoration of 1861. – PULPIT. 1861. Realistic carving; designed by *William Slater*, executed by *Forsyth*. – In the E end of the N aisle – the Saxon N porticus – a stone COFFIN LID with foliated cross; C14. – BRASSES. Sir John Cassey, c.1400. 3 ft 2 in. His wife has her feet on a dog, whose name Terri is inscribed, the only known pet dog to be so honoured. Above the canopies the figure of St Anne with the young Virgin and the matrix of the missing figure of St John the Baptist (said to have been taken in 1908 to America). On the r. the Cassey coat of arms, and in the border a wyvern; at the bottom, the Royal Arms. Cassey was Chancellor of the Exchequer to Richard II. – The other two brasses are of Ladies of the end of the first quarter of the C16. One Lady is 3 ft 5 in., the other 2 ft 11 in.

THE PRIORY HOUSE. Mainly a C14 building, but containing in a low room on the N a stone column with a capital with carved volutes, probably C11. On the w side of the house and on the s of the adjoining church are the corbels which once sustained the pentice of the cloister. The existing building therefore stands on the E side of the Benedictine cloister. It now contains a hall, built in with three floors, though the carved corbel heads and roof trusses remain. On the E side a tall window of the hall with reticulated tracery, obviously not *in situ*, as the chapter house must have been in this place. Most of the other windows are Tudor, and there is a stone fireplace and doorway inside, of Tudor date.

ODDA'S CHAPEL stands about 200 yds SW of the priory church. Its existence as an Anglo-Saxon church, in fact one of the most complete now surviving, was quite unsuspected until, during repairs in 1885 to what was regarded as an ordinary half-timbered house, an ancient window was brought to light by the removal of plaster. The nave was in use as a tall kitchen and the chancel had been divided by an intermediate floor. The chancel arch and other features had been mutilated. Two double-splayed round-headed windows were disclosed in the lateral walls of the nave, in good condition; the S window still retains part of a wooden mid-wall window-frame *in situ*. A medieval stone window-head was discovered to be a much earlier inscribed altar slab – 'In honour of the Holy Trinity this Altar has been dedicated'. This inscription provides a link with a large inscribed stone which had been discovered near the building in 1675, and is now in the Ashmolean. Its Latin inscription may be translated: 'Earl Odda has this royal hall built and dedicated in honour of the Holy Trinity for the soul of his brother Aelfric which left the body in this place. Bishop Ealdred dedicated it the Second of the Ides of April in the fourteenth year of the reign of King Edward of the English.' Aelfric had died at Deerhurst in December 1053; the chapel is therefore precisely dated – a unique fact for a pre-Conquest building – with a dedication on 12 April 1056.

The chapel now forms the W end of a half-timbered farmhouse from which it was 'disentangled' in 1965. It consists of a simple rectangular nave and a smaller rectangular chancel. Chancel arch with square-cut jambs built of through-stones with alternate stones laid flat to bond the intermediate uprights firmly into the wall. Plain, square-cut projecting bases and moulded imposts. The arch itself is wholly of through-stones and is outlined by a hood-mould of square section. It is of horseshoe shape, as is the N doorway. Externally the nave wall has well-defined long-and-short quoins, and the N doorway, although much mutilated, is nevertheless clearly of Late Saxon construction.

WIGHTFIELD MANOR, 1 m. S. A house on this moated site was

occupied by Sir John Cassey in the C14, and the family remained here till c.1670. The existing building appears to date
from the beginning of the C16. It is recorded that after the
dissolution of the monastery at Deerhurst, c.1547, the stone
from a chapel there was removed to Wightfield. The walls of
the house are partly built with this stone, and sufficient have
been removed to reconstruct a Norman porch with chevroned
arch and jambs with capitals as a garden entrance on the N.
The S entrance has an outer doorway with a Tudor arch and
spandrels enriched with the Cassey griffin head on the r.
Another Tudor arch is within. Two staircase towers, one on the
E and one on the NW, both with elm newel stairs. Stone gables
stepped in Flemish style. A number of Tudor mullioned
windows survive. In the S room on the r. of the entrance a fine
timber ceiling, and a stone hearth with an oven under a
moulded ogee arch. The window contains armorial glass of the
C16, one showing the arms of Cassey, and the other Cassey
impaling Fettiplace. (Henry Cassey married Dorothy Fettiplace in 1556.) Other rooms have C17 panelling.

VICARAGE. 1852. Of brick with stone dressings and very steep
gables, and tall chimneys. Wing added in 1859.

SCHOOL. 1856, by the same hand as the vicarage.

There are a few timber-framed COTTAGES in the village.

At DEERHURST WALTON, I m. SE, NOTCLIFFE HOUSE is late
C18 incorporating an earlier building, faced in stucco, three
storeys and four windows with cornice and parapet and pilasters either side. Tuscan portico and wrought-iron veranda.
Also one or two timber-framed COTTAGES.

DIXTON MANOR see ALDERTON

DOWNEND   6070

CHRIST CHURCH. 1831 by *Oliver Greenway*, member of a
Mangotsfield family of architects who had been charged with
forgery and bankruptcy.* Chancel 1914. Auditorium church,
of Pennant stone rubble with ashlar dressings, 'churchwarden' Gothic windows, buttresses, and embattled parapets.
Inside, a gallery supported on cast-iron columns continuous on
three sides. The added chancel has a rose window. Over the
chancel arch gable two stone turrets with open pyramidal
pinnacles; another smaller one on the apex of the W gable.

* Francis Greenway was transported to Australia in 1813, there to become
the father of that continent's architecture.

These give an otherwise almost featureless church its curiously satisfactory character.

DOWNEND HOUSE, North Street. Of *c*.1800, stucco, with parapet and stone coping. Three storeys, and three sash windows.*

CLEEVEWOOD, Cleeve Wood Road. Early C19. Good symmetrical ashlar elevation showing Greek Revival influence, with a central Ionic entrance, bows to full height either side, giant pilasters, cornice, parapet, and wings either side with three-light windows.

8020

DOWN HATHERLEY

ST MARY. Rebuilt in 1860 by *Fulljames & Waller*, except the C15 Perp w tower of two stages, with gargoyles and battlements, diagonal buttresses, Perp w window, and four-centred arched w doorway. The rebuilt church is Early Dec. Four-bay N arcade with capitals ornamented with carved foliage. The chancel arch is enriched with ballflower, and the chancel has a hammerbeam roof with arch-braced collars, and carved corbels. – FONT. One of Gloucestershire's nine lead fonts, but of late (Tudor) date, and decorated with branches of foliage of Renaissance type with Tudor roses, stars, and lozenges. At the bottom a band of Tudor cresting. It is mounted on a decorated stone base of 1860. – Two HATCHMENTS of Sir Matthew Wood † 1843. – MONUMENT. Thomas Turner † 1821, by *James Cooke*.

RECTORY, N of the church. Built at the same time as the church, by *Fulljames & Waller*.

HATHERLEY COURT. C17 stone house on a moated site, entirely re-faced in brick in the C19. The porch has re-used mullioned and transomed windows; otherwise there is no outside indication of its C17 and Regency interior fittings. At the rear a tall projecting staircase wing containing a C17 staircase with moulded balusters and ball-finials, and decorative plaster ceilings. A front room has C17 panelling with a frieze enriched with oval bosses, and a splendid Baroque chimneypiece with heraldry and swags of fruit. C17 panelling and a Regency fireplace in a bedroom. The drawing room is decorated in Regency style, and may date from the occupation of Pearson Thompson, the proprietor of the Montpellier Spa at Cheltenham.

LODGE. Neo-Greek, faced in stucco with Doric columns *in antis*.

* The birthplace in 1848 of W. G. Grace, Gloucestershire cricketer and founder of international games.

DOWN HOUSE *see* OLVESTON

THE DOWN HOUSE *see* REDMARLEY D'ABITOT

DOYNTON   7070

HOLY TRINITY. Mostly rebuilt in 1864–5, by *J. E. Gill* of Bath. Nave arcade and N aisle of this date, also the chancel; but the S wall of the nave retains a considerable amount of herringbone masonry of post-Conquest date, and the S doorway and a low-side window are C14. SE tower Perp with pinnacles and gargoyles. The organ chamber on the N also has Perp windows; the other windows are all C19 Perp. The church was again restored in 1893. – HATCHMENT, showing that the deceased fought at the battle of Talavera, 1809. – PLATE. Chalice, 1565 by *William Dyxson*; Plate and Flagon, 1743 by *William Williams*; Plate, 1750 by *John Wirgman*. – Good classical stone MONUMENT to Joseph Jackson † 1719.

DOYNTON HOUSE. A typical gabled C17 stone house with mullioned windows and conspicuous relieving arches, which are a feature of the district. The gables have finials, and the chimneys are set diagonally.

Several other houses in the village are C17, and there is later evidence of the influence of near-by Bath. COURT FARM-HOUSE is a rambling C17 building with a classical doorcase. THE OLD RECTORY is C18 with quoins of alternating lengths, cornice, and five sash windows with keystones and architraves, and a pedimented doorcase. RECTORY FARM is simple C17. Gables with ball-finials, five mullioned and transomed windows, and a contemporary staircase. OLD BREWERY HOUSE has a nice C18 front, and BROOK HOUSE a slightly more sophisticated elevation in ashlar, with a good cornice and a Tuscan doorcase with open pediment.

Outside the village, TRACY PARK, 1½ m. S, has a C17 nucleus but an early C19 classical front of two storeys and 2, 3, 2 bays. Additions were made in 1850, including a tower, and again in 1920. At the gates are a pair of large rubble COLUMNS carrying huge cornices with masonic emblems; at the other gates a similar pair of columns but without the emblems.

In 1865 a ROMAN VILLA was excavated at Tracy Park. It was enclosed in a rectangular earthwork, 2 acres in extent.

DRYBROOK

HOLY TRINITY. 1817. Broad nave, with short chancel, N and S porches, and embattled W tower. The plain Gothic windows have intersecting tracery. WEST GALLERY supported on classical columns with dentil cornice and panelling. – STAINED GLASS. E window 1922 by *Bewsey*. – MONUMENTS. Elizabeth Harper † 1837. White marble tablet by *Davis* of Bath. – The Rev. Henry Nicholls † 1867 and the Rev. Henry Berkin † 1847, both tablets in Gothic style, carved in stone, by *F. Morgan*.

DUMBLETON

ST PETER. The Norman remains include parts of the N and S walls of the nave, which retain sections of the Norman corbel table with carved grotesques, the N doorway with its chevroned arch and carved tympanum over a Tudor entrance, and the S arcade, which has re-set carved Norman stones in the soffit of the easternmost arch. Nave roof heightened to include a Perp clerestory. W tower late C13 with buttresses on the W, and a corbel table. Perp top stage with battlements. C13 S doorway with an inserted Tudor entrance, a plain parapet, and 'debased' windows. S porch added in 1905. The N transept has Dec windows, and next to it is a modern organ chamber. The SW window of the nave Dec, the NW a C13 lancet. Tower arch with three chamfered orders of the late C13. Perp windows in the chancel, and over the E window an inscription 'May 13, 1862', indicating a rebuilding. The walls are limewashed. – FONT. C17 Perp style; the octagonal bowl has the date 1661. – PULPIT, with panels of carved fruits, and SEATING, 1905. – STAINED GLASS. Two-light N chancel window by *H. J. Stammers*, 1947. – PLATE. Chalice and Paten Cover, 1685. – MONUMENTS. In the chancel: Sir Charles Percy † 1628 and wife. Painted stone monument with a Jacobean entablature over the kneeling effigies and one infant. By *John Guildon* of Hereford. – Charles Cocks † 1654. Classical, with bust by *Peter Bennier*. – Sir Richard Cocks † 1684. Gilded countrified Baroque stone monument with black marble columns and cherubs, by *Reeve* of Gloucester. – In the nave: Frances Lady Cocks † 1723. Marble tablet with a long inscription, by *Reeve*. – Sir Robert Cocks † 1765. By *Thomas Paty* of Bristol. – In the S aisle: Elizabeth Lady Cocks † 1749 and Dorothy Cocks

† 1767. Classical coloured marble tablets. – Hoptonwood stone tablet to Collins Ashwin, c.1938 by *Eric Gill*. – CHURCHYARD. Two Jacobean table-tombs. – Three well-preserved examples of a local type of excellent low-relief headstones with pictorial compositions of the Resurrection: Hester Clayton † 1792, Richard Clayton † 1793, and Robert Staight † 1792, all said to be by *Samuel Hob*.

DUMBLETON HALL. 1830 by *George Stanley Repton*. Tudor. Symmetrical entrance front with three projecting gabled wings crowned with tall finials, generally three storeys high, with mullioned windows. Additions to the N in keeping; the *porte-cochère* is a later addition. The GATES and LODGE were built c.1905.

OLD RECTORY. C16. Partly timber-framed, roughcast, with gables and a stone gable-end and chimney, on to which was added, in the late C17 or c.1700, a charming stone wing with overhanging hipped Cotswold stone roof, two storeys, and eight or nine wooden mullioned and transomed windows with moulded stone architraves; now divided into cottages.

Several timber-framed cottages in the village.

DUMBLETON MILL, 1 m. E. C18/19 corn-mill on the river Isbourne. Brick with stone dressings and mullioned windows, gables, and columbaria. Machinery *in situ*.

DYMOCK

6030

ST MARY. The church is supposed to incorporate Anglo-Saxon masonry in the lower parts of the wall. The building itself is Early Norman with excellent additions of c.1120–40.* The Early Norman church consisted of a nave, a central tower no longer in existence, a chancel, and an apse of which no more than the slight canting of the buttresses at its N and S start give evidence. To this building belong the two bays of very impressive, large blank arcading on the S side of the chancel, W of and above the canted buttress just referred to. The tympana have lozenge-shaped slabs, a typical Early Norman motif – cf. the Great Tower of Chepstow Castle and e.g. Westminster Abbey (Infirmary Cloister). Also to this building belong the flat buttresses and the string-course of small geometrical motifs outside and also a little inside. Again to this building

* The dating is controversial. I would call the additions c.1140. As for the building, the arcading outside to be mentioned presently is similar to the doorway to the Great Tower of Chepstow Castle, and that the Ministry of Public Building and Works dates 1067–71. But can so early a date be believed? (NP)

belong the responds of the sanctuary arch, with nook-shafts up
the angles. The S doorway of the nave cuts into this Early
Norman work. It is an addition of *c.*1120 or as late as *c.*1140
and has figured volute capitals, a Tree of Life tympanum, and
a chevroned arch. The chancel arch is so similar that it must be
of the same date and by the same hands. One can in fact speak
of a Dymock School characterized by these capitals.* The S
porch has a C14 doorway with an image niche above, containing a small sculptured Virgin by *Owen Wynniatt, 1927.* At
some period before the C14 the church became ruinous, and in
the C14 the E end of the chancel was rebuilt, a N transept and S
chapel added, and the W end of the nave rebuilt. The W tower
was added in the C15. The chancel E window is a C19 reconstruction. The tower is a good example of mid–late C15 work,
with W diagonal buttresses stepped in thickness and with
double-canopied niches; three stages, the lower two built in
red sandstone and the upper partly finished in greenish sandstone and with a dumpy shingled spire. In the wagon-roofed
Lady Chapel a C14 PISCINA. The church was restored in the
1870s by *John Middleton.* The whole of the interior has been
most disastrously scraped, revealing a disturbing patchwork
resulting from the many alterations. – The SCREEN was erected
in 1891, a date which represents further restorations by *Waller,*
which presumably include the introduction of the unsuitable
stone and alabaster PULPIT. – FONTS. One probably carved
by *Boulton,* who worked for *Middleton.* Another, made of wood
and found in the churchyard, dates from the time of the Restoration of Charles II. – COMMUNION RAILS. Laudian. –
STAINED GLASS. Fragments of medieval glass in the porch. –
Windows by *Kempe,* 1885, N transept; 1889, E window; 1893,
S chapel; and 1901, chancel S. – PLATE. Chalice and Paten
Cover, 1626 by *F. Terry.* – MONUMENT. William Hankins
† 1771, by *W. H. Stephens* of Worcester. – CHURCHYARD. A
good late C18 table-tomb of the Cam family.

The church is well placed with Wintour's Green in front.

OLD RECTORY, W of the church. Upstanding early C18 brick
house, of three storeys and five bays. Further W is the new
RECTORY designed by *H. Stratton-Davis, c.*1950.

* Other examples of the work of this school may be seen at Kempley and
Pauntley, along the Herefordshire border at Bridstow and Peterstow, and also,
so Mr Stratford informs me, at Rockford in Worcestershire. The capitals can
be compared with the ram's-head capital of the Preston pillar piscina, now in
Gloucester Museum, of which they are stylized versions. They probably all
derive from a common source.

ANN CAM'S SCHOOL. Rebuilt in 1825. Of brick, with pediment and 'churchwarden' windows.

Further NW along the village street two COTTAGES, both with exposed cruck trusses and thatched roofs.

OLD GRANGE, ¾ m. NW. A grange of the Cistercian abbey of Flaxley until the Dissolution, but occupied by the Wynniatt family from the C15 to 1965. The central portion of the house may be medieval, but it was remodelled in the C18 (and has some C18 fireplaces) and again in 1896, when a wing was added with gabled half-timbering and a porch. Two timber-framed BARNS to the W.

POUND FARMHOUSE, Tillers Green, ½ m. NE. Possibly C16. Exposed timber-framing, with remodelled hipped roof. Two storeys and gabled overhanging porch.

GREENWAY HOUSE, ½ m. N. The central gabled brick-built portion of the house may be C16, with a restored Tudor chimney. On the r. an C18 wing, three storeys high with hipped roof; lunette window in the top storey and Venetian windows below.

OLD NAIL SHOP. A timber-framed cottage, once lived in by the poet Wilfrid Gibson, associated with Rupert Brooke, 1913.

LITTLE IDDENS, Leadington, ¾ m. N. A timber-framed cottage, the home of the American poet Robert Frost at the outbreak of World War I.

HILL ASH, ½ m. N of the church. Rebuilt in the early C19. Three storeys, 1, 2, 1 bays. The central portion projects and is carried by Doric columns.

FARM MILL, ¼ m. N. Timber-framed house containing a little C17 panelling.

CALLOW FARM, 1¼ m. E of the church. C16/17. Timber-framed, with brick restoration. Brick chimneys with plaster enrichments.

EARTHCOTT GREEN FARM see ALVESTON

EASTINGTON

7000

ST MICHAEL. C14 embattled W tower of three stages, with a square stair-vice on the NE corner. The church otherwise is generally Perp, with a S aisle added by the Duke of Buckingham of Thornbury Castle before his execution in 1521. On the S doorway the carved initials SB for Stafford and Buckingham. Perp S aisle windows with straight heads; the E window of the aisle has an elaborate dripmould supported by angels with shields, and complicated tracery. The Perp N nave windows are divided only by a transom from the clerestory. Attractive small clerestory windows on the S above the aisle. E window restored Dec. On the E gable of the chancel a sanctus bellcote. N porch of 1653, N vestry C19. The church was restored in 1885 by *Waller, Son & Wood*. The weathercock is Elizabethan or older; repaired in 1673. Sundial on the S, dated 1737. Nave arcade of six bays with octagonal piers, of which two bays in the chancel are matched by two on the N of the C19, leading to the organ chamber. Elaborate chancel ceiling which, together with the PULPIT and the low stone CHOIR SCREEN, LECTERN, and PEWS, dates from 1885. – ALTAR, REREDOS, and metal RAILS by *S. E. Dykes Bower*, c.1950. The doors of the triptych are painted in Lent array on the back. – FONT. Norman, a plain tub with a band at the top. Cylindrical pedestal with a broad shelf of fifteen carved scallops, standing on a double circular base. – LECTERN. 1875. Brass with winged angels. – STAINED GLASS. Fragments of medieval glass in a N nave window, including the figure of St Matthew, and fragments of early C16 glass. – In the W window of the organ chamber the Duke's initials SB; C16 glass reset. – E window by *Sir Ninian Comper*, 1908. – SE window in the S aisle also by *Comper*, 1909. – Window in the N aisle by *F. C. Eden*, c.1936. – S aisle W window by *Wailes*, 1846. – BENEFACTION BOARDS. C18 stone tablets supported on acanthus-carved consoles. – ROYAL ARMS. Early Victorian. – PLATE. Chalice, 1622; Chalice, 1683. – MONUMENTS. Edward Stephens † 1587 and wife. Recumbent stone effigies with peculiarly small heads; country-work. – Elizabeth Knevet † 1518. Brass, 2 ft 5½ in., showing the Lady in a heraldic mantle. – Brasses on the floor of the S aisle, all of which have excellent lettering, and heraldry: Margaret Stephens † 1591, Catherine Stephens † 1632, Anne Stephens † 1722, Catherine Stephens † 1725, and Richard Stephens † 1705. – Edward Stephens † 1587. Stone Renaissance monument with heraldry, by the same hand as the Winston monument at Standish. – Two Baroque marble tablets, to Richard Stephens † 1660 and Robert Stephens † 1675. – Nathaniel Stephens, erected in 1792 by *Thomas King* of Bath. Marble, showing the Good Samaritan. – Henry Willis † 1794, veined grey marble, and Henry Stephens † 1795, draped urn; both by *King*. – Thomas Veel † 1821. Marble heraldry. By *King*. – John James † 1790. Oval medallion, by *Millard & Cooke*. – Robert Griffin † 1835, by *J. Hamlett* of Stroud (repeating a design frequently used by *W. Paty*). – Gothic monument (of excessive snobbery) to the Townshend family, by *F. K. Howell* of Thornbury, erected in 1906.

s of the churchyard flows the river Frome, with a stone terrace wall to the W, once part of the Stephens family mansion, demolished in the C18. CHURCHEND COTTAGES may be part of the buildings; they have four-centred-arched stone doorways, and mullioned windows.

EASTINGTON PARK. Late Georgian mansion faced in ashlar with cornice and blocking-course. Three storeys and five bays. The return elevations have segmental bows – on one side to full height. Tuscan portico.

EASTINGTON HOUSE. Tudor, with C18 alterations and fenestration. The front has three gables, and two storeys plus attics, with first-floor Venetian windows.

ALKERTON HOUSE. C18, rendered, with a hipped Cotswoldstone roof and pediment. ALKERTON FARM is of the C16. Timber-framed with overhanging first floor. ALKERTON GRANGE, C18, of brick, has in the garden an early C18 GAZEBO, also brick. The gazebo has stone dressings, pilasters, 71 moulded cornice, and broken segmental pediment with urns. Inside, good-quality oak panelling.

OLDBURY, ½ m. N. 1832 by *Rowland Paul*, built as a rectory. Stucco. Two storeys and seven bays with Ionic portico.

EASTWOOD PARK see FALFIELD

ELBERTON   6080

ST JOHN. C14 central tower, with Dec bell-openings, battlements, and a spire. Tower arches chamfered without capitals, with squints to N and S. The rest of the church, consisting of nave, N and S aisles, and chancel, was mostly rebuilt in 1858, E.E. – FONT. Norman, circular bowl, damaged and not used. – PLATE. Paten, 1770; Chalice, 1799 by *Peter & Ann Bateman*.

OLD MANOR HOUSE. C17, rubble, with three steep gables and a cupola. It contains a very fine Jacobean staircase with pierced finials and pendants.

ROCK HOUSE. Restored C16/17 house with projecting gabled wings, and windows with relieving arches. C19 chimneys, C18 stone gatepiers, with carved vase finials.

IRON AGE HILL-FORT. *See* Aust.

ELMORE

ST JOHN THE BAPTIST. The church contains E.E. architecture
of a sort rare in Gloucestershire. Nave and N aisle of exactly
the same width. The N aisle was the original chancel, and the
tower, at its W end, is of four stages, the lower C13, the top
Perp and embattled. Nave S and chancel windows Perp;
wooden S porch, and ogee-headed priest's door. E window of
the N aisle chapel with intersecting tracery. N porch timber-
framed with C15 cusped arches and restored balustraded sides.
Central arcade of five bays, with chamfered rectangular piers
and E.E. jamb shafts with good moulded capitals and bases on
the E and W faces of the piers. Chancel arch also E.E. Wide
chamfered arch between the chancel and the N chapel, now a
vestry. The church was restored in 1879–80 by *F. S. Waller*,
when the chancel was re-roofed and the nave and aisle roofs
repaired. – The FONT, PULPIT, and vestry SCREEN are of this
date.–AnotherFONT. C18.–HOLY TABLE. C17.–COMMUNION
RAILS. 1945. – PEWS. C17, with linenfold panels. – STAINED
GLASS. Large nave S window by *Heaton, Butler & Bayne*,
1903. – HATCHMENTS. Guise family, 1865, 1887, and another.
– PLATE. Pair of Chalices, 1631. – MONUMENTS. Tomb-chest,
1472, with incised-line portrait of a Knight in armour, and inscription commemorating Johannes Gyse and Alicia his wife.
The Knight has a canopy over his head and his feet rest on a
hound. – William Guise † 1716, by *John Ricketts* of Gloucester.
Gilded Baroque stone tablet with putti and heraldry. – Sir
William Guise † 1642, erected in 1653 by *Reeve* of Gloucester.
Renaissance detail with putti and heraldry. – Daniel Ellis
† 1797, by *W. Stephens* of Worcester.

68   In the CHURCHYARD one of the finest table-tombs in the
county, and several others nearly as good, of C17/18 date; particularly fine figure carving in relief, mourners, Time, Death,
and other symbolical and Renaissance details. Painswick stone,
suitable for deep undercutting, is used, with Minchinhampton
stone tops. – Also the ruined remains of an C18 mausoleum,
and many good headstones of local sandstone as well as limestone.

ELMORE COURT. Beautifully set in the first loop of the Severn
below Gloucester, on land which has belonged to the Guise
family since the C13. The existing house was built on a medieval site between 1564 and 1588, and consists of a central hall,

with its great mullioned and transomed bay window, an C18
classical portico marking the entrance to the original screens
passage, the solar wing on the r., and an additional five-bay
Georgian wing on the l. This does not result in a very distinguished elevation, and the outstanding features of the house
are to be found in the interior, which is rich in decoration
dating from 1564 to c.1636. The hall was remodelled in the
early C19 but retains a Late Tudor chimneypiece. The heraldic
STAINED GLASS in the great window dates from 1853, including the Guise arms showing forty-two quarterings. The
drawing room has Jacobean panelling, carved dragons running
round the frieze, strapwork on the chimneypiece, and a
Georgian bay window. The morning room is an addition in
late C18 or Regency style. Great Elizabethan staircase of outstanding quality, lit by a window with ovolo mullions. On the
first floor the Oak Room has a splendid unspoiled anti-
Renaissance chimneypiece, with its original colours and gilding, many caryatid figures, and the arms of Guise impaling
Pauncefoote.* Chimneypiece in another room with a crude
figure of Father Time.

The wrought-iron ENTRANCE GATES are by *William Edney*, 69
the greatest of Bristol's C18 blacksmiths, in the style of Tijou,
with acanthus and hart's-tongue fern motifs, and surmounted
by the swan badge of the Guise family. They were erected at
Rendcomb before 1712, and transferred here early in the C19.
In the village several old timber-framed cottages. Others survive
at ELMORE BACK, on the river opposite Minsterworth.
FARLEY'S END FARMHOUSE. A rectangular house of four
cruck-framed bays of which the two middle bays once formed
an open hall; the roof has massive curved wind-braces. The
hall was given an intermediate floor in the C17. Large BARN of
six cruck-framed bays, and a smaller building of two bays with
two surviving cruck-trusses. It was originally a manor house
belonging to Gloucester Abbey.

ELMSTONE HARDWICKE 9020

ST MARY MAGDALENE. An almost isolated church in the civil
parish of Uckington. It belonged to the Benedictine priory at
Deerhurst, and has a Perp tower like that at Leigh; otherwise
it consists of a nave, chancel, s aisle, and s porch. Ashlar tower
of three stages, with a Perp w doorway with a Perp window

* John Guise, builder of Elmore, married Jane Pauncefoote of Hasfield in
1564.

over. Below the w bell-opening a niche with a sculptured image *in situ*, presumably Our Lady. The bell-openings have hood-moulds with stops carved with figures, some playing musical instruments. Gargoyles and an embattled parapet. The s porch was rebuilt in the C19 – the church was restored in 1871–8 – and the s aisle largely refaced, but the beautiful E window with flowing tracery, and a hood-mould with stops carved with C14 heads were kept. Dec chancel windows. Small C19 N vestry. The windows on the N side of the nave C19 Dec.

Inside, a tall double-chamfered Perp tower arch. The two w bays of the nave arcade are Norman with plain arches on rectangular piers with chamfered imposts; the remaining three bays are C19. C13 PISCINA in the s aisle and another in the sanctuary. Chancel walls scraped. The overpowering stone REREDOS, erected in 1886, is elaborately carved with eight saints under crocketed canopies, with pinnacles and a tabernacle. – SCREEN. A good example of C15 work, probably *c.*1450, but covered in varnish. – PULPIT. C15 wooden carved Perp panels, similar to the screen. – FONT. C15. Octagonal bowl with panels containing quatrefoils with centres of four-leaf flowers and roses. C18 cover. – SAXON CARVED STONE. Decorated with double spiral ornament very similar to that on the bowl and stem of the font at Deerhurst, and therefore at least late C9. It could be the socket for a cross. – MONUMENTS. Tablet to John Buckle † 1794, white marble with draped urn, by *Bryan* of Gloucester. – John Buckle † 1818 by *T. Pitt* of Gloucester, a copy of the former. – Several C19 tablets by *G. Lewis*, and a Boer War one to Harry Brookes † 1901, by *Boulton*.

ENGLISH BICKNOR

ST MARY. From outside the church offers no expectation of the splendid Norman work within. The lower stage of the tower is mid-C13, the upper is Perp with battlements. The original Norman tower was central; so the w tower is a complete rebuilding. The church is of sandstone, which is soft and does not last well, and this partly explains the rebuilding of the exterior. Inside, the nave with wagon roof and clerestory has unaltered C12 N and s arcades, the piers, particularly on the s, with sculptured capitals.* The arch on the N at the E of the

* Enriched scallops, broad leaves ending in volutes. The arches are unmoulded, except for a slight chamfer to the nave. On the N side ordinary scallops (NP).

nave is even finer, with rich chevrons and beak-heads, and was probably the original s doorway.* Chancel and tower arches E.E., with slender shafts to the latter. The chancel is off-set and rather long, and the aisles continue on both sides, forming on the N a vestry, and on the s the Machen Chapel, which has a SCREEN of c. 1500 with an altered boarded dado. Priest's door on the N of the chancel. Dec E window; otherwise the fenestration is renewed. Early PILLAR PISCINA and STOUP in the vestry. – FONT. Scraped Norman circular tub. – ROYAL ARMS. George III. – STAINED GLASS. E window 1908 by *Percy Bacon*. – CHANDELIER. Reproduction, *c*.1900, of C18 Dutch work. – PLATE. Chalice and Paten, 1701 by *John Sutton*; Paten, 1723 by *Abraham Buteux*. – MONUMENTS. Two female effigies of *c*.1300 and 1350 said to be Cecilia de Muchegros, her feet on a dog, and Harwisia carrying a heart, indicating a heart-burial only; or is it an egg, symbol of the Resurrection ? Both have their long gowns caught up under the arms. Characteristic of the period but not good. – Effigy of a priest wearing a chasuble, in the N aisle vestry, not *in situ*. – In the Machen Chapel Edward Machen † 1778, a weeping child with portrait-bust medallion, by *T. Symonds* of Hereford. – Tablet in the chancel, 1664, with stone cherubs.

The church is in the outer courtyard of a MOTTE AND BAILEY with inner and outer bailey, of about 150 yds overall diameter. Norman masonry has been found in the motte, and the castle well is still identifiable. It may date from the reign of King Stephen – there are references to it in the early C13, but it is believed to have been destroyed soon afterwards. It is one of many such motte-and-bailey earthworks on the Welsh border.

BICKNOR COURT. Some remains of Tudor date; it was the house of the Wyrhalls, who were hereditary foresters. C18 stone front of three storeys and five bays. Central doorway with pediment. Tudor mullioned windows at the back. Small GAZEBO.

EASTBACH COURT. The house of the Machen family. C18, ashlar, stone roof, cornice and parapet, two storeys, five bays. The central portion breaks forward, and has a rusticated ground floor and a central pedimented door.

WHITEHOUSE FARMHOUSE dates from the C16, and has a two-storey gabled porch with arched entrance and some mullioned windows and gables.

* Heavy, big capitals with enriched scallops. The chevron is at r. angles to the wall (NP).

IRON AGE HILL-FORT, on the hill E of Symonds Yat. There are four ramparts on the S side (the fifth is part of Offa's Dyke); elsewhere it is defended by the natural scarp. The fort encloses about 650 acres.

ETLOE see AWRE

EVINGTON see LEIGH

6090
FALFIELD

ST GEORGE. 1860 by *S. W. Daukes*. Of cemetery-chapel type, with an octagonal turret with spirelet broached over the S porch. Plate tracery. Stone roof. Modern vestry at the W end. – STAINED GLASS. E window by *Lavers, Barraud & Westlake*, 1860. – Window in the S wall by *Ward & Hughes*, 1871. – W window by *Hardman*, good, with a Puginesque group at the bottom; 1892. – W window nave N by *Heaton, Butler & Bayne*, 1882. – SCREEN. 1915. – MONUMENT. Sir G. S. Jenkinson † 1892. Alabaster Gothic tablet with crocketed gable and angels.

CONGREGATIONAL CHURCH. 1813, rebuilt in 1843.

OLD WINDMILL. The tower has been converted into a dwelling.

EASTWOOD PARK. Begun *c*.1820 for the Earl of Liverpool Prime Minister, and rebuilt after 1865 for Sir G. S. Jenkinson, probably by *S. W. Daukes*. Stone dressings, modillion cornice, hipped sprocketed roof with dormers. Two storeys, the main elevation of 2, 5, 2 bays with the side wings projecting. The first-floor windows have pierced stone balconies. At the side a three-storey *porte-cochère* which has lost its turret.

HENEAGE COURT. C17, with additions by *E. P. Warren, c*.1913.

FIDDINGTON MANOR see ASHCHURCH

FIELDHOUSE see AWRE

6070
FILTON

ST PETER. Of *c*.1340. Enlarged and mostly rebuilt in 1845 by *Hicks*, and a new nave and sanctuary, orientated to the N, added in 1961, by *P. N. Taylor & A. W. Dickin*. C14 W tower with a Dec window over the entrance and gargoyles. New spire added in 1961. The old or C19 part of the church consists of nave, S aisle, and S porch. – FONT. C19 Perp. Octagonal. – PLATE. Chalice, 1633 by *William Shute;* Paten, 1723 by *Richard*

Bayley. – MONUMENT. Tablet to John Barnsley † 1789.
Classical.
New buildings for the BRISTOL AEROPLANE COMPANY by
Eric Ross: Assembly Hall *c*.1952; Apprentices' School *c*.1955.

FLAXLEY   6010

ST MARY. Rebuilt in 1856 by *Sir George Gilbert Scott*, of red
grit and grey Forest stone dressings. Early Dec. Chancel, three-
bay nave, N aisle, S porch, and a tower with a spire at the W end
of the N aisle. The interior is quite richly decorated with carved
hood-mould stops and corbels. Encaustic tiles. – FONT. Very
elaborate, of Painswick stone with marble columns on octagonal steps. – PULPIT. Somewhat similar. – REREDOS. Alabaster, carved by *J. Birnie Philip* (who carved the frieze on the
podium of the Albert Memorial). – MONUMENTS. Abraham
Clark † 1683. Baroque marble cherubs. – Some rather indiffer-
ent tablets to the Crawley-Boevey family, one † 1820 signed by
Cooke of Gloucester. – Long inscription on the S wall of the
nave to Catherine Boevey † 1726. (She also has a monument in
Westminster Abbey.)
FLAXLEY ABBEY. Some time between 1148 and 1154, the abbey
was founded for Cistercian monks by Roger, son of Milo, Earl
of Hereford, in memory of his father, who is said to have been
killed on the spot where it now stands while hunting on
Christmas Eve, 1143.

The fabric of the house now represents three different
periods of development: first the original monastic buildings
up to the Dissolution in 1536; second the Boevey period from
1647, when William Boevey bought it from the Kingston
family, to 1777 when the N part of the house was destroyed by
fire; and third the subsequent building of the S wing by the
architect *Anthony Keck*, 1777–83, and later C19 alterations.
The building is roughly L-shaped, the W wing consisting of the
W range of the claustral buildings considerably remodelled
during the Boevey period, and the S wing in the manner of
Adam by Anthony Keck, who had worked for Adam at
Moccas, in Herefordshire.

The ground floor of the W range survives substantially
unaltered. It consists of a fine C12 rib-vaulted undercroft,
perhaps the lay-brothers' REFECTORY, with, S of it (and off
the SW corner of the cloister), the two plain tunnel-vaulted
chambers of the REREDORTER. Above this is the C14 ABBOT'S

GUEST HALL, with an arch-braced roof, ceiled at upper collar level, and two rows of cusped wind-braces, an embattled cornice, gilded bosses, and timber battlemented corbels. The wood is said to be chestnut. The Gothic stone windows and stone chimneypiece are reconstructions made in 1913, when the four small C12 arrow-slit windows were discovered in the S wall. This indicates that the room had a different use before the Black Death in 1349, when lay help became no longer available, and was appropriated and altered by the Abbot for his guests, who included King Edward III. Under this hall is a mezzanine or secret chamber made possible by the difference in vaulting heights of the two chambers on the ground floor. The rooms over the C12 refectory have C17 fenestration of the rudimentary Venetian type, with timber arches within the glazing area. In 1961–2 these rooms were restored by *Oliver Messel*. The rainwater-heads here are dated 1751.

No other monastic remains are visible above ground except for two C12 jambs of the SOUTH PROCESSIONAL DOORWAY where it opened into the former nave of the abbey church from the NE corner of the cloister, now built into the rear wall of a plain early C18 orangery.

The extension N of the C12 portion, approximately balancing the Abbot's Guest Hall, is nondescript. To the E is a good robust mid-C17 staircase. The Georgian S block is not remarkable for its period, except perhaps for the method employed to line-out the rendering by inlaying 'joints' of rendering of a lighter colour, which seems to be original. The rooms, door, and staircase have pleasant decoration of Adam character, and the entrance hall is well organized in three bays with wall-arcuation. Front porch characteristically mean early C19 Gothic. Domestic offices re-designed by *Oliver Messel*.

The main parts of the abbey and church lie under the gardens to the E of the house. Some stones from the chapter house were uncovered during the excavations for a formal pond. The CHAPTER HOUSE was originally discovered in 1788, and was reported to have had an apsidal E end and a central column, the base of which was then found, together with six coffin lids. Foundations of the S and W walls of the SOUTH TRANSEPT have also been found.

At the Dissolution, the abbey was given to Sir William Kingston, who was Constable of the Tower of London and superintended the execution of Anne Boleyn in the same year, 1536. His son Sir Antony, the 'terrible Provost Marshal', was appointed to carry out the execution of Bishop Hooper at Gloucester. The most celebrated owner of Flaxley in later years was Mrs Catherine Boevey, the 'Perverse Widow' pursued by Addison's Sir Roger de Coverley.

GUNS MILLS. Old blast-furnace. In 1629 the Crown ordered six hundred and ten guns to be made there and sent to Holland. Some of the Flaxley guns were used in the Civil War. The buildings became a paper-mill, existing as such till the end of the C19.

FORTHAMPTON

ST MARY. A somewhat over-restored and much altered church consisting of a nave which surprisingly retains its plastered ceiling, chancel, N aisle, W tower, and S porch. The tower is C13 with massive diagonal W buttresses and stair-vice on the NE corner. Three stages, with a Dec W window with reticulated tracery, trefoil-headed single lights in the second stage, and two-light Dec openings above, with a plain parapet. Over the S doorway a mutilated Norman hood-mould with beast-head stops and a grotesque-head keystone. S porch C19. The plain C13 tower arch has two chamfered orders springing from the floor without capitals. N aisle and arcade added in 1847, and the short chancel restored or rebuilt in 1869, with a restored cinquefoil-headed lancet light on the S. The most interesting feature of the church is its stone ALTAR, a mensa of c.1300, complete with four chamfered stone supports and three consecration crosses. This has presumably survived *in situ*. – FONT. A memorial to Susanna Plumptre † 1849, elaborately fashioned in stone and marbles. – FURNISHINGS. Ancient pews at the W end with linenfold panels. – Former REREDOS, now placed against the S wall of the nave. Executed in pokerwork by the Rev. *W. Calvert*, c.1845. It depicts Christ and two disciples at Emmaus, in a frame which has a crocketed ogee arch and pinnacles. – The ALMS BOX is also the work of *Calvert*, carved in wood to illustrate the widow's mite. – The existing REREDOS of carved and gilded stone was erected in 1892. – ROYAL ARMS. Early C19. – STAINED GLASS. Beautiful E window with Pre-Raphaelite figures representing Virtues. – W window of the N aisle 1862 by *Clayton & Bell*. – MONUMENTS. John Rasteil † 1631, showing a small carved skeleton at the foot of the tablet. – The Hon. James Yorke, Bishop of Ely, † 1808. Tablet by *R. Blore* of London. – James Sommers Yorke † 1809, by *R. Blore*. – James Yorke † 1816, by *R. Blore Jun.* of

Piccadilly. – Mary Platt † 1833, by *Theakston* of Pimlico. – In the CHURCHYARD a simple C17 pedestal-sundial. – WHIPPING POST AND STOCKS, W of the church. Post with iron manacles and stocks for three.

YORKE ALMSHOUSES, E of the church. Stone, mid-C19, with gables bearing the Yorke coat of arms and finials the crest. Gothic windows.

FORTHAMPTON COURT, ¾ m. SE. A country house of the abbots of Tewkesbury and last used as such by the last abbot, John Wakeman, who became the first Bishop of Gloucester and died in 1549. The house, large and rambling, has undergone frequent alterations up to the present day. The most important part of the medieval buildings to survive is the GREAT HALL of c.1380. In the C18 it was divided up, and during the time that *Philip Webb* was doing alterations to the house, c.1891, a carpet and bookcase were designed by *Morris & Co.* for the upper room in the hall. In 1914 the floor was taken out and the hall restored to its original proportions, with the carpet still in use. The huge bay window which now lights the hall was then inserted by *Maurice Chesterton*. The medieval roof survives, with its trussed collar-beams supported from a moulded wall-plate, and with two tiers of wind-braces. A splendid open staircase designed by *Philip Webb* leads into the abbot's CHAPEL, which has Perp windows and contains a late C13 picture on wood of Edward the Confessor and St John the Baptist, which is thought always to have been here.

Plans were made in the C18 to regularize the façade of the house, but these were not carried out. Various additions were made in the C19, as well as the tower-like block, small hall, and library, designed by *Philip Webb* in 1891. The neo-Georgian drawing room was constructed in 1960.

At the time of the Dissolution, the abbey of Tewkesbury was bought by the town. Abbot Wakeman, retiring to Forthampton, brought with him a Crusader's tomb of c.1335. The TOMB CHEST survives on the terrace, and carries the effigy of a Knight, by tradition William de la Zouch.

In the village a number of timber-framed, thatched houses, originally with wattle and daub but now with brick infilling; BREWERS COTTAGE is one of these. Opposite is VINE FARM, C16, with close-set studding and overhanging gable, and a timber-framed thatched BARN.

THE SANCTUARY is timber-framed and has a C15 hall (now filled in with an upper storey) with carved wooden bosses on the

ceiling. Bargeboarded gable with carved vine-trail decoration.
Next is the VILLAGE HALL, *c*.1900, brick with stone dressings,
Tudor windows, and a stone shield of the Yorke arms. HILL
FARMHOUSE is timber-framed with gables either end.
FORTHAMPTON HOUSE is a substantial C18 brick house of
three storeys with five windows, and a door with fanlight;
contemporary staircase.

A lane in the opposite direction leads to ALCOCKS FARM, structurally much the same as when Edward Alcocke lived there in
the C17. It is timber-framed. The gable-end has a first floor
overhang.

In the lane leading to the Court stands SOUTHFIELD HOUSE,
formerly the vicarage, early C18, of brick, with modillion eaves
cornice, hipped tile roof, two storeys, and projecting wings on
the elevation facing the road. The garden front has two Venetian windows. Inside, a contemporary staircase with twisted
balusters. Early C18 brick DOVECOTE, with four gables with
stone ball-finials and lantern. On the river, the LOWER LODE
HOTEL is a neat Georgian brick house with two-storey bay
windows either side of a door with fanlight.

FRAMILODE   7010

ST PETER, on the banks of the Severn. 1854 by *Francis Niblett*.
Romanesque. N porch surmounted by a tower with a hipped
roof. Aisleless nave and sanctuary with rounded apse. Painted
open roof. – Contemporary FURNISHINGS. – STAINED
GLASS by *Rogers* of Worcester.

OLD VICARAGE. 1856–7. Stone-built with gables. Plain windows
with shoulder arches.

There were mills here for making iron-wire, and the village was
connected with Stroud by the Stroudwater Canal, begun in
1775. There is a typical terrace row of boatmen's cottages,
c.1800–20.

DARELL ARMS INN. Victorian Elizabethan with equal gabled
wings, painted to simulate timber-framing. Central iron
Gothic balcony, approached by an arched doorway on the first
floor, under the Darell coat of arms set in a quatrefoil.

FRAMPTON COTTERELL   6080

ST PETER. The church, except the W tower, was rebuilt in 1858
by *John Norton*, who had worked in Benjamin Ferrey's office.
The tower is Perp, three stages, diagonal buttresses, an embattled panelled parapet with pinnacles, and in the centre of

each side an ogee-canopied niche in which the images survive. The stair-turret is crowned with a crocketed spirelet. Norton built the rest of the church in Perp style in keeping with the tower. It consists of a nave with aisles, which have embattled parapets, chancel, and S porch. Five-bay arcades. – FONT. Norman octagonal bowl with scalloped stem, restored. – STAINED GLASS. A series, probably by *Bell* of Bristol, one commemorating Edward Pusey † 1882, indicating Tractarian persuasion. – Another window has Munich glass. – SANCTUARY LAMPS. Venetian. – MONUMENT. Brass to John Symes † 1661.

The church is now surrounded by suburban development. In Rectory Lane, STEP HOUSE, with an C18 front, survives; two storeys and five windows with keystones and voussoirs, and a door with a shell hood.

NORTH WOODS, 2 m. W. 1832. Ashlar-faced, the central block of two storeys and six bays has horizontal grooving on the ground floor, and a central segmental bow with a balustraded balcony on the first floor, with tall fluted Corinthian columns, cornice, and parapet. The windows are divided by pilasters; moulded panels above. Four-bay wings either side terminate in one-bay pavilions, and there are matching detached wings beyond.

FRAMPTON-ON-SEVERN

ST MARY. Mainly C14 (consecrated in 1315), with C15 additions. The church was restored by *Niblett c.* 1850 and in 1868–1870 by *Henry Woodyer*, who lengthened the chancel. W tower rebuilt in 1735, retaining the Perp style. Three stages, with diagonal buttresses terminated by crocketed pinnacles, and joined by an open panelled embattled parapet. W window Perp. Nave of four bays, with N and S aisles divided from it by C14 arcades with octagonal piers. Chapels were added to the E end of both aisles in the C15. The E end of the chancel was entirely rebuilt to form a sanctuary by *Woodyer*. The W end of the N aisle also appears to have been rebuilt. The E windows of the C15 chapels have hood-moulds with angel stops, and cusped tracery with quatrefoils and embattled transoms. C14 S porch with a chamber over it, rebuilt in the late C18 with a Churchwarden-Gothick window. On the N is a small doorway with an ogee arch. The windows generally are Perp. In the S chapel a C15 PISCINA, but the PISCINA and triple SEDILIA in the chancel are by *Woodyer*, restrained and pleasing in design. –

FONT. One of the six similar Romanesque lead fonts surviving [16] in Gloucestershire, the product of an Anglo-Norman school, possibly working locally, in the third quarter of the C12. – PULPIT. 1622; oak. – PEWS and STALLS. C19. Good, with linenfold panels at the end of each pew. – ROYAL ARMS. 1769. – CHANDELIER. A fine example of London work; 1756. – STAINED GLASS. The E window in the Clifford Chapel has fragments of a late C15 Seven Sacraments window, and an angel holding the quartered shield of the arms of Clifford. – More fragments in the tracery of other windows, including, in the N aisle, the arms of Berkeley. – E window by *Clayton & Bell*. – HATCHMENT. C18, bearing sixteen quarterings of Clifford. – MONUMENTS. Recumbent stone effigy of a Knight, made probably at Bath, but showing influence of Bristol craftsmen; *c*.1300. It rests on a low tomb-chest under a shallow cusped recess, and is supposed to be a member of the Clifford family. – Recumbent effigy of a Lady, *c*.1310, on a low tomb-chest in a shallow arched recess with two shields said by Bigland to have borne the arms of Clifford and de Malton. – Diminutive stone effigy of a Civilian, in a cusped recess on the floor of the N aisle. The bushy hair, curled over the ears, and the costume belong to the period of Edward II. – John Clifford † 1684. Baroque tablet. – Ann Wade † 1687. Baroque tablet. – Anthony Clifford. C17 tablet with arms. – William Clutterbuck † 1727. Classical marble monument. – Samuel and James Pearce † 1798–9, by *John Pearce*. Marble tablet. – Nathaniel Clifford † 1817. Marble tablet with arms. – Henry Barnard † 1813, by *T. King* of Bath.

FRAMPTON COURT. Built between 1731 and 1733 for Richard Clutterbuck, an official of the Bristol Customs House. It is most probable that he employed the Bristol architect *John Strahan*, who designed Redland Court. Strahan's architecture was called 'piratical' by John Wood, and it is evident that the main façade at Frampton is an interpretation of Colen Campbell's Stourhead (1722). The composition is somewhat overloaded with alternately blocked window surrounds of Palladio's Palazzo Thiene type. The windows between the pilasters of the three-bay pedimented central feature are cramped, and the thin quoins are too weak to emphasize the confines of the main block, which is unrelated to the plain boxlike wings. The Vanbrugh-inspired heavy arched chimneys make the total composition one of, architecturally speaking, naïve disharmony. The masonry of the house, however, is very fine; but perhaps its chief triumph lies in the splendid joinery of the interior. The wainscoting, the proportion of the doors, and the quality of the carving in the main rooms are exceptional, and in mint condition. Note the shell-cupboard, the most unusual piece of joinery in the dog gate at the foot of the main staircase, and the drawing room chimneypiece with Bristol Delft tiles.

76   ORANGERY. A rectangular canal to the NW of the house is terminated by a delicious Gothick bauble of a garden house in the style of Batty Langley, which may well have been designed by *William Halfpenny*, or his son *John Halfpenny*. Together they published *Chinese and Gothick Architecture Properly Ornamented* in 1752, and the resemblance of the orangery to some of these Bristol architects' known designs, such as a pavilion for Tsarskoe Selo, is unmistakable. The plan of the orangery is a pair of conjoined octagons of two storeys, with an octagon above, topped by a diminutive cupola. All the windows have pretty ogee arches, and the parapet has battlements and pinnacles. The interior is of the same high quality.

There are also an C18 octagonal DOVECOTE, and fine rusticated GATEPIERS with vase-finials and wrought-iron gates, the latter in Perry Way.

MANOR FARMHOUSE. Mid C15. The ground floor of the main building is of stone with some six-light mullioned windows; the upper storeys project and are timber-framed with close-set studding. Contemporary square-headed chimneypiece with continuous mouldings to jambs and head, tracery above, and carved flowers in the cornice. Another, in the hall, has good moulded splayed jambs. The house was thoroughly renovated in 1925. The BARN is also probably C15, timber-framed on a stone base. Rubble DOVECOTE.

The village green is wide, long, and flat, the *beau idéal* of a village green. The houses, timber-framed or Georgian, stand well back, with the mansion and the Manor Farm almost opposite each other about a quarter of the way along. At the N end of the E side FRAMPTON LODGE, a larger C18 house, brick, of three storeys and seven bays. At the S end EAST GABLES is a complete medieval house, timber-framed with cruck trusses. C18 alterations include windows with Gothick lights, and gables.*

Beyond this the houses come together either side of the road

* In 1821–3, *William James* made alterations to various farm buildings and cottages at Frampton.

leading towards the church. WALFORD HOUSE is late C18 with keystones and voussoirs to the windows, and an enriched frieze to the doorcase. GREYCROFT has an exposed cruck truss. Opposite, a timber-framed COTTAGE with a plaster shield of arms in a bedroom. TUDOR COTTAGE is timber-framed with first-floor overhang. BUCKHOLDT HOUSE, C18, has a bow to full height on the garden side. Further on are several timber-framed cottages, some with crucks. WILD-GOOSE COTTAGE is C15 (or possibly C14), timber-framed with three cruck trusses. The central portion was originally an open hall. OLD THATCH is a timber-framed C15 cottage with large braces, overhanging gable-end, and thatched roof. OEGROVE, timber-framed on a stone base, has a stone roof. The BARN opposite, of c.1550, is timber-framed with inter-laced wattle infilling. Behind it on the N is the last surviving fragment of the MANOR HOUSE of the early C16. It is now a farm shed, but retains first-floor chamfered joints with pyramid stops. The roof has wind-braces. Beyond the church, on the canal at SPLATT BRIDGE, is one of *Mylne*'s CANAL KEEPER'S HOUSES with the usual pedimented portico on fluted Doric columns *in antis*. Another, a bit mutilated, near 81 SAUL LODGE.

FROMEBRIDGE MILL, $1\frac{1}{2}$ m. E. C19, with C17 and C18 remains. There is an attractive cottage with a clock-turret. The mill building, which lies parallel to the leat, had an external under-shot wheel. It was an iron-mill in the C18.

FRENCHAY

ST JOHN THE BAPTIST. 1834 by *H. Rumley*. W tower, with spire restored in 1923 by *Hartland Thomas*. Embattled nave of five bays, with galleries on all sides, except the E, where there is a small sanctuary. The roof has a wide span, with ribbed plaster vaults over the nave. Galleries of the same height. The windows lighting the galleries are Dec; those in the aisles below are plain. The interior is much more successful than the exterior.

UNITARIAN CHURCH. Built in 1720 to an excellent design, 73 both restrained and dignified. Small tower of four stages with bell. The windows are round-headed. The interior is square on plan with a flat corniced ceiling, divided laterally by a beam supported on two slender Tuscan columns. Wide so-called 'Crinoline' entrance door. – Panelled GALLERY the full width

of the church on two wooden Tuscan columns. – Interesting
panelled PULPIT on a corbel in the centre of the facing wall.
– Some BOX PEWS. – GRAVEYARD. 'Body-snatchers'' stone.
FRIENDS' MEETING HOUSE. 1671, reconstructed in 1808–9.
Typical simple Quaker building with some original furnishings.
Frenchay is a green oasis on the outskirts of Bristol, with an
attractive group of fine Georgian houses built on the edge of a
common. The village proper consists of a charming un-
planned huddle of stone cottages on a steep slope facing s to
the river Frome and served by narrow stepped and paved
paths. Great care should be taken in its development.
FRENCHAY MANOR. 1736. Classical façade suggestive of John
Wood the Elder. Ashlar-faced, of three storeys and 2, 3, 2
bays. Modillion cornice and balustraded parapet with pediment. Rusticated quoins. The central portion breaks forward
with Corinthian pilasters through the upper floors, and the
first-floor windows have segmental pediments with a triangular
one in the centre. Rusticated ground floor with segment-
headed windows and a doorway which has Ionic columns and
segmental pediment. Either side a low pavilion. The staircase
fills an elliptical space at the rear of the hall. Parts of the interior were altered c.1813; the room on the l. of the hall has a nice
Regency marble fireplace with caryatids. – STABLES. C18,
with *œil de bœuf* windows and a pedimented doorway.
FRENCHAY LODGE WEST. C18 doorway with a rusticated
architrave, keystone, voussoirs, and pediment.
LAKE HOUSE. Early C19 villa, stucco, three storeys, two bays,
with pedimented one-storey wings either side with double
windows in segment-headed recesses. Earlier gabled house at
the rear.
RIVERWOOD HOUSE. C18. Stucco, cornice and parapet, two
storeys, three bays, and a door with fanlight and porch.
CEDAR HALL. C18, ashlar, with rusticated quoins, cornice, parapet, three storeys, and four bays. Two-storey wings either side
with bay windows. Attractive earlier stone STABLES.
FRENCHAY HOUSE. 1772. Ashlar-faced, with rusticated quoins,
modillion cornice, balustraded parapet, and two storeys. The
windows on the ground floor have keystone masks. Venetian
window in the return elevation, facing the garden.
NEW HOUSE. C18. Stucco-faced. Cornice and pediment and
chamfered quoins of alternating lengths. Three storeys, two-
storey bay windows, and a doorway with attached Tuscan
columns.

CLARENDON HOUSE. C18/19, faced in rendered ashlar. Three storeys and three bays. The windows have shaped architraves. Cast-iron Regency veranda on the first floor.

OLD HOUSE. C18. Roughcast, with chamfered stone quoins, cornice and pediment, and windows with shaped architraves and labels. Traditional four-gabled rear elevation.

FRENCHAY PARK, part of the hospital. Built c.1780, enlarged in 1804. The ashlar front has three storeys and five bays with moulded architraves to the windows, chamfered quoins, a balustraded parapet supporting eight carved urns, and a porch with Ionic columns. Two-storey, three-bay bows either side. The main block has panels under the window-sills, all joined vertically. The hall is panelled. Contemporary staircase with twisted balusters. In the park a large C18 stone URN carved with acanthus leaves and trailing vine. LODGE. 1870 by *John Birch*.

THE RECTORY and the house joined to it by lower wings are situated in a prominent position. They have stucco fronts of c.1800.

FRETHERNE
7000

ST MARY. 1847 by *Francis Niblett*, enlarged in 1857–9 by *J. W. Hugall*. It was commissioned by the Rev. Sir W. L. Darell, and no expense was spared; it is a small Victorian masterpiece which survives unaltered. N porch surmounted by a tower with pinnacles at the four corners, from which spring flying buttresses supporting the richly crocketed spire. Nave, chancel, N aisle, S aisle with two S chapels, organ chamber, and SE vestry. The style is Dec and very elaborate, particularly on Hugall's additional S chapels; the E window of the easternmost chapel has sculptured angels and crocketed pinnacles. The doors are guarded by wrought-iron gates. Each of the stone piers of the S arcade differs in plan; one has clustered shafts of polished granite, and a gilded capital. Painted nave roof, with braced collar-beams springing from carved corbels, lit by jettied gabled dormer windows. Almost everything is decorated, painted, and gilded. – REREDOS. Pyrographic picture by the Rev. *W. Calvert*. – STAINED GLASS. All the windows are by *George Rogers* of Worcester, 1859, except one of four angels by *Powell*, very insipid by contrast. – HATCHMENTS, bearing the arms of the Darell family. – PLATE. Chalice and Paten Cover, 1766. – MONUMENTS. Several C13 coffin lids with incised foliated crosses. – Bust of Sir Edward Tierney, erected 1857.

FRETHERNE LODGE, SW of the church. Early C19 classical front with Gothic detail. Brick. Two storeys and four windows with dripmoulds. Crowning pediment with a quatrefoil in the tympanum. Tuscan porch.

RECTORY, ¼ m. N. Early Victorian. Two bay windows, over-hanging eaves, and cast-iron veranda.

LUFFINGHAMS, on the road to Lower Framilode. Rectangular building framed with four pairs of crucks, smoke-blackened in the roof. It has an inserted floor and central stone chimney, two newel staircases, ovolo-moulded mullions to the ground-floor windows, several old doors and arched door-heads, and large curved braces in the E wall.

7000   # FROCESTER

ST ANDREW. Though largely rebuilt in the late C19, the church dates back to the C17. The medieval or earlier church of St Peter, on a different site, became ruinous and was abandoned in the C17, when this building, which still has the date 1637 carved in its ceiling and was then a chapel at Frocester Court, was removed to its present site and brought into use. In 1849 the old church was restored by *Francis Niblett*, and the services were transferred there; but in 1952 it was finally demolished (except for *Niblett*'s tower and the old S porch), and the stone given to Wycliffe College for the rebuilding of their chapel. St Andrew consists of an aisleless nave and chancel, with a bellcote. A small Norman window has been inserted in the N wall of the chancel. Interior walls scraped. – FONT. Octagonal bowl of *c.*1680, with octagonal plinth and circular base. – PULPIT. Jacobean. – MONUMENT. Ralph Bigland of Frocester, Garter King at Arms. Erected 1902.

ST PETER. N tower with broach-spire, 1849 by *Niblett*. S porch C14. Tudor windows.*

FROCESTER COURT. The manor was one of the earliest posses-sions of the monks of Gloucester, and was granted to them in 823 or soon after. The house is substantially medieval, with a C14 hall of cruck construction, now built in. In the roof the smoke-blackened louvre can still be seen. A later chimneystack has a small medieval window either side. At r. angles to this is part of another hall with a more elaborate roof with braced collar-beams and wind-braces. At the Dissolution of the monasteries the manor was bought by the Huntley family, and

* For Roman remains, *see* below.

the house was altered *c.*1554. In the principal bedroom is a moulded stone chimneypiece of this date. In the hall are two medallions with carved heads in wood which could represent Philip and Mary. The house was evidently restored in the early C19, and two of the principal living rooms have Gothic chimneypieces of this period.

GATEHOUSE. Timber-framed gateway with four gables and a stone roof. On one side is a rubble building with two gables and mullioned windows. The whole of this existed in the early C17.

TITHE BARN. A chronicle of Gloucester Abbey ascribes the [46] *magna grangia* at Frocester to Abbot John de Gamages, who ruled from 1284 to 1306. In view of its manifestly early features, the barn can be accepted as substantially built *c.*1300. It is one of the eight or nine most important barns in England, and the best preserved. Internally it is 30 ft wide and 186 ft long, of thirteen bays, including the passage-bays of two wagon-porches on the NW. Additional entrance-arches in the NW section; flying buttresses, to correct a settlement between the porches, support a lean-to roof. The walls, of coursed oolite, have buttresses of moderate projection. Some of the stone may be Roman in origin, as the barn is built adjacent to the site of the Roman villa (*see* below). The roof, carried in one span on raised base-crucks, is trussed above the heavy collars only by single-light collars over the trusses and in the middle of each bay. Wind-braces in two tiers but arranged in a reticulated pattern. Some of the other farm-buildings may be medieval in origin. There is a double DOVECOTE, and the SHEEP PENS existed in the C17. Several buildings have Gothic quatrefoil air vents.

The house which is now called the MANOR is C19, large and gabled.

NYMPSFIELD CHAMBERED LONG BARROW. *See The Buildings of England: Gloucestershire: The Cotswolds.*

Two ROMAN VILLAS are known here. Fragments of one were found beneath the church of St Peter. The other, at Frocester Court, is now being extensively excavated. It consisted first of a simple strip house, to which wings and a front corridor, together with back rooms and a bath block, were later added. Recent work has shown clear evidence of flower-beds laid out in front of the building.

FROMEBRIDGE MILL *see* FRAMPTON-ON-SEVERN

GARDNERS FARM see SANDHURST

GATCOMBE see AWRE

GAUNTS EARTHCOTT see ALMONDSBURY

GLENFALL see CHARLTON KINGS

GLOUCESTER

THE CATHEDRAL

INTRODUCTION

In 1022 the Bishop of Worcester introduced Benedictine rule to the monastery of St Peter which had been founded *c.*681 by Osric. The church was rebuilt in 1058. However, according to William of Malmesbury, 'zeal and religion had grown cold many years before the coming of the Normans'. In 1072, when the Norman Serlo was appointed abbot, the numbers were down to two monks and eight novices. The growth in wealth and importance of the religious houses in the first fifty years after the Conquest must have been remarkable; by 1100 Serlo had increased his numbers to sixty monks. He began rebuilding the church in 1089, and most of this building survives today, including the crypt. It was consecrated on 13 July 1100 and again in 1121. In 1122 a fire is thought to have destroyed the wooden roof of the nave, and there are signs of calcination on the piers. So by *c.*1120 the nave must have been ready, and that accords well with the

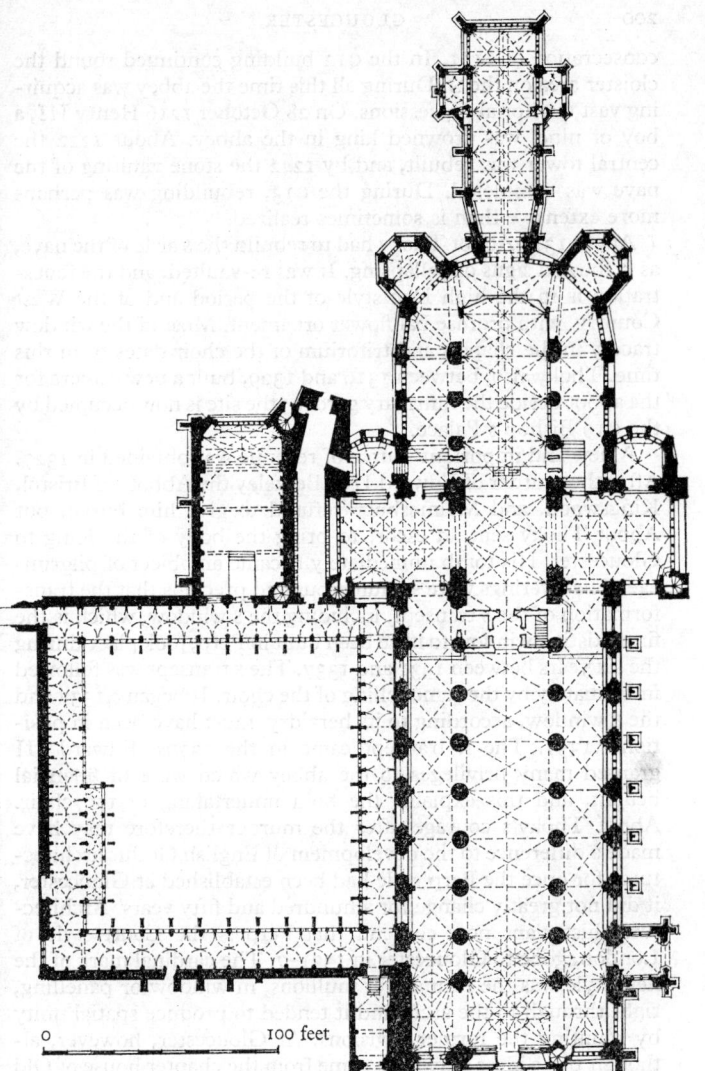

Plan of Gloucester Cathedral

consecration of 1121. In the C12 building continued round the
cloister area on the N. During all this time the abbey was acquir-
ing vast territorial possessions. On 28 October 1216 Henry III, a
boy of nine, was crowned king in the abbey. About 1222 the
central tower was rebuilt, and by 1242 the stone vaulting of the
nave was completed. During the C13, rebuilding was perhaps
more extensive than is sometimes realized.

About 1318 Abbot Thoky had to rebuild the S aisle of the nave,
as it showed signs of collapsing. It was re-vaulted, and the fenestration is in the high Dec style of the period and of the West
Country, with profuse ballflower ornament. Most of the window
tracery in the chapels and triforium of the choir dates from this
time. Thoky also, between 1316 and 1329, built a new camera for
the abbot beside the infirmary garden; the site is now occupied by
the C19 Bishop's Palace.

A new and important source of revenue was obtained in 1327.
After the murder of Edward II at Berkeley the Abbots of Bristol,
Kingswood, and Malmesbury refused to give him burial, but
Abbot Thoky sent an escort to bring the body of the King to
Gloucester. His tomb immediately became an object of pilgrimage. The offerings were so numerous and precious that the trans-
formation of the S transept, including the S window, which is the
first existing window to have been built in Perp, took place during
the six years between 1331 and 1337. The S transept was followed
immediately by the remodelling of the choir. It began c.1337 and
the E window, according to its heraldry, must have been in position c.1357. The N transept came in the 1370s. Edward III
granted many privileges to the abbey which were of financial
benefit, and this explains the bold undertaking of the choir.
Abbot Thoky's courage after the murder therefore may have
made a difference to the development of English Gothic architecture; for once the Perp style had been established at Gloucester,
it did not greatly change for a hundred and fifty years. Architectural historians now contend that Perp is the Court style of
London, gone to Gloucester in 1331–7. The cardinal mark of the
new style was the running of mullions, in window or panelling,
right through to the arch, and it tended to produce spatial unity
by blunting the former divisions. At Gloucester, however, although these ideas may have come from the chapter house of Old
St Paul's and St Stephen's Chapel, Westminster, whether
through the medium of Master William de Ramsey or not, the
execution is local, and the style is modified by the use of the
transom, so much so that the Court style itself henceforth is

strongly affected by the work at Gloucester. In other words, at Gloucester, the Court style passes into the hands of a perfectly independent school with a pronounced style of its own. In the Augustinian abbey at Bristol (1298–1332) as much stress was laid on the horizontal line as the London builders laid on the vertical. The heavy cross-beams of the s choir at Bristol Cathedral, perhaps imitating a wooden technique in stone, are an example. At Gloucester the triforium openings of the presbytery are deliberately crossed by horizontal tracery for no purpose except appearance, and thus the true Perp style was formed, producing a post-Gloucester Court style whose influence spread. This view is corroborated by the appearance in London of *Thomas of Gloucester* immediately after the completion of the great E window in 1350. Three years later Thomas of Gloucester was the King's Master Mason, and we can assume that his rapid promotion was due to his work at Gloucester.

There is another distinctive feature, besides the transom, that became part of the Court style: the ogee arch with cusps placed close together on each side of the arch. This detail is found in the very pretty ogee arches on the tomb of Edward II, and in the presbytery, and was not previously used in London, though it appears afterwards in St Stephen's Chapel, Westminster, destroyed in 1834. The three-dimensional ogee arch, though not particularly apparent in Gloucester Cathedral except perhaps in the C14 choir stalls, is also West Country, and can be found at Exeter as early as 1316. Gloucester's unique achievement, however, was the invention of the fan-vault. The date of the E range of the cloisters is between 1351 and 1377, and they are thought to be the first fan-vaults in Europe, though something similar was happening in the chapter house at Hereford.

Perp rebuilding continued in the C15. Abbot Morwent was evidently of a mind to rebuild the nave, and started at the w end some time between 1421 and 1437. His achievement consists of the w front and two westernmost bays, and the s porch, which was much restored in the C19. In the 1450s during Abbot Seabroke's time a monk named Robert Tully built the tower which replaced the E.E. structure. The Lady Chapel was rebuilt c.1450–99, also replacing the E.E. work. This was the last major alteration to the abbey, which was converted by Henry VIII into a college or cathedral with Bishopric and Chapter in 1541.

The second bishop was John Hooper, who was burnt at the stake in Gloucester in 1554 for holding Protestant opinions. When William Laud was dean in 1616 High Church principles were observed, and after the Table had been moved from the middle to the E end, there appeared the fine Jacobean altar rails which are now in the Lady Chapel; but the outraged Puritan Bishop Miles Smith is said never to have set foot in the cathedral again. During the Commonwealth the cathedral had a narrow escape, when its total destruction was planned; but it was eventually handed over to the mayor and citizens in 1657, by whom it was preserved. In the C18 Bishop Martin Benson (1734–52) spent vast sums on restoration and employed *William Kent* to design a Gothic choir screen (1741); this was removed in 1820. Kent wanted to 'flute' the Norman pillars in the nave. In the C19 *Sir G. G. Scott* destroyed almost everything which was not Gothic; but apart from this, Gloucester suffered much less than many cathedrals from C19 restorers. A major scheme of repairs started in 1953, consisting of the reconstruction of the roofs of the nave, choir, N transept, and cloisters. The cloister roof incorporates pre-stressed and light-weight concrete for decking to carry the re-cast lead outer covering. The pre-stressed concrete roof to the S walk was probably the first time (1956) this material had been used in the repair of a medieval cathedral in England. The architects were *N. H. Waller* and *B. J. Ashwell*.

The best printed account of Gloucester Cathedral is that by Sir William St John Hope in *Archaeological Journal*, LIV, 1897.

EXTERIOR

31 The first view of the cathedral, as it opens before one's eyes on
&
32 entering College Green from College Street, gives the impression that it is a Perp building. Closer inspection reveals its Norman bones in the rounded two-storey ambulatory with radiating chapels, and in the gabled ends of the transepts flanked in both cases by sturdy Norman turrets. The windows of the crypt, the ambulatory, and the ambulatory gallery also largely retain their round-headed Norman openings, though many are filled with later tracery. The radiating chapels are polygonal in plan, and E of either transept is a chapel too, of an oddly indistinct, rounded shape. Moreover, at gallery level are two small bridges which have blank Norman arcading with zigzag. These also are original, though they were not originally bridges.* Such details, however, cannot at first be apparent to the eye, overwhelmed as it must be by the immense mid-C15 Perp TOWER which soars 225 ft, piercing the sky with its

* That the blank arcading is not reset is proved by the fact that internally the bridges have blocked small Norman windows.

celebrated coronet of open parapet and airy pinnacles, and patterned all over with tier upon tier of blank arcading. The admirable effects of light and shade are produced by the bold projection of the buttresses, and the deep recessing of the windows and mouldings, and culminate in the openwork pinnacles at the top, each like the fantastic model of a church tower, and the openwork parapet and battlements. The coronet is a type of tower ornament more at home in Bristol and Somerset than at Gloucester.

Having returned to earth as it were, one finds oneself facing the SOUTH PORCH, which is the main entrance to the cathedral. This, as has already been noted, was built *c.*1420, but the niches are now filled with C19 figures by *Redfern*. Inside there are close wall panelling and a lierne-vault, and the inner DOORS have Norman hinge-work with trident-shaped iron strengtheners, thought to have been moved from the original Norman W door and adapted to fit the pointed doorway. The porch has an open parapet and pinnacles like the tower in miniature. The SOUTH AISLE is buttressed, and some of the niches retain sculpture, notably King Osric on the E, all much worn by the weather and contrasting with the over-restoration of the porch. This represents the only large extent of Dec work in the cathedral; all the windows which are early C14 are profusely ornamented with ballflower. Ogee arches are entirely absent, a noteworthy sign of conservatism. The tracery in each window has a horizontal emphasis, which is also to be seen at Bristol, and gives the impression of a large butterfly. There are seven bays altogether, and the easternmost window, although also decorated with ballflower, partakes of the Perp of the S transept. The clerestory windows above have ogee shapes and are placed under an embattled parapet; C15. But between the windows are the shallow Norman buttresses with chevron at the angles. They stop two bays from the W front. These two bays are Perp, as the W end was rebuilt in 1420 after the collapse of the Norman W end. What the latter looked like we do not know. Most probably there were two towers. The front has only one doorway, set with its surrounding masonry in front of the plane of the nine-light W window. The projecting wall ends in a pierced parapet. Against the W window stand two thin flying buttresses, and l. and r. are two dainty turrets with flying buttresses.

The Norman TRANSEPT FRONTS have turrets ornamented with arcading in two tiers (one with intersecting arches, the other with zigzag), and in the gable is a group of stepped, lancet-shaped, round-headed blank arches profusely provided with zigzag. Below, in spite of the Perp remodelling, are long vertical lines of chevron. These seem to be *in situ*, whereas the chevron round the great N window cannot be. Below this is the first Perp window, dating from *c*.1335. It is awkward as regards tracery, but a turning-point in the history of English architecture. (Can one detect the influence of the Bristol master mason with a penchant for non-vertical straight lines?) The transept windows to E and W must have been designed first, for in their tracery simple ogee motifs still survive, whereas the N window has strictly Perp panel tracery. In the AMBULATORY TRIFORIUM a Dec window with ballflower ornament is matched by a similar window in nearly the same position on the N. If the S aisle windows are *c*.1318, these, because they use ogees as well as ballflower, may be called *c*.1325-30. Perhaps the *tour de force* of the whole edifice is the EAST WINDOW with its fourteen lights, its canted side wings making the composition 3-8-3, with three transoms in the wings and five in the centre. The grid-frame gives strength against wind pressures. At its date, this was the largest window in the world. The outer hood-mould turns into ogee shape and rises to the perforated parapet of the gable, flanked either side by pierced pinnacles. In order to give full light to the window, the LADY CHAPEL is almost detached. This, the last alteration to the monastery, was not finished till shortly before 1500. Though about a hundred years later than the choir, the Lady Chapel is stylistically indistinguishable. The tracery patterns are pretty well the same. The E window has nine lights and three transoms, and an openwork parapet finishes the composition. Two identical chantry chapels project N and S, their fenestration in two tiers. On the N side of the cathedral the library is seen to bend round the N chapel of the transept where it was enlarged in the C14, and next to it is the large Perp window of the chapter house. Beyond this lie the cloisters (*see* p. 219).

Generally, the cathedral is built of pale cream Cotswold stone from Painswick, but the exposed battlements and pinnacles as well as the bottom courses of the walls are mostly of stone from Minchinhampton.

INTERIOR

9 The NAVE is dominated by the huge cylindrical Norman columns of the arcades, which have narrow, round, convex capitals

similar to those at Tewkesbury (consecrated 1121) and probably a regional invention. Seven bays with round Norman arches of three contrasting orders, a pair of strong soffit rolls, a straight edge, and chevron at r. angles to the wall; but the arches are not wide, as the massive columns are comparatively close together. Above this is a narrow band of triforium on a string-course with chevron. The triforium is remarkably small (cf. Tewkesbury) and has two twin openings with short columnar piers and responds, scallop capitals, and chevron at r. angles to the wall. The Norman clerestory seems to have had chevron set vertically, but of the Norman clerestory only traces remain; for springing from the line of the triforium is the E.E. rib-vault added in 1242, an elegant and graceful hat that hardly fits the rugged face below. The springings are supported on short clustered Purbeck shafts with sumptuous stiff-leaf capitals. In the early C15 the Norman W end of the nave, and the two most westerly bays, were altered in the Perp style and given lierne-vaulting. The longitudinal ridge-rib has two parallel subsidiaries l. and r., exactly as in the choir vault. The NORTH AISLE retains its Norman rib-vault with ribs of two rolls and a spur between, but the SOUTH AISLE was remodelled c.1318 and has a vault of that period with ribs decorated with ballflower in the three E bays. The most easterly bay of the Norman nave is blocked with the CHOIR SCREEN and organ chamber. In monastic times there was a second screen in line with the present nave altar, and there were altars in the two aisles (see the PISCINA in the S wall), so that everything E of this line was, in the peculiarly English fashion, completely screened off from the nave. The rather dull Perp panelling on the existing stone screen is C19. On its S side is the CHAPEL OF THE SALUTATION OF MARY, C15 Perp. To the E, the CHAPEL OF ST JOHN, with a Late Perp stone REREDOS, restored in 1964 by *Stephen Dykes Bower*. This chapel is against the back of the choir stalls and is protected on the S by a fine C15 wooden PARCLOSE SCREEN.

The SOUTH TRANSEPT, where, as has already been noted, the Perp style was first developed in the S window between 1331 and 1337, is Norman with a skin of Perp panelling threaded by the great flying buttresses of the tower; but isolated from the rest of the building. The slight movement of the E.E. tower southwards must have caused concern: on the NE corner the vertical of the Perp panelling has had to be rebated into the tower in order to keep truly vertical, and the huge

flying buttresses, which penetrate the rectilinear system, must
have been considered a necessity. The vault of the transept is a
complicated and early example of a lierne-vault, without the
benefit of any boss to cover up the sometimes inexact meetings.

On the E side is the CHAPEL OF ST ANDREW, Norman with
an irregularly rounded or three-sided apse. The WALL
PAINTINGS, representing incidents in the life of the saint,
and other decoration, are by *Thomas Gambier-Parry*, 1866–8.
Encaustic TILES on the floor. Perp stone REREDOS with figures
restored in the C19. On the l. of the entrance to the chapel is a
carved stone BRACKET with dowel holes for the figures which
stood on top of it.*

We must now turn to the NORTH TRANSEPT. This, like the
one on the s, was given a Perp veneer, but at a later date – between 1368 and 1373. The lierne-vaulting is also later and
more accomplished. The longitudinal ridge-rib has a parallel
rib either side, as in the choir, and the intersections of the ribs
are covered by bosses. The E.E. veranda SCREEN on the N
side is not *in situ*, and is probably part of the narthex of the
E.E. Lady Chapel, which was finished in 1227, i.e. dates from
c.1230–40. It is profusely enriched with Purbeck marble
shafts, the only place in the cathedral where this was done.
The elevation is tripartite with window-like openings l. and r.
The shaft capitals are of the most dramatic stiff-leaf types.
The centre bay has the doorway with a trefoiled head set under
a pointed gable, blank trefoils, and an eight-cornered star
whose diagonal corners are pointed-trefoiled and stiff-leaf
covering the spandrels. Inside are three little rib-vaults with
fillets on the ribs.

The Norman CROSSING survives, though the w and E piers
have been altered. To the N and s the piers have twin responds.
The masons of the C14 and C15 did a marvellous conversion of
the upper parts. It is as well to remember that what a building
looked like was always as important to the medieval mason as

53

* It is L-shaped, i.e. of the shape of the medieval equivalent of the architect's T-square, and so the bracket and the image for which it was put up may
be a gift of the master mason. The little figures below look convincing for that
role, and there is a little lierne-vaulting on the underside of the bracket. The
master of the transept was evidently a man of original ideas, and Bristol, as
Mr Verey suggests, is his most probable home, though the s window proves
of course that he absorbed the Court style of London while at work at Gloucester. Other typical Bristol touches are the small s doorway with side pieces
coming forward in a curve like the arms of a throne, and the frilly top of the
twin entrances to crypt and ambulatory. Above them are figures set in trefoils
which are carved detached from the wall (NP).

was structure and function. In order to vault the crossing in his lierne manner, the master mason needed in theory points of support in the middle of the crossing arches; but this cannot have been so in fact, for he threw across the wide space four-centred arches so flat and so thin that they are hardly capable of carrying any weight. On the not very pronounced apexes of each of them he placed a vertical mullion accompanied on both sides by counter-curves. The result is an ogee arch in mid-air from which rise the seven ribs of the vault. This is a very original stylistic conceit which by contrast emphasizes the spatial unity with the choir and isolates the transepts. The twin Norman respond mouldings at the crossing were joined together, and from them rise the mouldings of the mid-c15 tower arches.

An examination of the EAST END must begin below ground in the CRYPT; for the crypt was naturally the part with which building began, i.e. it dates from 1089 and the following years.* The crypt represents the Norman plan above, with ambulatory and three radiating chapels. England has six such crypts: St Augustine Canterbury, Winchester, Worcester, Canterbury Cathedral, and Gloucester. At Worcester the centre part is four-naved, at Winchester two-naved, at Canterbury, in both buildings, and at Gloucester three-naved. The Gloucester centre has columns with typical late c11 volute capitals and groin-vaults. The wall shafts have equally typical late c11 two-scalloped capitals. In the ambulatory and the chapels are elements of the same date, but very shortly after completion of the ambulatory the masons must have realized that for their superstructure, with the sturdy round piers of which more will be said presently, the ambulatory needed strengthening. So rounded responds were set below the upper piers and strong, elementary ribs were inserted, either of plain rectangular section or of one broad half-roll with two smaller quarter-hollows. There is no decoration, except somewhat later pieces of blank arcading in the SE and E chapels and some chevron at r. angles to the wall in the NE chapel. In the ambulatory is a piece of c14 SCULPTURE, a small stone Crucifix.

What the Norman CHOIR AND PRESBYTERY looked like, one can see better in the ambulatory than in the centre. The elevational system was completely different from that later adopted in the nave. It is the normal Norman system of arcade and gallery, both here with strong round piers. The piers have

* This and the next paragraph are by NP.

the same convex minimal capital bands as later in the nave.
The transverse arches are of plain rectangular section. The
wall shafts have single-scallop capitals, and the vaults are
groined. All this is still as in the crypt. The entries from the
transept to the ambulatory have twin shafts. On the gallery the
extremely interesting feature is the half-tunnel vaults, a feature
rare in England but frequent in France ever since Tournus of
about the year 1000. The radiating chapels have tunnel-vaults,
but the Norman E chapel is of course replaced by the present
Lady Chapel.

In the centre of choir and presbytery the Norman work is
33 entirely masked by the Perp panelling begun after 1337. The
Norman piers have been partly sliced off to make room for the
Perp shafts, which are anchored at the ground and gallery
stage. From the floor by the choir stalls to the apex of the vault
is about 92 ft. The vault with its longitudinal ridge-rib is
accompanied by two parallel ribs l. and r. – a motif invented
here and then, as we have seen, taken over in the N transept
and the W bays of the nave. The vault shows such a multiplication of liernes and tiercerons that it is to be considered more
textural than structural. Basically it is a tunnel-vault.* As the
points of crossing increase, so do the bosses. They intensify the
impression of texture, appearing to be heads of nails fixing a
net to the vault. The vault was painted by *Clayton & Bell*
c.1895. Note at the E end, centrally over the high altar, the
figure of Christ in Glory, and on the surrounding bosses
angels playing musical instruments, and carrying Passion emblems, an idea taken from the slightly earlier series at Tewkesbury, and much finer. The vertical lines of the shafts on the
walls are nowhere cut by the horizontals, nor are the main
mullions of the E window, so that the impression of soaring
height is intensified. The E window is canted against wind
pressures and the grid frame gives strength; all the same the E
bay of the vault looks as if it is held up by a glass wall. The
panelling runs blank over Norman wall surfaces, and open
where there were Norman openings. Some of the Dec spirit of
Bristol still survives at the foot of the wings, where a mullion
tiptoes on the apex of an arch. The Gloucester feature of close

* To find one's way through this seeming maze one ought to mark the
transverse arches between the bays first, then the normal cross-ribs, and the
ingenious device of cross-ribs across two bays together. The rest, apart from
the ridge-ribs, is infilling, simpler on paper than in reality; for often what is
straight if projected on paper appears broken owing to the varying curvatures,
e.g. of the penetrations from the windows into the main tunnel-vault (NP).

cusping is noticeable in the ogee arches of the stone panelling. It is also to be seen in the wooden tracery above the pinnacles of the C14 stalls. The sanctuary retains much of Abbot Seabroke's tiled PAVEMENT laid down in 1455 before the high altar. The HIGH ALTAR itself, and the recently painted REREDOS, were designed by *Sir George Gilbert Scott* in 1873, with realistic groups of figures carved by *Redfern*. The three upper turrets have statues of angels under the canopies. Everywhere *Scott* has seen to it that the cusping is of the Gloucester variety, echoing King Edward II's tomb. The restored or recarved quadruple SEDILIA are in detail much more commonplace, though the embattled parapet has three delightful angels sitting casually upon it and playing musical instruments, and these are original C15 sculpture.

Returning to the S ambulatory, we have not yet seen ST STEPHEN'S CHAPEL. It has a stone Perp SCREEN, windows, and panelled REREDOS.

The LADY CHAPEL is entered under the bridge which carries a small chapel and the passage running through the apse, which seems to have been three-sided rather than absolutely round. The chapel was finished *c.*1500 with a lierne-vault, and an E window very similar in design to that of the choir sanctuary, though nearly a hundred and fifty years later. N and S are CHANTRY CHAPELS with fan-vaults ingeniously adapted to an oblong plan. They support singing galleries which are held up by flying ogee arches across the open-panelled stone screens. In the S chapel a REREDOS with embroidery designed by *W. H. R. Blacking*. The sanctuary floor, separated by Dean Laud's COMMUNION RAILS (square, tapering balusters), has medieval TILES.* The REREDOS is late C15, but much muti- 41 lated. It is unusual in preserving contemporary graffiti or scribbled memoranda of the names of the saints whose statues once adorned it. The restored triple SEDILIA are contemporary.

Returning to the N ambulatory, the CHAPEL OF ST EDMUND AND ST EDWARD on the NE is dedicated as a War Memorial. It was formerly known as Boteler's Chapel, after Abbot Boteler (1437–50). It is also separated from the ambulatory by a Perp SCREEN. The C15 Perp REREDOS is mutilated; it was coloured. Stone ALTAR, restored. The floor is covered with medieval TILES.

By the Perp SCREEN between the N transept and N ambu-

* Both the rails and the altar were moved here by *Scott* from the high altar.

latory is a stone READING DESK. This was the entrance for the pilgrims who visited the shrine of Edward II, and also the entrance for the monks coming from the cloister into the choir, and the reading desk could well have been useful on either occasion for superintendence. The screen openings are similar to those on the S side in the same position. On the E side of the N transept is the CHAPEL OF ST PAUL, furnished in 1928. The REREDOS is C19. The date of the chapel is the same as that of the ambulatory – see the twin responds with single-scallop capitals and the groin-vault. So, to sum up, it looks as if the work of 1089–c.1100 went as far as the lower parts of the transepts. In their upper parts chevron has arrived, and so it has in the nave. However, nothing of the major work of the cathedral need be later than the dedication of 1121.

FURNISHINGS

The early C18 CHOIR STALLS and BISHOP'S THRONE in the NAVE were turned out of the choir in the C19 by *Sir George Gilbert Scott*. – PULPIT. C17, with stairs and sounding board designed by *Stephen Dykes Bower* c.1946. – Nave ALTAR also by *Dykes Bower*. – LECTERN. First half of the C17; wood. – FONT in the SW corner. 1878 by *Scott*. Polished granite, carved in the Romanesque style. – *Thomas Harris*'s ORGAN (rebuilt in 1920) has a fine case of 1665. The pipes were painted by *Campion*, a local man, in heraldic designs; on the nave side, initials of Charles II. – On the S of the organ chamber, above the chapel, is some Elizabethan wood PANELLING, similar to that in the Laud Room of the Old Deanery.

The CHOIR STALLS, of c.1370, are very perfect, with their three-dimensional ogee-arched canopies and a wonderful series of fifty-eight MISERICORDS, of which fourteen were made when this choir was restored by *Scott* in 1873. Some of the subjects are copied from those at Worcester. The carvings mostly consist of folk-tales, domestic scenes, and fabulous monsters rather than religious subjects. It is supposed that the carving was left to the carpenter's invention, and no one saw them thereafter except the monks. Generally the interest is more historical than aesthetic, giving an insight into the folk mind; medieval humour was coarse rather than keen. The sub-stalls, C19 by *Scott*, are very fine, with splendidly carved ends and finials. The choir stalls occupy the whole space of the crossing. Part of a C13 stall can be seen behind that of the vice-dean, on the N of the opening under the organ. The floor is covered in C19 encaustic TILES and MARBLES.

LADY CHAPEL. FONT. Lead. Late C12. One of nine lead fonts in the county, a large proportion, seeing there are supposed to be only thirty in the whole of England and Wales. This one, made from the same mould as five others, comes from Lancaut, situated on the banks of the Wye and now a ruin. An arcade in low relief surrounds the bowl, containing alternately figures and scrolls.

The sumptuous Art Nouveau CLOCK CASE in the NORTH TRANSEPT is by *Henry Wilson*, 1903.

MEDIEVAL GLASS

CHOIR EAST WINDOW. The great E window was probably finished by 1350. It was taken down and re-leaded by *Ward & Hughes* c.1862, under the superintendence of *Charles Winston*, and the stonework was repaired in 1914. No modern glass was added in 1862. With few exceptions the C14 glazier used white, blue, yellow, and red glass. The white glass is full of bubbles, giving that silvery light which is so apparent in this window. The blue was pure pot-metal, so that it is blue throughout. The ruby glass would have been nearly opaque if it had been red all through; so a different process was invented to produce flashed ruby glass. A yellow stain was also used which was lighter than the pot-metal and varied in many shades. For line-shading a brown enamel, made from iron, was used, or copper, if a greenish-black was required. It is not so much the development of technique, however, which is remarkable in this window, as the development of design. The great Perp window determined the design of the glass. It is the first as well as the grandest example of the window filled with tiers of full-length figures which became characteristic of the following century. The drawing of the cartoons seems closely connected with contemporary French manuscripts; the face's lack of a bottom eyelid is characteristic. The canopies, flat-fronted, are often surmounted with lofty spires; the side piers from which the arch springs run up either side into pinnacles. The background behind the figures is quite flat and richly coloured, with no attempt to produce by shading the effect of its being a hollow niche.

In this window the largest possible area for glass has been obtained by deflecting outwards the side walls of the easternmost bays of the choir and by making the window a 'bow', so that it almost suggests a triptych. The subject of the window is the Coronation of the Virgin, who is attended by the apostles and saints as well as by the founders and representatives of the abbey. The subject and its treatment are somewhat the same as Orcagna's contemporary triptych in the National Gallery. Above the central group of Christ and Mary (the best and least damaged figure left) enthroned are three pairs of angels holding palms. The second from the l. has been lost and replaced by a c15 Madonna from some other window. The figures on the same level as the central group represent the Twelve Apostles. The four outermost apostles on the s side have disappeared, with the exception of the feet of the last two, and have been replaced by four kings. The lower half of one of the apostles seems to have been used to replace the lower part of Christ; another may be found in the patched-up figure in the last light but one of the tier below. His large purple hat suggests St James the Greater, who was beginning to be represented as a pilgrim in the c14, with a small picture of the face of Christ set in front of the hat. The much damaged figure, two to the l. of this, may also be an apostle. The others in this row are canonized saints, in pairs, turning towards each other; in the l. half, including the central pair, four virgin martyrs alternate with four male martyrs: St Cecilia and St George, a virgin whose emblem is lost and St Edmund, St Margaret of Antioch and St Lawrence, St Catherine without her wheel and St John the Baptist. On the r. there is too much confusion for certain identification. The lower tier has figures without haloes, which shows they are historical personages. The place of honour in the centre is occupied by two kings, but the one on the r. has been replaced by St Edmund, who is an intruder, as the scale of the figure shows; so is the one to the r. of him. The other king (l. centre) may well be Edward II holding sceptre and orb, just like his recumbent effigy close by. His reputation as a quasi-saint was at its highest about this time. The inserted figures of the kings, on a larger scale but contemporary in style, may well have come from the clerestory windows. The quarries, a very large number of which survive, are ornamented with a star design or decorative insertions. The three principal tracery heads had gold flaming stars, though the central one has been replaced by a c15 figure of St Clement as pope. The four corresponding openings of the two wings are relieved by ornamental roundels. The quarry lights under the lowest tier of figures are varied by a series of roundels and heraldic shields which provide the chief evidence for dating the window shortly before 1350. The four shields on the l. and the four on the r. occupy their original positions, and their shape is the heater-shield of the C14. From the l. the arms are as follows: (1) Arundel, a beautiful example of streaky ruby and of a lion drawn with a lead outline. Arundel fought at the Battle of Crécy. (2) Berkeley. The greenish chevron is much later glass. (3) Warwick. Exquisite diapering of the ruby field and the yellow fesse. Warwick fought at Crécy. (4) de Bohun, also at Crécy. On the r. (1) Pembroke, an early instance of the deplorable quartering. (2) Talbot, fought at Crécy. (3) Sir Maurice Berkeley. fought at Crécy, killed at Calais in 1347. (4) Thomas Lord Bradeston; note the single rose of the C14. He fought at Crécy and is supposed to have given this window as a memorial to Sir Maurice Berkeley. The shields in the middle are (1) Ruyhale. (2) Edward I, but earlier than the rest. (3) Edward III, showing France quarterly, repaired in 1814. (4) The Black Prince, one of the original series. (5) Henry of Lancaster. (6) Instruments of the Passion; late C15. Below are (1) England; late C14. (2) Edmund Duke of York; late C14. (3) Edward III; late C14. (4) England, Henry of Lancaster, one of the original series.

LADY CHAPEL EAST WINDOW. The glass is now in such a confused and disordered state that one is hardly able to distinguish any definite subjects and carries away an impression of a mass of richly toned fragments, with here and there a face or a form dimly visible. The window generally contains work of the C14 and C15, and was reduced to this state early in the C19, when alien glass was also introduced. The chapel was built between 1450 and 1499, and one would therefore expect the glass to be late C15. As a rule, in cases of wholesale destruction, it is in the tracery openings and the cusped heads of lights that original glass has escaped and remains *in situ*, and that is so here. While the three central lights at the top of the window have been filled for the most part with imported glass, some at least of the contents of the smaller side lights immediately on both sides appear to be *in situ*. Both represent scenes in the open air, the blue sky or landscapes being continued into the cusped heads without any canopy or framework, a pictorial method characteristic of the late C15. The principal figure in the one on the l. is a crowned Madonna, and as there are remains of a similar figure in the small lights at both ends of the top tier, these four lights appear to be original, and illustrate miraculous stories about the Virgin. The nine main lights of the window, divided by two transoms into three tiers, again in the cusped heads, retain much original glass similar in character to that in the tracery lights. It seems likely that unframed scenes alternated with canopied figures, as in the E window of St Margaret, Westminster (before 1519); a compromise between the old and the new style. In the extreme r. hand light of the middle of the three tiers there are the substantial remains of a Madonna in a deep red mantle with jewelled border, standing on the crescent moon in the midst of a glory of gold rays. Her head has disappeared and the Child she carried has been replaced by a mass of alien fragments. At the bottom is an inscribed band of text reading 'S(an)c(t)a Ma(ria) cel(es)t(i) lumine'. This figure must have occupied a central light. In the eighteen round openings set between the lower transom and the heads of the lights in the bottom tier, a comb alternates with a barrel or tun, preceded on the l. by an initial E and followed in the case of the comb by the syllable 'to' and in that of the tun by 'co'. Here is the rebus for Edmund Compton, the donor, who died in 1493. He was the father of Sir William Compton, a ward of Henry VII and friend of Henry VIII, and also Constable of Gloucester Castle in 1512 and of Sudeley in 1513, and Chief Steward of the abbeys of Gloucester and Cirencester. With these Court connexions of the Comptons it is quite possible that this window was the work of *Barnard Flower*, the King's glazier. This would account for the advanced form of some of the fragments, both pictorial and realistic, with their considerable infusion of foreign character, particularly in the physiognomy of the full faces and the deep, rich colours of the draperies.

The three central lights at the top of the window, however, are not later than the middle of the C15 and are obviously an insertion from another window. They are characteristic English work and similar to the original glass left in the windows of the N aisle of the nave. Bits of glass from side windows in the chapel, depicting the Passion, are also included, particularly the fairly well preserved Precious Blood in the central light of the middle tier. Either side of this are soldier saints of the late C15. The Royal Arms of England is late C15 but of a different character. The bottom row of lights is mainly filled with C14 glass, from a Jesse Tree window, probably taken from the N transept. The kings, however, must date from nearer the middle of the C14, and they resemble the figures in the great E window of the choir, though they do not belong to it; but the bearded face of an apostle in light one from the bottom r. probably does.

There are also fragments of medieval glass in the windows of the CHANTRY CHAPELS.

NINETEENTH CENTURY GLASS

SOUTH PORCH. E window by *Heaton, Butler & Bayne* – angels ringing bells. – NAVE. Great w window by *Wailes* of Newcastle, to Bishop Monk † 1856, completed 1859. – SOUTH AISLE. w window by *Clayton & Bell*. – From w to E, first window by *Hardman*, 1864, second by *Bell* of Bristol, 1861, third by *Warrington*, fourth by *Clayton & Bell* (coronation of Henry III and heraldry), fifth by *Bell* of Bristol, c.1837, sixth by *Clayton & Bell* (Edward II), seventh by *Warrington*, c.1857, eighth by *Rogers* of Worcester, c.1853. – NORTH AISLE. w window by *Hardman* (life of King Lucius). – From w to E, first window by *Clayton & Bell*, second by *Ward & Hughes*, third old glass restored by *Hardman*, fourth by *Clayton & Bell*, fifth old glass restored by *Hardman*, sixth by *Clayton & Bell* (Bishop Hooper), seventh by *Clayton & Bell*, eighth by *Preedy* of London, c.1863. – CLERESTORY. Fragments of old glass, the third from the w on the N restored to the original design by *Hardman*. – NORTH TRANSEPT. w window by *Kempe*, 1874. – Great N window, Hicks-Beach memorial, by *Hardman*, 1876 (life of St Paul). – ST PAUL'S CHAPEL. Three windows by *Burlison & Grylls*, 1870. – NORTH AMBULATORY. Three windows by *Kempe*, c. 1892. – LADY CHAPEL. Excellent windows by *Christopher Whall* (1850–1924) in conjunction with his son and daughter *Christopher* and *Veronica Whall*. – GOLDSBOROUGH CHAPEL. Window by *Kempe*, 1895. – SOUTH AMBULATORY. Three windows by *Kempe*. – CHOIR. N clerestory, five windows by *Clayton & Bell*; s clerestory, windows in grisaille by *Hardman*. – SOUTH TRANSEPT. Great s window by *Hardman*.

PLATE

Two Chalices and two Patens, a Credence Paten and two Flagons, 1660. – Almsdish, 1661. – Two Altar Candlesticks, 1661. – Credence Paten, 1705 by *Humphry Payne*. – Bishop's Mace, 1737. – Two Maces, 1833. –Modern silver Cross and Candlesticks, designed by *S. Dykes Bower*. – On the N wall of the ambulatory a case containing the Art Nouveau Processional

Cross made by *Omar Ramsden* in 1922, and another with the staff carved with St George and the Dragon by *Leslie Durbin*, 1959. – Flagon, 1891, designed by *J. D. Sedding*. – Chalice, c.1900, designed by *Henry Wilson*.

MONUMENTS

PRESBYTERY (s side). C13 stone effigy thought to represent Abbot Serlo, the first Norman abbot and founder of the abbey church, supported on a cradle. The arch of the canopy over the head terminates in two diminutive heads. Below is a foliated boss representing maple leaves, naturalistic, not conventional. The monument cannot be earlier than *c.*1280. The effigy was moved from the N side when the original position was given over to Osric. – In the centre of the presbytery, resting on a
27 C14/15 wooden tomb, is the monument of Robert Courthose, Duke of Normandy, † 1134, eldest son of William the Conqueror. It is one of the very few existing wooden effigies made at Bristol in the C13, but it was broken during the Civil War and restored after the Restoration.

SOUTH AMBULATORY. The Rev. John Kempthorne † 1838. Gothic tomb-chest with angels and rich canopy. No effigy. The style is *c.*1300. – Bishop Ellicott † 1905. Alabaster tombchest and effigy, by *W. S. Frith*.

LADY CHAPEL. Tomb-chest and effigy of Bishop Goldsborough † 1604. He wears a white rochet and black chimere, with lawn sleeves, scarf, ruff, and black skull cap. – Elizabeth,
64 wife of W. J. Williams and daughter of Bishop Miles Smith, † 1622. The effigy lies on its side, with an infant on the pillow. – Margery Clent † 1623, another daughter of Bishop Miles Smith. Tablet with frontally kneeling figure. Both by *Samuel Baldwin*, of Stroud. – John Powell † 1713, signed by *Thomas Green* of Camberwell. Standing effigy of a judge, in marble, a noble figure by one of the outstanding statuaries of the first quarter of the C18. – Dorothea Beale. Inscription by *Eric Gill*, c.1907, on a bronze tablet by *Drury*.

NORTH AMBULATORY. Monument to Osric, which however only dates from *c.*1530. Osric was honoured by Abbot Parker as the founder of the monastery, and his sister Kyneburg was the first abbess, at the end of the C7. The effigy is rudely carved, perhaps in imitation of an earlier figure, and lies on a tomb-chest, above which is a Tudor canopy with a panelled soffit. In the spandrels on the N side the arms of Abbot Parker and the attributed arms of Northumbria.

The effigy of Edward II is of alabaster, London work of [28] c.1330. The canopy is fine-grained oolitic limestone from the Cotswolds, probably Painswick; plaster is used only for the joints. Restoration of the canopy was undertaken three times in the c18 by Oriel College, Oxford. The tomb-chest on which the effigy rests is made of Purbeck marble, with ogee-arched recesses, cinquefoiled with crocketed heads. The canopy consists of two stages of ogee-headed arches with close cusping at the sides of the arches and ogee foils – the work of a genius – surmounted by finials with buttresses placed diagonally and terminating in pinnacles. It may well be called the most thrilling of all tomb canopies. Large ogee-headed niches have been cut away from the Norman piers at either end of the shrine. The capitals were painted brown with a motif of white harts after the visit of Richard II in 1378.

The next monument is that of the last abbot, William Parker, the effigy carved of alabaster c.1535. It was prepared for him, but after the Dissolution he was not buried here; instead a Marian and an Elizabethan bishop lie below. Parker's effigy is vested in full pontificals, including his mitre (the abbots had been mitred since c.1381). It lies on a high tomb with three panels on each side, the first and third bearing emblems of the Passion and the middle one the arms of Parker. In the frieze above are the Tudor rose, the pomegranate, a lion's head, oak leaves, fleur de lys, and the initials W.M. for William Malvern (alias Parker). At the head, the Norman pier has been mutilated, and the abbot's arms are placed here surmounted by a mitre. The floor is paved with medieval tiles. The monument has close Perp screens to l. and r.

NORTH TRANSEPT. On the w side is the large painted stone monument to John Bower † 1615 and Ann his wife. The figures are painted. They kneel, the males facing the females.

SOUTH TRANSEPT. Tomb-chest with recumbent effigies of Alderman Abraham Blackleech † 1639 and his wife Gertrude, according to Mrs Esdaile by either *Epiphanius Evesham* or *Edward Marshall*, with faces like those by Evesham and hands like Marshall's. The recumbent effigies are carved in alabaster with very perfect attention to the details of the clothing. His feet rest on an eagle and hers on a mailed fist holding a dagger. They lie on a black marble tomb-chest and are good examples of the Nicholas Stone period, whoever they are by. – Next is the monument to Richard Pates, the founder of the Pates Grammar School in Cheltenham and builder of Matson

House, † 1588. The effigies have disappeared, but the painted stone Elizabethan canopy remains.

Other monuments in the S transept are as follows. Marble bust of T. B. Lloyd-Baker † 1886 by *W. S. Frith*, the bust in relief in a medallion above a relief of Justice. – Small brass and marble tablet to Canon Evan Evans † 1891, by *Henry Wilson*. – Tablet to Benjamin Baylis † 1777, by *Bryan* of Gloucester. – Mary, wife of Thynne Gwynne, † 1808, by *Reeves* of Bath. – Canon Trotter † 1913 and Canon Scobell † 1917, nice, rich tablets of the period.

CHAPEL OF THE SALUTATION OF MARY. Abbot Seabroke † 1457. Tomb-chest and alabaster effigy of a mitred abbot. – Francis Baber † 1669. Large tablet with twisted columns and emblems of death. Open segmental pediment.

In the SOUTH AISLE, near the S transept, the recumbent effigies of a Knight and Lady, in a C14 canopied tomb which has an ogee arch with foliated crockets and finial. It is panelled at the sides and back and has a vaulted roof without bosses, like the roof of the S transept. On either side is a canopied niche. The ogee arches are three-dimensional with pinnacles. The cornice has a splendid single rose and double roses and leaves. The Knight is said to be Sir John Brydges of Coberley and he wears the SS collar, a Lancastrian badge instituted by Henry IV; therefore the effigy must be early C15. The lady also has a SS collar. In the S aisle the following tablets. Mary Clarke † 1792, by *W. Stephens* of Worcester, and Richard Clarke † 1796, by the same. – Prebendary William Adams † 1789, by *T. King* of Bath. – Jane Webb † 1811, by *Wood* of Gloucester. – John Webb of Norton Court † 1795, by *Bryan* of Gloucester in classical taste. – Mary Singleton † 1761, by *J. and J. Bryan*. Coloured marbles, Baroque style. – Sir George Onesiphorus Paul † 1820. Free-standing bust by *Sievier* on a large marble sarcophagus. – Sir John Guise of Highnam † 1794, by *Millard* of Gloucester. A draped broken column. – Dame Mary Strachan † 1770, by *Ricketts* of Gloucester, who has produced a monument well above the usual provincial level; this one and the one to the Bishop of St David's near by are outstanding even for their date. A cherub holds Lady Strachan's portrait in a medallion, very elegant decoration, and underneath are the Baronet's arms with delightful little contemporary male supporters. – Richard Raikes † 1823. Gothic. – Eli Dupree † 1707. Bust on top in a broken pediment. – Bishop William Nicholson † 1671. – Anthony Ellys, Bishop of St David's,

† 1761, by *Ricketts*; excellent detail. – Jane Fendall † 1799, by *King* of Bath. – Alderman John Jones, *c*.1630. Painted, half-length upright effigy, by the Southwark workshops; a monument full of delightful details such as the packets of deeds as though in pigeonholes and dated 1581–1630, for he was registrar to eight bishops. – Hubert Parry, musician, † 1918. – Statue of Dr Jenner, who first used vaccination, by *R. W. Sievier*, London, 1825.

NORTH AISLE. W wall: Bishop Martin Benson † 1752. – Bishop Warburton † 1779, by *King* of Bath. – N wall: large monument to Charles Brandon Trye † 1811, with bust in a medallion held by two life-size angels. – Three pretty medallions to the bell-makers Abraham Rudhall † 1798, Charles Rudhall † 1815, and Sarah Rudhall † 1805. – Tablet to the Rudge family by *Millard*. – Col. Edward Webb † 1839, by *H. Hopper* of London. Conventional mourning female; Gothic. – Samuel Hayward of Wallsworth Hall † 1790, by *Bryan* of Gloucester. – Ralph Bigland, Garter Principal King of Arms, † 1784. – Hester Gardner † 1822, by *James Cooke*. The last three are good classical monuments in a group together. – Sarah Morley † 1784 at sea in passage from India. By *Flaxman*. 77 Three angels receive her and her baby from the rolling waves. Classical in style, Gothic in feeling. – Various tablets by *Millard & Cooke* of Gloucester. – Alderman Thomas Machen and his wife Christian. Painted monument of *c*.1615 (perhaps by *Samuel Baldwin* of Stroud). He was Mayor of Gloucester and kneels opposite his wife. Above them is a horizontal canopy supported by Corinthian columns. The monuments in the cathedral have been re-painted at different times, for instance for the Three Choirs Festival in 1797, but Machen the Mayor has his original red gown. – Canon E. D. Tinling † 1897. Bronze figure kneeling and marble details; a fine ex- 100 ample of the period by *Henry Wilson*.

In the NORTH CHOIR GALLERY, a splendid monument by *John Ricketts the Elder* of Gloucester with a bust of William Little † 1723 and a panelled plinth with gadrooned edge.

PRECINCTS

THE CLOISTERS

The E walk of the cloisters has the earliest fan-vaulting known; 34 the date is some time after 1351 and before 1377.* It was used as a passage communicating with other parts of the monastery.

* The demolished chapter house at Hereford had a fan-vault in 1364.

The side to the garth is divided into ten bays, nine containing a large Perp window of eight lights crossed by a broad transom projecting externally like a shelf as protection from the weather. The side to the wall has corresponding blank panelling. The other walks were vaulted between 1381 and 1412 and are almost but not quite identical. There are minor changes between the E and the other sides in the tracery as well as the fans, but the whole is yet of unmatched harmony and conveys a sense of enclosure such as no other Gothic cloister. The N walk contains the fan-vaulted LAVATORIUM at its W end, lit by eight two-light windows towards the garth and by a similar window at each end. Half the width is taken up by a stone ledge and trough, which originally carried a lead tank from which the water came out of spigots where the monks could wash. There was an excellent drainage system, which survives in the garth. Opposite on the N wall of the cloister is a groined recess or almery where the towels were hung. Against the N wall a stone bench on which traces of scratchings survive indicating that the novices here played a game called 'Nine Men's Morris' or 'Fox and Geese'. The W walk closely resembles the E, and like it was a mere passage, but it has a stone bench along the wall. At its S end is the Processional Door into the nave. The S walk was probably shut off by screens. It has ten windows towards the garth, but below the transom the lights are replaced by twenty little recesses or carrels. Each carrel, used for study, is lighted by a small two-light window and is surmounted within by a rich embattled cornice.

STAINED GLASS. E walk, S to N: first window by *Hardman*, and the following six windows all by *Hardman*, eighth window by *Ballantine*, ninth by *Hardman*, tenth by *Clayton & Bell*. – The ten small two-light windows in the LAVATORIUM by *Hardman*. – A few other windows by *Hardman* in the other walks. – The best glass is in the S walk, but this is not C19: it is mostly C16 glass from Prinknash Abbey, six panels having been taken to Prinknash by Abbot Parker, the last Abbot of Gloucester, and the rest by Lady Chandos of Sudeley. Woodforde writes: 'A much higher standard was maintained in the C16 in drawing of heraldry than figures. Representations of Royal Arms and badges are particularly good.' Here are excellent examples, including the badge of Katherine of Aragon (pomegranate). Before *Scott* caused the re-glazing of the cloisters, J. T. Niblett recorded seven examples of the Plantagenets' 'planta genista' in the lavatorium windows.

MONASTIC BUILDINGS ROUND THE CLOISTER

Beginning on the E, next to the cathedral is a wide vaulted passage leading to the monks' cemetery, which is chiefly of Early Norman date and was originally the same length as the width of the N transept against which it is built. It was entered from the cloister by a wide arch, later partly covered with Perp panelling. Norman wall arcade on each side, with fifteen arches on the N, but only eleven on the S, the space between the flat transept buttresses admitting no more than that number. The roof is a plain tunnel-vault without transverse arches. The capitals are of two scallops. In the C14, when the vestry and library over the passage were enlarged, the passage had to be extended to double its length. The original library stair was approached from this passage, but after the C14 a new stair from the cloister was made, intruding into the SW corner of the chapter house. The VESTRY communicates with the cathedral only through the chapel E of the N transept.

The LIBRARY* is C14, retaining much of its original open roof, which springs from beautiful wooden corbels. Eleven windows on the N, each of two square-headed lights which lit the bays, or studies. The large end-windows are Late Perp. None of the old fittings now survive. For several hundred years the boys from King's School (founded by Henry VIII) did all their academic work here.

The building N of the passage is the CHAPTER HOUSE. An earlier edition existed c.1080. It is said that William the Conqueror held 'deep speech' with his Witan here at Christmas in 1085, and the Domesday survey was finished in 1086. There was originally an apse, but this was replaced with a straight but canted end c.1380.‡ The roof is a tunnel-vault in three bays, carried by pointed transverse arches and so a second edition. The E bay lierne-vaulted. The side walls have blank Late Norman arcades, the W end a central door flanked originally by windows and surmounted by three more. The lower part of this wall is part of Abbot Serlo's original chapter house, reddened by the flames which destroyed the wooden cloister in 1102. Inside the chapter house is preserved a piece of early C10 SCULPTURE, of Christ Almighty or Pantocrator,

* The library contains the Chapter Act Book of which the first Act is the decree of Dean Laud for the moving of the communion table to the upper end of the choir.

‡ St John Hope says C14 (*Archaeological Journal*, LIV, 1897).

from an age when links with Carolingian art were to the fore.
It is a round medallion with a rim with the classical motif of the
running dog.

The next opening from the cloister led to the DORTER,
which no longer exists except for a fragment which can still be
seen on the outside of the NE corner of the chapter house. It is
a jamb of one of the windows built at the beginning of the C14,
with small ballflower decoration round the capital of a slender
shaft. It was there before the Norman apse of the chapter
house was removed; for the later E end, which is square externally, has the corner cut off so as not to block the window. A
Dec string-course also runs along the chapter-house wall. The
building more or less in its place, built in 1850 as an extra
schoolroom for the King's School, is now used as a gymnasium.

In the N walk of the cloister there are two E.E. doorways,
one at each end. The E one opens into a C13 vaulted passage
which led to the infirmary and at a later date the abbot's lodging.
The passage is rib-vaulted in four bays with elegantly profiled
arches and ribs. The W door now filled with a C19 window was
the entrance to the REFECTORY or FRATER. It has two orders
of colonnettes and a richly moulded arch. This building, which
was begun in 1246 on the site of the Norman one, has also
disappeared, except the S wall, which is common to the cloister,
and parts of the E end. Under the frater was the Norman
cellar; one of its responds with a fragment of the springing of
the vault survives in the SE corner of the LITTLE CLOISTER,
which is built against the E end of the frater. The garth wall is
Perp, with five traceried openings on each side. The S side is
covered by a lean-to roof, and the W walk forms part of a C15
timber-framed house which is built over to the W of it. The N
and E walks are now open, but were until quite late in the C19
joined to a complex of chambers and houses which had evolved
from the dividing up of the infirmary and lesser monastic
buildings, and which was known as Babylon. The INFIRMARY
hall stood E to W, built like the nave of a church. There was a
Chapter Order to pull it down in 1630; but in 1649 it was still
standing, and its W end and six arches of the early C13 S
arcade escaped because they had been incorporated into the
Babylon clutter of houses and were spared in 1860. The arcade
piers have fillets, the capitals are moulded or decorated with
stiff-leaf, and the arches have quite complex mouldings. It all
points firmly to the C13. LITTLE CLOISTER HOUSE, on the W

side of the Little Cloister, has C13 remains. An E.E. under-croft, probably used for storage, extends N and S beneath the western part of the house, and there is a good external C13 pointed-arched doorway with moulded hood facing N. Above this is the monks' MISERICORD, where they were allowed to eat meat. This building is now used by the King's School. Both it and the house next door, NO. 3 MILLERS GREEN, have back gardens on the site of the refectory. The latter house has later interest as well: the first-floor room has an early C17 plaster ceiling decorated with a swan, a crane, and what is now the device of the Cambridge University Press inscribed 'Alma Mater Cantabrigia'; so it is clear where the sacrist of those days received his education. This room also has a Jacobean over-mantel and panelling. The pretty staircase with twisted balusters is early C18, and the ground-floor rooms have typical Queen Anne panelling. The KITCHEN stood on the NW corner of the refectory, where No. 6 Millers Green now stands.

Immediately to the N was the ABBOT'S LODGING, built in the early C14. It subsequently became the BISHOP'S PALACE, was rebuilt in 1862 by *Ewan Christian*, and is now (since 1955) the KING'S SCHOOL. The private chapel incorporated in the palace was also rebuilt by *Christian* and is now a library. In the C18 it was shown to visitors by Bishop Benson, and Walpole particularly admired a stained glass window by *Price*. This however has not survived, though a quantity of C17 and C18 heraldic glass was put back into the Dec-style windows of the house. Part of the wall of the original palace with Tudor win-dows can be seen in Pitt Street. The stables have the date 1861 on the rainwater heads.

Before the abbot moved his quarters here *c.*1316 he lived in premises now represented by the OLD DEANERY, and which during monastic times became the Prior's Lodging. It is connected with the W walk of the cloister by two doorways, but now has its main front, largely Victorian Gothic, to the W, i.e. College Green. One doorway, about the middle of the walk, opens into the court of the prior's lodging, the other, at the S end, opens into a vaulted passage or slype of Norman date under part of the lodging. The passage is tunnel-vaulted, and the wall shafts have scalloped capitals. The E bay looks later in its details than the rest. The passage served as an OUTER PARLOUR where the monks could talk to visitors and strangers. It is on a lower level than the cloister, which is reached from it by a flight of steps. Over it is the ABBOT'S CHAPEL of *c.*1120–

35, which also has a tunnel-vault and Norman wall shafts with multi-scalloped capitals. C15 floor of TILES at the E end. The chapel is now used as the Secretary's Office of CHURCH HOUSE. Both the outer parlour and the chapel have been slightly shortened and their W ends rebuilt with the old masonry in the C15, but the tracery of the window is C19. The enriched flat-arched Perp external doorway into the outer parlour with its Gloucester type of cusping, though restored, is similar to the pairs of doorways in the N and S transepts leading to the ambulatory. The panelled DOOR is dated 1614. The buildings of the Old Deanery consist of two main blocks connected by the stair-case turret. The S block, apart from containing the chapel, has three large square Norman chambers one upon the other of which plenty of visual evidence survives within. The W gable preserves the original treatment of tall, shallow panels with zigzag ornament. The two windows on the top storey have tracery comparable with the Early Perp work in the S transept, but they are set under gables with arches and shafts of c.1200. Each chamber has in the NE corner a doorway for use into a garderobe which existed in 1807, when John Carter made his plan of the cathedral.* The two lower chambers have their SE corners crossed by segmental stone arches. The lower one is moulded, the upper has chevron. They must have carried something specially heavy. The ground floor is entered through a vaulted lobby with shafts of c.1200 with stiff-leaf and trumpet-scallop capitals. The main staircase was altered when the house was restored by *Fulljames* and *Waller* between 1863 and 1870 for Dean Law; but there are signs of C13 work, and a medieval stone lantern on the upper flight. The most beautiful room in the N block is the LAUD ROOM on the first floor, which was once part of a hall. The springing arches near the ceiling of this room reveal the original wooden structure of the roof, which may belong to the *camera hospicii* of Abbot Horton, who ruled in 1351–77. The panelling, which may not be *in situ*, was probably made late in the C16, before Archbishop Laud was Dean (1616–21), in a similar manner to Red Lodge at Bristol and by the same joiner; each panel contains a round-headed arched recess supported on miniature fluted pilasters and with enriched spandrels. The doorcases have fluted Ionic pilasters carrying an entablature, and the doors have the same motifs as the panels, on a larger scale, and

* The ground-floor doorway is larger than the others and has in the arch flat foliage panels and a pellet moulding (NP).

surmounted in the top panel by a fluted fan. The next room, known as the HENRY ROOM because traditionally Henry VIII and Anne Boleyn once used it, in 1535, has an exposed timber roof with a curious type of painted decoration and a stone Tudor fireplace. To the N of this and set at r. angles to it was once a much longer building, extending farther to the W than it does now, and of C13 date. It is thought that this may have been the Abbot's Hall. Some time before the end of the C15 it was cut down and an upper storey of wood built up on it, forming a long gallery of which the E end still remains and is called the PARLIAMENT ROOM, because it is thought that Richard II held his Parliament in the original building in 1378. The room, of exposed late C15 half-timber construction, has been restored recently by *Waller & Ashwell*. It contains a late C15 WALL PAINTING removed from the monks' misericord, in Little Cloister House, and a late C14 chimneypiece once used as a mason's setting-out table. The Old Deanery is now leased to the Diocesan Board of Finance and is partly used as a Church House Club.

COLLEGE GREEN in monastic times was divided into an outer court, which lay at the W end of the abbey church, a lay cemetery to the S, and a monks' cemetery and garden either side of the E end with a communicating tunnel under the Lady Chapel, as the precincts, which were surrounded by a wall, did not go beyond the E end of the Lady Chapel. The GREAT GATE, or St Mary's Gate, survives at the NW corner of the outer court, leading into St Mary's Square. It was about in the middle of the W wall of the precinct, a large part of which also still survives. On the outside it has C13 arcading over a C13 arched entrance with C18 wrought-iron GATES with gilded cherubs brought from Nuremberg, via Painswick church, in the early C20. The gateway, of three bays (two and one) of ribbed Transitional Norman vaulting, decorated with under- 18 cut chevrons, was restored by *Waller*. Next to it was the ALMONER'S LODGING, and there are signs of a window for distributing food. Above it is a C16 half-timbered house, used now for ecclesiastical archives and recently restored by *Waller & Ashwell*. The INNER GATE leading from the outer court into the inner court, now Miller's Green, has a lierne-vault. There were also two gates on the S side. KING EDWARD'S GATE is now represented only by one turret, and part of another with a stone newel stair inside, attached to which are later rooms. The rest of it was taken down when College Street was widened, and the end house of the Georgian terrace on the s side of College Green was demolished at the same time. The other gate, sometimes called ST MICHAEL'S GATE, at College Court, now consists of the remains of a small Late Perp arch surmounted by a modern brick-built bedroom.

The houses in College Green, which form a cathedral close, were mostly rebuilt in the C18, having been adapted from monastic to domestic use at the beginning of the C17.

Besides the buildings already mentioned there are three other notable houses, all of which now belong to the King's School, and are strictly speaking part of the precinct.

DULVERTON HOUSE, E of the infirmary and the demolished buildings of Babylon, is clearly part of the monastic buildings, connected with the infirmary. Buried in the house, which has had subsequent additions, there appears to have been a medieval building at least 50 ft long, running N to S. On its w side is a C13 chamfered stone doorway of the 'Caernarvon' type (a shouldered lintel). A great central beam carrying the upper floor is supported by oak pillars with chamfered edges and stops decorated with small trefoil-headed arches. The brackets each side of the capitals are enriched with carved figures which appear to be C15, and the pillars stand on moulded stone bases. An upper room has oak panelling (scratched date 1644). On the sw side is a projecting C18 ashlar wing, with a sundial and two scratched dates 1726 and 1743. The rest of the house was added to or rebuilt in the C19.

KING'S SCHOOL HOUSE is C16 in origin and post-Reformation. The front was rebuilt in ashlar in the late C18, of three storeys with seven windows and a doorway with reeded architrave, segmental fanlight, and shaped entablature. A first-floor room on this side has C17 panelling and a Jacobean fireplace with two tiers of Corinthian columns, made of stone. The interior structure is partly timber-framing.

WARDLE HOUSE (formerly Cathedral House). Built c.1686 but subsequently altered; it now has a conspicuous Georgian bow window, providing well-proportioned rooms with unsurpassed views of the cathedral. Rendered exterior.

OTHER MONASTIC BUILDINGS

BLACK FRIARS. Only three Dominican friaries, those at Gloucester, Norwich, and Newcastle, have survived in any degree of completeness. The site is just within the s wall which surrounded Roman and medieval Gloucester, accessible from Southgate Street and the river. The Dominican friars were established in Gloucester by 1239, and received large benefactions from Henry III. The church was consecrated in 1284. In 1539 the priory was granted to a clothmaker Thomas Bell, who altered the church into a house, known as Bell's Place, and used the claustral buildings as a cloth manufactory. The N transept of the church had been added in the C14; otherwise the buildings were generally C13, and in spite of their subsequent use considerable remains can still be seen.

The CLOISTER S of the church was 80 ft square. On the E side was the DORMITORY, above a centrally placed CHAPTER HOUSE. The S range was occupied by the rare example of a STUDY DORMITORY on the upper floor, which still exists with the remains of the cells. The REFECTORY was to the W. In 1721 the claustral buildings were virtually still complete. The most serious disruption now of the basic plan is the projection of a garage across the angle formed by the E and S ranges and into the cloister itself. Bell's Place does not occupy the full length of the CHURCH; the nave extended W of the gable wall of Friar's Lodge, and the choir extended at least 26 ft beyond the E gable of Blackfriars. The roof construction of the E range, of the collar-beam and scissor-braced type, is similar to those over the main body of the church and over the S range. The seventeen trusses are independent, without purlin or ridgepiece. It seems likely that these roofs are the original C13 construction. The C13 masonry is uncoursed rubble of thin slabs of limestone with ashlar dressings to doors and windows, contrasting with the coursed ashlar of the post-Dissolution rebuilding.

GREY FRIARS. Facing St Mary de Crypt churchyard is GREY-FRIARS HOUSE, of c.1800, with a stone façade of three storeys and five windows, central pediment, and portico with Roman Doric columns. This is attached to, and part of, the nave and N aisle of the Franciscan church, or GREY FRIARS, built in the early C16, although the house had been founded c.1230 on this site by Thomas of Berkeley. 'A goodly house, much of it new builded', it was delivered into the King's hands in 1538. The rebuilding had again been due to the benefactions of the Berkeley family. The friars' cemetery was on the N side of the church, the monastic buildings on the S. The nave and N aisle, which remain, are of nearly equal width, so that the building is divided (there being no S aisle) longitudinally into two equal compartments, with a central arcade of seven bays, supported on lozenge-shaped moulded piers with moulded capitals and bases, of which only four and the E respond survive. This arrangement has no parallel among English mendicant orders, though there are some Jacobin churches in France and many friars' churches in Germany which have the same feature. There were four-light traceried windows on the N and S, portions of which survive. The start of the N wall of the choir exists E of, and between, the nave and aisle. Reset on the outside of the S wall of the nave are two stone armorial shields, possibly from a former funerary monument: Chandos and Clifford of Frampton. SUFFOLK HOUSE is built on top of the site of the choir.

LANTHONY PRIORY, ¼ m. SW. Part of an embattled, buttressed gatehouse survives, leading to a now derelict timber-frame and stone Tudor house with a Victorian addition. Also the ruins of a great ashlar buttressed TITHE BARN with arched entrance under a gable. Fosbrooke, writing in 1819, says, 'the barn is the principal part remaining of the Priory. In digging the Berkeley Canal the foundations of the old church were discovered. Over the gateway are the arms of the Bohuns.' Fosbrooke published a plate of the gateway, which is not much more ruined today than it was then. It appears that the gateway is C14, and the remains of the barn may be as old. The connexion of the Bohun family as patrons lasted from 1175 to 1380, when the co-heiress Mary Bohun married the future King Henry IV.

The priory of Lanthony in the Monmouthshire mountains was founded c.1109 by a Norman baron as an Augustinian house. Surrounded by hostile people, the monks were very soon forced to flee, and this led to the building of a second Lanthony at Gloucester in 1136, under the patronage of Milo of Gloucester. To emphasize the fact that the new house was intended to be no more than a daughter-house to the mother-house in Wales, the new priory was also called Lanthony, or Lanthony St Mary to distinguish it from Lanthony St John in Wales. During the following centuries the Gloucester priory received many great endowments and lands in Gloucestershire and elsewhere, and, situated as it was under the shadow of Gloucester Castle, it prospered far more than the remote monastery in Wales. Writing in 1277 Queen Eleanor (of Aquitaine) says: 'At our instance and supplication the religious men of Lanthony granted us the one bridge to their garden, next the castle of Gloucester, through which same bridge, we and our household would be able to pass to the said garden for the sake of looking at it.'

St Oswald's Priory, outside St Mary's Gate. An Augustinian house. Only one wall with an arcade of round Norman arches on piers with scalloped capitals and two later and higher pointed arches survive from what must have been quite considerable ruins before they were used as a quarry for road-making. Owing to a peculiar historical sequence the priory came under the jurisdiction of the See of York. A new priory church built in the first half of the c12 was pulled down at the time of the Reformation, except the N aisle, which was converted into a parish church dedicated to St Catherine. These are the ruins that remain today.

CHURCHES

All Saints, Lower Barton Street. 1875 by *Sir G. G. Scott*. The finest c19 church in Gloucester and a good example of Scott's work. Dec. Nave of five bays with N and S aisles, chancel and S chapel. Vestry added in 1887. The fine lines and good furnishings are well displayed against the now painted walls. – In the five-light Dec E window stained glass by *Clayton & Bell*. – One window in the chancel and three in the S aisle also by *Clayton & Bell*, c.1875. – Broad English altar and excellent stone sedilia in the sanctuary. – The S chapel has a painted screen with serpentine curves between it and the choir, designed by *J. Coates-Carter* and carried out by *A. P. Frith*, the sculptor, c.1920.

Christ Church, Brunswick Square. By *Rickman & Hutchinson*, 1822, to serve people who lived in the newly developed Spa in houses with such names as Waterloo Villa. A preaching box, built in brick and stucco in the classical style still in favour at the time. The windows are filled with contemporary stained glass, decorated with honeysuckle motifs, regular and uniform, which mostly survives, though there are a few exceptions such as the window by *Edward Payne*, 1960. Later generations have done their best to change the atmosphere of the church, but with only partial success. The chancel was enlarged in 1865 and from 1899 to 1910 there were other alterations; the most amazing would-be Romanesque w end was added in red terracotta and brown roughcast. Goodhart-Rendel thought the effect 'exotic and revolting'. The flat ceiling of the broad nave was given a central cove or barrel-vault (perhaps influenced by the C18 St John the Baptist) which runs straight into the apse of the sanctuary. The apse was decorated *c.*1910 with a frieze of Art Nouveau angels and other MURALS. – MONUMENTS. A large number of tablets, signed by *Cooke* of Gloucester with dates between 1828 and 1844, *Lewis* of Cheltenham 1842, *J. Lewis* of Gloucester 1823, *W. Wingate* 1849, *T. Tyley* of Bristol, and *William Bussell* and *G. Sharp* both of Gloucester.

MARINERS CHURCH, The Docks. 1849 by *John Jacques*. E.E., with lancet windows. – STAINED GLASS. E window 1849 by *Clayton & Bell*.

101 ST ALDATE, Finlay Road. 1964 by *Robert Potter & Richard Hare*. The first 'modern' church in Gloucester; extremely confident, and specially designed to meet the needs of the Liturgical Movement. The texture of the concrete is often rough. The external outlines are impressive; a parabolic saddle of a roof contrasts with the pencil point of a triangular detached spire. The church is fan-shaped, so that everyone can feel he is a participator in everything that takes place, and the celebrant can conveniently adopt the westward position. The only concession to tradition seems to be a Laudian FRONTAL giving a welcome note of colour against the white walls of the apse, which rise with the roof to a point intended to be high enough to suggest transcendence and majesty.

ST BARNABAS, Tuffley. 1939–40 by *N. F. Cachemaille-Day*. Of reinforced concrete faced in brick. Good use is made of the new freedom of design due to concrete, but the arrangement is still traditional. Inside, the result is extremely dignified and calm, with tall intersecting arches of noble proportions in the chancel. English-style ALTAR. – STAINED GLASS. E window by *G. Webb*. – FURNISHINGS of original character by *Welch, Cachemaille-Day & Lander*.

ST CATHARINE, Wotton. 1915 by *Walter B. Wood*. There was a medieval church dedicated to St Catharine, and a C19 St Catharine's church (built by *James Medland* in 1868) on a different site; both were demolished. The new St Catharine, though C20, is C19 in character, and architecturally unsatisfactory. It is built in vermiculated stone, with a stone slate roof, a small flèche, and no tower. Broad, somewhat low nave and narrow aisles. Ashlar-faced inside, with rather elaborate detail, tame at its best, ignorant at its worst. Varnished deal roofs, STAINED GLASS of the type called cathedral glass, encaustic TILES on the floor, and two transeptal bays in each aisle with lean-to arches. The two-bay chancel is not divided from the nave, but there is an arch before the short sanctuary. The splendid painted REREDOS is by *Ellery Anderson*, 1937. The S chapel has a Gothic SCREEN of 1948.

ST JAMES, Upton Street. 1837–41 by *Sampson Kempthorne*, 'a good kind fellow' who designed workhouses. W front of ashlar, C13. Nave broad and undivided. N aisle, with a wooden arcade and lean-to roof, and short chancel added in 1879 by *F. S. Waller & Son*. A handsome C13-style REREDOS encloses the decalogue. – The STAINED GLASS in the N window of the N chapel is signed by *William Glasby*, 1934.

ST JOHN THE BAPTIST, Northgate Street. 1732–4. Designed and built by *Edward & Thomas Woodward* of Chipping Campden, with the exception of the C14 W tower and spire, of three stages, with Perp windows, diagonal buttresses, and a slightly truncated spire, topped with a ball-finial. The original top stands in a small churchyard near by. The E end presents a rich classical front to the street, but one which Goodhart-Rendel thought 'very Cotswoldy and making unintelligent use of the Orders'. The central portion has fluted Roman Doric pilasters, and a Doric entablature, enclosing a Venetian window with Ionic pilasters. Side wings with cornices which run straight into the pilasters of the central block, and quoins only on the outsides; large round windows over round-headed doorways. The stonework is very worn. Inside, the plaster ceilings, flat over the aisles and coved in the nave and chancel, are supported by four Roman Doric columns either side which have no entablature (the cove was later copied by the restorers of Christ Church, but in that case without visible support). Round-headed aisle windows. The church is surrounded by a panelled dado of 1734; splendid contemporary carved oak REREDOS and COMMUNION RAILS. – The PULPIT is part of the original three-decker preached in by George Whitefield and John Wesley. – PEWS and STALLS. C19. – The furniture also includes a medieval CHEST, a C17 TABLE, and wrought-iron MACE RESTS of 1734. – The church was restored in 1882, and the choir, which occupies the first bay of the nave, is floored with encaustic TILES. – STAINED GLASS. E window 1880 by *Camm Bros.* of Smethwick. – PLATE. Unusually splendid set of Cromwellian Communion Plate of 1659; eight silver-gilt pieces including 'two large flagons, two cups with covers, one gilt bason for the collection and one gilt plate for the bread'. It was given by Thomas Riche, merchant of the City of London, perhaps as a thankoffering for the dawn of the Restoration. – This parish with St Mary de Crypt also now holds the plate from St Michael, all given by Nicholas Webb, Alderman of the City of Gloucester: a pair of silver-gilt Chalices and Paten Covers, 1690; a Flagon of 1710 made by *Edward York*; and a Credence Paten and Almsdish, 1704 by *John Read* and *Daniel Sleamaker*. – Chalice, Paten Cover, and Flagon, 1730 by *John Eckford Jun.* – Almsdish, 1748 by *Henry Brind*. – MONU-MENTS. On the N wall of the sanctuary a Baroque gilded monument by *Reeve* with above-the-waist effigy of Thomas Price † 1678, Mayor of Gloucester and Master of Horse to Charles I. – Opposite, and also by *Reeve*, the recumbent effigy, much smaller than life, of Dorothy Price † 1693. – On the N wall of the nave two fragments of medieval BRASSES. – Later tablets include one signed by *Gardner* of Cheltenham in 1780. – Mary Nayler † 1790, by *Franklin*.

ST MARGARET, Wotton. Formerly the chapel of the leper hospital of St Margaret and St Sepulchre, which existed before 1163; now used by the United Almshouses. It appears not to be earlier than the C13 to early C14, however. Chancel and nave are divided by an arch of two chamfered orders. Dec E window with good STAINED GLASS probably by *Clayton & Bell*. Nave windows Perp. PISCINAS in chancel and nave. Restored in 1875 by *Waller & Son*.

ST MARK, Kingsholme. 1847 by *Francis Niblett*. Quite a success-ful town church. Stone, with W tower and spire. Five-bay nave with N and S aisles and lancet windows. Chancel 1891 by *R. Drew* of Torquay, Butterfield's nephew. – STAINED GLASS. E window 1895 by *Kempe*. – The W window in the N aisle by *Willement* with the emblem of St Mark in the tracery; the rest in geometrical patterns of 1847 and very decorative. It is a pity that all the other windows Willement did for this church have now disappeared. – Grisaille window by *Rogers* of Worcester. – PLATE. Good Elizabethan Chalice and Paten Cover, *c.*1575; Chalice, Paten, and Flagon, 1847.

ST MARY DE CRYPT, Southgate Street. Originally Norman, on a cruciform plan which has been retained, though the only Nor-man work to survive is some arches in the blocked-up portion of the crypt. The W doorway with its Agnus Dei tympanum is either entirely Victorian or totally recut. The church was restored in 1844 by *Daukes & Hamilton*. Evidence of C13 alterations and additions survives in the lancet windows, a group of three trefoil-headed and one single, in the S chancel chapel, in the semicircular W responds of the nave arcades with their semicircular moulded capitals and waterholding bases (were the responds heightened later?), and in the blocked N doorway. Dec windows were later inserted in the E wall of the S chapel, and in the N and S aisles. The church was largely rebuilt in the Perp period. The tower, the tall nave of three bays with slender cruciform chamfered piers, the slightly longer chancel, also of three bays, the rib-vaulted S porch of two storeys, and the windows in the chancel and N chapel were all built during this time. Once the Perp style was evolved, and this happened very early in Gloucester, it hardly changed at all for a hundred and fifty years, as we have already observed in the cathedral.

The enrichments in the chancel could be splendid examples of C14 Perp work, but the church is generally attributed in its new form to Henry Dene, Prior of Lanthony from 1461 to 1501; the unusual single SEDILE on the N side is said to have been made for him. Besides this there is an EASTER SEPULCHRE on this side, and on the S triple SEDILIA AND PISCINA, all with gorgeous ogee-shaped canopies. Note the small openings perhaps used as confessionals. Above them on both sides is a string-course which continues as a transom through the windows delightfully placed at the extreme ends, either side of the altar. On all these wall surfaces are remains of WALL PAINTINGS, now severely damaged, and said in the past by those who saw them to have been C14, an attribution which does not agree with the Henry Dene theory. On either side of the altar are restored canopied niches. Generally the walls throughout are fine ashlar. Perp stone SCREENS divide the chancel from the chapels, and these have openings with ogee arches which continue upwards to form the pier supporting the arch of the arcade, clearly reminiscent of the cathedral school of Perp architecture. The screens (without this feature) have been copied in the C20 at the W ends of both chapels. In the C16 the chancel roof was raised and a clerestory added so that it is taller than the nave. The roof was given carved wooden bosses and angels playing musical instruments. The very tall Perp E window completes an outstandingly beautiful though much restored chancel; on the exterior there are two niches in the gable and diagonal buttresses with pinnacles. The central tower has a lierne-vault, not unlike those of St Michael and St Nicholas. In the S transept, at one time perhaps a chantry chapel, a Perp PISCINA. At the restoration of 1844–5 the stone mensa was replaced on the high altar; but the REREDOS, with Venetian mosaics, surrounded by carved Caen stone, dates from 1889. In 1908 the tower battlements and pinnacles were taken down as unsafe. They were never replaced, much to the disfigurement of what is otherwise a splendid tower. – FONT. Early C18. – STAINED GLASS. The E window in the S chapel and one on its S wall are by *Rogers* of Worcester *c.*1857. – The chancel E window is said to be a copy of the medieval glass in Drayton Beauchamp church, Buckinghamshire. – W window typical of Rogers – subject and style. – SOUNDING BOARD of the old pulpit. From this pulpit Whitefield preached his first sermon in 1736. – Wrought-iron MACE REST, used by the Mayor and Corporation at the time of George II. – In the S chapel, commemorating Robert Raikes since 1939, oak PANELLING designed by *H. Stratton-Davis*. – PLATE. Chalice and Paten Cover, 1636; Credence Paten, 1684; Flagon, 1699 by *Francis Singleton*; two Chalices and Paten Covers, 1718 by *Anthony Nelme*, and two Salvers the same; Almsdish, 1718 by *Anthony Nelme*. – MONUMENTS. The S chapel contains a recessed monument, thought to be of Richard Manchester † 1460, again a possibly late attribution, with an ogee arch and Perp panels. – Tomb-chest (the effigies removed) of Sir Thomas and Lady Bell † 1567, with shields in lozenges and a moulded top. – Mrs Snell † 1746, by *Peter Scheemakers*. Marble mourning female figure and a portrait medallion on which leans a weeping putto with overturned cornucopia and torch. – C19 profile of Robert Raikes (who founded the Sunday School Movement in Gloucester) in boxwood; also the headmaster's desk Raikes used in the Crypt School. – In the N chapel kneeling effigy of Daniel Lysons † 1681, by *Reeve* of Gloucester. – On a window sill the bust from a former monument to Richard Lane, Mayor, † 1667. – In the N transept very much restored 3 ft brasses of John and Joan Cooke † 1544, founders of the Crypt Grammar School. – In the N aisle brasses of William Henshawe † 1519 and his two wives, 2 ft 1½ in., taken from St Michael in 1959. – Late C15 grave-slab with incised cross and inscription to Isabel wife of a Mayor of Gloucester called Pole.

ST MARY DE LODE. The church now stands in a modern precinct immediately W of the abbey gate leading to the cathedral. A broad nave supported by cast-iron columns was built on to the Norman building in 1826 by *James Cooke* of Gloucester, who was also a monumental mason. The style is typical rather impoverished Early Gothic Revival. The exterior, quite attractive, is rendered in stucco and has an embattled parapet. Inside, the difference in scale between the old and new is very marked, and the Norman arch appears like the entrance into a tunnel. The tower is central. The Norman arch is its W arch, the E belongs to the C13 (*see* below). The Norman arch has square responds with scalloped capitals. The angle shafts which carried the outer orders have been chopped off. The arch has chevron at r. angles to the wall. The E arch has clustered responds, foliated capitals, and a plain roll moulding. E.E. chancel with quadripartite vaulting ribs supported by clustered wall shafts with foliated capitals, largely restored or re-carved, as are the S capitals of the arch responds. The E window has three stepped, trefoil-headed C19 lancet lights. The two-light windows N and S are also C19. There was a restoration *c*.1912. The tower has pilasters at the angles, an open-work parapet, and pinnacles at each corner. On the S side the E arch is supported by a massive buttress. – PULPIT. Restored with old Gothic panels in wood. – Panelled wooden GALLERY at the W end. – STAINED GLASS. Windows in the chancel by *Rogers* of Worcester; the others have Art Nouveau glass. – PLATE. Paten, 1681; Chalice, 1736 by *Francis Spilsbury*; Paten, 1736 by *Joseph Smith*; Chalice, 1756. – MONUMENTS. On the chancel N side the effigy of a priest in eucharistic vestments, under a mutilated arched recess; early C14. It is said to be of William de Chamberlayne who died in 1304. – Among the monumental tablets in the nave are two signed by *James Cooke* himself in 1819.

ST MARY MAGDALENE, Wotton. Formerly the chapel of the leper hospital of St Mary Magdalene, and not now used. C12. The nave was pulled down and the chancel enclosed in 1861. The entrance is now through the mid-C12 chancel arch, and preserved inside is the former Norman S doorway of the nave. On the N side two blocked lancet windows, on the E a good example of intersecting tracery of *c*.1300. – MONUMENTS. On the floor the under life-size recumbent effigy of a Lady, *c*.1290. – Several monumental tablets, one of 1715.

ST MICHAEL, Southgate Street. Perp tower of 1465, left standing at the Cross, with a pedestrian way through it covered by a quite elaborate lierne-vault. The W window has STAINED GLASS of 1878. The rest of the church, which was rebuilt by *Fulljames* and *Waller* in 1851, was demolished in 1956. Small heraldic SHIELDS on the screen of the E archway by *Albert Cook*.

ST NICHOLAS, Westgate Street, has a conspicuous and pretty tower, near the cathedral. It is Perp, of three stages, with ogee-headed multiple windows under elaborate weather mouldings with crockets and pinnacles like those on the tower of North-leach. Diagonal buttresses, changing into smaller rectangular ones, lead into the embattled parapet with its traceried panels. In 1783, when the spire was repaired, *John Bryan* had to remove the top, as it was so much out of alignment; he replaced it with a coronet, pinnacles, and ball-finial. Inside, the tower is carried on three lofty arches. The belfry is lierne-vaulted. However, the church itself is much earlier than its tower. In the TYMPANUM of the Norman S doorway an Agnus Dei with foliage. Six-bay N nave arcade, the westernmost bay with a pointed arch, the next two with round arches on fat cylindrical Norman columns, and the last three with pointed arches supported by Transitional columns. The two capitals nearest the E are stiff-leaf. The S arcade has only four bays because of the porch. The S aisle itself is larger. It is an E.E. addition, with an arcade of pointed arches on cylindrical pillars with stiff-leaf capitals. The windows here are Perp in E.E. surrounds, with jamb shafts with moulded capitals and bases, except for the westernmost, which has C19 E.E. tracery. E window Dec, but also with E.E. surround. Chancel E window Perp, N aisle windows either Dec or C16. N and S of the chancel are quadruple squints from the aisles to the altar; on the S a large PISCINA and CREDENCE. The E.E. string-course remains. Gabled clerestory windows. No chancel arch. The 'Low Church' sanctuary has untouched C19 FURNISHINGS, encaustic TILES, and an unadorned HOLY TABLE. Good oak PANEL-LING on the E wall of the S aisle, and near it the plain octagonal FONT. On the S door a C14 bronze KNOCKER with a grotesque head holding the ring in its mouth, below a human head upside down. The church was restored in 1866 by *Jacques*, and again in 1927, when much work was done to stabilize the tower. – PLATE. Paten Cover, 1573; Chalice and Paten Cover, 1630; Flagon, 1632*; Chalice, 1638; Flagon, c.1668; Chalice by *Nathaniel Lock*, two Salvers by *Thomas Ewisden*, 1716. – MONUMENTS. In the S aisle tomb-chest with the painted stone effigies of Alderman John Wallton and his wife, † 1626, in contemporary costume; he has a red robe, and she a broad-brimmed tall hat. This is local work, with a crude Ionic arcade. – In the chancel, a portrait half-length effigy of a twenty-two-

* Sold to the City Museum.

year-old divine, Richard Green, † 1711. Local work under
London influence.

ST OSWALD, Coney Hill. 1939 by *Ellery Anderson*. A basilica, of
brick, with a tall S tower like an Italian campanile with hipped
flat-pitched pantile roof. Nave with narrow aisles, simplified
Byzantine-style arcades, and round-headed windows with clear
glass. – English ALTAR. – STAINED GLASS. Three-light E
window in the Lady Chapel by *Francis Stephens*, 1954.

ST PAUL, Stroud Road. 1882–3 by *Capel N. Tripp*, who had
been in Medland's office, and died in 1883, aged thirty-eight.
C13, of rusticated stone, with an unfinished S tower, now used
as the porch, plate-tracery windows, and tiled roof with a bellcote. The interior is much more handsome: nave and chancel,
arched sanctuary, nave arcades of four bays, three of which
have gabled transepts in addition to the aisles. One bay of the
nave is occupied by the choir, with chapels either side. In 1939,
W. E. Ellery Anderson completed the W end, which has a stone
gallery and organ loft. He also designed the English ALTAR in
a sanctuary which had already been provided with a dignified
Gothic screen and rood. A new rood was set much higher in
order to give a fuller view of the E window's new STAINED
GLASS by *Hugh Easton*.

ST PETER (R.C.), London Road. 1860–8 by *Gilbert Robert
Blount*. Chancel, nave, N and S chapels, N and S aisles, NW
tower with spire. Built in stone, the steeple has a real novelty in
the open bell stage, with coupled arches on each side giving a
splendid airy effect. The W end facing the street has good detail
and a rose window. Small two-light clerestory windows over
the piers, not the arches. Two gabled windows each side of the
sanctuary, which has a really enterprising wooden vault internally. Nave arcades rather low, with well moulded capitals to
octagonal piers, surmounted by larger octagonal blocks with
which the arch mouldings make a somewhat clumsy connexion.
Deep sanctuary, flanked by chapels, the Lady Chapel on the
Gospel side. Some exaggeration of scale in these arcades,
which have richly carved and gilded capitals and corbels.
Rather good rich rectilinear REREDOS placed under a five-light
E window which itself is too small in scale, but has excellent
STAINED GLASS by *Clayton & Bell*. In fact the whole sanctuary was formerly painted by *Clayton & Bell*, but this was
seriously modified and toned down by *Linthont* of Bruges in
1939. However, the Lady Chapel retains its original painted
walls by *Clayton & Bell*, and also windows by this firm, of

good design and bold colour. At the w end the organ is cleft in two to let in light from the rose window.

ST STEPHEN, Linden Road. 1895 by *Walter Planck*. w front added later by *H. A. Dancey*. Brick and stone, plastered and limewashed inside. This accomplished architect has built an original and good church, spoiled by the silly polygonal w baptistery added by *Dancey*. The transeptal windows have buttresses to the tracery evidently imitating the E window of the cathedral, but without excuse. In the nave a reasonable hammerbeam roof with vertical timbers, where might be vaulting-shafts, standing on mullion-like extra members of the columns. All the arches are four-centred. Clerestory and aisles. – The ALTAR has a dorsal and tester, all designed by *Stephen Dykes-Bower*. – The paschal CANDLESTICKS are by *Francis Stephens*.

CEMETERY CHAPELS, Cemetery Road. 1857 by *Medland & Maberly*. Dec, with tower and spire and flanking chapels.

CONEY HILL CREMATORIUM. Post Second World War. Stone, in neo-Norman, by *A. Morgan*.

NONCONFORMIST CHAPELS

BAPTIST CHAPEL. 1872–3, rebuilt by *Charles G. Searle & Son*. Classical ashlar elevation of one, three, one bays with pilasters and central pediment and rusticated treatment of the ground floor. Round-headed windows on the first floor.

CONGREGATIONAL CHURCH (Tyndale Chapel), Lower Barton Street. 1874–5 by *James Tait* of Leicester. E.E. Stone.

SOUTHGATE CONGREGATIONAL CHURCH. By *Francis Niblett*, c.1865. Dec style. GALLERIES on three sides. – STAINED GLASS. Three E windows by *Rogers* of Worcester. Texts and geometrical designs.

FRIENDS MEETING HOUSE, Greyfriars. Of c.1840. Plain, with contemporary FURNISHINGS.

METHODIST CHAPEL, Northgate Street. 1877 by *Charles Bell*. It seems to be a sort of eclectic exercise in the style of Wren. Flanking towers either side of a central gabled portion. Large rose window over the projecting segment of the portico, which is supported by pairs of round polished granite columns with Corinthian capitals. Behind it are two similar doorways with round heads, which would create a duality if they were not cut up (visually) by the columns of the portico. The ground floors of the towers horizontally rusticated, with windows with two round-headed lights. On the first floor the windows are the same but for circles over the two lights, a favourite mid-Victorian device. The windows have classical surrounds with panelled plinths, Corinthian pilasters, and moulded archivolts. Towers with Corinthian pilasters which then rise into Wrenish spires complete with vases, pediments, and circular louvres.

WHITEFIELD PRESBYTERIAN CHURCH, Park Road. 1871 by *Medland & Son*. Dec. Yellow brick with bands and patterns in brown and red brick; stone dressings. NW tower with ashlar spire. Rose window at the E end. The W entrance has double doors with a sculptured TYMPANUM of George Whitefield preaching 'The love of Christ constrains me to lift up my voice like a trumpet.'

UNITARIAN CHAPEL, Barton Street. Founded in 1699. Of brick, with a hipped roof covering its square proportions. Later classical ashlar front with round-headed openings and crowning pediment. Altered in 1893, when a proscenium was added at the N end; beyond this is a small graveyard.

PUBLIC BUILDINGS

SHIRE HALL, on the S side of Westgate Street. Designed by *Sir Robert Smirke* in 1816, with a recessed giant Ionic portico. The new blocks and alterations are the work of *R. F. Fairhurst*, the County Architect, and *Gilbert Jones*. In 1894 the Council Chamber was designed by *M. H. Medland*, who made further alterations in 1896. The Shire Hall was extended in 1909–11. Of Smirke's Shire Hall, built in Bath and Leckhampton stone, only the portico in Westgate Street and the polygonal assize courts at the rear now survive; the interior has been remodelled. Fairhurst's vast new extension of 1966, eight storeys high and mostly glass, is joined to the older buildings by a fly-over crossing Bearland, impressive and exciting.

GUILDHALL. 1890–2 by *George H. Hunt*. Cost approximately £31,000 Renaissance, of stone, with three storeys and one, three, one bays. Ground floor with horizontal grooving, first floor or *piano nobile* with a central three-bay arcade divided by Ionic columns, second or attic floor enriched with heraldry and carved cherubs with three circular windows. Ornamental stone vases on the parapet.

EASTGATE STREET MARKET ENTRANCE. Designed by *Medland & Maberly* in 1856. Of stone with three round-headed arches with giant attached Corinthian columns, modillion cornice, and pediment with a clock in the tympanum, surmounted by a bell tower. Excellent realistic carving of market produce and symbolic figures. This mid-C19 *tour de force* is unfortunately threatened by the proposed development in this area.

PUBLIC LIBRARY AND MUSEUM, Brunswick Road. 1897–1900 by *F. W. Waller & Son*. Rusticated Gothic. The Renaissance PRICE MEMORIAL HALL, adjoining, is also by *Waller*, 1892.

RAIKES MEMORIAL SUNDAY SCHOOL. 1884. By *Capel N. Tripp*.

ST BARTHOLOMEW'S HOSPITAL, Westgate Street. Built and designed by *William Price* of Gloucester in 1788–9 as almshouses with chapel and separate rooms for fifty-four people. Gothick, ashlar-faced, with an arcade of clustered shafts and roll mouldings; 6, 1, 3, 1, 6 bays. Projecting central portion with three pointed arches. Flat arches on the side wings. Thin diagonal buttresses, embattled parapet, and windows with flat chamfered arches and dripmoulds.

ST MARY DE CRYPT GRAMMAR SCHOOL. Erected in 1539, restored in 1862 by *Medland & Maberly* and again in 1880. Built on to the N wall of the church. Ashlar with mullioned windows. Tudor brickwork at the back. Oriel window with arms of Henry VIII.

ROYAL INFIRMARY. Built *c*.1755 by *Anthony Keck*, of brick, with central pediment and projecting wings. In the centre over the board room at the rear is a chapel (with STAINED GLASS by *Lavers, Barraud & Westlake*) in a projecting bay. The infirmary was enlarged in 1827 by *Thomas Rickman*, and again later in the C19.

H.M. PRISON. Built on the site of Gloucester Castle. Regular sums were spent on the castle from Henry II's to Edward IV's time, but by the end of the C17 the only remaining building, used as a county gaol, had been demolished. Sir George Onesiphorus Paul in 1783 urged the Grand Jury at Gloucester to order the building of five new county gaols at Gloucester, Northleach, Horsley, Little Dean, and Lawford's Gate, Bristol. The Paul committee did pioneering work in adopting Howard's principles. The gaol was built by *William Blackburn* and completed after his death in 1790 by the county surveyor *John Wheeler*. The cells open on to balconies supported by cast-iron snakes, an alteration of *c*.1810. It was enlarged in 1845–55 by *T. Fulljames*. Simple but impressive brick and stone buildings, surrounded by a high wall, with rusticated stone entrance archway and lodges. Near the entrance the OLD

BARRACKS or ARMOURY, 1854–7 by *Fulljames & Waller*, of stone, two storeys, with embattled parapets, central tower with stair-vice, and arched entrance with oriel window above. Perp windows. Most of this building has been demolished, but a portion was retained.

OLD CUSTOM HOUSE, at the end of Quay Street. Ashlar. Three storeys and two sash windows, and an arcade on the ground floor. Pilasters either side, cornice and panelled parapet; royal arms carved on the front. Some good WAREHOUSES, nine to the E of Victoria Dock, built in the first half of the C19. The brick-built DOCK OFFICE of c.1830 (now British Waterways Board) is the old office of the Gloucester and Berkeley Canal Company.

GLOUCESTER–BERKELEY SHIP CANAL. Opened in 1827. Many engineers had a finger in this unprofitable pie, chiefly *Robert Mylne*, whose estimate of £121,329 10s. 4d. for cutting the canal, 17¾ m. long, 70 ft wide at the top, and 15 ft deep from Gloucester to Berkeley Pill, proved totally inadequate. In 1823 *Telford* wrote, 'I have now nearly completed the working drawings', but these drawings do not seem to have survived, so that it is impossible to tell whether *Mylne* or *Telford* designed the charming little classical houses which are such a feature of the canal. 'Mylne most probably did', is the answer given by Telford's biographer, L. T. C. Rolt. One level is maintained from Gloucester to Sharpness, and it is still used. Telford designed the old canal entrance lock at Sharpness Point with its lock house. The dock at Gloucester covers eight acres.

H.M. CUSTOMS AND EXCISE OFFICE, Commercial Road. C19 classical, ashlar-faced, of two storeys and five grouped windows. Royal arms centrally placed on the parapet.

CENTRAL RAILWAY STATION. Opened by the G.W.R. in 1889; designed by *Lancaster Owen*.

EASTERN STATION. Built by the Midland Railway in 1891–6.

WESTGATE BRIDGE. Rebuilt in 1814–16 by *Sir Robert Smirke*, with one arch of 87 ft span.

OVER BRIDGE, across the Maisemore Channel. Designed in 1825 by *Thomas Telford*. Telford chose a single arch of stone based upon a design which the French architect Perronet had evolved in 1768 for his bridge over the Seine at Neuilly. The body of the arch is an ellipse, with a chord line of 150 ft and a rise of 35 ft, but the voussoirs, or external arch stones, are set to segments on the same chord with a rise of only 13 ft. The effect of this is that instead of being four-square the appearance of the arch is funnel-shaped, this shape being most pronounced at the springing and tapering off to the crown.

CATTLE MARKET, St Oswald's Road. Designed by *J. V. Wall* in 1955.

GIRLS HIGH SCHOOL, Denmark Road. By *Walter Bryan Wood*, early C20, brick and stone dressings.

UNITED ALMSHOUSES. By *Fulljames & Waller*, 1860–1. Patterned brickwork and Gothic details in stone. Trefoil-headed windows and pointed archways. Towers and turrets.

HORTON ROAD HOSPITAL. A vast early C19 stucco-faced building on a huge crescent, three storeys high, plus a basement faced in rusticated ashlar. Nineteen windows inside the crescent. Overhanging eaves and flat-pitched roof. The crescent is flanked by gabled blocks with two-storey bows. Central doorway with four Roman Doric columns. 1822–3 by *W. Starke*, supervised by *J. Collingwood*.

HATHERLEY ROAD SCHOOLS. 1899 by *Alfred J. Dunn*, in neo-Queen Anne style.

AMBULANCE STATION, Eastern Avenue. By *J. V. Wall*, c.1950.

DRILL HALL OF THE ROYAL GLOUCESTERSHIRE HUSSARS, Eastern Avenue. By *B. J. Ashwell*, c. 1950.

ROMAN CATHOLIC SECONDARY MODERN SCHOOL OF ST PETER'S. By *Peter Falconer*, c.1955. Its horizontal lines contrast with a delightful small open spire.

PUBLIC BATHS, Barton Street. 1888 by *J. Fletcher Trew*. Extension and new baths by *J. V. Wall*, finished in 1966.

PERAMBULATIONS

INNER GLOUCESTER

We start from MILLERS GREEN. THE DEANERY (No. 1
Millers Green) was built *c*.1730. It is a fine, square brick house,
three-storeyed with five windows. Pedimented stone doorway
of *c*.1770, approached by a flight of steps. The interior has a
good staircase and panelling. Regency balconies at the back. In
the forecourt GATEPIERS with handsome urns and wrought-
iron railings. THE OLD MILL HOUSE (No. 2) is late C18,
brick, on the site of the monastic mill. The original millstone
survives in the cellar, where there is a well. Besides No. 3 (already described, *see* p. 223), Nos. 4 and 5 incorporate, or are on
the site of, monastic buildings. No. 6 is an C18 brick house,
roughcast with Gothic glazed windows; gatepiers with urns.
No. 7 is C18, partly of stone, with a brick front in College
Green.

COLLEGE GREEN. A dignified cathedral close. The YEO-
MANRY WAR MEMORIAL is out of scale with the Georgian
houses, though in itself a good design, of *c*.1920. Bronze
panels by *Adrian Jones* on the plinth. The architects were
Cash & Wright. COMMUNITY HOUSE has a late C18 stuccoed
front, three storeys and five windows. Rusticated stone
ground floor. Modillion cornice and pediment. No. 14, next to
St Mary's Gate, is part of the monastic buildings used by the
almoner. The timber-framed upper storey may have been a
hall. Oriel window with carved bargeboards. All much restored
or rebuilt.

The remaining houses round College Green were mostly rebuilt
in the C17 and C18 on the sites of monastic buildings. No. 9 is
especially fine and early (*c*.1690); it is shown in Kip's drawing
of *c*.1700. Three storeys, of brick. Five windows with cambered heads, keystones, and brick arches. Brick pilasters either
side. Cornice, parapet, and pediment with a round window in
the tympanum. Nice portico with fluted columns and pediment. Inside, two excellent contemporary staircases and panelling. No. 7 was the monastic 'granarium'. It has a C19 Tudor
roughcast front with gables and mullioned windows. A ground-
floor room has a Renaissance chimneypiece of 1620 carved in
wood, and older panelling. No. 6 was the monastic 'camera de
la sexten', but was rebuilt in the C17 and enlarged in the early
C19. It has typical Regency interior fittings. Ashlar-faced.
Two storeys plus dormers ,five windows, crowning cornice and

parapet. Central door with fanlight and attached columns,
broken entablature, and pediment. The first-floor drawing
room has fine views of the cathedral.

The upper part of College Green, divided from the lower part by
a wall till the C18, consisted of the cemetery, now a car park.
On the s side a terrace of Georgian houses, and on the E three
or four C17 or C18 houses; No. 19 has a pleasant C18 brick
front with stone dressing.

Leaving College Green by St Michael's Gate in the SE corner we
enter a passage now called COLLEGE COURT. This was very
picturesque until the whole of the E side was demolished in the
1940s and replaced by the brick wall of British Home Stores.
The first house on the w side, No. 9, has also been rebuilt.
From here we enter WESTGATE STREET on the N side. This
was by far the longest and most important street in medieval
Gloucester, running up to The Cross, where it met the lesser
Northgate, Eastgate, and Southgate Streets. Owing to this
Roman grid arrangement, the medieval street plan of the city
has survived. Generally, however, Westgate Street now presents a sorry sight. Development always has been and still
continues piecemeal, so that opportunities for disclosing the
few good buildings left are never taken. Until the C18 there
were buildings in the middle of Westgate Street which
naturally had to give way to wheeled traffic. Earlier demolitions
included two medieval churches.

Turn r. and walk up Westgate Street. On the N side, No. 30 has an
overhanging gable indicating its concealed C16 timber-framing.
No. 26 (THE OLD JUDGE'S HOUSE) looks like a Georgian
shopfront, but that is merely a refacing on to the greatest
timber-framed building left in the city, visible only from the
very narrow Maverdine Passage. This historic house was
occupied by Governor Massey during the siege in 1643. Built
in the C16, it has a carved timber-framed elevation of four
storeys with five gables, overhangs, and oriel windows, which
have original wood mullions and transoms with ovolo mouldings and leaded lights. No. 14 at the corner of St John's Lane
is also a hidden old building. On the first floor at the back a
three-bay room with a decorated plaster ceiling of c.1600 with
small pendant bosses and coved sides. No. 8 also has an
interesting room on the first floor at the back which has C16
panelling and a series of Tudor carvings including heraldic
devices, the arms of Henry VIII and the pomegranate of
Katherine of Aragon, and the monogram T.P. for Thomas

Payne, a c16 Mayor of Gloucester. Some carvings were added by *G. A. Howitt* when he restored the room in 1890. The MIDLAND BANK, 1910, has a facsimile enlargement.

We now come to THE CROSS, where until 1751 stood a famous medieval High Cross. The earliest existing drawing of the Cross dates from 1455, and the last, made in 1750, was engraved by Vertue for the Society of Antiquaries. It shows eight canopied niches occupied by royal figures. Leland in his c16 *Itinerary* says: 'The beauty of the town lies in two crossing streets, and at the place of the middle meeting is an aqueduct incallated.' In 1751 the Corporation pulled down the High Cross and built a Tolsey House, designed by *William Roberts* and in its turn demolished in 1893–4, when a bank was built which has not survived today either. It is evident that the Cross has been subject to constant change since Roman times,* but its appearance today could hardly be more unworthy, except for the survival of the tower of St Michael.

Retracing our steps along Westgate Street, on the s side we come to the FLEECE HOTEL, which has a c12 vaulted chamber known as the MONKS RETREAT. However, it was probably built as a domestic, not an ecclesiastical building, a fireproof warehouse commonly found under merchants' houses in the Middle Ages; but it is a substantial building for a c12 merchant to have provided. Tunnel-vault of five bays with arches supported by round Norman pillars with concave-moulded capitals and chamfered abaci. In the c15, when the abbey provided inns for the pilgrims to Edward II's shrine, one such was on the site of the Fleece Hotel. The existing building, which has been altered several times, contains a dining room with an attractive curved bay window, probably late c18. Over the fireplace is a

---

* Gloucester was the Roman COLONIA NERVIA GLEVENSIUM. Recent excavations have shown that the site was first occupied by a rectangular legionary fortress, 43 acres in extent, defended by an earthen rampart and ditch, built in A.D. 49 when the Twentieth Legion was brought up from Colchester to be near the war in Wales. Subsequent troop movements removed the army from the region and allowed a colonia for retired veterans to be founded within the defences some time between A.D. 96 and 98. A stone wall was added to the front of the old rampart, and buildings of masonry were gradually erected within the enclosure. In Westgate a colonnade of Corinthian columns, serving as a monumental front to buildings behind, was traced for 200 ft along the N side of the street, and at the Cross the substantial foundations of a public building, possibly the forum, were found. Private houses are represented by more than twenty mosaic pavements recovered from time to time during the last 200 years. Outside the town traces of a quay, built of massive masonry, were seen between the town wall and the river Severn. See p. 457

picture of Westgate Bridge painted on the wall itself. The
bridge was taken down in 1813 and the picture is ascribed to
Frederick Seward, a painter living in Bristol in 1793. The
FOUNTAIN INN has been restored. In the courtyard is a small
bas-relief of William III on a horse and the inscription 'Dieu
defend le droit'. Nos. 59 and 61 have an impressive early C18
brick façade with a carved modillion cornice and chamfered
quoins.

On the opposite side, the entrance to COLLEGE STREET is
marked by Victorian Tudor brick and timber-framed buildings
by *F. W. Waller*, 1890, which look extremely picturesque from
Berkeley Street. The W side of College Street has old timber-
framed houses. Opposite the Shire Hall one old timber-framed
house with overhanging gables. The BOOTH HALL, immediately W of the Shire Hall, was demolished in 1957, but the
arms of the city carved in the C18 by *Thomas Ricketts* were
preserved and set up in 1961, re-painted by *John Drinkwater*,
on the corner of the modern block where Three Cocks Lane
enters the N side of Westgate Street. To the W of this, immediately to the E of St Nicholas' church, is ST NICHOLAS'
HOUSE. The rear part of the house is timber-framed, but the
street frontage is occupied by a two-storeyed C18 house of red
brick with stone dressings and with an Early Georgian façade
of considerable architectural pretensions. The ends and the
slightly projecting centre are emphasized by chamfered stone
quoins, and all the upper windows have moulded architraves
and keystones. The pediment is flanked by balustrading supporting five very handsome carved urns. This is a good example
of Georgian provincial architecture. W of the church is the
excellent, colourful block of modern flats, FOUNTAIN
SQUARE, designed by *J. V. Wall*, formerly City Architect, and
A. J. Ault, and distinguished by their human scale and feeling
for texture. In front of the York-stone-paved piazza modern
SCULPTURE by *John Whiskeard*.

On the opposite side of Westgate Street No. 91 is timber-framed
behind an C18 stucco front. It contains Queen Anne panelling and staircase. Shopfront with nice Victorian lettering.
60   BISHOP HOOPER'S LODGING, a folk museum since 1935,
has exposed timber-framing of *c*.1500. Three storeys with
double overhang. Next to it another timber-framed house, of
the early C17, with two gables and overhang and gazebo room
in the roof. This is a Regimental Museum. Nos. 109–123,
comprising a range of C17 and C18 houses including the

LOWER GEORGE INN, form an attractive street group. Beyond this, owing to the present state of change, the street deteriorates; but on the N side there still survives the DUKE OF NORFOLK'S HOUSE, early C18 and with the only stone elevation of this period in Gloucester. It is enriched with Corinthian pilasters, cornice, and stone balustrade, and the flanking walls to the forecourt are terminated by stone vases.

No less than about twenty-five buildings in Westgate Street which were listed as of architectural or historic interest under the Town and Country Planning Act after the Second World War, have now been demolished. Where this has been caused by private enterprise and the connivance of the local authority the results seem usually to have been disastrous; but no praise is too great for the Westgate Development Area undertaken by the City Architect's Department. Retracing one's steps thither, and turning l. in Archdeacon Street by Fountain Square, one comes into ST MARY'S SQUARE, dominated by the church of St Mary de Lode. To the E stands the beautiful MONUMENT by *Edward W. Thornhill* of Dublin, erected in 1862 to Bishop Hooper on the site of his martyrdom. It has a pretty Dec-style canopy, crocketed and pinnacled.

Apart from the backs of the houses in College Green, and MONUMENT HOUSE, an C18 house with a pretty ogee-arched Gothic doorcase, next to St Mary's Gate, all the old houses in St Mary's Square except one have been demolished. These included a remarkable group of C15 timber-framed cottages,* and twenty-two houses listed under the Town and Country Planning Act as being of architectural interest, including those in the former St Mary's Street. The only house to survive was built *c.*1690 with a lofty doorway of Dutch type with a large transom light. It is roughcast and has slightly projecting wings. It cannot be denied, however, that the new St Mary's Square is a success, with its carefully textured pavements and preserved trees. ST CATHERINE STREET till recently contained a remarkable group of C15 timber-framed houses on the corner of Park Street, one of which was where Robert Raikes held his first Sunday school in 1781. All these were demolished under a slum-clearance order.

Leaving this present scene of devastation it is best to walk along PITT STREET. The former Bishop's Palace (*see* p. 223) is on

*Some carved figure brackets are now preserved in the Folk Museum at Bishop Hooper's Lodgings.

the r., and on the l. a range of decent small Georgian houses, the largest and best of which is PADDOCK HOUSE, three storeys and five windows, a pedimented doorway, and a bow window at the back. This is one of the houses of King's School, whose new dining hall in adjacent Park Street was designed by *Bernard J. Ashwell*. Towards the end, on the r., is PALACE HOUSE, Neo-Georgian, by *Seely & Paget*, c.1958, containing a genuine Georgian staircase, disproportionately big for the house. The PROBATE REGISTRY is a fanciful Gothic Revival building of 1858 by *Fulljames & Waller*. Facing the end of the street in HARE LANE is the RAVEN TAVERN. Until Worcester Street was built at the beginning of the C19, Hare Lane was the Great North Road of the West of England. The Raven, built in the C16, was an important inn, and issued its own token coinage. Adjoining it was the Tanners Hall. In the early C17 the Raven belonged to the Hoare family, members of which emigrated to America, and it was partly for this reason that this timber-framed portion of a once larger building was restored by *H. F. Trew* c.1950, and is now an old people's club. A few doors away to the S is YE OLDE FISH SHOP, of c.1535, timber-framed with double overhang.

From here we enter NORTHGATE STREET. Turning to the r. towards the Cross, St John's church is on the r., on the opposite side is the New Inn, and beyond that and nearer the Cross a large, full-blooded, early C18 brick building of four storeys and nine bays; windows with wood architraves, keystones, bull-nosed sills, and chamfered quoins of alternating length between each house, as it is divided into three, Nos. 6, 8, and 10 NORTHGATE. Ground floor undercut with modern shops. The NEW INN was built c.1457 by the abbey (supposedly by a monk named *Twyning*) in order to accommodate pilgrims. It retains much of its original timber-framing, including C15 carving visible on the corner of the alley on the N side, a crocketed, pinnacled niche with a mutilated figure, carved braces, and Perp panels. The medieval plan with a courtyard and open galleries is retained. A Georgian façade in Northgate Street is altered to look in keeping, and in the courtyard 'New Inn' is written in bold Victorian lettering. Few inns in England can be so old and retain so much of their original character. Returning along the E side of Northgate Street, the BON MARCHÉ STORES, designed in 1926 by *Healing & Overbury*, has a modern extension in King's Square which is now a bus station and car park. Apart from the Methodist Chapel already

mentioned (p. 238) there is little to be said about the mostly
C18 and C19 houses in the rest of this street.

Turning l. into WORCESTER STREET, an early C19 development, and then r. into ALVIN STREET one comes to the
KINGSHOLME ESTATE development of the 1950s by *J. V.
Wall*. It consists of a splendid block of flats, eleven storeys
high, and the horizontal UNION STREET flats of three storeys,
black-painted boarded panels contrasting with brick very
effectively. KINGSHOLME SCHOOL includes an assembly hall
with a hyperbolic paraboloid roof also designed by *J. V. Wall*,
at the same time. From here one enters the LONDON ROAD
opposite WELLINGTON PARADE, a terrace of early C19 ashlar
houses with round-headed ground-floor windows with Gothic
glazing. Returning towards the city NORTHGATE HOUSE is
on the r., a good C18 house with modillion cornice and pediment and wrought-iron gates. Under the railway bridge and
beyond the Roman Catholic church is the BLACK DOG INN,
which has an enormous C19 plaster black dog lying on the
parapet. Turning l. in Market Parade, on the r. is the SPREAD
EAGLE HOTEL, by *Medland, Maberly & Medland*, 1864, with
a stepped gable and oriel window. Here is the old market, now
filled with a modern block of shops and offices (GROSVENOR
HOUSE) by *Gordon Payne & Preece*, c.1960, and a good new
Post Office Sorting House. From here one can return to the
Cross in order to explore the Eastgate Street quarter.

Nos. 1–15 EASTGATE STREET on the N side have all been rebuilt
since 1946. LLOYDS BANK of 1898 is by *Waller & Son*, of red
brick and terracotta, a tall Renaissance building with large
central gable and flanking gables either side with central bay
window and granite arcade on the ground floor. Next is the
NATIONAL PROVINCIAL BANK of c.1889 by *Charles R.
Gribble* of London, Baroque classical, of Cotswold stone, with
a great cambered pediment with a shell in the tympanum,
supported by scrolls. Three storeys; Ionic order on the two
lower floors. A section of ROMAN PAVEMENT is preserved in
the hall. EASTGATE HOUSE* was built by *John Ricketts Jun.*,
c.1781, on the site of the East Gate of the city, and on the
ROMAN WALL (*see* p. 245), which can still be seen under the
printing works at the back. Ricketts was one of the family of
monumental sculptors who did most elegant monuments in
the cathedral and elsewhere, and the low relief ornamental
vases on the façade are clearly designed by him. Facsimile

*To be demolished.

addition on the E. The DISTRICT BANK is by by *D. I. Stratton-
Davis*, dignified neo-Georgian, c.1950. BARTON STREET is
the continuation of Eastgate Street, with CLARENCE STREET
running N. The latter has good early C19 terrace houses faced
in ashlar or stucco, one particularly with Ionic pilasters.
ANNANDALE HOUSE, further along on the N side, is brick,
C18, with a stucco front, but not much better than the run of
the mill here. Returning on the S side, the houses are mostly
C18 and C19. Nos. 52, 54, and 56 are of slightly greater distinction, being ashlar-faced with pilasters, but buried by additional
shops. The former SIR THOMAS RICH'S SCHOOL (or Blue-
coat School), founded in 1666, is a late C18 brick house set
back from the street with a four-storey bow at the back. No. 14
has a well preserved early C19 classical ashlar façade built by
Estcourt,* the head of a long-established firm of Gloucester
masons who were afterwards employed by Philip Webb at
Clouds, in Wiltshire.

Turning l. into Brunswick Road and r. into BELL LANE, we
reach CONSTITUTION HOUSE, a large house built in 1759 on
the corner of QUEEN STREET. Brick with a parapet, three
storeys, seven windows with keystones and brick arches,
chamfered quoins. Doorcase with fluted Ionic three-quarter
columns and pediment. Bell Lane is in an area which is to be
redeveloped.

From here one enters SOUTHGATE STREET. Two doors away
from St Michael's church tower is a clock shop with a curious
chiming clock of 1904. It has large figures of Father Time,
flanked by an Irishwoman, a Scotsman, John Bull, and a
Welshwoman, made by *Baker*. No. 9 has a restored wooden
Jacobean front with two overhanging storeys. Panelled room
on the first floor with a fine carved fireplace of 1650 displaying
See
p. 457 the arms of Yate and Berkeley. The BELL HOTEL, mentioned
in 1544 under that name, has been gutted inside, and the
exterior looks C19. £10,000 was spent on it in 1864. It was the
birthplace of George Whitefield in 1714, but is due to be
demolished. Opposite in CROSS KEYS LANE the timber-
framed inn of that name survives. Continuing on the E side
there is a very nice C18 house, No. 31 SOUTHGATE STREET,
with a brick front of three storeys and five windows with stone
architraves and keystones on the first floor. Central Venetian
window with rusticated architraves and archivolt. Crowning

---

* Albert Estcourt of Gloucester had worked for Burges and was also
recommended by Sir T. G. Jackson.

stone modillion cornice. Central double entrance with four Ionic three-quarter columns supporting an entablature with pulvinated frieze and pediment. The doors have fanlights and are set in rusticated surrounds. Inside, a good mid-c18 staircase with enriched balusters and shaped dado, and, at the back, a chimneypiece of c.1600, carved with the so-called Tudor arms of the city. Nos. 36 and 38 Southgate Street form a splendid half-timbered house of the latter half of the c16, where Robert Raikes, founder of the Sunday School Movement, lived from 1768 to 1801. Three storeys, overhanging, with three gables to the street. On the island corner, where COMMERCIAL ROAD joins Southgate Street, the former SAVINGS BANK BUILDING, No. 1 Commercial Road. 1850 by *Hamilton & Medland*. Rusticated ground floor, the round-headed windows set in recesses which have crisply carved masks. Three storeys, bracket cornice, rusticated quoins. Opposite, the BLACK SWAN INN, a rather similar kind of building.

Further along on the E side is the turning into SPA ROAD, where we are confronted with the kind of houses more usually found in Cheltenham. The GLOUCESTER SPA was developed c.1812–25. In 1829 it is recorded of RIBSTON HALL (now the Gloucester College of Art) that a 'spacious and elegant mansion has lately been erected near the Spa by John Phillpotts, Esq.'. It later flourished as the Spa Hotel, and in 1860 became a 'Ladies School'. It is of three storeys faced in stucco with six windows; neo-Greek channelling and a portico with grouped Ionic columns. SHERBORNE HOUSE, of about the same date, was built by *John Chadborn*, a three-storey symmetrical stucco composition. Central portion with rusticated ground floor and central door with fanlight. First floor with a continuous wrought-iron balcony. Pilasters through the upper floors and wrought-iron window guards. The JUDGE'S LODGINGS were designed by *Sir Robert Smirke* for John Phillpotts, and originally called Somerset House. Faced in fine ashlar, the central portion breaks forward and has coupled Ionic pilasters through the upper floors, and a continuous wrought-iron veranda on the first floor. The rusticated ground floor has a similar continuous wrought-iron balcony. BEAUFORT BUILDINGS forms an asymmetrical stucco-faced terrace with Ionic porticoes, some with wrought-iron work. All these houses look out on to the Park or Spa Pleasure Ground, where till 1960 the Spa Pump Room was situated. This pretty one-storey building of 1815, with a veranda supported on wooden columns and a parapet adorned with carved lions and acorn vases, has been demolished. In the distance remains the STATUE of Queen Anne, carved in 1710 by *John Ricketts Sen.*, in return for which he was made a Freeman of the City. Unfortunately, however, it is now rather badly weathered.

Turning back into Brunswick Road one immediately enters BRUNSWICK SQUARE. On the E side beyond Christ Church is a terrace of early C19 stucco houses enriched above the second-floor windows with large laurel wreaths. The houses are divided in their upper floors by thin pilasters with running fret or key pattern and surmounted by anthemions. Generally the houses all round the square are early C19. Returning to Southgate Street, opposite is the entrance to the Docks, marked by one of the little neo-Greek canal houses by *Robert Mylne*, to be found quite often on the Gloucester–Berkeley Canal, and here a weigh-house. Now to the r. past the infirmary and l. in Kimbrose Way passing Black Friars on the r. (*see* p. 226) to enter LONGSMITH STREET by Ladybellegate. Opposite is LADYBELLEGATE HOUSE, now the Health Centre, but once the town house of the Guise family of Elmore. Early C18, with the most elaborate Rococo plasterwork inside, particularly in the hall and on the staircase. The swan crest of the Guises is everywhere in evidence. The ceiling of the staircase-well has a vigorous representation in high relief of Jupiter sitting on clouds with an eagle. The staircase itself is a fine piece of contemporary joinery with twisted balusters. The rooms have been partitioned off in several places, to the detriment of their proportions. One has a carved stone chimneypiece with a niche over it. The front of three storeys and seven windows is simple and flat, faced in plaster. It has a modillion cornice. On the opposite side of the street is BEARLAND LODGE, early C18, a very attractive brick house of two storeys and four windows. Modillion cornice and pediment with a group of figures carved in high relief, by *John Ricketts*, in the tympanum. Doorway with fluted Corinthian pilasters, entablature, and segmental pediment. BEARLAND HOUSE is a fine early C18 brick house of three storeys and 2–3–2 bays, the central portion breaking forward. Stone quoins of alternating length, modillion cornice, balustraded parapet with urns, and portico with detached Ionic columns. Interior with good staircase and panelling.

OUTER GLOUCESTER

KINGSHOLME ROAD has a group of early C19 ashlar, stucco, and brick houses of the Spa period, and an octagonal turnpike house. Kingsholme was the site of a royal palace.* Turning into DENMARK ROAD, further on on the r. is HILLFIELD, now used as local government offices, erected *c.*1867 for himself by the builder *Albert Estcourt* in the Italianate style of Barry. Ashlar-faced, two storeys, round-headed windows on the ground floor, pilasters with neatly carved foliated capitals, and keystones through the archivolts. First-floor windows with straight heads and entablatures with little carved panels and elegant consoles. The tall Italianate tower is not central. It has stone balustraded balconies on the third floor and a deep projecting stone bracket cornice. Inside, a hall with a balcony all round and top lighting. Much elaborate stone carving, very naturalistic, and stained glass windows on the stairs dated 1867. The S elevation has a ground-floor arcade like an Italian loggia. This is probably the most elaborate Victorian house in Gloucester, and it also has the best garden and trees. The garden is now public. The contemporary ashlar-faced LODGE in LONDON ROAD is carefully designed, with marked entasis on the ground floor. Small round-headed windows with pretty iron window guards, and ornamental gables in the flat-pitched overhanging slate roof. In the garden is the so-called KINGS BOARD, or BUTTER MARKET. Late C14, and thought to have been used for the sale of butter and cheese; but, as it is so small, it could have been a friars' preaching cross – it has carvings in the spandrels of scenes from Christ's ministry. It stood first in mid Westgate Street, but was taken down in 1780 and moved again three times, finally spending a hundred years at Tibberton Court, from whence it was returned to the city in 1938, shorn of its pyramidal roof, statues, and cross. It is a polygonal embattled building with five arched openings in front, with cinquefoil tracery and heavily restored carvings. The back is built in, and it is doubtful if much of the original remains. Another building preserved in the garden is SCRIVEN'S CONDUIT, built in 1636 by Alderman John Scriven in mid Southgate Street to supply water from Robin's Wood Hill. It was taken down in 1784, kept at Edgeworth Manor for a

* And earlier of a ROMAN FORT, probably occupied by auxiliaries before the legionary fortress was built at Gloucester.

hundred years, and returned to the city in 1938. It is a regular gallimaufry of Gothic and classical forms. The figure at the top, Jupiter Fluvius pouring rainwater on to Sabrina, is supported on a coronet of ogee ribs rising from a small embattled parapet, octagonal in plan, with a frieze containing medallions depicting industries in the Severn Vale (i.e. cider, fishing, corn, wool, etc.) and carved shells either side alternating with lions' masks. The whole is carried by a Gothic arcade, and is made of Painswick stone. Opposite is a Late Georgian terrace faced in stucco. Further along London Road on the r. is the OLD RECTORY in BARNWOOD ROAD, a timber-framed house, very much restored, with Victorian wooden casement windows. Jacobean staircase inside. A cupboard door has a wooden panel carved with the so-called Tudor arms of the city, which was superseded in 1652, when the new arms incorporated those of de Clare. Some of the carvings in this house may be the work of the sculptor *G. A. Howitt*, who restored the Tudor room at No. 8, Westgate Street, *c.*1890.

Returning and turning l. into HORTON ROAD, WOTTON HOUSE is C18, brick, with hipped roof, modillion eaves cornice, and a porch with fluted Corinthian columns and segmental pediment.

In DARWIN ROAD a new estate designed by *J. V. Wall*, an exciting layout, with brick and narrow weatherboarded houses, flat-pitched roofs, and attractively built-in garages. Open frontages with grass and paving-stones. Country gardens at the back, under Robins' Wood Hill. In STROUD ROAD a timber-framed COTTAGE with overhanging gable-end, and with a Cotswold stone-tiled roof. The HOUSING ESTATE further on has good-looking reconstructed-stone houses, with low-pitched pantile roofs. Returning along Stroud Road, into LINDEN ROAD, we come to the SECONDARY MODERN SCHOOL, designed by *Medland & Son*, 1893–5. Red brick with blue bands and a tall campanile. Addition of 1902.

GORSLEY

6020

2½ m. W of Newent

CHRIST CHURCH. 1892–3 by *Rollinson*. Of hideous but well executed stonework. Nave, chancel, shallow transepts, all low with bargeboarded gables except that at the W end. Bellcote; apsidal sanctuary at the E end. The roof internally has wall-posts, and hammerbeams connected by tie bolts, in spite of the solid collar-beams above. Small, squat lancet windows; plate tracery in the transepts.

GOSSINGTON HALL *see* SLIMBRIDGE

GOTHERINGTON

9020

COUNTESS OF HUNTINGDON FREE CHURCH. 1833. An inscription states: 'The gift of the Hon. Henry Augustus Berkeley Craven.' Gabled entrance front with a central doorway. Porch with pointed windows either side with Gothick glazing and a similar window-head over the entrance, all three having shaped archivolts with imposts and keystones.

There is a great deal of new building in the village; but several old houses both timber-framed and stone-built survive, the most attractive perhaps being ASHMEAD, which is said to have been held by one family since 1648. Small stone front of two storeys with two mullioned windows; rear wing timber-framed with a stone-built columbarium in the gable-end. The interior retains a dog-cupboard for turning a spit.

STONE HOUSE. A small ashlar-faced house of *c.*1800 with a moulded stone eaves cornice and two hipped dormers, two storeys, three windows with architraves and keystones, and a central door with fanlight and pedimented hood on brackets. BRICKHOUSE is C18, with two storeys and five wooden mullioned and transomed windows. At MANOR FARM a good square DOVECOTE with buttressed corners, and at MOAT FARM a rubble BARN, with cruck trusses.

IRON AGE HILL-FORT, on Nottingham Hill, 1½ m. SE. The fort encloses about 110 acres. It is bivallate on the SE (the best view) and along parts of the NE side. The original entrances were most likely at the SE and NW, where the remains are damaged by quarrying. The ramparts are largely obscured by trees and undergrowth.

GREAT WASHBOURNE

9030

ST MARY. A small Early Norman church. S doorway with a TYMPANUM carved with a Maltese cross and pellet ornaments in between the rays, a row of dogtooth, and a segment of six-leaved roses and stars. On the N, too, a Norman doorway, and a deeply splayed window. Small and plain Norman chancel arch with chamfered imposts. In the S wall of the chancel a lancet light, but the E end was rebuilt in the C17 and has a Perp-survival window with inscription above: 'James Cartwright did newly build up this chancel, 1642.' Rendered bell-turret over the w end of the chancel. w window Perp. s of the chancel arch a trefoil-headed squint; another on the N, blocked, has an AUMBRY with an old wooden door opening into the chancel. – FONT, in the chancel, in front of the altar. Perp octagonal bowl with quatrefoils and stem with niches. – WALL PAINTINGS. The walls are newly limewashed, carefully leaving patches of original wall painting of Norman and later date, including a consecration cross within a double circle painted in red. – PULPIT. C18 two-decker. – ROYAL ARMS. George III. – PLATE. Chalice and Paten Cover, 1571. – MONUMENT. Esther Martin † 1801. Slate tablet.

MANOR FARMHOUSE. C17. Rubble, with Cotswold stone roof and gables.

GREAT WASHBOURNE HOUSE, E of the church. Mid C19. Red brick with Dutch gables.

Most of the COTTAGES are timber-framed, some with curved braces.

GREAT WITCOMBE

9010

ST MARY. C12, with Late Norman nave and chancel. N aisle added in the C15, w tower rebuilt in the C18. The Norman chancel arch has a double band of chevron moulding and outer jamb shafts with small scalloped capitals. On the s of the nave are two enlarged round-arched windows, deeply splayed, as are the two windows on the s of the chancel; but these have lancets inserted. The E window is also a wide lancet. Priest's door with a pointed arch. The Perp N aisle has a three-bay arcade with octagonal piers, and straight-headed windows with very nice elaborate tracery, one to the E and two to the N. The tower was built between 1749 and 1752; *John Bryan* of Painswick and *Joseph Bryan* of Gloucester were the masons, and *William Clark* of Leonard Stanley the carpenter. Three stages, angle pilaster buttresses, battlements and pinnacles. Sundial dated 1752. The pretty s porch is also probably the work of the *Bryans*; it has a trefoil-headed opening under an ogee-shaped arch, and wrought-iron gates. A passage from the N aisle to the chancel originally led up a flight of steps to the rood loft. The rood beam remains *in situ*, and on either side are small windows to light the loft. The wagon roof of the nave is enriched as a canopy over the loft, with moulded ribs and carved bosses. – STAINED GLASS. Fragments of C15 glass in the N aisle windows. – FONT. A C19 copy of the Norman font at Lasborough.

1. *Scenery:* Looking across the Vale to the Malverns from Cleeve Hill

2. (above) *Scenery:* Little Dean
3. (below) *Village Group:* Ashleworth, Ashleworth Court (*left*),
c.1460, church tower, and tithe barn (*right*), 1481/1515

4. (above) *Village Group:* Standish, church, early fourteenth century, and Church House, sixteenth century
5. (below) *Townscape:* Cheltenham, The Promenade

6. (above left) Deerhurst church, nave, *c*.804 and tenth century
7. (left) Deerhurst church, corbel, *c*.804
8. (above) Deerhurst church, *c*.804, tenth century, and later

9. (above) Gloucester Cathedral, nave, finished c.1120
10. (above right) Tewkesbury Abbey, nave, probably finished by 1121
11. (right) Dymock church, south doorway, c.1120-40

12. (above left) Ruardean church, south porch, tympanum, *c.*1150
13. (left) Tewkesbury Abbey, tower *c.*1150
14. (above) Tewkesbury Abbey, west front, mid twelfth century, window 1686

15. (above) Bishop's Cleeve church, west front, *c.* 1160–90 and
Decorated
16. (above right) Frampton-on-Severn church, font, *c.* 1150–75
17. (right) Bishop's Cleeve church, arcading in the south porch,
c. 1160–90

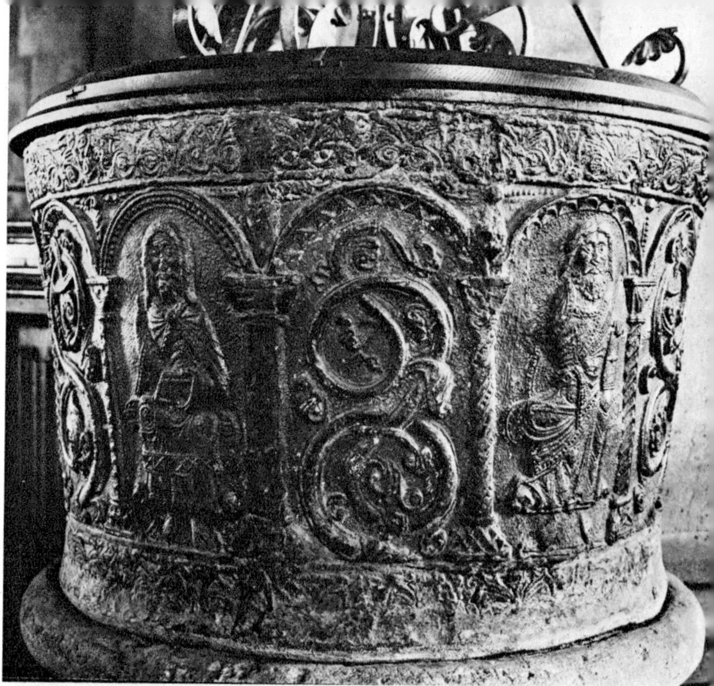
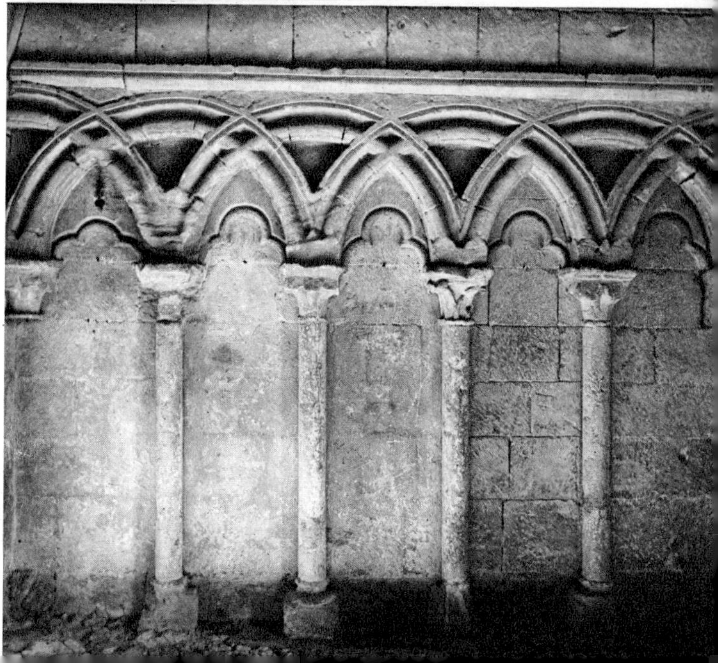

18. (above) Gloucester Cathedral, St Mary's Gate, Transitional
19. (above right) Deerhurst church, capitals, *c.* 1200
20. (right) Slimbridge church, capitals, *c.* 1200

21 and 22. Berkeley
church, capitals,
c. 1225–50

23. (left) Berkeley church, west front, mid thirteenth century

24. (below left) Newland church, thirteenth century and later

25. (left) Bishop's Cleeve church, chancel, south doorway, Decorated

26. (below left) Tewkesbury Abbey, choir, largely early fourteenth century

27. (right) Gloucester Cathedral, monument to Robert Courthose, Duke of Normandy, †1134, thirteenth century

28. (below right) Gloucester Cathedral, monument to Edward II, c. 1330, detail

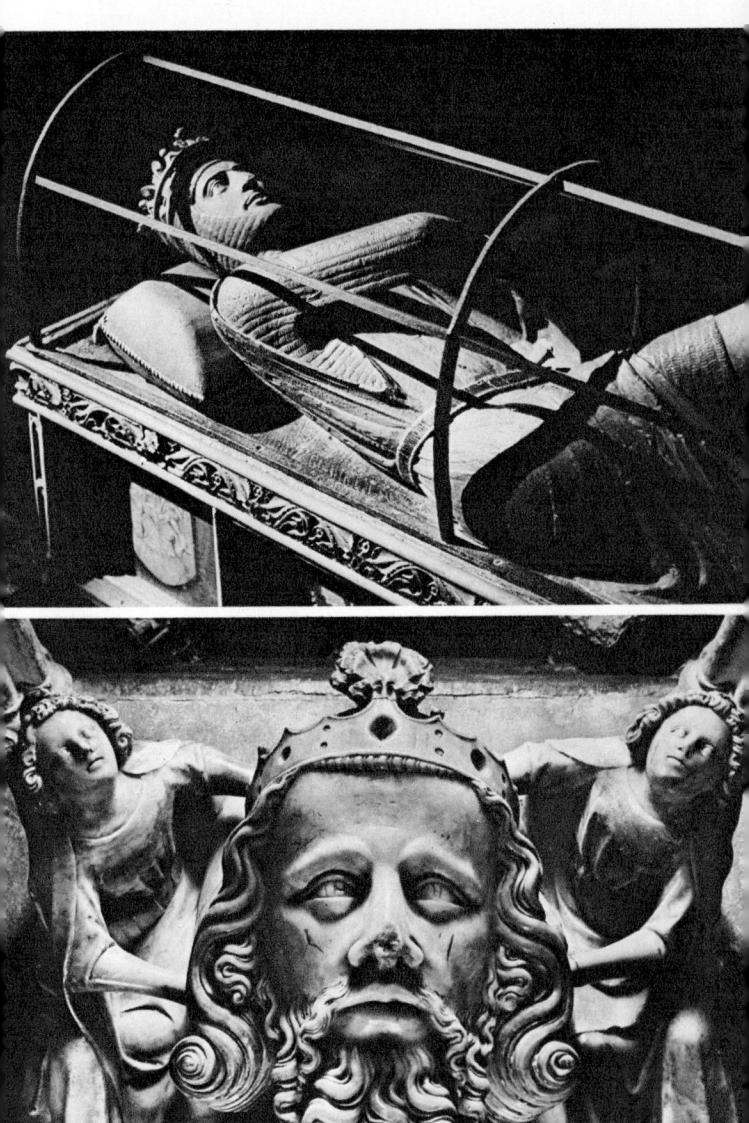

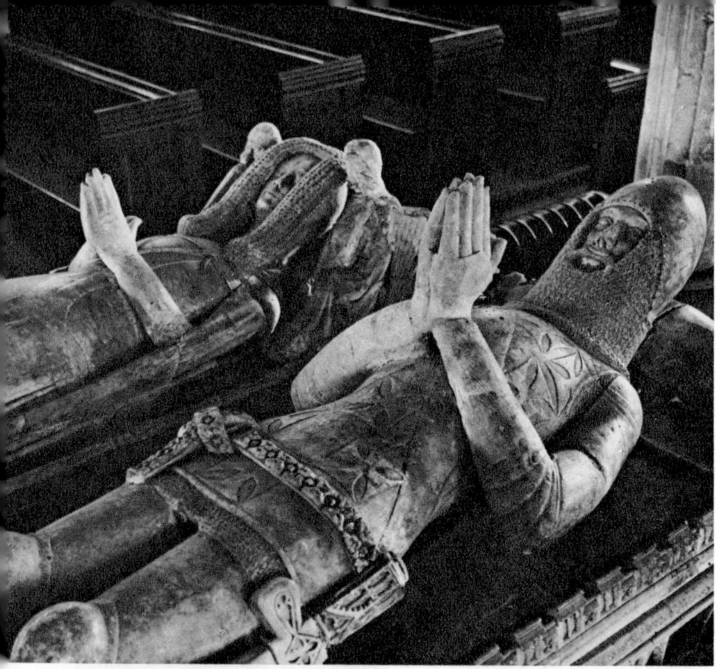

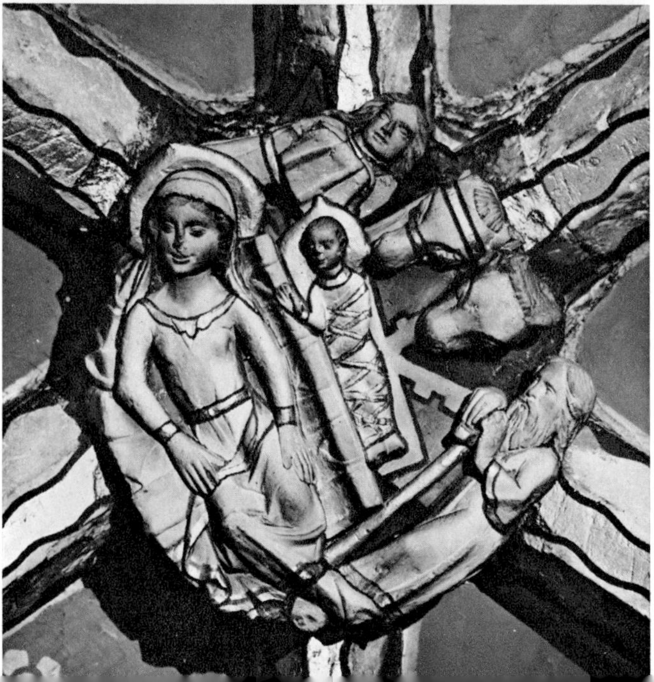

29. (above left) Berkeley church, monument to Thomas, eighth
Lord Berkeley, †1361
30. (left) Tewkesbury Abbey, nave, boss, c. 1340
31. (above) Gloucester Cathedral

32. (left) Gloucester Cathedral

33. (below left) Gloucester Cathedral, choir, begun *c.*1337

34. (right) Gloucester Cathedral, cloisters, between 1351 and 1377

35. (left) Westerleigh church, tower, Perpendicular
36. (right) Yate church, tower, Perpendicular

37. (left) Mitcheldean church, largely fourteenth century
38. (right) Abson church, tower Perpendicular, nave windows late
sixteenth-early seventeenth century

39. (left) Abson church, font, Perpendicular

40. (right) Ashchurch church, rood screen, Perpendicular

41. (below right) Gloucester Cathedral, tile with the Berkeley arms, fifteenth century

42 and 43. Tewkesbury Abbey, presbytery, stained glass, 1340/4

44. (right) Arling-
ham church, stained
glass, c. 1340

45. (below right)
Tredington church,
stained glass,
fourteenth century

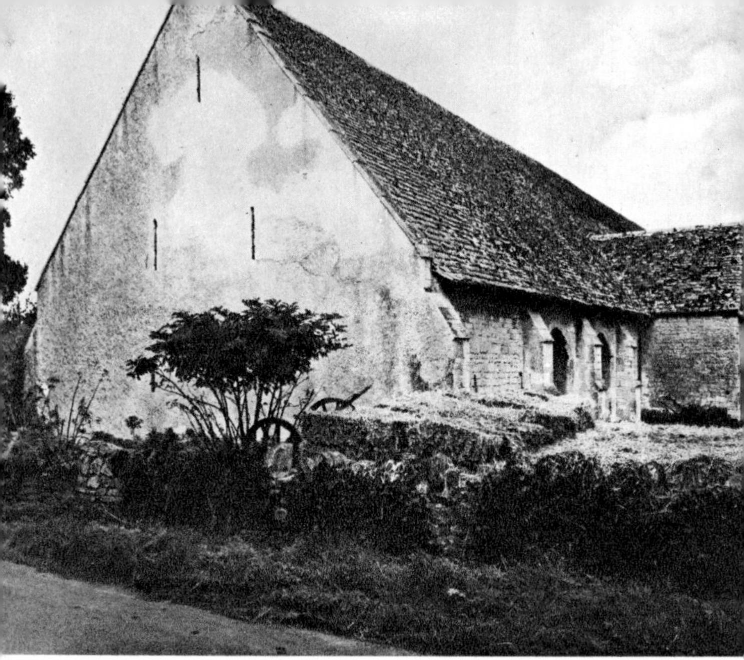
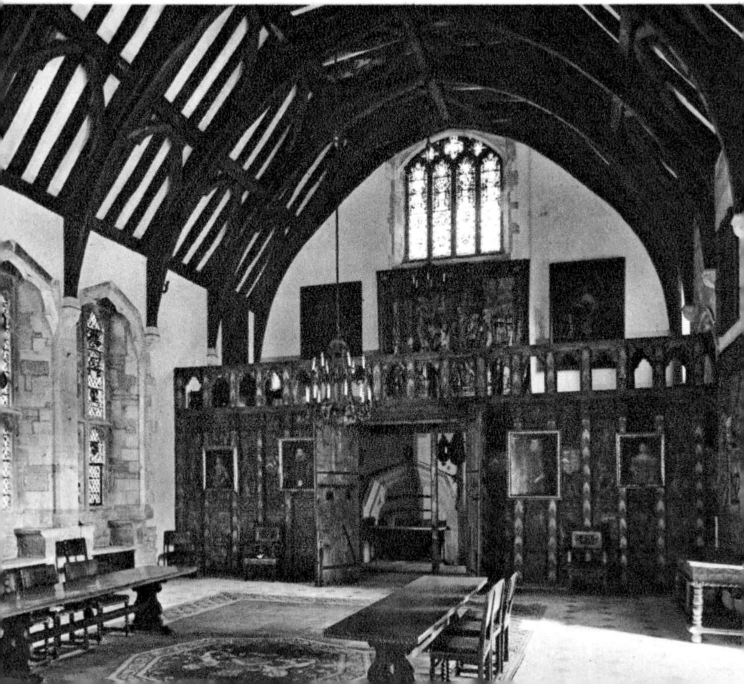

46. (above left) Frocester, tithe barn, *c.* 1300
47. (left) Berkeley Castle, Great Hall, *c.* 1340–50
48. (above) Berkeley Castle, doorway in Great Hall, *c.* 1340–50

49. (left) Iron Acton, churchyard cross, early fifteenth century
50. (above) Tewkesbury Abbey, Beauchamp Chapel, c. 1430

51. (above left) Tewkesbury Abbey, Wakeman Cenotaph, *c.* 1450
52. (left) Berkeley church, monument to James, eleventh Lord
Berkeley, †1463
53. (above) Gloucester Cathedral, crossing, 1450s

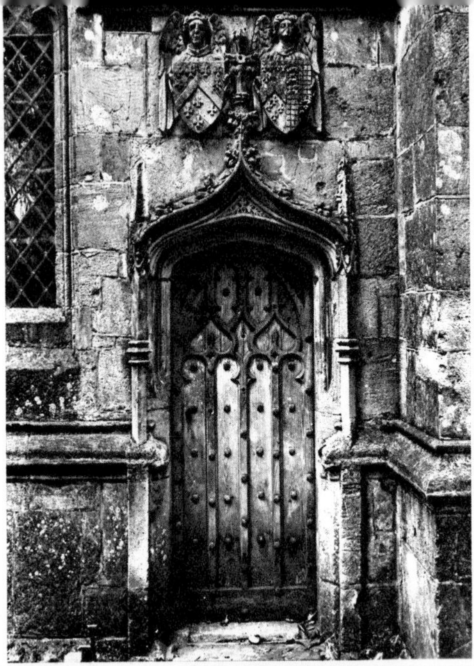

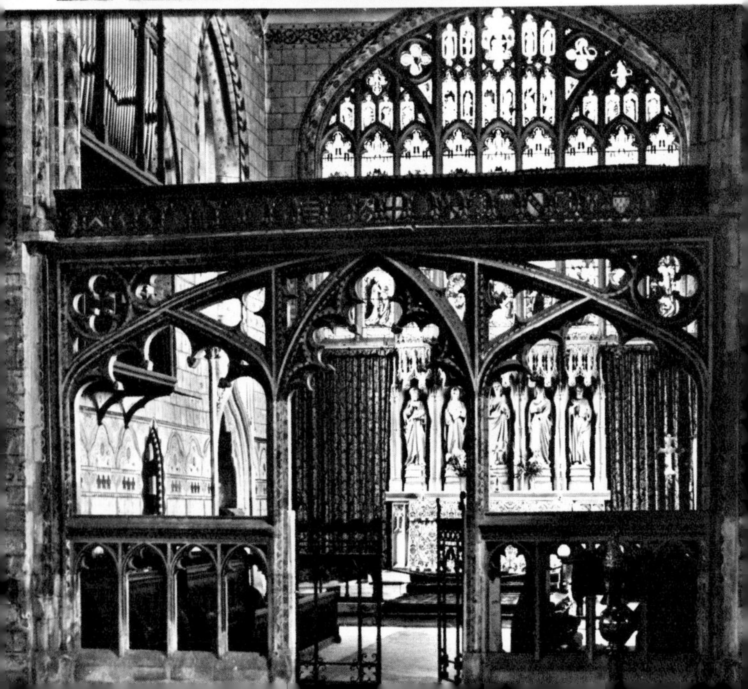

54. (above left) Berkeley church, priest's door, mid fifteenth century
55. (left) Berkeley church, screen, fifteenth century
56. (above) Tortworth church, stained glass, fifteenth century

57. (above left) Thornbury church, chiefly fifteenth century, tower
c. 1540

58. (left) Upleadon church, tower *c.* 1500

59. (above) Gloucester, The New Inn, *c.* 1457

60. (left) Gloucester, Bishop Hooper's Lodging, *c.* 1500 (*left*), and house of the early seventeenth century (*right*)

61. (below left) Thornbury Castle, begun *c.* 1511

62. (right) Kingswood near Wotton-under-Edge, window in abbey gatehouse, sixteenth century

63. (below right) Bishop's Cleeve church, west gallery, Jacobean

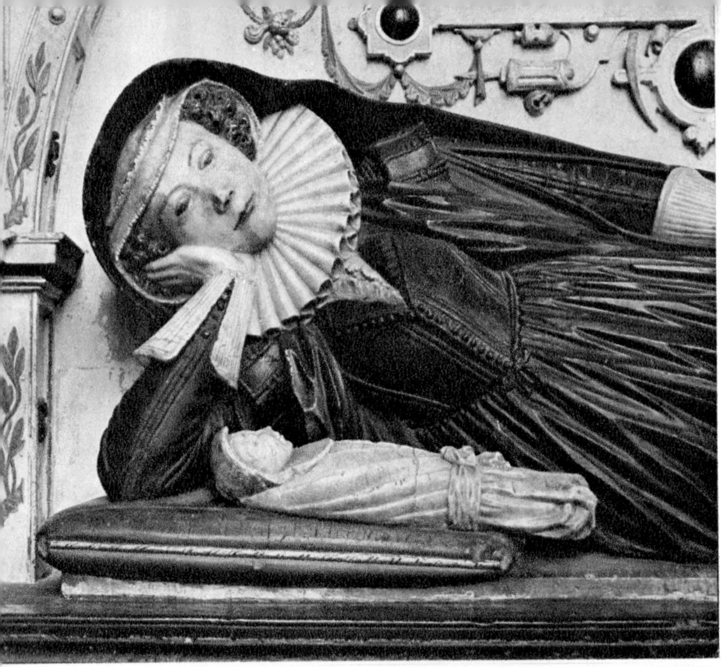

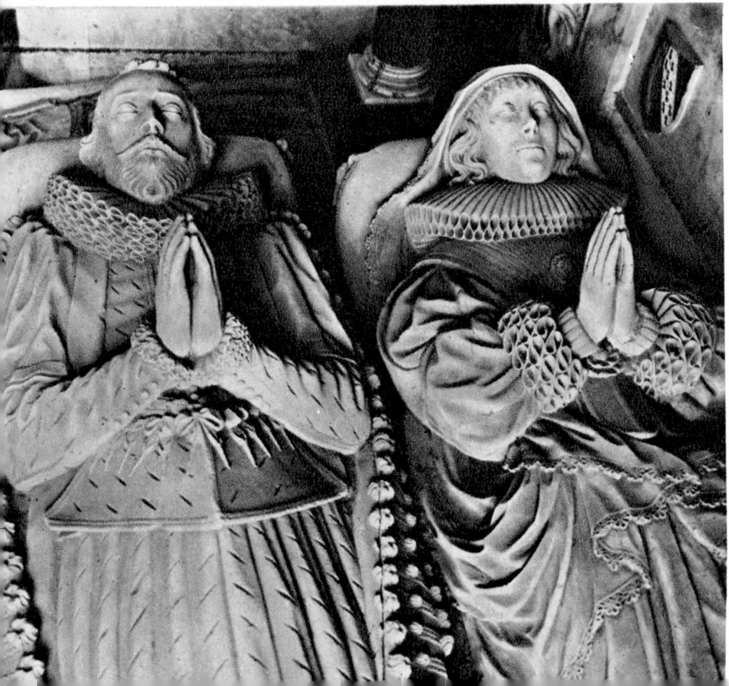

64. (above left) Gloucester Cathedral, monument to Elizabeth Williams †1622, by Samuel Baldwin

65. (left) Bishop's Cleeve church, monument to Richard de la Bere †1636

66. (above) Preston Court, complete before 1608

67. (above) Highnam Court, central doorcase, c. 1658
68. (above right) Elmore churchyard, table-tomb, seventeenth-eighteenth century
69. (right) Elmore Court, gates, by William Edney, before 1712

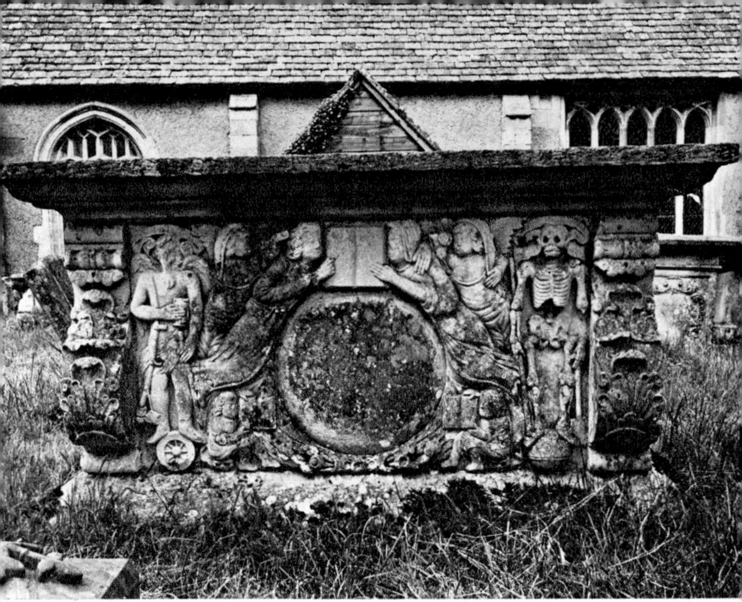

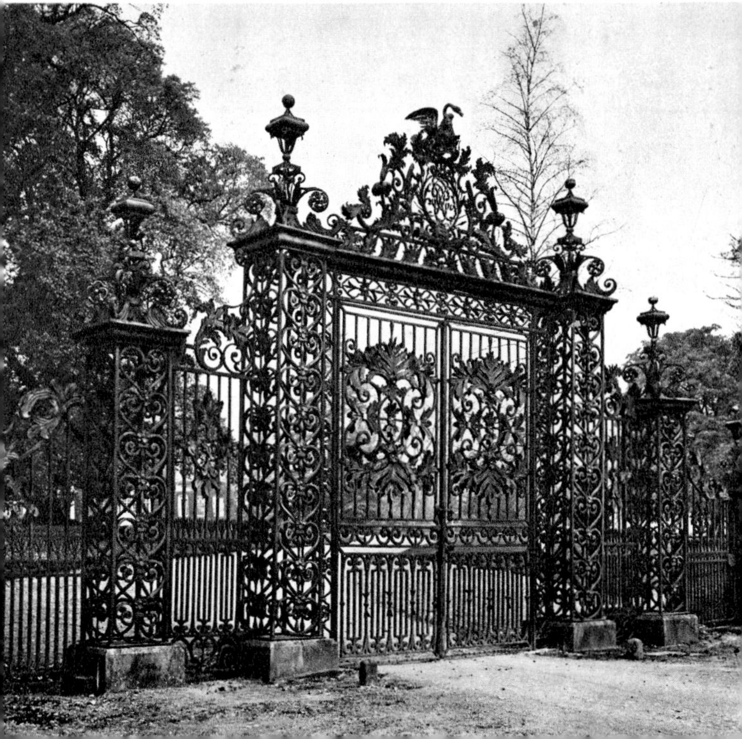

70. (left) Gloucester, Ladybellegate House, early eighteenth century, plasterwork on the staircase

71. (below left) Eastington, Alkerton Grange, gazebo, early eighteenth century

72. (right) Gloucester, Bearland Lodge, early eighteenth century

73. (below right) Frenchay, Unitarian church, 1720

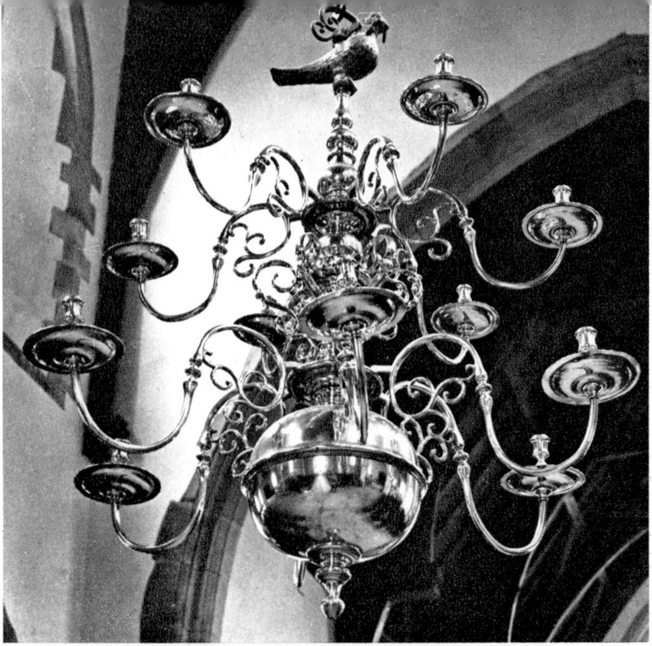

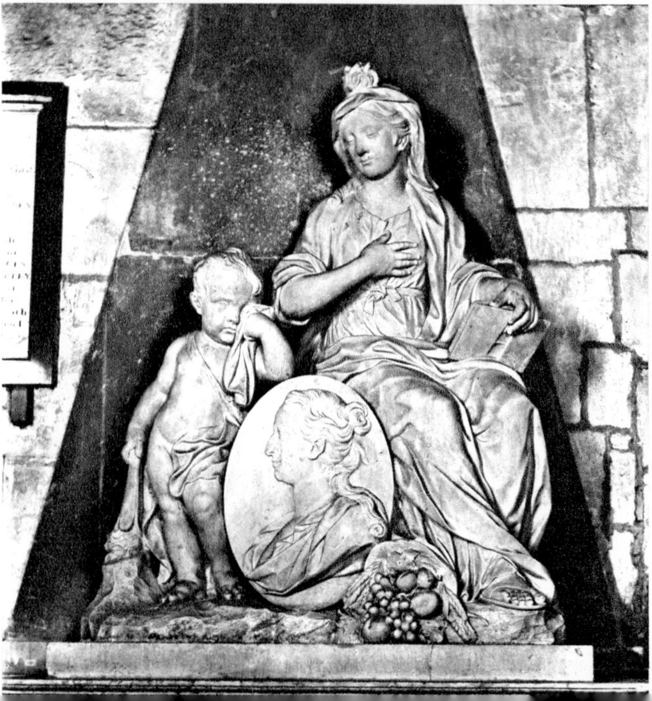

74. (above left) Newland church, chandelier, 1724–5
75. (left) Gloucester, St Mary de Crypt, monument to Mrs Snell
†1746, by Peter Scheemakers
76. (above) Frampton-on-Severn, Frampton Court, orangery, c. 1752

THE SEA SHALL GIVE UP THE DEAD

Sacred to the Memory of *SARAH MORLEY*, Wife of JAMES MORLEY Esqr of *Bombay* in the *East Indies*, and Daughter of Mr JAMES RICHARDSON, of *Newent* in this County.

Impelled by a tender and conscientious Solicitude to discharge her parental Duties in person, she embarked with her young Family when their Health and Education required their removal to England, and, having sustained the pains of Child birth at Sea, she died, a few days after that event, on the 25th of May 1784, in the twenty ninth year of her Age.

Of seven Children, the Issue of her Marriage, one Son and three Daughters survived to lament the untimely Loss of an invaluable Mother.

Her Husband erected this Monument, to testify his grateful and affectionate Remembrance of a Wife whose exemplary Virtues and amiable domestic Qualities endeared her to him beyond all that Language can express.

77. (above left) Gloucester Cathedral, monument to Sarah Morley
†1784, by John Flaxman
78. (left) Bishop's Cleeve, rectory, wall painting, 1810
79. (top) Tewkesbury, Mythe Bridge, by Thomas Telford, 1823–6
80. (above) Toddington Manor, by Charles Hanbury-Tracy, 1820–35

81. (above left) Frampton-on-Severn, canal house, by Robert Mylne
82. (left) Cheltenham, St Paul, by John B. Forbes, 1827–31
83. (top) Cheltenham, Christ Church, by R.W.& C. Jearrad, 1838–40
84. (above) Cheltenham, Montpellier Spa (Lloyds Bank), by G.A. Underwood, 1817, and J.B. Papworth, 1825

85. (above) Cheltenham, Municipal Offices, *c.* 1823
86. (above right) Cheltenham, Berkeley Place, before *c.* 1820, balcony
87. (right) Cheltenham, Oriel Terrace, 1824, balcony

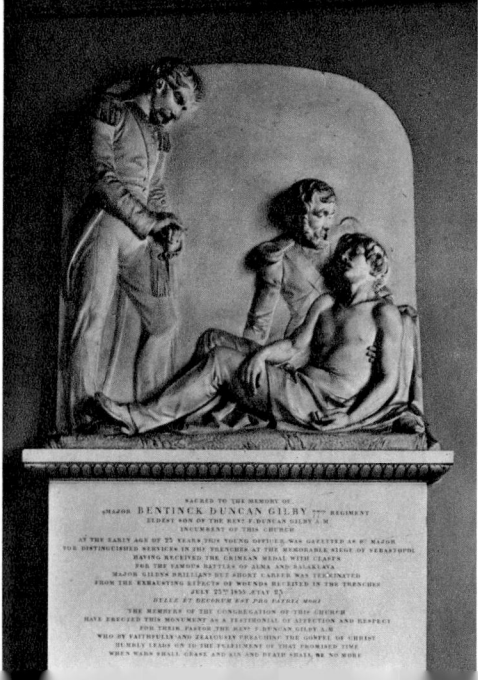

88. (above left) Cheltenham, Pittville Pump Room, by John Forbes, 1825–30
89. (left) Cheltenham, St James, monument to Bentinck Gilby, by Peter Hollins, 1855
90. (above) Cheltenham, Pittville Pump Room, by John Forbes, 1825–30

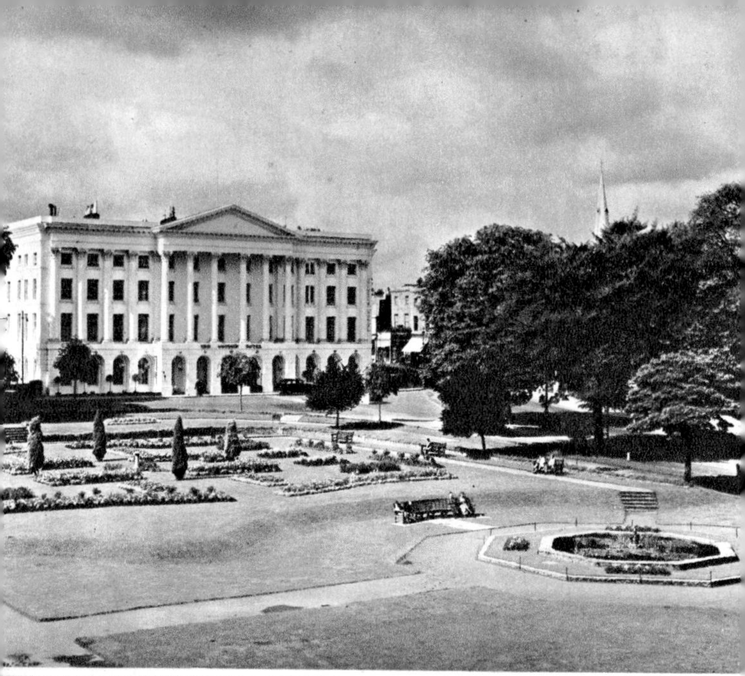

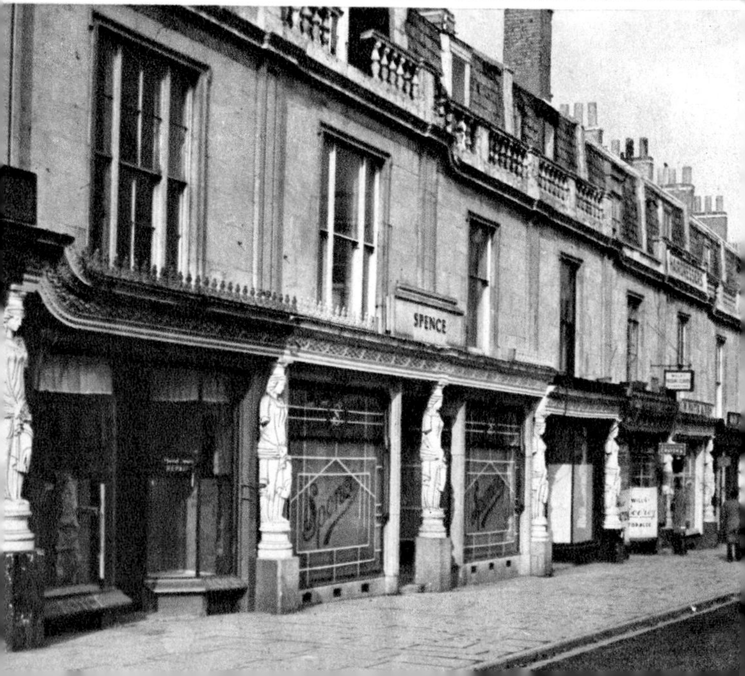
SPENCE

91. (above left) Cheltenham, Queen's Hotel, by R. W. & C. Jearrad,
1838
92. (left) Cheltenham, Montpellier Walk, by W. H. Knight,
c. 1840, caryatids by J. C. F. Rossi and W. G. Brown
93. (top) Coalpit Heath, vicarage, by William Butterfield, 1845
94. (above) Highnam, vicarage, by Henry Woodyer, 1852

95. (left) Highnam
church, by Henry
Woodyer and
Thomas Gambier-
Parry, 1847–51

96. (right) Tod-
dington church, by
G. E. Street,
1873–9

97. (below)
Huntley church, by
S. S. Teulon,
1861–3

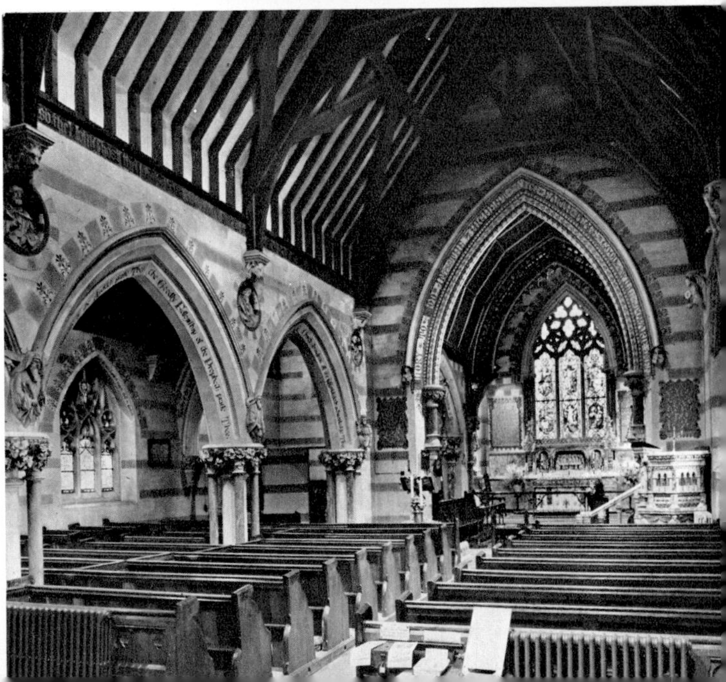

98. (left) Forthampton Court, staircase, by Philip Webb, *c.* 1891
99. (above) Kempley church, by Randall Wells, 1903

CANON OF THIS CATHEDRAL
AND H.M. INSPECTOR OF
SCHOOLS...

100. (left) Gloucester Cathedral, monument to Canon E. D. Tinling
†1897, by Henry Wilson
101. (top) Gloucester, St Aldate, by Robert Potter & Richard Hare,
1964
102. (above) Oldbury-upon-Severn, atomic power station, 1966–7

103. Aust, Severn Bridge, by Sir Gilbert Roberts (Freeman, Fox & Partners) and Mott, Hay & Anderson, opened 1966

Witcombe's C15 font was given to St Andrew, Churchdown. –
PULPIT. Made up from C17 banisters and panels from the old
manor house. – HOLY TABLE. C17 inscription: 'Love as breth-
ren 1688'. – REREDOS. Made in 1904 from panels from a house
in Gloucester. – ROYAL ARMS. George III. – CANDELABRA.
C18, blacksmith's work; in the chancel. – Three-light brass
candlesticks in the nave. – MONUMENTS. Sir Michael Hicks
† 1710. Baroque tablet. – Howe Hicks † 1727. – Sir Howe
Hicks † 1801 by *Millard*. – Sir William Hicks † 1834 by *G.
Lewis.*

WITCOMBE PARK. The house built by Sir Michael Hicks, who
died in 1710, was pulled down shortly before 1891, when a
new house was built. All that remains of the C17 house is a
GAZEBO or summer house, dated 1697, with its polygonal
ogee-shaped roof of Cotswold slates, and a pair of handsome
stone gatepiers with finials. The C19 house is jerry-built and
really unworthy of its setting in this park-like combe below the
wooded edge of the Cotswold escarpment. At the rear is the
domestic wing of an earlier house.

THE COTTAGE IN THE PARK. C16. Stone. Two gabled dormer
windows, one with a sundial and date-stone 1617. Round
stone chimney; stone spiral stairs.

RECTORY. 1828, with later additions.

SCHOOL. 1845. Now a private residence.

GREEN FARM. Picturesque timber-framed building with a
cruck truss visible on the N end. The similar frame at the S end
is hidden by additional rooms.

WITCOMBE FARM. C16. Stone, with mullioned windows.
Panelled dining room. One room has a carved stone chimneypiece with a plaster frieze with the initials C.H. and date 1665.
On the S front a stone is inscribed 'Love the truth, Sin God
doth hate and be content with thine estate.'

ROUND HOUSE. Built by Sir William Hicks, who died in 1834,
as a lodge for Witcombe Park, with pointed windows and
originally a conical thatched roof; now modernized.

Great Witcombe is the site of a ROMAN VILLA of courtyard type,
first excavated by Lysons, and re-excavated in 1938–9. Dating
evidence suggests that occupation began in the late C1, but the
visible building, consisting of two wings linked by a corridor,
is later.

GREET

MANOR FARMHOUSE. Built *c*.1600. The rear wing is original
with Tudor mullioned windows, but the front has been greatly

altered in the C19 and has a Jacobean style porch and large mullioned windows.

DOVECOTE. C17. Tall building with steep gables and lantern.

MANOR COTTAGES, opposite. Partly stone and partly timber-framed.

GRETTON

CHRIST CHURCH. 1868 by *John Drayton Wyatt*. 'A quintessentially Victorian building by Sir Gilbert Scott's trusted draughtsman, and one that would have pleased his master. All the detail is Gilbert Scottish (early C13 style) of the kind considered in its age to be thoroughly contemporary and untraditional. Alarmingly experienced: how can so much expertise lead only to aesthetic nullity?'; so wrote Goodhart-Rendel. It consists of an aisleless nave, apsidal chancel with single lights stretching up into semi-dormers, s transept with internal arch, cinquefoiled by heavy unmoulded cusps, and a s porch carried up into a modest octagonal tower and spire. In the w gable a rather good four-light window. Roofs internally with close-set scissor trusses, extremely complicated in the apse. The interior is unaltered and has typical Gilbert Scott FURNISHINGS. – STAINED GLASS. Three E windows by *Hardman*.

TOWER OF MEDIEVAL CHURCH. Probably C15, with a Tudor w window, diagonal w buttresses, a simple pointed tower arch with chamfered imposts, and a hipped Cotswold stone roof. The remainder of the church was demolished in 1868. Several old timber-framed and thatched cottages stand very close round the tower, forming a picturesque group.

TITHE FARMHOUSE. Early C18. Ashlar with Cotswold stone roof and modillion eaves cornice, chamfered quoins, mullioned and transomed windows, and a Tuscan pedimented doorcase. Inside, a good contemporary staircase.

GRETTON FARMHOUSE. C17. Ashlar, Cotswold stone roof with two gables, ground-floor mullioned windows, and small wooden oriels above. Doorway with carved archway dated 1656.

GUBBERHILL see TWYNING

GUBSHILL MANOR see TEWKESBURY, p. 378

HAGLOE see AWRE

THE HAIE see NEWNHAM-ON-SEVERN

HALLEN

ST JOHN. 1854 by *C. S. Fripp*. Small nave and chancel, Dec, with bellcote. – STAINED GLASS. E window by *Bell* of Bristol, 1854.

HAMBROOK *see* WINTERBOURNE

HAMFALLOW

A parish in the Berkeley Vale without a village, but with scattered isolated farms and cottages, set among small flat fields and many elm trees.

WANSWELL COURT. The original building was a hall-house of *c.*1450–60. The hall has three bays and an open roof supported on stone head corbels with datable head-dresses, and three tiers of wind-braces. Arched entrance to the former screens passage, and on the l. four-centred arches, one leading to a stone spiral staircase, another to a small panelled room. At the other end of the hall, which is almost square, is an embattled wall-plate. The high-table window comes down low and has window seats, and cinquefoiled tracery. The second lateral window has trefoiled tracery, and is narrower, to allow it to be placed between the entrance doorway and the former fireplace, now removed to the Great Hall in Berkeley Castle. The mid-C15 parlour projects, with the original spyholes in position facing outdoors diagonally. Another squint at the back of the hall. The parlour has moulded beams. Early C16 addition at the back, with a moulded stone fireplace and moulded beams. The other additions are late C17.

ACTON HALL. Late C18, of brick, with a stone cornice, parapet, and pediment with an elliptical window in the tympanum. Three storeys and five bays with a central stone Venetian window on the first floor. Stone Tuscan portico.

OLDLANDS FARM. On an irregular plan. Possibly C16 with later additions. Round stone chimney.

BREADSTONE MANOR FARM. Medieval in origin, partly stone and partly timber-framed, with a four-centred arched stone doorway. The C18 rusticated gateposts have ball-finials.

GREEN FARM has a curious outbuilding with a pyramid roof. – Early C16 TILES from Thornbury Castle.

BREADSTONE HOUSE. Early Victorian Gothic. Gables with bargeboards, oriel windows, and a broad porch with castellated turrets.

HANHAM

CHRIST CHURCH. 1842 by *Thomas Foster* for the Rev. H. T. Ellacombe. An auditorium church almost on a Nonconformist plan, with pews in the centre of the nave. Neo-E.E., with W bellcote. Chancel added in 1897. – FONT. 1842. Stone octagon enriched with diaper-work on clustered shafts. Crocketed wooden cover.

OLD BAPTIST CHAPEL, Hanham Street. Built *c.*1721 (foundation 1714) – the oldest existing Nonconformist chapel in the district. Stone, with parapet and round-headed windows. (Derelict in 1965.)

THE GRANGE, Hanham Street. Early C19 classical. Symmetrical two-storey, three-bay façade with a Roman Doric portico covering the central bay.

HANHAM MOUNT COTTAGES. Pre-1739; the cottages in which the preachers John Wesley and George Whitefield congregated for the earliest open-air sermons.

HANHAM ABBOTS

ST GEORGE. The church consists of nave, chancel, S aisle, N porch, and W tower, which is attached to the E wing of Hanham Court. It dates from the C14 but was extensively restored in 1909 by *Bligh Bond*; previous restoration by *Pope, Bindon & Clark*, 1854. C15 tower. Pierced parapet with large angle pinnacles and smaller ones in between, and gargoyles at the corners. In the N porch a C14 arch and original timber roof; the inner door has good C14 enrichments, a crocketed arch surmounted by an elaborate finial and with crocketed pinnacles either side and a trefoil-headed niche above. Inside, C15 S arcade of three bays. Plastered wagon roof in the aisle, the E end of which is now a vestry but may have been a Lady Chapel. The Perp windows all appear to be C19 or later restorations. Nave and chancel roofs also renewed. In the sanctuary a beautiful C13 PILLAR PISCINA. The pillar is fluted and has a sculptured capital of conventional foliage. – FONT. Norman, with a plain four-sided scalloped bowl resting on a roll and circular mouldings with four spurs on the plinth. It and the piscina probably came from Keynsham Abbey. – FURNISHINGS. Bishop's Chair, 1616. – Kneeling stools made by *W. Craymen*, 1854. – BELL. Pre-Reformation. – PLATE. Chalice, 1572; Paten, 1690.

HANHAM COURT has the reputation of being on medieval if not Norman foundations; the manor was given to Keynsham Abbey c.1330. The present house consists of a main block with a wing running E to the church tower. The former has two storeys plus basement plus gabled attics; the latter has three storeys, with a five-storey octagonal turret in the angle with a C19 cupola. The entrance, approached through an arch in the E wing, is in the main block facing E, and this elevation looks c16/17, with its gables, finials, and mullioned windows. E wing with dentilled cornice and parapet and C18 fenestration; the windows over the archway have niches either side. In the dining room C16 oak panelling and screen. The drive is railed off from the church by wrought-iron railings and gates; the gates on the opposite side have an overthrow with heraldic shield.

Adjacent is the TITHE BARN, probably C15, of Pennant stone rubble with angle buttresses. Central two-storey porch to the W, with pyramidal roof and a wide four-centred arched opening. Open timber roof with tie- and collar-beams, two purlins, and arched wind-braces.

SALLY-ON-THE-BARN, ¼ m. NE. A barn at Court Farm, called thus because of a stone statue of Ceres placed on the coping. Of limestone rubble with Pennant stone dressings, it has C18 features; the porch has a wide segmental arch with a keystone, and doors with original ironwork.

In WEST HANHAM, CASTLE INN FARM and the house next door have polite Georgian fronts. At HANHAM MILLS a Georgian house on the bank of the Avon dated 1726.

HANHAM HALL, Whittucks Road, 1 m. NW of the church. C17. Projecting gabled wings to the S with lunette windows and a recessed central portion with six gabled dormers. Central clock turret with wooden arcaded lantern and cupola. The fenestration is mostly C18. Inside, a late C17 staircase with twisted balusters, and moulded and ramped handrail. The rear elevation is confused by attached hospital buildings at the back.

HARDWICKE   7010

ST NICHOLAS. C13, but much altered in the C19, when the E window was introduced from Haresfield. C13 SW tower with Perp battlements. S porch with a good E.E. S doorway with jamb shafts having stiff-leaf capitals. Nave and chancel with N and S aisles. The S nave arcade of three bays was rebuilt c.1840, and the N aisle added by *Waller* in 1876 with an arcade copying that on the S. The broad C13 chancel, cleared of all choir stalls, opens into the S chancel aisle or chapel with a classical archway; the chapel has a charming little geometrical Dec E window. The E.E. chancel arch, rebated for a screen, has a pretty double Perp squint on the S side, with an image bracket on the mullion. Two PISCINAS side by side in the chancel, with a window above which now opens into the S chapel. Apart from the chapel, the walls are plastered and limewashed. – FONT. C13 arcaded bowl with a pedestal of eight shafts. – COMMUNION RAILS. Laudian. – STAINED GLASS. E window by *O'Connor*, 1854. Heraldic shield in the tracery. – ORGAN CASE, at the W end of the N aisle. By *Stephen Dykes Bower*, c.1937. – PLATE. Chalice and Paten Cover, 1572; Chalice, Paten, and Flagon, 1842. – MONUMENTS. Recumbent stone effigy of John Trye † 1591, in armour, and his small son Peregrine, who only comes up to his knee. Crude figures; but the whole monument, which has a Renaissance canopy, columns with Ionic capitals, and a shield of many quarterings, is differently treated each side in every detail, and has an admirable countryfied directness. It is also very well placed between the chancel and S aisle. – In the S aisle five more C16 and C17 tomb-chests to the Trye family, with Baroque ornament and heraldry and often with very snobbish inscriptions. – In the N vestry tablet to Richard Martin † 1818, by *T. King* of Bath. Neo-Greek, with draped urn.

HARDWICKE COURT. Only the cellars of the C17 house remain. In the C18 it was the seat of a Lord Chancellor, the Earl of Hardwicke. The main block was rebuilt by *Sir Robert Smirke* in 1818, for Thomas Lloyd-Baker.* Front of three storeys and five sash windows. One-bay, two-storey wings either side, with three-light windows. The central portion of one bay breaks forward and has a simple pilastered porch. The entrance hall is well contrived, with a stair-well completely in the rear, and with wrought-iron balusters. The room on the l. has a Chinese wallpaper with bamboo surrounds. Victorian addition at the back of the house. In the C19 Thomas Fulljames made plans for the aggrandisement of the house, but they were luckily not carried out. The remains of a late C17 formal GARDEN survive, with a straight canal.

THE OLD HALL. Now two cottages, restored by *C. D. Carus-Wilson*. Timber-framed, with three C15 cruck trusses not

* Information supplied by Col. A. Lloyd-Baker.

visible from the outside. HARDWICKE FARM is also of cruck construction.

On the Gloucester–Berkeley Canal opposite the Pilot public house is a CANAL KEEPER'S HOUSE (one of many; cf. Gloucester, p. 241) with a portico with fluted Doric columns and pediment; designed by *Mylne*.

MADAM'S END FARMHOUSE still has a thatched roof.

HARESFIELD
8010

ST PETER. The church was granted to the Prior of Lanthony, Gloucester, in 1161. As at Painswick, there are two chancels. On the N of the chancel adjoining the nave a small, much restored Norman window. The N door also has a restored Norman TYMPANUM. W tower C14. Three stages, battlements and a spire. Stair-vice on the NE similar to that at Eastington. C14 stone tierceron-vault. The windows generally are Dec, though the E window is Perp, and there is an ogee-headed lancet in the sanctuary. Aisleless nave with N and S porches. On the quoin of a N buttress a possibly Norman fertility SCULP-TURE. The church was restored and largely rebuilt after *c.*1841. Victorian diapering survives on the chancel arch, but other decoration was limewashed over in 1966. The nave roof has trussed collar-beams, with open Gothic arcading above, and in the spandrels. – FONT. One of the nine lead fonts in the county; but this one is probably C17, ornamented with simple cusped arcading, and buttoned vertical shafts. – ROOD SCREEN and other furnishings C19. – STAINED GLASS. E window by *Herbert Bryans*, 1899. – The Norman window has glass by *T. Willement*, 1846. – The sanctuary windows, St Paul on the N and St Peter on the S, are by *Willement*, 1847. – Also an excellent heraldic window by *Willement* in the S chancel, of three lights, with eleven shields of arms. – A nave N window by *Hardman*, 1887; very good. – PLATE. Almsdish, 1674; Chalice and Paten, 1737 by *Thomas Mason*; Flagon, 1750 by *John Wirgman*. – MONUMENTS. Recumbent effigy of a Lady, *c.*1320, in an ogee-arched recess with open cusped foliations. – About 1845 a second effigy of a Lady, also early C14, was placed in front of it, and the monuments were restored. – John Rogers † 1698, by *Reeve* of Gloucester. Painted stone, with vigorous sculpture of cherubs, clasped hands, symbolic figures, and heraldry. – Blanche Quiatt † 1592. With epitaph and heraldry. – John Rogers † 1683. Very homely rustic sculpture, and poem by Dryden. – John Rogers † 1670. Tablet with good lettering. – John Niblett † 1794, by *Millard*. Excellent 'Adam' urn, striped coloured marbles. – CHURCHYARD. Splendidly carved table-tombs.

VICARAGE. Built in 1846, for D. J. Niblett. Excellent romantic Tudor composition, set at the edge of the park near the church.

HARESFIELD COURT stands well in its flat park. The older part of the house dates from the Restoration of Charles II; a typical stone gabled manor house. It was enlarged in the 1860s when occupied by the antiquarian D. J. Niblett, who employed his younger brother, the architect member of the family, *Francis Niblett*.* The best feature of this addition is the beautifully French bow window of the former billiard room. The heraldic STAINED GLASS in this window is signed by *Swaine Bourne*, of Birmingham. The house was generally much altered and enlarged in 1892–3 by *Waller & Son*. The new drawing room then built remains a perfect period-piece. Waller was a thoroughly derivative architect, and his elaborate fireplace in this room is a *tour-de-force* comprising motifs from many sources. The beautiful sunflower tiles by *William de Morgan* may be a slightly later insertion. The bay window has yellow STAINED GLASS by *Lavers & Westlake*, with the words 'Musica, Concordia and Poesis'. Other windows in the house have similar glass, and another fireplace also has de Morgan tiles.

The RAILWAY INN, 1855, and MOUNT FARM, 1861, are both by *Francis Niblett*. Tudor; brick with stone dressings. Two-storey gabled porch at the farm.

ROUND HOUSE FARM. C17 timber-framed house with an C18 roughcast front and hipped stone roof. Half-timbered and thatched BARNS.

IRON AGE HILL-FORT, 1¼ m. SE. The W part, on Ring Hill, encloses Haresfield Beacon and about 15 acres (but the continuation SW of the Beacon is doubtful; RCHM). The E part, on Haresfield Hill, encloses about 20 acres; it was perhaps this only that was formerly known as Eastbury. The earthworks are univallate. A hoard of 3,000 Roman coins was found in 1837 'inside the s entrance'.

---

* *Francis Niblett* was born in 1814 and died in 1883; he is buried at Haresfield. Despite his sincere belief in the ideals of the Cambridge Camden Society, *The Ecclesiologist* slated Niblett's work and he was never an 'in' architect with them.

HARTPURY

St Mary. A possession of St Peter's Abbey, Gloucester, from Norman times. Norman w window in the nave; the tower added against it in the C14 has three stages and a Perp embattled top. C15 timber-framed w porch. On the nave s side some herringbone masonry survives, and a Norman doorway. Nave windows Dec. Large chancel also rebuilt in the C14, a beautiful early C14 E window with 'butterfly' tracery. Plain Norman chancel arch. The church was restored by *Waller* in 1882, and the walls are scraped. – FONT. C14 Perp. Octagonal bowl with pairs of quatrefoils in each face, and traceried panels on the stem. Wooden cover dated 1668. – PULPIT. Jacobean. – STAINED GLASS. Fragments of medieval glass in the nave. – Chancel window 1862 by *Clayton & Bell*. – PLATE. Chalice and Paten Cover, 1571. – MONUMENTS. Thomas Pulton † 1778. Classical marble tablet. – Catherine Canning † 1813, by *Cooke*. Neo-Greek. – Ann Webb † 1701. Vigorous countrified Baroque stone tablet, with torch, cherub-heads, flowers, and drapery.

Barn, formerly a Roman Catholic CHAPEL, built for French refugee nuns in 1830.

Tithe Barn. Very large stone barn, possibly C14. Eleven bays supported by buttresses, and two gabled porches on the s with pointed-chamfered arches and diagonal buttresses. Heraldic finials on the gable-ends. Massive roof timbers, with braced tiebeams carrying king-posts.

Hartpury Court, or Abbot's Place, has been rebuilt as a farmhouse in Tudor style.

Hartpury House. Late Georgian (the original garden side has a wrought-iron veranda), greatly enlarged by *Guy Dawber* in the early C20. His front is neo-classical, of brick with stone dressings. Two storeys with a central pediment and a projecting porch with segment-headed windows either side. On the l. a projecting one-storey wing.

Vicarage. Of brick, 1856 by *William Cullis*, builder of Tewkesbury.

School. 1869, possibly by *Woodyer*. Picturesque stone building with hipped gables and a turret.

Hill House. Probably C16, timber-framed gabled farmhouse, enlarged. Partly built on a rubble plinth and partly with close-set studding. Brick-nogged chimneys and stone tile roof. C18 brick garden GATEPIERS with ball-finials and wrought-

iron gates. In a rural situation with timber-framed COTTAGES
in the neighbourhood.

HASFIELD

ST PETER. The lower stages of the W tower are C13 and rather
similar to those at Tirley and Chaceley, the top stage C14 or
C15 with battlements and gargoyles. Stair-vice on the NE; Dec
W window. On the S face a shield with the date 1719, marking a
restoration. The Dec and Perp windows generally are restorations; the E window has flowing tracery in early C14 style. N
aisle by *Thomas Fulljames*,* 1850, with Dec windows and a
characteristic corbel table, or eaves cornice, decorated with
ballflower. The four-bay arcade, with octagonal piers, also has
ballflower on a bandcourse round each capital. Pointed arches
stopped by carved-angel corbels. S porch timber-framed.
Tower arch C13 or C14, of two chamfered orders. A C14
wagon roof survives in the nave, but the church is over-
restored. – FONT. Norman tub-shaped bowl on a chamfered
rectangular plinth. – PULPIT. Made up with Jacobean carved
wooden panels. – BENCH ENDS. Carved; C15/16. – STAINED
GLASS. E window by *Hardman*, c.1850. – S window in the
chancel by *A. Gibbs*, 1859; another by *G. Hedgeland*, 1852. –
PLATE. Chalice and Paten Cover, 1685; Almsplate, 1699 by
John Sutton; Flagon, 1719 by *Francis Garthorne*. – MONU-
MENTS. Tomb-chest of Dorothy Pauncefoote † 1568, with inscription round the lid, and shields of arms in the panelled
sides. – Henry Brown † 1620. Jacobean-Renaissance marble
monument with Corinthian columns and heraldry. – John
Barnes † 1820, by *Gardner*. – Thomas Fulljames † 1847.
HASFIELD COURT. Owned by the Pauncefoote family from
1200 to 1598, when they were obliged to sell owing to the per-
secution of recusants. The medieval or Early Tudor house was
probably moated. It is said to have had a separate gatehouse,
the ARCHWAY of which still exists, built into the stable block.
It is of excellent masonry and appears to date from c.1500.
Either side is a little quatrefoil opening. The house is L-shaped
and essentially of the later half of the C17, though at the back
there are signs of Early Tudor features. The exterior was completely changed c.1860, when it was bought from Thomas

* *Thomas Fulljames*, the architect, 1811-71, is buried in Hasfield church-
yard. He rebuilt the N aisle in memory of his father Thomas Fulljames of
Hasfield Court, who died in 1847. At this time he was in partnership with
Waller.

Fulljames by William Meath-Baker, who refaced the stone walls and added a neo-Renaissance porch, bow windows, and the fanciful silhouettes now presented by the gabled dormers. Two rooms contain C16 remains. An oak-panelled room has round the cornice a series of biblical texts in black lettering, the likely date of which is c.1550, for the inscription is interrupted by the initials R.P. and D.P. for Richard and Dorothy Pauncefoote, who died in 1559 and 1568. In the library Late Tudor panelling and pilasters rearranged to form bookcases. The Corinthian pilasters have arabesque enrichments, the chimneypiece male and female caryatids, and the panelling is decorated with double-tailed mermaids. – SCULPTURE. In a niche on the stairs a bust of the Duke of Wellington, by *Turnerelli*, 1814.

THE GREAT HOUSE, ¼ m. NE. L-shaped, partly timber-framed, and partly faced in stone or small bricks. C16/17. The N front of the E wing has exposed close-set studding and gables. The S and W fronts are partly stone and partly brick. On the S is a projecting stone garderobe next to the splendid Jacobean staircase. To the W four gables, two stone and two brick, with mullioned and transomed windows. Inside some Late Tudor or early C17 furnishings, including four-centred arched wooden doorways with carved spandrels, two good staircases with turned balusters, Jacobean pendants, and finials, a C17 panelled bedroom, and another with a plaster ceiling ornamented with *fleurs-de-lys*.

HEMPSTED

ST SWITHUN. Rebuilt in 1467–77, when Henry Dene, afterwards Archbishop of Canterbury, was Prior of Lanthony. Mostly ashlar-faced, with a central Perp tower with battlements enriched with panels of trefoil-headed tracery, and gargoyles. Normal buttressing, deeply moulded string-courses, and large Perp openings in the upper stage. In 1885–6 the Dec chancel was given a new roof and a new E window, and the N vestry built on. S porch Perp. The nave, lengthened by 12 ft in 1885, is well lit with restored or rebuilt Perp windows N, S, and W. Limewashed walls. Restored Perp roof with embattled tie-beams with pierced and enriched spandrels, ribs with carved bosses, and carved corbel heads, one of which shows a mitred head said to represent Henry Dene. The floor is now paved with stone flags. The tower is narrower than the chancel, so that the E arch responds are peculiarly constructed to project over the supporting piers. – FONT. Transitional with a pedestal of six shafts. – STAINED GLASS. A fragment of medieval glass in the tracery of the N window under the tower, showing a small mitred head, again said to be Henry Dene. – HATCHMENT. Samuel Lysons, rector of Rodmarton, † 1804, father of Samuel Lysons the antiquary. Arms impaling Peach of Chalford. – PLATE. Salver, 1697; Chalice and Paten, 1721; Flagon, 1721. – MONUMENTS. Brass to the children of Arthur Porter, 1548. – Painted recumbent stone effigy of Judge Richard Atkyns of Tuffley † 1610, great-grandfather of the county historian. – Good Baroque marble monument to Thomas Lysons † 1713. – Tablet to Samuel Lysons, the antiquary, † 1819, in neo-Greek taste. – Daniel Lysons † 1789, by *T. King* of Bath. – Sarah Lysons † 1808. – Tablets of 1824 and 1828 by *Cooke* of Gloucester; 1847 by *Tyley* of Bristol; 1826 by *W. Bussell* of Gloucester; 1816 by *Wood* of Gloucester; and 1821 by *J. Cale* of Hempsted. – In the CHURCHYARD the table-tomb of John Freeman, a Cavalier officer killed by a musket ball at the siege of Gloucester in 1643.

VILLAGE CROSS. Medieval, restored and re-positioned.

HEMPSTED HOUSE, formerly the rectory. Inscribed on the doorway:

> Who'er doth dwell within this door
> Thank God for Viscount Scudamore 1671.

Doorway of carved stone with Jacobean strapwork and finials and a pretty ogee Gothick arch (revival or survival?). Viscount Scudamore was a friend of Laud, and the inscription was set up by a grateful rector to honour the builder of the rectory a few years earlier. Brick, roughcast, with mullioned and transomed windows. Cruciform plan. At the head a three-storey projecting gable.

HEMPSTED COURT. Built by the Lysons family in the late C17 but demolished *c.*1959.

HEWELSFIELD

ST MARY MAGDALENE. One of the ancient churches on the edge of the Forest of Dean, 600 ft above the Wye. Norman nave, narrow N aisle, central tower, E.E. chancel, and N transept enlarged in the C16. The E.E. S porch has an outer chamfered arch on moulded corbels. Over the inner door is a Norman image niche. An E.E. W doorway leads into a small chamber on the s of the nave. The low central tower retains a Norman corbel table. On the N the nave roof continues in one slope over the aisle to within a few feet of the ground. In the chancel a priest's door on the s, and an Early Dec two-light window; the E window has plate tracery. Late Norman or Transitional four-bay arcade with cylindrical piers with round moulded capitals and round arches of two chamfered orders. Small lancet windows in the aisle, mostly restored. The tower arches E and W are plain E.E. with two chamfered orders which die off; the N arch has a single continuous chamfered order, with a trefoiled PISCINA in its E jamb, which must have belonged to an altar in the N transept. This transept was enlarged to the N in 1558. Arched entrance from the N aisle, wider than the aisle. The rood steps open out of the transept. – FONT. Early C13 octagonal scalloped bowl on a circular pedestal. – STAINED GLASS. E window by *Horace Wilkinson*. – PLATE. Chalice and Paten Cover, 1695. – MONUMENTS. Edmund Bond † 1742. Stone tablet with heraldry. – Anne Eddy † 1768. Stone and marble tablet with heraldry.

At BROCKWEIR, a hamlet 2 m. w, the following:

MORAVIAN CHAPEL. C19 with pointed windows, Art Nouveau glass, and a bellcote.

MANOR HOUSE. C16, facing the bridge over the Wye. Three-storey gable, and Tudor windows with arched lights and carved stops to the dripmoulds. Opposite, another probably Tudor house, GLENWYE. The OLD MALT HOUSE also has mullioned windows and a Tudor-arched stone doorway.

HEWLETTS see PRESTBURY

HIGHLEADON see RUDFORD

HIGHNAM 7010

HOLY INNOCENTS. 1847–51 by *Henry Woodyer*,* his first 95 major work after he left Butterfield's office, though it is not particularly Butterfieldian. It is, according to H.-R. Hitchcock, the 'most important Anglican example of painted internal polychromy, rivalling Pugin's St Giles, Cheadle'. Goodhart-Rendel thought it the 'fulfilment of the Pugin ideal'. It is certainly a very notable monument of the Oxford Movement.

* *Woodyer* was a man of flamboyant Bohemian manner, habitually dressed in an Inverness cloak and a crimson tie, and smoking a rare cigar. He was the kind of person who would not have been able to cross Butterfield's office doorstep in later years.

Thomas Gambier-Parry, the client, was himself responsible for the WALL PAINTINGS. He made a study of the technique used by Italian painters of the C14 and C15, and invented 'spirit fresco', suitable for wall painting in the English climate. His hopes have proved well founded, and the frescoes have retained their freshness to a remarkable degree.

A very large church for a country park, it has a magnificent W tower and spire, a very tall nave, with N and S aisles and chapels, and a chancel which completes an immensely impressive ensemble. The style is Dec and in some instances, particularly in the FONT and PULPIT, the detail is rather florid; but generally every detail reveals the best and costliest work of the period, especially the spire with its wonderful crocketed pinnacles. The interior is religiously dim. – The rood WALL PAINTING, with figures with golden haloes in low relief, is lit only by a single dormer either side. The walls are painted to simulate drapery, below a complete system of paintings by *Gambier-Parry*.* – The STAINED GLASS has a jewel-like quality and is seen to great advantage, comprising work by the best artists of the period. – E window by *Clayton & Bell*, 1859; nine scenes from the Life of Christ. – The N aisle has a complete set of windows by *Wailes* of Newcastle, 1850, and the S aisle a matching set by *Hardman*, from designs by *Pugin*. – The less good W window, and those in the S chapel, are by *O'Connor*, 1850. – PLATE. Chalice, Paten, and Almsdish by *Keith*, 1850; Butterfield pattern. – MONUMENTS. Bust of Annamaria Gambier-Parry † 1848. – Brass to Thomas Gambier-Parry † 1888. – Sir Hubert Parry † 1918.

Other buildings designed by *Woodyer*, N of the church, include a lodge, school, and vicarage with stables. The LODGE is of stone with a pretty round turret. Trefoil-headed windows, some with quatrefoils above, and without dripmoulds. The SCHOOL is similar, with slightly sprocketed eaves. The VICARAGE, of 1852, is full of characteristically original invention, with a polygonally arched porch. STABLES with a charming two-bay arcade.

HIGHNAM COURT. A large rectangular C17 house of brick with stone dressings, and two main storeys. Neither the exact date nor the architect‡ are known, though according to tradition it

---

* Gambier-Parry painted the roof of Ely Cathedral in 1865, and decorated a chapel in Gloucester Cathedral.

‡ According to information given by Mark Gambier-Parry, it was designed by *Edward Carpenter* (Murray's Guide says *Francis Carter*) in 1658.

was built in the later years of the Commonwealth, which would
appear to be correct. Characteristic of this period are the
prominent bracketed eaves cornice, and in particular the design
of the central garden doorcase with its broken scroll pediment, [67]
and heavy carved drops to the jambs. The details of the door
surround are typical of what Sir John Summerson calls
Artisan Mannerism. Above this is a stone niche with a carved
shell hood. The original plan of the house is still relatively
speaking intact, except on the first floor, where there are C19
changes, and on the ground floor as the result of the change of
entrance; but the most important interiors date from the mid
C18, and of these there are two rooms which are particularly
good. The plaster decoration of the Music Room is of a very
high order – wall panels with musical instruments in high relief
and elaborate swags and drops, Rococo in style, and probably
by *William Stocking* of Bristol, together with a ceiling in the
Adam manner. The neighbouring Gold Drawing Room also
has a good gilded Rococo ceiling with plasterwork modelled in
high relief, representing eagles, dolphins, and lions. The other
rooms are more restrained, but generally have good doorcases
and fireplaces; there is a particularly good fireplace on the first
floor with Bossi work of *c.*1770. Also a large main staircase with
an ornate wrought-iron balustrade, besides a smaller dog-leg
stair surviving in parts from the C17. Alterations and additions
were carried out in the C19; *c.*1840 by *Lewis Vulliamy* and
again in the 1870s. The new entrance was given a large pedimented portico on the N, with flanking walls and later a large
billiard room. This has hidden the N elevation of the original
house. Other alterations included the addition of ponderous
central dormers on the S, E, and W fronts and the renewal of the
other dormers; there are signs that the window surrounds and
cornices, and the string-course of the main storeys, are also
later additions. To the W is a large but relatively unobtrusive
office wing. NW of the house is an attractive STABLE BLOCK in
the Gothick style with battlements. The gardens, specially a
rock-garden, were laid out by *James Pulham*, who used a
Portland stone cement of his own, called Pulhamite, before
1850.

HILL   6090

ST MICHAEL. Situated almost in the garden of Hill Court and
approached only by a path across the park, the church retains
its Georgian atmosphere. It is medieval in origin. C14 W tower

and spire, with a tower arch of two chamfered orders, and a rib-vault springing from corbels ornamented with ballflower. The C13 chancel is raised four steps above the nave. One lancet window survives on the S. The other chancel windows are C14, mostly restored in 1870 with new tracery by *Ewan Christian*. Rebuilt Perp sanctus bellcote over the E gable of the nave. The Fust mortuary chapel, added to the S of the chancel in the early C18, was restored or rebuilt in the C19. The brass fixed to the door of the chapel has the arms of Sir Edward Fust † 1713. Nave rebuilt in 1759 by Sir Francis Fust. In 1909 *William Weir* and *Temple Moore* advised on the repair of the nave and reported that the windows had been rebuilt with old materials in the C18 and had never possessed tracery. The S porch had to be rebuilt and buttresses added; but it was due to them that the plastered walls were not interfered with, and the interesting family pew and furniture were retained. – FONT. Norman bowl cut down *c.*1550 into a hexagon, leaving the circular top untouched, and mounted on a Late Perp moulded plinth. – PULPIT. 1629, oak, enriched with carving and surmounted by a sounding-board. – MANOR PEW. C18, with a large panelled canopy. – SEATS. Early C16, with finely carved rectangular ends in excellent condition. – CARVINGS. Two heraldic fragments preserved loose in the chapel: a sinister hand clenched, the Poyntz crest, and the rebus of Abbot Newland (Nailheart) of Bristol; early C16. – PLATE. Chalice and Paten, 1576. – MONUMENTS. Lancelot Law † 1650, with Latin inscription describing his accidental death when shooting. – Tablet commemorating Sir Francis Fust, who 'in 1759 new modled and repaired this church'. – Sir John Fust † 1779. Classical coloured marble tablet. – Thomas Hobby † 1781, by *T. Paty* and Sons of Bristol. – Sarah Jones † 1812, by *Lancaster* of Bristol. – Flora Fust † 1841, by *J. M. Payton*. – Sir John Colt † 1845, by *Daw* of Berkeley. – Elizabeth Hamilton † 1855, by *Tyley*.

HILL COURT. Rebuilt in 1863–4, in rather a modest way compared with what it had been before. Classical. Two storeys, six bays, with a central pediment and hipped roof. Tetrastyle porch with bay windows either side. In the hall a fine wooden Renaissance chimneypiece, carved and gilt, with a central panel representing Diana reclining on a couch with stag and hounds near by, and emblematic carvings. The heraldry indicates a date *c.*1631. On the terrace in front a collection of stone urns of the C18 and C19 with arms showing the marriages of the Fust family. Centrally placed early C18 rusticated stone gatepiers with pulvinated friezes and ball-finials.

VICARAGE. Early C19 painted brick, with a long wing in the rear with Gothick windows. In the garden the ruins of a late C15 TITHE BARN.

HINTON 6000

A civil parish with no nucleus except at Purton and Sharpness.

ST JOHN, Purton. Mid C19. Consists only of a nave and apsidal sanctuary, with an elaborate timber roof.

The village of PURTON, on the Gloucester–Berkeley Canal, has several early C19 brick houses. Opposite the church is one of *Mylne*'s neo-Greek CANAL HOUSES, for bridgemen, with Doric columns *in antis*. MIDDLETON HOUSE is late C18, of brick, with a parapet, two storeys, and three bays. The windows have keystones and voussoirs. Fanlight over the doorway. Wrought-iron porch.

SHARPNESS. Even if *Robert Mylne* designed the charming bridgemen's houses which are such a feature of the Gloucester–Berkeley Canal, it is almost certain that *Telford* designed the old canal entrance LOCK at Sharpness Point, with its lockhouse. The canal was opened in 1827.

SEVERN–WYE RAILWAY BRIDGE. 1875–9 by *Keeling & Owen*. The existence of hard Devonian rocks, which outcrop in the red cliffs of Sharpness and Gatcombe, determined the location of this iron bridge. It consisted of two main spans of 327 ft over the main channel of the river, and nineteen lesser spans with a steam-operated swinging span over the Gloucester–Berkeley Canal. It was struck by an oil barge in 1960, and two of the spans were brought down; it has now been demolished.

SANIGER FARMHOUSE. C17, roughcast, with three gables, and a charming two-storey porch with three gables with ball-finials, and a plaster date inscription of 1718. Rusticated gateposts with ball-finials and scroll supports on the wall.

HOWN HALL *see* TAYNTON

HUCCLECOTE 8010

ST PHILIP AND ST JAMES. 1850 by *John Jacques & Son* of Gloucester. Chancel, nave, s porch, w turret with spirelet, and N aisle added by *F. W. Jones* in 1911. E. E., of stone, with trefoil-headed lancet windows. The N aisle has five transverse gables with grouped lancet windows. The nave is buttressed round the outside; inside it is quite spacious, with high king-post roof trusses. N arcade of five bays, with the choir in the first bay of the nave separated by a low screen wall. – FONT. Designed by *David Stratton-Davis* in 1965. – STAINED GLASS. E window by *William Warrington*, 1860, in violent purply-blue and hot red colours. – The side windows in the sanctuary by *J. Eadie Reid*, 1922. – PLATE. Chalice, Paten, and Flagon, 1849 by *John Keith*, probably Butterfield design.

Most of the older houses are situated in Barnwood Road, the old Ermine Street; but they are rapidly being demolished to make way for modern development.

FOLEY HOUSE, on the corner of Green Lane, is an extraordinary mid-C19 building with a three-storey tower, and an attic in a steep, pointed roof of bands of fish-scale tiles. Brick-built, it has long-and-short stone quoins and an arcaded frieze. One-storey pavilion wing with a hexagonal pointed roof, flanked by square projections set diagonally and linked by a veranda with three trefoil-headed arches.

PARSONAGE COTTAGE, next in Green Lane, is a one-storey timber-framed building of the C16. No. 117 BARNWOOD ROAD is also timber-framed, probably C17 but much restored and altered. Further towards Gloucester a group of early C19 villas. THE CEDARS is stuccoed and has a veranda; HUCCLE-COTE COURT is rather earlier, of painted brick, with a central pediment and lower matching wings either side.

There is at Hucclecote a ROMAN VILLA of corridor type. The site was occupied in the C1 to C2, possibly by a wooden building. About 150 the centre part of the masonry building was erected; later the N and S wings were added. Alterations continued late: a coin of c. A.D. 395 was found beneath a tessellated floor.

HUNTLEY

ST JOHN THE BAPTIST. The C12 church was demolished in 1861, except for the ancient tower, which was restored, and a spire of equal height added by *S. S. Teulon*, whose new church in his own Dec style was consecrated in 1863. The very large sum of money provided came from the rector, Daniel Capper. Teulon used the old red sandstone of the district and Pains-wick stone for the spire. The church has a nave, N aisle, S porch, transepts, and chancel. Goodhart-Rendel called it 'one of the most interesting buildings in England', and it certainly shows Teulon in a very enterprising mood. The s transept window, blocked internally by the organ, has some of Teulon's most flamboyant tracery. On the outside NE corner a pretty turreted stair leading to the vestry. Interior decoration very rich, with carving by *Earp;** in the spandrels of the three-bay arcade on the N are the four evangelists, brilliantly sculptured, in medallions, and above them the evangelistic symbols carved on corbels supporting the roof trusses. The nave roof is open, but the chancel roof is polygonal and panelled with painted and gilded ribs and carved bosses over the sanctuary. Fretted and painted wooden sanctuary arch, a kind of proscenium arch which gives a dramatic and theatrical effect when the altar is lit up. The capitals of the arcade have deeply carved flowers, and those in the chancel have symbols of the Passion. Texts are inscribed on all the arches and elsewhere. The internal walling is of red and white stone with profuse red mastic inlays in the white. – LECTERN, PULPIT, and REREDOS of alabaster and marble. On show at the Great Exhibition of 1851. – STAINED GLASS by *Lavers & Barraud*, but the windows in the nave and aisle are glazed with glass of a peculiar kind designed by Teulon. They represent biblical scenes drawn in brown line with coloured shading and have line illustrations enriched with grisaille ornamentation and coloured borders. – CHURCH-YARD. A fair collection of c18 and c19 Forest-stone headstones.

SCHOOL. Dated 1875, and not a bad neighbour for the church.

RECTORY. 1866, Elizabethan, but with stepped gables. Brick with Bath stone dressings.

HUNTLEY MANOR. Built by *S. S. Teulon* at the same time as the church. The rainwater-heads are dated 1862. The style is usually described as 'French Château', but it shows much of Teulon's characteristic originality. The mansard roof is enlivened with turrets and ornamental iron finials – thoroughly spiky and blending beautifully with the coniferous trees planted round about. Inside, ceilings with ribs and bosses. The carved fireplaces in Teulon's brand of Gothic are highly inventive. The sash windows are not Gothic; so there is no gloom. Splendidly coloured stained glass armorial window with an Art Nouveau touch on the staircase. The house was sympathetically restored in 1964 by *Sir Percy Thomas & Partners*.

* *Earp* was Street's principal sculptor and worked at St John, Kennington, and also for Scott and many others.

INGST *see* OLVESTON

6080

IRON ACTON

ST JAMES. The w tower was presumably built by Robert Poyntz, who died in 1439.* Three stages, diagonal buttresses, pinnacles, and gargoyles. In the lower stage a large blind arcade with trefoil-headed ogee arches supporting shields, and divided by pinnacles. The middle stage on the N has two image niches, and on the panelled parapet on this side is the sculptured waist-length figure of a knight, thought to represent Sir John Poyntz who died in 1376, and to have been placed here by his son when he built the tower. The rest of the church is Perp. Clerestoried nave with s aisle and chapel, chancel, and N porch of two storeys with a squint in the upper chamber, a pillar stoup in the lower, and an embattled gabled parapet with a band of panelling below the window, renewed when the church was restored in 1878-9 by *Sir T. G. Jackson*. N projection for the rood stairs. Perp s aisle, buttressed. Tall nave of three bays and with wagon roof; Perp arcade on the s. Perp chancel arch, and arcade of three bays with flat Perp arches to the chapel. Chancel and chapel have ceiled wagon roofs with ribs and carved bosses and an embattled wall-plate. Grotesque capitals to the tower arch. Fan-vault under the tower, and on the N a small chamber once used as a lock-up. – FONT. C19, with attached stone reading desk. – PULPIT. 1624, with sounding-board. – TEXTS, now in the porch, probably C18, with ornamental triangular frames. – FLOOR in the chancel. 1880, an admirable copy of a Roman mosaic pavement. – BENCHES. C16 linenfold ends, some original. – CHANDELIER. 1725; Bristol style. – REREDOS behind the high altar, carved and painted, to the designs of *F. C. Eden*, c.1930, with images in restored niches either side. – Classical SCREEN behind the s altar, by *F. C. Eden*, painted wood simulating marble. It is half-way into the Poyntz chapel, the PISCINA for the original aisle being further w, in the s wall. – STAINED GLASS. In the N window of the chancel fragments of glass of the time of Edward IV, including a crowned king, a pope, and a bishop. – Window in the s aisle in memory of Agnes King † 1894, by *Bewsey*. – PLATE. Pair of Chalices and Patens,

* The tomb inscription reads: 'Here lyeth Robert Poyntz Lord of Iron Acton and this stepyl here maked.' Lysons conjectured from this that he built the tower, but it could mean the church or the churchyard cross, or all three.

1792 by *Peter & Anne Bateman*. – MONUMENTS. Effigy of a Knight *temp*. Edward III, and therefore possibly Sir John Poyntz † 1376. – Effigy of an unknown Lady, early C15. – Three incised slabs, representing Robert Poyntz † 1439 and his two wives Anne and Katherine, the latter defaced with an inscription of 1631. – Early C16 canopied tomb without inscription. On the tomb-chest lozenge panels with roses surrounded by acanthus leaves. Three shields with heraldic animal supporters at the back. Pierced canopy with cresting and finials. – C17 funeral helmet, spur, and piece of leather surcoat. – Jacobean two-tier tomb-chest in the chancel with crude balusters. – William Machin † 1716. Classical tablet. – Mary Senior † 1814, by *Tyley*. – Thomas Richardson † 1834, by *Tyley*. – Bluett Jones † 1836, by *O. Greenway*. – John Alway † 1842, by *J. Thomas* of Bristol.

CHURCHYARD CROSS. Probably a memorial cross to a mem- 49 ber of the Poyntz family of the early C15. Square, on a base of three octagonal steps, with four-centred arches with ogee hood-moulds and four clustered shafts, supported by light buttresses which originally terminated in pinnacles. There was also an octagonal shaft in the centre, the base and cap of which only remain; from it sprang a rib-vault. Upper stage with two shields on each face, four charged with the symbols of the Passion, and two bearing the arms of Acton, and Acton impaling FitzNicoll.* This supports a four-sided shaft with cinquefoiled panels and canopies. The cross itself has disappeared. Open panelling on three sides; the fourth facing the church is blank. – FONT. Remains of an early C18 font, in the churchyard.

OLD RECTORY. Rebuilt in the early C19 on the SW side of the church. Some arched doorways and walls of the earlier house remain to the W of the church. The parson put a public footpath through a tunnel to prevent it crossing the approach to his new house.

The village has several old houses. The LAMB INN is dated 1690 and has two three-storey gables. A house opposite with two gables is dated 1688.

HILL HOUSE. C18 ashlar front of two storeys and seven bays. Pedimented doorway and window above.

IRON ACTON COURT. The Poyntz family were Lords of the Manor from 1344 to 1680. Their house was probably rebuilt in

---

* Robert Poyntz's second wife was Katherine FitzNicoll, and his grandmother was Maud Acton.

the C16 and altered in the C17. The large courtyard E of the house is entered by a four-centred archway under an elaborate Renaissance pediment, with low-relief carving in the spandrels. The house itself consists of a rectangular block with a NW wing, and a projecting stair-turret in the angle with a newel staircase. C15 Perp window on the E. A central passage with Tudor arched openings runs through the house. The house has not been restored, and in 1966 it was in a poor state of repair.

ALGARS MANOR. Tudor in origin.

At LATTERIDGE, a hamlet 1 m. NW, several C17 and C18 farmhouses.

6020   KEMPLEY

99 ST EDWARD THE CONFESSOR. 1903 by *Randall Wells*, who was Lethaby's resident clerk-of-works at Brockhampton-by-Ross church in 1902; aged about twenty-five, he was given a free hand at Kempley by Lord Beauchamp. He employed direct local labour and material. The brown sandstone came from the Forest of Dean and the roof timbers from the estate; the ironwork was made by the village blacksmith, *Jack Smallman* – a personification of the Arts and Crafts Movement. Nave with a steep pitched roof which has enormous stone slates. These proved unsatisfactory and, at the time of writing, are being replaced by pantiles. The large W window has a diagonal stone grid, the idea taken from Brockhampton. No E window. On the N side of the nave a chapel, vestry, tower with saddleback roof, and a porch under. The E wall of chancel and N chapel has patterns of random projecting stones. The heavy scissor-beam roof-trusses, with grape-vine trails painted on the rood beam, are typical of Wells's taste in decoration, as is the SCULPTURE of Christ the Peacemaker over the N doorway, drawn out by Wells and executed by the village carpenter, *Walter James*. – ROOD FIGURES by *David Gibb*, a carver of ships' figureheads. – FURNISHINGS from the workshop of *Ernest Gimson*, and LECTERN and CANDLESTICKS by *Ernest Barnsley*, with mother-of-pearl inlaid in oak.

The LYCHGATE has a gabled roof with a rather low deep arch, giving a great sense of perspective. The stones above are all set as voussoirs.

ST MARY. Early Norman. Tunnel-vaulted chancel containing an almost complete cycle of contemporary frescoes, nave with tempera paintings of the C13 and later, W tower of *c.*1276, built for defence with no entrance from the outside, and C14 wooden

porch. The porch almost hides but has certainly protected the
s doorway, which has capitals possibly carved *in situ* with confronted volutes and tongues, a Tree of Life TYMPANUM
similar to the one at Dymock and presumably by the same
hand, and an inserted chevron-carved arch. The capitals and
the tympanum appear to be the work of a local 'school'
centred at Dymock. On the pillar to the E of the door is a
broken holy water stoup, and on an adjacent jamb a small incised cross.* The DOOR itself is of very early date, with original
ironwork. Inside the nave, the early W window opening had
steps cut into its base in the C17 to give access to a no longer
existing gallery. Plain flat ceiling with long C17 wooden corbels,
one dated 1670. Opposite the s door a C17 window, with a
consecration cross partly cut away by the splay. Early Norman
zigzag work on the chancel arch. Triple piers with cushion
capitals on the E, scallops on the W, and confronted volutes with
tongue motifs on the bulbous main capitals. In the chancel N
and s walls are original narrow Norman windows with very
deep splays. The E window was enlarged in Norman times (the
original narrow sill can still be seen on the outside). – The
FRESCOES of *c.*1130–40 in the chancel, whitewashed over at
the time of the Reformation, were rediscovered in 1872 when
the Cheltenham architect, *John Middleton*,‡ hurriedly uncovered them, treating them with a coat of transparent shellac
varnish whereby he hoped to preserve them. From 1921 onwards they appeared to be fading rapidly, until in 1955 Mrs
Eve Baker found that the varnish could be safely removed.
Underneath she discovered a beautiful complete fresco on hard
dry plaster in good condition.§ In the centre of the ceiling,
surrounded by a cusped round-headed vesica, is Christ seated
upon a rainbow in the act of Benediction. In his left hand an
open book showing the Greek monograms IHC and XPS.
Around the vesica are the sun, moon, and stars, seven golden
candlesticks, and the symbols of the Evangelists – the winged
ox is particularly splendid; on the NW the Virgin, on the SW
St Peter. In the four corners of the vault are tall Seraphim. On
the N and s walls below the Revelation scheme: seated under
an arcade are the Twelve Apostles, but only two of their faces

---

* The tower has a pyramid roof which reads very happily with the steep
roofs of nave and chancel (NP).

‡ *Micklethwaite*, according to Hobart Bird.

§ The colours are actually seen better when the walls are slightly damp
after rain.

are clear, the rest having been scraped either inadvertently by
Middleton or deliberately by the Reformers. Some of these
figures are exceedingly beautiful. Over the N and S windows
are buildings with towers, and the splays are given delightful
perspective with chequer patterns. Between these windows and
the E wall are lay figures with pilgrim's staff and hat. On the S
of the E window is a bishop; on the N the figure has been lost
owing to a past memorial tablet. Over the window are three
roundels enclosing angels holding scrolls, over the chancel
arch ten roundels. The colours are generally the earth pig-
ments, reds, ochres, and whites. In its completeness the
Kempley cycle is unique in England. Of the TEMPERA
PAINTINGS in the nave, the most visible is the Wheel of Life
on the N wall, depicting the ten stages of man as in the C14
Arundel Psalter. Near the wheel is an original Norman window
with on one splay St Anthony of Padua, on the other St
Michael weighing souls, with the Virgin and the Devil. Over
the chancel arch a fresco chequery pattern and above that a
Doom; but more uncovering, it is hoped, will be done here.
On the S wall some can see Balaam and his ass.

The church has no foundations, and a reinforced concrete
U-bolt has been placed under the chancel to prevent any dis-
turbance to the frescoes, evidence of which can clearly be seen
in the reconstructed stone buttressing. – PISCINA, nave S.
C14. – FONT. C16; from Blaisdon. – PULPIT and BENCHES.
C17/18. – ROYAL ARMS. George III. – STAINED GLASS. E
window by *Kempe*; its realistic sweetness goes extremely ill
with the frescoes. – A Norman GABLE CROSS is preserved in
the vestry under the tower, and a C14 CHEST. – PLATE. Paten,
1634. – MONUMENTS. Dorcas Lewes † 1672. Painted stone;
typical Welsh border country style. – C18 marble monument
to the Pyndar family.

Near the church the OLD VICARAGE, late C18, with three
storeys of plain Gothic windows. KEMPLEY COURT, S of the
church, has a date-stone 1689 with crest. It is a painted brick
farmhouse of two storeys, with six wooden mullioned and
transomed windows, hipped roof, and a door with a hood on
carved consoles. The forecourt gatepiers have ball-finials.
Otherwise the village has moved away from the old church to
the hamlets of Kempley Green and Fishpool, where the new
church was built.

KILCOT *see* NEWENT

KINGSHOLME see GLOUCESTER, p. 232, 249, 253

KINGSWOOD
Near Bristol

6070

HOLY TRINITY. 1820–1 by *James Foster & Son*. Quite an
attractive exterior, of ashlar. Castellated w tower with a big
cornice and pinnacles and diagonal buttresses, and round
quatrefoil windows in the first stage. The windows generally
have simple Dec tracery. The interior is dull; a broad auditorium with w gallery of 1821. N porch (now a chapel) and organ
chamber added by *C. P. Pritchett*, 1872. Chancel, painted inside, of 1899 by *E. H. Lingen Barker*. Vestries 1933 by *Sir G.
Oatley*.

MORAVIAN CHURCH. 1856, Gothic.

KINGSWOOD TABERNACLE, Park Road. Inscription: 'This
building was erected by George Whitefield and John Cennick
A.D. 1741. It is Whitefield's first Tabernacle, the oldest existing
memorial to his great share in the 18th century revival.' Enlarged in 1802. Return elevation with tall round-headed windows, but the Park Road front very plain.

The Gothic CONGREGATIONAL CHURCH, behind the Tabernacle, was built in 1851. Three lancet windows symmetrically
arranged in the gable-end and flanked by turrets.

WESLEYAN METHODIST CHAPEL, Blackhorse Road. 1843.
Classical, with wide angle-pilasters, and moulded eaves cornice
breaking forward round the pilasters. Entrance front with open
pediment with date inscription and three tall round-headed
windows set close together on the upper level. Central porch
with doors on three sides with fanlights. The SUNDAY
SCHOOL and MEETING ROOM are in a similar style.

n DEANERY ROAD, several C18 and C19 houses. THE YEWS is
an C18 stone house with nice doorway and C19 additions.

KINGSWOOD
Near Wotton-under Edge

7090

ST MARY. 1723. Stone-built nave with sanctuary, and a large N
transept, with chamfered quoins of alternating lengths. The w
end has two contemporary little oval windows with keystones
top and bottom and at the sides, rather high up. The church
has been altered and was restored in 1900. It now has plain
Gothic windows and an E.E. arch to the transept. w bell-turret

faced in hung tiles, with a hipped sprocketed roof. – FONT. C18 carved bowl on a fluted base. – ROYAL ARMS. George I. – DECALOGUE behind the altar. – CHANDELIER. 1723, made in Bristol. – PLATE. Chalice, 1566; Paten Cover, 1581; Salver 1737 by *Robert Abercromby*; Chalice, 1738 by *Thomas Mason*; pair of Flagons, 1738; Paten, 1745. – MONUMENTS. Persis Webb † 1659. Baroque marble and slate tablet with heraldry – Thomas Thomas † 1834, by *Reeves* of Bath.

GATEHOUSE OF KINGSWOOD ABBEY. All that survives of the Cistercian abbey is the C16 gatehouse, one of the last pieces of monastic building in England, together with a range of precinct wall on each side incorporated on the W in cottages. Nothing of interest survives behind the façade, except the pretty lierne-vaulting, with carved bosses, over the passage. The dove descending between the arch and canopy of the niche above the porter's door implies that this niche held a carving of the Annunciation. The lily-plant formed by the mullion of the central window also signifies the Annunciation to the Virgin, to whom the abbey was dedicated. The mullion is Renaissance in character, daringly placed in a Gothic setting. On the finial crowning the gable, a Crucifixion has escaped vandalism. The gable-verge is crocketed, and either side are buttresses terminating in crocketed pinnacles.

CONGREGATIONAL CHAPEL. C18. Almost square rubble building, with a hipped roof, segment-headed windows, and a fanlight over the door.

SCHOOL. 1891 by *W. L. Bernard* of Bristol.

BOUNDARY HOUSE. Formerly a rectory; mid C18. The imposing front has three storeys, and 2, 1, 2 bays, with chamfered quoins of alternating lengths, the central portion breaking forward with a crowning pediment; parapet with ornamental panels above a modillion cornice. First-floor central window Venetian with Ionic pilasters and Gothick glazing in the central light. The doorway has windows either side, and a segmental pediment on consoles. Wings either side. At the back a projection with a Venetian window lighting a fine contemporary staircase.

MOUNTENEYS FARMHOUSE, 1½ m. S. C17, with early C19 alterations. Two storeys, roughcast. Inside, a fine mid-C17 staircase with twisted balusters.

NEW MILLS, ¾ m. NW. Built c.1820, of brick with a hipped slate roof, four storeys and dormers, and eighteen bays with segment-headed windows and brick arches. The central projection has an ogee-shaped gable, with clock and weather-vane.

KNOLE PARK *see* ALMONDSBURY

KYNETON *see* THORNBURY

LANCAUT *see* TIDENHAM

LANSDOWN *see* CHELTENHAM, pp. 129, 134, 141, 142

LANTHONY PRIORY *see* GLOUCESTER, p. 228

LASSINGTON 7020

St Oswald. w tower possibly CII, with later top stage and hipped roof. In 1875 this Norman church was thoroughly restored and mostly rebuilt in the same style by *Medland & Son*. – PLATE. Chalice and Paten Cover, 1576.

LATTERIDGE *see* IRON ACTON

LEADINGTON *see* DYMOCK

LECKHAMPTON 9010

St Peter. C14 central tower carrying a graceful octagonal spire; C14 chancel. Apart from these and a few other ancient features the church was rebuilt and enlarged in 1866–8 by *John Middleton*, who studied under J. P. Pritchett of Darlington and married his daughter. Originally a Norman church, the Norman s arcade of the nave was destroyed *c.*1830. Its piers must have been very low, as one respond survives at the E end of the s aisle with a round capital carved with foliage of Transitional character. The E wall of the s aisle also is ancient, and there was an altar here, as marks of a long stone altar slab are visible. On either side of the E window there was a stone bracket for an image. The square-headed Perp window here seems to be the prototype for the C19 copies round the church. The early C14 tower has plain rib-vaulting with chamfered ribs, angels' heads carved at the stops of the wall ribs, and a circular opening broken through for the bells. N and s walls below the vaulting are thinned to a bare foot in thickness, additional thickness above being carried by pointed arches ranging with the wall ribs of the vault. The sanctuary has a simple quadripartite vault in one compartment, with carved heads at the springing and stops of the wall ribs. Central boss carved with a large nimbed head of Christ. AUMBRY in the E wall, and on the N side an internally blocked priest's doorway. Over the vaulting is a room with a rude tiebeam roof, lit from the E by a two-light Dec window. A room in this position is very unusual. E and N windows Early Dec of two lights. Outside the sanctuary, by the sill of the S window, is a DEDICATION CROSS which is said to be Norman, 8½ in. across and well preserved. Sundial on the S buttress. The C19 rebuilding consists of the nave, N and S aisles, and S porch. N porch Perp, rebuilt in its new position; one of the label stops appears to be a bearded Victorian portrait, perhaps of Middleton. – The most obvious Norman feature is the FONT, which has cable ornament at the top and bottom of the bowl, on a cylindrical pedestal with a base of two stages and a rectangular plinth. – STAINED GLASS. Windows in the N porch, dated 1903, by *Lavers & Westlake*; also two in the S aisle dedicated to Baron de Ferrières, and the E window of the N aisle. – N sanctuary window by *Heaton, Butler & Bayne*. – All the W windows by *Wailes*. – The westernmost window in the N aisle, the E window in the S aisle, and that in the crossing are by *Hardman*, and there are *Clayton & Bell* windows in both aisles. – PLATE. Chalice and Paten, 1574; Flagon, 1627; Salvers, 1759 and 1765. – MONUMENTS. E of the N porch four sepulchral slabs lying in the open, with effigies of the C13 and C14. – At the W end of the N aisle effigy of a priest in eucharistic vestments carrying a chalice in his hands. It is of the late C15 or early C16 and much decayed, as it has been out of doors, but, unlike the others, it has now been given shelter. – The effigies of Sir John Giffard † 1327 and his wife are among the best preserved and most delightful in the county. The knight has fringed garments, apparently peculiar to the western counties, with the uncommon and perhaps rather awkward addition of mamellieres, which are chains attaching the nipples of the breasts on his surcoat to his sword-hilt and scabbard. His twirling moustaches, exaggerated costume, and pretty wife well become one of this exuberant race from near-by Brimpsfield. Unfortunately they have been removed from their rightful resting place on the N side of the S chapel and poked into the corner at the back of the S aisle. – At the E end of the same aisle on the S wall is a late C16 BRASS to Elizabeth Norwood † 1598, with incised figures of her husband, nine sons, and two daughters. – Bust in the N aisle: 'Near Nazareth, 1877, aged 19, "He fell among robbers".' – In the CHURCH-YARD a granite cross on which is recorded the death of Edward Wilson during the expedition with Captain Scott to the South Pole. He lived at The Crippetts near by.

ST PHILIP AND ST JAMES. Designed in 1870 by *J. Middleton*, replacing a church of 1844 by *Shellard*. Plainer than All Saints, but somewhat similar. Good saddleback steeple astride the ridge of the W end of the S aisle, with a copper roof surmounted by a flèche. Built of hard rusticated stone; but the interior is of ashlar and much more pleasing, with arcades of six bays. E.E. Nave, clerestory, chancel, N and S aisles, S chapel, and N organ chamber. Tremendously rich chancel. Obviously no expense was spared, but building was then comparatively cheap. – Iron chancel SCREEN and carved stone REREDOS both by *H. A. Prothero*. – STAINED GLASS. The E window and those in the S chapel are by *Heaton, Butler & Bayne*. – Side windows in the sanctuary by Kempe. – W window of the N aisle by *Hardman*. – One window by *Geoffrey Webb*.

CHURCH LADS' BRIGADE. Previously a church school by *J. Middleton*, with the same vermiculated stone arches over the windows as over the C19 windows of St Peter.

LECKHAMPTON COURT. Built on three sides of a courtyard. The E side facing the entrance gates consists of a C14 hall now divided from the central passage by an C18 screen, and other rooms formed on the S of the passage. The hall has C14 windows on the W side which now look into a corridor built much later, and similar windows on the E, now blocked up by C18 panelling. The large N window of the hall was put in *c*.1840, and the roof is also C19. Central embattled porch with a C14 doorway with a C17 window above it. The semicircular steps were moved from the lower gateway. At the S end of the E range is a small projecting wing with a doorway inscribed with the date 1582. Most of the S wing has medieval timber-framing. At the W end of the N wing, let into the wall, a small late C14 or early C15 carving of an angel holding a shield. This part of the house is certainly C16 and has mullioned windows, four-centred arched openings and an oriel window on the N front, buttresses, and twisted brick chimneys. The link between the W end of the N wing and the E range has seen most change, as it was destroyed by fire in 1732, rebuilt in the Georgian style, and again completely rebuilt in the late C19 to the designs of

H. A. Prothero, who did the large library which now occupies most of the interior of this portion on the ground floor. The C17 coach-house shown in the Kip engraving of c.1712, S of the S wing, still survives, and the form of the layout and garden is unaltered. On the whole this house is a remarkable survival of medieval domestic architecture. It passed from the Giffards on the marriage of the heiress to John Norwood, who died in 1509. The last Norwood died at the end of the C18, and the manor went to the Trye family of Hardwicke. It is now a private school.

LODGE, on Leckhampton Hill. Early C19 embattled stone-built lodge with Tudor windows.

PARISH HALL. 1901 by H. A. Prothero. Cotswold Tudor style with mullioned windows with dripmoulds and stops. Octagonal cupola. Iron gates.

In CHURCH ROAD two timber-framed COTTAGES, one of which retains its thatched roof.

BARTLOW, Leckhampton Hill. Designed by J. Middleton in 1868. Brick, with bands of dark grey brick, and ashlar dressings to the windows. Steep pitched tiled roof with one large projecting gable and two smaller dormer gables; but the original ornamental bargeboards are now replaced by plain ones. The upper windows have pointed trefoil-headed lights with transoms. Under the large gable is a two-storey ashlar bay, and over the porch a stone balcony pierced by trefoil openings, from which a panoramic view is obtained of Cheltenham, where Middleton was to build no less than five churches.

IRON AGE PROMONTORY FORT, on Leckhampton Hill. The fort is defended by a precipitous rock-face on the W and N. It is univallate, with a rock-cut outer ditch on the E and S. The core of the rampart was vitrified probably by enemy attack. The entrance, near the N end of the E rampart, contained a 'guard-room' on each side. The area enclosed is 8 acres. About 350 yds E is a bank with a ditch on the E, perhaps an outwork. Excavation in 1925 and earlier finds revealed evidence of occupation in the Iron Age and Roman periods, and a scattered hoard of Anglo-Saxon coins dating from A.D. 835 to 901.

ROUND BARROW, within a square enclosure, just E of the promontory fort on Leckhampton Hill. Excavation in 1925 revealed only the central pit, which had been robbed. The square enclosure has sides about 75 ft long. It is uncertain whether this is one of the distinctive Iron Age barrows within square enclosures which occur mostly in Yorkshire, or whether the square enclosure is a later addition.

LEIGH

ST CATHERINE. The church belonged to the Benedictine priory at Deerhurst; a chapel here was first mentioned in 1225. The oldest parts of the church are C13. It consists of a nave, chancel, S transept, S porch, small N vestry, and a Perp W tower similar to that at Elmstone Hardwicke, which was also a possession of Deerhurst. It is enriched with sculpture. W side faced in ashlar, with a Late Perp doorway with ornamental stops and an old oak DOOR, its head carved with Perp tracery. The Perp window above has stops to the hood-mould carved with winged angels bearing shields. Image niche with crocketed canopy containing the headless image of St Catherine carrying her wheel. Perp windows in the top stage below an embattled parapet with gargoyles; diagonal buttresses to the lower stages. The other faces are of blue lias rubble with ashlar quoins, string-courses, and band courses also of ashlar. Nave and chancel windows mostly Perp. The S window of the nave and the S doorway are C19; the porch is of restored timber-framing. The church was restored in 1885. S transept C13, with a Dec S window and a lancet E window.

Inside, plain chamfered arch into the transept, which has a C13 PISCINA and two corbel brackets either side of what must have been an altar. The Perp tower arch is very tall and has three chamfered orders. No chancel arch; the C14 roof, with braced collar-beam trusses and chamfered tiebeams, carries straight through. In the chancel a good C14 PISCINA, with CREDENCE SHELF and crocketed canopy. The walls are lime-washed. – FONT. C15, octagonal, carved with quatrefoils with foliated centres. C17 cover. – C18 Commandment Boards. – PLATE. Elizabethan Chalice; Paten, 1664; Flagon, 1760 by *Sam. Wood*. – MONUMENTS. Janet Lady Grant † 1836, by *E. Physick*. Mourning female figure. – William Hill † 1812, by *Gardner*. – Anne Jones † 1860, by *Lewis & Son* of Cheltenham.

In the hamlet of EVINGTON are several old timber-framed cottages, such as DANIELS ORCHARD; CIDER PRESS FARM-HOUSE, which may be medieval, has herringbone masonry in a small lean-to structure. TUDOR COTTAGE is a particularly attractive timber-framed building, with an additional early C19 wing with simple Gothick windows.

LITTLE DEAN

St Ethelbert. A nice church for West Gloucestershire. C14 tower; the spire was destroyed in a gale in 1894. C14 nave and chancel. The chancel arch has Norman jambs and capitals with small pellet enrichments; the pointed arch is slightly later. N aisle and chamfered arcade of four bays Perp, as is the N chapel built c.1411 by the Brayne family. Mass dials on the s porch, which is now blocked and used as a vestry. The walls are limewashed, and the C14/15 wagon roofs in nave and chancel, with ribs and bosses, are intact. Part of the rood-loft stairs is visible. The floors are all on one level. Opening over the tower arch. The windows are chiefly Perp, though the E window and others in the chancel are C19, and some are Dec. – STAINED GLASS. The E window in the N chapel and others on the N have fragments of medieval glass in the tracery. – FONT. C18, octagonal, with Gothic panels, on a C17 base and possibly earlier plinth. – Medieval VESTMENT in its case; a pair of tunicles sewn together to make a pall or altar cloth, c.1500 or earlier – they were the same shaped garments as the tabard. – HOLY TABLE in the N chapel. C17. – HIGH ALTAR and REREDOS. 1948. – MONUMENTS. In the chancel, tablet to Thomas Pyrke † 1752, by *T. Ricketts* of Gloucester; another Pyrke monument high up in the nave. – In the CHURCHYARD an excellent collection of Forest of Dean stones, at the time of writing in urgent need of protection. One has a delightful boy in semi-relief on a large headstone, the only part of the inscription now legible reading 'suffer the little children'; another records the local tragedy of four youths killed in a pit, and another that of a policeman killed whilst apprehending poachers. Many highly original carvings characteristic of the area.

Congregational Chapel. Founded in 1796.

Dean Hall. C16; N wing added c.1609; top storey added in 1852. Cement rendered, with three storeys, and mullioned windows. Oak-panelled rooms inside. A fight took place in the house during the Civil War in which two Royalist officers were killed. The drive GATEWAY is of 1852.

The village is compact. RED HOUSE comprises a very early settlement, and possibly has a Norman core. C16 mullioned windows with arched lights. Tudor panelling inside. The house was used as a pin factory in the C18. DEAN CROFT is C17; a gabled house faced in stucco. The house opposite the

King's Head is C18, of stone, with a pediment and a bull's eye window, three windows with keystones, and a door with a coved hood on brackets. Beyond it on the same side, a rendered timber-framed house with overhanging first floor. Further on towards the church, FROGMORE, C18, painted brick with five wooden mullioned and transomed windows and a central door with a coved hood on brackets.

GAOL. Now the police station and County Records Office; one of Sir George Onesiphorus Paul's four identical gaols built in the county in 1791, and the best preserved. By the London architect *William Blackburn*. Great care was taken in the layout and in the detailed design of the fittings; in particular the iron adjustable louvres, cell signalling-flaps, and centre-pivoted barred doors are remarkable for their appropriateness. It combines function and style to a marked degree.

MOTTE-AND-BAILEY, on a hill ¼ m. E of the church. Excavation has shown the period of occupation to have been from the late C11 to the early C12.

LITTLETON-UPON-SEVERN   *5080*

ST MARY OF MALMESBURY. Largely rebuilt in 1878 by *Pope & Bindon*. Nave with S aisle and S W tower, and chancel. Four-bay S arcade, partly C14, with compound piers with bell-shaped capitals. The tower arches are also original or rebuilt with old material, as are some of the windows. C15 PISCINA in the S aisle. – FONT. Norman, the bowl ornamented with large chevrons, on an octagonal pillar with spurs at the corners. – TILES. Round the font are set a number of heraldic tiles brought from Thornbury Castle, showing the arms and badges of the Duke of Buckingham; early C16. – ROYAL ARMS. Victoria. – PLATE. Chalice and Paten Cover, 1576. – MONUMENTS. Thomas Archard † 1580. Fine ledger stone. – John Allin † 1768. Painted stone tablet.

CORSTON FARM. C17 farmhouse with gables, and diagonal chimneys.

ROCK FARMHOUSE. C17, of manor type, with two gables.

CENTRAL FARM is surrounded by medieval garden walls.

LITTLE WASHBOURNE   *9030*

ST MARY. An isolated little Norman church with interesting fittings, untouched since Georgian times. The W wall retains its original shallow buttresses and string-course; later buttressing on the other sides. The small chancel arch has jamb shafts with scalloped capitals. N window in the chancel Norman; otherwise what few windows there are, are plain late C18 or early C19 insertions with arched heads like the S doorway. The chancel roof has a braced collar-beam truss, and supports a bell-turret. The walls are plastered and the floor stone-flagged. – WALL PAINTING. In the N chancel window splay a rectangular red pattern with rosettes. – HOLY TABLE. C18, with a marble top. – COMMUNION RAIL. Plain; C18. – BOX PEWS. C18. – PULPIT, with reading desk and sounding-board; C18. – On the chancel floor a BELL, dated 1583. – The LIGHTING is by candles. – MONUMENT. William Hill † 1786. Tablet with coat of arms.

LITTLE WITCOMBE

9010

BAPTIST CHAPEL. 1869. Stuccoed box with central reading desk.

CHESTNUT COTTAGE and THE COT. Two partly timber-framed and partly rubble cottages, near the chapel, with thatched roofs.

WITCOMBE COURT. Late C18. Rendered façade with cornice and blocking course. Central block of two storeys and three windows. Early C19 fluted Doric porch. Either side are two-storey one-bay wings.

CHANDLERS. The nucleus of the house is probably C15, but it is now encased in brick and much altered. LITTLE WITCOMBE HOUSE was also a C15 timber-framed cottage, but it now has a modern additional gabled wing.

LONGHOPE

6010

ALL SAINTS. C13, but severely restored in 1869 by *A. W. Maberly*. W tower of four stages, with a small Transitional window on the S, and pilaster buttresses to the lower stages. Top stage with embattled parapet and crocketed pinnacles. The aisleless nave and chancel are spacious, and the church is cruciform with small transepts. Transept arches C13, with two chamfered orders which die off into the responds. The tower arch also is of this period, and has two chamfered orders. In the S nave wall C13 splays filled with a two-light Dec window; other windows have renewed Dec tracery. Chancel arch and E window C19, but on the S side are a C13 priest's doorway, a lancet window, and a Perp window. – STAINED GLASS. E window 1861 by *Clayton & Bell*. – ROYAL ARMS. William III. – COMMANDMENT BOARDS. Early C19. – MONUMENTS. Recumbent effigy of a Priest in eucharistic vestments; C13/14. – Josiah Bright † 1777. Painted stone tablet with flat obelisk and urn. – In the CHURCHYARD a domestic MORTAR used as the FONT from the Restoration till 1860. It is mounted on pillars resting on the socket of a cross.

RECTORY. Early C19, with a recessed porch with Tuscan columns *in antis*; its bow windows have been demolished.

MANOR HOTEL. Late C18. Hipped roof, three storeys, five bays, and a central doorway with fanlight.

HARTSBARN FARMHOUSE. An attractive early C18 brick front, of two storeys and seven bays, with crowning pediment and bull's eye window. Central doorway with a segmental hood on carved consoles. Part of the house is older and timber-framed, with a late C17 staircase.

Several old timber-framed cottages in the village. KNAP HOUSE is probably C15. It has massive beams, with rudely chamfered stops.

LONGLEVENS

8020

HOLY TRINITY. 1935 by *H. Stratton-Davis*. Of brick, with Perp-style windows. The nave has N and S aisles with five-bay arcades of stone, with octagonal piers, no capitals, and pointed chamfered arches. Chancel and N Lady Chapel. – STAINED GLASS. Fragments of medieval glass, and some foreign medallions.

GLOUCESTER TEACHERS' TRAINING COLLEGE. The Training College of Domestic Science was designed by *S. E. Urwin* in 1956. Splendid extensions and hostels designed in 1963, by *Leslie Tucker*, of *Farmer & Dark*.

LONGNEY

7010

ST LAURENCE. Mostly C13, with Perp adjuncts. Restored by *F. S. Waller* in 1873. S tower with C13 lower stages and a Perp top stage, with gargoyles and battlements. W of this on the S side is a beautiful Perp porch, with a panelled arcade, image niche, and battlements; E of it is a C13 chapel with a Perp S window and Dec E window. E window of the chancel of three pointed lights with Early Dec tracery. Chancel N windows Dec. N porch timber-framed, probably C15, with arched braced collars carved with stars and an ornamented bargeboard; the sides have open panelling with rough Perp tracery. W window of the nave late C13. The Tudor S doorway has a four-centred arch with carved spandrels. Long, tall nave with plastered walls and an open wagon roof with moulded tiebeams. The chancel arch is C19, but on the S it has a Transitional arcade of two bays. Both the chancel and S chapel have C13 PISCINAS, and on the N of the chancel is a C14 tomb recess, with medieval TILES, including one with the Berkeley arms. – FONT. C14, octagonal, with a panelled and buttressed stem. – PLATE. Chalice, 1805 by *Thomas Halford*; Plate, 1804, also by *Halford*. – MONUMENTS. Richard Littleton † 1713. Rustic painted stone monument with a portrait bust. – John Fryer † 1783, by *J. Pearce* of Frampton. Charming classical marble tablet. – John Fryer † 1799, by *J. Pearce*. Classical tablet with sarcophagus, urn, and weeping willow.

INDEPENDENT CONGREGATIONAL CHAPEL. 1838.

There are several old timber-framed COTTAGES in the parish. DOWNINGS, YEWTREE, and HILL FARMHOUSES are all old and partly timber-framed.

LONGWELL GREEN see OLDLAND

LOWER LEY FARMHOUSE see WESTBURY-ON-SEVERN

6010   LYDBROOK

HOLY JESUS. 1851 by *Henry Woodyer*. W tower in C14 style with saddleback roof. Clerestoried nave of five bays, N and S aisles, chancel, and S porch. Geometrical Dec windows. The arcades have cylindrical columns and pointed arches, and the roof is a forest of wind-bracing with scissor-beam trusses in the chancel. Double SEDILIA under the traceried rere-arch of the S window. Restored in 1904 by *M. H. Medland*. Organ chamber added in 1913 by *A. H. Pearson*. – PLATE. Chalice, Paten, and Flagon, 1850 by *John Keith*; probably Butterfield design.

OLD HOUSE. C16, timber-framed on a stone base. Traditionally said to have been the home of Sarah Siddons, the actress.

LYDE GREEN see PUCKLECHURCH

6000   LYDNEY

ST MARY. Aesthetically dull; but the nave has archaeological interest, and the tower considerable landscape value. A large church, mostly E.E. but much restored generally, consisting of nave, N and S aisles, chancel, N chapel, W tower, and N and S porches, the latter a vestry. The most outstanding feature is the splendid nave with matching C13 arcades of five bays with slender cylindrical piers with round moulded capitals. The great C13 tower arch has three chamfered orders. The chancel is also E.E. and has an E window with three trefoiled lancets with an inner order supported on detached shafts. Unusual plate tracery in the E window of the S aisle. The C13 tower's medieval spire was rebuilt in the late C19 after the top fell off. N doorway E.E. with later trefoiled niche above it; C13 holy water stoup inside. Good wagon roofs in nave and aisles, with carved bosses. The mutilated ARMS over the four-centred arch from the chancel to the N chapel are those of the Wynter family. N chapel added c.1500. Chancel SCREEN C19, reduced in size. – STAINED GLASS. Windows by *Hardman*. – Good E window by *G. E. R. Smith*, 1946. – Chapel E window with glass depicting the Franz Josef Glacier in New Zealand, designed in 1941, by *G. E. R. Smith*; also a four-light window by *Joseph Bell*, 1938. – PLATE. Chalice, C16; Chalice and Paten, 1813. – HATCHMENT and BANNER. Lord Bledisloe. – FONT. Perp octagonal bowl with quatrefoils; scraped. – ROYAL ARMS. William and Mary. – MONUMENTS. C14 stone effigy of a Lady carrying a heart; a later date 1630 is inscribed on it. – Mourning female by *T. King* of Bath, to Poole Bathurst † 1792. – Mrs Bragge † 1793. Tablet by *William Paty* of Bristol. – CHURCHYARD. Good collection of Forest-stone churchyard monuments, nearly all highly original and expertly carved.

VICARAGE. 1841. Neo-Tudor.

Opposite the lychgate, which has a sundial, there is a large barn, and further behind it is the site of WHITECROSS, the house built by the Elizabethan Admiral Sir William Wynter and destroyed by Sir John Wynter rather than let it fall into Parliamentary hands, after it had been defended in his absence by his wife.

VILLAGE CROSS. C14, restored in 1878. Many steps and original base with ogee-headed niches.

SCHOOL. By *Ewan Christian*. Stone. Windows with plate tracery. Steep slate roof, round ashlar chimneys, and wooden bell-turret. Quite an attractive design.

TOWN HALL. 1888 by *Seth-Smith*. Rusticated stone. Symmetrical front with a flat arched entrance under a crocketed hood-mould.

Nos. 6 and 8 HIGH STREET. C16. The original manor house of

Sir William Wynter. Stone faced in roughcast; two gables, three storeys. Inside, a C17 staircase, with twisted balusters and ball-finials.

POST OFFICE. 1896 by *Howard Howell*. Rusticated stone with elaborate ashlar dressings.

ALTHORPE HOUSE. C18. Two storeys; six windows with quoins of alternating lengths and keystones with voussoirs. Portico with four Roman Doric columns.

Down the road adjacent to the new paper mill is the structure of the early C19 TINPLATE WORKS built for Richard Thomas & Co., which stopped production in 1956. On the opposite side of the road are the empty ENGINE SHEDS built in 1865 for the Severn and Wye Railway. At Lydney Junction Station, COOKSON TERRACE has eighteen gables in a row with the Railway Hotel in the middle.

LYDNEY PARK, ¾ m. w. 1877 by *C. H. Howell*. A mansion of rusticated stone with gables and gabled dormers, mullioned windows, and a castellated tower at one corner.

The OLD STABLES of the earliest manor are early C18; hipped slate roof, pediment with dentil cornice, and cupola. This is near the site of the Bathursts' early C18 manor house.

1 m. w of Lydney, on a wooded spur overlooking the Severn, is a late C4 ROMAN TEMPLE dedicated to the worship of the god Nodens. The temple and the buildings associated with it were built within the defences of an Iron Age hill-fort* which, augmented by a stone wall, continued to form the boundary on the N, S, and W sides. The foundations of the temple are still visible on a raised platform in the S part of the enclosure. A flight of steps leads up to the central cella, a rectangular room, at the far end of which is a three-roomed sanctuary. The cella is surrounded by an ambulatory enlivened at intervals by recesses, presumably side-chapels, not at all a common feature of Roman temples but probably necessary here to satisfy some unknown ritual connected with the worship of Nodens. Close by was a large guest-house with ranges of rooms laid out around a central courtyard. Many of the pilgrims would no doubt have stayed here; others needing isolation for meditation or divine aid would have slept in the cubicles of a long building sited

---

* This was originally univallate except on the W, where it was defended by the natural scarp. It enclosed about 5 acres, and was probably built during the C1 B.C. The entrance at the SE is pre-Roman in origin. Finds from the excavations by [Sir] R. E. M. Wheeler, T. V. Wheeler, and others are in the museum at Lydney Park (private).

close to the temple. The pilgrims were also supplied with a substantial suite of baths of normal Roman type, probably used more for ritual bathing than recreation.

N of the temple group are traces of earlier Roman iron mining.

In the Deer Park SE of the Roman temple are a MOTTE AND BAILEY with foundations of a castle built in the C12.

NAAS COURT, 1 m. E. C16. Rubble; one Tudor window survives on the first floor with three arched lights, Perp traceried heads, and ornamental stops to the dripmould. On the l. a gabled GRANARY and BARN project. Good stone FARM BUILDINGS with cylindrical rubble columns, and a buttressed BARN.

NAAS HOUSE, 1¼ m. SE. In a remote situation near Lydney harbour. Built c.1580 by the Jones family, one of whom was William Jones, a rich Hamburg merchant and prominent member of the Haberdashers' Company, who are the trustees of his charities which still exist in Gloucestershire. The house is of the same date as Whitecross, and is the only important house of this period surviving in the district. Main block with three gables, joined by a parapet, with oval openings high up, carved finials, and wooden mullioned and transomed windows; below this, two storeys with seven identical wooden mullioned and transomed windows with original bead mouldings on the first floor, and a central doorway on the ground floor with a wooden bolt dated 1573, and a much weathered cambered stone pediment. Hexagonal cupola in the centre of the roof. On the r. is a three-bay additional wing, with a hipped roof. The rear has projecting gabled wings, with a tower-like block in the centre with mullioned windows, six or seven half-storeys high, in which is a magnificent contemporary staircase with carved pendants. The house remained in the Jones family till the C20, and is unrestored.

PURTON MANOR, 2½ m. NE, on the bank of the Severn. C16. Stone, faced in cement rendering to imitate masonry, with three storeys and some mullioned windows with dripmoulds. The side has a two-storey bay with four-light stone mullions, and a porch with a four-centred arched entrance. Another porch is gabled and has a moulded stone surround to the entrance and oak doors. The interior contains a panelled room with a modelled plaster ceiling of the period, and a fireplace dated 1618.

SOILWELL, 2 m. NE. C17. Stone, cement-rendered. Grouped chimneys with diagonal stacks. Front of two storeys with later windows, and a basement with a four-light mullioned window. The porch has steps up and a flat-arched stone entrance and date-stone 1661. Inside, a room with late C17 panelling, and a carved stone fireplace and simple plastered ceiling; also a circular oak staircase. Conversion into flats may have spoiled some of the features.

SEVERN RAILWAY TUNNEL, opened in 1886; 4½ m. long.

8020   MAISEMORE

ST GILES. Apart from the Perp w tower of three stages, with gargoyles and battlements, and the Perp s porch with an image niche over the entrance, the church was mostly rebuilt in 1869 by *Fulljames & Waller*. Nave with a characteristic hammer-beam roof, N arcade of four bays with octagonal piers, hood-mould stops carved with foliage, N aisle, N vestry, and chancel. – FONT. Norman tub cut into an octagon in the C15. – PULPIT. Jacobean. – REREDOS, *c.*1918, with panelling. – ROYAL ARMS. George III. – STAINED GLASS. Window in the s aisle by *Jones & Willis*, 1916. – N aisle by *S. Evans*, 1905. – PLATE. Paten, 1723; two Chalices, 1813. – MONUMENTS. C17 tablets – James Pitt † 1784, by *Bryan*. – Richard Raikes † 1823, by *Cooke*.

MAISEMORE COURT, SE of the church. C17, with C18 and C19 alterations, and additions. Roughcast, with two projecting gabled wings and a few mullioned windows.

SCHOOL. 1859 by *H. Woodyer*. Brick with stone dressings, trefoil-headed windows, sprocketed roofs and boarded dormers.

MAISEMORE PARK, ¼ m. N. Early C19, stucco. Two storeys with cornice and parapet. Porch with Ionic columns *in antis*.

MAISEMORE BRIDGE. Rebuilt in 1956, with a commemorative plaque, and a C19 CROSS from St Michael, Gloucester.

6070   MANGOTSFIELD

ST JAMES. C13, C14, and C15, but altered and repaired by *James Foster* of Bristol in 1812, and again in 1851 by *Pope, Bindon & Clark*. The form, and some old bits, survive. The church, of Pennant stone rubble with freestone dressings, consists of nave, chancel, N aisle, N chapel (now filled up with the organ), vestry, and tower abutting the s side of the nave with the entrance porch under. s doorway E.E. with deeply undercut mouldings, detached shafts with waterholding bases, and small

dogtooth ornament to the capitals. C14 tower of three stages
with an embattled, pinnacled, freestone parapet and octagonal
spire which was raised in 1851, having been stunted like St
Mary Redcliffe. Inside, an arcade on the N which was rebuilt
Perp in 1851. – FONT. Perp. – PLATE. Chalice and Paten, 1716
by *Richard Bayley*. – MONUMENTS. Edward Andrews † 1758.
Marble tablet. – Several tablets of the 1850s signed *W. Emett*
of Frenchay.

RODWAY HILL HOUSE. C16 with some restoration. Pennant
stone rubble with freestone dressings. Three storeys; tiers of
three-light Tudor windows with straight heads and arched
lights, and dripmoulds with carved stops. Porch, restored, with
arched entrance and coat of arms in the gable. Two-storey
wing on the l. with curvilinear parapet. Contemporary staircase.

MATSON

ST KATHERINE. The original church, said to have been C13,
was rebuilt in 1739. The chancel was added in 1852 by *F. S.
Waller* and the Georgian nave replaced in 1893, by *Waller &
Son*, E.E. and quite elaborate. – The PEWS of 1893 are notice-
ably comfortable. – WALL PAINTING on the s wall by *Hugh
Arnold*, 1909. – PLATE. Paten, 1699 by *John Sutton*; Chalice,
1717 by *Joseph Clare*, 'ex dono Albinia Selwyn'; Chalice and
Paten of Spanish workmanship removed from Cuba *c*.1762 by
the third Earl of Albemarle. – MONUMENTS. A Selwyn child's
monument – mid-C17 – on the w wall of the nave, and several
Selwyn family brasses, some showing the arms which were
subsequently borne by Selwyn College, Cambridge.

ST AUGUSTINE (R.C.). 1962 by *Egbert Leah*. – SCULPTURE.
Crucifix by *Patrick Conoley*. – STAINED GLASS. Five-light
window by *Whitefriars Studios*, 1962.

MATSON HOUSE. Built *c*.1575 by Richard Pates, Recorder of
Gloucester and the founder of Pates Grammar School, Chel-
tenham, on the site of a manor which had belonged to
Lanthony Priory. About 1597 the estate was bought by Jasper
Selwyn, son of a clothier, of King's Stanley, who had married
Margaret Robins, heiress of the other manor at Matson, and
the Selwyns lived here for two hundred years. The house is
situated on the NE slopes of Robins Wood Hill, whence
Gloucester obtained its water supply from medieval times.
The old reservoir which supplied Gloucester's conduits is in
the fields just above the house. The house was chosen by

Charles I for his headquarters when he laid siege to the city, so
that he could cut off its water supply. His residence from 10
August to 5 September 1643 is attested by letters and documents, and the young princes (both subsequently kings of
England) were left here for even longer. The King slept in the
first-floor room in the E wing, still called the King's Room,
with a view looking s up the hill, and the princes are said to
have cut furrows with their knives in the window sill of the
room above. In the C18 George Augustus Selwyn, a man of
fashion, made some alterations to his house, and pulled down
the Robins' Old Manor, using the stone for his new stables. On
the wall dividing the garden from the stable court the Selwyn
coat of arms appears with the date 1755. He was also a collec-
tor and had a bust of Charles I by Roubiliac which he showed
to George III in 1788; a brass plate in the hall commemorates
this visit. Selwyn adopted Maria Fagnani, who subsequently
married Lord Hertford and was reputed to be the mother of
Sir Richard Wallace, which explains why Selwyn's bust of
Charles I and other things are now in the Wallace Collection.
At Matson Maria had a little ORATORY, the window of which
contains three painted glass figures of saints perhaps by *Francis
Eginton*.

The house is typical Cotswold-style of the late C16. It has
two projecting gabled wings set close together leaving room
for only one gable over the entrance. At the back two gables,
part of the main range, all with finials. Sundial on the s gable
dated 1596. The original mullioned windows remain only in
the gables; elsewhere sash windows have been introduced,
with pretty cusped Gothick tracery, the result no doubt of two
visits by Horace Walpole to George Selwyn. The chimneys are
of brick, and so is the C18 office wing. The interior retains
much original panelling. Hall with three segmental arches,
early C18, as is the staircase. In one window two shields of
arms of C18 Selwyns, impaling Betenson and Farington. In
the grounds a canal-shaped lily pond, and a C17 stone urn.
The house is now used as a girls' school, known as Selwyn
School, and was recently restored by *Brian S. Tait*.

SAINTBRIDGE HOUSE. A square brick house of *c*.1800, with
characteristic reeded doorcases and fittings. Now an old
people's home with an additional wing, by the *City Architect's
Department*.

There is a new HOUSING ESTATE. The MOAT PRIMARY
SCHOOL is by *J. V. Wall*, *c*.1960.

MINSTERWORTH

St Peter. Rebuilt by *Henry Woodyer* in 1870, twenty years after his great church in the next-door parish of Highnam. This is a much simpler church, as obviously there was very much less money. Nevertheless it exemplifies Woodyer's considerable genius, and shows up the neighbouring churches of his local contemporaries Fulljames & Waller for the much lesser works of art that they are. The plan of the medieval church on the site was more or less followed, and the church has a nave and a fairly large N aisle with a N chapel, now the vestry. The window heads without dripmoulds are carved out of polygonal chunks of freestone without regard for symmetry, but with a feeling for texture. In the E window Dec tracery like a butterfly, faintly reminiscent of the Dec windows in the cathedral. E window of the N chapel with reticulated tracery. W window very tall and elegant, with two little lights above. NW tower with three stages and battlements. The four-bay N arcade has cylindrica columns and pointed arches, with sculptured corbels added in 1884 (one particularly delightful one shows fish caught in a net, very suitable for a Severn-side church). The two-light windows in the N aisle have C13-style shouldered rere-arches. In the chancel, the PISCINA has a most original cinquefoiled head with ballflower instead of a hood-mould. Roof with scissor wind-braces. – Marble REREDOS, and a splendid E.E.-style wooden chancel SCREEN. – FONT. C15 Perp, with a panelled and buttressed octagonal stem. – PULPIT. Jacobean. – ALTAR FRONTAL, or COPE. Early C16, incorporating C14 figures. – PEWS. C19, with linenfold panelling. – STAINED GLASS. E window and two on the S of the chancel *c.*1870 by *Clayton & Bell*. – E window by *Capronnier* of Brussels, 1876. – W window by *Hardman*, 1880. – PLATE. Chalice, 1833. – MONUMENTS. Tablet commemorating the rebuilding – 'retaining the best features of the old'. – Charles Barrow † 1789, by *Ricketts* of Bath, with a portrait medallion.

MINSTERWORTH COURT. C17 gabled house with carved barge-boards and wooden mullioned windows. Added to this is a late C18 wing, with an entrance doorway with half-pilasters with feathered capitals and a cornice enriched with rosettes.

MITCHELDEAN

St Michael. Chancel, clerestoried nave of four bays, one S and two N aisles, S porch, and tower with spire at the W end of the S aisle. The s aisle, nave, and N aisle are probably C14, but the outer N aisle was added *c.*1460; also the clerestory and remarkable roofs. The church was restored by *Henry Woodyer*, in 1853, when the sanctuary was rebuilt. The C13 or C14 tower has a fine slender spire rebuilt by *Nathaniel Wilkinson* of Worcester *c.*1760. Entering the church through the late C13 s porch, one passes under the tower into a spacious but not particularly beautiful church, in spite of its great width. Very high nave with a C15 wagon roof with ribs, plastered panels, and one hundred and thirty three bosses. The roofs of the two N aisles are also outstanding features with their rich carvings, including angels holding shields. Windows mostly Perp, including several large examples. Originally a rood screen ran right across the church at the first bay of the nave; the loft stairs project on the s of the s aisle. No structural division between nave and chancel. The existing sanctuary SCREEN is late C19. Above it and below the roof is a late C15 PAINTING on wooden panels depicting the Last Judgement, with scenes from the life of Christ beneath. At the E of the s aisle on the s side are a C14 priest's door and a PISCINA with a flying ogee arch under a pointed arch. The steps continuing down from the rood-loft stair lead to a C14 tunnel-vaulted OSSUARY which communicates with the churchyard, from where bones could be thrown into it. The church is dominated by an enormous REREDOS, erected in 1911 and carved by *W. G. Storr-Barber* with life-size white marble figures illustrating the text 'Come unto me'. – FONT. A copy of the original Norman work with figures of the Apostles, which resembles that at Hereford Cathedral and elsewhere. – The original C15 wooden, wineglass-shaped PULPIT is not used. The seat from it, of *c.*1480, is now fixed on a wall. – STAINED GLASS. Fragments of medieval glass in the tracery on the N. – The W five-light window looks like *Walter Crane*, 1911, the W six-light like *Warrington*. – SE window in the s aisle by *Kempe*, 1887. – Window partially screened by the organ, by *Rogers* of Worcester. – E window by *John Hayward*, 1968. – PLATE. Elizabethan Chalice and Paten Cover. – MONUMENTS. Brasses of Margaret † *c.*1477 and Alice † 1518, the two very different wives of Thomas Baynham; 2 ft 6 in. – Tablet in the chancel, C18, by *Bryan* of Gloucester. Classical coloured marbles, with a draped urn and obelisk shape behind. – Tablet in the s aisle, local Baroque work, to Elizabeth Holmes † 1758. – Thomas Blunt † 1811, by *Cooke*. Neo-Greek. VICARAGE. 1850. Tudor.

OLD TOWN HALL. Early C18, of stone, with a three-bay arcade of round-headed arches, now filled in. The upper storey has restored wooden mullioned and transomed windows and a hipped roof.

GEORGE INN. C17; but it has had its high gables taken down, and been given a flat roof, with curious effect.

In MILL END STREET, S of the church, a row of C16 timber-framed houses survives. The central one has exposed timber-framing and an arched wooden entrance formerly leading to an alleyway. The next-door house has a pronounced overhang, but is plastered over.

Most of the old houses of Mitcheldean are disappearing rapidly, and there is a great deal of new building, including flats quite close to the church.

MORETON VALENCE

7000

ST STEPHEN. Norman nave and chancel; C15 Perp S aisle and W tower. The S aisle has three Perp windows with four-centred arched heads, and three cusped heads to the lights with tracery above; it is buttressed, and the four-centred arched doorway has enriched spandrels. Tower of three stages with battlements, Perp bell-openings, diagonal buttresses, and gargoyles. The N porch has a timber-framed gable, and protects a Norman doorway, which has a sculptured early C12 TYMPANUM representing the Archangel Michael fighting with a dragon. It has animal motifs of Scandinavian type. Scallops and dogtooth on the lintel. The arch has a roll-moulding supported on jamb shafts with round capitals and chamfered abaci. Small Norman window in the N wall of the chancel. E window Perp. The Early Norman chancel arch has a plain inner order, and an outer order with roll-moulding on jamb shafts with scalloped capitals. Two-bay nave arcade with tall octagonal piers with concave mouldings, and exaggeratedly quirked capitals, like some of the Late Perp wool churches on the Cotswolds. The arch between aisle and chancel is similar, but lower. Plain PISCINA in the chancel. Another PISCINA is preserved in the church, which may later have been used as a font; but it was originally fixed against a wall, as one side of the bowl is straight. It is Norman and stands on a cylindrical column. Chancel roof C19. The church was restored in 1880–4. – FONT. The bowl is a moulded octagon, which stands on a plain octagonal pedestal on a circular plinth chamfered to each face of the stem; c.1700. –

STAINED GLASS. Fragments of C15 glass in the tracery of the
E window of the S aisle. – The ELECTRIC LIGHT has pendant
bulbs from iron hoops. – PLATE. Chalice and Paten Cover,
1569. – MONUMENTS. John Harris † 1727. A countryfied
Baroque stone tablet. – Daniel Willey † 1768, by *Pearce* of
Frampton. – Daniel Palmer † 1827, by *T. Bennett*.

CANAL KEEPERS HOUSE, Parkend Bridge. Early C19, probably
designed by *Mylne*; one of several similar houses with a large
portico and pediment supported by fluted Doric columns *in
antis*.

MORTON see THORNBURY

MYTHE see TEWKESBURY, p.378

NAAS HOUSE see LYDNEY

7020   NEWENT

ST MARY. A church with an interesting nave rebuilt in 1675–9
after the collapse of the earlier nave in 1674. The rebuilding
was undertaken by a Newent carpenter, *Edward Taylor*, who
had worked under Wren in London, and the masons were
Francis Jones of Hasfield and *James Hill* of Cheltenham. Taylor
designed a roof with a broad span without pillars. This auditorium was built across the entrances to the chancel, and Lady
Chapel on the S. The arches between chancel and Lady Chapel
are C13, probably the surviving portion of an arcade which ran
the length of the original church. In the chapel a C14 PISCINA
with ballflower decoration. SW tower C14 with an octagonal
sandstone spire;* it is entered through a S doorway, and the
ground-floor stage forms the porch, with a fan-vault. The C17
nave has an embattled parapet with classical finials at the corners and buttresses. Windows of three segment-headed lights
with transoms, under segmental arches. The outer S wall of the
Lady Chapel appears to have been re-faced in the C19, and
there is a timber-framed porch. Chancel E window inserted in
1881, Late Dec, but the N chancel windows are C17. At the W
end two great five-light C17 windows with a three-light window above. Vestry added in 1912.

When the nave was built the church was re-orientated away
from the altar and towards the pulpit, which stood against the
N wall, and had galleries all round and high pews; but in 1865

* The spire was partially taken down in 1968, when it was discovered to
be dangerous.

the long gallery across the chancel and Lady Chapel openings was taken down, and later the BOX PEWS were lowered and reset to face E. The result is not altogether happy, owing to the visual duality caused by the large pier in the centre between the equally wide and straight-headed openings into the chancel and Lady Chapel. Furthermore, the walls have been horribly scraped of all plaster, probably by *John Middleton*, who had an exaggerated feeling for texture and did the restorations mostly between 1881 and 1884. However, the ashlar pilasters with their Ionic capitals are delightful, even though they stand on plinths designed to accommodate the high C17 pews, and now of course much too high and out of scale with the lowered seats. Nave roof restored in 1906. – CROSS SHAFT. Anglo-Saxon, possibly early C9, with carvings of Mercian type; now set up in the porch. – FUNERARY TABLET. C11. The stone is 8 in. by 6½ in., and 1¼ in. thick, with carvings, and the name 'Edred'; it probably imitates a metal or ivory prototype. – FONT. C17, with acanthus carved on the bowl, and swags on the stem. – REREDOS. C17. Not now *in situ*. Stone panel with carved cherub heads, and ironwork scroll. – PULPIT. C17. – WEST GALLERY. 1839. – ORGAN CASE. Of *c*.1740. Finely carved, and surmounted by an ornamental urn and finials. – PLATE. Paten, 1680; Paten, 1760; Chalice, 1762; two Flagons, 1769 by *Francis Crump*. – MONUMENTS. Tomb-chest with alabaster recumbent effigies of a Knight and Lady; 1370–85. – Brass to Roger Porter † 1523, showing a figure 1 ft 6 in. long, in Tudor armour (E wall of the Lady Chapel). – Tablet to Walter Nourse † 1652. – Coloured marble pyramid tablet to Elizabeth Nourse † 1757. – In the nave, high above the S door, Barbara Bourchier † 1784, by *Flaxman*. An angel with a book floating on a cloud above the sea. – In the chancel, William Rogers † 1690. Renaissance and symbolism. – Miles Beale † 1713. Baroque tablet with flowers, putti, and heraldry.

CEMETERY CHAPELS AND LODGE, Watery Lane. 1863 by *Jacques & Son*. Asymmetrical block with central turret and gabled buildings either side with Dec windows.

OLD COURT. An old house next to the church, though the exterior appears to have been rebuilt in the early C18. Brick with hipped roof and windows with flat brick arches.

Apart from a quantity of new building, Newent consists of a charming dog-legged main street with some old timber-framed houses, and a lot of mostly C18 houses with neat brick frontages.

On the s side of CHURCH STREET, the BLACK DOG INN has an early C18 front with a pretty segmental hood with carved brackets over the door. The back part is gabled and timber-framed. Alterations were carried out in 1910 by *H. A. Dancey*. ALMA HOUSE, late C18, has windows with keystones and voussoirs and a doorcase with fluted pilasters and a transom light. OAKWOOD is C17, timber-framed and plastered. PORCH HOUSE, C18, has a doorway with an open pediment supported on free-standing Ionic columns. OAK DENE is probably C16 and has a timber-framed gable jettied out on the first floor, and two other gables with C19 bargeboards. The GEORGE HOTEL is early C19, brick, with eaves cornice, three storeys, and four windows – three-light on the ground floor. At the back an early C19 Assembly Room with reeded doorcases and fireplaces.

The MARKET HOUSE is a restored late C16 or early C17 timber-framed building with one large room approached by outside stairs, and supported about ten feet above ground on twelve posts.

In BROAD STREET, the pretty, Dec, ashlar-faced CONGREGA-TIONAL CHAPEL was built in 1846. Embattled gable with pinnacles and buttresses. The door and three windows have ogee arched hood-moulds with finials and stops. The doorway is richly crocketed. LLOYDS BANK is C18, brick with modillion eaves cornice, pediment with lunette in the tympanum, two storeys and five bays. The central portion breaks forward and has a Venetian window. Fine Doric doorcase with fluted columns.

In CULVERT STREET, TAN HOUSE is an attractive late C17 house with wings which project forward, all with hipped roofs and coved eaves cornices, two storeys, seven wooden mullioned and transomed windows, and sashes on the ground floor. The doorcase with fanlight has a hood high up on consoles, and the gateposts have ball-finials in scalloped vases. Contemporary staircase inside, with twisted balusters. The BARN adjacent is dated 1695; by the same builder as the barn at Taynton.

On the E side of HIGH STREET, the ALMSHOUSES are of C17 foundation, brick-fronted with timber-framing at the back.

SCHOOL, Watery Lane. 1964 by *Peter Ryland*.

CROOKES FARMHOUSE, formerly CROOKES PARK, 1 m. w. The estate belonged to Thomas Hooke at the time of Agin-court, and it still belongs to the Hooke family. Part of the house is C15, but it was evidently altered in the early C17, and remodelled in the early C19. The main block, which faces NW, has a large umbrella roof. This masks a lower medieval roof on the w side, which has carved arched braces, and was probably the exposed roof of a small hall, with a circular stair and rooms to the s w of it. Under the medieval roof now is a bedroom with a coved plaster ceiling, and a front bedroom into which has been inserted – rather awkwardly – a Regency window to match the others on the front. The Regency front has a wooden Doric portico, with a doorway complete with side-lights and large fanlight, leading to a hall with one principal room either side, all with reeded doorcases and Regency-style fireplaces. From the hall rises a contemporary staircase joining an early C17 staircase, which rises the full height of the house, with turned balusters and newels with ball-finials.

CONIGREE COURT, 1 m. SW. Elizabethan E-shaped house, but with only one original timber-framed wing surviving; the remainder was rebuilt in the same style in 1897.

COMMON FIELDS FARMHOUSE. Late C18. Brick, with dentil eaves cornice and hipped roof, three storeys, two windows of three lights with wooden pilasters, dentil cornices, and flat brick arches with keystones.

STARDENS, ¼ m. NE. Built in 1872–3 on to an old house, Gothic, with Dec traceried windows, steep roofs, and a castellated tower.

COMPTON HOUSE, 2 m. NE. Early C19; two storeys and 2, 1, 2 bays. Faced in stucco, with a Roman Doric porch.

THE MOAT, 1 m. S. Rebuilt in 1802, on the site of an earlier house; the moat survives, and a fire-back dated 1648. Of brick, three storeys and five bays, hipped sprocketed roof, and a central doorway with fanlight. The contemporary staircase is lit by a tall round-headed window with Gothick glazing. The bridge over the moat has gateposts with ball-finials.

BRIERY HILL, Kilcot, 1¼ m. SW. Early C18. Brick faced in stucco. Two storeys, three bays, with a coved eaves cornice. Georgian portico with grooved columns. Gateposts with ball-finials.

NEWLAND

5000

ALL SAINTS. Sometimes nicknamed 'The Cathedral of the Forest' because of its broad aisles and splendid proportions. It is entrancingly situated in hilly, tree-clad country, on the shoulder of a little hill which falls away sharply on the s. The flat rectangular churchyard is surrounded on all sides by houses, mostly C17 and C18, which form a close. The late C14 upper stage of the tower, with its five exceptionally pretty pinnacles and pierced parapet, shows up well from every possible direction of approach. From the s it is soaring and elevated, and from the N it appears as the centre of a broad and fertile plain.

Newland is not such an old place as neighbouring Clearwell, and the church was first built when Robert de Wakering was rector, in 1215–37. In 1247 Walter Giffard, subsequently Archbishop of York, was rector, and he was succeeded by John of London (1264–1302), a Westminster monk afterwards historian of Edward I. The early builders of this remote church therefore were all men of consequence in the kingdom. Much of the best work in the church is in fact of c.1280–1300 (N aisle windows, lower stages of the tower, s aisle E window). The c13 church consisted of a long chancel, an aisled nave, s porch and w tower. The aisles are spectacularly wide, almost as wide as the nave, a feature which began to appear in major English churches in the c13. Five-bay nave arcades with octagonal piers. The three windows of the N aisle, with exterior corbel heads and a fragment of ballflower, appear to be original. They have three stepped lancet lights. In 1305 Edward I added the small chapel adjoining the s porch and founded the chantry of King Edward's Service.* The chapel at the E end of the s aisle has a tall five-light window with intersecting tracery – again a motif of c.1300 – and a two-bay arcade into the chancel. Late in the c14 or early in the c15 the Perp chapel on the N side was added, with openwork parapet with cusped diagonals and a Perp E window, and entrance to the rood stair. John Chinn, who died in 1416, founded this Chantry of Our Lady's Service to support the 'morrow mass' priest, who was to 'go from one smith to another and from one mining pit to another twice a week to say them Gospels'. The morrow mass was a specially early mass for those engaged in early morning duties.

The tower was begun in the late c13 or the earliest c14 – see the arch to the nave with continuous sunk-quadrant mouldings and the beautiful w window of four lights with Y-tracery and very delicate mouldings. The tall, many-windowed upper stage, not added till the end of the Dec period, is now the chief glory of the church. The spires of the four corner pinnacles are elaborately fluted, but the fifth and larger one over the belfry staircase is plain, an admirable restraint which enhances the

* But its windows are Perp, and the arch to the aisle has two broad continuous hollow chamfers.

effect. It is said that when *William White* restored the almost ruinous church in 1861 the tower was in perfect condition. White only wished to do what was absolutely necessary. In the event, the E window was completely re-designed, with tracery similar to that of the great W window at Tintern Abbey, a wholly new and high clerestory was inserted, buttresses were added where required, particularly on the N side, and grievous damage was done to the Joce tomb-chest. – FONT. Dated 1661. Of crude local workmanship, but none the less full of character. Shields in cartouches and, on the shaft, plain leaves and elementary geometrical motifs. – CHANDELIER. 1724–5.⁷⁴ Thought to have been made in London, and this is consistent with the apparent use of London patterns for the branches, scrolls, and finial, and does not agree with the theory that it was made by one of the local Coster family. – STAINED GLASS. The E window is by *Clayton & Bell*, but the extensive mural paintings by this firm have now been obliterated. – Window in the small S chantry chapel by *Kempe*, 1898. – A few fragments of medieval glass. – On the floor of the S chancel chapel some medieval TILES with the 'Bohun swan', etc. – The dignified sanctuary has a broad HIGH ALTAR, Carolean communion rail, and a black and white marble floor. – The N and S chapel ALTARS have stone MENSAS, at one time used as gravestones. – HATCHMENTS. Thomas Wyndham † 1752 and Charles Wyndham † 1801. – PLATE. Chalice and Paten Cover, 1606; Flagon, 1802.

MONUMENTS. Newland has the richest collection of early effigies in the district. In the S aisle the tomb-chest of Sir John Joce and his lady, † 1344 and 1362 respectively. The knight is in armour similar to that of the Black Prince at Canterbury. His head rests on a helm carrying an immense Saracen's head with flowing hair and beard. The lady wears a square head-dress like that of Queen Philippa in Westminster Abbey. At the restoration William White apparently thought there was sufficient left of the canopied panels round the tomb for them to be reproduced, but unfortunately the stone-cutter renewed the whole panelling and re-cut the surface of the effigies. – In the S chancel chapel are the effigies of two priests, both probably removed from the chancel. One is C13 and is thought to be the founder, Robert de Wakering. It is stiff, angular, and primitive but with impressive features suggesting a portrait. The other dates from *c.*1365 and is the work of an accomplished sculptor, well rounded and admirably composed in a lifelike manner.

The drapery is gracefully arranged, especially about the feet, which rest on a small dog of the greyhound type, beautifully modelled. – To the w of the font lies the unique effigy of the Forester of Fee, which was brought into the church from outside in 1950, and shows interesting details of the hunting costume of the mid C15. On his r. hangs his hunting horn and on his l. his sword and knife. His cap is drawn back in plaits and tied. The sides of the tomb-chest are divided into four panels with quatrefoils within a circle, and there is an inscription in English giving his name, Wyrall, Forster of Fee, and the date MCCCCLVII. – At the E end of the s aisle a flat slab with the incised figure of a bowman, complete with bow, horn, and dagger and large-brimmed hat. He is early C17. – In the s chancel chapel, brasses of c.1445 to Robert Gryndour (2 ft 8 in.) and his wife. The husband's brass shows him in armour, but the head is bare, showing a luxuriant beard; another rare feature is the pauldron used in tilting instead of a shield. The words 'Sir Christopher Baynham Knt' have been incised on the slab between the figures, but this was in 1557. – Also on this slab a separate brass plate of later insertion but unknown origin, which is generally considered one of the most curious. It is a helmet, mantling, and crest which represents a medieval miner of the Forest of Dean with hod and pick in hand and a candlestick in his mouth. I ft overall. It is unique, not only for its subject but also for its technique, as the figure is shown in relief. – Classical tablet to John Coster † 1718, 'Aerariae inter Britannos Restaurator Artis', a reference to the founder of a brass-working company in Bristol which first used brass from the mines in Cornwall. – In the small chantry chapel on the s are several tablets to the Probyn family. The largest is by *T. Ricketts* of Gloucester and has a bust of Sir Edmund Probyn, Lord Chief Baron of His Majesty's Court of Exchequer, † 1742. – In the N chapel good Baroque marble monument to Benedict Hall of Highmeadow † 1668 and his wife Anne Wynter of Lydney with the arms of Hall impaling Wynter. – Christopher Bond † 1668. Stone Baroque tablet under the tower; laughing cherubs carrying cornucopia. – The CHURCHYARD CROSS was rebuilt in 1864 on five old steps.

w of the churchyard is the old GRAMMAR SCHOOL, which has an inscription to Edward Bell, 1639, with his arms. The three-light windows have arched heads and dripmoulds with ornamental stops. Running almost the whole length of the s side of the churchyard are the ALMSHOUSES founded in 1615 by

Miner's Brass

William Jones, citizen and haberdasher of London. Long and low, with thirteen windows on the first floor. Ten doors on the ground floor, but some have been converted into windows, the hoods remaining and the windows wood-mullioned. The range terminates on the W with a larger house. At the E end several early C18 houses. DARK HOUSE is attractive, with a hipped roof, and the OSTRICH INN forms part of the group. BIR-CHAMP HOUSE, set back, is a good Georgian house. OAK HOUSE, on the road out to Clearwell, is early C18, square, with parapet, three storeys, three bays, keystones and voussoirs to the windows, and a S wing with a hipped roof. The hall has a Queen Anne panelled dado and swags of carved fruit over the doorways. ROSE COTTAGE appears to be a converted early C19 stable. TANHOUSE FARM is early C18, like a doll's house, with hipped and sprocketted roof.

NEWLAND RAILWAY STATION. Built of Forest of Dean stone. Converted into a house in 1967.

NEW MILLS see KINGSWOOD, p. 282

6010

NEWNHAM-ON-SEVERN

ST PETER. The original church on this site was built in 1380 on land near the castle, given by Humphry de Bohun. A previous church on the Nab existed in 1018 and was re-dedicated in 1360, soon afterwards suffering disaster from floods. Some of the material from this church was re-used in the new church, such as the tracery of a C13 window in the porch, an ogee trefoil-headed niche of c.1300 on the E of the porch, and a Norman window over the N door; and of course the font. The lower stages of the tower date from 1380, but the church was completely restored by *Waller* in 1874, and the top stage of the tower, with its spirelet, replaced early C19 battlements. Shortly afterwards the church was burnt. It was rebuilt by Waller in 1881, except for the N porch and the tower, which survived. It now has a nave, S aisle and arcade of polished granite piers with C13-style foliated capitals, chancel, and N vestry. The two windows in the N and one in the S wall of the chancel appear to be original C14 with Dec tracery. Painted boarded ceiling to the chancel with ribs and bosses. Carved REREDOS, 1881. – PULPIT. Elaborate carving with pink marble columns; 1881. – FONT. One of a group of four, the others being in Hereford Cathedral, Mitcheldean (largely a replica), and Rendcomb (originally at Elmore). It has an arcade of twelve niches, the pillars enriched with a variety of Norman motifs, containing the figures of the Apostles. Band of 'honeysuckle' round the bottom. The font is the product of a local Late Norman school of sculptors. – One or two loose CARVED STONES are preserved in the church which also belong to this school. – Near the pulpit lies part of a stone Norman TYMPANUM carved with the Tree of Life. – HATCHMENT. 1855. The wife of Sir Humphry Davy, Bart., inventor of the miners' safety lamp, showing the arms of Kerr in pretence. – STAINED GLASS. E window 1881, N window in the chancel (St Tabitha and St Anne) 1894, E window in the s aisle 1881, by *Kempe*. – The other N window in the chancel is by *Bell* of Bristol; s window by *Ward & Hughes*. – The s aisle windows are by *G. Webb*, 1946, and *Anthony Westlake*, 1900. – Nice roundel of Our Lady in the porch. – PLATE. Credence Paten, 1714 by *William Gamble*; Chalice and Paten Cover, 1806. – MONUMENTS. Mosaic and alabaster St George; 1919. – Brass to John Hill † 1894, by *John Hardman & Co.*, Birmingham.

The (medieval?) EARTHWORKS just W of the church are most likely the remains of a castle occupied in the reign of Edward I.

Up till the middle of the C19 Newnham was the chief town in Gloucestershire W of the Severn. It was on the main coach route to the W, and many trackways from the Forest converged on the river here. One of the earliest tramroads was tunnelled under Haie Hill in 1807.

The High Street has a grassy bank in the middle which represents the foundations of houses facing both ways; for there were two streets here originally. Starting from the upper end, which generally has later houses than the lower end, between the church and the castle site, is CASTLE HOUSE (once a bank), late C18, brick, with three windows with keystones and voussoirs. The VICTORIA HOTEL of the early C18 has a good staircase which divides at the first half-landing under a window with rusticated architrave and a small panel of glass dated 1622. The front has a painted stone centre with quoins of alternating lengths, and an entrance with attached Roman Doric columns under a portico, the mouldings of the capitals of which have been clumsily plastered over. Either side are pairs of windows with pediments on the ground floor. The wings each side are later additions. At the back a fine dining room with a stone façade with classical pilasters and pedimented windows, containing a good C18 fireplace with overmantel. Further on the l. a pair of early C19 brick terrace houses with pedimented gables either end. A turning on the l., LITTLE DEAN ROAD, has a former NONCONFORMIST CHAPEL, square, with over-hanging eaves and round-headed windows with Gothick glazing. Adjacent to this is HILL COTTAGE, timber-framed and roughcast, probably C16, with a central chimney and a staircase which divides to serve the bedrooms either side of the chimney (one of the re-erected cottages at St Fagans Folk Museum has a similar arrangement). Higher up this road is an animal POUND, and the VICARAGE built by *Waller* in 1888, with his usual complicated arrangement of roof ridges and valleys. Returning to the N side of High Street, the OLD VICARAGE, early C18, was refronted in the early C19. The Queen Anne interior was destroyed in 1965. The OLD LAMB AND FLAG is faced in stucco but is timber-framed, with wattle and daub; gables with Victorian bargeboards. The CONGREGATIONAL CHAPEL is late C19 Dec; rusticated stone. WILCOX HOUSE is C17, roughcast, with later sash windows, and doors with cambered hoods on wooden pillars. The interior has interesting modelled plaster ceilings; in a ground-floor room, panelling of *c.*1690, with a shell cupboard, a plaster ceiling showing crossed swords, and a fireplace with a fluted keystone. Front room upstairs with a Jacobean geo-metrical pattern on the ceiling with slight pendant bosses and thistles; back room with geometrical and nail-head patterns on the ceiling and a carved date-stone S.W.:I.H.:1665. CLOCK TOWER of 1875. The TOWN HALL (now the Club) is early C19. Dignified symmetrical stone façade and a recessed en-trance with Roman Doric columns *in antis*. Beyond this are some pretty Georgian elevations: the RED HOUSE, red brick, three storeys, three windows with white-painted keystones and painted stone quoins of alternate lengths; and THE OLD HOUSE, larger, with windows widely spaced, keystones and voussoirs, string-courses, parapet, small quoins, and a Roman Doric portico – evidence of Newnham's status in the C18. The gatepiers to the stableyard have pretty carved stone vase-finials; when they were built this was the end of the road as the pill came up between Old House and Unlawater House, the coach road going through a splash nearer the river. UNLAWATER HOUSE is mostly C18. The river front has two bows to full height, modillion cornice, and parapet pierced with ovals. In-side, a good staircase, with Queen Anne panelling, Ionic col-umns, and arches. It is on the site of an earlier house, as a fireplace was found dated 1547. In 1779 Robert Pyrke was in possession of this house, 'very pleasantly situated upon the river'.

Returning on the SE side of the High Street, BANK HOUSE is C18, brick, with a modillion cornice, and a doorway with an enriched frieze. Nos. 1, 2, and 3 MORNINGTON TERRACE represent one C17 house, better seen from the Severn side. MANSION HOUSE has a rendered façade to the street with an elegant wrought-iron porch and railings brought from Cheltenham in the early C19 by one Clifford, who had a rope-walk going down to the river behind. A front room has early C18 panelling and a shell-cupboard. At the back is a garden room quite separate from the house. BRITANNIA HOUSE, formerly an inn, is timber-framed with two gables facing the street. The newel post of the staircase-well is an adze-trimmed tree trunk. KINGSTON HOUSE has C17 mullioned windows on the first floor, an added second floor, and modern windows replacing the original shop windows on the ground floor. The doorway has a shell-hood on consoles. The UPPER GEORGE INN is medieval, with a half-timbered front now plastered over.

Turning down SEVERN STREET, the former BEAR INN is on the r., a coaching inn, and used by people crossing on the horse-ferry. At the Unlawater end of CHURCH STREET some COTTAGES partly built with black blocks of dross from the old glass works. In 1620 there was a factory, the first, it is said, to make glass in England using coal as fuel. The QUAY WAREHOUSES are also partly built of this material; note the remains of projecting pulley-beams. NEWNHAM HOUSE, Regency, is said to be the original house of *East Lynne* in Mrs Henry Wood's novel.

Outside the village, 1½ m. SW, THE HAIE is situated up a very long drive. Large porte-cochère with glazed windows, dated 1883, and the arms of the Kerr family. This is an addition, together with the hall and a vast stone staircase with a wagon roof, ribbed and bossed, and a large window with geometrical Gothic tracery. The earlier house has a symmetrical front with Flemish gables and Tudor-style windows, and would seem to have been built c.1840, in a far more reasonable manner than the monstrous additions. The house commands a panoramic view.

STEARS FARMHOUSE, ¼ m. NW, on the road to Little Dean. There was an independent manor of Staure in the time of Domesday. The existing building appears to be Tudor. It is of stone and rather high, having three or four storeys with gables.

The exterior is now roughcast, with some wooden mullioned windows and original wooden doors with ironwork. The interior has several original doors, beams, and floorboards, a room with Jacobean panelling, and a very good C17 staircase. An additional porch has C13 windows from Newnham church.

NEWPORT see ALKINGTON

NORTHWICK see REDWICK

NORTH WOODS see FRAMPTON COTTERELL

8020

NORTON

St Mary. E.E. chancel with an excellent, though restored, C13 E window, a pair of trefoiled lancets within moulded arches, with a central shaft below a quatrefoil, all within a moulded arch, and jamb shafts with capitals and bases. Priest's doorway on the s. The nave has Dec features, particularly the N and s doorways, which have unusual cusped tracery, coarsely restored. The good Perp w tower of three stages has diagonal buttresses, gargoyles, and battlements. The church was restored by *Waller* in 1875–6. The walls are limewashed. – MONUMENT. Richard Browne † 1636. Painted stone tablet with heraldry.

WESLEYAN CHAPEL. 1841. Square brick building with round-headed windows set in recesses.

NOVERTON see PRESTBURY

OAKLANDS PARK see AWRE

6090

OLDBURY-UPON-SEVERN

St Arilda. On a hill with a splendid view over the river including the Severn Bridge and Oldbury Power Station. Apart from the tower and porch, the church was rebuilt by *Waller* in 1899. NE tower Perp, with a pierced parapet, pinnacles, gargoyles, and diagonal buttresses. N porch also Perp, with a panelled parapet and image niche. The C19 building consists of a nave with N and s aisles, arcades of four bays without capitals, and a chancel. The textured plaster walls are quite successful. – FONT. A replica of the Norman font destroyed by fire in 1897. – STAINED GLASS. Art Nouveau glass in the E window. – PLATE. Chalice, Paten, and Flagon without hallmarks.

POWER STATION. A new 600 megawatt nuclear power station of 102 the Central Electricity Board; 1966–7.

COWHILL has a cider press still used in 1966.

THE TOOTS, NE of the village crossroads, is an Iron Age hill-fort. It is univallate, with rampart and ditch clear in the NE sector. The W sector coincides roughly with the village street. The area enclosed covers about 10 acres. The site may have given the name to the parish. The church, ½ m. S, stands on what has been claimed to be an EARTHWORK, but is probably a natural knoll.

OLDEND see STONEHOUSE

OLD GRANGE see DYMOCK

OLDLAND

6070

ST ANNE. 1829 by *James & Thomas Foster*. Nave, chancel, W porch, N and S transepts. Flat ribbed plaster ceiling. Porch probably the Rev. *H. N. Ellacombe*'s addition. – FONT and PULPIT. c.1880, by *Ellacombe*. – STAINED GLASS. E window by *Joseph Bell*, 1931.

ALL SAINTS, Longwell Green. 1908 by *Prothero, Phillott & Barnard*. Competent Perp. Stone with Bath stone dressings. Nave, S aisle, chancel, and S chapel.

OLDLAND HALL. Late C18; ashlar, with hipped slate roofs. Two-storey, slightly projecting central block with a lower two-storey wing either side; four central sash windows to the ground floor, three on the first floor, with a round-headed window in the middle; pilasters carrying a fluted frieze and moulded cornice on tall consoles. Central rusticated porch with dentilled pediment. Rusticated ground floor. Side wings similar, with two windows, rusticated quoins, and acorn finials at each angle.

OLVESTON

6080

ST MARY. The massive low central tower is Late Norman, with an embattled parapet and large pinnacles of 1606, rebuilt after the tower was struck by lightning, which also damaged the chancel. Two-storey C14 S porch bearing an inscription stating that the church was enlarged and repaired in 1841. It was restored in 1888–9. Nave with N and S aisles. C14 five-bay arcades, octagonal piers with moulded capitals, and pointed arches of two chamfered orders. Either side of the crossing transeptal chapels with C14 arched openings to the aisles. The tower is supported on Transitional Norman arches springing from piers with scalloped capitals and keel-moulded jamb shafts. The arch on the s is later and springs from the floor with deeply hollowed mouldings. The chancel, which must have been largely rebuilt in the C17 and restored in 1841, has Perp-style windows, and a coved plaster ceiling. – FONT. Copy of a Norman one, made before 1872. – STAINED GLASS. E window by *A. Gibbs*. – SW window 1893 by *Kempe*. – Window on the N 1846 by *Willement*. – CHANDELIER. Three tiers, surmounted by a bird; C18. – PLATE. Two Chalices, 1634. – MONUMENTS. C14 tomb recess in the s transept. Ogee-crocketed arch with pinnacles. – Brass of *c.*1505 to Morys Denys and his son Sir Walter Denys † 1496. Two kneeling figures wearing tabards, 12½ in. high; arms and inscription. – There are a quantity of C18 and C19 tablets, as one would expect in an old-established residential village near Bristol. – Rachel Turton † 1775, by *H. Wood*. – Samuel Peach † 1785, by *T. Paty*. Mourning female figure. – Elizabeth Bailey, 1785, and John Camplin † 1799, both by *Drewett*. – Clarissa Peach † 1836, by *Daw*. – Robert Charleton † 1844, by *Reeves*. – William Tongue † 1844, by *H. Wood*. – Adela Lawrence † 1851, by *T. Tyley*; figures of three children.

METHODIST CHAPEL. 1820.

OLVESTON COURT FARM. Even in the time of Sir Robert Atkyns's history this ancient manor house of the Denys family was in ruins, and his description would more or less fit it now. There is still a very high wall inside the moat, and an Early Tudor gatehouse survives with a four-centred archway and a stone spiral staircase. Several of the farm buildings have unmistakably Tudor-arched doorways and must be part of the original ensemble.

DOWN HOUSE, ½ m. E. Late Georgian stucco house, with overhanging eaves and projecting wings.

WESTONS. Inscribed 'Miss Weston's Infant School, 1857'. Rubble, gabled dormers, bellcote; converted into a residence.

LOWER HAZEL MANOR, 1¼ m. E. C17, with three gables and sashed windows.

TOCKINGTON MANOR, ¾ m. SE, dates originally from the C16. The asymmetrical s entrance front was built *c.*1712 by a Mayor of Bristol, but the parapet has been removed and the roof altered. Three storeys, and some seven bays with grouped windows with segmental heads and brick arches built into rubble walls. Two-storey porch, polygonal, buttressed, with a dentil eaves cornice. The W front of two storeys and five bays, cornice and parapet, was added c.1780. Entrance hall and drawing room have painted pine panelling, dentil cornice, and chair rail. The room on the E has Jacobean panelling, and the principal bedroom is oak-panelled. N of the entrance is a staircase hall, late C18, and lit by a lantern with geometrical glazing bars. The formal garden W of the house has carved stone urns on moulded plinths.

A ROMAN VILLA was excavated here late in the last century. It appears to have been of courtyard type. One of the ranges included a basilican building for stores, animals, or labourers.

SHEEPCOMBE FARM. C17. Irregular gables. Six bays.

VALLEY FARM, Ingst. Small C18 house of two storeys and three bays. Windows with moulded stone architraves and keystones. Central pedimented doorway opposite stone gateposts bearing large pineapple finials.

OVER COURT see ALMONDSBURY

OXENHALL 7020

ST ANNE. Rebuilt by *John Middleton*, 1865, except for the early C14 embattled W tower with its octagonal spire, and diagonal buttresses on the W. The church is in the E.E./Dec style typical of Middleton. The chancel arch has ballflower decoration and bands of different coloured stone on polished granite shafts with deeply carved floriated capitals, supported on corbels with groups of sculptured angels. E window and chancel windows oranmented in the same manner. The nave roof is supported by corbels with rich naturalistic carving of leaves, flowers, fruit, and birds; the chancel roof by angels. The REREDOS has a richly carved and diapered arcade. – FONT. One of the important Gloucestershire group of six late C12 lead fonts, with an arcade enriched with chevron, cable, and sunk pellet mouldings and containing six apocalyptic figures and six scrolls. The top band has rather damaged anthemions. – PULPIT. Jacobean. – MONUMENTS. Sculptured tablet in the chancel, signed *M. K. Potter*, 1901. – Early C19 tablets under the tower.

OXENTON 9030

ST JOHN THE BAPTIST. An almost unspoiled medieval church, dating from the C13 and tactfully restored in 1905. It was a

possession of the abbey of Tewkesbury, and consists of a fine
Perp tower built inside the w end of the nave, nave, N aisle,
chancel, s porch, and N mortuary vault. The tower has three
stages, with diagonal buttresses to the lower stages, and angle
pilasters with moulded panels on the top stage, which has an
embattled parapet and angle pinnacles. w window Dec, bell-
openings Perp, with ogee hood-moulds with finials. Sanctus
bell in the s face of the top stage. Nave and chancel have one
continuous roof, though there is a break on the s side with a
buttress and a high window to light the original rood loft. s
window of the nave Dec. The s window of the chancel has a
cinquefoil head and ogee arch, with a Perp window to the E, and
a Dec E window. In the N aisle a Dec window on the E, another
on the N, and a C13 N doorway; its w window is a trefoil-
headed lancet. s porch C13 with lancet windows; C13 s doorway.

Inside the church the tower has four-centred Perp arches on
N, E, and s. N arcade of three bays; C13 Transitional round-
headed arches and no capitals. Under the rood window a
trefoil-headed PISCINA, indicating the existence of a nave
altar on the s. C13 PISCINA and AUMBRY in the chancel.
Chancel roof C15, with two moulded cambered collar beams
on arched braces springing from finely carved corbels. The
sides have curved wind-braces. The nave roof was restored
facsimile in 1905 with braced kingposts. On the chancel floor a
charming lozenge pattern in possibly Elizabethan TILES, the
colours red, yellow, and blue, so arranged as to give it the
appearance of a third dimension. – FONT. C14. Octagonal
bowl with two trefoil-headed panels on each face. – WALL
PAINTINGS. The interior seems to have been entirely covered
with paintings. On the N wall are three layers of various
periods. Under the tower is a Catherine wheel. The s wall has
remains of two or three layers; the latest shows the head of a
lion, part of a Royal Arms, probably C17. The N doorway has
C14/15 painting on the jambs. – Two wooden SCULPTURES:
one, showing the Virgin and Child with St Anne, has considerable merit, and would appear to be C15 Flemish; the
other represents the Resurrection. – HOLY TABLE. Very nice
Late Elizabethan work; bulbous legs with Ionic capitals, and
winged cherub heads in the frieze. – Linenfold panelled
PEWS in the choir; the PULPIT and low choir SCREEN also
have linenfold panelling, possibly re-assembled in 1905. –
Oak BENCHES. Perhaps C14. – STAINED GLASS. A small win-

dow at the w of the N aisle has brightly coloured decorative
glass with Lord Ellenborough's cypher and coronet, similar to
the windows at Southam. – PLATE. Paten, 1629; Chalice, 1796
by *Sam. Godbehere* and *Edward Wigan;* Almsdish, 1848. –
MONUMENT. On the N wall of the N aisle, a tablet to the Earl of
Ellenborough † 1871, which states among other things that his
'almost unrivalled powers of oratory were the admiration of
the British Senate'. Immediately behind this wall is his mausoleum, which has neither window nor door; here he is buried
with his illegitimate son Captain Richmond.

Several timber-framed farms and cottages in the village.

PIKE HOUSE. Early C19 toll-house with three-sided two-storey
front with pointed Gothic windows, the central one filled in
with a list of fees and inscribed 'Tolls to be taken at the Gate'.

THE KNOLLS, on a hill 1 m. E, is an Iron Age hill-fort. The
ramparts are well marked on the SW and SE and enclose about
8 acres. Trial excavation in 1932 yielded Iron Age A, linear-
tooled B, and stamped B pottery which is now in the Cheltenham Museum.

OXWICK FARMHOUSE *see* YATE

PARKEND   *6000*

ST PAUL. 1822 by *Richard James*. Octagonal plan with cruciform
arms formed by the sanctuary, N and S transepts, and w end.
Each arm has an extension; the transepts have porches and the
sanctuary a vestry, all the same size. Tower beyond the w end.
The large central space of the nave is roofed by crossing ridge
beams and diagonal ribs, meeting in a central rose-like boss.
The tower, similar to James's other towers in the Forest, at
Coleford and Berry Hill, has three stages, with diagonal buttresses, embattled parapet, and pinnacles. The windows are
Late Georgian Gothic. Gallery and organ chamber at the w
end, and each transept has a gallery, all approached by steps
with delicate cast-iron balusters and handrails. Original
REREDOS in the sanctuary, with a central painting of Christ
Mocked, flanked by the Commandments, in a Gothick setting.
Doors either side of the altar lead to the vestry. Restoration,
redecoration, and COMMUNION RAILS 1958 by *R. W. Paterson*. – ROYAL ARMS. George IV. – PLATE. Chalice, two Patens,
and Flagon, 1821. – MONUMENTS. Rev. Henry Poole † 1857
and John Langham † 1855 in the Crimea, both by *Cade* of
Bristol.

This remarkable church is set in the heart of the Forest of Dean, and the only other building close to it is the RECTORY. The house was presumably built at the same time as the church, in more or less the same Gothick style and Forest stone. Square plan with ground-floor projections and an oriel window. Inside, a nice staircase and some plaster vaults. The drawing room has Gothick panelled walls and ceiling.

OLD ENGINE HOUSE, Parkend Coke Furnaces (now School of Forestry). Mid-C19 four-storey house, with a slate-hung two-storey projection supported on classical columns.

PATCHWAY see ALMONDSBURY

7020

PAUNTLEY

ST JOHN. A red-sandstone church consisting of a Norman nave with S doorway and chancel arch, chancel, Perp S chapel dedicated to St George and built c.1430, C14 timber-framed N porch, and short, broad, Late Perp W tower, with battlements and gargoyles, and diagonal buttresses on the W. The S doorway has shafts with the Dymock type of capital with tongued volutes, a chevroned arch with billet hood-mould, and a fish-scale tympanum under a segment of pellet mouldings and over a diapered lintel. The windows in the S wall on either side are Dec. The S chapel has angle buttresses and a Perp S window. Both the E windows and the N window of the chancel are Perp. N doorway C13, with an old DOOR with iron hinges, and a niche or stoup on the E side. The magnificent large chancel arch is double-chevroned, with outer shafts having grotesque-head capitals and an inner order with diapered band on shafts with splendid (restored) capitals of tongued volutes. Nave roof supported on carved corbels, two of which have crowned heads. Plastered wagon roof in the chancel. Both chancel and S chapel have PISCINAS, that in the chapel being the C13 pillar type. The church interior is limewashed and beautiful, owing to a recent restoration, and financial help from the Lord Mayor. – STAINED GLASS. In the tracery of the chancel N window C14 shields of arms including Whittington, and in the W window of the tower two impaled shields of Whittington arms. Releaded in 1928 by *Sydney Pitcher*. – ROYAL ARMS. George III; 1817. – MONUMENTS. Brass to Elizabeth Pole † 1543. – Brass to William Pauncefoote † 1616. – Marble monument to Anne Somerset † 1764, by *Thomas Symonds* of Hereford; impressive architectural work. – Catherine Hodges † 1825, by *Cooke* of

Gloucester. – Various fine ledger stones: John Diggs † 1713; Philip Petre † 1704; William Wall † 1652; Elizabeth Dabitot † 1660.

PAUNTLEY COURT belonged to the Whittingtons till 1545 (the family of Dick Whittington, Lord Mayor of London, c.1400). The house may date from the C16 and has three gables with exposed timber-framing; it is otherwise mostly C18 and rough-cast. – DOVECOT. Stone, four-square, with gables.

WALDEN COURT, Pool Hill. C16/17. Timber-framed with close-set studding. Gabled cross wing. C19 roof. Brick BARN with two gabled porches.

PILNING see REDWICK

PITTVILLE see CHELTENHAM, pp. 124, 126, 133, 137, 150

PRESCOTT
9020

There is no village.

PARDON HILL FARM. The C17 farmhouse is timber-framed, but it has been much enlarged in stone. Well preserved stone ICEHOUSE on a steep bank under an artificially terraced lawn. At PRESCOTT HILL FARM the earliest building is the large BARN built in 1807, one end of which is a columbarium. Two cart-houses beside the barn, built c.1860, are inscribed 'E E' for Lord Ellenborough, who also enlarged PRESCOTT HOUSE in Tudor Gothic style.

PRESTBURY
9020

ST MARY. An early possession of Lanthony Priory, Gloucester. A church was consecrated in 1136; but the oldest part of the existing building would appear to be the lower stages of the w tower, which have E.E. lancet lights. Top stage Perp with battlements and gargoyles. Outside flight of steps on the N. The tower had to be buttressed in the C19. The church other-wise consists of a nave with N and S aisles, S porch, chancel with C19 organ chamber on the N, chapel on the S, and C19 S vestry. The drastic restoration of 1864 was carried out by *G. E. Street*, who removed the Perp E window and set it in the organ chamber, giving the chancel a new E window with five lancet lights. The other windows are Dec but all mostly restored, and the S aisle was lengthened by Street to match the N with a very nice C19 Dec window in the w. The sanctus bell turret, which is still used, is early C15. The fine nave arcades with clerestory

above are C15. Splendid large chancel arch of the same period.
The rood stairs have survived almost intact. The chancel is
mostly the work of Street; stone screens divide it from the
organ chamber and S chapel, and semi-arched buttresses have
been introduced to support the great chancel arch. In the S
chapel or Lady Chapel a good double PISCINA, with cusped
heads and quatrefoil over. The walls generally are scraped.
– FURNISHINGS. All C19 or later. Since 1860 there has been a
High Church tradition, though the vicar was forced to resign
in 1881 on this account. – STAINED GLASS. W window in the
N aisle by *Kempe*, 1877. – Three windows by *Lawrence Lee*
1963–7. – PLATE. Chalice and Paten, 1638; Flagon, 1734. –
MONUMENTS. Christopher Capel † 1740. A nice tablet with
cherubs, swags of flowers, and coat of arms. – Thomas de la
Bere † 1821, by *G. Lewis* of Cheltenham. – Mary Christie
† 1827 and others also by *G. Lewis*. – Edward Southouse
† 1829, by *Gardner*.

THE PRIORY, W of the churchyard, dates from the C14, when
the Prior of Lanthony had a house here. The older part is a
long rectangular structure of timber-framing and stone with a
Cotswold stone roof. It incorporates a C14 hall of four bays,
formerly single-storeyed and open to the roof. Most of the
arch-braced collar-beam trusses were later cut back, but one
brace on the S side retains a bowtell moulding and springs from
a semi-octagonal wall post with a moulded capital. At both
ends of the hall are additional two-storeyed bays, probably
C16 or early C17. The insertion of a floor in the hall and a
chimney in its E bay presumably took place during the same
period. In the C18 the house was largely cased in stone, con-
cealing most of the timbering, though it is visible in the W
gable-end; a stone wing was added on the N, and extended in
1886. Later, casement windows were introduced on the S.
Square stone DOVECOTE with stone slate roof and lantern.

PRESTBURY HOUSE stands further to the W, in BURGAGE
STREET. It is early C18, of rubble, with ashlar quoins, cornice,
and parapet. Three storeys and five windows with moulded
stone architraves and continuous entablature over the ground-
floor windows. Late C18 wing to the E with a two-storey bow.
There are other attractive houses in this wide and ancient street.
Part of the ROYAL OAK INN is a C17 cottage faced in stone
with gabled dormers and mullioned windows. BURGAGE
CLOSE is partly timber-framed, and so is FOUR WAYS. The
MANOR HOUSE on the corner of LAKE STREET has the date

1770 on the gable. At the other end of Burgage Street, THE
LINDENS is early C18.

Prestbury is very near Cheltenham, and now a suburb of that
town, with much new residential building. For two hundred
years at least it has been a favoured residential area, set as it is
at the foot of the Cotswolds, and very close to the racecourse.
The HIGH STREET reflects this atmosphere. The OLD MAN-
SION looks like part of a Cheltenham terrace on the S side,
stucco with wrought-iron window guards. MANSARD
HOUSE, late C18, is faced in ashlar. GEORGIAN HOUSE is a
Regency villa with a neo-Greek cornice and triangular parapet.
The KINGS ARMS INN, a restored C16 timber-framed house,
has an inscription which begins: 'At this Prestbury Inn lived
Fred Archer, the jockey who trained on toast, Cheltenham
water, and coffee . . .'. The BAKERY STORES, originally of
three bays, retains a pair of large crucks internally, but tiebeam
trusses were later inserted to support the roof; at the W end
shortened cruck-blades have been re-used in the gable of an
additional timber-framed bay.

In CHURCH STREET, the continuation of High Street on the
Cheltenham side, the THATCHED COTTAGE is what survives
of several timber-framed cottages, now roughcast but still
thatched. On the opposite side is a row of old stone cottages.
REFORM COTTAGE is weatherboarded and thatched. It is
probably a converted barn, and may be the tithe barn of the
priory.

At NOVERTON, DARK'S FARM is C16, timber-framed, and has
a large moulded stone Tudor fireplace. LOWER FARM and
HOUGHTON COTTAGES are also timber-framed. UPPER
NOVERTON FARM, at the foot of the Cotswold escarpment
and at the E end of the hamlet, is a long, two-storeyed stone
building with a Cotswold stone roof and mullioned windows
with segment-headed lights. Near the centre, the N and S doorways to the former screens passage survive, with four-centred
arches and massive oak doors which appear to be original. In
the roof above the former hall, E of the passage, is an arch-
braced collar-beam truss, probably built by the Baghott family
in the early C16. The N and S gables are not original features.
Stone N porch added in the C19.

HEWLETTS, 1 m. SW but further by road, is a substantial ashlar-
faced house of the first half of the C18. Central block of three
storeys and five windows, with moulded architraves and sills,
the centre breaking forward with chamfered quoins; pediment.

Two-storey wings either side with shaped parapets. The house is high up the hill, overlooking the CHELTENHAM CEMETERY, which has CHAPELS designed in 1864 by *W. H. Knight* of Cheltenham. They are Dec, of rock-faced stone with freestone dressings, and flank a central tower with spire.

6030

PRESTON
2½ m. NW of Dymock

ST JOHN THE BAPTIST. Norman nave, E.E. chancel, s aisle added in 1859. The C14 timber-framed porch protects the Norman N doorway, which has plain jambs and a late C11 Agnus Dei TYMPANUM with a Maltese Cross instead of the more usual Flag. Near this doorway is a narrow Norman light. E window with a pair of trefoiled lancets and the other chancel windows E.E., restored in 1885. PISCINA on the N, SEDILIA below the s window, which is blocked by the vestry. w bellcote restored in the C19. – STAINED GLASS. Medieval Crucifixion with the Virgin and St John, inserted into one of the C19 windows in the s aisle. – PLATE. Chalice, 1805. – MONUMENTS. Anne Robbins † 1658. Painted Baroque stone and slate monument with broken pediment, cartouche of arms, and a bust of the lady, supported by angels; country work. – Thomas Hanbury † 1708. Marble tablet. – Robert Pauncefoote † 1843, by *E. Gaffin.*

66 PRESTON COURT. A well preserved and unspoiled large timber-framed house finished before 1608. Three storeys; the front has six gables and a two-storey gabled porch with overhang. Wooden mullioned and transomed windows. On the return elevation close-set studding, second-floor overhang, and two small gables. Restored diagonal brick chimneys. Good panelling in one of the rooms, probably C16.

6000

PRIMROSE HILL
Near Lydney

HOLY TRINITY. 1903. Small brick church with round-headed Romanesque windows. w bell-turret. – STAINED GLASS. E window by *Crombie.*

PRIORS LODGE *see* ST BRIAVELS

6070

PUCKLECHURCH

ST THOMAS OF CANTERBURY. Chancel, nave, N aisle, s porch, and w tower. Blocked Norman N doorway; but generally a large

C13 church. E.E. chancel with an E window with restored geometrical tracery. Chancel arch C13, its jamb shafts with stiff-
leaf capitals. C14 N arcade of four bays. Octagonal piers with
moulded abaci and arches with two chamfered orders. The
aisle has an ancient roof, and a C14 stone tomb-chest which is
used as an altar, beautifully carved with cusped quatrefoils;
fenestration of three plain lancets, an E window of three
cinquefoiled lights, and a Late Dec window next to it, of three
lights with flamboyant tracery. Tower C13 and C14 with
diagonal buttresses; renewed parapet and pinnacles. Rectangular transomed window on the S of the nave, perhaps C17. High
window to light the rood. C14 S porch. The church was restored in 1846 by *R. C. Carpenter*, and again in 1889 by *J. D.
Sedding*. Low C19 stone choir SCREEN. – FONTS. C19 font said
to be a copy of one in All Saints Church, Leicester, which is
E.E. – Also the original post-Reformation font, baluster-
shaped. – PULPIT. 1846. E.E. arcading. – STAINED GLASS. E
window in the N aisle by *Clayton & Bell*, 1886. – S window in
the chancel signed by *Wailes*, 1852. – PLATE. Chalice, Paten,
and Flagon, 1852. – MONUMENTS. Effigy of a Lady, *c*.1325,
with a later flat-topped Perp canopy above which rises a high
ogee canopy with crockets and pinnacles, forming a rere-arch
to the NE window. Said to have been put up in 1888, when the
figure may have been brought in from the churchyard. – The
other recumbent effigy is also probably by a Bristol craftsman:
an excellently preserved Civilian. *c*. 1360, under a similar flat-
topped canopy with ogee arches either side. Battlemented
moulding running round the edge of the top, Perp panelling
in the spandrels. The head of this figure is a fine piece of
sculpture, with a calm, peaceful expression, long hair in curls,
and a beard. – John Dennis † 1638. Renaissance marble tablet
with heraldry. – Interesting C17 epitaph by Thos. Cam to a
nameless deaf woman. – Thomas Ridley † 1714. Baroque
marble. – Edward Hathway † 1798. Tablet with draped urn
signed by *Jones, Dunn & Drewett* of Bristol.

DENNISWORTH FARMHOUSE. A splendid example of a large,
almost untouched C17 farmhouse. Of rubble, with tile roof,
gables with ball-finials, moulded mullioned and transomed
windows with continuous dripmoulds, projecting staircase
wing housing a fine contemporary staircase with large twisted
balusters, and a front door with bolection architrave and broken
pediment with cartouche of arms.

HARWOOD FARMHOUSE. C17, rubble with ashlar quoins, three

gables linked by a parapet, and mullioned windows with relieving arches. Doorcase with Roman Doric columns and open
pediment.

MOAT HOUSE. Another C17 gabled rubble house with mullioned
windows. Three gables with moulded verge stones and finials
linked by a small parapet.

THE GREY HOUSE. C17, large and gabled. Three storeys.
Mullioned and transomed windows, oval windows in the tops
of the gables, and grouped diagonal chimneys.

Pucklechurch is still an attractive country place, though there is
a lot of new building going on, both industrial and residential.
At LYDE GREEN, WHITE HOUSE, roughcast, has three C17
gables, diagonal chimneys, five windows, and a doorway with
an open pediment.

PUCKRUP HALL see TWYNING

PURTON see HINTON

PURTON MANOR see LYDNEY

QUEDGELEY

ST JAMES. Until the Dissolution the church belonged to
Lanthony Priory. C14 tower with broach-spire, S arcade and
chapel; otherwise rebuilt by *H. Woodyer* in 1856. It was one of
Goodhart-Rendel's favourite churches. He wrote: 'An extremely lovable church. The S side, with an ancient aisle running into the tall SW tower and solid broach spire, is a perfect
specimen of the picturesque. The rest is Woodyer at his best, a
nave, chancel and N aisle, simple, idiosyncratic but not egotis-
tic; some delightful fun in squints.' The most idiosyncratic
feature is perhaps the tracery in Woodyer's windows. Entrance
to the organ chamber on the N an addition by *S. Gambier-Parry*
c.1880, with two 'shoulder-arches' supported by a single shaft.
– FONT. C19, with Jacobean cover. – BENCH ENDS. C16. –
PULPIT. Jacobean. – STAINED GLASS. Fragments of medieval
glass in the S window. – W window by *Kempe*. – PLATE. Almsdish, 1674; Chalice, 1694. – MONUMENTS. Brass to the children of Arthur Porter, 1532 (another at Hempsted). – In the S
chapel, monument with a broken pediment and barley-sugar
columns; 1684.

RECTORY. By *Francis Niblett*, c.1840. Symmetrical Cotswold
style; stone, with a central gable and three three-light

mullioned windows. Tudor doorway. Added to soon afterwards, and now somewhat reduced again in size.

QUEDGELEY HOUSE. Early C19, very plain, with overhanging
slate roof.

FIELD COURT. The N wing is a former open hall of the C14 or
C15; the N gable-end of large squared oolitic blocks may be
earlier. Side walls of coursed maelstone rubble, roughcast. The
E wall has two tall windows with quatrefoil tracery, and a third
similar window blocked between them. Floor inserted at the
level of the window tracery, roof rebuilt, probably higher,
perhaps c.1600. Reset in the porch of c.1840 is a carved wooden
panel (perhaps a frieze from a fireplace or doorway), and two
corbel heads of c.1600. The long S wing was added early in the
C17, with a timber-framed upper floor. It was the manor house
of the Field family from the C12 to the C14.

QUEDGELEY MANOR FARM. The central block, roughcast, said
to be of close-studding, with a window on each side at the
modern floor level, appears to represent a medieval hall. N wing
early C16, timber-framed, of four bays on a high stone plinth.
Ground-floor room on the E side with heavily moulded ceiling
beams; the upper room lofty, with two pairs of well-carved
braces. S wing added c.1810.

Several other timber-framed and thatched houses in the parish,
such as READS FARM and PACKERS COTTAGE.

REA BRIDGE CANAL HOUSE. One of *Mylne*'s canal houses.
Portico with fluted Doric columns *in antis* and pediment.

R.D.C. HOUSING SCHEME. By *C. D. Carus-Wilson*. Brick;
traditional.

RANGEWORTHY 6080

HOLY TRINITY. Norman in origin. S doorway with chevron-
moulded arch, pellet mouldings, and jamb shafts with scalloped
capitals, and a niche or stoup in the E corner of the porch. The
C19 vestry has a similar doorway rebuilt or copied. Chancel
arch also Norman, with similar mouldings. In the chancel a
small C15 PISCINA and CREDENCE. The church was restored
in 1851, and the N aisle added with an arcade of three bays.
E.E.-style bellcote at the W end. – FONT. C13 irregular octagonal bowl with the corners chamfered off later. – PULPIT.
C15. On the N side of the chancel arch, as at Cromhall, and
approached from the back by steps from the vestry, originally
the rood-loft stair. Massive stone pedestal ornamented with
bands of foliage and traceried panels. – STAINED GLASS. Five

windows by *Sir Ninian Comper*; E window 1919, with a typical young beardless Christ; chancel S window 1945; nave S window 1919; w window 1928; N window 1952. – PLATE. Chalice and Paten, 1576.

RANGEWORTHY COURT. C17 gabled house with a porch added by the Lord Chief Justice Sir Matthew Hale in 1664. Most of the windows mullioned with ovolo mouldings. Several rooms have moulded stone C17 fireplaces, one bedroom overmantel having ornamental plaster roses.

VICARAGE. 1858 by *John Hicks*.

RAYMEADOW FARMHOUSE see TODDINGTON

5000
REDBROOK

ST SAVIOUR, on the beautiful wooded banks of the Wye. 1873 by *J. P. Seddon*. Small, Early Dec, and of stone. Wide chancel and nave with small transepts, S porch, and S turret with spire. Plate tracery in the w window, geometrical Dec in the E. – STAINED GLASS. E window 1902 by *W. Tower*; very good. – CHOIR STALLS. Contemporary, with carved finials. – Nice Victorian TILES on the sanctuary floor.

7030
REDMARLEY D'ABITOT

ST BARTHOLOMEW. w tower rebuilt in 1738 in ashlar, with three stages, an embattled parapet, and simple Gothick windows. The rest of the church – nave, N aisle, and chancel – rebuilt in E.E./Dec in 1854–5 by *Francis Niblett*. In the N aisle Lady Chapel an ALTAR and tester designed by *Stephen Dykes Bower* in 1932. – COMMUNION RAIL. C17. – STAINED GLASS. 1857 by *Wailes*. – PLATE. Chalice and Paten Cover, 1571. – MONUMENTS. Brass to George Shipside † 1609. – John Moreton † 1789, by *King* of Bath. – Judith Hicks † 1787, by *Millard*. – John Howe † 1799, by *Millard*. – Richard Morley † 1793, and another to his wife. Classical marble monuments with obelisks, urns, and heraldry. – Joseph Cooper † 1831, by *Cooke*.

Several timber-framed cottages near the church. CHURCH HOUSE is C16, ROCK FARM C16/17, timber-framed, with jettied upper storey.

OLD RECTORY, ¼ m. E. A Queen Anne house on a moated site. Brick, two storeys and attics, 1–3–1 bays, segment-headed windows with ornamented keys, and a crowning pediment with a later lunette window in the tympanum. The return elevation has a Late Georgian bow, with larger windows. C18 staircase with moulded balusters.

BURY COURT, 1 m. NE, contains a late C12 undercroft with a quadripartite rib-vault of three bays with moulded corbels; but of the hall itself no original features remain. The house was remodelled in the C18 and later.

THE DOWN HOUSE, 1¼ m. SE. 1823 by *Rickman*. Neo-Greek. Faced in stucco, with cornice and parapet, two storeys, and three bays. Doric portico with four fluted columns, below a central Venetian-type window. STABLES. Fine contemporary block with an archway surmounted by a round cupola with small Doric columns.

REDWICK AND NORTHWICK   5080

ST THOMAS, Northwick. Closed. 1840. Neo-Romanesque. W tower with gabled parapet on a slight corbelled arcade, nave, transepts, and chancel. – FONT. Norman; plain rectangular bowl with the lower corners chamfered off, and retooled.

ST PETER, Pilning. 1855 by *H. Crisp*. E.E. Large triple lancet window at the W end under an open bellcote. Nave and chancel. – STAINED GLASS. Single lancet window by *Joseph Bell*, 1951.

ROCKHAMPTON   6090

ST OSWALD. C14 W tower of three stages with a Perp parapet pierced with tracery; the pinnacles have disappeared. The Dec bell-openings have hood-moulds linked by a string-course which continues round the top set-offs of the diagonal buttresses. Dec W window. NE stair-turret. The tower arch has three chamfered orders which die off into the responds, and the tower was vaulted, though only the springings survive. Nave and chancel rebuilt in 1860–1 by *Kempson* of Hereford, with Perp windows and hood-moulds which have unfinished stops. S porch ancient, surmounted by a sundial. The oak SOUTH DOOR C15 with Perp panelling, but now cut in half to make a double door. In the S chancel window-sill SEDILIA made up from a C14 tomb-chest. Ogee-shaped canopies with crocketed finials and shields for coats of arms. On the N a restored PISCINA with a cinquefoil head. – FONT. Perp; octagonal bowl with quatrefoils in panels. – PLATE. Chalice, 1751; two Almsplates, 1816 by *William Bateman*.

RODFORD see WESTERLEIGH

RODLEY see WESTBURY-ON-SEVERN

6010

RUARDEAN

ST JOHN THE BAPTIST. Set in the high part of the Forest of
Dean, one of the series of ancient churches on its fringe, the
church lies near the green mounds of a former fortified house
and commands a spectacular view. It dates from c.1110.
Chancel, nave of three bays, s aisle, w tower with spire, and s
porch. Restored in 1890 by *Waller & Son*. C14 spire with conspicuous flying buttresses to support it, crocketed pinnacles,
and a small band of quatrefoils higher up. The porch has a c13
outer door with a sculptured head over its hood-mould; the
inner doorway is Norman and has an outstandingly well pre-
12 served sculptured TYMPANUM of St George and the Dragon,
which belongs to the Herefordshire school of sculpture and can
be compared with those at Brinsop and Stretton Sugwas; an
alive and moving work of art. The Herefordshire school was
active between 1140 and 1160, and is strongly influenced by
the sculpture of western France. A local knight, Oliver de
Merlimond, while building Shobdon church made a pilgrimage
to Compostela, and must have included one of the sculptors in
his retinue. The subject of St George on horseback is taken
from that at Parthenay-le-Vieux, where the subject is actually
Constantine; but the treatment is the same there as at Brinsop,
Stretton Sugwas, and Ruardean. In a house in Ruardean a
small carved stone of two fishes (Pisces of the zodiac) was discovered c.1956; this was probably a jamb of the s doorway of
the church and is another link in the artistic relationship with
Aquitaine. Over it is an ogee-arched cinquefoil niche.* C13
four-bay arcade of round piers with plain, strong, moulded
capitals and beautiful waterholding bases. Tierceron-vault
under the tower. C13 PISCINA in the chancel with moulded
trefoil head. Rood-loft entrance. The walls are limewashed. –
FONT. 1657, a rare date for a font. Octagonal with a splayed
shaft. No decoration. – PULPIT. C17 with carved wooden
panels. – PLATE. Chalice, 1744 by *Henry Brind*. – MONU-
MENTS. Recessed tomb on the N wall, with trefoil and cusping.
In the chancel, a Rococo carved stone tablet with painted
lettering on slate, to Richard Jelfe † 1769. – In the nave: John

* Is it not the top of a window reset? (NP)

Hankinson † 1637. Countryfied Renaissance tablet. – Alice
Smith † 1776. Painted stone tablet with obelisk. – Charles
Bennett † 1829. Primitive angel with trumpet. – Hannah
Davis † 1860, by *Tyley*. White marble; book, palms, and cross.
– CHURCHYARD. A very fine collection of carved Forest tomb-
stones has unfortunately been moved to facilitate grass-cutting.
Some, however, survive, propped against the churchyard wall,
and these show great skill in their execution combined with a
charming naïve symbolism in the choice of subject, such as
weeping willow trees and heavenly crowns.

RUDFORD 7020

ST MARY. Early Norman, of nave, narrower square-ended
chancel, and a s and w doorway, as at Postlip. The chancel has
a ribbed quadripartite vault of two bays, and originally a
chamber above. Two small Norman windows above the E window, which has externally a mutilated outer order, and a chevroned inner order supported on attached jamb shafts with
scalloped capitals. s chancel wall rebuilt. Nave s doorway with
attached jamb shafts with scalloped capitals, a plain tympanum, and two orders of chevron moulding on the arch. Large
Perp window. w doorway similar but without a tympanum;
above it a Dec window, and two Norman windows higher up.
Bellcote rebuilt in Norman style. The N side of the church
retains its original windows. The chancel arch has jambs with
scalloped capitals, two roll-mouldings underneath the arch,
and a double band of chevrons. The arch dividing the two bays
of the vault is supported on piers with scalloped capitals.
Double PISCINA in the sill of the s chancel window; C14. The
interior of the church is painted in a very uncompromising
manner. – FONT. C14. Deep octagonal bowl, on a short octagonal shaft. – PLATE. Chalice, 1663; Paten, 1663.

BARBERS BRIDGE CROSS. C19 memorial, made partly with old
stones from the walls of Gloucester, commemorating the
Welsh forces who fell on 24 March 1643.

HIGHLEADON TITHE BARN. 100 ft by 24 ft with 2 ft thick stone
walls up to plinth level, above which is a timber-framed construction of seven bays, with an original four-centred opening.
It was a grange of St Peter's Abbey, Gloucester.

ST BRIAVELS 5000

ST MARY. Originally cruciform and Norman. Norman s arcade
of five bays, a Norman clerestory complete with windows, and

a narrow s aisle with lean-to roof. Arcade of low round piers with scallop capitals (and one with a battlement motif), square abaci, and unmoulded arches. The windows are above the spandrels, not the arches. The equally narrow N aisle has an E.E. arcade of four bays, and another lean-to roof. The octagonal piers have curiously retracted capitals and double-chamfered arches. The original central tower was taken down, but the fine Transitional-Norman arches of the crossing remain. Four of the capitals are elementarily moulded, the other four have leaf motifs. One is odd, with broad, rounded, diagonally placed leaves (cf. e.g. Abbey Dore). The arches have inner continuous roll-mouldings. In many ways the church is similar to Staunton and English Bicknor, and like them it has a long and beautiful chancel, E.E. but rebuilt in the restoration of 1861 by *J. W. Hugall*, retaining the trefoiled PISCINA on the N. The Transitional-Norman arches into the transepts from the aisles have arches including rolls with fillets, brackets with broad, simple moulded capitals, and hood-moulds with snake-head stops. Rood stairs on the s. A new tower was built over the s porch *c.*1830 to the designs of *John Briggs*, a 'builder'. The bell stage is approached by a circular C19 cast-iron staircase. – FONT. Norman, on a shelf of sixteen lobes projecting horizontally, which may be unique; made of the same stone as the nave s arcade. – STAINED GLASS. E window 1899 by *Powell*. – ORGAN. Exceptionally good; 1922, made by *Nicholson* of Worcester. – ROYAL ARMS. Elizabeth II. – PLATE. Chalice and Paten Cover, 1795. – MONUMENTS. In the s transept an early C14 carved slab with sculptured head above a cross in foliage, and a form of ballflower on the rim. – Remains of a late C16 tomb with complete semi-reclining effigies of William Warren and his wife and children. – Tablet to Charles Court † 1819, by *Woolcott* of Bristol.

ST BRIAVELS CASTLE. The most conspicuous part of this castle is the magnificent GATEHOUSE, built *c.*1292–3 and a very fine example of the royal masons' work of the period. Two large D-shaped towers flank a strongly defended passage, and unite above to form a roomy block of building. It seems out of proportion to the remainder of the castle, and in view of the relatively modest strength of the enclosure it is not surprising to find that it was designed as a 'keep-gatehouse', i.e. a gatehouse which could be closed and defended against attack from the rear as well as the front. It thus resembles some of the great North Welsh castles of Edward I. There were three main port-cullises, and a remarkable feature is the use of smaller port-cullises to defend the doorways from the passage into the porter's lodges. An unpleasant pit under one of these lodges was probably the Forest of Dean prison. The castle however has nothing to do with the defence of the Border, and has no military history.

The remainder of the castle consists of an irregular polygonal ward in very poor repair. Its plan seems to indicate that it was built on an early earthwork. It appears in history in 1131, though this first reference may apply to a small EARTH-WORK near Stowe Grange, $1\frac{1}{4}$ m. or so to the N, which is likely to be the first St Briavels Castle. (A medieval iron snaffle-bit found here is in the Gloucester City Museum.)

Inside the area are some fallen fragments of a separate tower, probably of the C12, which collapsed and was demolished in the C18. The hall range of c.1200 remains, adjoining the gatehouse, although much altered.* It contains a number of original features. A fine hooded fireplace of the C13 in the Jury Room and a probably C14 chimney were apparently moved to their present position from elsewhere in the castle. The fireplace has moulded lamp brackets. The stiff-stalk capitals with small leaves suggest a date c.1240. Chimneystack with trefoil heads with crocketed gables and a short spire crowned by the Horn of the King's Forester or Constable, as a finial. On the E wall of the State Apartments, a chapel was built at the end of the C13. This was long used as a Court Room, but retains its PISCINA. The accommodation here was for the king, when hunting in the Forest. The gatehouse was a prison, and graffiti on the walls of one of the cells show that it was so used up to the C17: 'Robin Belcher. The Day will come that thou shalt answer for it for thou hast sworn against me, 1671.'

The village has several elegant early C19 façades, including a COTTAGE with charming Gothic glazed windows, opposite a cottage with date-stone 1829. Another old stone cottage is said to retain the remains of a CHANTRY CHAPEL OF ST MARY, though there is little to show. CHURCH FARMHOUSE, NW of the church, is certainly old, probably C16; of stone, with a stone roof and a blocked doorway with a four-centred arch.

GREAT HOGGINS FARMHOUSE, 1 m. E. C17. Three gabled dormers and gabled porch. Date-stone 1767 on a wing at the back.

* It is now used as a Youth Hostel.

RODMORE, 1¾ m. SE. Also C17. Tall gabled staircase projection at the back.

STOWE GRANGE, 1¼ m. N. In the farmyard a BARN and remains of a CHAPEL OF ST MARGARET, consisting of two walls some 2 ft high. C16 house with moulded stone archway with four-centred arch, and another arched stone opening. Gabled porch wing, with moulded wooden doorway inside, oak spiral staircase, and chamfered beams. Opposite and down the hill, MORK FARMHOUSE, C16/17, stone, with gables, on an irregular plan. Mullioned windows with dripmoulds and relieving arches.

BIGSWEIR HOUSE, 1 m. W. In a fine situation overlooking the Wye. Of c.1740. Stone, with hipped roof, two storeys, and five windows. Doorway with stone pediment and pilasters approached by a pretty flight of steps. The interior is quite richly decorated, with panelled rooms, elaborate cornices and architraves, and contemporary fireplaces and staiacase. A room off the hall has a fine doorcase with Corinthian columns. It was the seat of the Rooke family, and their arms appear in the hall.

AYLESMORE COURT, 1 m. S. Early C19.

PRIORS LODGE, 2½ m. E. Late C18. The side elevation has a pediment; contemporary staircase.

SANDHURST

8020

ST LAWRENCE. Rebuilt in 1858, presumably by *Fulljames & Waller*, except the W tower, probably C14, with a later embattled upper stage. Old masonry on the S of the chancel, and a blocked four-centred arched priest's doorway. The style is E.E./Dec. N aisle of four bays and transverse gables. The chancel has decorative corbels and a hammerbeam roof. The walls are limewashed. – FONT. One of the six late C12 lead fonts in Gloucestershire. An arcade of eleven compartments in low relief surrounds the bowl, containing alternately five figures and six scrolls. – PULPIT. Jacobean. – STAINED GLASS. W window of the N aisle, commemorating the Second World War, by *H. J. Stammers*. Very good, delicate, small scale. – PLATE. Chalice, 1606; two Chalices, 1715 by *Nathaniel Lock*; Paten, 1730. – MONUMENTS. Hester Gyse † 1673 and Joan Gyse † 1680. Slate tablets with stone surrounds. – Walter de Winton † 1851, by *T. Gaffin*.

The houses in the parish are scattered over a wide area.

GARDNERS FARM, ½ m. S. Perhaps C15, with three cruck trusses.

Mayfield, a cottage opposite, has an exposed cruck in the gable end.

Base Lane Cottage, 1 m. s. Timber-framed cottage with cruck truss and thatched roof.

Wallsworth Hall, ¾ m. e. A mid-c18 mansion, of brick with stone dressings. Front of two storeys and 3–3–3 bays, with quoins of alternating length and windows with keystones – those in the centre have moulded architraves. Balustraded parapet, raised in the centre, with three bull's eye attic windows. Central doorway with rusticated Roman Doric columns, an enriched frieze, and a pediment curiously ornamented with dripping icicles, more usually found in a grotto. The sw elevation is also original. It has a pedimented portico with rusticated columns, and a Rococo shield of arms. The skyline, altered in the c19, has a mansard roof with pedimented dormers and a tower. The house has been divided into tenements, but a very fine c18 mahogany* staircase, with twisted balusters, moulded under-treads, and shaped dado, survives.

SAUL   7000

St James. Perp embattled tower, and nave with Perp windows on the s. Altered and enlarged in 1863–5 by *T. Fulljames*, who rebuilt the chancel and added the n aisle. The chancel has a corbel-table with stiff-leaf decoration, trefoil-headed lancets with elaborate rere-arches, and an e window with geometrical tracery. Four-bay c19 n nave arcade. – Reredos. Made in 1883 of Caen stone, with sculpture by *H. C. Frith* and *W. S. Frith*. It was part of the reredos in St Michael, Gloucester, and was moved to Saul in 1956. The new setting was successfully designed by *Cecil Thomas*. – Font. Norman tub-shaped bowl, drastically cut down; modern circular pillar. – Pulpit. Jacobean. – Plate. Chalice, 1697 by *John Sutton*.

Almost opposite the church Alma Cottage, 1865; two doors away a cottage has its central window blocked, and a carved lion on the sill. Further towards Framilode, Prospect Place is dated 1852 and Victoria Place 1854. Next is a cottage with the painted carved figures of twin sailors and a pair of doves, like figures on a Victorian barometer. Clifton Place, 1864, and Prince of Wales Terrace, 1863, are small brick terrace houses, with painted keystones and voussoirs to the windows, and doorways with hoods surmounted by

* First imported from Jamaica in 1753.

carved wooden acorns. The JUNCTION INN, where the Stroudwater Canal crosses the Gloucester–Berkeley Canal, is a typical C19 canal public house. Brick. Two storeys, six bays, windows with brick arches, and doors with segmental hoods.

THATCHED COTTAGE, Saul Corner. Timber-framed gabled house of four bays. Parts of three cruck pairs are visible. It has an inserted floor and central stone chimney.

SCOWLES see COLEFORD

SEDBURY PARK see TIDENHAM

SEVERN BRIDGE see AUST

SHARPNESS see HINTON

9010
SHURDINGTON

ST PAUL. The best part of the church is its early C14 tower with its spire, which is exactly like the neighbouring ones at Leckhampton and Cheltenham, octagonal, very steep, and broached on to the tower. The date 1797 on the spire must refer to a repair, as does the 1843 on the tower, which is of two stages with a Perp w window and diagonal w buttresses. Otherwise the church consists of a nave, chancel, N aisle, and wooden C19 s porch. The s window of the nave is Dec. Sundial dated 1655. Chancel with two trefoil-headed lancets on the s, a two-light Dec E window and a lancet on the N. The N aisle has a Perp E window, a C19 vestry, and a C19 Norman N doorway. The church was restored in 1852.

Inside, the nave has a four-bay C14 N arcade, a tall, plain, chamfered tower arch, and rib-vaulting under the tower. Chancel arch C13 with two chamfered orders both sides. The rood beam survives, and there are signs of a WALL PAINTING in the tympanum above. The nave and N aisle roofs are wagon-shaped, the former with good moulded ribs and carved bosses; but the short chancel has been given a new roof, and internally is completely C19. – FONT. C14. Octagonal bowl with quatrefoils and sprays of foliage. Pedestal divided into two tiers of eight attached circular shafts placed round a central pillar; the lower part is probably C13. – ROYAL ARMS. George III. – STAINED GLASS. E window by *Christopher Webb*.

Shurdington is becoming a built-up area; the old part of the village straddles the main road. POPLAR FARMHOUSE is C17, partly built of rubble; one gable-end has mullioned windows and a finial. The front is plastered and has a timber-framed two-storey gabled porch and gables either side with small wooden oriel windows. Opposite is THE LAWN, an early C19 Cheltenham-type of small stucco villa.

THE GREENWAY HOTEL. The Kip drawing in Atkyns's *Ancient and Present State of Gloucestershire* shows Mrs Dulcibella Laurence's handsome seat in 1712, and from this it can be seen that the NW front has not been greatly altered. It is C17, with projecting gables either side of a central gabled portion with smaller gables in the angles, all surmounted by finials. Tower over the centre with windows and dome. The SE front was rebuilt c.1910 by *Ernest Newton*, with new gables and fenestration. Good late C17 Baroque stone fireplace in the entrance hall, but the interior has been much altered.

High up on the hill behind the Greenway stands THE CRIPPETS, approached by an avenue of Spanish chestnuts. The house is late C19, brick painted black and white to imitate half-timber work. Gables with pierced bargeboards and iron finials. This was the home of Edward Wilson the Antarctic explorer.

LITTLE SHURDINGTON COURT. Late C17, stone, with hipped roof and mullioned and transomed windows.

SHUTHONGER MANOR *see* TWYNING

SISTON

ST ANNE. Nave, chancel, S porch, S transept, and W tower. Elaborate C12 Norman S doorway with chamfered and diapered jambs, their shafts with scalloped capitals. Chevron-moulded arch with, carved in the TYMPANUM, the Tree of Life, which has five branches with trefoil leaves at each extremity. Norman N doorway filled in with a window. The small nave is Norman and the chancel E.E., with a triplet of trefoiled lancets. Openings in the tower with straight pointed arches in the upper stage (not unlike the windows in the N aisle of St Mary Redcliffe). The S transept has the inscribed date 1796. On the porch a C17 sundial. The church was restored in 1887. – FONT. One of the six lead fonts in Gloucestershire all cast from the same pattern probably towards the end of the C12. It has twelve arcades, six filled with scrollwork and six with figures for which two patterns are used, enthroned, and with the hand raised in benediction. The treatment of the figures suggests that the craftsman may have been copying Saxon work, but the architectural details preclude a date much before *c.*1170. Frieze decorated with anthemions. – PULPIT. C17, with wooden panels. – BOX PEW. C18. – WALL PAINTINGS. All over the chancel arch; *c.*1907. – PLATE. Paten, 1664. – MONUMENTS. Tablets to Samuel Trotman † 1788 by *T. King* of Bath. – Richard Ivyleafe † 1814, a sculptured mourning female by *J. Kendall* of Exeter. – George Nutt † 1828, by *Reeves* of Bath.

SISTON COURT, 7 m. E of Bristol. Late C16, built by the Dennys family, whose arms appear on the bay windows and who sold it in 1598. It is constructed round three sides of a square. The central portion has three gables and the projecting wings each have three gables facing inwards, all with verges and ball-finials. In the two corners of the open court are tall octagonal turrets crowned with ogee-shaped roofs ending in a ball-finial. The house is built of coursed rubble and the straight-headed mullioned and transomed windows have relieving arches showing above, a local characteristic. Two storeys and gabled attics, with dripmoulds above the windows forming continuous string-courses. The inside elevations of each wing have three square-headed chamfered doorways, and at the E end on the first floor a coved shell-headed niche with bolection-moulded surround and flat moulded cornice over. The end elevations of the wings have two-storey, six-light angular bays with battle-mented parapets and carved heraldic shields in recessed panels between the ground- and first-floor window lights. Although the house has been divided into flats, the central block retains an original plaster ceiling with ribs and pendants, a C17 well-type staircase with twisted balusters, and a Jacobean fireplace and oak chimneypiece.

LODGES. Twin C19 lodges which look as if the top stages of the turrets on the mansion had been cut off and placed one each side of the drive gate, complete with their ogee-shaped roofs. Gothic Revival windows alternate with cross-loops, and the doorways have ogee-shaped heads.

CHERRY ORCHARD FARMHOUSE, Goose Green, 1 m. SW. A simple little house distinguished by a broad shell-hood sup-ported on carved scroll brackets, and large ball-finials on the forecourt gatepiers.

WEBBS HEATH FARM, ¾ m. E, is notable for a projecting timber-framed gable and oriel window.

At BRIDGEYATE two public houses, the GRIFFIN and WHITE

HART, both appear to be C17 in origin. EBENEZER CHAPEL is dated 1810.

SLIMBRIDGE   7000

ST JOHN. Probably the best example in the county of the Early Gothic style of the C13. The nave with its four-bay N and S arcades was built *c*.1200, and the foliage carvings on the capitals of the columns, and on the S doorway, are of a high standard of mason-craft and great beauty. The bold stiff-leaf ornament runs continuous up the jambs and over the round arch of the S doorway. The piers of the arcades have a square core chamfered at the angles and four keeled shafts. The bases are of the waterholding type. The capitals are variously carved: some have in-curved scalloped or truncated cones, others have foliage curved into knobs, or lobed, and rising from stiff stalks. One is of the trumpet kind, but it may well be that this was 20 never carved but was intended to receive foliage as well. There are no neckings for any of the capitals, always a disturbing feature. It is a West Country fashion (Wells, St Davids). The capitals support pointed arches of complicated section with a roll label. The W tower and spire and the windows of the chancel with their geometrical tracery were added before 1300. Tower of three stages with diagonal buttresses; on its W face is a window with cusped intersecting tracery and image niches either side, and three more above. Pierced parapet, pinnacles, and a fine recessed spire. Below the parapet is a blank, pointed, elongated quatrefoil, probably originally with a painting inside. The rib-vault of the tower can be seen through the tall C14 tower arch. Chancel arch E.E. In the chancel C14 triple SEDILIA, and a PISCINA; also a nave PISCINA and CREDENCE SHELF by the chancel arch. The E window has minor flowing tracery. On the N side of the chancel is a two-storey sacristy, detached from the N aisle, which has flowing Dec tracery in its E window. The sacristy, of the same date as the chancel, is entered by a doorway similar to the priest's door on the S. On the S is a two-storey porch, and a string-course with ballflower ornament, running round and below the parapet of the aisle. Aisle windows Perp; gargoyles on the parapet on the N side. The handsome clerestory windows, by *Francis Niblett*, date from 1845, and the parapet above is pierced with mouchettes. The building is largely faced with blocks of tufa. Good collection of C14 carved corbel heads in the aisle roofs. – FONT. Lead bowl, decorated with cherubs and roses and kinds of balusters a little like exclamation marks. Dated 1664. – PULPIT. Made up with Jacobean panels. – STAINED GLASS. Fragments of medieval glass, particularly in the N aisle E window, and some heraldry in the chancel windows. – PLATE. Credence Paten, 1679; Chalice and Paten Cover, 1719 by *Richard Green*; Flagon, 1734. – MONUMENTS. Several pretty tablets. William Cradock † 1727. – William Davies † 1742. – Sarah Smith † 1763, by *Pearce* of Frampton. – John Cowley † 1793, by *Pearce*. – Robert Awood † 1734. – Drusilla Richens † 1805, by *Tyley*. – William Davies † 1810, by *Tyley*.

RECTORY. 1818–20 by *William James*. Brick, with a hipped roof, two storeys, and a three-bay front.

RESEARCH CENTRE, WILDFOWL TRUST. By *Peter Bicknell*, 1965.

HURST FARMHOUSE. C17; part may be older. It is one of the traditional birthplaces of William Tyndale.

GOSSINGTON HALL, 1 m. S. Early C18 brick house with a hipped stone roof, two storeys, five bays, and hipped dormers. The side has a centre breaking forward with a small pediment. On the garden side is a later C18 bay window to the full height. The outbuildings attached to the house are attractively built on a curve. Contemporary BARN with projecting hipped wings.

At CAMBRIDGE, a hamlet ½ m. E on the Gloucester–Bristol road, is a CONGREGATIONAL CHAPEL of 1807.

SNIGS END see CORSE

SOILWELL see LYDNEY

SOUDLEY see CINDERFORD

6070

SOUNDWELL

ST STEPHEN. 1903 by *H. M. Bennet*. Nave, N and S aisles, but no chancel. Built of rusticated Pennant rubble with freestone dressings. Bellcote at the W, and turret at the E. A drastic and inspired scheme of interior decoration has transformed it into a dignified and beautiful place of worship.

STAR INN. By *R. C. James & H. E. Meredith*, 1938.

9020

SOUTHAM

CHURCH OF THE ASCENSION. A small Norman church of nave, chancel, and S transept; subsequently used as a barn, it fell into disrepair and was drastically restored in neo-Norman style as a private chapel by the Earl of Ellenborough, c.1862. The early C12 N doorway has megalithic stone jambs, chamfered imposts, and a straight head. A small Norman window survives in the N wall of the chancel, and there is a two-light Perp window in the S wall; otherwise all the windows are elaborate neo-Norman. The chancel arch and archway into the S transept, though probably rebuilt, have megalithic jambs and simple chamfered imposts. Ancient ironwork on the NORTH DOOR. – Stone ALTAR with neo-Norman legs and stone COMMUNION RAIL, supported by an interlaced Norman-style arcade. An oak-panelled DADO runs round the nave and chancel, and on the N of the chancel are three foreign Renaissance CHOIR STALLS with carved MISERICORDS. – LECTERN. Carved wooden eagle, probably C17. – FONT. Marble pedestal not made for a font, with beautiful carved lotus ornament. – STAINED GLASS. Brightly coloured heraldic and decorative glass, memorials to Lord Ellenborough's friends and relations; one window for instance commemorates 'the brave who fell at Sinde and in Gwalior, 1843'. – PICTURE. St Veronica; Flemish school. – MONUMENTS. On the S wall of the chancel in two neo-Norman niches, the busts of the Earl of Ellenborough † 1871, and Octavia, his first wife, † 1819. – In the SW corner of the nave, a small equestrian bronze memorial to the Duke of Wellington. – Brass tablet to Edward Law, first and last Earl of Ellenborough, † 1871.

TITHE BARN. Late C14 or early C15. The timber frame, mainly original, is of seven bays with crucks rising from a stone plinth. The roof is now covered with concrete imitation stone slates. At the E end a small stone chamber with an arched doorway, a small cusped window, and a stone chute for grain.

THE PIGEON HOUSE. A picturesque medieval house forming a group with the church and barn. Part of the house may date from the C14 or C15. NE wing of stone with traceried mullioned windows. W wing timber-framed, with close-set studding. Most of the oriel windows are quite modern.

MANOR FARMHOUSE. A good C17 stone frontage with two gables and mullioned windows; inscribed date 1631. The back is a nice example of fairly elaborate half-timber work.

SOUTHAM DELABERE. In 1478 Sir John Huddleston of Cumberland, an associate of Richard, Duke of Gloucester, was made Constable of Sudeley Castle. He died in 1512, having acquired the Southam estate, which was inherited by his son, another Sir John, who built or rebuilt the house. This Sir John died in 1547 and was succeeded by his daughter Eleanor, who had married Kenard de la Bere before 1554. It remained in the de la Bere family till shortly before it was bought c.1831 by Lord Ellenborough, Governor General of India from 1841 to 1844.

Of the original early c16 house there remain the hall, two ranges at the S end of the hall, and considerable buildings round the E and N sides of the courtyard; it is therefore one of the largest houses of this period to survive in the county. It completely escaped alteration in the Georgian period, and whatever may be thought of Ellenborough's additions, the main features of the W front have remained almost unchanged since it was first illustrated c.1700 by Kip. Lysons's view in 1798 shows that a barn has temporarily appeared in front of the S range. By 1840 Lord Ellenborough's Gothic NW tower had been built, but the end of the N range is still timber-framed; this was later faced in stone and another tower built in the angle of the main block. The final addition was the great semi-detached neo-Norman tower on the E side, erected by Lord Ellenborough after his return from India.

The house is now entered through a c19 porch and screens passage into the HALL, which has two original four-light windows, and ceiling beams which may have been inserted in Elizabethan times if the hall was once open to the roof, but this is by no means certain. Part of a braced collar-beam roof is visible in the school dormitory above the hall. The original PORCH has been made into a small room which has medieval tiles from Hailes Abbey on the floor, linenfold panelling, and a moulded four-centred arched doorway. The main suite of rooms lies to the S of the hall. The GREAT PARLOUR, now the DINING ROOM, is the first of an impressive range. It has an original Perp bay window, with Tudor glass medallions including the arms or badges of Henry VII and Elizabeth of York, the Tudor rose, and the pomegranate. More examples of Tudor heraldic glass in other windows. The panelling is of good quality, with a frieze decorated with early strapwork and dragons. The splendid overmantel showing the arms of de la Bere impaling Huddleston (gules, fretty argent) presumably dates from the marriage of c.1554. The ceiling looks as if it was an introduction of Ellenborough's, but in the *Beauties of England and Wales* (1803) it is stated that the ceilings are 'of oak frames, fretted, in allusion to Sir John Huddleston's coat of arms', a perfectly appropriate description of what is there now. In the adjoining LIBRARY the frieze over the panelling has winged angels, and the overmantel the de la Bere arms and a helmet in high relief with a crest of eleven ostrich feathers. The STATE BEDROOM is the SW room on the ground floor; this also has a dragon frieze and the de la Bere arms in the glass. The adjoining DRESSING ROOM has a fireplace with bolection mouldings of *c*.1700. The LESSER DRAWING ROOM is again panelled with the dragon frieze, but the arms over the fireplace are Lord Ellenborough's. The main STAIRCASE, of *c*.1700, has turned balusters and a panelled dado. Original roofs survive above the two S ranges; they are only visible in the roof spaces and are not complete, but they are of unusual form and have considerable interest.

The original courtyard is now filled in with later building, but the timber-framing of the E range is visible on its W face. STABLE YARD to the N with mostly C19 buildings, in particular a neo-Norman game-larder.

SUMMER HOUSE. Built by Ellenborough to commemorate the staff who served him in India; a curious square stone building with pendant Gothic cusping under a hipped roof.

Southam is now becoming a residential area with a great number of new houses built in reconstructed stone.

IRON AGE PROMONTORY FORT, at the W end of Cleeve Common. Defended by the edge of the cliff on the W and SW, bivallate on the N, E, and SE. The outer rampart, enclosing about 5 acres, is in good condition and under grass. The circles in the centre and to N and S are probably the result of planting tree-clumps in the C17 and C18. A LINEAR DITCH with its main bank on the N side, ½ m. N, is undated.

STANDISH

ST NICHOLAS. A possession of St Peter's Abbey, Gloucester, the church is all of one period, the first part of the C14. It is aisleless, with a wide nave, an only slightly less wide but somewhat lower chancel, and a disproportionately narrow W tower surmounted by a graceful spire with rolls up the edges. The church was presumably built before the death of Edward II in 1327, but the E window looks *c*.1340 rather than *c*.1320. This very beautiful window has five lights, forming two intersecting arches, which are filled with reticulated tracery and many cusps; the contrasting flow of the tracery in the space above is horizontal, forming a kind of horizontal cross. The other win-

dows have two lights with Dec tracery, and are all the same
Mouldings are universally very simple, in contrast to the show
made by the E window. Small priest's doorway on the S, with
plain chamfer. No buttresses except at the junction of nave and
chancel; on the S a slight thickening of the wall marks the
protrusion of the rood-loft stair. S vestry C19. N porch with a
plain chamfered arch of two orders down to the ground. The
chancel is more than half the size of the nave and is divided
from it by a large plain chamfered arch. Nave roof covered in
panelling with one hundred and eighty differently carved
bosses. On the N wall the PISCINA of an old nave altar, with a
depressed ogee arch. The chancel roof looks like a fairly recent
restoration. The chancel PISCINA has a trefoil-headed ogee
arch. The church was restored in 1869 by *J. P. St Aubyn*,* and
most unhappily the walls were scraped of their plaster. –
FONT. 1860 by *F. Niblett*. – PULPIT. Of *c.*1700. Oak, with inlaid panels and carved mouldings. The sounding-board and
other adjuncts have been removed. – BOX PEWS. Designed in
1764 by *Anthony Keck*; oak panelling and delicate mouldings.
– WEST GALLERY and ORGAN CASE. By *S. E. Dykes Bower*,
1950. – ALTAR. By *Dykes Bower*, 1927. – STAINED GLASS. E
window by *Clayton & Bell*, 1879. – S window in the chancel by
Kempe, 1888. – PLATE. Chalice and Paten Cover, 1573, which
formerly belonged to St Mary Magdalene, Colethrop, now
demolished; Chalice, 1651; Almsdish, 1721. – MONUMENTS.
Sir Henry Winston † 1609. Rustic classical monument with
short fluted Ionic columns supporting an enriched entablature
and pediment flanked by ball-finials. It was painted and restored in 1965, under the supervision of *S. E. Dykes Bower*,
and now presents a most gorgeous appearance, with an inscription commemorating the fact that Winston Churchill was
a descendant of Winston. – GRAVE SLAB, beneath the nave
piscina. Early C14, with a woman's head and a foliated cross
carved in low relief. – LEDGER STONE with coat of arms, on
the N of the altar, to Robert Frampton, Bishop of Gloucester,
† 1708.‡ – In the CHURCHYARD a good collection of C17 and
C18 TABLE TOMBS. – LYCHGATE. Designed by *S. E. Dykes
Bower*, 1932.

* *James Piers St Aubyn*, 1815–95. Educated chiefly at Gloucester and a pupil
of *Thomas Fulljames*.

‡ He was one of the famous Non-juring bishops of 1689, who refused to
swear allegiance to William III. Pepys thought he preached 'most like an
apostle . . . it was much the best time that I ever spent in church'.

CHURCH HOUSE, running N–S along the W side of the N part of
the churchyard. C16. Built by the churchwardens for parochial
purposes. At the N end is a room traditionally known as the
kitchen which has two doorways with four-centred arches.
Two other doorways have spandrels ornamented with leaves.
The building is buttressed, and has Tudor mullioned windows.

STANDISH COURT, SW of the church. Originally C14 and built
for the Abbot of Gloucester (though not necessarily used by him
as a residence), the house has undergone many alterations and
additions. It is H-shaped in plan, with additional buildings on
the E and N sides of the N courtyard. The hall was in the central
portion of the H. Buttery on the N with a small vaulted cellar.
On the NE corner a Tudor addition, called the Abbot's Wing,
which contains in the ground-floor room a fine chimneypiece
with moulded splayed jambs, and lintel. Main N elevation of
two storeys with five C17 mullioned and transomed windows.

GATEHOUSE. C14. Two plain chamfered arches survive, together with buttresses and part of a stone spiral staircase.

STANDISH VICARAGE, ½ m. N. The site of the vicarage dates
from 1348, but the oldest part of the house appears to be C15.
This consists of the N portion of the existing building, which
now has two ground-floor rooms with moulded ceiling beams,
originally divided by a passage. The entrance on the S survives,
inside the building, with a splendid moulded stone ogee archway. On the W is an original moulded Tudor window with
mullions. On the N are two wide buttresses, one of which contains a garderobe. A wing on the SW was added in Tudor times.
This house was restored by Bishop Frampton in the C17;
there is a sundial on the SE buttress with the arms of the See of
Gloucester. About 1839 the hall and study were added on the
S, in the style of the original building, by *William James*. The
windows are copies of the original Tudor windows. At the back
of the house an ancient stew pond.

STANDISH HOUSE, near Stonehouse. Built in 1830 as a hunting-
box, and now the centre of a large hospital. Square stucco house
with a classical porch.

COTTAGE, in Standish-Moreton Lane. C17, gabled, of stone;
the back is timber-framed.

STANLEY PONTLARGE

PARISH CHURCH (dedication unknown). A small Norman
building, but with mostly C19 neo-Norman fenestration.* N

* According to Murray's Guide, in 1884, there was no E window at all.

doorway Late Norman, with two orders of chevron moulding, a billet hood-mould, plain tympanum with a band of dogtooth ornament round it, and jamb shafts with scalloped capitals. s doorway simpler, with a plain tympanum. w window Late Perp. Bellcote for two bells on the E gable of the nave. The chancel arch, which has moved outwards, has chevron mouldings and jamb shafts with scalloped capitals. Perp PISCINA. The nave roof was reconstructed in 1923–4 with undressed oak from Chedworth. Two beams at the w perhaps supported a gallery. Stone-flagged floor. – FONT. A Norman bowl cut into octagonal shape, symbolizing re-creation, in the C13. It rests on three circular rolls of diminishing circumference. – PLATE. Chalice, 1610; Flagon, 1758 by *Thomas Whipham* and *Charles Wright*; Chalice, 1792 by *Henry Chawner*; Paten, 1827.

THE COTTAGE. Partly Tudor, but most of the windows are C19 copies.

STAPLETON *see* STOKE GIFFORD

STAUNTON
Near Coleford

ALL SAINTS. One of the ring of older churches round the Forest of Dean. Norman with central tower, the same form as at English Bicknor and St Briavels. The windows in the second stage of the tower are Norman, and the corbels in the upper stage indicate its original height. Perp embattled top with C19 pinnacles. An angel on the SW corner holds the arms of the Walwyns, patrons in the late C15. The N aisle, three bays of which are blocked, has an arcade of two bays with round Norman arches, and three bays with early pointed arches. S aisle arcade of five bays with pointed arches and beautiful E.E. capitals, some with stiff-leaf ornament. Perp windows in the aisles. The N chapel in the transept, or Lady Chapel, has two E.E. image brackets and a trefoiled PISCINA. In the s chapel an E.E. PISCINA and s window; otherwise the transept chapels are C15. Crossing arches E.E., that on the s having rounded or keeled mouldings with waterholding bases. Broad chancel. Limewashed walls. Re-seated in 1872. – PULPIT. Built off the stairs to the rood and belfry, with ogee arches; c.1500. – Two FONTS. One is very Early Norman, a rough cube with a band of pellet mouldings; the other is Late Perp, but re-tooled. – STAINED GLASS. Small window high up in the E wall with medieval glass. – Lurid E window probably by *Bell* of Bristol, 1862. – E window in the N chapel by *Kempe*. – PLATE. Chalice and Paten, 1684. – Altar ornaments in the N chapel by *Kempe*. – MONUMENT (chancel). A flat C13 gravestone with incised cross and chalice, apparently re-used in the C17. – CHURCHYARD. NE of the church the grave of David Mushet, the metallurgist whose experiments with those of his son at Coleford revolutionized the steel industry.

VILLAGE CROSS, s of the church. Shaft, plinth, and steps of a medieval cross.

CHURCH FARMHOUSE, opposite and s of the church. C17, stone, with a pretty oval window in one gable. VICTORIA COTTAGE has a date-stone 1719; THE STEPS, C17, has stone mullioned windows. ANIMAL POUND, SW of the church. Octagonal; stone walls 7 ft high; possibly C18.

HIGHMEADOW. The site of the great C17 house of the Hall family, once offered to the Duke of Wellington but turned down on the grounds that the landscape too much resembled the Pyrenees. A farm building retains some Tudor windows.

STAUNTON

7020

6 m. NE of Newent

ST JAMES. Norman herringbone masonry survives in the s wall of the nave; otherwise the church is mostly C14, over-restored in 1860 by *G. Row Clarke*, who rebuilt the chancel, added the s porch and N vestry, and remodelled the N aisle. Embattled C14 W tower with diagonal buttresses, a NE stair-vice, and a spire. Perp W window. E of the N aisle is a pretty transeptal chapel, with transverse gabled wagon roof enriched with panels and bosses, a trefoil-headed PISCINA, and a Dec window. Four-bay N arcade with octagonal lozenge-shaped piers supporting unusually straight-sided pointed arches. Nave PISCINA s of the restored chancel arch, and the entrance to a former rood loft on the N. Lancet windows in the chancel. – FONT. On the pedestal are the heads of a King, Queen, Bishop, and Rector. – STAINED GLASS. E and W windows 1870 by *Alexander Gibbs*. – PLATE. Chalice, 1645; Flagon, 1729. – MONUMENTS. C14 recessed tomb in the s wall of the nave. – William Horton † 1612. Kneeling effigies of his family in painted stone, with heraldry. – Francis Walker † 1829, by *Daniel Hewlett* of Gloucester.

STAUNTON COURT. Probably built in the latter half of the C16, but much altered. Modern additions. Timber-framed, with a great brick chimney. The outbuildings include a square timber-framed DOVECOTE.

CHARTIST HOUSES. Part of the settlement founded by Fergus O'Connor at Snig's End (*see* Corse) and Lowbands. Built *c.*1847. There are sixteen of these houses s of the road between the Swan Inn and the church, and nine others adjacent to BROOK FARM.

STAVERTON

ST CATHERINE. Nave, chancel, N transept, with tower opposite on the s, and s porch. The exterior has a somewhat patched-up appearance, particularly in the nave, where C18 brick has been used (dated before 1736). Restored in 1884 by *H. M. Townsend* and again in 1897. Short truncated ashlar tower with embattled parapet dated 1712, which is presumably when an upper stage was taken down. Good Dec window with reticulated tracery, large diagonal buttresses on the s, and a sundial over the s bell-opening. N transept of ashlar. E chancel window Dec. In the E side of the (modern) s porch is a low pointed C13 doorway into the tower. The interior of the narrow nave has a C14 braced collar-beam roof, and moulded tiebeams with braced king-posts. C19 flat plastered ceiling in the N transept. Arch into the tower C18, with plain imposts and keystone. Under the tower on the s is a C13 PISCINA, and signs of springers for a stone vault, also probably C13. C19 chancel roof; the floor is raised on steps. – FONT. C19. – PULPIT. C19 or later. – STAINED GLASS. Tracery in the E window has fragments of medieval glass including the top of a Crucifixion. – The two lights of the E window have glass designed by *J. Eadie Reid* in 1914, and carried out by the *Gateshead Stained Glass Co.* – PLATE. Almsdish, 1678; two Chalices, Paten, and Flagon. 1852. – MONUMENTS. Tablets in the chancel: Thomas Banester † 1627. – Rev. John Kipling † 1794, by *Bryan* of Gloucester. – Henry Wyndowe † 1772, a nice Baroque marble monument with a pun in the Latin inscription and a carved eye. – Thomas Pearce † 1808, by *Lewis* of Gloucester. – Joseph Pearce † 1807, by *Lewis* of Cheltenham. – In the N transept: Elizabeth Home † 1848, by *G. Lewis*, showing a conventional resurrection scene. – William Pearce † 1818, by *Gardner* of Tewkesbury. – Rhoda Pearce † 1827, by *E. Gaffin*.

MANOR, SW of the church. A good L-shaped timber-framed

house, C16 or earlier. The N wing has a modern Stuart coat of arms carved in stone in the overhanging gable-end, and the initials C.R. Inside over a large open fireplace is an original Carolean Royal Arms. Gabled E wing with elaborate half-timber work.

STAVERTON HOUSE. Faced in stucco, like many Cheltenham houses, with cornice and blocking course, two storeys, 1, 3, 1 bays, and a peculiar tall ashlar porch.

STAVERTON PRIORY. Early C19, stucco, with hipped slate roof, overhanging eaves, two storeys, two windows, and a Doric portico in stone, the frieze enriched with wreaths.

STAVERTON COURT. Set slightly to the E of the village in a park-like field. Early C19, ashlar-faced, two storeys, four windows, cornice and parapet with vase finials. Return elevation with a shaped parapet, Doric porch, and C19 wooden veranda.

STAVERTON AIRPORT is about 1 m. to the S.

STOKE GIFFORD

ST MICHAEL. The existing building, with the exception of the font, does not appear to be older than the C14; it was greatly altered in the C18. N porch with a pretty ogee-arched entrance with crocketed finial and pinnacles. S tower of coursed Pennant stone with flush ashlar quoins of alternating lengths. Three stages with diagonal buttresses on the lower stage, and a Perp embattled parapet with pinnacles. Plain blocked round-arched S doorway. Most of the windows are Late Perp or later, with straight heads and cusped lights, though the E window of the N aisle is C14 Dec. C18 N arcade of three bays with classical fluted piers, C18 chancel arch. The N chapel, now the vestry, was open to the chancel in the C18, when it was known as the Duchess of Beaufort's room, and an C18 fireplace survives at the E end. The church was restored c.1894–7 by *E. H. Lingen Barker*. – FONT. Norman, with one scallop on each face; partially built into the N wall of the N aisle in the C18. – COMMUNION RAILS. Early C18, with turned and twisted balusters. – PANELLING. A fragment of C18 panelling survives behind the organ at the W end. – STAINED GLASS. E window by *Joseph Bell* of Bristol, c.1900. – ROYAL ARMS. Georgian. – HATCHMENT. Arms of Parsons. – PLATE. Flagon, 1720 by *John Bignell*; Chalice and Paten Cover, 1775 by *Andrew Fogelberg*; two Plates, 1775 by *Frederick Kandler*. – MONUMENTS. Painted stone Jacobean-style monument, dated 1662, with brass plates commemorating Mary Berkeley † 1615 and Richard Berkeley † 1661. – John Berkeley † 1736. Marble tablet on a gadrooned sill, with Corinthian pilasters, a broken pediment, cherubs, and heraldry. – William Willcox † 1819, by *Greenway*.

STOKE PARK. The original manor house, built by the Berkeleys in the C16, on a great artificial platform, was rebuilt by *James Paty* c. 1760, for Norborne Berkeley, Lord Botetourt, Governor of Virginia in 1768–70. Central block with wings on an H-shaped plan, with bay windows each end. Octagonal rooms on the S and W, constructed so as to exploit the splendid views, with an artificial lake and the remains of an obelisk in the foreground. Early C19 Gothic porch and castellated parapet, also added later, but there are no Gothic touches inside, where all is classical. The two best rooms on the SE corner have Rococo plaster ceilings of 1763 by *William Stocking*, who did work at the Royal Fort, Bristol. One room has fluted Roman Doric columns, with an elaborate cornice, the metopes carved with masks, and trophies, and Bacchanalian masks on the ceiling. The staircase ceiling is somewhat later and has the Greek-key pattern, with Ionic pilasters on the landing. The house is now a hospital.

The ORANGERY (now a CHAPEL), of c.1700, has a central portion with four fluted Corinthian pilasters. It is at one end of the great TERRACE, which retains its original Jacobean or late C16 stone balustrade, ornamented with strapwork.

Besides the remains of the OBELISK, which is a memorial to a member of the Berkeley family of c.1732, there is a SARCOPHAGUS in the near-by wood commemorating a winner of the St Leger, c.1834.

The grounds were laid out by *Thomas Wright*, c. 1760.

BEAUFORT HOUSE, No. 52 PARK ROAD, 1 m. S, in Stapleton.* C17, refronted in the classical style of 1860. A living room retains a splendid plaster ceiling of c.1690, with a broad oval wreath of fruit and flowers, and corner panels decorated with oak and broom. Staircase also of c.1690, with early C19 shafts added to the newels. Rear altered in the early C19. The forecourt gatepiers have original stone pineapple finials. The house next door, No. 54, has a C17 chimneypiece carved in the manner of *Grinling Gibbons*.

* Strictly speaking these houses are just in Bristol; but they have not hitherto been mentioned in these volumes.

STOKE ORCHARD

ST JAMES THE GREAT. An ancient chapel-of-ease attached to Bishop's Cleeve. A very interesting, small, mostly Norman building of *c*.1170, consisting of nave and chancel, and a single bell-turret over the chancel arch. Plain Norman S doorway with tympanum and two scratch dials on the E jamb. Ancient NORTH DOOR with original C12 ironwork, with animal heads (like those in some of the wall paintings inside) of Scandinavian origin. The chancel arch is supported by exterior buttresses and the chancel itself is a rebuilding, with a lower-pitched roof than formerly. The chancel windows are Perp but the PISCINA is Norman.

C13 chancel arch, pointed and later than the plain Norman responds, with their capitals (one enriched with scallops, the other with trumpet-scallops) and chamfered abaci; the original arch must have moved owing to poor foundations. The nave walls also lean outwards and have round-arched, deeply splayed Norman windows N and S. The WALL PAINTINGS which cover all four walls of the nave were discovered before 1889, and further restored in 1953–5, by *Clive Rouse*. Five successive schemes were identified dating from between *c*.1190–1220 and 1723. The most important is the earliest, comprising a cycle of the life of St James of Compostela, the only one in England of that subject. The only comparable series on the Continent is found in one of the windows of Chartres Cathedral. It is set between borders which change all the way round the nave. The paintings, of twenty-eight scenes, are of poor artistic quality and often fragmentary. The decorative borders are striking, and in their motifs provide a link with the curious school of sculpture in the Hereford region of Kilpeck, derived from a wide variety of sources. Bristol was a port for pilgrims going to Compostela. – FONT. Norman, with intersecting arch ornament. – BENCHES. C16. – COMMUNION RAIL. C17. – PULPIT. Jacobean. – PLATE. Chalice and Paten Cover, 1618.

Opposite, utilitarian buildings of the NATIONAL COAL BOARD. MILL FARMHOUSE, ¼ m. S. C16/17 with a medieval wing at the back. Timber-framed, partly faced in brick, and with Cotswold stone roofs. The rear wing has a good roof with arched braces. The chief front room has fine moulded beams and oak panelling. The brick DOVECOTE, with a date-stone 1741, has a gabled stone roof and lantern.

STONE

ALL SAINTS. Mostly C13/14. W tower with diagonal buttresses, an open pierced parapet with pinnacles, and a spire. The windows of the nave are Dec, and it has an embattled parapet which masks the lowered roof. Small chancel E window, rebuilt in 1831 in Dec style. N vestry of 1846. The W window and door in the tower are Perp insertions. Chancel arch of two chamfered orders. Either side are round windows with tracery, to light the rood, the steps to which survive. Also a PISCINA, high up for a rood altar. The chancel has an embattled wallplate, priest's doorway, and AUMBRY. – STAINED GLASS. Fragments of medieval glass in the tracery of two windows on the N, showing the Berkeley arms, and one on the S with the badge of Edward IV. – Two-light N window by *Joseph Bell*, 1960. – PEWS. 1857. – ROOFS. 1894. – CHANDELIER. Brass; 1754. Bristol style. – PULPIT. 1755. – ROYAL ARMS. 1789. – PLATE. Chalice, Paten, and Flagon, 1795; two Almsplates, 1736. – MONUMENTS. N and S of the nave are matching tomb recesses with cusped ogee arches, and low tomb-chests carved with five panels of quatrefoils, that on the N having a cross in low relief on top. – John Morse † 1728. Marble Baroque tablet. – John Cox † 1795, by *J. Pearce* of Frampton. Nice classical tablet with a draped urn. – William James † 1818, by *Reeves* of Bath. – George Jenner † 1846, by *Tyley*.

VICARAGE. 1743 by *Ephraim Hale*, mason. Altered in the C19.

STONE MILL. 1796. Painted brick, three storeys and five bays.

MIDDLEMILL FARM. Early C18. Two storeys, five bays. Inside, contemporary panelling, chimneypiece with Roman Doric order, and staircase. The back is older, and one bedroom has fine Jacobean panelling.

PEDINGTON MANOR, 1 m. NW. C17 gabled house, rendered, with an C18 wing.

STONEHOUSE

ST CYR. Embattled Perp W tower with NE turret; otherwise rebuilt in 1854 by *Henry Crisp*, Perp, with nave, N and S aisles of five bays, chancel and chapels. – STAINED GLASS. E window by *Wailes*. – Sanctuary windows by *Payne*, 1965. – PLATE. Two Chalices and Credence Paten, 1819. – MONUMENTS. Louise Davies † 1819, by *Tyley* of Bristol. – Elizabeth Dimock † 1854, by *Hamlett*. – Samuel Spencer † 1790, by *Franklin*.

ROMAN CATHOLIC CHURCH. 1966 by *Peter Falconer.* –
Stations of the Cross by *Bryant Fedden.*

STONEHOUSE COURT. Elizabethan mansion with gables and
mullioned and transomed windows. The two-storey gabled
porch has the modern inscription, 'E.R. 43. 1601'. s front with
two projecting gabled wings. The house was completely
gutted by fire in 1908, after having been altered by *Sir Edwin
Lutyens* in 1906; but Lutyens's oriel window on the s survives,
and many other features. He has repeated the form of the
Tudor windows on the N side.

WYCLIFFE COLLEGE. A public school founded in 1882. The
Senior School is a conglomeration of buildings of all dates.
The CHAPEL has a late C19 tower with heavy pinnacles and a
spire; otherwise it was altered in 1911 and rebuilt in 1952, by
H. F. Trew, and has lancet or round-headed windows, and a
fine open roof with scissor-beam trusses. The STAINED GLASS
in the E window is by *Hugh Easton,* 1956. E of the chapel is a
C16/17 house, L-shaped in plan, with two gables facing the
street, either side of a three-storey porch. The gables have good
carved finials, and the windows have concave-moulded mullions. The SIBLEY MEMORIAL HALL was designed by *Peter
Falconer,* 1964–5. The Junior School has part of an C18 house
incorporated in later building.

HAYWARDSEND. C16/17 gabled house with mullioned windows.
s front Georgian with date-stone 1789. Two storeys and eight
bays. The centre breaks forward with a pediment; portico
with four Tuscan columns.

BRIDGEND BRUSH WORKS. A cloth mill till the mid C19. The
brick buildings with stone dressings, and a tower, were erected
*c.*1876. The tower has a tall sprocketed Welsh slate roof,
surmounted by ironmongery. BRIDGEND FARM was the
clothier's house; early C19, of brick, with a stone cornice, and
pediment. On the road from Bridgend to Stanley Downton the
FLEECE INN. This has an unusual early C19 façade with a
shaped parapet with concave sides and a flat top, in which is a
rusticated niche with an inscription in good Victorian lettering.

WAREHOUSE, Stonehouse Mills. 1889 by *W. Clissold.*

WEAVING MILL, Ryford Mills. 1948 by *S. S. Careless.*

OLDEND, ¾ m. NW. C17 or earlier stone-built house with gables,
and a doorway with a large C18 segmental hood on brackets.

STOWE GRANGE *see* ST BRIAVELS

SWINDON

ST LAWRENCE. Apart from the extremely rare hexagonal Norman tower, which resembles one at Ozleworth, this church was treated shamefully c.1845, when it was rebuilt by *T. Fulljames*. Even at the time, the *Gentleman's Magazine* deprecated Fulljames's plans, which entailed the removal of the internal massive Norman walls and piers and the s and w walls of the s aisle, and severe restoration of the chancel and N aisle, all in order to gain fifty-seven extra seats.

The irregular hexagonal w tower has no two sides quite alike. The top stage has two-light Norman openings divided by round columns with cushion capitals, set in splayed round-headed recesses. On the N side, within a neo-Norman arch, is the tall original Norman doorway, with single jamb shafts and cushion capitals, and an arch with two orders of roll-mouldings and hood-mould. The tower arch also survives inside. It is 11 ft wide and has shafts with plain capitals on the w and is perfectly plain on the E. The nave is a shocking example of neo-Norman work, with three-bay arcades and thin piers, and a chancel arch ornamented with mean neo-Norman motifs. Hammerbeam roof supported on corbels with ugly grotesques. The original C13 E window of the s aisle is preserved, and the s window of the chancel is also C13. On the N of the chancel a lancet window and a small blocked Norman window. N aisle N windows C19 Dec. – FONT. C15; octagonal bowl enriched with quatrefoils. – PULPIT. Scraped stone; possibly C16. – STAINED GLASS. E window by *T. Willement*, 1843. A brass by *Percival* of Cheltenham, commemorating the erection of the window, is under the tower. – PLATE. Chalice and Paten Cover, 1576. – MONUMENTS. As one would expect in a church so near Cheltenham, there are a number of early-mid C19 tablets. William Long † 1815, by *J. Hale*. – Captain Edward Stopford R.N. † 1834, by *Gardner* of Cheltenham. – Sarah Elliott † 1838 and Henrietta Ricketts † 1838, neo-Greek and quite good, both by *Lewis*. – John Cox † 1847, by *Blackwell*. – And a large tablet to the family of Admiral Sir Cornwallis and Lady Caroline Ricketts, c.1898.

MANOR HOUSE. C17 and C18. Pretty s front with brick gables. Three storeys and two windows either side of a two-storey centre with three windows and parapet. The central ground-floor room has Regency doorcases and a marble fireplace. The

back is older and includes a timber-framed part. Diagonal
stone chimneys with moulded caps.

MAUD'S COTTAGE. A timber-framed, thatched cottage in the
churchyard. OLD SWINDON HOUSE is late C18 with a stucco
front in the Cheltenham manner. Attached to it is a house with
Gothic windows.

The village identity is now almost lost, as it becomes swallowed
up in the Cheltenham spread of new housing estates (though
most of the new housing here is attractive) and small factories.

TALBOT'S END see CROMHALL

TAYNTON   7020

ST LAWRENCE. The ancient church was destroyed during the
Civil War (1643), and a new one was built by order of Parliament in 1647–8; a simple hall-church, orientated N and S. It
was restored by *Thomas Fulljames* in 1864, and the chancel
added in 1894. – Restoration FONT, with cherub-heads and
acanthus-leaf. – HOLY TABLE. C17, but altered in the C19. –
PULPIT. Early C17, with Renaissance detail. – WEST DOOR-
WAY. C17, classical, oak, with fluted pilasters and Corinthian
capitals. – PLATE. Chalice and Paten Cover, early C17. –
MONUMENTS. John Holder † 1734, by *Ricketts* of Gloucester.
Baroque marble tablet. – Elizabeth Holder † 1765. Oval marble
tablet surmounted by a shell. – Joseph Clark † 1808, by
Millard & Cooke. Attractive small tablet with urn and palms.

TAYNTON HOUSE. C16, with three gables. The house was remodelled in 1810, and has a pleasant contemporary staircase
with Gothick windows, and Regency doorcases. BARN. 1695
Of brick, with a stone roof. Six bays with queen-post trusses,
and two gabled porches with stone cartouches containing Latin
tags and John Holder's initials. A few years later, Holder
added a two-storeyed MILL HOUSE, in which he installed cider
presses, and opposite, an OX HOUSE. They are at r. angles to
the barn and form a very nice group, with an enclosed garden
in front. The same rose-red brick is used in the other garden
WALLS which he continued building up to 1719.

THE GROVE. The oldest part is Late Tudor, partly timber-
framed, with white-painted brick, and gables. Enlarged c.1630;
Jacobean timber porch. It was the home of Thomas Pury,
M.P. for Gloucester during the Civil War and the Long Parliament; his coat of arms is at the back of one of the fireplaces. In

the early C18 one gable was rebuilt and one of the rooms was panelled in pine. A matching gable was added in 1925 by *H. F. Trew*. Next to the oldest part of the house is a CIDER MILL and GRANARY, in red brick and stone slate, which looks contemporary with the barns at Taynton House, only on a much smaller scale.

HOWN HALL. Early C18 farmhouse; brick, two storeys, five bays. Forecourt wall with pretty sweeping lines and stone caps. Situated in delightful undulating country, with hedgerow trees, under the shadow of May Hill and its tree-clump top.

TEDDINGTON

9030

ST NICHOLAS. The oldest part of the church is the tall Early Norman chancel arch, and the wall in which it is built contains other fragments of worked Norman stones. The fabric of the nave seems to have been rebuilt in the C13 and the chancel altered and lengthened in the C13 and C14. On the N side of the nave is a small window with a trefoil head. The N doorway must date from *c.*1200. This is indicated by the pointed arch, the continuous roll-moulding, and the hood-mould on a human and a beast's head. Chancel E window Dec. The four two-light square-headed windows in the side walls have the same jambs and mullions but must have lost their tracery. The N porch is also a C14 addition. N doorway of the chancel C15. The S nave windows are dated 1624. The W tower is also dated: it was built in 1567, when the splendid E.E. tower arch and W window were brought here from Hailes Abbey. The arch opening into the nave is too grand for a simple country church, and in any case it does not fit its position and has no bases. The responds, however, are identical on plan with the piers of the ambulatory round the apse of the abbey church built in 1270–7, to receive the shrine of the Holy Blood. They represent a mighty round pier shape with four attached shafts. The window, too, is a fine example of Late E.E. work, of two lights with cinquefoiled heads above which is a richly moulded and cusped circle. The jambs have shafts with delicately cut capitals and bases. Here then can be seen fragments of beautiful work far exceeding anything that now remains on the abbey site.

The walls of the chancel are scraped, but the nave walls are plastered and have WALL PAINTINGS of which the most conspicuous is a large and important ROYAL ARMS of William and Mary, 1689, enclosed with draped architectural features. On the opposite and N wall are traces of the Lord's Prayer and Creed painted in C16 lettering. – FONT. Bowl modern, but the base and circular shaft are C14 with eight small attached shaft and between them ballflower similar in design to the font at Tewkesbury. – STAINED GLASS. In a N window of the chancel, fragments of C15 quarries of flowers. – FURNISHINGS. The seat ends have well-moulded top rails of the C15 or C16. – PULPIT and READING DESK. 1655 – an unusual period for church furniture. The pulpit has the names of the Commonwealth churchwardens, and the desk has texts 'Pray continually', the Genevan rendering of 'Pray without ceasing', and 'Quench not ye spirit, Despise not prophecying'. The pulpit has a sounding-board. – COMMUNION RAILS. Also C17. – PLATE. Chalice and Paten, 1571.

TEDDINGTON CROSS HANDS. Stone guide-post with a pyramidal top and ball-finial, erected by Edmund Attwood in 1676.

TEWKESBURY

8030

THE ABBEY CHURCH OF ST MARY

INTRODUCTION

The Benedictine abbey was founded by a Norman nobleman, Robert FitzHamon, who died in 1107, before the completion of the building, which was consecrated in 1121. The nave may have been finished at this date; the tower appears to have been built during the second quarter of the C12. In the ambulatory plan and in the elevation of the nave, the church bore a close resemblance to the sister church at Gloucester. In all probability W towers were designed at the ends of the nave aisles, but they were not carried on with, and the turrets on either side of the lofty arch, which fills the whole height of the W front, appear to have been substituted for them. After FitzHamon's death, the building work was carried on by his son-in-law, Robert FitzRoy, Earl of Gloucester, a bastard son of Henry I. From him the 'Honour of Tewkesbury' descended to the great Norman family of de Clare, and it was during their ownership that the two chapels adjoining the N transept were built, towards the middle of the C13, that on the E side taking the place of an apsidal chapel similar to that in the S transept. Eleanor de Clare married Hugh Le Despencer,

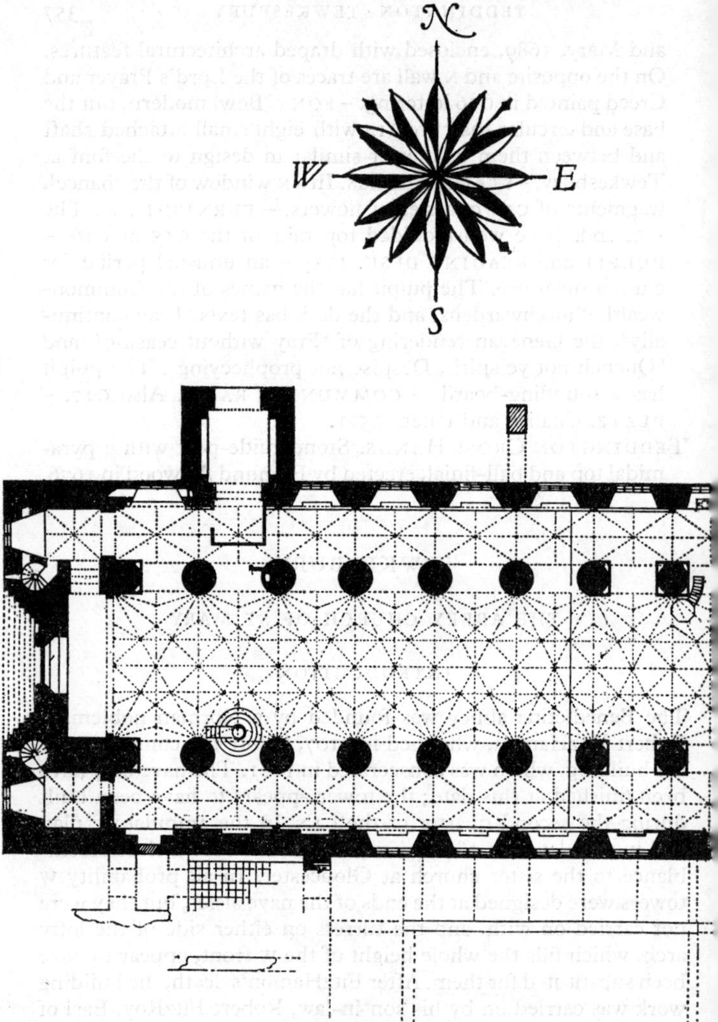

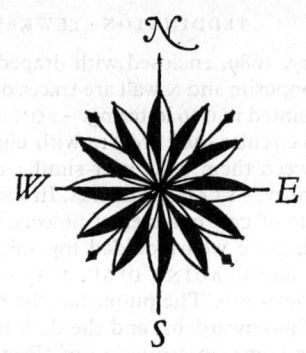

N
W E
S

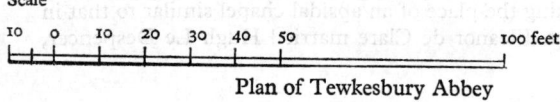

Scale

10   0   10   20   30   40   50   100 feet

Plan of Tewkesbury Abbey

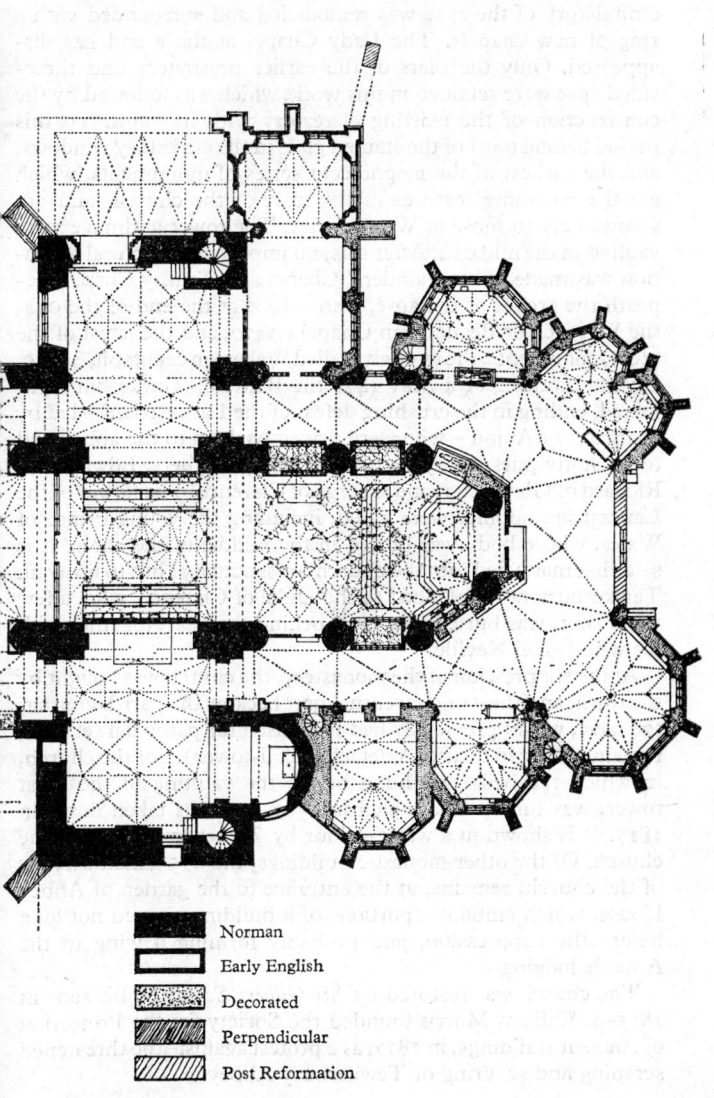

Norman

Early English

Decorated

Perpendicular

Post Reformation

whose evil influence on Edward II led to his execution in 1325.
It was during the life-time of Eleanor and her son Hugh that the
ambulatory of the apse was remodelled and surrounded with a
ring of new chapels. The Lady Chapel at the E end has disappeared. Only the piers of the earlier presbytery and three-
sided apse were retained in this work, which was followed by the
construction of the existing clerestory with its vault. To this
period belong most of the stained glass in the clerestory windows,
and the earliest of the magnificent series of monuments, which
are the crowning features of this part of the church, and are
second only to those at Westminster. The tower and nave were
vaulted in the mid C14. After this, no important structural alteration was made. The Founders' Chapel and Trinity Chapel, beneath the arches of the apse, were added at the end of the C14,
the Warwick or Beauchamp Chapel c.1430, and the latest of the
great monuments, the wrongly-called Wakeman cenotaph, c.1450.
On the morning of 4 May 1471 the Battle of Tewkesbury was
joined, ending in the crushing defeat of the Lancastrians – led by
Margaret of Anjou – who were driven back on to the abbey and
town, hotly pursued by the three Yorkist brothers, Edward IV,
Richard of Gloucester, and George of Clarence. The flower of the
Lancastrian nobility were killed, including the young Prince of
Wales, whose body was buried in the middle of the choir. It is
said that many fled into the church for sanctuary; but to no avail.
Tewkesbury now belonged to the Duke of Clarence, who, a few
years later, was buried in a vault behind the altar, together with
his wife Isabel Neville.

At the suppression of the monastery, the church was bought by
the town, and the E or conventual part became the parish church;
the nave, which previously had been used for parochial services,
remained long in disuse. A detached bell-tower NE of the church,
in which the bells had hung before the vaulting of the great
tower, was turned into a gaol in 1582, and was taken down in
1817. It is shown in a water-colour by *Turner*, preserved in the
church. Of the other monastic buildings, the C15 gatehouse, SW
of the church, remains, at the entrance to the garden of Abbey
House, which embodies portions of a building erected not long
before the suppression, and probably forming a wing to the
Abbot's lodging.

The church was restored by *Sir Gilbert Scott* and his sons in
1875–9. William Morris founded the Society for the Protection
of Ancient Buildings, in 1877, as a protest against 'the threatened
scraping and scouring of Tewkesbury Abbey'.

EXTERIOR

The church is approached on the N through fine wrought-iron churchyard GATES erected by Lord Gage in 1734, and attributed to *William Edney*. The whole length of the Norman nave is visible, dominated by the huge C12 Norman TOWER, probably 13 the largest and finest Romanesque tower in England. The three top stages are enriched, the upper and lower with shafts and chevroned arches – the upper pierced by double and the lower by single bell-openings – and the middle with a small blind arcade of interlacing arches. The whole of the outer facing of the tower was repaired in 1935–9 by *Thomas Overbury* and *Sir Charles Peers*. On the sides of the lower portion can be seen the ridge lines of the original high gabled roofs, which were taken down in 1593, when the much lower-pitched roofs were substituted. The pinnacles and battlements of the tower were added in 1660; the wooden spire had fallen in 1559. The nave windows are C14 Dec insertions, as are the clerestory windows, which break the Norman arcade of small round arches irregularly.

We can now look at the WEST FRONT. The great Norman 14 recessed arch, with its six orders of roll mouldings supported on shafts with scalloped capitals, is 65 ft high. It is one of the finest original Norman fronts now existing, in spite of alterations. The presence of a seventh inner order was discovered by *Sir George Gilbert Scott*. The window was inserted in 1686 – an example of Gothic Survival or copying – after an earlier window had been destroyed in a gale in 1661. On either side of the arch the wall surface is enriched with a double arcade of small Norman arches, and at each end is a turret, the lower portions of which are Norman, though the pinnacles and spires are altered. A straight parapet replaces the C12 gable.

The S wall of the nave shows traces of where monastic buildings were built on to the church, including the CLOISTER, the one existing bay of which is mostly a C19 reconstruction. The cloister had been rebuilt early in the C15, in close imitation of that at Gloucester, and the panelled Perp arcading, at the back of the N and part of the E walks, remains as added to the walls of the church. The doorway from the cloister to the church is part of this work. Passing round the C18 SW buttress of the TRANSEPT, we see on its S wall some corbel stones which probably supported the roof of the dormitory, while the original arcading survives high up on its E face. In the apsidal end of the transept chapel is a Dec window, inserted when the original E window was blocked by the building of the buttressed sacristy in the C14. We can now walk round the chevet of C14 chapels at the E end. The three-light Dec windows, of stepped lancet lights, in several cases have the distinctive feature of many cusps in the centre lights. Above the chapels rises the CHOIR with its ornate windows, enriched by ballflower and crowned by gables, and its embattled and pierced Dec parapet and flying buttresses. The level of the roof was lowered in 1603. The blank E wall, now pierced by two windows and with a few clustered shafts and springings, indicates where the Lady Chapel was. There are two arches, that of the entrance to the chapel and that of the chapel high vaults. Also there is a clear difference between the shafts and capitals of c.1300 and a Perp re-management. Continuing along the N side, beyond the chapels and under the flying buttress, we come to a confusing area. The N transept has an E.E. N doorway of five orders of shafts with crocket capitals. This led originally into a chapel of which some of the vaulting springers survive. From this chapel a fine big arch, also with crocket capitals, led eastward into the Chapel of St Nicholas. This survives and has a Dec window to the E. Then the area between this chapel and the ambulatory was filled in by the Chapel of St James. The E wall of this has two Dec windows.

Finally the NORTH PORCH. It is high and tunnel-vaulted, and the long shafts of the outer and inner entrances all have small single-scallop capitals. The lintel of the inner doorway has two hogback lintels, one on top of the other. All this is clearly of before 1121. Over the arch is a modern image of Our Lady by *Darsie Rawlins*.

INTERIOR

10 The great Norman NAVE, probably complete at the time of consecration in 1121, is contemporary with the nave of Gloucester, and has many similar features. In both cases the columns are so huge that little more than abaci suffice for capitals. These round capitals seem to be a regional characteristic, as they are found also at Pershore and Malvern. The eight bays of cylindrical columns, here and at Gloucester, are double the height of those at Hereford, yet the diameters are practically the same (6 ft 6 in.) in all three churches. The arches at Tewkesbury are of two orders, the outer with a roll on the edge, the inner

broad on the underside and unmoulded. When columns, and not piers, support arches of more than one order, there can be little harmonious relationship between column and arch. Owing to the great height of the arcade there is a somewhat insignificant triforium, which has two twin openings in each bay, square-edged round arches over a cylindrical shaft. The capitals are treated in a variety of ways. The openings are unusually placed, on either side of the middle of the arch below. The form of the clerestory is partly obscured by the C14 vaulting, but blocked traces of the Norman clerestory wall-passage are recognizable. There is no indication of a Norman nave vault, nor of an intention to vault. The wooden roof was replaced by the existing lierne-vault c.1340. Beautiful though this vault is, it springs directly from the Norman capitals, producing a somewhat crushing effect. In the centre of the roof are fifteen bosses illustrating the Life of Christ; on each side 30 bosses bear angels playing musical instruments, as well as other designs. The W bay of the nave differs from the other bays. Instead of arcading there is solid wall to S and N, with one long demi-shaft which breaks off higher up. These solid walls and the arches across the aisles separating the W bays of the aisles from the rest indicate that a pair of W towers was intended. The aisles have some more interesting Norman features. In the outer walls are niches, oblong in section and much higher than wide. Their purpose is not known. Also the aisles connect with the transepts not by arches, but by half-arches, and it looks as if a beginning was made of half-tunnel-vaulting – a motif to be found e.g. at Tournus in Burgundy, the only church in France with giant columns older than those of Tewkesbury and Gloucester. If these vaults were projected, they were not carried on with, and the present vault with diagonal and ridge ribs is of c.1300. The monastic part of the church originally extended two bays W of the crossing with a pulpitum and rood screen; the position of the front of the rood screen is now marked by a difference in floor level. The TOWER was designed as a lantern, with triforium and arcading on the inner wall surfaces, intended to be seen from below, but since obscured by the splendid C14 lierne-vault, which is decorated with bosses bearing the arms of Sir Guy de Brien, and Yorkist badges added after 1471.

The TRANSEPTS pose a particularly interesting problem. They have to the E the entrance arch to the chancel aisle and above it the arch to a chancel gallery. There is next to these two the large opening to a former E chapel, and this also had an upper storey with its own arch opening to the transepts. Above this stage is again a tiny triforium with twin openings, and if one can assume that where the masonry now changes there was, as usual, a clerestory, then that makes a four-tier elevation, which would be internationally unique about 1100.* The C14 vaults have progressed towards the fan-vault, but as they have not abandoned the horizontal ridge rib, or struck off the arched ribs on the same curve, the fan-vault has not materialized. The S transept still retains its small apsidal chapel, and this has a vault with radiating ribs, though a Dec window is inserted on the S. The arches rest on twin jamb shafts with scalloped capitals. The N transept was originally constructed in the same way, but c.1237 the alterations began here to which reference has already been made (p. 362). A new chapel was built on to the E side, approached from the transept through the original Norman arch, and from the ambulatory by a wide new arch, later filled in with a Dec stone screen. To the N of this chapel is the Chapel of St Nicholas, divided from it by another fine E.E. arch. A beautiful E.E. arcade, originally with Purbeck marble shafts, runs round the walls, with broad stiff-leaf in the spandrels, but the rib-vaulting bears the de Clare and Despencer arms indicating a date a hundred years later. This is a good example of E.E. architecture, generally rare in Gloucestershire.

Returning to the AMBULATORY, which was remodelled during the first half of the C14, we can see the original Norman half-columns, with their capitals nearly similar in design to those in the nave, from which the C14 rib-vaulting now springs. The first radiating chapel on the N is that of ST MARGARET of Scotland, from whom the de Clares and Despencers were descended. It was, like the others in the chevet, wholly rebuilt in the Dec style, though only a little earlier in date than the Early Perp work at Gloucester. It has a Dec stone screen with delicate carved panels and open reticulated tracery above, into which is set the tomb and effigy of Sir Guy de Brien (see Monuments). Delightful lierne-vaulted roof with carved bosses. The recess on the N W is said to have been a Holy Well. The next chapel is a double one, containing altars to St Edmund and St Dunstan, Patron Saint of Bell Ringers. Bosses in the vault show the martyrdom of King Edmund.

---

* Unless one allows for the nave of Tournai Cathedral a yet earlier date (NP).

The stone screen running behind the high altar is nearly similar to that which guards St Margaret's Chapel. Centrally on the E is the blocked-up archway which led to the Lady Chapel. The iron grating on the floor leads to the vault where the Duke of Clarence was buried after his drowning in a butt of malmsey wine. The first chapel on the S is dedicated to St Faith and the next to St Catherine (now used as a museum); then comes the SACRISTY. Here we find the only extensive use of ballflower in the church, on the doorway, and round the string-course. The door itself is covered with iron plates, hammered flat, which are parts of the *brigandine* worn by the soldiers in the Battle of Tewkesbury.

Having left the best to the last, we now enter the PRESBY- 26 TERY. Six short round Norman piers with moulded Dec capitals support pointed arches, above which are seven Dec windows, and over all the marvellous lierne-vaulting of the C14, later peppered in the centre with the Yorkist badges of the 'Sun in Splendour'. The Norman piers pose yet another problem, to which the late Sir Alfred Clapham's solution is here accepted. It is probable that these piers were originally the same height as those in the nave. Their diameter is the same, and the bays are of the same dimensions. The string-course running below the choir windows is at the same height as the nave capitals, and this would mark the original height of the choir piers. We have seen on the other hand that there was a proper gallery at normal height (*see* p. 363). Such a gallery can only be reconciled with giant columns if an arrangement was adopted such as it is found later at Jedburgh, Romsey, and Christchurch, Oxford. In the C14 remodelling the new capitals were inserted three courses above the ambulatory vault springers, and moulded arches were thrown across the bays, thus reducing the height of each bay. The upper portions of the Norman piers were then encased in walling. Everything above the piers was removed, and replaced by the series of large Dec windows. S of the altar are mutilated Dec SEDILIA which still show traces of rich gilding and colour. The ALTAR is a mensa, consecrated in 1239, and made of Purbeck marble.

MONUMENTS

It is best next to study the MONUMENTS, as they form an important architectural feature of the choir. There are three CHANTRY CHAPELS of the stone-cage type, all of them within a few feet of the high altar. On the N side, in the second bay from the W, is the CHAPEL OF ROBERT FITZ HAMON, founder of the Abbey, who died in 1107, though the chapel was not built till c.1395. The enclosing walls are stone screens, each consisting of two large Perp five-light windows above a panelled base, and crowned with oak-leaf cresting. The chapel is entered by a small doorway at the SW, and within is a lovely little fan-vault. In every way the chapel is a delightful specimen of Perp Gothic. – On the S side is the TRINITY CHAPEL, built between 1375 and 1380 as a chantry for Edward Despencer † 1375. It closely resembles the later Fitz Hamon chapel. Above a base faced with a series of canopied niches are two Perp windows, each of five lights; cornice with cresting above. The chapel is roofed with a true fan-vault, built up out of separate pieces of stone, and traces of wall-painting survive inside. The unique feature is the canopied niche that rises from the middle of the roof and contains the life-like kneeling effigy of Lord Despencer praying towards the altar. He was described by Froissart as the 'most honourable, gallant and valiant Knight in all England, much beloved of ladies, for the most noble said that no feast was perfect if Sir Despencer was not present'. – The third, and architecturally most splendid, of the chantry chapels is on the N, that erected c.1430 by Isabel Despencer, Countess of Warwick, for the celebration of masses for her first husband, Richard Beauchamp, † 1421. The design of the BEAUCHAMP CHAPEL is not unlike that of the Wykeham Chapel at Winchester, though it is less lofty, and is divided into two storeys, of which the lower is fan-vaulted and the upper has a miniature lierne-vault. The lower stage is enclosed with stone screens of Perp windows above a panelled base. In the panels are figures of angels holding heraldic shields. The vault of the lower stage covers only the W half of the chapel, and is supported by two slender shafts. The vaulting is intricate with delicate tracery covering its surface and pendants. The upper storey is quite open except for the buttress-mullions carried up from the screens below. Against the W wall are three niches which perhaps once formed a background for the kneeling figures of Isabel and her two Beauchamp husbands, the Earls of Worcester and Warwick; otherwise the purpose of the upper storey is a matter of conjecture, for there is no stair.* – The tomb on the NE nearest the altar is that of Hugh, Baron Despencer, † 1348, and his wife Eliza-

* *Thomas Porchalion* made a design and model for a statue of Isabel, Countess of Warwick, for her tomb, according to a Will of 1440.

beth Montacute † 1359 (who together with his mother, Eleanor de Clare, was responsible for the remodelling of the abbey). Recumbent effigies in white alabaster; tall, lean figures. The Knight is encased in a mixed suit of chain and plate as worn c.1350, youthful and beardless. The Lady's head-dress is square at the top, forming a frame to the face reaching below the chin. The canopy above, which can be compared with that of Edward II in Gloucester Cathedral, is Late Dec, and consists of four tiers of open arches, diminishing upwards, and richly decorated with crockets, finials, and high pinnacles. The roof of six square bays is made of inverted conoids, and supported by shafts between the effigies.

Immediately to the N, on the other side of the ambulatory, is the tomb of Guy de Brien, who married the widowed Elizabeth Montacute c.1350, thus becoming a patron of the abbey. He was standard-bearer to Edward III at the Battle of Crécy, and a Knight of the Garter. He died in 1390, but the tomb was presumably prepared before, and the effigy appears to come from the same possibly Flemish school as that of Edward Despencer. Above the tomb is a Late Dec canopy, obviously suggested by the monument opposite, but less fine in detail. A beautiful blue colour still remains on the vaulting of the canopy, and traces of gilding.

To continue with the monuments round the ambulatory, the next one is the so-called Wakeman Cenotaph, but it dates from 51 a century earlier than John Wakeman, the last abbot, who died in 1549. The architecture of the monument is mid-c15, and the cadaver is placed on top of the altar tomb instead of below. It lies in an open shroud, as it might appear a little time after death with the body crawled over by vermin, under a canopy decorated with a profusion of tabernacle work. The altar part of the tomb is hollow, with a fine panel of perforated tracery forming three stars. The canopy is said to have been copied for the throne of the House of Lords. – Archdeacon Robeson † 1912. Altar tomb with recumbent effigy by *Bryant Baker*, 1913. – Tablet designed in 1939 by *G. Kruger Gray*, to record the gift of the land at the E end of the church by an American lady, Miss Woodhull. – Abbot Cheltenham, who ruled from 1481 to 1509. Altar tomb with four panels decorated with quatrefoils bearing shields, and surmounted by an arched canopy with enriched spandrels, showing shields with scallop-shells and pilgrim's staves. Opposite are two tombs, at the back of the sedilia. That on the l., greatly mutilated by Puritans, as the canopied niches must have contained many images, is the burial place of Hugh Despencer, who was hanged in 1325. The Purbeck marble coffin, however, is that of John Cotes, abbot during the remodelling (1328–47). The tomb on the r. has a crocketed ogee cinquefoil arch. Turning w, the tomb on the l. is that of Abbot Robert Forthington † 1254. The ogee canopy is carved with spirited little figures, and ballflower ornament placed at intervals within the mouldings of the arch, in the cusps, and along the front of the tomb. The crockets and finials consist of finely carved oak-leaves and acorns with doves. The Purbeck marble coffin slab has a diminutive figure within the head of a floriated cross, in low relief. – Abbot Alan † 1202. Biographer of Thomas Becket. This is the only tomb in E.E. style. – Next is an early C14 tomb. Note the medieval encaustic tiles. – On the opposite side is a Renaissance style marble tablet by *H. H. Armstead* to Mrs Craik, author of *John Halifax, Gentleman*, erected in 1890. – In the s transept: alabaster tablet with portrait in low relief of the builder, Thomas Collins, † 1900. – Classical marble tablet with cherub heads and torches, to the Mann family, by *Richard Squire* of Worcester, 1749. – In the s aisle of the nave: C14 Dec tomb with recessed, slightly ogee arch, and cusped inner arch; very elaborate. – Charles Wynde † 1716. Marble with bust, painted arms, and cherubs. – Neo-Greek marble tablet to Catherine Price, erected in 1844 by *Gardner* of Tewkesbury. – Kenelm Chandler † 1809. Neo-Greek marble tablet, erected in 1833, by *Gardner*. – In the N aisle: a Knight's recumbent stone effigy, c.1350, surmounted by an ogee-shaped crocketed arch, later than the effigy, with a quatrefoil in the centre, and ending in a finial of four sets of foliage. – On the N wall of the N transept: half-length upright effigy of John Roberts of Fiddington † 1631. Like the bust of William Ferrers at Ashchurch, it is London work, and probably came by sea from the Southwark marblers' workshops. – Joseph Reeve, 'Artist, whose works in several parts speak his praise', † 1651. Stone and slate Baroque tablet. – In the N ambulatory: Ann, Lady Clarke, † 1800, by *Flaxman*. White marble slab flanked by Faith and Charity in full relief. – Dr George Peyton † 1742, by *Thomas White* of Worcester. Classical marble tablet with drapery.

FURNISHINGS

NAVE. FONT. C14 stem of eight attached shafts with five ballflowers between each; c.1320. The marble base may be earlier.

The bowl is C19, dating from the restoration of the church by *Scott*. – INNER S PORCH. A Gothic oak lobby, designed in 1913 by *W. D. Caröe*. – STAINED GLASS. W window 1886 by *Hardman* of Birmingham. – Five windows in the S aisles *c*.1888, and five windows in the N aisle, *c*.1892, all by *Hardman*. – The CHAPEL OF THE HOLY CHILD JESUS, at the W end, has a C16 altar picture after *Innocenzo da Imola*. Either side are C18 Benefaction Boards. – PULPIT. 1892. – LECTERN. 1878. – SCREEN, W of the tower. Of poor workmanship, fussy design, and unhappy proportions. By *John Oldrid Scott*, carried out by *Thomas Collins* in 1892.

CHOIR. SCREEN, on the N (with small foreign figures on top), and MISERICORDS, C14. Tip-up seats on the N, but only two on the S. The three outside the screen are the best examples. – ROYAL ARMS. Queen Anne. – STALLS. 1875–9 by *Scott*. – The MILTON ORGAN dates from *c*.1580. It has the best examples anywhere of embossed tin pipes, and a contemporary case. It formerly belonged to Magdalen College, Oxford. Made by *Thomas Dallam*, rebuilt *c*.1607–36 by *Robert Dallam*.

PRESBYTERY. STAINED GLASS. The seven windows in the clerestory were glazed between 1340 and 1344. Everything points to Eleanor de Clare as donor, though the royal arms of Edward III shows that the glass must have been painted after 1340, and, as Eleanor had died three years before, we may suppose her intentions were carried out by her son Hugh Despencer. The arms of Fitzalan and de Warenne would not have been used in this context after 1344. The glass has all the characteristics of windows of the second quarter of the C14, particularly the use of a beautiful green, never more beautiful than here. The tall and elaborate canopies have carefully patterned shafts, and delicate designs decorate the coloured background of the figures. Very skilful use has been made of silvery white glass and yellow stain to give lightness and brilliance. The windows were restored in 1923 by *Walter E. Tower* of *C. E. Kempe*'s workshops. Care was taken in the reassembly that glass which had been added from other windows in 1820 was extracted, and placed in a window in the sacristy. The disposition of the glass in the seven windows, therefore, is now, as closely as possible, the original one. Heads of figures that were lost were left blank, and the missing parts of their drapery were made up in outline, or blocks of plain glass. The principal lights contain a series of full-length figures of prophets, patriarchs, kings, and historical personages connected with the church. The figures in the E window, the subject of which is the Last Judgement, are more varied in composition. The central figure is Christ, seated and displaying the Five Wounds. On his r. is Mary and on his l. probably the Archangel Michael. The outer lights contain the Apostles, and St John the Baptist. The small scenes below depict the Resurrection, the lost and the saved, but the fifth light is occupied by the nude figure of the donor, kneeling, stripped of all earthly trappings. The rose of the E window has a special treatment, its subject being the Coronation of the Virgin, set in the central quatrefoil. The two westernmost windows contain men in the armour of the period, and with heraldic surcoats which show that they represent, on the N, from l. to r., FitzRoy, de Clare, Despencer, and Fitz Hamon, and on the S, de Clare, Zouch (Eleanor de Clare's second husband), and two more de Clares, Earls of Gloucester. Such a series of portraits of a great family is without parallel at this period.

SOUTH TRANSEPT. Mosaic over the altar by *Salviati* of Venice, 1893. The modern sculpture of the Virgin (this is now the Lady Chapel) is by *Alec Miller*. – STAINED GLASS. Window by *Geoffrey Webb*, 1945.

NORTH TRANSEPT. GROVE ORGAN. Built for the Inventions Exhibition of 1885; designed by *Carlton Michell* and *William Thynne*.

ST NICHOLAS'S CHAPEL. REREDOS. Painted by *Thomas Gambier-Parry*, c.1880.

ST MARGARET'S CHAPEL. ALTAR. White marble mensa by *John Ricketts*, 1726. – STAINED GLASS. Fragments of medieval glass, arranged by *Tower* in a window by him, 1906.

ST DUNSTAN'S CHAPEL. The REREDOS is a C15 Flemish painting.

ST FAITH'S CHAPEL. STAINED GLASS. E window by *Geoffrey Webb*, 1941. – S window by *Kempe*, 1896.

SACRISTY. STAINED GLASS. Medieval fragments; slight remains of a Tree of Jesse window; figures of prophet and patriarch; portions of names; Lombardic lettering.

PLATE. Cross and candlesticks on the high altar by *Sir Ninian Comper*, designed for a smaller altar and therefore too small; Chalice and Paten Cover, 1576; Chalice and Cover, 1618; Credence Paten, 1618; Flagon, 1660; Flagon, 1723, by *Thomas Ffarrer*; Credence Paten, 1725; two Almsplates, 1729.

GATEHOUSE. C15/16, restored in 1849 by *J. Medland*. Two
storeys, of stone, with embattled parapet, string-course with
angels and gargoyles, and on the N two Tudor windows and a
central niche over a wide outer arch. A central arch is divided
from the outer arches by compartments with sexpartite vaults.
W of the gatehouse is part of a timber-framed BARN which may
represent the almonry barn, and two cottages which may survive from the almonry house.

ABBEY HOUSE. A long stone range – timber-framed internally –
between the gatehouse and the W end of the church. A number
of medieval features survive, sufficient to establish a monastic
origin, but not sufficient to be able to say whether it was the
abbot's lodging or the guest house. The ground-floor hall has
close-studded partitions with three adjacent doors at the
screens end, and windows with fragmentary C15 cusped heads.
The oriel window on the N is early C16 and has the initials of
Abbot Henry Beoly (1509–31), shields of arms, an inscription
on the sill, and six mullioned and transomed lights with close-
cusped cinquefoil heads; inside it has pendant ornament on the
ceiling. Restored in 1966.

On the N side of Church Street, the abbey's buildings included
the abbey MILLS, on the Mill Avon, and the abbey BARTON
or BARN, part of which can still be seen at the lower end of
Mill Street, with its heavily buttressed stone wall. Running SW
from the barton is a wall including fragments of an ancient
stone wall that may have marked the edge of both the town
and the abbey precincts.

OLD VICARAGE. 1846 by *S. W. Daukes*. Tall, symmetrical elevation, faced in ashlar, with three gables with ornamental
wooden bargeboards, Tudor windows, and central gabled
porch.

CHURCHES

HOLY TRINITY. 1837 by *Ebenezer Trotman*. Red brick con-
venticle, with a 'great arch' at the W quoted from the abbey.
Goodhart-Rendel considered rightly that it is 'artist's work of
a sort. Combination of diagonal buttresses with octagonal
turrets; all done sensitively'. The interior has good proportions and retains its original pews and W galleries. – STAINED
GLASS. E window by *Horwood Bros.* of Mells, 1862. – MONU-

MENTS. William Sandilands † 1867. Stone tablet, hatchment shape, inlaid with a band of small encaustic tiles. – Two others like it, 1863 and 1865.

ST JOSEPH (R.C.), Mythe Road. Simple brick building of c.1870 with Early Dec stone windows.

NONCONFORMIST CHAPELS. BAPTIST CHAPEL, Old Baptist Chapel Court, Church Street. 1623. One of the oldest Nonconformist Chapels in the county, retaining some old features. Panelled dado and coved ceiling. Late C17 furnishings; panelled pulpit; gallery. – BAPTIST CHAPEL, Barton Street. 1805. Brick with round-headed windows. – CONGREGATIONAL CHURCH. 1830. Brick with round-headed windows. Plain porch. – METHODIST CHAPEL, The Cross. 1878. Dec. On the site of the C18 market.

PUBLIC BUILDINGS

TOWN HALL, High Street. Built in 1788, enlarged c.1840, and altered in 1891 by *Medland & Son*. Georgian tradition and Medland's inclination – it can be compared with his entrance to the Eastgate Market, Gloucester, and his Corn Hall, Cirencester – have produced a happy result. Ashlar-faced. Three round-headed openings, archivolts with keystones carved with wheatsheafs, and a central shield of arms. Tuscan columns support an entablature and pediment with sculptured figures and a clock in the tympanum, and a bell-turret with urns above.

WATSON HALL, Barton Street. 1909.

PERAMBULATION

The site of the town was so confined by the rivers, and the abbey and manorial estates, that expansion after the later Middle Ages was impossible. Any increase that was required in the number of houses was achieved by raising the density of building, and particularly by making, behind the houses fronting the three main streets, rows of cottages approached by the alleys that had originally given access to the stores, workshops, and gardens. In this way the characteristic arrangement of picturesque but insanitary alleys and courts evolved. Most of the houses in the alleys are of the late C17 or C18, and are associated with the increase of population owing to the change from the cloth industry, in which most of the work was done in the master's house, to that of knitting, carried on in the homes of the workers. There was hardly any new building in Tewkesbury between the 1850s and the 1930s.

Opposite the churchyard gates stands the BELL HOTEL, largely rebuilt in 1696. It is timber-framed with a double overhang and three gables. A section of C17 wall painting is preserved in the dining room. MILL STREET leads down to the Mill Avon water-front and the site of the ABBEY MILLS, now an early C19 mill, said to be the 'original' of Abel Fletcher's Mill in *John Halifax, Gentleman*; Tewkesbury is the Nortonbury of Mrs Craik's famous Victorian novel. The first house on the s side of CHURCH STREET is the former NATIONAL SCHOOL, enlarged in 1842. It is somewhat of an interloper, square and stone-built and out of scale with the street. Behind it are a row of Tudor Gothic cottages of 1831. The main block of houses, Nos. 34–50, on this side of the street, between it and the abbey, and stretching from the school to Gander Lane, are of considerable interest. There is every reason to suppose these timber-framed cottages were not part of the abbey precincts; the abbey wall in fact ran at the back, against which the cottage privies and outbuildings have been built. The conventual buildings of the Benedictine abbey were on the s and the abbot's lodgings on the w. These cottages however are pre-Reformation, and possibly represent one of the earliest surviving examples in the country of uniform medieval town development. It appears they were built by the monks and let to tenants in the town as a speculative development. This is proved by the existence of the abbey rent roll, taken by the Crown in 1539. There were twenty-nine tenements, some of them quite large by the standards of the time: No. 39, for instance, was quite a large house, perhaps originally with a detached kitchen. The many doors with ogee-headed lintels suggest an early C15 origin. On the N side of Church Street the houses, like almost all the other houses in old Tewkesbury, are timber-framed with mostly Georgian frontages. These houses still retain a slightly more residential air than those in the other more commercialized streets. Nos. 61 and 62 has quite a handsome tall Georgian façade, with pedimented and fanlit doorways, next to the alley to the old Baptist chapel. No. 65 is faced in Georgian brickwork – all headers – and has windows with carved stone keystones and bull-nosed sills.

The turning called St Mary's Lane leads back to the water-

front, which is faced by small, mostly altered houses. SOUTH-
END HOUSE has three storeys and five windows in its C18
façade. Nos. 67 and 68 have Georgian brick three-storey fronts,
with good doors with fanlights and slender columns and pediments. No. 73, combined with No. 1 SMITH'S COURT, is
timber-framed with two gables, though much restored. No. 75,
together with MAYALL'S COURT, is also timber-framed. No.
77 has an early C18 front of brick, two storeys, three windows
with keystones, hipped roof, modillion cornice, and chamfered quoins. Almost opposite there is a break where a house
on the S side has been demolished, providing a glimpse of the
NE end of the abbey church, by Gander Lane. Here there are
some Georgian houses built as though part of a crescent, with
pedimented fanlit doorways. Beyond them No. 27 (NEWTON
HOUSE) has an C18 front, and a carriage-way leading to a
much older house at the back, which contains a medieval hall
with a fine timbered roof. On this side of the road, between
here and the Cross, there are several buildings of interest. Nos.
15 and 16 is a C16 timber-framed house with double overhang
and two gables. No. 13, though much restored, has four
storeys with overhangs. No. 10 has an C18 front masking a
medieval timber-framed house; there are signs of a cruck-
truss in the rear wing, and the front room, now a shop, has C17
panelling. There follow on the r. two intriguing alleys.
LILLEY'S ALLEY leads past a timber-framed cottage with
pronounced overhang, to a fine medieval barn with end-crucks
and two bays with queen-post trusses. No. 9 has three storeys
with continuous mullioned windows on the first floor of sixteen
pointed Gothic lights, though much restored. ANCIL'S
COURT and the BERKELEY ARMS comprise medieval timber-
framed buildings with a mullioned window on the first floor of
fourteen lights.

The houses on the other side of Church Street, from opposite
Gander Lane, are equally interesting. Nos. 78–81 have various
C18 brick elevations. Nos. 82 and 83 is probably C15, with a
double overhang and first-floor openings – now filled in – with
cusped-headed lights and Perp tracery. TURNER'S COURT is
another alley. Nos. 88 and 88A is timber-framed with overhang.
Continuous windows with transoms and twelve lights, over
close-set studding. On the corner of ST MARY'S LANE, No.
90 has a rib-vaulted basement of the C14/15. Nos. 91 and 92
have a double overhang and two gables and the sign of a Penny-
farthing Bicycle. The ROYAL HOP POLE HOTEL has an C18

painted brick front of three storeys and four windows, next to
a restored timber-framed portion. No. 97 has a Georgian façade
of three storeys and five bays, the centre breaking forward
under a hipped roof with eaves cornice. No. 100 is timber-
framed with a double overhang and a fourteen-light window
with transoms. The door lintel is carved R.B.K. 1664. Early
C19 sign of a Cocked Hat. The very fine and tall CROSS
HOUSE is probably C15, but has been much restored. The
TOLZEY LANE elevation has three gables. The CROSS marks
the site of the market, which was established in the C11. At
the junction of the roads stood the High Cross, demolished in
1650. The existing Cross is a 1918 War Memorial.

HIGH STREET. This street was built-up for virtually the whole
of its length by the late C14. In 1672 it had the highest share of
the large houses. On either side it is flanked by narrow tenements running back. Apart from small alleys, each within the
width of the tenement to which it belonged, only SMITH'S
LANE, QUAY LANE, and RED LANE, which existed in 1393,
break the street frontage on the W side between the Cross and
King John's Bridge; the E side remained unbroken until the
C19. We will first look at the houses on the l. Nos. 1 and 2 have
fine early C18 brick fronts of three storeys and three bays each
with ornamented parapets with urns. No. 9 is timber-framed
with four overhanging storeys on carved brackets, two gables,
leaded casements, and oriel windows. In the first-floor front
room a charming C17 plaster ceiling ornamented with mermaids, vines, and acorns. Sign of a Golden Key. The SWAN
HOTEL is C18, three storeys and five plus three bays. Venetian
window over the central carriage-way. OLD FLEECE INN.
Built c.1519, restored in 1897. Timber-framed with double
overhang, and also jettied out in the alley. No. 15 (the OLD
GRUDGE) is a timber-framed house with Tudor details, and
double overhang. The Tudor-arched wooden doorway has
Early Renaissance dragons carved in its spandrels, and the
ground-floor front room has fine moulded ceiling beams and a
stone Tudor fireplace inscribed R.P. LLOYDS BANK, built in
1921, has imitation half-timber work. No. 21 has four storeys
with overhangs and two gables. Nos. 27, 28, and 29 are timber-
framed with pleasing C18 fronts. The GARAGE occupies a C19
brewery. The houses hereafter, though mostly timber-framed,
have been refronted. Nos. 39 and 40 is a larger C18 house with
a central carriage-way and Venetian windows above on the
upper floors. Much further along is TUDOR HOUSE HOTEL,

one of the most charming houses in the town in spite of the fact that in 1897 its façade suffered the indignity of being covered with floorboards in pseudo-timber-frame style. It is a timber-framed C17 house altered and enlarged in 1701, the date on the cast lead rainwater-heads. As a piece of architectural design and proportion it was a small masterpiece. Three storeys, mullioned and transomed windows, string-courses at the floor levels. Triangular pediment on the first floor. Fluted Doric doorcase with a segmental pediment. The hipped roof has a modillion cornice. On the r. is a classical stone gateway with fluted frieze, pediment, and ball-finials. The interior has excellent details of 1701, including archways with rusticated keystones and voussoirs, panelled rooms, and a splendid staircase with twisted balusters. The older part of the house has a C17 staircase with turned balusters, and is gabled with exposed timber-framing at the back. Added on to this is an early C19 room with a bow window overlooking the river. At the very end of the street is the BLACK BEAR INN, said to have existed in 1308, but apparently a much restored C15 timber-framed building, with double overhang and oriel window of six mullioned and transomed lights. KING JOHN'S BRIDGE, really two bridges across the Avon, was, according to tradition, built by King John; but until the C19 it was called the Long Bridge. A bridge existed in 1205, however, and there are remains of ribbed stone arches. It has frequently been repaired, and the whole was rebuilt in stone and concrete, retaining some of the old features, in 1962.

We must now return along the High Street on the opposite side. Most of the timber-framed houses at this end have been demolished, though there are plenty of Georgian houses; but nearer the Cross more interesting ones survive. No. 124 is C16/17 with a Tudor front of 1845. A beam in the alley has the old Elizabethan inscription: 'DEV: REG: AMIC' – meaning God, Queen, and Friends. Good panelling inside and the date 1606. The NOTTINGHAM ARMS is C16, timber-framed, with a fine alleyway with a Tudor arch with carved spandrels. The WHEATSHEAF INN, also probably C16, has four storeys and a central projecting bay window through the upper floors, surmounted by an ogee-shaped gable. The side entrance has a good doorway with Early Renaissance carving in the spandrels and the initials I.V. No. 135 is timber-framed with four storeys, all overhanging. C17 panelling in the front first-floor room. No. 137 is timber-framed behind the early C19 front, and has a small panelled ground-floor room with an interesting medieval carved wooden corbel representing a man holding a dragon. The back upper room has exposed timber-framing with wind-braces. Nos. 138 and 139 have early C18 brick fronts. CLARENCE HOUSE. C15 (Gothic sunk cusps to the framework on the first floor), but altered at the beginning of the C17, when the gables were replaced by the deeply moulded cornice with carved modillions. Four storeys with triple overhang, and continuous ten-light mullioned and transomed windows with a central projecting bay. The front first-floor room has an ornamental plaster ceiling of the early C17, with wreaths, raspberry pendants, cherubs, and a cornice with acanthus leaf and egg and dart mouldings.

Having arrived back at the Cross we may now turn l. along the humbler BARTON STREET, so called in 1257 from the barton or grange of the Earls of Gloucester (*see* p. 371) which was situated in the w angle of Chance Street and Barton Street from the C13. The first houses on the l. are mostly timber-framed with C18 brick fronts. Nos. 9, 10, and 11 have rather elegant façades with three storeys, Venetian windows, a cornice and pediment with a bull's eye window in the tympanum, and a tall parapet. There follow several timber-framed houses, and the picturesque alley of ALEXANDRA COURT. No. 22 has a triple overhang and gables. It is probably not worth walking any further beyond the turning to ORCHARD STREET, as the houses get later and later in date. On the opposite side Nos. 64 and 64A BARTON STREET is a timber-framed building with double-jettied front, typical of the early C17 Tewkesbury houses. The front has scarcely been altered; the wooden railings on the pavement are original, and so is the oak door at the entrance to the passage that runs right through to the back, and thus divides the single L-shaped building into two parts. Mullioned and transomed windows run the length of the first floor, and the second floor has two leaded casement windows. In No. 64, the C17 oak panelling has survived intact in the ground-floor and first-floor front rooms. The second-floor room has a late C17 oval-wreathed plaster ceiling. The first floor is used as a museum. Nos. 78, 79, and 80 must once have been an inn. Timber-framed, with an C18 brick front. Carriageway leading through a courtyard, which has part of the wooden balustrade of a first-floor balcony. A rainwater-head is dated 1715. The PLOUGH HOTEL has been altered and has gables behind a modern front.

OUTER TEWKESBURY

79 MYTHE BRIDGE, ¼ m. N of the town. 1823–6 by *Thomas Telford*.
A splendid example, surviving intact. Cast iron, with a single
span of 170 ft, complete with its charming miniature toll house
at the E approach. On the W is an extended masonry abutment
pierced by a series of narrow Gothic arches to allow the passage
of flood water. Before this there was no bridge over the
Severn, only a ferry.

KING JOHN'S CASTLE, Mythe Road. This building is more
likely to have been associated with the abbey than with King
John, who would have occupied the now vanished Holme
Castle, SE of the abbey. It may have been a lodging of the
abbots, though the building was leased to Richard Wakeman,
brother of the last abbot, in 1534. A square rubble tower with
massive walls rises to three storeys, lowered and stepped back
at each floor in the C19. Staggered windows. Blocked doorways, with arches apparently of the C15, at ground- and
second-floor levels. Against the W face a C17 gabled wing with
mullioned and transomed windows.

THE MYTHE. 1812. Of brick. Ashlar façade, with Gothic windows with Perp tracery added symmetrically *c.*1825. The arms
in the parapet are those of Charles Porter. Typical Regency
fittings, with mahogany doors and reeded doorcases. The
Gothic windows have coloured glass in the tracery.

MYTHE END. Of *c.*1865. Possibly the house *John Middleton* is
known to have designed at The Mythe. Of brick, with poly-
chromatic bands at floor and eaves levels, and on the chimneys.
Windows with carved stone lintels and sills. Hipped gables, one
with bargeboards. Pitch-pine staircase; in the window a painted
glass Last Supper. Gothic stone fireplaces.

TEWKESBURY PARK, 1 m. SW of the town. On the site of the
late C14 house of Edward Despencer. The present house was
largely built in the late C18, a narrow building of rendered
brick with three storeys and two bow windows to full height on
the S. On the N a central entrance, with fanlight and later porch,
leading into a hall with a Tuscan colonnade and a nice C18
staircase built on the curve; moulded balusters. The chief
rooms are panelled.

GUBSHILL MANOR, 1 m. SW, on the Gloucester road. Part of the
house may be C16 or even earlier, but substantially it is C17,
timber-framed with two storeys and attics, overhanging at
first-floor level. It has been restored, and bears the probably

misleading inscription '1438, restored 1707'. It was converted for use as a public house in 1955 by *G. H. Ryland*. C17
doorway at the back with carved spandrels and frieze. Inside,
moulded beams and the remains of stone tracery in the bar. It
is traditionally associated with Queen Margaret's camp at the
Battle of Tewkesbury.

THORNBURY

6090

ST MARY. Somewhat apart from the town and next to the castle. 57
The noble tower is crowned by pierced battlements and
turrets like St Stephen, Bristol. No trace remains of the Norman church granted to Tewkesbury Abbey, though the N and
s doorways are Transitional Norman re-inserted in later walls.
The (over-restored) chancel is Dec, *c.*1340, and a s aisle or
chapel was added later in the C14. Richard II's badge, the
peascod, is carved on one of the stops of the hood-mould over
the E window of the chapel. At the end of the C15 the church
was mostly rebuilt, except for the chancel. The tower is latest
of all; *c.*1540. The church is therefore mainly Perp, with a
clerestoried nave of six bays with N and s aisles, and s porch.
Parapet above the clerestory, with battlements and pinnacles.
The windows on the s are arched, those on the N have straight
heads. The tracery of the s windows is very curious, with drop-
shapes vertically bisected by mullions, a Dec conceit rather
than a Perp, one is tempted to say. The s aisle and its continuation, the Stafford Chapel, display on the hood-mould stops the
Stafford Knot, the badge of Edward Stafford; Duke of Buckingham (*see* below), who intended to found a college here.

The s doorway has a round Norman arch with dogtooth enrichments supported on E.E. shafts with stiff-leaf foliage on
the capitals. The DOOR itself has original ironwork. Tall and
graceful Perp nave arcades of the familiar four shafts and four
waves section. Above them runs a horizontal course in the
form of a roll, and up each spandrel vertically runs a roll as
well, meeting the other. The large clerestory windows are
recessed and have blank panelling beneath. Chancel arch C19.
The church was restored in 1848 by *Francis Niblett*, and the
stone corbels which support the nave roof are also of this date.
The tower was restored facsimile in 1889 by *F. W. Waller*.
Vestry by *Robert Curwen*, 1876.

In the s wall of the chancel are a Dec PISCINA with cinquefoiled arch and triple SEDILIA under similar arches with narrow

lobed trefoils in the spandrels, but all are now too low for convenient use, as the chancel floor has been raised. The s chapel also has a PISCINA under a moulded arch, and a tomb recess with crocketed and pinnacled arch. – FONT. Transitional Norman; square bowl on a massive clawed pedestal. – PULPIT. Stone, Perp, with panels. – STAINED GLASS. N window in the chancel by *Thomas Willement*, 1846, for Henry Howard, with arms, supporters, crests, mottos, mantlings, and badges. – W window also by *Willement*, 1855, with Evangelists under Gothic canopies. – ROYAL ARMS. Period 1816–37. – HATCHMENT. – PLATE. Chalice and Paten Cover, 1683; Paten, 1711; Paten, 1786; Flagon, 1813. – MONUMENTS. Brass in the chancel to Thomas Tyndall † 1571. Only the wife's brass survives. – In the s chapel, within the tomb recess, a C17 monument: Roger Fowke † 1648. – Several tablets of the C17 and C18, and later ones, some by *Tyley* of Bristol.

THORNBURY CASTLE. The home of the Staffords since the early part of the C12, and, till recently, of the Howards. The present castle was begun *c.*1511 by Edward Stafford, third Duke of Buckingham, but before his plans were completed he was executed, in 1521, when only the s, w, and N sides had been built. The old hall of the original house was on the E. The plan indicates a quadrangle, 120 by 110 ft, to be enclosed by buildings. For two hundred years it remained uninhabited, but in 1720 it was partly roofed and in 1811 Lord Henry Howard restored portions of the building, including the s tower. It was finally restored in 1854, by *Anthony Salvin*.

Much of the original Tudor building remains; a castle without, a palace within – or even, regarding the outside only, a castle on the w, i.e. the entrance side, a palace on the s, i.e. the privy garden side. In 1521 the w front was left much as it is now. The w gate is dated 1511. The broad polygonal s tower was completed with its machicolated parapet, but the central part and the N end of the w front were only built to the first floor. The s range was finished and still retains its splendid features, specially the moulded brick chimneystacks (evidently a snob material here) with heraldic decoration and dated 1514. The s elevation shows Tudor or Perp domestic architecture at its very best, carefully restored by *Salvin*. Embattled parapet to the main block, with three bays to full height, each different and with Tudor mullioned and many-transomed windows with cusped heads to the lights, perhaps the most perfect in existence, particularly the easternmost bay, which is cinquefoil in plan on the upper stage, and comes out to five points on the ground floor with concave mouldings, contrasting with the convex mouldings above. This skilful use of Perp mouldings, as in Henry VII's Chapel, Westminster, is a *tour de force*, which became widely appreciated after Pugin published his measured drawings of the castle in 1832, and was not without its influence on C19 architecture. One of the state rooms has in addition another large, many-transomed window towards the courtyard. The rooms inside are on the small side; some of the windows have heraldic glass, 1858 by *Thomas Willement*. The doorway leading into one of the main rooms on the ground floor has a flat Tudor arch and concave-moulded jambs enriched with sculptured armorial badges, the Stafford Knot included. Some medieval tiles survive on the ground floor, and a fine Perp fireplace on the first floor.

The outer or base-court on the W is marked by low ruinous buildings, but the garden to the SE is a rare example of an Early Tudor layout, with its clipped hedges and sheltered walks. A very curious feature and one apparently without parallel is the walling of the garden towards W and S. To the W it is pierced by windows, to the S by bay windows. The assumption is that there was here a wooden gallery running from the big SW tower to the S, then along the N boundary of the churchyard, and then back to the E end of the S range.*

THORNBURY PARK. 1832–6. Square, classical, with an Ionic portico.

The town is approached from the church by CASTLE STREET, which has C18 and C19 houses standing in their own grounds, and then becomes a regular street with mostly residential buildings. THE HATCH is C17, with gables and mullioned windows, three-light with transoms on the garden side. THE PRIORY is probably C16, roughcast and with C19 alterations. PORCH HOUSE is also C16, with a two-storey gabled porch with arched entrance, and an old wooden door. THE CHANTRY is C18 with a Gothic Revival doorway, and WIGMORE HOUSE is also C18, with two storeys and parapet and door with hood on carved consoles. Near this is a C16 timber-framed house with two gables and C19 bargeboards, and other alterations.

In the HIGH STREET, on the N side the NATIONAL PROVINCIAL BANK, mid-C19 Italianate. The METHODIST CHAPEL is neo-E.E. OLD REGISTER OFFICE. 1839 by *S. W. Daukes*;

---

* Or can this have been the beginning of an L-shaped building for the members of the projected college? (NP)

a small neo-Greek building of ashlar with pediment and four pilasters. The shaped doorway has edges leaning inwards. The C18 WHITE LION HOTEL is distinguished by a splendid painted cast lion over the portico. THE OLD MARKET HOUSE, C18, is roughcast, with a hipped slate roof and lantern. Ground-floor arcade with stone Tuscan columns, now filled in with modern shop windows, and one Venetian window above.

There follows a good group of C17 and C18 houses higher up the street. 100 yds N of the White Lion is a C19 Italianate ashlar-faced house with a modillion eaves cornice and windows with entablatures and blind balustrades; on the r. a two-storey wing with date-stone 1766. The house opposite SOAPERS LANE has Venetian windows. On the E side of HIGH STREET the SWAN HOTEL, C18 with a C19 cast swan over the portico. In ST JOHN'S STREET the old QUAKER CHAPEL has a date-stone 1794. In ST MARY'S STREET the CHURCH INSTITUTE has a carved wooden porch dated 1679, and four gables.

MORTON GRANGE, 1 m. NE. The nucleus of the house is medieval, with a filled-in hall of cruck construction. The screens passage survives with the date 1594 carved on its E doorway. A projecting stair-turret has been added on the W, with spiral stairs. The room on the N has a Tudor fireplace. The dining room S of the passage has C17 panelling and a simple Renaissance fireplace carved with the initials T.P. Beyond this is a good Regency drawing room of c.1815, with a bay-window added in 1918.

KYNETON, 1 m. W. The house has a C17 nucleus (date-stone 16?5 over an outside doorway now inside the house). Stone, with mullioned windows. Altered and enlarged in the C19, when Flemish gables and an embattled tower were added.

FEWSTERS FARMHOUSE. C17 with five gables.

WILLOW FARMHOUSE. C17 with two gables.

SPRING FARMHOUSE, Lower Morton, 1 m. N. C18, rubble, with hipped roof and small pediment with a lunette opening, two storeys and three bays.

TIBBERTON

7020

HOLY TRINITY. Nave, chancel, W tower, and W porch. Herringbone masonry in the N and S walls of the nave and N wall of the chancel; also the nave has alternating quoins which almost amount to long-and-short work, all indicating an Early

Norman date. Blocked Norman doorway and remains of windows on the S. The tower is probably a little later – perhaps
C13; it is now capped with a hipped roof and has a Perp W
window above the porch. C14 tower arch of two plain chamfered orders. Springers for a vault with carved head corbels.
The very primitive chancel arch is Norman. Nave windows
Dec. Plastered wagon roof. Low Perp chancel roof with carved
bosses. Dec window on the N, two lancets on the S, and a
restored E window of three lancets. The walls are limewashed,
except under the tower. Restored in 1908. – FONT. 1920. –
PLATE. Chalice and Paten Cover, 1571. – MONUMENTS.
Quite attractive small marble tablets in the chancel. Richard
Donovan † 1816 ('the imperious command of parental duty
urged him to visit Antigua'), by *Cooke* of Gloucester. – Sarah
Donovan † 1813, by *Cooke*. – Francis Donovan † 1811, by
Millard & Cooke. – Gilbert Elton † 1803, by *Millard*. –
CHURCHYARD. Table-tomb of William Church † 1754,
signed: 'cut by *Giles Samson*, Westbury'.

TIBBERTON COURT. A five-bay Georgian house refaced and
altered in 1852 by *James Medland*,* who also added the wings
and Italianate tower. The main block of three storeys has
crisply carved stone enrichments including a modillion eaves
cornice, alternating triangular and segmental pediments over
the first-floor windows, and a five-bay veranda with Corinthian
columns supporting a balustraded balcony. The two-storey,
one-bay projecting wings either side have three-light windows
with first-floor balconies on carved consoles. Set back on the
NE corner is a *campanile* of four stages; the top has pairs of
round-headed windows with imposts, keystones, and blind
balustrades.

RECTORY. 1851 by *Eugene Sweny*.

MEREDITH. 1893. Brick with stone dressings and some simu-
lated timber-framing, gables with fanciful bargeboards, oriel
windows, and a Perp bay window with stained glass.

TIDENHAM

5090

ST MARY. E.E. and Dec. The rugged E.E. W tower, which in
the past has served as a beacon for navigation in the Severn
estuary, has small single lancets in the S and W faces of the

---

* *Medland* came to Gloucester as chief assistant to S. W. Daukes, later,
.1842, Daukes & Hamilton. When Daukes went to London, the firm became
Hamilton & Medland, and later Medland, Maberly & Medland. Medland
died in 1894 aged 86.

lower stage. N aisle with trefoil-headed lancet windows. S porch, with an upper chamber, rebuilt in the C19. The church was over-restored in 1858, by *John Norton*. S doorway E.E., the jamb shafts with stiff-leaf capitals. A window on the S side of the nave has two lights with a flowing ogee head; similar one-light Dec window on the S of the chancel. E window C19. E.E. arcade of four bays; a fifth bay in the chancel has a C13 arch leading to a chapel with a cinquefoiled PISCINA. No chancel arch. – FONT. One of Gloucestershire's six late C12 lead fonts.* – STAINED GLASS. Fragments of medieval glass in the tracery of a S nave window. – E window by *Geoffrey Webb*. – MONU-MENTS. Early C19 tablets include Sarah Lowder † 1802, by *Drewett*. – Selwyn James † 1805, by *Tyley*. – Anna Camplin † 1812, by *Lancaster* of Bristol. – Frances Morgan † 1831, by *Reeves* of Bath. – Drummond Thatcher † 1835, by *Woolcott* of Bristol.

ST MICHAEL, Tidenham Chase. 1888 by *S. Gambier-Parry*. O rock-faced stone, with nave, chancel, S porch, and W bellcote E.E. The windows mostly pairs of lancets. – REREDOS with mosaics, and E window, c.1889, in Pre-Raphaelite taste.

ST JAMES, Lancaut. Ruins of a small Norman church, on the banks of the Wye. A Transitional chancel arch and E window remain. – The lead FONT is in Gloucester Cathedral (*see* p. 211).

SEDBURY PARK, 1¾ m. S. C18 (some enriched doorcases of early to mid-C18 date survive in the hall), entirely refaced and re-modelled by *Sir Robert Smirke*, c.1825. Three storeys, faced in ashlar, with balustraded parapet. Six bays on the garden side, with a Greek Doric arcade continued on the entrance front, which has a projecting centre with a three-light window over a *porte-cochère*. The great central hall, lit by a dome, has late C19 embellishments.

THE MEAD, 1 m. S. A plain C18 ashlar-faced house with cornice, parapet, and blind balustrading. Three storeys and five bays, with band courses at floor levels. The central door, with a fan-light and segmental hood, is approached by a flight of steps.

STROAT HOUSE, 2 m. NE. C18. Three storeys, with modillion eaves cornice, chamfered quoins of alternating lengths, and rusticated pilasters to full height either side of a central window also treated with quoins. Pedimented doorcase with rusticated surround. Classical stone entrance archway in the garden wall.

OFFA'S DYKE. This linear earthwork was built as a negotiated

* For full description *see* Siston.

political boundary roughly between Wales and England by Offa, King of Mercia (757–96). The dyke was probably built between 784 and 796, and the mound known as Buttington Tump formed part of it. The Gloucestershire portion crosses the Beachley peninsula ESE of Chepstow, and is just under a mile in length.

TIRLEY

8020

ST MICHAEL. Built of blue lias. The tower is roughcast, and the lower stage probably dates from the C13. Diagonal W buttresses. W window with C14 reticulated tracery. Upper stage with embattled parapet and pinnacles. Dec and Perp windows in the nave; two on the N are C19 Dec replacements. Chancel windows Perp, except the E window, which is C19 Dec. The church was restored in 1894. S porch timber-framed and restored. The aisleless nave has limewashed walls. Plain C13 chancel arch with two chamfered orders. Both nave and chancel have medieval wagon roofs. Over the chancel arch the remains of a pre-Reformation WALL PAINTING. Trefoil-headed PISCINA in the chancel. – FONT. Scraped Norman tub. – STAINED GLASS. E window by *Clayton & Bell*, 1873. – HOLY TABLE. C17. – BENEFACTION BOARDS. C18 and early C19 slate tablets. – PLATE. Chalice, 1640; Paten, 1704 by *John Sutton*. – MONUMENTS. William Hurdman † 1684. Countrified Renaissance monument of painted stone, with twisted Purbeck marble columns, Corinthian capitals, and an inscription on slate. – Mary Browne † 1717. Painted Baroque stone tablet with heraldry, and inscription on marble. – Anne Turton † 1642. Classical painted stone tablet with heraldry. – Robert Gittos † 1724. Marble tablet. – Thomas Hopkins † 1789. Coloured marble tablet.

TIRLEY COURT, 1 m. W. C17 or earlier, faced in brick, with mullioned and transomed windows; re-roofed.

GREAT CUMBERWOOD, ¾ m. N. C17, timber-framed and gabled. S front added in the C18.

HILL FARM, ½ m. SW. Partly C17. Timber-framed and brick, with a brick GAZEBO in the garden.

HAW BRIDGE. Designed in 1961, by *S. C. Brown*.

HAW FARM. C18. Of brick. Attractive GAZEBO with pedimented doorcase.

MALT HOUSE. Late C18 or early C19, with a classical front facing the river.

TOCKINGTON see OLVESTON

0030
TODDINGTON

ST ANDREW. Completely rebuilt in 1873–9 by *G. E. Street*, in his Early Dec style, i.e. with geometrical tracery. This large church would be more suitable in London than in this remote country park. The noble exterior, faced in ashlar, described by Goodhart-Rendel as 'of that terrible orange yellow colour that Gloucestershire sometimes provides', has a fine tower, with broach-spire, on the S side. Interior of magnificent white ashlar. Aisleless nave with an elaborate oak hammerbeam roof. The W bay, which has a pointed tunnel-vault, is boldly screened off from the nave by a large stepped tripartite giant arcade, with the W window appearing dramatically behind. It is the most original as well as a highly successful feature. Equally success-
96 ful is the management of the E parts. Chancel with S aisle and N mortuary chapel, all with stone rib-vaulting supported by slender Purbeck marble shafts. The shallow E end of the S chancel aisle is divided from the rest by a two-bay arcade, again an unexpected touch. Sanctuary arcade of trefoil-headed arches on marble shafts, incorporating a PISCINA and SEDILIA. – FONT, PULPIT, and FURNISHINGS contemporary. – In the N chapel various carved bosses, tablets, and a late C17 FONT, from the earlier building. – STAINED GLASS. E window by *Clayton & Bell*. – PLATE. Chalice, Credence Paten, and Flagon, 1671. – MONUMENTS. Tomb-chest with recumbent effigies of Charles Hanbury-Tracy, 1st Lord Sudeley of Toddington, † 1858, and his wife, by *J. C. Lough*, 1872.* – Viscount Tracy † 1756. White and grey marble monument with a bust in relief on a medallion. The inscription states that he rebuilt the church in 1723. – Recumbent effigy of a Tudor Lady. – Bust of a C17 man in armour, his hand resting on a skull. Immediately W of the church are the ruins of the gatehouse of the old MANOR, consisting of a Jacobean carved stone overthrow, and the walls of the lodges, with mullioned windows. After the Dissolution the Tracys first lived in the abbot's lodgings at Hailes Abbey. They then built this house, which was abandoned in the early C19 owing to its damp situation. The STABLES are possibly by *Charles Beazley*, who is known to have done alterations to the old manor, *c.*1800. Symmetrical

* Lord Sudeley allocated £5,000 in his will for the erection of this memorial.

ashlar block on one side of a courtyard, with Gothick windows on the ground floor and bull's eye windows above. Cornice and central broken pediment.

TODDINGTON MANOR. Designed by the amateur architect *Charles Hanbury-Tracy*, afterwards first Lord Sudeley of Toddington (1778–1858), and built by him in 1820–35, at a cost of more than £150,000. Hanbury-Tracy also designed the alterations to Hampton Court, Herefordshire, in 1834–42.* In 1835 he was appointed chairman of the commission to judge the designs for the new Houses of Parliament, and it was largely due to his persistence that Barry's plan was proceeded with, though at one time he produced a plan of his own as a substitute for that of Barry. Hanbury-Tracy was far from being a romantic like Beckford; 'his enthusiasm for what was then considered the national style sprang from his proper sense of the value of historical tradition', writes his biographer, M. J. McCarthy. Toddington is proof of his accurate knowledge of the Gothic style and his sense of the picturesque. From the extent of his borrowings from the Oxford colleges, it would seem that he used his eyes during his undergraduate days, and later referred to the 'specimen' examples of Gothic detail taken mostly from Oxford and published by the elder Pugin in 1821 and 1823. His adherence to the principles of the Picturesque presupposes a knowledge of the publications of Price and Knight. As early as 1823, a date which rules out all possibility of Barry having had anything to do with it, Mrs Arbuthnot recorded a visit to Toddington: 'Unlike other gentlemen architects, he seems to have built what will be a very comfortable as well as a good house.'

In plan, Toddington consists of three rectangles, each ranged round an open court and connected diagonally one with another. This disposition ensures that from all sides to which there was an approach, the main part of the building could be seen in relief against the lower ranges of the offices and stables. To the viewer walking round the house, the relations of mass to mass change frequently about the one stabilizing element, the Great Tower; turrets and pinnacles appear in continually varying relationship to the tower and to each other. Main block of two storeys, except on the E wing, which has a basement, ground floor, mezzanine, first floor, and attic. Vaulted cloisters,

* In *The Buildings of England: Herefordshire*, p. 142, this work is attributed to Wyatville, without knowledge of the Arkwright correspondence existing in the Hereford County Records Office.

a refined edition of those at Christ Church, surround the court. The N entrance is a cubic hall; opposite it on the s under the tower is the Grand Staircase. The s and w ranges, with large bay-windows, contain the principal rooms. Each front is completely different, the N serving as a transition between the castellated Gothic of the E and the Flamboyant of the s. The tower is modelled on Magdalen College; above the tracery of the Grand Staircase window is a statue of Henry VIII. The sculpture generally is by competent anonymous craftsmen, though the statue of St Bruno at the foot of the grand staircase is signed by *J. C. Lough*. For some of the windows Hanbury-Tracy bought C15 and C16 STAINED GLASS, mostly from German Switzerland, but much of it was sold in 1911. The large window on the staircase is a late C16 Cologne School Last Judgement. Heraldic glass in the cloisters, reset by *Clayton & Bell* in 1928, includes the arms of local families like Berkeley and Chandos. There is nothing gloomy, however, about the Rococo Gothic decoration of the principal living rooms; gold leaf is liberally used on the bosses of the plaster vaults, particularly in the Drawing Room and Music Room; doorcases, marble fireplaces with their great mirrors, all reproduce Gothic forms. In the history of English domestic architecture the house stands alone, the product of an original mind, influenced only by the taste of the time which preceded A. W. N. Pugin and the Camden Society; it was consequently ignored by Eastlake, but more surprisingly by Sir Kenneth Clark also. It is now used as a Christian Brothers Training College. It was damaged by fire in 1965.

TODDINGTON GRANGE. Built for the estate agent in the mid C19. Symmetrical Tudor brick with stone dressings. The central staircase is top-lit and has elaborate cast-iron balusters.

RAYMEADOW FARMHOUSE, 1 m. N. Rubble-built house with freestone dressings, and quoins, which also follow the eaves line of the gables. Attractive STABLES with gables, similar quoin stones, and a turret. The pair of COTTAGES situated on the N of the drive entrance have similar treatment of quoins, but the eaves-course follows the line of the gables in a straight line instead of being stepped. The windows have mullions. All of 1876, by *William Eden Nesfield*.

TORTWORTH

ST LEONARD. Perp w tower with a C19 open balustraded parapet with pinnacles; but the combination lacks good proportions, and the church is much better inside than outside. Apart from the C14 arcade of five bays, which divides the nave from the almost equally wide s aisle, the church was largely rebuilt in 1872 by *R. H. Carpenter & W. Slater*, with Perp windows. The tall arcade has clustered shafts and an image niche on the easternmost pier. N porch with the date 1853 and the arms of Oriel College, Oxford. – FONT. Norman; octagonal bowl with incurved cones growing out of a cylindrical base. C17 cover. – ROYAL ARMS. George I. – STAINED GLASS. In the tracery of the E window in the s aisle C15 glass with the portrait of [56] Edward IV, and angels bearing shields with emblems of the Passion. – The excellent E window is by *Powell*, c.1872. – w window in the s aisle also by *Powell*, 1895. – N nave window by *Clayton & Bell*, 1886. – SANCTUARY ORNAMENTS dedicated in 1886. – PLATE. Salver, 1736 by *John Tuite*; Chalice, Paten Cover, and Flagon, 1758. – MONUMENTS. Thomas Throckmorton † 1568. Tomb-chest and canopy, Gothic verging into classical. The tomb-chest has panels with shell hoods and the canopy a Tudor arch below a segmental pediment. – Sir Thomas Throckmorton † 1607. Alabaster effigy resting on a tomb-chest below a splendidly decorative alabaster panel full of ingenious carved devices and symbols, and surmounted by a dramatic Renaissance canopy. – John Bosworth † 1785, by *Wood* of Bristol. – Monument of 1896, giving a list of the Ducie family in Art Nouveau lettering on copper. – In the CHURCHYARD a large neo-Jacobean stone canopied seat by *W. D. Caröe* in memory of Julia, Countess of Ducie, † 1895. – CROSS. C14 steps, base, and shaft, with C19 head.

TORTWORTH COURT. 1849–52 by *S. S. Teulon* for the 2nd Earl of Ducie. Teulon's career was only just getting under way when he undertook Tortworth. He is generally thought of as the most outrageous of the Gothic Revivalists, and it might therefore be presumed that he would appeal to the middle-class client who no longer felt bound by 'good taste'; on the contrary, his clientèle belonged to the least *nouveau riche* section of patrons, the royal family and aristocracy. Tortworth appears far more interesting and significant than many other large houses designed at exactly this time, such, for example, as Hardwick's Aldermaston. It is built round an enormously tall square central hall, whose wooden Gothic staircase winds round all four walls, with balconies on each floor and large octagonal newels, supported on huge carved pierced brackets. Ceiling panelled with octagons and quatrefoils. Above this is a large gazebo chamber, now used as a chapel, lit by clerestory windows of bold and uncompromising geometrical tracery intended to be seen at a distance. The entrance front is approached through an archway which once had carved on it the word WELCOME, removed when the house became a prison. Rib-vaulted porte-cochère, dated 1850. This side is dramatic, possibly chaotic, with Tudor Gothic windows, oriel windows, corbelled-out gables, turrets with onion domes, castellated bays, and steep fish-scale-tiled roofs. The material is local stone with Bath stone dressings. The garden front by contrast is symmetrical and ordered. Large service wings, all displaying here and there an inspired detail which arrests one's attention, though it is nowhere profuse, and has a characteristic Victorian seriousness. The principal rooms on the ground floor are magnificently fitted, particularly the double dining room divided by a painted Gothic screen, and lined with china cabinets. It has two fireplaces elaborately decorated with brass ornament, including foliated brass capitals to the columns, and china tiles moulded in relief. Ceilings with carved bosses. The bedrooms however are generally austere, badly proportioned, and often aesthetically indefensible.

CONSERVATORY. By *Ewan Christian*. E.E., with glass dome.

LODGES to the earlier manor, which was situated next the church. The lodges designed by *Sir John Soane* in 1796 were presumably not built, and this pair is castellated and roughcast, with hipped slate roofs, two storeys, and casement windows with dripmoulds.

COTTAGE, N of the entrance to the mansion. 1854 by *Teulon*.

TORTWORTH HOUSE (former Rectory). C18 two-storey five-bay house, with an early C19 wing.

TRACY PARK *see* DOYNTON

TREDINGTON

9020

ST JOHN THE BAPTIST. Norman, with a long chancel rebuilt in the C13, but preserving an original Norman window on the S. Timber-framed belfry rebuilt in 1883. The windows generally are Dec or Perp. On the N side of the chancel a trefoil-headed lancet. Norman N doorway with an early C12 sculptured TYMPANUM, badly weathered, with three figures. On the S porch a date-stone 1624. On the floor a fossilized ichthyosaurus, 9 ft long.* s doorway Norman. Arch with two orders of chevron-moulding and a hood-mould with pellet decorations and a dragon-head stop on the w. The jamb shafts have twisted and chevron ornament and capitals with primitive volutes. Low Norman chancel arch with two plain orders and an enriched hood-mould. The rood beam survives. The nave has an Elizabethan coved plaster ceiling with ornamental rosettes and heads; the chancel also has a plastered wagon ceiling, but without decoration. Stone seat on the N side of the chancel. The walls are scraped. The C19 reredos is unsuitable in its surroundings. – FONT. Of c.1700. – FURNISHINGS. Excellent C17 COMMUNION RAILS and HOLY TABLE. – Elizabethan BENCHES, the ends carved in the C19. – PULPIT. Made up of bench ends with similar carving. – COMMAND-MENT BOARDS. Probably early C19. – HATCHMENT. Surman family arms. – STAINED GLASS. Fragment in the N window in the chancel, showing the beautiful crowned head of a C14 king. – N window under the tower by *Kempe*, 1882. – PLATE. Chalice with Paten Cover, 1576. – CHURCHYARD CROSS. Steps and base with fine attenuated shaft of the C14, over 12 ft high, and surmounted by a modern Maltese cross. – A C17 TABLE TOMB opposite the s doorway has a flat stone top which could be the medieval mensa.

MANOR FARMHOUSE, next to the churchyard, is timber-framed with projecting gables.

TREDINGTON COURT. A fine C16/17 gabled timber-framed house with matching gabled wings on the front, brick-faced in the centre. Two storeys plus dormers, Cotswold stone roof, and a central C19 stone porch with the crest of the Surman family. The forecourt walls have ball-finials.

MILL FARM is also a picturesque building, timber-framed and gabled.

TUFFLEY see GLOUCESTER, p. 230

TUTSHILL

5090

ST LUKE. 1853 by *Henry Woodyer*. Nave with bellcote on its SE buttress, chancel, s porch, and N aisle. Dec windows with ogee foils and pronounced cusping. The four-bay N arcade appears to be a copy of the one at Tidenham. N vestry and organ cham-

---

* The muddy seas of the Lower Lias clay lasted for about ten million years, and in them, 180 million years ago, lived many kinds of reptile including the Ichthyosaurus, viviparous and up to 30 ft long.

ber, with a two-bay E.E. arcade from the chancel; on the opposite side double SEDILIA. This is quite a successful church. – STAINED GLASS. Contemporary E window probably by *O'Connor*. – N aisle windows by *Cakebread, Robey & Co.*, c.1894.

Tutshill was evidently a favoured residential village at the beginning of the C19. There are a number of houses and villas of this date. Communication with Bristol by water, and an ideal situation overlooking the Wye gorge must have been contributing factors. The best of the houses is TUTSHILL HOUSE, stucco, with cornice and blocking course. Two bows to full height and a wrought-iron balcony. Inside, an elegant contemporary staircase and fittings.

CHEPSTOW RAILWAY SUSPENSION BRIDGE.* 1849–52 by *Brunel*.

CHEPSTOW ROAD BRIDGE. 1816 by *John Rennie*. Cast-iron arched ribs.

EASTCLIFF. Early C20 stone house by *Eric C. Francis*, a pupil of Guy Dawber.

8020
TWIGWORTH

ST MATTHEW. 1842–4 by *T. Fulljames*. Chancel and S aisle 1891 by *Waller & Son*. Elegant yet prim. The tower with its small but sharp spire stands in front of a box-nave. Built of carefully roughened stone. E.E. The additions are more accomplished, but not more interesting, with detail breaking away into the semi-Dec.

8030
TWYNING

ST MARY MAGDALENE. Norman, but considerably restored in 1867–8 by *John Middleton*. Perp embattled W tower. The long nave has Norman walls with flat pilasters on both N and S, and remains of a few blocked original windows. The existing windows are C19 Norman. Genuine Norman N doorway with jamb shafts with cushion capitals and a plain arched roll-moulding. The piers have niches either side and a stoup. Large chancel arch with similar jamb shafts with cushion capitals, but the arch itself is C13. Plastered walls. Chancel rebuilt by *Middleton*, with Dec windows, roof trusses supported by short wall shafts with corbels, and capitals carved with deeply undercut foliage in Middleton's usual manner, probably executed by

* Partly in Gloucestershire.

Boulton. – PULPIT in the same style. – FONT. C15 with plain octagonal bowl. – The BELFRY contains a wooden bell-frame of *c.*1450–75. – PLATE. Credence Paten, 1723 by *James Smith*; Chalice and Paten Cover, 1745 by *Henry Brind*; two Flagons, 1745. – MONUMENTS. Sybil Clare † 1575. Recumbent effigy of a Lady with an infant, executed in alabaster, with black marble pillars with Ionic capitals supporting a classical pediment. – William Hancock † 1676 and two sons. Three half-length upright effigies; provincial work. – Edward Baldwyn † 1669. Painted stone tablet. – George Maxwell † 1779. Tablet by *Harris* of Bath. – James Olive † 1826, by *G. Gardener*. – Anne Young † 1858, by *T. Collins*.

In the village proper, N of the church at Twyning Green, several timber-framed cottages, one of which shows crucks in the gable-end. TWYNING PARK is C18, of brick, two storeys, three windows with fluted keystones.

MANOR HOUSE, in a small park on the N. Mid-C19, of stone. Two-storeyed, with gabled attic dormers, and an oriel window over the Tudor entrance.

GUBBERHILL, 1½ m. NW, on the county border at Ripple, is probably C16, timber-framed, with a good oak staircase.

PUCKRUP HALL, ½ m. NW. A classical C19 house faced in stucco, with Ionic order, and lower matching wings with balconies.

TOWBURY, 1 m. NW, W of the A38 on a hill spur just E of the Severn, is an Iron Age hill-fort. Univallate, it encloses about 20 acres. There is a possible entrance in the NE corner. The fort has been partly destroyed on the SW by quarrying.

SHUTHONGER MANOR, ½ m. SW. C18. Brick, with parapet and hipped roof with dormers. Two storeys, five windows with segmental heads and keystones, and larger central window with balcony.

TYTHERINGTON 6080

ST JAMES. Mainly E.E. and Perp. Restored in 1884 by *Pope & Paul* of Bristol. Perp W tower with diagonal buttresses, and an embattled parapet with pinnacles. Nave with a narrow S aisle and a broader N aisle. Over the S doorway an image niche. Stoup; PISCINA not *in situ*. S arcade of three bays. Octagonal piers with feet at the four corners, and moulded capitals. N arcade also of three bays, with slender shafts to the piers and a continuous E.E. hood-mould. The W window of the S aisle is a lancet, and at the E end is a chapel with the remains of an E.E. reredos, and a PISCINA. S of the rebuilt C19 chancel arch a fragment of an impost of a former Norman arch. Wagon roofs to nave and aisles. Windows mostly Late Dec, with geometrical tracery in the E window. Perp E window in the S chapel with a Late Perp window on the S. – FONT. Post-Reformation. Octagonal bowl with a nicely proportioned stem. – PLATE. Chalice and Paten Cover, 1694. – MONUMENTS. William Pullin † 1729. Classical stone tablet. – Martha Hobbs † 1777. Classical marble tablet, typical of several others. – William Cullimore † 1829, by *Emett*.

THE GRANGE. C16/17 house with four gables. Stone relieving arches over the windows. Porch and bargeboards added in the C19. Lanthony Priory had a grange here in the C14.

THE CASTLE, ¼ m. W of the church. Univallate Iron Age hill-fort enclosing about 5 acres. The S side has been destroyed by quarrying, but the rampart still rises 10 ft high on the E.

There are C17 farms at STIDCOT and ITCHINGTON.

9020   UP HATHERLEY

ST PHILIP AND ST JAMES. 1885 by *Prothero & Phillott*. Originally commissioned as a private chapel by Mrs Laura Gretton. The exterior is faced in uncompromising rusticated stone. Nave with rounded apse in the sanctuary, SW bellcote, N porch, and S vestry. Plate tracery in the W window; the other windows are pairs of trefoil-headed lancets with rere-arches. The interior is much better, with a High Church flavour. It has a wagon roof, and, dividing the nave from the sanctuary, a wrought-iron screen by *Prothero*. The sanctuary is enriched with wall paintings by *J. Eadie Reid*, depicting the Annunciation and Apostles in mitres. – STAINED GLASS. E and W windows by *Clayton & Bell*. – PLATE. Credence Paten, 1713. – CHURCHYARD. Discarded FONT of post-Reformation date, consisting of a stone vase-shaped bowl enriched with hart's tongue ferns hanging downwards under the rim, and octagonal plinth; pedestal missing. To be placed inside the church.

7020   UPLEADON

58 ST MARY. C12, but the most remarkable feature is the timber-framed W tower, possibly of *c.*1500. The church otherwise consists of a Norman nave and a C19 chancel. The Norman string-course survives with two windows in both the N and S walls of the nave. N doorway with a C12 chevroned and moulded arch, jamb shafts with carved capitals and abaci, and a

sculptured TYMPANUM with a crude Agnus Dei within a cabled vesica and grotesque animals either side. The sandstone Norman work has been patched with limestone; their mutual incompatibility has resulted in shaling. The rare half-timbered tower is of great interest. Long, close-set studding, infilled on the E with stone, otherwise mostly with C18 brick. No bracing is visible on the exterior, enhancing the appearance of height – a trick often used successfully for this purpose in Early Tudor domestic architecture. Inside, massive cross-bracing with carefully adzed timbers, crossing each other at the junction of the first floor of the belfry. The king-posts of the nave roof are probably a little later. The church is built on a mound of clay, which has caused constant anxiety and necessitated many repairs. It was restored in 1850, and again in 1879, when the very early chancel arch was removed, and rebuilt much bigger by *Ewan Christian*. Vestry added in 1884. – PULPIT. Of oak panels; dated 1661. – STAINED GLASS. E window by *Rogers* of Worcester, 1850.

UPTON CHENEY *see* BITTON

UPTON ST LEONARD'S

ST LEONARD. The church was very much altered and enlarged at different times during the C19, with the exception of the fine Perp W tower, which has three stages, diagonal buttresses to the lower stages, rectangular above, and a panelled embattled parapet with panelled pinnacles surmounted by crocketed finials. S aisle added in 1835, Late Perp, with an arcade of three bays with four-centred arched openings and windows. The Norman doorway, re-set at the same time at the W end, has an arch with roll-moulding and dogtooth ornament, and jamb shafts with scalloped capitals. In the nave N arcade one possibly Transitional Norman pier supporting pointed arches, but the N aisle was rebuilt in the 1850s by *Francis Niblett*, together with the N porch. Chancel rebuilt in 1849 by *Henry Woodyer*, retaining the E.E. style, including the lancet windows at the E end, and the C14 N chapel, which has restored windows of that period. SEDILIA on the S of the sanctuary, a nice piece of E.E. design by *Woodyer*. The double sanctus bellcote was moved from over the chapel to the E nave gable. The church was restored in 1889, by *Waller & Son*, who added the S chancel chapel and vestry. – FONT. Norman tub-shaped bowl. – RERE-

DOS. By *Woodyer*; gold mosaic. – COMMUNION RAILS and CHOIR STALLS by *Woodyer*. – PULPIT and PEWS by *Waller*. – STAINED GLASS. E window 1849 by *William Wailes* of Newcastle. – Two lights over the sedilia by *Thomas Willement*. – S chapel E window by *Bosdet* of Chiswick, 1905. – N aisle W window by *Evans*★ of Shrewsbury, 1859. – PLATE. Paten, 1672. – MONUMENTS. Sir Thomas Snell † 1745, by *Thomas Ricketts* of Gloucester. Huge tomb-chest with gadrooned edge, supporting a sarcophagus, putti, vases, and heraldry, squeezed into the N chapel along with the organ and protected by an iron screen designed by *Woodyer*. – James Steers † 1817, by *Wood* of Gloucester. – John Dearman Birchall † 1897. Alabaster tablet with inlaid mosaic. – Sydney Ancrum † 1906. Marble tablet and mosaic work. – In the CHURCHYARD a rectangular SUNDIAL, possibly C18, on a C19 base.

SCHOOL. 1850 by *Woodyer*. An outstandingly original design. Two blocks are linked by a one-storey wing or cloister behind which is a small, almost medieval garth with a stone well-cover and pump. The N block has large windows with reticulated tracery, and sprocketed gable-ends. Two tiers of gabled dormers in the roof with small pointed windows in wood boarding. The S block has a gabled bell-tower with louvres in the gables. Windows generally with trefoil-headed lights.

BIRCHALL MEMORIAL INSTITUTE. 1898 by *Waller*. Rock-faced stone and half-timber. Gables with bargeboards, and Tudor windows.

VILLAGE HALL. 1920 by *Fletcher Trew*. Of concrete blocks.

WINDSWAY. By *H. F. Trew*, 1930s. Freestone, with mullioned windows and Tudor porch.

There is a considerable amount of new housing going up in the village. A few old timber-framed houses and cottages survive at BONDEND and PORTWAY. MANOR FARM has a good BARN.

ST LEONARD'S COURT. Of *c*.1840.

GROVE COURT, Upton Hill. C16. Timber-framed and gabled, with first-floor overhang.

BOWDEN HALL, ½ m. E. 1770. Brick, now faced in stucco. Three storeys and two bow windows to full height on the garden front. The entrance has a wide pedimented porch with Ionic columns.

WHITLEY COURT, 1 m. E. A small C18 brick house with ren-

★ *David Evans*, † 1861, tried to revive medieval methods of construction and design with vigorous if crude results.

dered front and chamfered stone quoins, and a hipped stone roof; two storeys and five bays.

VINEY HILL 6000

ALL SAINTS. 1867 by *Ewan Christian*. Chancel, three-bay nave, and s aisle. Rather a hard exterior, but good inside, with pleasing clear-cut windows with clear glass. Built of local sandstone. Apsidal sanctuary.

HAYES MANOR FARM. c16/17. Timber-framed, partly rebuilt or refaced in stone, with mullioned windows. Projecting porch with an arched wooden head to the entrance. First-floor overhanging timber-framed room with gable. The s and w walls are stone-faced, and in the sw corner is a stone spiral staircase, which may be part of some kind of tower with a commanding view of the Severn estuary. On the N side of the main block is one massive chimney, and an L-shaped one-storey wing.

WALLSWORTH HALL *see* SANDHURST

WALTON CARDIFF 9030

ST JAMES. Rebuilt in 1869 by *John Middleton*. Small, of stone, with nave and apsidal sanctuary and a bell-turret on the NW. The windows lancets, except for a simplified rose window at the w. Transitional N doorway. The sanctuary arch has short shafts supported by corbels with angels holding heraldic shields, and with Middleton's usual carved floral capitals probably executed by *Boulton*. – PLATE. Chalice, 1699 by *Francis Singleton*; Paten, 1699; Paten, 1720 by *James Smith*.

WANSWELL COURT *see* HAMFALLOW

WAPLEY 7070

ST PETER. Nave, chancel, s chancel chapel, s tower, and s porch. In the N wall of the nave a blocked c13 doorway and a rectangular three-light Tudor window. The chancel has a blocked priest's door on the N, and restored Perp windows, with older rere-arches. c13 tower of four stages with a Perp top stage, embattled parapet, crocketed pinnacles, and w stair-turret with a pyramidal roof rising from a small embattled cornice. Bellopenings with Perp tracery filled in with beautiful pierced stonework. The s porch has a c15 entrance. Tudor w door to the nave, blocked. Tower arches C13, the arch between the tower and the S chapel with E.E. corbelled shafts. The chancel arch is a restoration. On the N is a squint. The church was restored in 1897 by *C. E. Ponting*. In contrast to the very plain and ordinary nave, though it has a nice wagon roof, the area between the sanctuary and the S chapel is very rich. A C15 arch has elaborate panelling on its soffit and a pair of image brackets in its E jamb. To the E of this a smaller, similar arch over a C15 tomb-chest. Next on the E wall of the chapel is a C15 corbel, carved with a winged angel, to support an image; on the S a trefoil PISCINA. – FONT. Perp; octagonal bowl carved with quatrefoils. – HOLY TABLE. C17. – REREDOS. Jacobean panelling from elsewhere, enriched with shields of arms, those of Berkeley on the N. – Other bits of Jacobean carving are worked into the COMMUNION RAIL, LECTERNS, and PULPIT. – ROYAL ARMS. Stuart; 1661–89. – MONUMENTS. Between the sanctuary and the S chapel John Codrington † 1475, a tomb-chest with five panels carved with enriched quatrefoils, and two incised crosses on the top. – Thomas Hooper † 1675. Painted stone tablet. – Richard Oseland † 1769. Tablet by *S. T. Emett*.

CHURCH FARMHOUSE. Simple C17 house with a two-storey porch dated 1636.

⁶⁰⁷⁰

WARMLEY

ST BARNABAS. 1849 by *James Park Harrison*; like Hursley (for John Keble) but skinnier. Dec. Nave, N and S aisles, chancel, W tower with broach-spire. Five-bay nave arcades with octagonal piers. Vestry and organ chamber added by *H. C. M. Hirst*, 1909. – STAINED GLASS. E window by *Hudson*. – Single window in the choir by *Joseph Bell & Son*, 1950.

WARMLEY RAILWAY STATION. Built of wood with horizontal grooving. Round-headed windows. Hipped overhanging slate roof. Separate waiting room and signal boxes to match. Early railway period charm.

WARMLEY HOUSE (now R.D.C. Offices). Built in the 1760s for William Champion, a Quaker, who started the copper and spelter works here. Ashlar, three storeys, with crowning cornice and pediment. 1, 3, 1 bays with sash windows, the central ones in recessed reveals. Chamfered quoins, and rustication on the ground floor round the pedimented doorcase. On the garden side a two-storey balustraded bow. The STABLE buildings are contemporary and charming. In the grounds a STATUE of

Neptune still exists, formerly in a lake but now surrounded by a caravan site.

SUMMER HOUSE, formerly in part of the layout of Warmley House grounds. Mid-C18, in the form of a square two-storey battlemented tower built of black slag (a by-product of spelter) with freestone dressings. It stands on the crown of a stone archway spanning a small stream.

THE POTTERIES embodies the surviving portion of Champion's brass foundry. Original block roughly oblong on plan, rubble with black slag quoins; hipped pantile roof. A square tower projects, rising to ridge level with gabled pantile roof and housing a bronze bell dated 1764 and clock with external octagonal dial. In 1767 two thousand people were employed here. Several rows of COTTAGES, built partly of black slag, survived in 1965.

BRIDGE HOUSE. C18. Painted coursed rubble, moulded stone coping, quoins, two storeys plus attics, five sash windows with flat brick heads to the openings. The central door has a portico with a pediment on columns; garden forecourt with wrought-iron railings and gate. Abutting the l. hand end elevation of Bridge House are three nice early C19 houses, the central house, SHETLAND VILLA, projecting forward slightly from the house on each side.

WESTBURY-ON-SEVERN

ST PETER, ST PAUL, AND ST MARY. The detached tower was built c.1270 as a garrison or watch-tower, heavily buttressed at the angles. The C14 spire, 160 ft high, is framed with a network of great oak beams from the Forest, like gigantic spiders' webs, and covered entirely with wooden shingles held in place by copper nails. It was re-shingled in 1937. The E face of the tower shows the ridge line of a former chantry chapel of St Mary, later used as the school and taken down in 1862.

The church, which stands some 50 ft away to the S, is not earlier than c.1300, which would appear to be the date of the N aisle and porch. Nave arcades of seven bays, S very similar to N, with octagonal piers alternating with others of quatrefoil plan. Dec chancel with good Dec windows S and N; the E window is a C19 restoration. The church is built of Severn Valley lias stone, which breaks down under severe frost when wet. It was restored by *Medland & Maberly* in 1862, and again in 1878. Chancel arch, with deeply cut floriated capitals, vestry, and organ chamber are all C19. S aisle windows of three lights with trefoil heads and straight lintels, the arches apparently having been cut off. S porch with a Tudor entrance arch. On the W wall of the church a Calvary in a canopied niche with a C14 cinquefoiled arch. W window Perp. Rose PISCINA sunk in the S window-sill of the sanctuary. – FONTS. Old octagonal bowl standing on an interesting pedestal which has the arms of Elizabeth I carved on it, and the date 1583. – Also a C19 font. – REREDOS. 1878; carved stone and alabaster. – PEWS. The bench ends have carved linenfold panels. – CHANDELIERS. Two, Bristol style; c.1730. – STAINED GLASS. E window by *Clayton & Bell*. – N and S chancel windows 1864 and 1866 by *Powell & Sons*. – N aisle E window 1906 by *Jones & Willis*. – S aisle SE widow by *Kempe & Tower*. – The S aisle window further W has the extraordinary inscription: 'This church, built A.D. 1530, was dedicated to the Virgin Mary.' This is clearly a misunderstanding and can only refer, if it has any meaning at all, to alterations to the S aisle and porch at that date. – PLATE. Chalice, 1570; Paten, 1672; Paten, 1719. – MONUMENTS. Upper half of a medieval stone coffin, found in the demolished chantry chapel attached to the tower; it may therefore be late C13. Now in the N porch. – In the chancel, a plain marble tablet to Maynard Colchester † 1715, by *Thomas Green* of Camberwell, and other tablets to the Colchester family. – Neo-Roman tablet to Joseph Boughton † 1782, by *Bryan* of Gloucester. – White marble tablet with violin and bow to Thomas Sinderby † 1812, by *J. Pearce* of Frampton. – Neo-Greek tablet to Ann Lane † 1848, by *G. H. Cooke* of Gloucester.

WESTBURY COURT GARDEN. Created by Maynard Colchester between 1696 and 1705. Of the fifty-eight houses illustrated by Kip in Atkyns's *Present State of Gloucestershire* (1712), twenty have variations of the water-garden; but only this one was completely to survive the picturesque cult of later generations. Probably in Holland and certainly in England very few 'Dutch gardens' still exist. This one has a straight CANAL with a PAVILION at one end, and a parallel canal with a T-shaped end opposite. The pavilion was originally built on six Ionic columns, had a room above, and was surmounted by a cupola. No architect seems to have been employed, though a model was made by a Mr *Pyke*. The arms of Maynard Colchester and his wife Jane Clarke, daughter of a Lord Mayor of London, appear in the tympanum of the pediment. At the other end of the canal are wrought-iron CLAIRVOYEES flanked by pillars with original pineapple finials. Near them *c.*1743 a SUMMER HOUSE was built, with French quoins, round-headed windows, and keystones. The brook is diverted round the garden in order to feed the canals.*

At the time of the making of the Dutch garden there was an Elizabethan house near the churchyard. Council houses for old people were built on this site in 1967. Another house was built in the C18, but from 1800 to 1895 there was no house; the family lived elsewhere, though the garden was maintained and a cottage was attached to the pavilion for the gardener. In 1895 a house was built on the site of the cottage. This was demolished in 1961. The canals were restored in 1969.

LOWER LEY FARMHOUSE, 3 m. NE. C16. Timber-framed with overhanging gable. BARN. Timber-framed with upper crucks.

DOVE HOUSE, Rodley, 2½ m. SE. Early C19, with hipped roof and pediment containing a crude plaster shell ornament with a dove; comparable to some of the houses on the other side of the river at Saul.

WEST DEAN

SPEECH HOUSE. During the Middle Ages the Forest of Dean was divided for administrative purposes into bailiwicks with courts held at St Briavels Castle, where disputes might be settled. Charles I sold the Forest without reservation to Sir John Wynter of Lydney, who tried to enclose it. In 1661 a Commission was set up to inquire into the state of the Forest, and in 1675 it was formed into six Walks. The lodge in the King's Walk housed the Court of Speech, and this was the original Speech House. In 1680 the new Court Room was first used for a session of the Mine Law Court. The original building includes the present façade overlooking Cannop Valley, but the width did not extend further than the small bay window on the entrance side, with the ground-floor window next it. It has two storeys and five mullioned and transomed windows, with deeply overhanging eaves and a hipped roof. The Court Room retains a dais with carved balusters, and a moulded stone chimneypiece. Over the side entrance to the Court Room is an

---

* Accounts for planting in 1702–4 include 2,000 yews, 1,500 hollies, Scots firs, filberts, laurestinus, tuberoses, phillyreas, fruit trees espalier and standard, plums, cherries, pears, peaches, apricots, nectarines, red and white grapes, tulips, iris, crocus, jonquil, hyacinth, narcissus, honeysuckle, mezereum, bay, asparagus, anemones, ranunculus, and payments to the Weeder-woman.

13**

escutcheon with the initials of Charles II and the date 1680. The house was an inn in 1858. It had grown into one owing to the need to cater for the people attending the court, and was enlarged in the later part of the C19.

MONUMENT. 1861 by *Benfield*. Stone; commemorating the planting of an oak tree by the Prince Consort.

6070   WESTERLEIGH

35 ST JAMES. Good Perp w tower, though built of Pennant stone, an unattractive material, with ashlar dressings. Diagonal buttresses, stair-turret with spirelet, open balustraded parapet, and crocketed pinnacles. N side of the nave C13 with an E.E. N doorway and window next to it on the E; otherwise the church was largely rebuilt in the C15, when the S aisle was added, almost as wide as the nave, with a five-bay arcade to the nave, and two bays to the chancel. In the spandrel over a pier in the nave a richly carved image niche. N porch C15 with an image niche over the entrance; C13 oak DOOR. The S chapel has a C13 priest's doorway and a late C13 E window which is not authentic. The church was restored in 1896, when the chancel arch was rebuilt. C15 SEDILIA; not very elegant. – FONT. A Norman forgery of the C17. – PULPIT. C15. Stone, vase-shaped, and panelled, with foliated heads to the panels. – WEST GALLERY. C18, with panelling of 1638 underneath. – ROYAL ARMS. George II. – STAINED GLASS. Fragments of medieval glass in the tracery of the Perp window on the N of the nave. – PLATE. Chalice and Paten, 1690. – MONUMENTS. Mary Jones † 1661. Renaissance tablet with heraldry. – Thomas Roberts † 1673. Another of the same type. – Elias Dolling † 1728. Painted stone; cherubs and drapery. – Edward Clent † 1735. Classical marble tablet.

THE OLD INN and a range of C17 COTTAGES w of the church form a group, though the architectural features of the cottages are all but lost under very dark-coloured rendering.

RODFORD is a hamlet ¾ m. N, with a couple of Tudor or C17 farmhouses. RODFORD HILL FARM is a medieval hall-house.

8010   WHADDON

ST MARGARET. Nave and chancel C13. C15 Perp w tower of three stages, with diagonal buttresses and battlements. The N porch has a four-centred arched entrance; the N doorway of the nave is C13. Windows mostly lancets. The church was

generally restored in 1855, and the chancel in 1880. Restored
C13 PISCINA. – FONT. Early C14. Octagonal bowl with trefoil-
headed niches on a panelled stem. – ROYAL ARMS. George III.
– STAINED GLASS. E window by *Sir N. Comper*, 1920. –
PLATE. Pair of Chalices, 1718.

WHITESHILL *see* WINTERBOURNE

WHITMINSTER

ST ANDREW. Nave, N aisle, chancel, W tower, and S porch.
Perp tower with battlements and a taller embattled turret over
the stairs, gargoyles, and diagonal W buttresses. The date 1763
must refer to a repair. The porch has a C14 outer archway, but
the inner doorway is C13 and the DOOR has fine original ironwork. The porch windows E and W are single lights with
cusped heads; wagon roof with carved bosses and wall-plates;
also a stoup. W of the porch a straight-headed Perp window, E
of it a Dec one. In the chancel a Late Perp or Tudor priest's
door with P and B (probably for Byrd) carved in the spandrels, a
nice Perp window, and a restored Dec window on the S; on the
E the window is C19 Perp, and the E window of the N aisle is also
Perp. The three of the N aisle are Dec or restored. Interior
with a three-bay C14 N arcade. The chancel arch is C19, and
the chancel was restored so that it is mostly C19, by *Sir A. W.
Blomfield*, 1884–5. Reredos by *Heaton, Butler and Bayne*.
Wrought-iron CHANDELIERS. – FONT. C19 Perp. – PULPIT.
Jacobean. – PLATE. Chalice and Paten Cover, 1597. – MONU-
MENTS. Rebecca Lloyd † 1625. Small kneeling effigy with her
elbow on a desk. – Another large C17 Baroque monument to
the Lloyd family. – John Bray † 1797, by *J. Pearce* of Frampton. – Charles Owen Cambridge † 1847, by *William Bussell*.
– Jasper Hawkins † 1856, by *T. Bennett* of Frampton.

WHITMINSTER HOUSE. An extremely interesting example of a
small country house which has developed through the different
stylistic periods from Tudor to Victorian. The nucleus is C16,
and the mullioned windows with concave mouldings on the l.
of the front door show this. The house is built of local blue lias
stone, which always had to be rendered, with Cotswold freestone dressings. The main block to the r. of the front door is
C17. It has mullions with convex mouldings and a Jacobean
doorway enclosed in an C18 porch with a small room above (now
used as a little oratory). Fine, large C17 fireplace in the kitchen.
The three gables facing E all have C17 pargeter's decorations

with flowers, very unusual in Gloucestershire and a unique survival. Over the porch the words 'Per Dominum', carved in Jacobean style. C18 projecting wings with bay windows to full height. In the C18 the house was remodelled by the Cambridge family, and what they left is by no means negligible. The library on the SW corner has C18 panelling and fireplace. Fine main staircase of c.1740 with twisted balusters and shaped dado. A NE bedroom has C18 panelling, and the bell on the N roof is dated 1739 and engraved: 'come away, make no delay'. In the 1860s the S and W fronts were refaced. The S front has recently been given a large plain gable, as it must have had before 1860; but the W front is frankly Victorian. The main room on this side is the drawing room, which has an exceptionally fine plastered cornice and Victorian fittings made for the room.

The setting of the house, close to the Perp church tower, is very good. In the grounds is the river Frome, and almost parallel the Stroud Water Canal; one still can imagine the days when Frederick, Prince of Wales, was able to board a gondola in the garden.

PARKLANDS. C19 neo-Greek villa with additional wing.

WEIR LODGE. One of *Mylne*'s canal houses. Early C19, with the usual portico with fluted Doric columns *in antis* and pediment.

The Stroud Water Canal (now mostly disused) crosses the navigable Gloucester–Berkeley Canal in this parish.

The major part of the village is 1½ m. SE of the church, straggling along the main road. It has one or two surviving timber-framed cottages.

WICK

ST BARTHOLOMEW. Chancel, nave, S porch, and W tower. Begun in 1845 from plans by *Charles Dyer* of Bristol, but finished by *William Butterfield*, and consecrated in 1850. There is nothing much to indicate the Butterfield touch except the tower and lychgate. Built of freestone with Bath stone dressings. The rough interior walls are now painted; they were an early example of rough walls being built and left bare. The best thing is the trussed timber roof. Dyer's nave, much broader than Butterfield would have wished, is aisleless with quite well proportioned lancets (having the freak that one on each side only is cusped, and those not opposite). The chancel also, with its correct triplet window, must have seemed to Butterfield too short, but it has characteristic 'brutal' furniture. Goodhart-Rendel wrote: 'rather a key building for its epoch – pray heaven it is not damaged ever by stupid men'. – STAINED GLASS. *Powell*'s quarries in every window. – PLATE. Complete service by *Keith*, 1848; Butterfield design. NATIONAL SCHOOL. 1853.

WICK COURT. Built *c*.1615–20, probably by Sir Edward Wynter. Stone, covered in traditional yellow ochred plaster. Three-storeyed projecting wings, their gables facing inwards and with large oval windows in the apices, all with moulded stone verges and finials; mullioned and transomed windows. The rear has three flush gables. Early C18 room added over the door, and supported on pillars. C17 panelling in the entrance hall, and a Jacobean staircase, with newel-posts and open finials and pendants. Good panelling in other parts. The house is rather like Cold Ashton Manor.

STANDING STONES, ½ m. SE. These two are probably the remains of the burial-chamber of a destroyed LONG BARROW.

WICK COURT *see* ARLINGHAM

WICKWAR

HOLY TRINITY. Good Perp w tower; otherwise the church was practically rebuilt in 1881, when it was restored by *W. L. Bernard*. The tower, of three stages, has diagonal buttresses with attached pinnacles on the set-offs, a panelled embattled parapet with crocketed pinnacles and gargoyles, image niches on each face of the middle stage, and large bell-openings with tracery and pierced stonework. Stair-turret on the NE corner. w doorway with enriched spandrels. Under the tower is a fan-vault springing from carved corbels. Perp nave and s porch with embattled parapets. The N aisle, arcade, chancel arch, chancel, and N chapel are C19 rebuilding. The projecting organ chamber of 1929 has on its outer N wall a SCULPTURE of St John the Baptist, dated 1496, and removed from Pool House (*see* below). The date-stone 1749 over the E window perhaps refers to some other restoration. Perp PISCINA in the N chapel. – FONT. Perp, with enriched octagonal bowl. – PULPIT. Jacobean. – HATCHMENT. Arms of Purnell. – CHANDELIERS. One of 1728, Bristol style, a large and fine example. The other is Austrian, of *c*.1929. – STAINED GLASS. W window 1911 by *Christopher Whall*. – Two-light window on the s, nearest the pulpit, by *Horace Wilkinson*. – PLATE. Elizabethan Chalice and Paten Cover; Credence Paten, 1707; Almsplate, 1743, and Flagon, 1730, both by *Robert Brown*. – MONUMENTS. Elizabeth Yate † 1721. Baroque tablet. – John Purnell † 1726. Coloured marble tablet. – Brass to John Biddle, a Socinian vicar, † 1733. – George Hobbs † 1740. Classical marble. – William Giles, High Sheriff, † 1750. Baroque coloured marble tablet. – Thomas Stokes † 1762, by *W. Paty*.

The terraced garden SW of the church is all that remains of Pool House,* which formerly stood on the edge of a lake. The round building is an air vent for the railway tunnel. The SUNDAY SCHOOL, on the N of the churchyard, was built in 1837. The OLD RECTORY is of 1864 by *George Devey*, of rubble, on an irregular plan. Gables with bargeboards, mullioned and transomed windows, stone dressings, an oriel window, and a doorway with enriched spandrels surmounted by the Earl of Ducie's coronet.

The OLD GRAMMAR SCHOOL, dating from 1684, is a good building with a hipped roof, coved eaves cornice, and projecting wings. 2–3–2 bays. The HIGH STREET continues from here on a slight uphill bend, turning into a straight street with decent, mostly C18-fronted, rendered or stuccoed houses. On the l. is a good group of such buildings, HALL HOUSE, SOCIAL CLUB, ALBERT HOUSE, and the POLICE STATION, all with nice doorways. Next is a CONGREGATIONAL CHAPEL, dated 1817, altered in 1919. On the r. is No. 30, two storeys and five bays, with a pediment with an *œil-de-bœuf* window in its tympanum. No. 38 has Georgian shop windows. The TOWN HALL is of rubble, c.1795, with arched openings on the second floor and a bellcote with pinnacle. On the opposite side No. 59, C17, has an oak door with a moulded stone architrave and segmental hood. At the end on this side CASTLE FARMHOUSE is more distinguished, with an C18 stone front. Moulded cornice and parapet with carved panels. The centre breaks forward with a crowning pediment. Three storeys and seven bays, the windows with dripmoulds added in 1880. At the side is a Venetian window on each floor.

HILL HOUSE. A Queen Anne house with a hipped roof, two storeys and five bays, restored in 1968 by *Claud Phillimore*.

---

* A Tudor house illustrated in Lysons' *Antiquities*, with the statue of St John the Baptist visible in the gable-end. The existing inscription reads 'STE. JOHES. BAPTISTA. ORA', and under the figure, 'IN THE YERE OF OURE LORDS GOD M.CCCC. IIII SCORE XVI. TRINITE MONDAY XXII DAY OF MAY'.

WILLSBRIDGE *see* BITTON

WINTERBOURNE

St Michael. The chancel dates from the C12; pilaster buttresses survive on its E wall. Priest's door and chancel arch Transitional. The s tower, set transept-wise, is E.E. and Dec. Three stages, with diagonal buttresses, a pierced parapet, and pinnacles, and a spire which had to be rebuilt *c.*1870. Image niches on the buttresses about 7 ft from the ground; Dec window on the s. E.E. s doorway to the nave with a cinquefoiled arch supported on jamb shafts with floriated capitals, a chamfered order, and a roll-moulded hood. Nave N aisle arcade of four bays rebuilt in 1843. N tower arch E.E., with attached cylindrical shafts, roll-mouldings, and a hood-mould with head stops. On its E respond is a PISCINA, and what was originally a deeply splayed window to light the nave altar, now blocked by the organ chamber added in 1895. The early C13 chancel arch has jamb shafts with floriated capitals, the inner ones stopped on corbels. E wall of the chancel rebuilt in 1856 and raised to allow the insertion of a loftier E.E.-style window. On the N is a chantry chapel, founded in 1351 by Thomas, Lord Bradeston, but largely rebuilt in 1880. On the E wall are corbels to support images, embattled and bearing shields of arms, that on the l. being the arms of Bradeston (argent, on a canton gules, a rose or, barbed proper).* – FONT. Late C17. Rectangular bowl with scalloped or gadrooned sides, on an octagonal stem. – WALL PAINTINGS. Under the tower is a scheme of painting carried out after alterations in the Dec period. The corbels are painted with roses, and the splays of the s window and the soffits of the arches have indistinct patterns. The figure of a Knight has been recorded. – PULPIT. Stone; 1877. – STAINED GLASS. E window 1856 by *Thomas Willement*. – PLATE. Salver, 1711; Flagon, 1722; Chalice, 1811; Salver, 1812. – MONUMENTS. Brass of *c.*1370, the oldest in Gloucestershire. Figure of a Lady, 4 ft 5 in. high, possibly Agnes, widow of Lord Bradeston, † 1369. – Against the N wall of the chapel effigies of a Knight and Lady, possibly Sir Robert Bradeston † *c.*1356. By the l. shoulder of the knight, hidden against the wall, is a badge carved in high relief showing the head of a fish. The knight is cross-legged with his feet on a lion; their heads are supported by angels. The effigies were

* Lord Bradeston's arms appear in the great E window of Gloucester Cathedral.

Winterbourne church, brass to a lady, *c* .1370

made by Bristol craftsmen. – Effigies of a Knight and Lady, *c*.1400. Camail and jupon, suit of plate armour with pointed bascinet, straight legs resting on a lion; attributed to Sir Edmund Bradeston † *c*.1395. Effigies made by Bristol craftsmen. – Effigy of a Lady, C14. – In the N aisle, effigy of a Knight with head on helm, cross-legged, his feet resting on a lion with a long paw. Under a cinquefoil crocketed canopy, also C14. – Brass inscriptions to Matthew Buck † 1631 and Thomas Buck † 1658. – James Buck † 1612. Renaissance detail. Tomb-chest with Ionic pilasters, and a canopy with Corinthian columns. – Amy Symes † 1662. Provincial Renaissance monument with twisted columns and Composite capitals supporting a broken pediment. – Arthur Tucker † 1785, by *T. Paty*. Classical tablet. – Thomas Mountjoy † 1797, by *Emett* of Downend. – William Perry † 1807, by *Wood* of Bristol. – William Rickards † 1827 and Thomas Whitfield † 1834, by *O. Greenway*. – Mary Brydges † 1826, by *T. Clark*, of Bristol.

NW of the churchyard is a raised FOOTPATH built between two walls, laid out equally to E and W of two central flights of steps. This may be part of the garden of the original manor house, though the existing house, COURT FARM, is modern. The round rubble DOVECOTE survives.

WHITESHILL CONGREGATIONAL CHAPEL. 1816 – date-stone in bold figures, under a shaped parapet. Painted stone pilasters and round-headed windows.

OLD RECTORY. Plain Georgian house of ashlar, with cornice and parapet. Two storeys, three bays, and door with a large fanlight.

In the village, WINTERBOURNE HOUSE (Collegiate School) is originally possibly C16, but was remodelled in the C18, and is roughcast. It contains an excellent mid-C18 staircase with twisted balusters, and Queen Anne panelling and a shell-cupboard in the drawing room. Dining room added in 1920, with a Jacobean style plaster ceiling. In the garden an C18 GAZEBO, with carved urns.

CROSSLEY HOUSE. C18. Chamfered quoins, three storeys, five bays with central round-arched windows, and parapet.

The following houses are in HICKS COMMON ROAD. HICKS FARM. 1650. Two gables. THE MOUNT. C18 front with older house at the back. Front of two storeys and three bays with bay windows either side. Wooden Tuscan porch at the side. HARCOMBE FARM. C17. Two gables and a two-storey gabled porch. Mullioned windows and diagonal chimneys.

HAMBROOK GROVE, 1 m. s. C18. Three storeys, five bays, ashlar cornice and parapet. Stone portico with Ionic columns *in antis*. At the back two two-storey bow windows. Either side are two-storey rubble wings.

HAMBROOK COURT. C18. Two storeys, seven bays, chamfered quoins and parapet.

GROVE VIEW. C18 terrace.

HAMBROOK HOUSE. C17 in origin, but re-fronted and altered *c.*1784. Front of three storeys and 2, 1, 2 bays, the centre breaking forward with a crowning pediment containing a lunette window. Three-light windows on each floor with pilasters, fluted friezes, and cornices; central doorway similarly treated. The crowning parapet carries sculptured urns. The central grand staircase divides at the first landing, though thereafter it continues only on one side. Moulded oak balusters and a panelled dado. The rooms have ornamental plaster cornices and beams.

FABERS PLACE. Date-stone 1698. L-shaped, with two gables, and a two-storey gabled porch in the angle.

BURY HILL, 1 m. SSE, S of the river Frome. Bivallate Iron Age hillfort, but with only one ditch(?); quarried away on the N. It encloses about 6 acres. Excavation within the enclosed area revealed Iron Age B occupation, and a continuance or recurrence of occupation in Roman times.

₆₀₇₀
WINTERBOURNE DOWN

ALL SAINTS. 1858 by *G. E. Street*. Nave, N aisle, chancel, S porch, and lead-covered bellcote. The windows have plate tracery. N arcade of three bays with cylindrical columns bearing large floriated capitals; the responds are plain. Chancel PISCINA and E.E.-style double SEDILIA. Organ chamber added on the N in 1894 by *E. H. Edwards*. – STAINED GLASS. The E window is Pre-Raphaelite in character, perhaps by *Morris & Co*. – Three-light window on the S by *J. F. Bentley*, 1876.

MOOREND FARMHOUSE. Date-stone 1676 on the porch. Roughcast. Two gables, and a two-storey gabled porch. One of the most likely sites in the Bristol area of an early vineyard.

₉₀₂₀
WOODMANCOTE
1 m. E of Bishop's Cleeve

COUNTESS OF HUNTINGDON CHAPEL. 1854. Pointed Gothic windows. Symmetrical gable-end with bell-turret.

MANOR HOUSE. C16. Of stone with Cotswold stone roofs and many gables with moulded verges and ball-finials. The mullioned windows are typically Tudor, with four-centred arched lights and concave mouldings. Timber-framed wing with attached BARN. Inside, the main rooms have Tudor or C17 panelling, and over a large moulded stone fireplace is a carved overmantel bearing the arms of the Cocks family. C17 staircase with moulded balusters and hand-rail.

WOOLASTON

ST ANDREW. Originally a Norman church with a possibly C13 tower on the NE, almost completely rebuilt in 1859 by *J. W. Hugall*. A new aisle was built by *John Briggs* in 1839, but this must also have been remodelled. N vestry added in 1903. The church now consists of a fairly spacious nave, chancel, S aisle with transverse gables, S porch, and NE tower. W window C13 with interlacing tracery. The porch has a Norman-style entrance and S doorway. S aisle with polished granite columns and elaborately carved capitals with foliage. – FONT. C14 plain octagonal bowl on a modern pillar and plinth. – SCULPTURE. Mutilated medieval crucifix. – PULPIT. Of c.1750; moved from Claycoton, Northamptonshire. – SCREEN. Of c.1860; moved from the Church of the Venerable Bede, Sunderland. – STAINED GLASS. Two windows in the chancel by *Francis Skeat*, 1963. – MONUMENTS. Blanche Woodroffe † 1831. Painted stone tablet. – John Powles † 1844. Neo-Greek. – CHURCHYARD. The doorway leading to the rectory has C14 corbel heads.

RECTORY. A large house W of the church. Originally possibly C16/17, remodelled in the C18. Square, with bow windows; three storeys high. On the l. a wing was added c.1830, and in 1860 a matching wing was added on the r. by *John Gwatkin*, of Chepstow. He also moved the staircase so that it descends in an alcove at the rear of the entrance hall, and has cast-iron ornamental balusters.

Several C17 and C18 houses at BROOKEND, ¼ m. NE. The OLD INN has stone gatepiers with enriched ball-finials, dated 1713. PLUSTERWINE HOUSE is C18. HIGH WOOLASTON is a C16/17 farmhouse built on three sides of a courtyard. WOOLASTON GRANGE, an early C19 house, has in the farmyard the remains of a chapel with a tunnel-vaulted undercroft. At The Chesters is a ROMAN VILLA of corridor type, lying at the E side of a walled enclosure, with outbuildings to the S and W.

All were contained within a courtyard *c.*210 ft square enclosed by a stone wall and outer ditch. The original main house was 90 ft long, with a simple bath suite at the W end of the S wing. C4 reconstruction increased the size and elaboration of the baths.

WOOLSTONE

St Martin. C14, with C15* Perp tower which has moved dangerously owing to the clay sub-soil. The exterior is mostly faced in ashlar, but the interior rubble walls were ruthlessly scraped of plaster in the severe restoration by *John Middleton* in 1873. Nave with the C14 blocked arcade of a former aisle showing in the N wall, which now has C19 Dec windows; chancel with an off-centre C14 Dec E window with nice flowing tracery, Late Perp windows on the S side, and a priest's doorway on the N; C19 S porch; tilting W tower with battlements, pinnacles, gargoyles, diagonal buttresses, and Perp openings. S doorway Perp. Dec chancel and tower arches and C19 roofs. In the chancel E wall to the S of the E window is a C14 image niche with pinnacles and vaulted canopy, much mutilated by iconoclasts. The enriched carved stone bracket is supported on various stones including a carved capital upside down. On the other side is a smaller niche, also mutilated. Stone-flagged floors. – FONT. Late C14. Tall octagonal bowl with deep chamfered base, each face decorated with a plain rectangular moulded panel. – MONUMENTS. Recumbent effigy of a priest in eucharistic vestments; *c.*1425 (chancel N). The church was attached to Deerhurst Priory. – Ledger stone in the sanctuary to John Roberts † 1650(?). – Tablets of the mid C19 by *G. Lewis.*

In the village are several old timber-framed COTTAGES.

The Grange. C17, with late C18 addition. The older part carries the date 1637 and the initials of John Roberts and his wife, with a double heart similarly carved to that on the ledger stone in the church. This side of the house is gabled and has mullioned windows. The C18 front has a parapet, two storeys, and three windows. In the garden a SUNDIAL, dated 1741.

The old RECTORY, designed by *W. H. Knight*, was damaged by fire in 1889. A HOUSE S of the church is by *Norman Collins*, 1967.

WORMINGTON

St Catherine. This small church, said to have been built by the Abbot of Hailes in 1475, is mostly Perp or later; but there

* Atkyns says the church was rebuilt in 1499.

are a few Norman corbels not *in situ* below the wooden bell-turret, which was probably built *c.*1800 on the w gable. Nave with N and s aisles with three-bay Perp arcades. Chancel with a Tudor arch leading into a N chapel now used as the vestry. E window Late Perp; w window C18. In the chancel a restored trefoil-headed PISCINA. The walls are limewashed. – FONT. C15. Octagonal bowl enriched with quatrefoils in circles, and octagonal pedestal with trefoil-headed niches on four sides. – SCULPTURE. Set at the E end of the s aisle an Anglo-Saxon Crucifixion of *c.*1020–50, found at Wormington Grange; it may therefore have come from Winchcombe Abbey. It shows Eastern, as opposed to Byzantine, influence in the contorted head and thin straining arms, though crudely followed. The *Dexterae Dei* above is a non-Celtic feature and typically English. – STAINED GLASS. Good fragments of medieval glass in the westernmost windows of the N and s aisles. – Early C19 borders to the windows in the N vestry. – E window. Excellent glass by *William Morris & Co.,* 1912. – Tapestry CURTAINS in the N chancel arch from a design by *William Morris.* – Ancient BENCHES in the choir. – Good modern PEWS. – HATCHMENT. Mid C19, with the arms of Gist and Baron Rossmore. – PLATE. Chalice, Salver, and Flagon, 1836. – MONUMENTS. Early C15 incised grave slab, depicting a man flanked by two wives; very worn inscription round the border. – Anne Savage † 1605. Brass showing a Lady in a four-poster bed. – Hon. Mary Ann Gist † 1844, and two other tablets, by *Lewis.* Several timber-framed COTTAGES in the village.

WORMINGTON GRANGE, 1¼ m. SE. A Late Georgian bow-fronted house with a large addition in refined neo-Greek, 1826–7 by *Henry Hakewill.* The ashlar-faced front has two storeys, three bays with three-light windows, and a moulded stone cornice and parapet, the sides breaking forward with panelled pilasters. Central tetrastyle portico with fluted columns with Ionic capitals and pediment. The gardens were planned in the early C20 by *Guy Dawber.*

WOTTON *see* GLOUCESTER, pp. 230, 232, 235, 254

YATE   7080

ST MARY. Of Pennant stone, with Cotswold stone roofs. Magnificent Perp w tower, of three stages, with different-coloured freestone dressings and diagonal buttresses. The tall, slim, blind windows in the middle stage have image niches with

small projecting ogee-cusped canopies, and crocketed pinnacles. Stair-turret spirelet and pierced parapet rebuilt in 1896
by *W. D. Caröe*. The C13 church incorporates part of the
Norman fabric; there is a Norman window in the w wall of the
s transept. Early Tudor priest's doorway on the s of the chancel
with a sculptured angel above it, cut by a mass-dial. No s aisle.
The s porch has a round-headed entrance with restored Perp
niches above, and over the s door is a mutilated image of the
Virgin(?). The collapse of a central tower, causing damage to
the E part of the nave, would explain the change of style in the
N arcade, which has four bays; the two to the w have C13 keel-
moulded piers with crude floriated capitals, the two to the E
were rebuilt in the C15 without any attempt to unify the design.
The two-bay chancel arcades are C13 and similar to those in the
nave, but the chancel arch and the arches to the transepts are
Perp. Either side of the chancel are balancing chapels of almost
equal size; all the fenestration is Perp or Tudor. The interior
walls are limewashed. Chancel restored in 1879 by *Ralph
Nevill*. It has deep yellow encaustic tiles. – FONT. C15. Octagonal bowl with quatrefoils. – STAINED GLASS. E window by
Burlison & Grylls, c.1879. – Fragments of medieval glass in
the E window of the N chapel. – Three-light window on the s
side, nearest the E, by *Horace Wilkinson*. – WALL PAINTING.
On the nave N wall a small portion of a St Christopher and a
water-mill. – PLATE. Two Salvers, 1764 and 1765; Flagon,
1772; Chalice, 1811 by *Samuel Hennell*. – MONUMENTS. Small
brass showing Alexander Staples † 1590, with two wives and
eleven children. – Thomas Stokes † 1786. Classical tablet of
coloured marbles with draped urn, by *Reeves* of Bath. –
Augusta Bradshaw † 1810, by *T. King* of Bath. Pretty small
white marble monument on a slate background.

Yate is to be a new overspill town for Bristol and Bath. A
SHOPPING CENTRE was begun in 1965 by *Stone Toms &
Partners*. – Proposed SCULPTURE, by *Franta Belsky*.

YATE COURT FARM, 2 m. N. On the site of a fortified house of
the time of Edward I. Any remains of interest are said to have
been taken to Berkeley Castle.

OXWICK FARMHOUSE, 2 m. NNE. Built c.1702 for Mr Oxwick,
Citizen and Fishmonger of London, on an earlier plan.
Rubble with brick dressings. Five unequal gables, segment-
headed windows, a three-storey bow to the side, and an enriched escutcheon of arms over the front door, with vertical
brick piers and a stone pediment. Altogether the house is

curious and unsophisticated. Contemporary interior fittings include oak spiral staircases.

The STABLE BLOCK is an echo of the house; symmetrical with three gables, arched carriage-ways, and a central doorway with rusticated brick columns, segmental head, cornice, and illegible inscription.

HILL HOUSE FARM, HALL END FARM, and FRITH FARM, close together in the N of the parish, are all picturesque C17 houses with gables.

GLOSSARY

ABACUS: flat slab on the top of a capital (q.v.).

ABUTMENT: solid masonry placed to resist the lateral pressure of a vault.

ACANTHUS: plant with thick fleshy and scalloped leaves used as part of the decoration of a Corinthian capital (q.v.) and in some types of leaf carving.

ACHIEVEMENT OF ARMS: in heraldry, a complete display of armorial bearings.

ACROTERION: foliage-carved block on the end or top of a classical pediment.

ADDORSED: two human figures, animals, or birds, etc., placed symmetrically so that they turn their backs to each other.

AEDICULE, AEDICULA: framing of a window or door by columns and a pediment (q.v.).

AFFRONTED: two human figures, animals, or birds, etc., placed symmetrically so that they face each other.

AGGER: Latin term for the built-up foundations of Roman roads; also sometimes applied to the banks of hill-forts or other earthworks.

AMBULATORY: semicircular or polygonal aisle enclosing an apse (q.v.).

ANNULET: see Shaft-ring.

ANSE DE PANIER: see Arch, Basket.

ANTEPENDIUM: covering of the front of an altar, usually by textiles or metalwork.

ANTIS, IN: see Portico.

APSE: vaulted semicircular or polygonal end of a chancel or a chapel.

ARABESQUE: light and fanciful surface decoration using combinations of flowing lines, tendrils, etc., interspersed with vases, animals, etc.

ARCADE: range of arches supported on piers or columns, free-standing; or, BLIND ARCADE, the same attached to a wall.

ARCH: round-headed, i.e. semicircular; pointed, i.e. consisting of two curves, each drawn from one centre, and meeting in a point at the top; segmental, i.e. in the form of a segment;

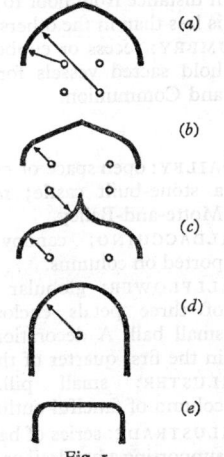

(a)

(b)

(c)

(d)

(e)

Fig. 1

pointed; four-centred (a Late Medieval form), see Fig. 1(a); Tudor (also a Late Medieval form), *see* Fig. 1(*b*); Ogee (introduced *c.* 1300 and specially popular in the C14), *see* Fig. 1(*c*); Stilted, *see* Fig. 1(*d*); Basket, with lintel connected to the jambs by concave quadrant curves, *see* Fig. 1(*e*).

ARCHITRAVE: lowest of the three main parts of the entablature (q.v.) of an order (q.v.) (*see* Fig. 12).

ARCHIVOLT: under-surface of an arch (also called Soffit).

ARRIS: sharp edge at the meeting of two surfaces.

ASHLAR: masonry of large blocks wrought to even faces and square edges.

ATLANTES: male counterparts of caryatids (q.v.).

ATRIUM: inner court of a Roman house, also open court in front of a church.

ATTACHED: *see* Engaged.

ATTIC: topmost storey of a house, if distance from floor to ceiling is less than in the others.

AUMBRY: recess or cupboard to hold sacred vessels for Mass and Communion.

BAILEY: open space or court of a stone-built castle; *see* also Motte-and-Bailey.

BALDACCHINO: canopy supported on columns.

BALLFLOWER: globular flower of three petals enclosing a small ball. A decoration used in the first quarter of the C14.

BALUSTER: small pillar or column of fanciful outline.

BALUSTRADE: series of balusters supporting a handrail or coping (q.v.).

BARBICAN: outwork defending the entrance to a castle.

BARGEBOARDS: projecting decorated boards placed against the incline of the gable of a building and hiding the horizontal roof timbers.

BARROW: *see* Bell, Bowl, Disc, Long, *and* Pond Barrow.

BASILICA: in medieval architecture an aisled church with a clerestory.

BASKET ARCH: *see* Arch (Fig. 1e).

BASTION: projection at the angle of a fortification.

BATTER: inclined face of a wall.

BATTLEMENT: parapet with a series of indentations or embrasures with raised portions or merlons between (also called Crenellation).

BAYS: internal compartments of a building; each divided from the other not by solid walls but by divisions only marked in the side walls (columns, pilasters, etc.) or the ceiling (beams, etc.). Also external divisions of a building by fenestration.

BAY-WINDOW: angular or curved projection of a house front with ample fenestration. If curved, also called bow-window; if on an upper floor only, also called oriel or oriel window.

BEAKER FOLK: Late New Stone Age warrior invaders from the Continent who buried their dead in round barrows and introduced the first metal tools and weapons to Britain.

BEAKHEAD: Norman ornamental motif consisting of a row of bird or beast heads with beaks biting usually into a roll moulding.

BELFRY: turret on a roof to hang bells in.

BELGAE: Aristocratic warrior bands who settled in Britain in two main waves in the C I B.C. In Britain their culture is termed Iron Age C.

BELL BARROW: Early Bronze Age round barrow in which the mound is separated from its encircling ditch by a flat platform or berm (q.v.).

BELLCOTE: framework on a roof to hang bells from.

BERM: level area separating ditch from bank on a hill-fort or barrow.

BILLET FRIEZE: Norman ornamental motif made up of short raised rectangles placed at regular intervals.

BIVALLATE: Of a hill-fort: defended by two concentric banks and ditches.

BLOCK CAPITAL: Romanesque capital cut from a cube by having the lower angles rounded off to the circular shaft below (also called Cushion Capital) (Fig. 2).

Fig. 2

BOND, ENGLISH or FLEMISH: see Brickwork.

BOSS: knob or projection usually placed to cover the intersection of ribs in a vault.

BOWL BARROW: round barrow surrounded by a quarry ditch. Introduced in Late Neolithic times, the form continued until the Saxon period.

BOW-WINDOW: see Bay-Window.

BOX: A small country house, e.g. a shooting box. A convenient term to describe a compact minor dwelling, e.g. a rectory.

BOX PEW: pew with a high wooden enclosure.

BRACES: see Roof.

BRACKET: small supporting piece of stone, etc., to carry a projecting horizontal.

BRESSUMER: beam in a timber-framed building to support the, usually projecting, superstructure.

BRICKWORK: *Header:* brick laid so that the end only appears on the face of the wall. *Stretcher:* brick laid so that the side only appears on the face of the wall. *English Bond:* method of laying bricks so that alternate courses or layers on the face of the wall are composed of headers or stretchers only (Fig. 3a). *Flemish Bond:* method of laying bricks so that alternate headers and stretchers appear in each course on the face of the wall (Fig. 3b).

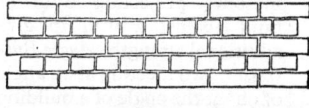

(a)

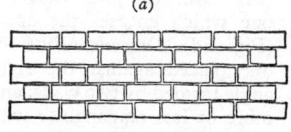

(b)

Fig. 3

BROACH: see Spire.

BROKEN PEDIMENT: see Pediment.

BRONZE AGE: In Britain, the period from c. 1600 to 600 B.C.

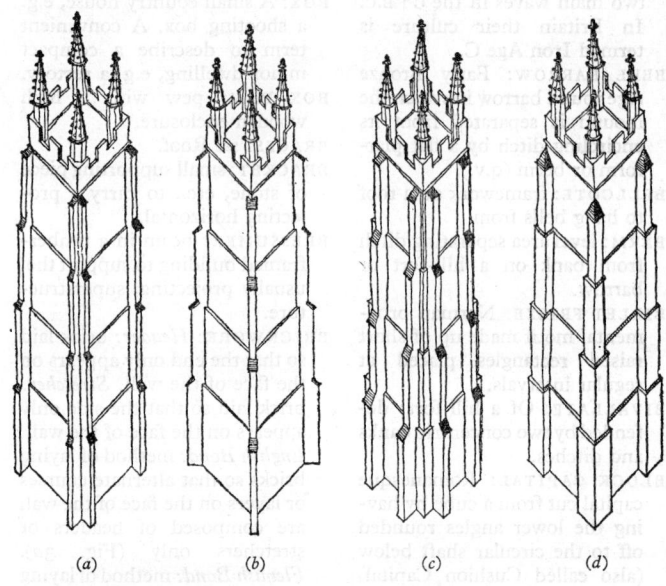

(a)   (b)   (c)   (d)

Fig. 4

BUCRANIUM: ox skull.

BUTTRESS: mass of brickwork or masonry projecting from or built against a wall to give additional strength. *Angle Buttresses:* two meeting at an angle of 90° at the angle of a building (Fig. 4a). *Clasping Buttress:* one which encases the angle (Fig. 4d). *Diagonal Buttress:* one placed against the right angle formed by two walls, and more or less equiangular with both (Fig. 4b). *Flying Buttress:* arch or half arch transmitting the thrust of a vault or roof from the upper part of a wall to an outer support or buttress. *Setback Buttress:* angle buttress set slightly back from the angle (Fig. 4c).

CABLE MOULDING: Norman moulding imitating a twisted cord.

CAIRN: a mound of stones usually covering a burial.

CAMBER: slight rise or upward curve of an otherwise horizontal structure.

CAMPANILE: isolated bell tower.

CANOPY: projection or hood over an altar, pulpit, niche, statue, etc.

CAP: in a windmill the crowning feature.

CAPITAL: head or top part of a column.

CARTOUCHE: tablet with an ornate frame, usually enclosing an inscription.

CARYATID: whole female figure

supporting an entablature or other similar member. *Termini Caryatids:* female busts or demi-figures or three-quarter figures supporting an entablature or other similar member and placed at the top of termini pilasters (q.v.). Cf. Atlantes.

CASTELLATED: decorated with battlements.

CELURE: panelled and adorned part of a wagon-roof above the rood or the altar.

CENSER: vessel for the burning of incense.

CENTERING: wooden framework used in arch and vault construction and removed when the mortar has set.

CHALICE: cup used in the Communion service or at Mass. *See also* Recusant Chalice.

CHAMBERED TOMB: burial mound of the New Stone Age having a stone-built chamber and entrance passage covered by an earthen barrow or stone cairn. The form was introduced to Britain from the Mediterranean.

CHAMFER: surface made by cutting across the square angle of a stone block, piece of wood, etc., at an angle of 45° to the other two surfaces.

CHANCEL: that part of the E end of a church in which the altar is placed, usually applied to the whole continuation of the nave E of the crossing.

CHANCEL ARCH: arch at the W end of the chancel.

CHANTRY CHAPEL: chapel attached to, or inside, a church, endowed for the saying of Masses for the soul of the founder or some other individual.

CHEVET: French term for the E end of a church (chancel, ambulatory, and radiating chapels).

CHEVRON: Norman moulding forming a zigzag.

CHOIR: that part of the church where divine service is sung.

CIBORIUM: a baldacchino.

CINQUEFOIL: *see* Foil.

CIST: stone-lined or slab-built grave. First appears in Late Neolithic times. It continued to be used in the Early Christian period.

CLAPPER BRIDGE: bridge made of large slabs of stone, some built up to make rough piers and other longer ones laid on top to make the roadway.

CLASSIC: here used to mean the moment of highest achievement of a style.

CLASSICAL: here used as the term for Greek and Roman architecture and any subsequent styles inspired by it.

CLERESTORY: upper storey of the nave walls of a church, pierced by windows.

COADE STONE: artificial (cast) stone made in the late C18 and the early C19 by Coade and Sealy in London.

COB: walling material made of mixed clay and straw.

COFFERING: decorating a ceiling with sunk square or polygonal ornamental panels.

COLLAR-BEAM: *see* Roof.

COLONNADE: range of columns.

COLONNETTE: small column.

COLUMNA ROSTRATA: column decorated with carved prows of ships to celebrate a naval victory.

COMPOSITE: *see* Order.

CONSOLE: bracket (q.v.) with a compound curved outline.

COPING: capping or covering to a wall.

CORBEL: block of stone projecting from a wall, supporting some horizontal feature.

CORBEL TABLE: series of corbels, occurring just below the roof eaves externally or internally, often seen in Norman buildings.

CORINTHIAN: *see* Order.

CORNICE: in classical architecture the top section of the entablature (q.v.). Also for a projecting decorative feature along the top of a wall, arch, etc.

CORRIDOR VILLA: *see* Villa.

COUNTERSCARP BANK: small bank on the down-hill or outer side of a hill-fort ditch.

COURTYARD VILLA: *see* Villa.

COVE, COVING: concave undersurface in the nature of a hollow moulding but on a larger scale.

COVER PATEN: cover to a Communion cup, suitable for use as a paten or plate for the consecrated bread.

CRADLE ROOF: *see* Wagon roof.

CRENELLATION: *see* Battlement.

CREST, CRESTING: ornamental finish along the top of a screen, etc.

CRINKLE-CRANKLE WALL: undulating wall.

CROCKET, CROCKETING: decorative features placed on the sloping sides of spires, pinnacles, gables, etc., in Gothic architecture, carved in various leaf shapes and placed at regular intervals.

CROCKET CAPITAL: *see* Fig. 5. An Early Gothic form.

CROMLECH: word of Celtic origin still occasionally used of single free-standing stones ascribed to the Neolithic or Bronze Age periods.

Fig. 5

CROSSING: space at the intersection of nave, chancel, and transepts.

CROSS-WINDOWS: windows with one mullion and one transom.

CRUCK: big curved beam supporting both walls and roof of a cottage.

CRYPT: underground room usually below the E end of a church.

CUPOLA: small polygonal or circular domed turret crowning a roof.

CURTAIN WALL: connecting wall between the towers of a castle.

CUSHION CAPITAL: *see* Block Capital.

CUSP: projecting point between the foils in a foiled Gothic arch.

DADO: decorative covering of the lower part of a wall.

DAGGER: tracery motif of the Dec style. It is a lancet shape rounded or pointed at the head, pointed at the foot, and cusped inside (*see* Fig. 6).

Fik. 6

DAIS: raised platform at one end of a room.

DEC ('DECORATED'): historical division of English Gothic architecture covering the period from c.1290 to c.1350.

DEMI-COLUMNS: columns half sunk into a wall.

DIAPER WORK: surface decoration composed of square or lozenge shapes.

DISC BARROW: Bronze Age round barrow with inconspicuous central mound surrounded by bank and ditch.

DOGTOOTH: typical E.E. ornament consisting of a series of four-cornered stars placed diagonally and raised pyramidally (Fig. 7).

Fig. 7

DOMICAL VAULT: see Vault.

DONJON: see Keep.

DORIC: see Order.

DORMER (WINDOW): window placed vertically in the sloping plane of a roof.

DRIPSTONE: see Hood-mould.

DRUM: circular or polygonal vertical wall of a dome or cupola.

E.E. ('EARLY ENGLISH'): historical division of English Gothic architecture roughly covering the C13.

EASTER SEPULCHRE: recess with tomb-chest usually in the wall of a chancel, the tomb-chest to receive an effigy of Christ for Easter celebrations.

EAVES: underpart of a sloping roof overhanging a wall.

EAVES CORNICE: cornice below the eaves of a roof.

ECHINUS: Convex or projecting moulding supporting the abacus of a Greek Doric capital, sometimes bearing an egg and dart pattern.

EMBATTLED: see Battlement.

EMBRASURE: small opening in the wall or parapet of a fortified building, usually splayed on the inside.

ENCAUSTIC TILES: earthenware glazed and decorated tiles used for paving.

ENGAGED COLUMNS: columns attached to, or partly sunk into, a wall.

ENGLISH BOND: see Brickwork.

ENTABLATURE: in classical architecture the whole of the horizontal members above a column (that is architrave, frieze, and cornice) (see Fig. 12).

ENTASIS: very slight convex deviation from a straight line; used on Greek columns and sometimes on spires to prevent an optical illusion of concavity.

ENTRESOL: see Mezzanine.

EPITAPH: hanging wall monument.

ESCUTCHEON: shield for armorial bearings.

EXEDRA: the apsidal end of a room. See Apse.

FAN-VAULT: see Vault.

FERETORY: place behind the high altar where the chief shrine of a church is kept.

FESTOON: carved garland of flowers and fruit suspended at both ends.

FILLET: narrow flat band running down a shaft or along a roll moulding.

FINIAL: top of a canopy, gable, pinnacle.

FLAGON: vessel for the wine used in the Communion service.

FLAMBOYANT: properly the latest phase of French Gothic architecture where the window tracery takes on wavy undulating lines.

FLÈCHE: slender wooden spire on the centre of a roof (also called Spirelet).

FLEMISH BOND: see Brickwork.

FLEURON: decorative carved flower or leaf.

FLUSHWORK: decorative use of flint in conjunction with dressed stone so as to form patterns: tracery, initials, etc.

FLUTING: vertical channelling in the shaft of a column.

FLYING BUTTRESS: see Buttress.

FOIL: lobe formed by the cusping (q.v.) of a circle or an arch. Trefoil, quatrefoil, cinquefoil, multifoil, express the number of leaf shapes to be seen.

FOLIATED: carved with leaf shapes.

FOSSE: ditch.

FOUR-CENTRED ARCH: see Arch.

FRATER: refectory or dining hall of a monastery.

FRESCO: wall painting on wet plaster.

FRIEZE: middle division of a classical entablature (q.v.) (see Fig. 12).

FRONTAL: covering for the front of an altar.

GABLE: *Dutch gable:* A gable with curved sides crowned by a pediment, characteristic of c.1630–50 (Fig. 8a). *Shaped gable:* A gable with multi-curved sides characteristic of c.1600–50 (Fig. 8b).

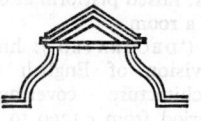

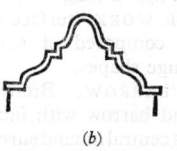

(b)

Fig. 8

GADROONED: enriched with a series of convex ridges, the opposite of fluting.

GALILEE: chapel or vestibule usually at the W end of a church enclosing the porch. Also called Narthex (q.v.).

GALLERY: in church architecture upper storey above an aisle, opened in arches to the nave. Also called Tribune and often erroneously Triforium (q.v.).

GALLERY GRAVE: chambered tomb (q.v.) in which there is little or no differentiation between the entrance passage and the actual burial chamber(s).

GARDEROBE: lavatory or privy in a medieval building.

GARGOYLE: water spout projecting from the parapet of a wall or tower; carved into a human or animal shape.

GAZEBO: lookout tower or raised summer house in a picturesque garden.

'GEOMETRICAL': see Tracery.

'GIBBS SURROUND': of a doorway or window. An c18 motif consisting of a surround with alternating larger and smaller blocks of stone, quoin-wise, or intermittent large blocks, sometimes with a narrow raised band connecting them up the verticals and along the face of the arch (Fig. 9).

Fig. 9

GROIN: sharp edge at the meeting of two cells of a cross-vault.

GROIN-VAULT: see Vault.

GROTESQUE: fanciful ornamental decoration: see also Arabesque.

HAGIOSCOPE: see Squint.

HALF-TIMBERING: see Timber-Framing.

HALL CHURCH: church in which nave and aisles are of equal height or approximately so.

HAMMERBEAM: see Roof.

HANAP: large metal cup, generally made for domestic use, standing on an elaborate base and stem; with a very ornate cover frequently crowned with a little steeple.

HEADERS: see Brickwork.

HERRINGBONE WORK: brick, stone, or tile construction where the component blocks are laid diagonally instead of flat. Alternate courses lie in opposing directions to make a zigzag pattern up the face of the wall.

14 + V.F.O.D.

HEXASTYLE: having six detached columns.

HILL-FORT: Iron Age earthwork enclosed by a ditch and bank system; in the later part of the period the defences multiplied in size and complexity. They vary from about an acre to over 30 acres in area, and are usually built with careful regard to natural elevations or promontories.

HIPPED ROOF: see Roof.

HOOD-MOULD: projecting moulding above an arch or a lintel to throw off water (also called Dripstone or Label).

ICONOGRAPHY: the science of the subject matter of works of the visual arts.

IMPOST: bracket in a wall, usually formed of mouldings, on which the ends of an arch rest.

INDENT: shape chiselled out in a stone slab to receive a brass.

INGLENOOK: bench or seat built in beside a fireplace, sometimes covered by the chimneybreast, occasionally lit by small windows on each side of the fire.

INTERCOLUMNIATION: the space between columns.

IONIC: see Order (Fig. 12).

IRON AGE: in Britain the period from c. 600 B.C. to the coming of the Romans. The term is also used for those un-Romanized native communities which survived until the Saxon incursions.

JAMB: straight side of an archway, doorway, or window.

KEEL MOULDING: moulding whose outline is in section like that of the keel of a ship.

KEEP: massive tower of a Norman castle.

KEYSTONE: middle stone in an arch or a rib-vault.

KING-POST: see Roof (Fig. 14).

KNOP: a knob-like thickening in the stem of a chalice.

LABEL: see Hood-mould.

LABEL STOP: ornamental boss at the end of a hood-mould (q.v.).

LACED WINDOWS: windows pulled visually together by strips, usually in brick of a different colour, which continue vertically the lines of the vertical parts of the window surrounds. The motif is typical of c. 1720.

LANCET WINDOW: slender pointed-arched window.

LANTERN: in architecture, a small circular or polygonal turret with windows all round crowning a roof (see Cupola) or a dome.

LANTERN CROSS: churchyard cross with lantern-shaped top usually with sculptured representations on the sides of the top.

LEAN-TO ROOF: roof with one slope only, built against a higher wall.

LESENE or PILASTER STRIP: pilaster without base or capital.

LIERNE: see Vault (Fig. 21).

LINENFOLD: Tudor panelling ornamented with a conventional representation of a piece of linen laid in vertical folds. The piece is repeated in each panel.

LINTEL: horizontal beam or stone bridging an opening.

LOGGIA: recessed colonnade (q.v.).

LONG AND SHORT WORK: Saxon quoins (q.v.) consisting of stones placed with the long sides alternately upright and horizontal.

LONG BARROW: unchambered Neolithic communal burial mound, wedge-shaped in plan, with the burial and occasional other structures massed at the broader end, from which the mound itself tapers in height; quarry ditches flank the mound.

LOUVRE: opening, often with lantern (q.v.) over, in the roof of a room to let the smoke from a central hearth escape.

LOWER PALAEOLITHIC: see Palaeolithic.

LOZENGE: diamond shape.

LUCARNE: small opening to let light in.

LUNETTE: tympanum (q.v.) or semicircular opening.

LYCH GATE: wooden gate structure with a roof and open sides placed at the entrance to a churchyard to provide space for the reception of a coffin. The word *lych* is Saxon and means a corpse.

LYNCHET: long terraced strip of soil accumulating on the downward side of prehistoric and medieval fields due to soil creep from continuous ploughing along the contours.

MACHICOLATION: projecting gallery on brackets constructed on the outside of castle towers or walls. The gallery has holes in the floor to drop missiles through.

MAJOLICA: ornamented glazed earthenware.

MANSARD: *see* Roof.

MATHEMATICAL TILES: Small facing tiles the size of brick headers, applied to timber-framed walls to make them appear brick-built.

MEGALITHIC TOMB: stone-built burial chamber of the New Stone Age covered by an earth or stone mound. The form was introduced to Britain from the Mediterranean area.

MERLON: *see* Battlement.

MESOLITHIC: 'Middle Stone' Age; the post-glacial period of hunting and fishing communities dating in Britain from *c.* 8000 B.C. to the arrival of Neolithic communities, with which they must have considerably overlapped.

METOPE: in classical architecture of the Doric order (q.v.) the space in the frieze between the triglyphs (Fig. 12).

MEZZANINE: low storey placed between two higher ones.

MISERERE: *see* Misericord.

MISERICORD: bracket placed on the underside of a hinged choir stall seat which, when turned up, provided the occupant of the seat with a support during long periods of standing (also called Miserere).

MODILLION: small bracket of which large numbers (modillion frieze) are often placed below a cornice (q.v.) in classical architecture.

MOTTE: steep mound forming the main feature of C11 and C12 castles.

14*

MOTTE-AND-BAILEY: post-Roman and Norman defence system consisting of an earthen mound (the motte) topped with a wooden tower eccentrically placed within a bailey (q.v.), with enclosure ditch and palisade, and with the rare addition of an internal bank.

MOUCHETTE: tracery motif in curvilinear tracery, a curved dagger (q.v.), specially popular in the early C14 (Fig. 10).

Fig. 10

MULLION: vertical post or upright dividing a window into two or more 'lights'.

MULTIVALLATE: Of a hill-fort: defended by three or more concentric banks and ditches.

MUNTIN: post as a rule moulded and part of a screen.

NAIL-HEAD: E.E. ornamental motif, consisting of small pyramids regularly repeated (Fig. 11).

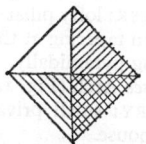

Fig. 11

NARTHEX: enclosed vestibule or covered porch at the main entrance to a church (*see* Galilee).

NEOLITHIC: 'New Stone' Age, dating in Britain from the appearance from the Continent of the first settled farming communities *c.* 3500 B.C. until the introduction of the Bronze Age.

Fig. 12–Orders of Columns (Greek Doric, Roman Doric, Tuscan Doric, Ionic, Corinthian) E, Entablature; C, Cornice; F, Frieze; A, Architrave; M, Metope; T, Triglyph.

NEWEL: central post in a circular or winding staircase; also the principal post when a flight of stairs meets a landing.

NOOK-SHAFT: shaft set in the angle of a pier or respond or wall, or the angle of the jamb of a window or doorway.

OBELISK: lofty pillar of square section tapering at the top and ending pyramidally.

OGEE: *see* Arch (Fig. 1c).

ORATORY: small private chapel in a house.

ORDER: (1) *of a doorway or window:* series of concentric steps receding towards the opening; (2) *in classical architecture:* column with base, shaft, capital, and entablature (q.v.) according to one of the following styles: Greek Doric, Roman Doric, Tuscan Doric, Ionic, Corinthian, Composite. The established details are

very elaborate, and some specialist architectural work should be consulted for further guidance (*see* Fig. 12).

ORIEL: *see* Bay-Window.

OVERHANG: projection of the upper storey of a house.

OVERSAILING COURSES: series of stone or brick courses, each one projecting beyond the one below it.

PALAEOLITHIC: 'Old Stone' Age; the first period of human culture, commencing in the Ice Age and immediately prior to the Mesolithic; the Lower Palaeolithic is the older phase, the Upper Palaeolithic the later.

PALIMPSEST: (1) *of a brass:* where a metal plate has been re-used by turning over and engraving on the back; (2) *of a wall painting:* where one overlaps and partly obscures an earlier one.

PALLADIAN: architecture following the ideas and principles of Andrea Palladio, 1518–80.

PANTILE: tile of curved S-shaped section.

PARAPET: low wall placed to protect any spot where there is a sudden drop, for example on a bridge, quay, hillside, housetop, etc.

PARGETTING: plaster work with patterns and ornaments either in relief or engraved on it.

PARVIS: term wrongly applied to a room over a church porch. These rooms were often used as a schoolroom or as a store room.

PATEN: plate to hold the bread at Communion or Mass.

PATERA: small flat circular or oval ornament in classical architecture.

PEDIMENT: low-pitched gable used in classical, Renaissance, and neo-classical architecture above a portico and above doors, windows, etc. It may be straight-sided or curved segmentally. *Broken Pediment:* one where the centre portion of the base is left open. *Open Pediment:* one where the centre portion of the sloping sides is left out.

PENDANT: boss (q.v.) elongated so that it seems to hang down.

PENDENTIF: concave triangular spandrel used to lead from the angle of two walls to the base of a circular dome. It is constructed as part of the hemisphere over a diameter the size of the diagonal of the basic square (Fig. 13).

PERP (PERPENDICULAR): historical division of English Gothic architecture covering

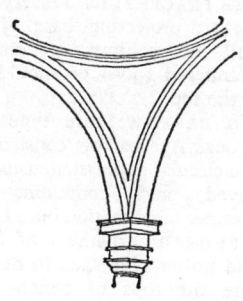

Fig. 13

the period from c.1335–50 to c.1530.

PIANO NOBILE: principal storey of a house with the reception rooms; usually the first floor.

PIAZZA: open space surrounded by buildings; in C17 and C18 England sometimes used to mean a long colonnade or loggia.

PIER: strong, solid support, frequently square in section or of composite section (compound pier).

PIETRA DURA: ornamental or scenic inlay by means of thin slabs of stone.

PILASTER: shallow pier attached to a wall. *Termini Pilasters:* pilasters with sides tapering downwards.

PILLAR PISCINA: free-standing piscina on a pillar.

PINNACLE: ornamental form crowning a spire, tower, buttress, etc., usually of steep pyramidal, conical, or some similar shape.

PISCINA: basin for washing the Communion or Mass vessels, provided with a drain. Generally set in or against the wall to the S of an altar.

PLAISANCE: summer-house, pleasure house near a mansion.

PLATE TRACERY: *see* Tracery.

PLINTH: projecting base of a wall or column, generally chamfered (q.v.) or moulded at the top.

POND BARROW: rare type of Bronze Age barrow consisting of a circular depression, usually paved, and containing a number of cremation burials.

POPPYHEAD: ornament of leaf and flower type used to decorate the tops of bench- or stall-ends.

PORTCULLIS: gate constructed to rise and fall in vertical grooves; used in gateways of castles.

PORTE COCHÈRE: porch large enough to admit wheeled vehicles.

PORTICO: centre-piece of a house or a church with classical detached or attached columns and a pediment. A portico is called *prostyle* or *in antis* according to whether it projects from or recedes into a building. In a portico *in antis* the columns range with the side walls.

POSTERN: small gateway at the back of a building.

PREDELLA: in an altarpiece the horizontal strip below the main representation, often used for a number of subsidiary representations in a row.

PRESBYTERY: the part of the church lying E of the choir. It is the part where the altar is placed.

PRINCIPAL: *see* Roof (Fig. 14).

PRIORY: monastic house whose head is a prior or prioress, not an abbot or abbess.

PROSTYLE: with free-standing columns in a row.

PULPITUM: stone screen in a major church provided to shut off the choir from the nave and also as a backing for the return choir stalls.

PULVINATED FRIEZE: frieze with a bold convex moulding.

PURLIN: *see* Roof (Figs. 14, 15).

PUTTO: small naked boy.

QUADRANGLE: inner courtyard in a large building.

QUARRY: in stained-glass work, a small diamond or square-shaped piece of glass set diagonally.

QUATREFOIL: *see* Foil.

QUEEN-POSTS: *see* Roof (Fig. 15).

QUOINS: dressed stones at the angles of a building. Sometimes all the stones are of the same size; more often they are alternately large and small.

RADIATING CHAPELS: chapels projecting radially from an ambulatory or an apse.

RAFTER: *see* Roof.

RAMPART: stone wall or wall of earth surrounding a castle, fortress, or fortified city.

RAMPART-WALK: path along the inner face of a rampart.

REBATE: continuous rectangular notch cut on an edge.

REBUS: pun, a play on words. The literal translation and illustration of a name for artistic and heraldic purposes (Belton = bell, tun).

RECUSANT CHALICE: chalice made after the Reformation and before Catholic Emancipation for Roman Catholic use.

REEDING: decoration with parallel convex mouldings touching one another.

REFECTORY: dining hall; *see* Frater.

RENDERING: plastering of an outer wall.

REPOUSSÉ: decoration of metal work by relief designs, formed by beating the metal from the back.

REREDOS: structure behind and above an altar.

RESPOND: half-pier bonded into a wall and carrying one end of an arch.

RETABLE: altarpiece, a picture or piece of carving, standing behind and attached to an altar.

RETICULATION: *see* Tracery (Fig. 20e).

REVEAL: that part of a jamb (q.v.) which lies between the glass or door and the outer surface of the wall.

RIB-VAULT: *see* Vault.

ROCOCO: latest phase of the Baroque style, current in most Continental countries between c. 1720 and c. 1760.

ROLL MOULDING: moulding of semicircular or more than semicircular section.

ROMANESQUE: that style in architecture which was current in the C11 and C12 and preceded the Gothic style (in England often called Norman). (Some scholars extend the use of the term Romanesque back to the C10 or C9.)

ROMANO-BRITISH: A somewhat vague term applied to the period and cultural features of Britain affected by the Roman occupation of the C1–5 A.D.

ROOD: cross or crucifix.

ROOD LOFT: singing gallery on the top of the rood screen, often supported by a coving.

ROOD SCREEN: *see* Screen.

ROOD STAIRS: stairs to give access to the rood loft.

ROOF: *Single-framed:* if consisting entirely of transverse members (such as rafters with or without braces, collars, tie-beams, king-posts or queen-posts, etc.) not tied together longitudinally. *Double-framed:* if longitudinal members (such as a ridge beam and purlins) are employed. As a rule in such cases the rafters are divided into stronger principals and weaker subsidiary rafters.

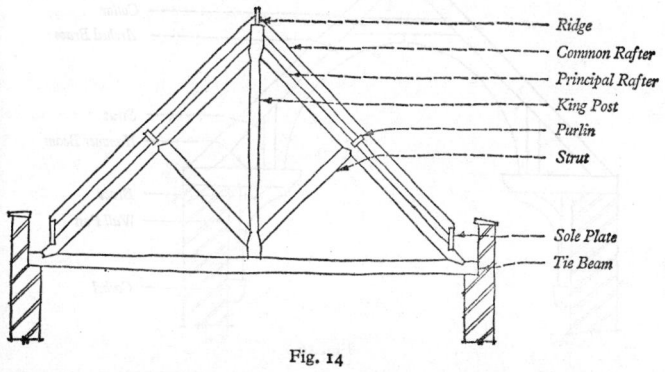

Ridge
Common Rafter
Principal Rafter
King Post
Purlin
Strut
Sole Plate
Tie Beam

Fig. 14

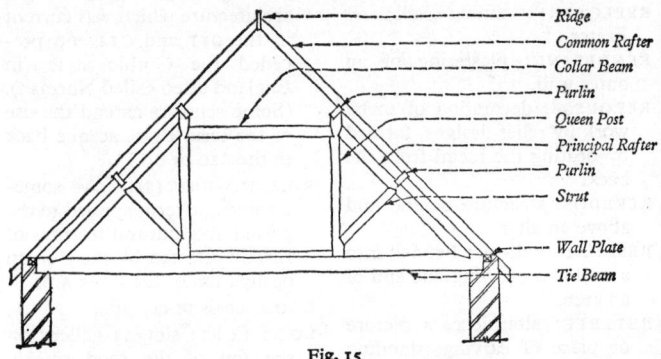

Fig. 15

Ridge
Common Rafter
Collar Beam
Purlin
Queen Post
Principal Rafter
Purlin
Strut
Wall Plate
Tie Beam

Hipped: roof with sloped instead of vertical ends. *Mansard:* roof with a double slope, the lower slope being larger and steeper than the upper. *Saddleback:* tower roof shaped like an ordinary gabled timber roof. The following members have special names: *Rafter:* roof-timber sloping up from the wall plate to the ridge. *Principal:* principal rafter, usually corresponding to the main bay divisions of the nave or chancel below. *Wall Plate:* timber laid longitudinally on the top of a wall. *Purlin:* longitudinal member laid parallel with wall plate and ridge beam some way up the slope of the roof. *Tie-beam:* beam connecting the two slopes of a roof across at its foot, usually at the height of the wall plate, to prevent the roof from spreading. *Collar-beam:* tie-beam applied higher up the slope of the roof. *Strut:* upright timber connecting the

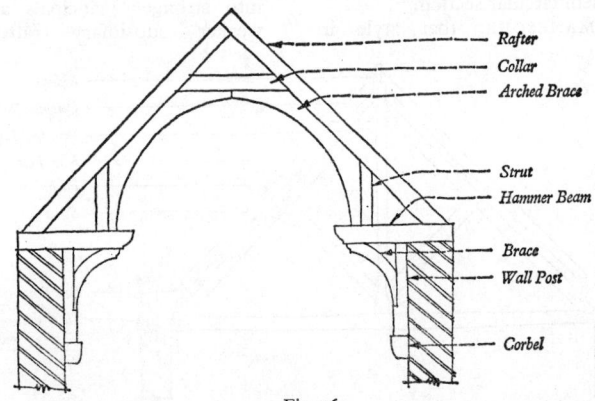

Rafter
Collar
Arched Brace
Strut
Hammer Beam
Brace
Wall Post
Corbel

Fig. 16

tie-beam with the rafter above it. *King-post:* upright timber connecting a tie-beam and collar-beam with the ridge beam. *Queen-posts:* two struts placed symmetrically on a tie-beam or collar-beam. *Braces:* inclined timbers inserted to strengthen others. Usually braces connect a collar-beam with the rafters below or a tie-beam with the wall below. Braces can be straight or curved (also called arched). *Hammer-beam:* beam projecting at right angles, usually from the top of a wall, to carry arched braces or struts and arched braces. (*See* Figs. 14, 15, 16.)

ROSE WINDOW (or WHEEL WINDOW): circular window with patterned tracery arranged to radiate from the centre.

ROTUNDA: building circular in plan.

RUBBLE: building stones, not square or hewn, nor laid in regular courses.

RUSTICATION: *rock-faced* if the surfaces of large blocks of ashlar stone are left rough like rock; *smooth* if the ashlar blocks are smooth and separated by V-joints; *banded* if the separation by V-joints applies only to the horizontals.

S

SADDLEBACK: *see* Roof.

SALTIRE CROSS: equal-limbed cross placed diagonally.

SANCTUARY: (1) area around the main altar of a church (*see* Presbytery); (2) sacred site consisting of wood or stone uprights enclosed by a circular bank and ditch. Beginning in the Neolithic, they were elaborated in the succeeding Bronze Age. The best known examples are Stonehenge and Avebury.

SARCOPHAGUS: elaborately carved coffin.

SCAGLIOLA: material composed of cement and colouring matter to imitate marble.

SCALLOPED CAPITAL: development of the block capital (q.v.) in which the single semi-circular surface is elaborated into a series of truncated cones (Fig. 17).

Fig. 17

SCARP: artificial cutting away of the ground to form a steep slope.

SCREEN: *Parclose screen:* screen separating a chapel from the rest of a church. *Rood screen:* screen below the rood (q.v.), usually at the w end of a chancel.

SCREENS PASSAGE: passage between the entrances to kitchen, buttery, etc., and the screen behind which lies the hall of a medieval house.

SEDILIA: seats for the priests (usually three) on the s side of the chancel of a church.

SEGMENTAL ARCH: *see* Arch.

SET-OFF: *see* Weathering.

SEXPARTITE: *see* Vault.

SGRAFFITO: pattern incised into plaster so as to expose a dark surface underneath.

SHAFT-RING: motif of the C12 and C13 consisting of a ring round a circular pier or a shaft attached to a pier.

SHEILA-NA-GIG: fertility figure, usually with legs wide open.

SILL: lower horizontal part of the frame of a window.

SLATEHANGING: the covering of walls by overlapping rows of slates, on a timber substructure.

SOFFIT: underside of an arch, lintel, etc.

SOLAR: upper living-room of a medieval house.

SOPRAPORTE: painting above the door of a room, usual in the C17 and C18.

SOUNDING BOARD: horizontal board or canopy over a pulpit. Also called Tester.

SPANDREL: triangular surface between one side of an arch, the horizontal drawn from its apex, and the vertical drawn from its springer; also the surface between two arches.

SPERE-TRUSS: roof truss on two free-standing posts to mask the division between screens passage and hall. The screen itself, where a spere-truss exists, was originally movable.

SPIRE: tall pyramidal or conical pointed erection often built on top of a tower, turret, etc. *Broach Spire:* spire which is generally octagonal in plan rising from the top or parapet of a square tower. A small inclined piece of masonry covers the vacant triangular space at each of the four angles of the square and is carried up to a point along the diagonal sides of the octagon. *Needle Spire:* thin spire rising from the centre of a tower roof, well inside the parapet.

SPIRELET: *see* Flèche.

SPLAY: chamfer, usually of the jamb of a window.

SPRINGING: level at which an arch rises from its supports.

SQUINCH: arch or system of concentric arches thrown across the angle between two walls to support a superstructure, for example a dome (Fig. 18).

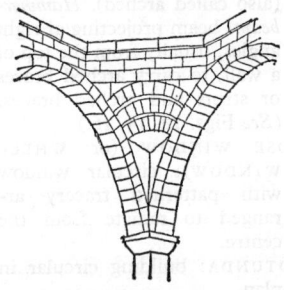

Fig. 18

SQUINT: hole cut in a wall or through a pier to allow a view of the main altar of a church from places whence it could not otherwise be seen (also called Hagioscope).

STALL: carved seat, one of a row, made of wood or stone.

STAUNCHION: upright iron or steel member.

STEEPLE: the tower of a church together with a spire, cupola, etc.

STIFF-LEAF: E.E. type of foliage of many-lobed shapes (Fig. 19).

STILTED: *see* Arch.

STOREY-POSTS: the principal posts of a timber-framed wall.

STOUP: vessel for the reception of holy water, usually placed near a door.

Fig. 19

STRAINER ARCH: arch inserted across a room to prevent the walls from leaning.

STRAPWORK: C16 decoration consisting of interlaced bands, and forms similar to fretwork or cut and bent leather.

STRETCHER: *see* Brickwork.

STRING COURSE: projecting horizontal band or moulding set in the surface of a wall.

STRUT: *see* Roof.

STUCCO: plaster work.

STUDS: the subsidiary vertical timber members of a timber-framed wall.

SWAG: festoon formed by a carved piece of cloth suspended from both ends.

TABERNACLE: richly ornamented niche or free-standing canopy. Usually contains the Holy Sacrament.

TARSIA: inlay in various woods.

TAZZA: shallow bowl on a foot.

TERMINAL FIGURES (TERMS, TERMINI): upper part of a human figure growing out of a pier, pilaster, etc., which tapers towards the base. *See also* Caryatid, Pilaster.

TERRACOTTA: burnt clay, unglazed.

TESSELLATED PAVEMENT: mosaic flooring, particularly Roman, consisting of small 'tesserae' or cubes of glass, stone, or brick.

14**

TESSERAE: *see* Tessellated Pavement.

TESTER: *see* Sounding Board.

TETRASTYLE: having four detached columns.

THREE-DECKER PULPIT: pulpit with Clerk's Stall below and Reading Desk below the Clerk's Stall.

TIE-BEAM: *see* Roof (Figs. 14, 15).

TIERCERON: *see* Vault (Fig. 21).

TILEHANGING: *see* Slatehanging.

TIMBER-FRAMING: method of construction where walls are built of timber framework with the spaces filled in by plaster or brickwork. Sometimes the timber is covered over with plaster or boarding laid horizontally.

TOMB-CHEST: chest-shaped stone coffin, the most usual medieval form of funeral monument.

TOUCH: soft black marble quarried near Tournai.

TOURELLE: turret corbelled out from the wall.

TRACERY: intersecting ribwork in the upper part of a window, or used decoratively in blank arches, on vaults, etc. *Plate tracery: see* Fig. 20(a). Early form of tracery where decoratively shaped openings are cut through the solid stone infilling in a window head. *Bar tracery:* a form introduced into England c. 1250. Intersecting ribwork made up of slender shafts, continuing the lines of the mullions of windows up to a decorative mesh in the head of the window. *Geometrical tracery: see* Fig. 20(b). Tracery characteristic of c. 1250–1310 consisting chiefly of circles of foiled circles. *Y-tracery: see*

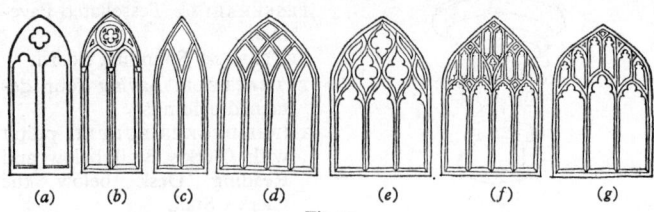

(a)   (b)   (c)   (d)   (e)   (f)   (g)

Fig. 20

Fig. 20(c). Tracery consisting of a mullion which branches into two forming a Y shape; typical of c. 1300. *Intersecting tracery: see* Fig. 20(d). Tracery in which each mullion of a window branches out into two curved bars in such a way that every one of them is drawn with the same radius from a different centre. The result is that every light of the window is a lancet and every two, three, four, etc., lights together form a pointed arch. This treatment also is typical of c. 1300. *Reticulated tracery: see* Fig. 20(e). Tracery typical of the early c14 consisting entirely of circles drawn at top and bottom into ogee shapes so that a net-like appearance results. *Panel tracery: see* Fig. 20(f) and (g). Perp tracery, which is formed of upright straight-sided panels above lights of a window.

TRANSEPT: transverse portion of a cross-shaped church.

TRANSOM: horizontal bar across the openings of a window.

TRANSVERSE ARCH: *see* Vault.

TRIBUNE: *see* Gallery.

TRICIPUT, SIGNUM TRICIPUT: sign of the Trinity expressed by three faces belonging to one head.

TRIFORIUM: arcaded wall pas-
sage or blank arcading facing the nave at the height of the aisle roof and below the clerestory (q.v.) windows. (*See* Gallery.)

TRIGLYPHS: blocks with vertical grooves separating the metopes (q.v.) in the Doric frieze (Fig. 12).

TROPHY: sculptured group of arms or armour, used as a memorial of victory.

TRUMEAU: stone mullion (q.v.) supporting the tympanum (q.v.) of a wide doorway.

TUMULUS: *see* Barrow.

TURRET: very small tower, round or polygonal in plan.

TUSCAN: *see* Order.

TYMPANUM: space between the lintel of a doorway and the arch above it.

UNDERCROFT: vaulted room, sometimes underground, below a church or chapel.

UNIVALLATE: of a hill-fort: defended by a single bank and ditch.

UPPER PALAEOLITHIC: *see* Palaeolithic.

VAULT: *Barrel-vault: see* Tunnel-vault. *Cross-vault: see* Groin-vault. *Domical vault:* square or polygonal dome ris-

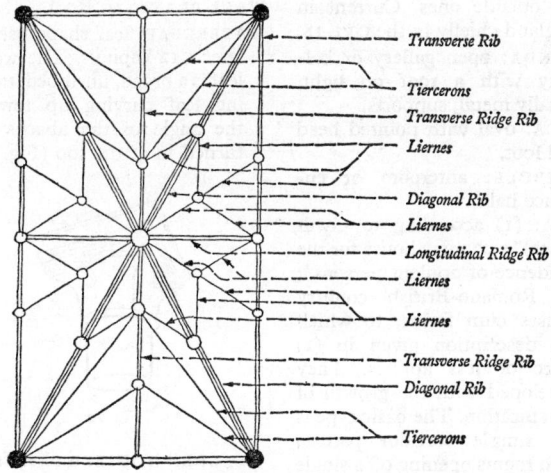

Transverse Rib
Tiercerons
Transverse Ridge Rib
Liernes
Diagonal Rib
Liernes
Longitudinal Ridge Rib
Liernes
Liernes
Transverse Ridge Rib
Diagonal Rib
Tiercerons

Fig. 21

ing direct on a square or polygonal bay, the curved surfaces separated by groins (q.v.). *Fanvault:* Late Medieval vault where all ribs springing from one springer are of the same length, the same distance from the next, and the same curvature. *Groin-vault* or *Crossvault:* vault of two tunnelvaults of identical shape intersecting each other at r. angles. Chiefly Norman and Renaissance. *Lierne:* tertiary rib, that is, rib which does not spring either from one of the main springers or from the central boss. Introduced in the c14, continues to the c16. *Quadripartite vault:* one wherein one bay of vaulting is divided into four parts. *Rib-vault:* vault with diagonal ribs projecting along the groins. *Ridgerib:* rib along the longitudinal

or transverse ridge of a vault. Introduced in the early c13. *Sexpartite vault:* one wherein one bay of quadripartite vaulting is divided into two parts transversely so that each bay of vaulting has six parts. *Tierceron:* secondary rib, that is, rib which issues from one of the main springers or the central boss and leads to a place on a ridge-rib. Introduced in the early c13. *Transverse arch:* arch separating one bay of a vault from the next. *Tunnelvault* or *Barrel-vault:* vault of semicircular or pointed section. Chiefly Norman and Renaissance. (*See* Fig. 21.)

VAULTING SHAFT: vertical member leading to the springer of a vault.

VENETIAN WINDOW: window with three openings, the central one arched and wider than the outside ones. Current in England chiefly in the C17–18.

VERANDA: open gallery or balcony with a roof on light, usually metal, supports.

VESICA: oval with pointed head and foot.

VESTIBULE: anteroom or entrance hall.

VILLA: (1) according to Gwilt (1842) 'a country house for the residence of opulent persons'; (2) Romano-British country houses cum farms, to which the description given in (1) more or less applies. They developed with the growth of urbanization. The basic type is the simple corridor pattern with rooms opening off a single passage; the next stage is the addition of wings. The courtyard villa fills a square plan with subsidiary buildings and an enclosure wall with a gate facing the main corridor block.

VITRIFIED: made similar to glass.

VITRUVIAN OPENING: A door or window which diminishes towards the top, as advocated by Vitruvius, bk. IV, chapter VI.

VOLUTE: spiral scroll, one of the component parts of an Ionic column (see Order).

VOUSSOIR: wedge-shaped stone used in arch construction.

WAGON ROOF: roof in which by closely set rafters with arched braces the appearance of the inside of a canvas tilt over a wagon is achieved. Wagon roofs can be panelled or plastered (ceiled) or left uncovered.

WAINSCOT: timber lining to walls.

WALL PLATE: see Roof.

WATERLEAF: leaf shape used in later C12 capitals. The waterleaf is a broad, unribbed, tapering leaf curving up towards the angle of the abacus and turned in at the top (Fig. 22).

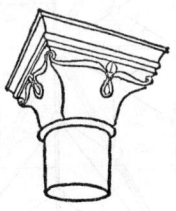

Fig. 22

WEALDEN HOUSE: timber-framed house with the hall in the centre and wings projecting only slightly and only on the jutting upper floor. The roof, however, runs through without a break between wings and hall, and the eaves of the hall part are therefore exceptionally deep. They are supported by diagonal, usually curved, braces starting from the short inner sides of the overhanging wings and rising parallel with the front wall of the hall towards the centre of the eaves.

WEATHERBOARDING: overlapping horizontal boards, covering a timber-framed wall.

WEATHERING: sloped horizontal surface on sills, buttresses, etc., to throw off water.

WEEPERS: small figures placed in niches along the sides of some medieval tombs (also called Mourners).

WHEEL WINDOW: see Rose Window.

INDEX OF PLATES

INDEX OF ARTISTS

INDEX OF PLACES

ADDENDUM
(APRIL 1969)

pp. 245 and 250 [Gloucester]. The Bell Hotel has now been demolished, and excavations at Nos. 11–15 SOUTHGATE
STREET have uncovered 1,000 sq. ft of paved courtyard which is almost certainly the ROMAN FORUM.
On the E stood a colonnade, shops, and a street, and
on the S a floor 2 ft higher is from the evidence of past
discoveries the probable site of the basilica. The
rectangular base of a bronze equestrian statue stands in
the courtyard. Pottery beneath the courtyard and floor
is all of C1 type. From the C4 to the C11 the site was
apparently completely empty, as a deposit of 12–15 in.
of sterile soil separates the latest Roman from the
earliest medieval layers. From the C11 to the C13
leather-workers occupied the site, but C18 and C19
cellars have destroyed later medieval stratification.